In this wide-ranging and challenging book, Ruth Smith shows that the words of Handel's oratorios reflect the events and ideas of their time and have far greater meaning than has hitherto been realised. She explores literature, music, aesthetics, politics and religion to reveal Handel's works as conduits for eighteenth-century thought and sensibility. She gives a full picture of Handel's librettists and shows how their oratorio texts express key moral-political preoccupations and engage with contemporary ideological debate. British identity, the need for national unity, the conduct of war, the role of government, the authority of the Bible, the purpose of literature, the effect of art – these and many more concerns are addressed in the librettos. This book enriches our understanding of Handel, his times, and the relationships between music and its intellectual contexts.

HANDEL'S ORATORIOS AND EIGHTEENTH-CENTURY THOUGHT

HANDEL'S ORATORIOS AND EIGHTEENTH-CENTURY THOUGHT

RUTH SMITH

CAMBRIDGE
UNIVERSITY PRESS

Published by the Press Syndicate of the University of Cambridge
The Pitt Building, Trumpington Street, Cambridge CB2 1RP
40 West 20th Street, New York, NY 10011–4211, USA
10 Stamford Road, Oakleigh, Melbourne 3166, Australia

First published 1995

Printed in Great Britain at the University Press, Cambridge

A catalogue record for this book is available from the British Library

Library of Congress cataloguing in publication data
Smith, Ruth, 1947–
Handel's oratorio librettos and eighteenth-century thought / Ruth Smith.
p.   cm.
Includes bibliographical references and index.
ISBN 0 521 40265 4 (hardback)
1. Handel, George Friederic, 1685–1759. Oratorios. Librettos.
2. Oratorios – 18th century – Librettos – History and criticism.
3. Great Britain – History – 18th century.
I. Title. II. Title: Handel's oratorio librettos and 18th-century thought.
ML 410.H3S58   1995
782.23′0268   1995
782.23′0268–dc20   94–20603 CIP MN

ISBN 0 521 40265 4   (hardback)

To the memory of
Hilary M. Gornall
(1922–1979)
teacher and friend

Contents

Acknowledgements   page xi

Introduction   1

PART I ENGLISH ORIGINS OF ENGLISH ORATORIO   41

1   Artistic norms   43

2   The purpose of art   52

3   Music, morals and religion   81

4   The biblical sublime   108

5   The survival of epic   127

6   The defence of Christianity   141

7   Towards oratorio   157

PART II THE PATRIOT LIBRETTO FROM THE EXCISE BILL
TO THE JEW BILL: ISRAELITE ORATORIOS AND
ENGLISH POLITICS   171

8   Political events and political thought   173

9   Allegorical politics   202

10 Moral politics   233

11 *Esther* to *Athalia*   276

12 In time of war   288

13 Images of government   304

x   *List of contents*

14   The conflict of public and private interests   335

15   Coda: the end of Handel's Israelite oratorios   346

Appendix 1   Libretto authors and sources   351
Appendix 2   The oratorios and Methodism   354
Notes   361
Bibliography of sources cited   438
Index   467

Acknowledgements

Like the author of a much more substantial work, 'I must frankly own, that if I had known, beforehand, that this book would have cost me the labour which it has, I should never have been courageous enough to commence it.'[1] The topic was patently a piece of the jigsaw of eighteenth-century intellectual history waiting to be dropped into place; but I would not have had the confidence to persevere without the help and encouragement of many friends and academics.

This book originated with its dedicatee, who lent me (when I was a pupil in her English class) the Peter Pears/Anthony Lewis recordings of *Acis* and *L'allegro* and, later, tapes of Douglas Brown's Third Programme talks on Handel's English word-setting. To her I owe both the impulse for all my academic work and the educational grounding which made it possible. Jeremy Prynne supervised my initial research and likewise gave me lasting stimulus and an example of intellectual and scholarly standards to try to live up to. As an undergraduate at Girton I benefited from the humane teaching of Joan Bennett, Anne Barton and Mary Ann Radzinowicz, who allowed me to read texts in preference to textual criticism.

David Armitage, Michael Burden, Donald Burrows, Merlin Channon, Jane Clark, Alun David, Christine Gerrard and Murray Pittock kindly let me read their work in progress, to the great benefit of this book. I am very much indebted to Gill Allen, David Armitage, Jeremy Black, Philip Brett, Donald Burrows, Ted Buttrey, Merlin Channon, Christine Gerrard, Mark Goldie, Paul Langford, Jeremy Maule, Tom McGeary, Murray Pittock, Curtis Price and Mike Smith for the time and thought they gave to reading parts of my text and for their helpful suggestions and encouragement. I am

[1] Mrs Isabella Beeton, *The Book of Household Management* (1861), preface.

grateful too for the support and assistance of Brian Allen, Lord Aylesford, Anne Barton, Ruth, Frances and Frank Benatt, Lorenzo Bianconi, Derek Brewer, Paul and Liz Chipchase, Jane Clark, the late Gerald Coke, the late Peter Croft, Eveline Cruickshanks, the late Charles Cudworth, Rosemary Dooley, Howard Erskine-Hill, George Haggerty, Anthony Hicks, the late Earl Howe, Ann Johnston, Jonathan Keates, Emily Lane, Richard Luckett, Malcolm MacDonald and Libby Valdez, Shan Millie, Arthur Sale, Stewart Sinclair, Brian Skeet, Elsa Strietman, Brian Trowell, Brian Vickers, Marie Wells, Andrew Wilton and my colleagues at Cambridge University Careers Service. The book has been written without the benefit of official faculty or college affiliation, so support from more informal contacts has been proportionately more important and welcome.

I am deeply indebted to the existence, holdings, borrowing regulations and staff of Cambridge University Library (including, of course, its (former) tea room). I am likewise grateful to the staff of the British, Bodleian, and Pendlebury Libraries; to Jacky Cox, archivist, King's College, Cambridge; to Stephen Parks, Curator, Osborn Collection, Yale University Library; and to Frank Stubbings and the staff of Emmanuel College Library, Cambridge, for their help and hospitality. Like many other Handel students I have greatly benefited from the generous welcome of the late Gerald Coke and Mrs Coke, and I gratefully acknowledge permission to quote from material in the Coke Collection.

The Leverhulme Trust has twice sustained this enterprise with a generous research award, for which I am most grateful, not only on account of the financial benefits, but because of the encouragement implied. Grants for scholars in the humanities who are over the age of thirty and who do not have an academic position are not plentiful, and the Trust's enlightened policy and liberality in this regard are keenly appreciated.

At Cambridge University Press Penny Souster's supportive combination of patience and pressure enabled the book to come into being, while Linda Bree's eagle eye saved it from many subeditorial lapses. To both I am very thankful.

This is also the place to mention the two books which I have used most, and which prompted this one. Otto Erich Deutsch's *Handel: A Documentary Biography* (1955) is an inestimable and pioneering collection of contemporary reaction to Handel and his works, and the first half of this book is greatly indebted to it. Winton Dean's *Handel's Dramatic Oratorios and Masques* (1959) set new standards in Handel studies; it brings together a huge amount of essential information in wonderfully accessible style, and remains indispensable. This book is intended to complement it.

Ruth Smith
3 April 1994

Abbreviations

BJECS	*British Journal of Eighteenth-Century Studies*
Dean, *Oratorios*	Winton Dean, *Handel's Dramatic Oratorios and Masques* (1959)
Deutsch	Otto Erich Deutsch, *Handel: A Documentary Biography* (1955)
ECS	*Eighteenth-Century Studies*
GHB	*Göttinger Händel-Beiträge*
HJ	*Historical Journal*
HJb	*Händel Jahrbuch*
HMC	Historical Manuscripts Commission
J/H	Correspondence between Charles Jennens and Edward Holdsworth, Coke Collection
M&L	*Music & Letters*
MT	*Musical Times*
PMLA	*Publications of the Modern Language Association of America*
PQ	*Philological Quarterly*

DATES

Until 1752 the Julian calendar was used in England and the new year began on 25 March; dates for the period 1 January to 24 March are given as in the eighteenth century, in the form '1 January 1742/3'.

Unless otherwise indicated, place of publication is London

Where possible, the edition cited is contemporary with the period of the oratorios' genesis

Introduction

A knowledge of the context remains necessary to a knowledge of
the innovation
      J. G. A. Pocock, *Virtue, Commerce, and History: Essays on Political*
Thought and History, chiefly in the Eighteenth Century (Cambridge, 1985)

PURPOSE AND SCOPE

This book is about the words of Handel's oratorios. In recent
decades concern for historical authenticity has transformed our
reception of baroque music, Handel's included. Scholarly performers strive to recreate for modern ears the sounds that the
composers' first audiences would have heard; music historians
increase modern understanding and enjoyment of the music by
explaining its historical contexts. This book aims to bring a com-
plementary historical perspective to our understanding of the
librettos – the verbal texts – of a mainstay of western culture,
Handel's English oratorios.

It might be thought that such familiar works do not need this
treatment. After all, what is obscure or recondite about, for
example, *Messiah* or *Judas Macchabæus*? Their continual performance
by people of every kind from the date of their composition to the
present proves their accessibility. But though the music is accessible,
the point of the words which Handel set frequently eludes us. To
some of us they are so familiar that we tend not to hear them, far less
think what they mean. Those who have listened to them critically in
the twentieth century have often damned them as worthless. Robert
Manson Myers' comment is representative of this response: 'When
one reads the words of some of Handel's oratorios in cold blood, it
seems nothing short of a miracle that Handel should have been
inspired to write music around them.'[1] Large portions of the ora-

1

torios have been judged defective even by their most enthusiastic
advocates because of their verbal texts. In the major modern study
of Handel's English theatre works Winton Dean writes that *Samson*,
a work which he admires, 'suffers from an excess of diversionary airs:
no fewer than fourteen – exactly half the total – are sung by
anonymous Philistines and Israelites or by Micah [a bystander to
the 'action']. At least eight of these are better omitted if the oratorio
is to retain its shape in modern performance.'[2] Leaving aside the
question of licence to cut according to taste, this proposed rejection
by a leading interpreter of a substantial portion of a major work in
the corpus on grounds of verbal rather than musical text – one of
several such recommendations in Dean's book – fairly indicates that
there is much in the librettos that the twentieth-century audience
finds difficulty in appreciating.[3] Apparently our judgement of what
makes an effective oratorio is often opposed to Handel's. And
Handel's estimate was frequently endorsed by his audience, in
opposition to our own response. For example, *Joseph and his Brethren*,
in modern opinion an almost complete failure largely because of its
dreadful libretto, was popular in his own day.[4] Evidently appreciating the oratorios is not plain sailing, and we still have something to
learn about them. Why did Handel accept those texts which he
chose to set? Why are they constituted as they are? What are the
'diversionary' passages about, and why are they there? Did the
original audiences see things in them that we do not? It is part of my
aim to raise such questions and suggest answers to them.

   This book develops ideas first outlined in 1983, when I argued
that we would enlarge our understanding and enjoyment of
Handel's oratorios and his other English theatre works if we took
account of their intellectual contexts.[5] This approach gives a different perspective on the compositions from that afforded by previous
studies, which are grounded in biography or music criticism and
scholarship.[6] Handel is no longer the focus; the words and the ideas
in and behind his compositions come to the fore. The basic method is
familiar: looking at a body of creative work against its intellectual
background, relating it to the relevant ideas and preoccupations of
the time.[7] The procedure is routine for the creative literature of the
period but has only recently begun to be adopted for its musical-
literary works. The novelty of approach is in the particular combination of work and background: there has been no previous attempt
on this scale to examine the words of Handel's oratorios in relation

to the thought of their time.[8] It is long overdue. Dean called for a study of Handel's English librettists in 1959 but, before and since, they have been neglected, to an astonishing extent: witness the many accounts which give the impression that Handel wrote his own oratorio librettos. When I outline my subject-matter to educated non-specialists, their most frequent first response is 'Didn't Handel write them himself, then?'; they can hardly be blamed for their ignorance on this score when both specialist musicologists and leading cultural historians still give the impression that he did.[9]

This book discusses the librettos but only occasionally touches on the music. Happily it is no longer necessary to argue the importance of librettos and their authors in the study of major words-and-music compositions, an importance acknowledged in, for example, the prominence given them by *The New Grove Dictionary of Opera*. In the case of Handel's oratorios and other English theatre works the separation of text and music for the purpose of increased under-standing seems to me legitimate. Handel did not, so far as we know, write any of the librettos (see Appendix 1 for librettos, authors and sources). He was not a proto-Wagner. Nor was his collaboration with his librettists of a Strauss–von Hofmannsthal intensity (it would have been very unusual for its time if it had been). In the very scant surviving correspondence of composer and librettists we have only a single indication of his suggesting new verbal material: Charles Jennens reported that he wrote 'Il Moderato' to conclude his rearrangement of Milton's *L'Allegro* and *Il Penseroso* 'at Mr Handel's request'.[10] More usually, so far as we can tell, Handel's involvement with his librettists' texts consisted of editing them, principally cutting them (to what extent this was a collaborative exercise we are often uncertain). As Dean has shown, Handel and his librettists often seem to have had different ends in view; this reflects not only the circumstance of the collaborators working independently for at least some of the process, but also, as this book will suggest, differing priorities, which need to be more clearly distinguished than studies concentrating on the music have allowed. Handel's working relationship with his librettists is outlined in the second part of this introduction. Finally, there is more than enough to say in one book about the librettos and the ideas which shaped them without attempting discussion of their musical setting. But new findings about the librettos bring new light to Handel's treatment of them, and I invite musicologists to go on from here. The initial survey which I made of this material was drawn on by a musicologist and a literary historian to show Handel's response to what the librettist provided; the present book will have succeeded if it prompts further studies of the same kind.[11]

But analysing the librettos is not easy. Handel's impact on his librettos is so powerful, there is so much to notice and say about his settings of the words (and about all the additional music), that the words themselves have tended to be viewed as it were backwards. Our understanding of the words is coloured, often distorted, by the impression which the music makes on us and, as Dean in particular pointed out, the music often imposes its own flagrant distortion (one of the major themes of his book is Handel's readiness to override the apparent meaning of the librettist's words with the music to which he set them). Once one knows the music it is hard to read the words without hearing the transforming musical versions of them in one's head, as one scholar candidly admits in his own approach to *Messiah*: 'it is impossible to-day to separate the text from the music'.[12] But I believe the effort to separate the text from the music is worth making, since it will increase our understanding and appreciation of these literary-musical compositions. Handel's English librettos were compiled or written by English men of letters who drew on major literary sources, including Sophocles, the Bible, Dryden and Milton. The process of clarifying the oratorios' make-up is served by identifying the texts the librettists chose to adapt, the selections they made from them and the alterations they effected; asking the reasons for their preferences and changes; and recognising the ideas which their productions express. These lines of enquiry are central to the present undertaking. They yield the conclusions that Handel's oratorio librettos made considerably more meanings available to their original audiences than we now realise, that these meanings can be identified by reference to ideas current at the time, and that the librettos, and hence Handel's English works, encapsulate views current in their time on major issues of their day. What these ideas and views were is worth identifying. In the same way that 'authentic' performance reveals unsuspected musical vitality, so the recovery of verbal meanings in the oratorios enables us to understand what captured the interest of the original audiences and so increase the depth and range of our own responses.

The sense of the words has been muffled not only by the power of Handel's music but by conceptions of the nature of the oratorios influenced by subjective response. The pioneering work of Young, Dean and some of their successors rescued Handel from his distorting and bowdlerising nineteenth-century editors, but remade him to suit their own tastes. The work which has dominated the study of Handel's English theatre music since its publication and which will continue to be indispensable on account of its vast quantity of illuminating information, Dean's *Handel's Dramatic Oratorios and Masques* (1959), proclaims in its title that the key element sought and found in its subject is the ability to dramatise. And for Dean, drama chiefly means the portrayal of characters reacting and interacting, the interplay of motive and emotion within and between characters, and strongly plotted action. This is what he most admires, what he looks for, what he rejoices to find and regrets to find lacking. The very human inclination, shared by all generations of interpreters, to define their subject according to their own preferences, is positive in that it helps to engage their contemporaries' enthusiasm on their subject's behalf (as Dean has done for a whole generation of listeners and interpreters), but it risks several kinds of distortion.

Firstly, to make dramatisation of character the defining element imposes a particular definition on the corpus. Of Handel's twenty-five English theatre works Dean selected for detailed discussion only the eighteen with named characters, relegating the others – *Israel in Egypt, Alexander's Feast*, the *Ode for St Cecilia's Day, L'allegro, il penseroso ed il moderato, Messiah*, the *Occasional Oratorio* and *The Triumph of Time and Truth* – to the margins. This selection gives the sense that parts of the corpus, including works generally regarded as among Handel's greatest achievements, do not merit the highest regard because they do not match the criterion 'dramatic'. Secondly, while selection on these terms has proved invigorating to enjoyment and performance of Handel's music, it negates the strong connections between works discussed and works excluded. The selection runs counter to, and so has tended to obscure, the major distinction drawn in Handel's own time, not between works with and without *dramatis personae* but between sacred and secular works. Handel's advertisements for his premières use the designation 'oratorio' consistently and exclusively for those works with religious subjects. Thirdly, the 'dramatic' criterion leads to the dismissal from serious consideration of large tracts of the librettos even of the selected works, and even whole librettos. Dean writes of *Joseph and his Brethren*: 'The essential requirements for a composer, firm construction, distinct characters, interesting situations, and concrete imagery, are wholly to seek.'[13] Whether they were of prime importance to the librettist, even whether he thought in such terms, is not considered; what the librettist's aims and criteria actually were, and what he did provide, remains to be objectively elucidated. In fact (fourthly), Dean himself constantly shows that these 'essential requirements' were not necessary for Handel to produce great music, and the existence of *Messiah* proves it. The librettist often provided, and Handel often responded magnificently to, elements other than character and plot. These elements often spring from the concerns of the collaborators' own time, from beliefs, standards and principles to which Dean is unsympathetic.[14] His contempt for mid-eighteenth-century moral and cultural canons, particularly moral didacticism in art, leads him to find that Handel persistently 'transcends' the 'limited sympathies and narrow didacticism of his librettists'.[15] The inference (for which I am unaware of any non-musical evidence) is that Handel did not share the artistic and moral assumptions of his contemporaries and (a fifth form of distortion) deflects serious attention away from these assumptions and their presence in the oratorios. Finally, while it is true that many of the oratorios are dramas, it is even truer if we use the criteria of their own time rather than ours to define 'dramatic'. For the eighteenth-century audience, more of Handel's English works, and more within them, would have seemed dramatic than Dean allows. *Acis and Galatea, Esther, Athalia, Semele, Joseph, Hercules, Alexander Balus, Susanna, Theodora* and *Jephtha* all exhibit characteristics of eighteenth-century sentimental drama, and a study of Handel's English works as *eighteenth-century* theatre is overdue (Brett and Haggerty have shown how satisfying it would be[16]). The ahistorical stance of Dean's appraisal has had its critics. William C. Smith, for example, commented that 'scholars and writers . . . are not fair to the subject when the Handel they create for us is a present day figurehead fashioned out of their own philosophy'.[17] The balance is beginning to be redressed, but much remains to be done.

My enquiry, following eighteenth-century definitions of oratorio, focuses on the librettos with religious themes (but many of its findings are relevant to the librettos of Handel's secular English theatre works). It attempts to recover the eighteenth-century perspective by making an objective survey of the ideas in the librettos, and to yield a fuller understanding of the completed works by understanding what they could have meant in their own day. Much in the oratorios which seems irrelevant or insipid to us would have been, on the contrary, fully engaging for Handel's first audiences. In order to recognise the librettos' meanings we need to recognise the impact on them of the thought of their time and to appreciate the artistic and moral criteria that influenced their authors. Contemporary aesthetic prescription, religious discourse, moral teaching and political ideology provide the entry points. (There is a parallel in our need to appreciate the primacy which the eighteenth century accorded to the constituent elements of 'history painting' – a genre that leaves many modern viewers cold – before we can respond fully to its art.) Hence this study occupies what Pat Rogers – to my mind with excessive deprecation – has called 'not so much musicology as the humbler province of contextualization'.[18] It evaluates the librettos not as satisfying artistic constructs or as vehicles for the composer's skill but as reflections and embodiments of the *ideas* of their time. By 'their time' I mean the time of their creation and first performance, not of their later reception (much study of the ideas in the oratorios has been confused by back-projection from the reception accorded them in the later eighteenth century[19]). Part I locates the oratorios' English origins in contemporary prescriptions for literature and music and contemporary religious debate. Part II first establishes the forms of discourse available to and used by the librettists, then identifies major contemporary concerns – moral, religious and political – which are apparent in the oratorios, and finally discusses the reflection of these concerns in individual librettos.

It was Dean's contention that Handel was strikingly independent of the received opinions of his time and that his oratorios are highly original works. In his account of Dryden's political poetry Stephen Zwicker comments that 'Literary historians who find Dryden innovative ... more often than not reveal uncertainties in their grasp of seventeenth-century literary and intellectual contexts'.[20] Correspondingly, once we know the context, we usually have to revise our view of an artist's 'originality'. This has happened with Handel in the twentieth century and even in his own time when informed listeners recognised his use of other composers' material and models. Handel was no maverick, and the absorption of his society's ideas into his works is consistent with his compositional practice of building on its musical forms.[21] Some readers may feel that the oratorios, or at least the librettos, are diminished by an awareness that their verbal texts embody received ideas, and for them this second-handedness will widen the gap which they already perceive between what they regard as the librettos' artistic inferiority and Handel's genius. I find that, on the contrary, it is immensely satisfying to understand why the librettos are as they are, and to recognise in them the intellectual, emotional, political and spiritual preoccupations, questions and solutions (however well or ineptly handled) of eighteenth-century authors and audiences. Analysing the subsoil in which the librettos have their taproots, and as a result understanding the components of the plant itself, makes a performance of *Messiah, Joshua* or *Alexander's Feast* (or any of the oratorios, odes and dramas) a richer experience; and seeing in the librettos the reflection of much eighteenth-century thought is to put another piece in place in the jigsaw of eighteenth-century intellectual history. Past attempts to explain Handel's oratorios by categorising them have proved hazardous, the categories being overwhelmed by the number of qualifications they entailed.[22] But setting the librettos in the light of contemporary ideas illuminates common themes in oratorios which have previously seemed widely diverse in subject and quality. This yields a more satisfactory description of the genre than we have so far achieved – establishes it, in fact, *as* a genre, on the grounds of consistency of ideas and their expression, and shows it to be not a thing apart but a signal repository of the prevailing ideas of its time and a major conduit of eighteenth-century sensibility and thought.

The dominant influences on mid-eighteenth-century English thought were religion and politics. They permeated life and art, and they permeate this book. This was still a culture in which (as much recent historiography has reminded us) religious belief and the morality taught by religion informed prescriptions for the content of works of art and the works themselves. The pulpit was the major public-address system. Sermons addressed and influenced every aspect of private and public life (including art), religious debate was a major element of intellectual life, religious publications dominated book production, and people believed that God supervised their lives and could and would intervene with punishment on a personal or national scale if provoked by wrongdoing.[23] It has been persuasively argued that the arts, including music, were fostered by the Church of England in order to increase piety and religious orthodoxy.[24] Creating a Handel who speaks to the secular mid twentieth century made it fashionable to dismiss as apocryphal anecdotes from his own time illustrating his commitment to Protestant belief.[25] Edward Fitzgerald's phrase that he was 'pagan at heart'[26] has been supported with interpretations of his music, usually without acknowledgement that the music in question illustrates a dramatic fiction. For Dean and many successors influenced by him, religion in Handel's oratorios is closer to ethical humanism than to Protestant Christianity: 'the God of the greater oratorios is not the jealous Jehovah of the Old Testament, still less the Christian God of the Atonement, but rather the remote and impartial controller of man's destiny'.[27] Besides being a reading that is impossible if *Israel in Egypt* and *Messiah* are taken into account, this is to suggest that the oratorio authors had and expressed beliefs which would have been considered freakish, if not blasphemous, in their own time, and would have set them completely apart from the society they were addressing. But the writers of the librettos were members, or even ministers, of the Church of England. Unsurprisingly, comparison of their texts with contemporary Anglican writing reveals the very considerable extent to which Handel was given conventional doctrinal material to set, and endorses Larsen's observation that 'Oratorio acknowledges two masters, the church and the theatre.'[28] Separating artistic concerns from those of religion and morality in a way which would have been incomprehensible to the eighteenth century, Dean stated of Handel's concern in the oratorios: 'The voice of the moralist, the preacher, and the propagandist he rejected'.[29] But these are precisely the voices which we will find resounding through the librettos. If Dean is right, Handel was even further at variance with his librettists and his contemporaries than Dean himself has suggested. Or maybe Handel was more attuned to the evangelical Protestantism of his librettos than his secularised portrait suggests.

In the mid eighteenth century religion was bound up with politics: 'There was no conceptual separation between issues of Church and state, religion and politics'.[30] Full participation in citizenship depended on conformity to the Church of England. The Stuart claimants to the British throne were Catholic and, it was feared, would impose Catholicism if they regained power. The (Lutheran) Hanoverians were accepted as rulers of Britain by many of their subjects because they safeguarded Protestantism and supported the

Church of England. European and international politics tended to be aligned according to Protestant versus Catholic national identity. Linda Colley has convincingly argued that Protestantism was the chief defining characteristic of British nationhood (including Handel's oratorios in her evidence): 'Protestantism determined how most Britons viewed their politics. And an uncompromising Protestantism was the foundation on which their state was explicitly and unapologetically based'.[31] It was not only conservative members of the Church of England who connected political stability with the dominance of Protestantism. Low Church and Dissenting opponents of 'priestcraft' (a key trigger word, connoting attempts by the clergy to take over political power) were equally ready to suspect that those 'endeavouring to root out the Christian Religion' from British minds were 'making their utmost Efforts for the bringing back Popery, Slavery, and the Pretender' (in other words, fomenting anarchy). It was generally agreed that 'the establish'd Religion in every Country, and especially every Free Country, is the Foundation and Basis of the Publick Spirit and Publick Virtue of that Country', and that 'The Original Contract . . . between the Prince and the People', which is 'the very Life and Soul of the Constitution of *Great Britain*' unquestionably 'depends upon the Influence and Efficacy of the Christian Religion'.[32] The national (Protestant) religion and the national (non-arbitrary) government were mutually dependent. National celebrations (for example anniversaries of royal accessions) and national crises (war or natural disasters) were the occasions for special church services and special sermons and these, time and again, as later chapters describe, delivered their messages by comparing the British nation with the biblical Israelites. Secular political discourse, from tracts on statecraft to speeches in Parliament, used the same analogy.

The meshing of religion and politics in the fourteen oratorios about the Israelite nation would have seemed entirely natural to their first audiences. The presence of political themes in these works of art and entertainment would also have been unsurprising. As at no other period before or since, politics pervaded literature and music theatre, and, as much contemporary testimony asserts, the nation was unusually politically aware and opinionated, from top to bottom of society. From the moment that Handel first arrived in England, he was involved in producing music for national events. The librettists would have been unusual if they had excluded political themes from their texts, and oratorio audiences would have been behaving anachronistically if they had not found political themes in them.

To read specific meaning in texts is to raise questions about the authors' and audiences' apprehension of those texts: *did* the authors intend, did the audiences perceive, these meanings? In the period of the oratorios' creation literary meaning was famously multiple, ambiguous and variously received. I do not wish to claim that all members of Handel's oratorio audience received all the meanings identified in the librettos in the course of this book; rather I suggest that these meanings were perceptible and available to them, on the grounds that they were common currency and were often embodied and recognised in other literary productions available to them. I have already mentioned the authors' subscription to the commonly accepted religious and moral tenets of their time. The more complicated questions of their attitude to prevailing political ideologies in relation to the presence of these ideologies in the librettos, and their audience's perception of them there, are discussed at the beginning of Part II.

BOUNDARIES

It is necessary to specify the limits of this study. The 'oratorios' of my title are English, Handel's single German and two Italian oratorios (the *Brockes-Passion, Il Trionfo del Tempo e del Disinganno* and *La Resurrezione*) being excluded from the discussion. By excluding the non-religious theatre works (*Acis and Galatea, Alexander's Feast,* the *Ode for St Cecilia's Day, L'allegro, il penseroso ed il moderato, Semele, Hercules, The Choice of Hercules* and *The Triumph of Time and Truth*) from detailed consideration I have left a major, distinct (and in my view most attractive) topic to be pursued by a literary historian with an understanding of music: the relation of the dramas and odes to contemporary literary prescription and practice, and – a desirable extension of the topic on account of their emotiveness – Handel's treatment of their librettos. The topic could also include related aspects which are excluded from my discussion, the detail of the librettos' versification or paraphrase, their critical standing and their affectiveness.

The 'eighteenth-century thought' of my title is likewise English, and mainly the common currency of its time – thought which was

readily available, if not second nature, to the librettists and their
intended audiences. My aim being to read the librettos with the eyes
of their contemporaries, I have not taken account of unfamiliar
continental, minority-view or obscure publications, or of works in
manuscript which were not widely circulated, with the exception of
the librettists' own writings. An omission here is the possible influence of freemasonry (Solomon and Cyrus, both oratorio heroes, are
also potent figures in masonic culture).[33] A scholar tough enough to
take on this difficult area of eighteenth-century studies might like to
test my guess that freemasonry did not influence the librettists or
public understanding of their works.[34] My cut-off date being 1752
(the date of the first performance of *Jephtha*, Handel's last English
theatre work to a 'new' text), I have not taken account of contemporary writing much after the early 1750s.

There is no one authoritative text for any of the librettos or
oratorios. My basic text, unless otherwise stated, is the wordbook –
the printed libretto – for the first performance (British Library
and/or Rowe Library, King's College, Cambridge). This is also my
source for the title by which I refer to an oratorio.[35] 'Repeated and
extensive revising is a very Augustan habit',[36] and Handel was
wholly Augustan in this regard. The substantial second thoughts
that (as Dean showed) preceded many first performances and the
revisions which Handel made to nearly every work for nearly every
season are outside the scope of this book, but performances after the
first could and sometimes did involve the librettist, and any complete study of a librettist or of the genesis of an individual work
should take account of them.[37]

I am concentrating on the genesis of the oratorios up to and
including their first performance. With one exception (*Athalia*) this
was always in a capital city (London and, exceptionally, Dublin); so
my focus neglects the importance of the provinces which, recent
studies have shown, must be taken into account in any whole view of
eighteenth-century Britain.[38] My interest is in texts, ideas and
events rather than social setting (but the questions raised by location
are discussed in Part I). The social class of the audience is important
to reception but less so to conception, and I do not explore it in
detail (it is outlined at the end of this Introduction).

According to Paul Langford's standard survey of eighteenth-
century Britain, 'The potential of eighteenth-century music studies
beyond musicology itself has yet to be exploited.'[39] I hope this book
will join other recent studies to render his comment dated, will help

to answer Linda Colley's call for someone to explore the connection between music and the identity of eighteenth-century Britons,[40] and will contribute to the erosion of the boundaries between disciplines which the proliferation of knowledge obliges experts to draw. In this respect it should have a twofold result, showing audiences and students that the intellectual concerns of mid-eighteenth-century England are relevant to an appreciation of Handel's English works, and showing historians of eighteenth-century English thought that these texts are part of their material. But an interdisciplinary work of this scope is unlikely to be exhaustive. Citations of secondary sources in literary, theological and political fields are selective. Nor are primary sources comprehensively charted: for example, many major eighteenth-century writers, additional to those already cited, could have been invoked to endorse my arguments. My intention is not inclusiveness, rather to open up the terrain and point out its major features, encouraging others to continue to explore it. Correspondingly, in a book spanning academic disciplines it is impossible to avoid telling some readers, some of the time, what they already know. Political historians will be familiar with many of the themes of Part II, and their interpretations; music historians will recognise some of the material in Part I. I hope both will find enough novelty to carry them over the familiar ground. To help with orientation in unfamiliar territory, references include overviews and syntheses. I hope this book will lead to a more digestible one on the same subject, but first its arguments need to be laid out on the usual academic basis of supporting evidence. That said, some of the conclusions I draw from the evidence are suggestions, not proofs, and need further testing and investigation.

THE COMPOSER, THE LIBRETTISTS, THE PRODUCT

In order to understand the nature of the librettos we need to try to understand Handel's compositional aims, the resources available to him and the demands of his audiences. What can we discern about his rationale?

Handel's oratorio career

Handel is credited with introducing oratorio to England, but the first public performance of one of his own oratorios apparently happened without any initiative on his part. There was a preliminary. In

February 1732, probably to celebrate Handel's birthday, his friend Bernard Gates, Master of the Children of the Chapel Royal, mounted a performance, under the auspices of the Philarmonic [sic] Society (also known as the 'Society of the Gentlemen Performers of Musick'), of *Esther*, which Handel had written in 1718 for private performance at Cannons, the country estate of his then patron, the Earl of Carnarvon (James Brydges, later Duke of Chandos).[41] This revival (repeated in March) was private, but the music must have been 'leaked', because in April there was a public performance – unauthorised by the composer – at York Buildings, London's main concert venue.[42] Likewise the first public performances of Handel's secular masque for Chandos, *Acis and Galatea*, were given without his involvement, also around this time, by John Rich at Lincoln's Inn Fields in March 1731 and in May 1732 by the Arne–Lampe company at the New Theatre in the Haymarket. This latter company was pulling audiences away from Italian opera with the biggest and most successful run of English operas London had ever experienced, as a pamphleteer reported: 'I left the *Italian* Opera, the House was so thin, and cross'd over the way to the *English* one, which was so full I was forc'd to croud in upon the Stage, and even that was thronged ... This alarm'd *H—l*, and out he brings an *Oratorio*.'[43] According to this author and in the view of later interpreters, Handel's own first production of an oratorio for the British public was a response to competition: a reactive and oppor-tunist move which yielded a hybrid, patchwork result, the rapid revision of *Esther*. However, as Part I of this book shows, there were also strong currents of musical, literary and moral opinion encour-aging such a venture and creating a favourable climate for its acceptance.

From 1719 to 1738 Handel's prime commitment was to Italian opera. But he was an entrepreneur, and he acted swiftly to capitalise on the apparent vogue for English works and on public interest in his domestic products by mounting his own performances of both *Esther* and *Acis*. Even so he might not have responded to the provo-cation of piracy had he not had a mandate from the highest quarter. According to the eighteenth-century music historian Charles Burney, his *Esther* of May 1732 was prompted by his music-loving pupil Princess Anne, the Princess Royal, 'who was pleased to express a desire to see it exhibited in action at the Opera-house in the Hay-market'.[44] The royal family attended several of his performances in 1732, both his first, on 2 May, and a revival on 12 March 1733 being advertised as 'By his Majesty's command'.[45] What they heard was not Chandos' *Esther* but an altered, unacted and distended version, tactfully padded with two of the four anthems Handel had written for George and Caroline's coronation in 1727 and music from the Birthday Ode for Queen Anne – the current royal family's illustrious predecessor on the British throne, during whose reign their own succession to it had been established. The composition was billed as an oratorio, and further padding was drawn from oratorios Handel had written for other countries, *La Resurrezione* (Rome, 1708) and the *Brockes-Passion* (performed Hamburg, 1719). For the additional words Handel turned to his current literary assistant, Samuel Humphreys, who had been providing English translations for his Italian opera wordbooks and who was also employed by the competition as an English opera librettist.[46]

Interestingly, both the Cannons *Esther* and the Cannons *Acis*, like their 1732 revivals, can be seen as responses to current musical fashion. They were written at what turned out to be the end of three years of exceptional activity in the virtually new field of all-sung English masque (opera in all but length) among composers of German extraction working in England. This yielded four works by Handel's Cannons colleague J. C. Pepusch and two by John Galliard. Galliard's earlier *Calypso and Telemachus* (1712) was reputedly admired by Handel and had a libretto by John Hughes, the author of probably the first English words Handel himself set.[47] The urge to respond in kind to new music theatre developments, and master them, is traceable throughout Handel's career. There may also have been influences at work from an early and particularly formative stage. During the years 1707–9, when he was in his early twenties, he worked in Rome in the household of Marquis (later Prince) Francesco Ruspoli, primarily as a composer of cantatas for meetings of the Arcadian Academy. This club in which noblemen and artists mixed, the one sponsoring the work of the other, was professedly dedicated to restoring the simplicity and naturalness of the pastoral ideal to opera (hence the production of cantatas with pastoral themes), but its immediate models were the highly formal and moral dramas of Racine and Corneille.[48] Handel's social context at Burlington House and Cannons a decade later – again a mixture of noblemen, intellectuals and artists – was more like the Ruspoli milieu than any he had experienced in the interim, and it is possible that his admission to these sophisticated, close-knit communities would prompt him to pass the creative ideas of the Roman group on to the English one, yielding both a pastoral work and one drawn from Racine (Ruspoli himself had commissioned Handel's first, Italian, version of the story of Acis and Galatea).[49]

The original *Esther* was typical of the majority of later oratorio librettos in being a newly written text dramatising the biblical and apocryphal narratives (sometimes paraphrasing Scripture, sometimes inventing incidents). The use of an intermediary source (Racine's *Esther*) also set a pattern adopted by some later librettists, for example Newburgh Hamilton, who used *Samson Agonistes* and thirteen other poems and psalm paraphrases by Milton for his *Samson*. The anthems inserted in the later version of *Esther* represent another and less frequent strain of libretto composition, using actual scriptural text (only *Israel in Egypt* and *Messiah* consist entirely of biblical words or the versions of them in the Book of Common Prayer). The venue in 1732, as for nearly all Handel's subsequent oratorio performances, was a theatre. The decision to dispense with stage action was probably not his (according to Burney, it followed from a fiat by the Bishop of London before his first performance); but he does not seem to have tried to reverse it. As we shall see, it accorded with some aesthetic prescriptions of the time. Several other facts about his relationship with his first oratorio also pertain to the rest of his English output. He never regarded his works as inviolable; he habitually altered them for revivals. He had no fixed policy about the structural detail or verbal content of a libretto. He did not, so far as we know, compile or write the words himself; and though it appears that once an author had provided him with a workable text Handel went back to him for more librettos or accepted further offers from him, there is no indication that he had a programme for selecting a librettist.

The *Esther* formula proving successful, Handel repeated it for *Acis*, mounting his own performance but trumping the piratical competition by offering, under the same title, a work on a much larger scale, with far more performers and in two languages. Fewer than half the resulting numbers belonged to the Cannons original.[50] This too was successful, and next year he capitalised on *Esther* again by producing *Deborah*, this time with wholly new words but again with Humphreys as librettist, again meeting the challenge of competition (his rival Maurice Greene's *The Song of Deborah and Barak*, 1732)[51] with a bigger work, again invoking royal patronage (the libretto was dedicated to Queen Caroline), and again celebrating an Old Testament heroine who saves her nation from destruction by foreign oppressors. In this last respect he and Humphreys were picking up the gauntlet recently thrown down by James Thomson in his tragedy *Sophonisba*: 'A female patriot! – Vanity! – Absurd!' (Act IV scene 2), and supporting Thomson's more direct plea, in the play's epilogue addressed to the women in the audience, to set the men an example and act like patriots. Again he gave patriotism a royalist Hanoverian slant by recycling the Coronation Anthems. Indeed the bulk of *Deborah*'s music, like *Esther*'s, was reused from previous compositions. So far he had not actually composed an oratorio *ab initio*.

When *Deborah* severely dented his reputation among his potential patrons in the capital (though for non-musical reasons, see chapter 9), he responded accordingly. His next English work, the oratorio *Athalia* (1733, based on Racine's other sacred drama), was written for Oxford and not produced in London until 1735. Charles Jennens, who was present at the first performance of *Athalia*, sent him an oratorio libretto in July 1735 (of what is unknown), but Handel launched no new oratorio in London until 1739. *Alexander's Feast* (1736), his first secular English setting since *Acis*, was a huge success but an unrepeatable *mélange*: Dryden's ode, a text recognised by contemporaries and put forward by Hamilton in his preface to the libretto as a masterpiece of English verse which had been waiting forty years for adequate realisation, was spliced with an Italian cantata and several instrumental pieces to make up an evening's entertainment.[52]

Handel's performances in the following season, 1736–7, similarly aimed to please every taste: six Italian operas, an Italian serenata, an Italian oratorio, an English ode, and an English oratorio.[53] The year 1737 was also a climacteric. Handel suffered what seems to have been a stroke, partial paralysis and a nervous breakdown, audiences flocked to the burlesque operas which ridiculed Italian opera, and the Opera of the Nobility folded.[54] When Handel returned to composing, he devoted more energy to English works. After capitalising on the public response to Dryden by setting his other St Cecilia ode (not, however, a full-length work) he produced three very different English settings in 1739–40 – *Saul*, based on Scripture but wholly written by Jennens, *Israel in Egypt*, wholly selected (probably by Jennens) from Scripture, and *L'allegro, il penseroso ed il moderato*, arranged by Jennens from Milton with additional text supplied by Jennens at Handel's request.[55] Then there was another pause in the production of new English works, the next one, *Messiah*, being launched in Dublin in 1742. Until now Handel's theatre seasons had comprised a mixture of Italian operas and English settings. He was already 55 when he presented a new Italian opera for the last time, and a letter of 1743 reports him as still vacillating about whether to write one or two more.[56] It was twenty-five years after composing his first English oratorio and only nine years before his last, in 1743, that he began offering new English works in the British capital every year. In the two years following his final rejection of Italian opera he produced *Semele* and *Hercules*, the nearest he ever came to English opera. They were his last secular dramas and they failed to gain public approval.[57] Thereafter he wrote only oratorios and two near-oratorios, the moral allegories *The Choice of Hercules* (1750) and *The Triumph of Time and Truth* (1757, a revision of an earlier work). As others have pointed out, Handel does not appear to have had anything approaching a long-term 'vision' or 'mission' or even 'programme' for his English settings, and oratorio as we commonly think of it evolved by fits and starts, driven by what seem to have been his contending interests – concern for box office returns, ambition to be London's leading composer by dominating current fashion, determination to out-manoeuvre competition, and the urge to write to his strengths as he perceived them.

Responding to public taste

Market forces were crucial to Handel in his ventures addressed to the paying public, because his only regular income, from the court, could not cover serious losses on them. While his contractual arrangements for opera and oratorio production in this early period of oratorio are still opaque, though much clarified by Judith Milhous and Robert Hume,[58] we know that he bore some of the financial risk and could not rely on a profitable return. In the course of his English career he took increasing responsibility for the management of his theatre performances, to the extent of acting as his own impresario – hiring the theatre, singers and orchestra, determining the method of ticket-buying (initially a mix of seasonal subscriptions and casual sales, later dispensing with the subscription system), fixing the prices and organising the publicity. His riposte to his singer Alexander Gordon, who had threatened to jump on the harpsichord in protest against his accompaniments – 'Let me know when you do that and I will advertise it; for I am sure more people will come to see you jump than to hear you sing' – if apocryphal, was nevertheless perpetuated presumably because it was highly characteristic, and is eloquent evidence of Handel's grasp of the rules of financial management. His first, immediate thought was for market value and market share. High-art music theatre, even unstaged, was (then as now) expensive to put on. Oratorio, in the pattern initiated by *Esther*, used larger forces than Italian opera: a chorus in addition to soloists and a more massive and varied orchestra. But it did not need (though initially it had) the exorbitantly priced Italian stars, new costumes and fancy sets expected by the Italian opera's public. Moreover, unacted works, unlike opera, could be performed on Wednesdays and Fridays during Lent (and oratorio was not confined to Lent).[59] In 1732 Handel's theatre company, assembled to perform Italian opera, starred Italian singers (for musical and box-office reasons),[60] and for some of his audience at least, this reduced the viability of works in English; the pamphleteer already quoted was quick to complain of Handel's first performances of *Esther* that '*Senesino* and *Bertolli* made rare work with the *English* Tongue you would have sworn it had been *Welch*; I would have wish'd it *Italian*, that they might have sung with more ease to themselves, since, but for the Name of *English*, it might as well have been *Hebrew*'. His rehashed *Acis*, and revivals of other works in the 1730s, in which his Italian and English soloists sang in their own languages, may indicate a response to this criticism. He lost most of his Italian singers in 1733 and replaced them with English ones, so this problem was on the way to being met; however, the concerted attempt to establish English opera in 1732–3 fizzling out, he also lost one major spur to English word-setting, and for the next season he reassembled an Italian cast, now responding to the competition mounted by the Italian opera productions of the Opera of the Nobility (1733–7), to which most of his previous singers had deserted. For Handel to run two separate companies, one English and one Italian, would have been economically impossible; however, a compromise was gradually reached on the language issue. His public began to accept Italian singers of English words, and he increasingly cultivated English singers.[61] English music theatre was virtually annexed meanwhile by ballad operas – over a hundred were composed in the ten years following the huge success of *The Beggar's Opera* in 1728 – but Handel was not interested in bettering comic or part-spoken productions on their own ground.

The messages Handel received from the public response to his works in these early years of oratorio were confusing. The taste for virtuoso Italian artists co-existed with fierce xenophobia, while experiments in composition, encouraged by a constant demand for variety and novelty, risked being rejected as too newfangled. Nor did competition cease once he had embraced English texts: he had to contend with spoiling or copycat productions by other exploiters of the oratorio vein. In 1740 Lockman and Smith's *David's Lamentation over Saul and Jonathan* was put on at Hickford's rooms while his own *Saul* played at Lincoln's Inn Fields, and in 1745 De Fesch's *Joseph* at Covent Garden coincided with his own *Joseph* at the King's Theatre.[62] While we have no firm evidence for Handel's motivation, most scholars agree that it was his love for Italian opera which chiefly delayed his readiness to satisfy the public demand for English works. It is possible to make out a musical rationale for Handel's loyalty to Italian opera in the 1730s. English singers were unable to sing such elaborate music as he wanted to compose; only Italian singers had the technique for what was currently the most complex solo vocal music being written (a sore point for nationalists such as Defoe, who urged the foundation of an English music school to make expensive Italian talent redundant[63]). But the Italians could not sing English convincingly. On the other hand there were no English singers available who had the theatrical talent for the parts he enjoyed writing for male leads, such as the heroic pathetic (the kind for which Senesino was famous), let alone the musical capacities of the castrato which afforded scope for the thrilling effect of several high voices set off against each other. (It is significant in this connection that, as Dean pointed out, Handel selected several of his principal English singers for their *acting* ability.[64]) The ideal form of opera which Aaron Hill had proposed at the start of Handel's English career, in the preface to the libretto of their *Rinaldo* – which, unlike that opera, would be musically Italian but verbally English – had a daunting battery of circumstances ranged against it.

The complexity and elaborateness of much of Handel's aria writing had always distinguished him in the London opera public's view, not always favourably, from his fellow composers of Italian opera. Though he was capable of exquisite simplicity, he was evidently not inclined to adopt to any large extent the more homophonic style of Neapolitan composers writing for the Opera of the Nobility or the 'modern' *galant* style. But in English ode and oratorio his penchant for complexity found another kind of fulfilment, transferred from aria to chorus. This was an immensely practical move, in that while the English did not train opera singers they did train chorus singers, in the choirs of the Chapel Royal, St Paul's and Westminster Abbey, and these were the institutions which provided Handel's oratorio chorus members. His first oratorios for London were marked by heavy injections of anthems, which these choirs specialised in performing, and Handel's were exceptionally varied, elaborate, dense and weighty by comparison with earlier English music for choirs. His experiment in this direction culminated in an oratorio which was mainly anthem, *Israel in Egypt* (as Larsen pointed out, even the 'solos' in this work are choruses, partly because the text is descriptive narrative which, as Silke Leopold noted, could not sensibly be transmitted in a da capo aria[65]). This amount of choral music was too much for his public, but he continued to use the chorus to satisfy his desire to compose highly wrought, extended movements, even in contexts where dramatically they seem (at least to later listeners) inappropriate;[66] and contemporary comments repeatedly acknowledge that the complexity, density and scale of his choruses and accompaniments were unprecedented in English music.[67] The first sustained critique of his style, the conclusion to the account of his life published in 1760,[68] sees this and the pathetic power of his solos as the distinctive features of his musical style, as do many individual remarks of the time. This is not to say that Handel turned to oratorio simply because he saw the potential of the chorus as the only available vehicle for music of a kind he wanted to write, rather that this may have been a strong contributory motive. Adopting a large and prominent chorus as a fixed element of his English theatre works obviously had major consequences for the compilation of any libretto (on the contemporary critical encouragement to revive the use of the chorus in drama and music drama see chapter 2).

Handel's apparent lack of consistent artistic purpose in setting English texts may be partly responsible for our own lack of clarity about the defining qualities of the resulting works. *Acis* (a masque),

Alexander's Feast, the *Ode for St Cecilia's Day* and *L'allegro* (odes), *Semele* and *Hercules* (unacted dramas) and *The Choice of Hercules* (allegorical unacted drama) are still often referred to as oratorios because, like his oratorios, they are in English, were unacted, and are sung throughout by soloists and chorus with orchestral accompaniment, the singers often representing *dramatis personae*. Musically, it was above all the chorus which distinguished Handel's English theatre productions from his Italian operas in his public's ears and eyes – its size, its prominence in the action, the volume it generated together with the enlarged accompanying orchestra, and the often 'solemn', churchly, weighty, contrapuntal textures of its music. (His Italian operas, and those of his competitors, generally followed the conventions of the genre in having only vestigial choruses, sung by the small cast of soloists at the end of the last act.) Textually, it was the religious subject-matter which distinguished oratorio from Handel's Italian operas and his secular English settings, in his own and his contemporaries' eyes. In his preface to *Samson* Newburgh Hamilton defined oratorio as 'a musical Drama, whose Subject must be Scriptural, and in which the Solemnity of Church-Musick is agreeably united with the most pleasing Airs of the Stage'. This succinct account needs only minor qualification to cover Handel's whole oratorio output (*Theodora* is not scriptural). The fact that a work was unacted did not prevent its being a drama by eighteenth-century canons. Nor, apparently, did a lack of named characters (which distinguishes *Israel in Egypt*, *Messiah* and the *Occasional Oratorio* from the other oratorios for some modern listeners): the appreciative critic of *Israel in Egypt* writing in the *London Daily Post* of 18 April 1739, who has read the libretto and urges patrons to read it in advance of a performance and take it with them, calls the work a drama (see below, p. 169). The sacred/secular distinction, which was clear enough to contemporaries, has been blurred in modern times by the delighted recognition of Handel's ability to portray human character and emotion. While it is obviously true that this ability cuts across the sacred/secular divide, it is also the case that to make this the defining feature of his output is to impose a view of it that differs from that of his contemporaries – and, perhaps, himself. There is no historical evidence to support a modern interpretation of the musical text according to which Handel's views and tastes were at variance with those of his contemporaries.

The librettos and their authors

The printed libretto – the wordbook – was an indispensable part of attendance at the oratorio. Members of Handel's audience bought copies of the text in the theatre in order to read the words during the performance, as Fielding's Amelia attests: her unknown admirer in the first gallery 'procured her a Book and Wax-Candle, and held the Candle for her himself during the whole Entertainment' (book IV chapter 9). Wordbooks were also sold in advance of the performance so that they could be studied beforehand. They contained information essential to full understanding and enjoyment of the performance. Some, after the manner of the similarly marketed opera librettos, which often gave the larger narrative context of the part of the story being presented, provided a synopsis, including parts of the story which the librettist had chosen to omit. James Miller's *Joseph* is an example, obviating the charge occasionally made by modern critics that the librettist rendered the 'plot' unintelligible (in any case, most oratorio stories were very familiar to the audience, enabling the librettist to dispense with details of the action and provide a commentary on it instead). Printed 'stage directions' often compensated for the lack of visible action. Frequently the apportioning of text to characters had to be clarified by reference to the libretto, because soloists doubled minor and even major roles. For example, Esther Young created the roles of both Juno and Ino in *Semele* (aptly, since the plot entails the disguising of the former as the latter); given the absence of costume and action, this doubling would have been extremely confusing to the audience but for the wordbook.[69]

But what the audiences read did not always match what they heard. Frequently Handel chose not to set some parts of the libretto but, to make sense of the action, they were printed with the rest, their omission usually indicated by inverted commas. Conversely, as Handel's autograph material in the British Library shows, the librettist sometimes provided text which never appeared in print, because Handel did not set it or because, despite being set, it was discarded before the libretto was printed.[70] Such passages can adjust our idea of the librettist's contribution. Comprehensive study of any individual libretto (a task not undertaken in this book) must entail consideration of the early musical sources, including the autograph, as Dean has shown: a complete investigation of the evidence which the autographs provide of the authors' critical judgement of their creations is long overdue. When Handel revised an oratorio after its first appearance a new libretto seems usually to have been printed, and we have evidence of the involvement and contribution at this stage of at least two of his principal librettists, Jennens and Thomas Morell.[71]

The choice of theme was seldom novel. Precedents for the librettists' subjects (besides their immediate sources, for which see Appendix 1) can be found among Italian oratorios, Italian sacred cantatas, German Passions, European sacred drama, recent and contemporary English drama and verse – including fair-booth drolls – or English oratorios by other composers, or a combination of these. *Deborah*, *David and Jonathan*, *Jephtha* and the choice of Hercules had all been subjects of English oratorios before Handel treated them. The Exodus, Joseph, David, Solomon and the Messiah were subjects of English eighteenth-century verse and drama. Saul and the witch at Endor and Jephtha were subjects of drolls performed at London fairs (at which all classes of society mingled) during the early eighteenth century. Saul's meeting with the witch at Endor was the subject of Purcell's *scena* 'In Guilty Night'. Some topics were mooted in poems of praise addressed to Handel, or in critiques of his work.[72] The contemporary Milton cult is reflected in the choice of *L'Allegro* and *Il Penseroso*, *Samson Agonistes* and *Paradise Lost*, and the use of Milton's psalm translations for the *Occasional Oratorio*; as Jennens wrote sourly of the latter, 'it is transcribed chiefly from Milton, who in his Version of some of the Psalms wrote so like Sternhold and Hopkins that there is not a pin to choose betwixt 'em. But there are people in the world who fancy every thing excellent which has Milton's name to it.'[73]

All Handel's known oratorio librettists were published authors in other spheres by the time they collaborated with him (except Jennens, who, however, collaborated in the Virgil commentary of his friend Holdsworth and in later life published innovative editions of Shakespeare's plays), though none of them except Humphreys was a writer to the exclusion of other occupations. Jennens was a connoisseur and heir to large estates; Hamilton was steward to the Earl of Strafford and his family; Miller and Morell were clergymen. Where we have information about Humphreys' successors as Handel's librettists, it shows that they either came to him of their own accord (Jennens), or were suggested to him by others (Morell);

and that the majority who volunteered or agreed to write for him were admirers of his music, or members of his circle of acquaintance, or both (Jennens, Mary Delany, John Upton, Edward Synge, Hamilton, Thomas Broughton, Miller), as indeed his very first English librettists had been (Gay and his literary friends in Burlington's and Chandos' orbit, the authors of *Acis and Galatea*). The authors of three of the late librettos are unknown (*Joshua, Solomon* and *Susanna*) and the author of one is conjectural (*Israel in Egypt*); but in no instances is Handel known to have been his own librettist, and we do not even have any record of his suggesting the topic of an existing work (there is an intriguing note in his hand for an oratorio about Elijah,[74] but this idea had to wait another century to be realised). Not that he set everything he was offered. Neither Upton nor Mrs Delany managed to persuade him that an oratorio taken from Milton's *Paradise Lost* had possibilities,[75] nor did he warm to Bishop Synge's proposal and draft synopsis, inspired by *Messiah* and *L'allegro*, for a work to be titled *The Penitent*. But he did not have to be in at the start or even the progress of a libretto's composition for it to be acceptable. *Messiah* was Jennens' idea, and the libretto was complete before it was offered to Handel.

The collaboration

We have only a tiny number of letters from Handel, and the correspondence of only one of his librettists written at the time of active collaboration, so it is impossible to reconstruct a fully reliable picture of the working relationships of composer and librettists. But a series of five letters about *Belshazzar* to Jennens (who is also the librettist whose correspondence survives) illuminates the process so tellingly that it is worth quoting in full once more. Handel writes:

Now should I be extreamly glad to receive the first Act, or what is ready, of the new Oratorio with which you intend to favour me, that I might employ all my attention and time, in order to answer in some measure the great obligation I lay under. This new favour will greatly increase my Obligations ... (9 June 1744)[76]

At my arrival in London, which was Yesterday, I immediately perused the Act of the Oratorio with which you favour'd me, and, the little time only I had it, gives me great Pleasure. Your reasons for the Length of the first act are intirely Satisfactory to me, and it is likewise my Opinion to have the following Acts short. I shall be very glad and much obliged to you, if you will soon favour me with the remaining Acts. Be pleased to point out these passages in the Messiah which You think require altering . . . (19 July 1744)

The Second Act of the Oratorio I have received Safe, and own my self highly obliged to You for it. I am greatly pleased with it, and shall use my best endeavours to do it Justice. I can only Say that I impatiently wait for the third Act . . . (21 August 1744)

Your most excellent Oratorio has given me great Delight in setting it to Musick and still engages me warmly. It is indeed a Noble Piece, very grand and uncommon; it has furnished me with Expressions, and has given me Opportunity to some very particular Ideas, besides so many great Choru's. I intreat you heartily to favour me Soon with the last Act, which I expect with anxiety, that I may regulate my Self the better as to the Length of it. I profess my Self highly obliged to You, for so generous a Present . . . (13 September 1744)

I received the 3ᵈ Act, with a great deal of pleasure, as you can imagine, and you may believe that I think it a very fine and sublime Oratorio, only it is realy too long, if I should extend the Musick, it would last 4 Hours and more.

I retrench'd already a great deal of the Musick, that I might preserve the Poetry as much as I could, yet still it may be shortned. The Anthems come in very properly. but would not the Words (tell it out among the Heathen that the Lord is King [part of Chandos Anthem Vb]) [be] Sufficient for one Chorus? The Anthem (I will magnify thee O God my King, and I will praise thy name for ever and ever, vers). the Lord preserveth all them that Love him, but scattreth abroad all the ungodly. (vers and chorus) my mouth shall speak the Praise of the Lord and let all flesh give thanks unto His holy name for ever and ever Amen. [part of Chandos Anthem Va]) concludes well the Oratorio. I hope you will make a visit to London next Winter. I have a good Set of Singers. S. Francesina performs Nitocris, Miss Robinson Cyrus, Mrs. Cibber Daniel, Mr. Beard (who is recoverd) Belshazzar, Mr Reinhold Gobrias, and a good Number of Choir Singers for the Chorus's. I propose 24 Nights to perform this Season, on Saturdays, but in Lent on Wednesday's or Fryday's. I shall open on 3ᵈ of Novembʳ next with [?] Deborah. (2 October 1744)

The picture of the collaboration given by these urgent messages may surprise anyone used to the idea that Handel called all the tunes. He is prepared to begin composing an oratorio without having seen the whole text. He is willing to accede without discussion to his librettist's plan for the relative proportions of the major parts. He is willing to consider making alterations to an existing work according to his librettist's judgements. He is willing to adapt his ideas, even jettisoning his music, to accommodate to the librettist's plan: his plaintive remarks about retrenchment were genuine – his original Act I was oratorio-length.[77] His tone is obliging even by eighteenth-century standards and, by comparison with his own attestedly forthright style, positively ingratiating. His main stated concern about the implications of the text is its *extent*. This last is the only point he discusses in detail. 'Ideas' are mentioned but they are not canvassed (and the sense seems restricted to musical ones), and there is no mention at all of *dramatis personae*. When he asks for Acts II and III he does not suggest what they might contain. The libretto of *Belshazzar* can be read as an assertion of the validity of Christian revelation, a contribution to the many contemporary depictions of the ideals and person of the Patriot King (politically a theme dear to the Whig opposition) and an allegory of the restoration of the exiled Jacobites to their rightful home.[78] None of these themes, nor any other religious or political inference, nor even the behaviour of the characters, elicits comment from Handel. This of course is not to say that he failed to register or think about any elements in the libretto but those which he mentions. However, while the broad outlines may have been discussed previously, he did not wait to settle the text to his satisfaction before beginning on it and he can hardly have given himself much time to think about it: what he does not tell Jennens is that between the second and third letters – in the space of one month – he composed *Hercules*, and that he started setting *Belshazzar* two days after sending the third letter.

Sadly we do not have the other side of the exchange, but most of it can be deduced, and what we do have is perhaps more illuminating – comments by Jennens to his friend Holdsworth, which provide a gloss for Handel's politeness, especially if we take account of one written before *Belshazzar* was conceived:

His Messiah has disappointed me, being set in great hast, tho' he said he would be a year about it, & make it the best of all his compositions. I shall put no more Sacred Words into his hands, to be thus abus'd. (J/H 17 February 1742/3)

Handel has promis'd to revise the Oratorio of Messiah, & He & I are very good Friends again. The reason is, he has lately lost his Poet Miller [by death, 26 April], & wants to set me at work for him again. Religion & Morality, Gratitude, Good Nature & Good Sense had been better Principles of Action than this Single Point of Interest but I must take him as I find him, & make the best use I can of him. (J/H 7 May 1744)

I have been prevail'd with once more to expose my self to the Criticks, to oblige the Man who made me but a Scurvy return for former obligations; the truth is, I had a farther view in it; but if he does not mend his manners, I am resolv'd to have nothing more to do with him. But the reason of my mentioning this was to excuse my delay of answering your letter dated almost 4 months ago. For my Muse is such a Jade, & Handel hurry'd her so, that I could not find time for writing Letters. (J/H 26 September 1744)

[The libretto of *Belshazzar* was] a very hasty abortive Birth, extorted out of due time by Handel's importunate Dunning Letters ... the additional Nonsense he had loaded it with under pretence of shortening it ... (J/H 21 February 1744/5)

This was a flammable partnership of two strong-willed, intelligent men, with totally opposed working habits, each convinced of the soundness of his own judgement. Besides, Jennens was doing Handel a favour in giving him the libretto and they were having to patch up a quarrel as well as embark on a new and uncomfortable collaboration; this partly accounts for Handel's careful courtesy and Jennens' irritation at his intransigence. It is unlikely that Handel had such combative relationships with his other librettists: none had so much to offer as Jennens. But Morell's recollections show the composer exercising similar insistence on speed, complaisance as regards narrative content and indifference to verbal detail (metre excepted), and causing pique by demanding alterations to the text. After Handel's death he recalled:

And now as to Oratorio's: – 'There was a time (says Mr Addison), when it was laid down as a maxim, that nothing was capable of being well set to musick, that was not nonsense.' And this I think, though it might be wrote before Oratorio's were in fashion, supplies an Oratorio-writer (if he may be called a writer) with some sort of apology; especially if it be considered, what alterations he must submit to, if the Composer be of an haughty disposition, and has but an imperfect acquaintance with the English language. As to myself, great lover as I am of music, I should never have thought of such an undertaking (in which for the reasons above, little or no credit is to be gained), had not Mr Handell applied to me, when at Kew, in 1746, and added to his request the honour of a recommendation from prince Frederic. Upon this I thought I could do as well as some that had gone before me, and within 2 or 3 days I carried him the first Act of *Judas Maccabaeus*, which he approved of. 'Well,' says he, 'and how are you to go on?' 'Why, we are to suppose an engagement, and that the Israelites have conquered, and so begin with a chorus as
Fallen is the Foe
or, something like it.' 'No, I will have this,' and began working it, as it is,

upon the Harpsichord. 'Well, go on', 'I will bring you more tomorrow.'
'No, something now,'

'So fall thy Foes, O Lord'

'that will do,' and immediately carried on the composition as we have it in
that most admirable chorus ... as to the last Air [in *Alexander Balus*] ...
when Mr Handell first read it, he cried out '*D—n your Iambics*'. 'Don't put
yourself in a passion, they are easily Trochees.' '*Trochees, what are Trochees?*'
'Why, the very reverse of Iambics, by leaving out a syllable in every line, as
instead of

Convey me to some peaceful shore,
Lead me to some peaceful shore'

'That is what I want.' 'I will step into the parlour, and alter them
immediately.' I went down and returned with them altered in about 3
minutes; when he would have them as they were, and set them ...[79]

In this account Handel again accepts the first act of a libretto
without knowing how it is to go on, and once composition is under
way he gets so far ahead of his librettist as to have the metre of an
aria determinedly in mind before its words exist. As Dean points out,
the autograph scores provide further proof of Handel's tendency to
compose settings of the text before the libretto took its final shape,
and then to cut, retrench or adapt.[80] A final piece of evidence which
fills out the picture of his collaborations most tellingly comes in
another letter from Jennens, this time to his young cousin Lord
Guernsey, about work in progress on *Saul* and Handel's various
'maggots' (aberrations) which are obstructing it:

His third Maggot is a Hallelujah which he has trump'd up at the end of his
Oratorio since I went into the Country because he thought the conclusion
of the Oratorio not Grand enough; tho' if that were the case 'twas his own
fault, for the words would have bore as Grand Musick as he could have set
'em to: but this Hallelujah Grand as it is, comes in very nonsensically,
having no manner of relation to what goes before. And this is the more
extraordinary, because he refus'd to set a Hallelujah at the end of the first
Chorus in the Oratorio, where I had plac'd one, & where it was to be
introduc'd with the utmost propriety, upon a pretence that it would make
the Entertainment too long.[81]

For all Handel's dramatic insight and Jennens' overriding concern
for religious truths, in this instance it was the librettist who had
dramatic sense on his side. The climax of the last act, to which this
hallelujah was to be appended, is David's lament over Saul and
Jonathan, and a chorus of rejoicing would indeed have 'come in
very nonsensically'. The words of Jennens' conclusion to the ora-

torio, also a chorus, look confidently but grimly towards continuing
struggle, and he was justified in believing that they 'would have bore
as Grand Musick as he could have set 'em to'. But Handel, apparently, was more interested in having an unqualifiedly rousing,
positive conclusion – which might well have better suited his audience's taste – than in subscribing to dramatic logic (and the dis-
ingenuousness which Jennens detects in his colleague with reference
to the work's length gives some credence to his later complaints
about Handel's changes to *Belshazzar*, 'the additional Nonsense he
had loaded it with under pretence of shortening it'). Jennens won his
point; in the completed work the hallelujah is where he intended it
to be and there is no concluding hallelujah. Anthony Hicks has
shown that this was not the end of the composer's readiness to take
account of his librettist's views. He gave the autograph score, the full
score and the partbooks of *Saul* to Jennens for comment, and
implemented some of his suggested amendments to the music itself.
Jennens also altered his own words in some places, seeing that the
music to which Handel had set them required their adjustment in
order to make their intended point. As Hicks notes, this strikingly
illustrates Jennens' intense involvement in the collaboration and
Handel's regard for his views.[82] No comparable example of consultation has yet come to light in respect of Handel's other librettists
and it seems unlikely that this level of interchange was typical, even
between Handel and Jennens,[83] but it shows how far Handel was
willing to submit his judgement of a work, in both major construction and fine detail, both verbal and musical, to his librettist's
opinion.

   The question arises: why did people write oratorio librettos for
Handel? In England librettos had been regarded, ever since Dryden
first provided and deprecated them, as one of the lowest forms of
literary creation.[84] Charles Gildon's scorn (and explanation) are
representative of the attitude of men of letters in the first part of the
eighteenth century:

One of the greatest obstacles, perhaps, to the perfection of our songs, is the
slavish care or complaisance of the writers, to make their words to the goust
of the composer, or musician; being oblig'd often to sacrifice their sense to
certain sounding words, and feminine rhimes, or the like; because they
seem most adapted to furnish the composer with such cadences which most
easily slide into their modern way of composition: And it is very observable,
there is scarce one master of musick, who has set a song, composed with art

and fine sense, to any tolerable tune; but have generally exerted their musical faculty most upon such trifling words, as are scarce remov'd one degree from nonsense.[85]

Both Morell, in the recollection cited above, and Miller in his dedication of *Joseph*, deprecated libretto writing on the grounds of subservience to the musician and inevitably second-rate results. On his own account Morell good-naturedly obliged the composer, in part because he was flattered by princely encouragement. However, this apparently candid admission was not the whole truth – he needed the money, as did Miller (see chapter 8). While we do not know to what extent libretto-writing was a money-earning activity (whether, for example, there was a royalty arrangement on the sale of wordbooks), it is clear that some financial return could be envisaged. Handel's acknowledgement to Jennens (cited above) for the libretto of *Belshazzar* as 'so generous a Present' implies gratitude for something not ordinarily given. Morell expected, and received, the customary monetary reward for his dedication of *Judas* to the Duke of Cumberland, and was given the proceeds of its third performance by the composer. But the librettists for whom money may have been a motive had other sources of income and were able to earn by other forms of writing, so why did they diversify into oratorio?[86]

The authors did not really view their librettos as negligently as – in the time-honoured fashion of the gentleman practitioner – they pretended. It is no surprise to find Morell, an energetic and esteemed classical philologist, vigilantly scrutinising revisions of *Judas Macchabæus*. From his study of successive printings of the text Merlin Channon deduces that Morell 'kept a sharp eye on what went into Watts' [the printer's] books', and 'did not approve of any deviation from his own libretto'.[87] Similarly Jennens was incensed by the 'Bulls' (printing errors) in the first edition of the libretto of *Messiah* and determined to expunge them in time for the first London performance: 'I have a copy, as it was printed in Ireland, full of Bulls; & if he does not print a correct one here, I shall do it my Self, & perhaps tell him a piece of my mind by way of Preface.'[88] Winton Dean points to an errata slip in the first issue of the libretto of *Susanna*, and corresponding corrections in the second, as evidence of 'a finicky author with a passion for minute accuracy'.[89] Morell describes himself as willing to alter his metre at the composer's whim, but this should not lead us to suppose that he had a tin ear; a letter in the archives of his old college (King's, Cambridge) on

Sophocles' versification proves his sensitivity to metrical variation and other details of aural effect.[90] In fact English librettos for Handel negated much of the conventional contempt for song texts, because they consisted of or derived from the greatest literature: the Scriptures, Dryden, Milton. Gildon's complaint continues:

I shall only give one instance of the contrary, tho' many might likewise be found of that, I mean Mr. *Drydens Alexander's feast*, admirable in its sense, and the most harmonious in its numbers, of any thing in the *English* tongue: Numbers so harmonious, that had one of the ancient masters been to compose it, it had been one of the most transporting and ravishing pieces of musick that had been seen in the world these thousand years.

But Gildon despairs of any modern composer having the requisite talent; what is to us the obvious answer may have eluded him because at this date (1721) Handel was setting English texts only as church music.

Handel was recognised by his English contemporaries as the country's leading composer. He achieved remarkable prominence on the London scene by any standards, and as Deutsch's great *Documentary Biography* attests, he was written about to a degree surely unmatched by any British composer until the twentieth century. It would appear that the many enthusiasts of high culture among his librettists wrote for him at least in part because they admired his work and wanted to join in creating great art. This seems to have been what principally motivated such devotees as Mrs Delany and Newburgh Hamilton – the splendid project of allying the music of their favourite composer, famed for his capacity for the sublime, with the highest achievements of the sublime in verse, the poetic masterpieces of Dryden and Milton. In selecting *Alexander's Feast* to 'give Satisfaction to the real Judges of *Poetry* and *Musick*', Hamilton was convinced that, as he claimed in the jubilant conclusion to his libretto's preface, 'it is next to an Improbability, to offer the World any thing in those *Arts* more perfect, than the united Labours and utmost Efforts of a *Dryden* and a *Handel*'. Miller deprecated his own efforts, but described Handel's oratorios as 'Refined and Sublime Entertainments' and the composer as 'the Great Master, by whose Divine Harmony they are supported'. The attachment of several of the librettists to Handel's music can be traced in the subscription lists to his works: Hamilton, Broughton and Jennens all subscribed to his published scores, Jennens (who could best afford it) with unwavering loyalty.[91] Of all Handel's librettists Jennens emerges as the most fervent admirer of his music, so it is no surprise to find him actively trying to promote the composition of a masterpiece by providing the words for it, as his letters to Holdsworth explain: 'Handel says he will do nothing next Winter, but I hope I shall perswade him to set another Scripture Collection I have made for him . . . I hope he will lay out his whole Genius & Skill upon it, that the Composition may excell all his former Compositions, as the Subject excells every other Subjcct. The Subject is Messiah.' Some months later, 'I heard with great pleasure at my arrival in Town, that Handel had set the Oratorio of Messiah; but it was some mortification to me to hear that instead of performing it here he was gone into Ireland with it. However, I hope we shall hear it when he comes back.' His subsequent chagrin is largely due to his sense of Handel's failure to do *himself* justice in failing to do justice to the subject.[92] A contemporary writer attests that Jennens, at least, achieved the aim of propagating great art. According to Joseph Warton in his essay on Pope, 'L'Allegro and Il Penseroso . . . are now [1756] universally known', but this was not so before Jennens and Handel produced their ode; they 'lay in a sort of obscurity, the private enjoyment of a few curious readers, till they were set to admirable music by Mr Handel'.[93]

Handel was not only a masterly artist, he was a famous one. Writing oratorio librettos for him might not increase one's reputation in the world of letters, but it increased one's audience. Handel's public ranged from the royal family to the patrons of Vauxhall Gardens and from London to Dublin to Edinburgh, and his work lasted (the repeated performance of his oratorios and operas was a novelty in early-eighteenth-century England; musical works were seldom revived in their entirety). The theatre was the most popular forum for serious secular writing, and hence the most sought-after arena for writers with a message; and serious music theatre works were less vulnerable to censorship than stage plays. For a writer with something to say to the educated, influential upper- and middle-class London public Handel's music could be an ideal vehicle. It is interesting that Miller turned to writing for Handel only after his own hitherto successful plays had been permanently denied a hearing by an offended claque. The most astonishing phrases in Jennens' remarks about his willingness to collaborate once more with Handel, on *Belshazzar*, suggest that he did have a specific, individual purpose beyond the creation of great art. His statements that 'I must take him as I find him, & make the best use I can of him' and 'the truth is, I had a farther view in it' imply that he had an axe of his own to grind; and I have suggested elsewhere that Jennens did indeed 'use' Handel's oratorios to promulgate his deeply felt religious and political views.[94] As the case of *Messiah* shows, the topic and source of an oratorio could be the librettist's choice; and Hamilton's prefaces to *Alexander's Feast* and *Samson* imply that he suggested these texts for setting. Librettists other than Jennens may have had 'a farther view' in the words they provided for Handel to set.

One admirer of Handel's work who, though not a librettist, put the plan of a libretto to Handel, certainly wished to convey a message to the composer's public through his oratorios. Edward Synge, Bishop of Elphin, attended Handel's Dublin performances and was so impressed by *Messiah* that he wrote down why, in his view, 'As Mʳ Handel in his oratorio's greatly excells all other Composers I am acquainted with, So in the famous one, called the Messiah he Seems to have excell'd himself'. His reasons naturally include the subject, 'which is the greatest & most interesting, It seems to have inspir'd him'. But he recognises that the rhetorical handling of this subject, by both librettist and composer, is crucial: the words 'are all Sublime, or affecting in the greatest degree', and the music is immediately accessible, for 'tho' the Composition is very masterly & artificial [elaborate], yet the Harmony is So great and open, as to please all who have Ears & will hear, learned & unlearn'd', a feature of the work which he acutely singles out as 'particularly remarkable'. The audience's response, which for him will be the happy result of this affecting way of writing, is not aesthetic pleasure but moral resolve: 'Many, I hope, were instructed by it, and had proper Sentiments impres'd in a Stronger manner on their minds.' Hoping that Handel will draw on his observations when meditating future oratorios, he lays out a synopsis embodying his idea of morally useful oratorio:

Plan for an oratorio
Title the Penitent.
Part 1. To be made up of passages describing the Righteousness of God. That He is of purer Eyes than to behold iniquity – is just to punish Sinners, mercifull to them that repent, loves & cherishes the good, but Shews indignation against them that do evil – a number of particulars will easily offer themselves here

Part 2ᵈ. Two Characters to be introduc'd 1. a Good man obedient to the Laws of God, flourishing like a green bay tree, enjoying peace of mind & prosperity, & on a reverse of fortune patient & resign'd in adversity, trusting in God, and by him Supported & reliev'd & 2. a wicked man acting in defiance of God, Saying Tush I shall never be mov'd Strengthening himself in his Wickedness for a time, but at last visited with Evils, under which He falls into misery & Some horrors, at first without any compunction or thought, of returning to God. These two Characters may be mix'd, as the L'Allegro ed il Penscroso are, which would have a very good effect, & it would not be amiss to introduce the wicked man as insulting the good in affliction & tempting him to forsake God. The Book of Job will furnish variety of fine passages for this purpose.

Part.3. To begin with the good man exhorting the wicked loaded with afflictions, and Sunk under them, to return to God by repentance, then on these Exhortation[s] having their effect, The wicked man to address himself to God, Confess his guilt, beg pardon & forgiveness. The Psalms commonly call'd the Penitential Psalms will furnish variety of fine passages for this. Lastly to conclude with the joy of the Penitent on his prayers being heard, and the Good man & He joyn in Celebrating yᵉ mercy & goodness of God, who pardons Sinners on Sincer[e] Repentance & Reformation. This to be further carried on into the Grand Chorus.[95]

Handel sent the bishop's comments and synopsis to Jennens (which is why we still have them), with the endorsement: 'I send you this Sʳ only to show you how zealous they are in Ireland for oratorio's. I could send you a number of Instances chose from others in Print and in writing.' Reading between the lines, we can infer that he wanted to share the pleasure of being praised, but was keen to head Jennens off any notion of implementing Synge's proposal.

We will return to the salient assumptions which Synge makes about the ingredients of a libretto; here we should note his overwhelmingly didactic purpose – to deliver, through the emotional power of Scripture verse and Handel's music, the message that belief in God and virtuous conduct are to be preferred to atheism and vice. A printed tract on this theme would risk being as ineffectual as the dozens published yearly which failed to make a mark, but oratorio could carry the message to its intended audience and lodge it in their minds and hearts. The bishop was pleased to note, during the performance of *Messiah* which inspired him, that 'tho the young & gay of both Sexes were present in great numbers, their behaviour was uniformly grave & decent, which Show'd that they were not only pleas'd but affected with the performance'. A solely verbal defence of the divinity of Christ would, like the dozens of similar defences, quickly be overtaken by the latest crop of theological publications; but, set to music by Handel, its sound would (in the words of *Messiah*) 'go out into all lands, and its words unto the ends of the world'. And, as this book will suggest, his music could be used to convey lessons for civic as well as spiritual life.

The exact composition of the audience that the librettists hoped to reach is hard to gauge. For consumers oratorio was, with or after opera, the most expensive form of entertainment in the capital. In 1742–3 Handel's oratorio prices were more than double theatre prices – first gallery seats cost more than three times as much, and the cheapest seat was only 6d less than the most expensive seat at the theatre. The pit was customarily floored over and made into boxes, reducing capacity and raising the quality of the seats (and audience); and 'A. D.' complained in *Common Sense* on 10 April 1738 that 'every Body knows his [Handel's] entertainments are calculated for the quality only, and that People of moderate Fortunes cannot pretend to them'.[96] However, a seat in the first gallery cost (to compare it with other luxuries) no more than a long book and much less than a pound of tea and, unlike modern opera prices, only a third of a London labourer's weekly wage.[97] It is frequently said that Handel opened oratorio to the 'new middle class' when he abandoned subscription sales from 1747 onwards, but, as Smith pointed out, seat prices did not change;[98] rather, having overreached himself with a double-length season in 1745–6, Handel finally saw that selling tickets for individual performances was less risky than pledging himself to a definite number of performances for the sake of an uncertain number of advance sales. Season tickets for oratorio in any case involved considerably less outlay than those for opera. For example, in 1742–3 Handel's patrons paid six guineas for three box seats every night of the first six performances, with the option of the same for the next six, while the normal opera subscription was twenty guineas (though for more performances). Moreover, season ticket holders had never filled the house to the exclusion of casual buyers. The theatre audience for opera and oratorio was not restricted to the aristocratic and rich: witness the patronage by Handel's own less well-off friends such as Mrs Delany and Newburgh Hamilton and, in the world of lifelike fiction, Amelia's attendance at the oratorio and Joseph Andrews' leadership of opinion among the footmen in the second gallery at the opera. Furthermore, through publication of scores and extracts, the librettists reached a far wider audience outside the theatre (such as – to take another instance from

Fielding – the country-bound but discriminating Sophia Western).
In making the libretto an essential ingredient of full enjoyment of
the performance, the oratorio authors addressed themselves principally to the educated, minimally the literate, part of their audience. But the Bishop of Elphin noted 'great numbers' of the 'young
and gay' at *Messiah*, and Fielding describes (this time as reality) 'two
ingenious Gentlemen' studying the libretto of *L'allegro* before a
performance in blissful ignorance that the words were taken from
Milton.[99] In other words, though the audience probably consisted
chiefly of people who were educated, sober and genteel, it had a
leavening of people who were not. It is also probably safe to assume
that the audience of English oratorio was less likely than the opera
audience to have come principally to hear the singers and more
likely to pay attention to the words being sung. The serious-minded
Mrs Pendarves (later Mrs Delany) regretted that 'most of the people
that hear the oratorio make no reflection on the meaning of the
words, though God is addressed in the most solemn manner', but the
date was 1734, the oratorio in question was in Italian, Porpora's
Davide e Bersabea, and the leading soprano was an Italian described
by Mrs Pendarves as making the most of her voluptuousness.[100] In
1743 Faulkner's *Dublin Journal* reported from London that 'Our
friend Mr Handell is very well ... for the Publick will be no longer
imposed on by Italian Singers, and some Wrong Headed Undertakers of bad Opera's, but find out the Merit of Mr Handell's
composition and English Performances: That Gentleman is more
esteemed now than ever.'[101]

Handel's letters about *Belshazzar* remind us of the practical con-
straints within which he had to work and which took precedence for
him over any librettist's message. He had to write to the expected
length of an evening's entertainment; he had to accommodate first
to his planned company of singers and then to the forces actually
available on the night (the cast of *Belshazzar* he describes to Jennens
had to be changed because Mrs Cibber dropped out); he had to
survive at the box office; and after 1737 he had to get his works past
the censor of stage performances (according to one press report, he
courted trouble with *Israel in Egypt*, see chapter 12). We have only
one certainly authentic statement from him about his intention in
writing oratorios:

As I perceived, that joining good Sense and significant Words to Musick,
was the best Method of recommending *this* [music] to an English Audience;
I have directed my Studies that way, and endeavour'd to shew, that the

English Language, which is so expressive of the sublimest Sentiments is the best adapted of any to the full and solemn kind of Musick.

This is part of a letter to the *Daily Advertiser* (17 January 1745) written at a time of personal crisis, to explain to his subscribers his proposed cancellation of the remainder of an over-ambitious and financially disastrous season of English works; it is a public statement. So naturally Handel stresses the ways in which he has tried to please his public. Nevertheless, it is striking that the elements which he selects as significant are the use of English words, 'sublime sentiments' and 'the full and solemn kind' of music, and that (unlike some of his twentieth-century admirers) he makes no claim for his works on the grounds of plot or characterisation. This accords with what we learn from the *Belshazzar* letters and can deduce of his working practice. His chief concerns in considering a libretto's viability appear to have been extent and structural balance (variation of solo roles, disposition of solo, ensemble and chorus numbers, proportions of recitative to aria). Once he began setting, verbal detail, including metre, was important.[102] He did not have a Romantic concern for his works' 'integrity': his changes for revivals were often drastic, altering or even scuppering the rationale of plot and characterisation in the interests of practical and musical considerations.[103] In bringing a work to completion for its first performance, he was as ready to add words-and-music that weighted it with religious and moral commentary as to jettison music he had already composed, as the second thoughts that shaped *Samson* demonstrate.[104] His imagination was fired by anything which could give rise to emotional affectiveness: not only conflict of characters, individual and mutual feeling, or national fear and exultation, but the onset of dusk (*L'allegro*), the turning of the spheres (*Semele*), an abstraction (the 'envy' chorus in *Saul*) or simply the word 'Amen' (*Messiah*). His letter to the *Daily Advertiser* mentions none of this. Variety of emotional affect had after all been the essence of all his operas, and Handel chooses to highlight the differences between the operas which he has given up composing and his oratorios, which have unprecedented elevation and grandeur. His statement that English is peculiarly capable of expressing 'sublime sentiments' and that these in turn are peculiarly suited to his kind of 'solemn' music refers to and builds on current aesthetic polemic, and he was shrewd to proffer his music as the perfect vehicle for lofty concepts. But modern critics have found him frequently disregarding or overriding the import of the text in his musical setting of it, and there is no oratorio in which we can feel sure that the finished work was the outcome of a common aim of textual and musical author. The librettist might use his text to convey a 'message', but Handel did not necessarily notice or co-operate with it. (Jennens regretfully interpreted Handel's motivation in asking him for another libretto after *Messiah* as self-interest rather than adherence to the cause of 'Religion & Morality'.) This is important with regard to what follows in this book about the librettos' possible meanings. We should not be inhibited in our readings of the librettos by a notion that Handel would not have set a text containing ideas to which he did not personally and fully subscribe. Equally, we should not assume that Handel did not subscribe to the commonplace ideas of his time simply because he did not leave us authenticated verbal statements in support of them.

PART I

English origins of English oratorio

To judge rightly of an author, we must transport ourselves to his time, and examine what were the wants of his contemporaries, and what were his means of supplying them.

Samuel Johnson, 'Life of Dryden', *Lives of the English Poets* (1779–81)

CHAPTER I

Artistic norms

When the English public was introduced to *Esther* in 1732 it also encountered the designation *oratorio* for the first time. The advertisements for both the 'pirated' York Buildings version and Handel's own performances referred to the work as such. The former helpfully added 'or Sacred Drama', but this may have raised false expectations. The commentator who objected to Handel's Italian singers mangling the English words, though carefully warned in Handel's advertisement that 'There will be no Action on the Stage', complained that 'I saw indeed the finest Assembly of People I ever beheld in my Life, but, to my great Surprize, found this Sacred *Drama* a mere Consort [concert], no Scenary, Dress or Action, so necessary to a *Drama*'. Preferring Handel's new operas, *Ezio* and *Sosarme*, he confesses:

(I am sorry I am so wicked) but I like one good Opera better than Twenty *Oratorio*'s: Were they indeed to make a regular *Drama* of a good Scripture Story, and perform'd it with proper Decorations, which may be done with as much Reverence in proper Habits, as in their own common Apparel; (I am sure with more Grandeur and Solemnity, and at least equal Decency) then should I change my Mind, then would the Stage appear in its full Lustre, and Musick Answer to its original Design.[1]

Should the Scriptures be used for entertainment, and if so, as full drama, or not; the distinctions between opera and oratorio; the effect of Scripture, and the music it requires; the proper nature and purpose of music – all these themes, raised here, were debated by Handel's contemporaries, and their discussions of them are explored in the following chapters. In two respects the writer's attitudes are characteristic of the period and its responses to the arts, Handel's music included. The author-critic is prescriptive and genre-conscious.

43

'Self-consciousness about genre', writes Margaret Anne Doody, 'affects all Augustan writers',[2] and when an artist breaks through the bounds of existing genres as Handel did with English oratorio, contemporaries are likely to address the resulting work in terms of familiar generic elements rather than on what appear to be its own terms. Another early commentator on *Esther*, Viscount Perceval, recorded the performance in his diary entirely in terms of accepted categories of place and style: 'I went to the Opera House to hear Handel's "oratory", composed in the church style'.[3] Newburgh Hamilton was explaining *Samson* to listeners in a way which they could readily assimilate when in the preface to his libretto he described oratorio as 'a musical Drama ... in which the Solemnity of Church-Musick is agreeably united with the most pleasing Airs of the Stage'. This sense of oratorio's disparate parentage was not idiosyncratic: James Grassineau, in his *A Musical Dictionary; being a Collection of Terms and Characters, as well Ancient as Modern* (1740), a work endorsed opposite the title page by a trio of leading practitioners (Pepusch, Greene and Galliard), called oratorio 'a sort of spiritual opera'.

Music for the church and music for the stage were thought of as separate genres, and the mingling of generic elements was not a light undertaking. From the point of view of both theoreticians of music and moral aestheticians it could be subversive or even impossible. Conversely, once a genre was established, a certain style was expected of it – its own; innovations risked being received as undesirable deviations (hence in 1749 the Countess of Shaftesbury objected to the 'light *operatic* style' of Handel's new oratorio *Susanna*[4]). It is well known that the English public was slow to accept oratorio *as a genre*, and complaints from Handel's contemporaries about his musical and non-musical oratorio practices on the basis of the distinctiveness of established genres were frequent. They range from James Bramston's satirical remarks in 1733, pretending to approve fashionable taste:

> The Stage should yield the solemn Organ's note,
> And Scripture tremble in the Eunuch's throat.
> Let *Senesino* sing, what *David* writ,
> And *Hallelujahs* charm the pious pit.
> Eager in throngs the town to *Hester* came,
> And *Oratorio* was a lucky name ...[5]

to Catherine Talbot's gentle regret in 1756 at having to hear *Messiah* in a theatre, leading her to conclude that 'the opera and oratorio taste are, I believe, totally incompatible'.[6] Modern commentators have been inclined to dismiss such responses as philistine and primitive,[7] but they have a strong theoretical base.

Objectors to oratorio practice such as Bramston and Talbot were complaining about a perceived mismatch between music, subject-matter and location.[8] They were countered by an answer which seems obvious to us: 'The Theatre, on this occasion, ought to be enter'd with more Solemnity than a Church', because 'These hallow'd Lays ... sanctify the Place'.[9] But this was not the majority view. The writer who wanted a fully staged version of *Esther* was opposed by a large body of critical opinion as well as the Blasphemy Act of 1605, which prohibited Scripture plays. The perceptive librettist John Lockman quoted Charles de Saint Evremond, an influential director of English dramatic taste, to the effect that 'the Stage loses all its Charms, when sacred Subjects are brought upon it; as sacred Subjects suffer greatly in the religious Opinion which ought to be entertained of them, when they are brought upon the Stage'.[10] Even without action, *Esther* and subsequent oratorios were transgressing rules of art by bringing religious subject-matter into the theatre. The prevailing critical orthodoxy was 'decorum', or *appropriateness*. Certain kinds of words and music were considered appropriate to certain circumstances, occasions and purposes: sacred or secular, entertaining or edifying, private or public, to be heard in a theatre or in a church. Kinds of musical style considered apt to these differing ends existed, and writers of the first half of the eighteenth century continually referred to them as norms.[11] Not for the mid-eighteenth century the metaphysical poet's delight in transposing elements from one conceptual world into another. Heartfelt critical outrage at the blurring of generic distinctions underpins Pope's objection to the dilution of musical language, which he puts into the mouth of the mincing harlot Opera as a description of music in the reign of Dulness:

> One Trill shall harmonize joy, grief, and rage,
> Wake the dull Church, and lull the ranting Stage;
> To the same notes thy sons shall hum, or snore,
> And all thy yawning daughters cry, *encore* ...[12]

As might be expected, the preachers of music sermons, for St Cecilia festivals or at Three Choirs meetings, all agree with Pope that sacred music can and should sound different from its secular counterpart. They do not condemn secular music – religious persons can enjoy stage music and church music in their proper place and proportion.[13] But 'There is and ought to be a great difference, an essential disparity between the compositions formed for the Stage and for the Sanctuary'; 'a Divine Hymn set to wanton Notes is most vilely abus'd by such a wrong Emphasis.' Sacred music 'should be not only good Musick, but good Church Musick'.[14] There is agreement on *how* church music should sound: solemn, stately, grave, majestic. Sermon after sermon makes this recommendation in the eighteenth century. Not all the preachers seek to restrict variety of effect. George Lavington (future Bishop of Exeter) requires only that the music be apt for the words, not necessarily grave. He devotes four pages to suggesting a gamut of rhetorical variety in music; but even he concludes this part of his discourse with a caveat against '*robbing the Play-house*, only to dress up the *Spouse of Christ* in the *attire* of a *harlot*'.[15] Even within the realm of devotional music, according to one of the Three Choirs preachers, further distinctions were to be kept, corresponding to the literary-theological differentiation of psalms, hymns and spiritual songs. The urge to classify and discriminate was strong and all-pervading.[16]

Mingling of styles was identified as a recent (post-Restoration) innovation in musical practice. The Nonjuring clergyman and writer on church music Arthur Bedford laments current fashions in a passage which has particular resonance for readers of *Alexander's Feast* (its core is a quotation from one of the sources for Dryden's poem, Jeremy Collier's essay 'Of Musick'):

The *Humour* of the Age is turn'd from every thing that is solid to that which is vain, and our grave *Musick* vanishes into *Air* ... Our antient *Church-Musick* is lost, and that solid grave *Harmony*, fit for a Martyr to delight in, and an Angel to hear, is now chang'd into a Diversion for *Atheists* and *Libertines*.[17]

The distrust of modern musical styles and the sometimes apparently automatic preference for old music *because* it is old reflects the wider cultural clash of the ancients and moderns, and was not confined to the Church.[18] Thomas Tudway is an interesting example of a musician who supported modern innovations in practice but condemned them as modern degeneracy in principle. As Christopher Hogwood has shown in his publication of the prefaces which Tudway wrote to his collections of church music for the Harley family, Tudway was no musical bigot. He considered Italian opera 'ye greatest of all secular performances in Music' and looked forward to the time when English composers would be capable of it. But he was certain that secular and sacred music should have distinct styles: 'As to Church-music, I'm afraid, some have mixt, too much of ye Theatrical way, thinking therby to make it more Elegant and takeing; But by this means, the peculiarity, & gravity of style is lost, wherby it was always, worthily distinguish'd, from ye secular.'[19]

A stylistic difference between sacred and secular music was, moreover, not just promulgated as ideal by theorists, but described as real by scholars. In 1740 James Grassineau could still assert that 'The *Style* of church music is very different from that for theatres.'[20] It was even accepted as real by composers; they may not always have practised it, but they respected it as a valid convention. Watkins Shaw (among other twentieth-century writers on baroque music) contended that 'on the question of whether the style of writing ... is secular or not, we must remember that neither Bach nor Handel, nor any composer of the day, would concede any distinction between a sacred and a secular style', but composers' comments do not bear him out.[21] For example, William Croft commended his anthems to his public on the grounds that they embodied 'the Solemnity and Gravity of what may properly be called the *Church-Style* (so visible in the Works of my Predecessors) as it stands distinguish'd from all those light Compositions which are used in Places more proper for such Performances'. Here again, the place as well as the occasion is a determining factor.[22] Similarly Charles Avison, a practising composer with up-to-date tastes, writing his theoretical *Essay on Musical Expression* at the end of Handel's oratorio career, still accepted the conventional distinctions, pointing out that the cultivated listener's sense of appropriateness is so strong that attempts to override them are likely to fail:

The different Species of Music for the *Church*, the *Theatre*, or the *Chamber*, are, or should be, distinguished by their peculiar Expression. It may easily be perceived, that it is not the *Time* or *Measure*, so much as *Manner* and *Expression*, which stamps the real Character of the Piece. A well wrought *Allegro*, or any other quick Movement for the Church, cannot, with Propriety, be adapted to theatrical Purposes, nor can the *Adagio* of this latter Kind, strictly speaking, be introduced into the former: I have known several Experiments of this Nature attempted, but never with Success. For, the same Pieces which may justly enough be thought very solemn in the Theatre, to an experienced Ear, will be found too light and trivial, when they are performed in the Church: And this, I may venture to assert, would be the Case, though we had never heard them but in some Anthem, or

other divine Performance: And were, therefore, not subject to the Prejudice, which their being heard in an Opera might occasion.[23]

Church, chamber and theatre were the conventional main categories of musical style; they were the ones used to catalogue
Handel's compositions in the first study of his life and works, in
1760.[24] But Avison's discriminations go into more detail than this.
He suggests a fineness of differentiation in musical style to which the
modern listener is now unaccustomed, complaining for example that
in some movements of his *Stabat Mater*, despite his mastery of the
'sorrowful style', Pergolesi fails, in deploying it, to make 'the just
distinction, which ought always to be observed, between the tenderness or passion of a theatrical scene, and the solemnity of devotion'.[25]

Clearly, the early-eighteenth-century audience had preconceptions about the way a biblical text or a text dealing with biblical or
other religious topics should be set. A distinctively devotional style,
though losing ground, was still considered both identifiable and
proper. Audiences for whom Handel's oratorios constituted an
unprecedented form, having perused the librettos before and during
the performance, would have expected compositions in a different
style from his operas or other secular works on the one hand, and on
the other would have been taken aback to hear such words in a
secular setting, especially a theatre. Italy, whence Handel imported
much of his practice in oratorio composition, did not observe such
strict conventions: opera and oratorio shared musical styles, and
oratorio was performed in sacred and secular settings (though not in
theatres).[26] In the passage just quoted Avison endorses the distinctions he makes with a reference to the Bolognese theorist Tosi, who,
however, writing in 1723, describes them as the principles of former
generations, 'to very many [Italian] Moderns ... quite unknown'.[27]
Handel, having absorbed modern Italian styles at his most formative period, used anthems in *Esther* (and in later oratorios) which he
performed in theatres, and Italian love duets for *Messiah*, which he
performed in the Foundling Hospital chapel.[28] What we now take
for granted as his oratorio style was to its first listeners a highly
innovative mix. To some this was excitingly admirable. Viscount
Perceval, who noted that Handel's *Esther* was an 'oratory' in church
style in an opera house, had previously recorded, without demur,
the opinion of Caspar von Bothmer (Hanoverian Representative in
London, and an amateur oboist) that Handel gained musical

ascendancy in Britain not only for 'the great variety of manner in his compositions, whether serious or brisk, whether for the Church or the stage or the chamber' but for 'that agreeable mixture of styles that are in his works'.[29] For others, the disturbance of sensibilities was perhaps as shocking as that experienced in our own times by a churchgoer attached to traditional forms of worship when first confronted with guitars in the aisles.

In other aspects of oratorio composition Handel responded unequivocally to the prescriptions of contemporary aesthetic theory. In the passage just quoted Perceval mentions the most important principle governing eighteenth-century art besides decorum: variety. In his *Analysis of Beauty, Written with a View of Fixing the Fluctuating Ideas of Taste* (1753), Hogarth lists the 'fundamental principles, which are generally allowed to give elegance and beauty, when duly blended together, to compositions of all kinds whatever': the first is 'fitness' (or 'decorum'), the second, which includes all the others (uniformity, simplicity, intricacy and quantity), is 'variety'. His dictum that 'the art of composing well is the art of varying well' is a description of eighteenth-century creativity as well as a prescription for it. The kind of variety he specifies is also generally agreed on. 'When you would compose an object of a great variety of parts, let several of those parts be distinguish'd by themselves, by their remarkable difference from the next adjoining.'[30] According to John Nichols' *Literary Anecdotes*, one of Handel's librettists, Morell, a friend and neighbour of Hogarth, was instrumental in the writing of his *Analysis*.[31]

The principle of contrast (rather than fine shading off from one style or topic to another) had been prescribed for poetry by Samuel Say in *An Essay on the Harmony, Variety and Power of Numbers* (1745). Say's detailing of the elements of verbal variety suggests that the more sensitive members of Handel's audience listened to his word-setting with great acuteness:

Variety arises from the different Length and Form of the Periods; the different Structure and Composition of the Parts; the different Quantity of Time in which they move; the Force of Consonants or Sweetness of Vowels ... And a proper Mixture, Exchange, Agreement, or Opposition of such a Variety of Parts, Sounds and Numbers; and sometimes a Sudden and Seasonable Start from all Rules.[32]

The extent to which the principle of variety through contrast was accepted, and that of 'a Seasonable Start from all Rules' over-exploited, is indicated by one of Handel's librettists, James Miller, in *Harlequin Horace: or, The Art of Modern Poetry*, which he satirically dedicated to the impresario John Rich for having popularised diversions lacking all sense of decency. Miller's mock instructions point to current abuses:

> A thousand jarring Things together yoke . . .
> Consult no Order, but for ever steer
> From grave to gay, from florid to severe.
> Thus ne'er regard Connection, Time, or Place,
> For sweet Variety has every Grace . . .
> Take then no Pains a Method to Maintain,
> Or link your Work in a continu'd Chain,
> But cold, dull Order gloriously disdain.
> Now here, now there, launch boldly from your Theme,
> And make surprizing Novelties your Aim.[33]

In fact Miller's one libretto for Handel, *Joseph and His Brethren*, does have more consistency of mood than most of the oratorio librettos, which generally show the composer and his librettists fully accepting and deploying the variety-through-contrast principle. Textures are varied by alternation of recitative, aria, ensemble, chorus, varying weight of instrumental accompaniment, and varying obbligato instruments. Vocal registers are varied rather than matched within a scene; characters with the same vocal register who do coincide are given contrasting natures (in *Athalia*, for example, the fierce Athalia, the maternal Josabeth, the child Joash). The action moves through change, rather than progression, of mood. The first act of *Samson*, for example, often described as static, swings between Samson's recurrent despair and unanswered prayers, a vision of God's wrath, confident optimism, pity, self-pity, rapturous anticipation of heavenly bliss and a lesson in stoical faith. *Susanna* presents in turn (to take only the emotions) connubial, parental and filial love, the sorrow of parting, the pain of absence, mourning, compassion, lust, fear, unmerited suffering, the joy of reunion and relief at escape from mortal danger. Contrast is the principle that shapes the main part of *L'allegro, il penseroso ed il moderato*: Milton's two poems about opposite temperaments are cut up and dovetailed with each other to provide a series of changes of mood. The liking for variety in the sense of contrast appears at its simplest in those librettos which alternate, but do not mix, the concerns of love and war, such as *Joshua* and *Alexander Balus*. The critic Hugh Blair, praising one of the period's greatest poetic successes, James Macpherson's pretended ancient Celtic epic by Ossian, *Fingal*, particularly admires its 'agreeable diversity', its mixing of 'war and heroism, with love and friendship, of martial, with tender scenes'.[34] This is also the scheme on which the libretto of *Joshua*, like *Fingal* a celebration of early national history, is based. The librettists met the requirements of their period for contrast; they also, as the rest of this book will show in more detail, shared the prevailing enthusiasm for its corollary, inclusiveness.[35]

CHAPTER 2

The purpose of art

THE CONTENT OF ART

One basis of the shocked reaction to the performance of oratorio in the theatre was the widespread view that the theatre was a principal purveyor of vice and encourager of vicious habits. The severest members of the moral majority, for example the Nonjuring clergymen Jeremy Collier and William Law, whose writings on the subject were seriously read and responded to, wanted the playhouses closed.[1] But the belief that public performances were matters of public concern, because they influenced behaviour, was not confined to churchmen; it was universal. Even the popular weeklies agreed that 'Public Diversions are by no Means Things indifferent; they give a Right or a Wrong Turn to the Minds of the People, and the wisest Governments have always thought them worth their Attention.'[2] Art affected individual and civic well-being, so it was a matter of national importance. A number of writers, including several friends of Handel and his librettists, and some of the librettists themselves, campaigned for a reform of the stage. Sensitivity about differences of genre co-existed with a very flexible attitude to the uses to which different kinds of art could be put. As Part II of this book shows in more detail, music and drama were arenas for political debate. They had always been vehicles for moral and religious instruction, and some recent commentators have recognised positive campaigns by establishment groups in the seventeenth century and the first half of the eighteenth to exploit them more vigorously to this end.[3] In putting onto the theatrical stage works that endorsed Christian teaching and advocated public and private virtue, Handel and his librettists were fulfilling many elements of the programme being pursued by a variety of groups to produce a

52

reformed, public art that would revitalise the nation's morals, religious belief, spirituality and patriotism.

It would be wrong to think of this reform movement as inimical to art. Many of its leading spokesmen were artists eager to enhance the remit, standing and influence of art, at a national level as well as among individuals. Their advocacy was rooted in the accepted classical humanist view (represented in eighteenth-century England in particular by Horace) that to be more than mere diversion art must be moral, that is, instructive and rational, and that it has an unmatched capacity to be instructive. Their sights were set not only on the drama, but on poetry, epic and music theatre as well. The arts were to be rescued from practitioners who debased them; invested again with serious, elevated subjects which would rouse the reader's noblest emotions, they would regain their rightful, beneficial, educative power in the nation. Dryden, echoing Milton and his English Renaissance forerunners, had claimed that 'A HEROICK POEM, truly such, is undoubtedly the greatest work that the soul of man is capable to perform. The design of it is, to form the mind to heroick virtue by example; it is conveyed in verse, that it may delight while it instructs.'[4] He was echoed in turn by the doyen of early-eighteenth-century critics, John Dennis: writing a tragedy or epic is 'perhaps the greatest thing that a Man can design', and not only is 'The End of Tragedy, and of Epick Poetry ... to instruct', but 'It belongs to Poetry only, to teach publick Virtue and publick Spirit'.[5] Dennis passed these principles on to the circle of reformers whom he influenced, notably James Thomson and Handel's first English librettist, Aaron Hill.[6] Handel's remark that he intended *Messiah* not only to entertain his audience, but 'to make them better',[7] is anecdotal but credible as a claim, in keeping with the standards of his time, that his work was worth the name of art.

Hill is still a rather shadowy presence in most accounts of Handel's work but, as Christine Gerrard has shown, he was a pivotal figure in mid-century literary life, a friend and encourager of writers just as he was of Handel, and immensely productive himself. He was greatly and deservedly respected, and the subscription list for his posthumously published *Works* filled twenty-six double-column pages with illustrious names.[8] He will be mentioned several times in this book, and we can trace the main thrust of the movement to reform the arts through him.

Hill worked ceaselessly to refresh, invigorate and ennoble art. His literary periodicals, *The Plain Dealer* and *The Prompter*, regularly provided constructive criticism of the literary and musical stage. As soon as Handel arrived in England Hill seized on him – the rising European master of his own art, specialising in a public form of it with boundless possibilities for good influence – and wrote the scenario of *Rinaldo*, Handel's first London opera. As the historians of Handel's early operas attest, 'Hill was in effect the only begetter. He chose the subject, laid out the plot, and, when Rossi had versified it, translated the result.'[9] Twenty years later, when English opera was showing its strongest promise since Purcell and badly needed a composer of comparable stature to realise its potential, Hill acted on the new readiness which Handel had shown (by putting on *Esther*) to set English words for the theatre, and wrote him a letter urging him to make the switch from Italian to English opera (see below, p. 79). After forty years of active literary life his preface to the 1744 edition of his play *Alzira* (dedicated to Frederick Prince of Wales, champion of native artistic endeavour) shows him still unsatisfied, still campaigning, still hopeful: 'It may be at present a *fruitless*, but it can never be an *irrational* wish, that a Theatre intirely *new*, (if not rather the old ones, *new-modelled*) professing only what is *serious* and *manly*, and made sacred to the interests of *wisdom* and *virtue*, might arise'. He was a principal activist in the high-minded group (vainly) urging Pope to write his serious epic, *Brutus* (see chapter 5).

The time-honoured union of delight and instruction was similarly the goal of another keen reformer who was close to Handel, his oratorio librettist James Miller: 'To make Instruction Partner with Delight, / Shall be our care.'[10] But Hill, following Dennis, sought not just to bond but to fuse emotion and instruction, and advocated writing which leads to virtue by treating great subjects in a way that profoundly stirs the readers' emotions and hence engages their minds. He complained that

The most obvious Defect in our Poetry . . . is, that we study Form, and neglect Matter . . . and under a full Sail of Words . . . we leave our Sense fast aground . . . our Poetry has been degenerating apace into mere Sound, or Harmony . . . whatever Pains we take, about polishing our Numbers, where we raise not our Meaning, are as impertinently bestowed, as the Labour wou'd be, of setting a broken Leg after the Soul has left the Body . . . with an unsinewy Imagination, sent abroad in sounding Numbers.

Although 'the Loftiness of the Expression will astonish shallow
Readers into a temporary Admiration, and support it, for a while',
the impact is only on the ear, and 'The Heart remains unreach'd'
because of 'the Languor of the Sentiment'.[11] The true poet is 'an
Exalter of what is most dignified, and substantial, in Nature', and by
reconciling his passions with his reason 'can restore Himself to a
Harmony, like That, we fell from, in the Loss of Paradise'. Poetry
should concern itself with human worth, national achievements,
and religion. Hill is every bit as ambitious as Sidney or Shelley in his
claims for the poet's potential power:

> Learn, *Poets*, learn, th'Importance of your Name;
> And, conscious of your Power, *exalt* your Aim.
> Soul-shaking Sovereigns of the Passions, *you*
> Hold wider *Empire*, than the *Caesars* knew.
> While clam'rous *Rhet'ric* but suspends the Mind,
> And whisp'ring *Morals* sigh, unheard, behind;
> While frail *Philosophy* but starts Designs,
> And *Revelation's* Light, too distant, shines,
> Ardent, and *close*, The *Muse* maintains Her Sway . . .
> Tho' faint, through modish Mists, *Religion* shines
> Oft, let Her sacred Soarings lift your Lines:
> Oft, let your Thoughts take Fire, at That *first* Flame,
> From whose bright Effluence Inspiration came.
> Th'Almighty *God*, who gave the Sun to blaze,
> *Voic'd* the *Great Poet*, for his Maker's Praise.[12]

As Hill's friend James Thomson urged in the preface to the second
edition of his *Winter* (1726):

let POETRY, once more, be restored to her antient Truth, and Purity; let
Her be inspired from Heaven, and, in Return, her Incense ascend thither;
let Her exchange Her low, venal, trifling, Subjects for such as are fair,
useful, and magnificent; and, let Her execute these so as, at once, to please,
instruct, surprize, and astonish . . . Nothing can have a better Influence
towards the Revival of POETRY than the chusing of great, and serious,
Subjects; such as, at once, amuse the Fancy, enlighten the Head, and warm
the Heart. These give a Weight, and Dignity, to the Poem . . .

As these passages make clear, morally elevated themes implied a
framework of religion – Christian religion. Dean and Knapp,
pointing out Hill's deviations from Tasso in his libretto of *Rinaldo*,
call attention to 'the absurd conversion [of Armida and Argante] to
Christianity, no doubt a concession to English taste'.[13] Rather it was

a blow for the improvement of English taste, in keeping with the reformers' programme. Poetry, they argued, is most satisfying when it most affects us, by treating a subject in which we have the deepest concern; therefore poetry should treat subjects drawn from religion. Hill was particularly active in carrying out his mentor Dennis' teaching that 'the use of Religion in Poetry was absolutely necessary to raise it to the greatest exaltation, of which so Noble an Art is capable', as 'an effectual way of Reconciling People to a Regulated Stage'.[14] Art, according to these reformers, is not only legitimised but given the means to realise its full potential when, and only when, it embraces moral and religious themes – as oratorio was to do.

THE EIGHTEENTH-CENTURY VIEW OF GREEK TRAGEDY

The reformers looked to the example of Greek tragedy, on several counts. It was a public art form instilling consciousness of national history and an aspiration to public service. 'The true Poet is a *Patriot*', as were the Greek tragedians. They were 'the only *State Pensioners* of those Days' (as distinct from the yes-men nowadays rewarded with government pay), and, 'From the *moving* Enthusiasm of their Stage', Athenian youth

grew up in a Spirit of Greatness, and Liberty, an Aversion against Tyranny, a Propensity to Arms, and Eloquence; a Contempt of Danger, and Death, and an impatient *Emulation* of what they daily heard, and saw, so *provokingly* praised, and represented; – The Actions, and Sentiments of the *Brave*, and the *Virtuous*: By whose Remembrance, therefore, the Scene was *politically inflam'd*, that the Fire might expand itself, and kindle up the Souls of the Audience.[15]

Athenian theatre was publicly funded, providing a venerable precedent for the national sponsorship of the arts which the reformers advocated (Hill follows the above paragraph with a plea for a government-funded national theatre).[16] It united the arts and combined their effects of sound, sense and spectacle; modern art was the weaker for dividing them.[17] Above all, it taught morality, a morality firmly based in religion.

Over and over again the translators of Aristotle, the translators of the plays and the literary reformers commend Athenian tragedy because it teaches us to behave better. 'The aim and business of the *Greek Tragedy* was, by some fable or other, to teach and inculcate some moral maxim.'[18] Each tragedy is admired for teaching a plain moral lesson: *Ajax* warns against anger, *Oedipus Tyrannus* against rashness and curiosity, *Antigone* against severity and *Trachiniae* against jealousy; *Philoctetes* and *Hecuba* teach patience.[19] But this was not seen as some kind of ethical humanism; the plays were recognised as religious-political events imbued with religious belief. John Brown, in common with many critics, traced their origins in religious song, in a passage with resonances for students of oratorio:

Their *Songs* . . . being drawn chiefly from the Fables or History of their own Country, would contain the essential Parts of their *religious, moral*, and *political* Systems . . . the *Celebration* of their deceased Heroes would of Course grow into a *religious* Act . . . would naturally become the *Standard* of *Right* and *Wrong*; that is, the Foundation of *private Morals* and *public Law*: And thus, the whole Fabric of their *Religion, Morals*, and *Polity*, would naturally arise from, and be included in their *Songs*.[20]

Some commentators linked the religion of the Athenian plays with that of modern Britain. Handel's librettist Thomas Morell, like other classicists of his time, asserted its concordance with Scripture: 'It has been proved by many writers, antient and modern, if not to demonstration, to the highest moral certainty, that the chief parts of human literature had their derivation from the sacred oracles; that the choicest contemplations of Gentile philosophy were derived, originally, if not immediately, from the sacred scriptures and Jewish church.'[21] Morell may have felt obliged to make this case for the religious value of the plays because he was producing school texts, but it was not idiosyncratic, and literary critics agreed that ancient tragedy, a pinnacle of dramatic achievement, sets the modern dramatist an example to recommend 'the Human and Christian Virtues'.[22]

Tragedy can more readily provide a moral lesson, as critics of the time required, if it shows Providence to be firmly in control. Moral aspiration depends on optimism about the nature of man and needs to be ratified by optimism about the powers that control him. Much of the dramatic criticism of the period and all the treatment of Greek tragedy, whether criticism or adaptation, is dominated by the need to show that there is a God and that He is benevolently interested in the fate of humanity and of the individual. The idea of a benevolent deity is incompatible with a sense of man hopelessly pitted against an incomprehensible destiny, and a major source of fear, the unknown, is largely absent from eighteenth-century tragedy. Conversely a tragedy which suggests a blind or evil-eyed destiny is condemned as outrageous, and those who could not accept Greek tragedy as a 'publick lesson' rejected it as too shocking on these grounds. The possibility of an amoral Providence was not entertained; the explanation for it when it was found, by a few critics, in the Greek tragedies was the barbarous primitivism of the dramatists and more particularly of the society in which they lived.[23]

In the twentieth century several of Handel's oratorios and secular music dramas have been likened to Greek tragedy – to a twentieth-century view of Greek tragedy which, as the above remarks suggest, tends to be remote from that of Handel's time.[24] It is instructive to distinguish here between the effect of Handel's music and the texts he was setting. In their treatment of tragic conflict, what did the librettists actually provide? The comparison with Greek tragedy has been made in relation to some of the oratorios, for example *Saul*, but if we turn to the secular English dramas we can compare a libretto with a source which is actually a Greek tragedy. Several of the librettos have classical settings, but one is taken directly from an Athenian play: Thomas Broughton's *Hercules* (1744) is based on Sophocles' *Trachiniae*. Of all the plays available as a model, this seems the least likely to be chosen by an eighteenth-century divine (Broughton was a prebendary of Salisbury Cathedral and wrote in defence of Christian doctrine[25]). It is shocking even to the twentieth-century reader, and was evidently shocking, or at least unacceptable, to its adapter, who altered every incident of its plot but one, and changed the characters out of all recognition.

A modern humanist reading of the play derived simply from the text might plausibly go like this. The central character is Heracles' suffering wife Deianira, who is fearful, sorrowful, neglected and overawed, but not jealous or rancorous. She finally kills herself. Heracles appears only in the final quarter of the play, when he suffers excruciating pain without restraint and rages against his wife (he wants to tear her apart) and against his blameless son. Hyllos, the son, mistakenly accuses his mother and thus becomes the immediate cause of her suicide. He is ordered – by his father – to marry his father's concubine, whom he sees as responsible for his parents' death, and to burn his father alive. According to the last lines of the play, all this is impassively presided over by the gods. Nor is the conclusion relieved by any demonstration of man's capacity for nobility, dignity or sensibility in the face of suffering. Heracles himself embodies complete disregard of conventional morality. He

has sacked the city of Oechalia in order to acquire Iole, whom he has
abducted and sent home ahead to share his wife's bed as an alternative consort. His lust is described as an overmastering sickness,
and when he appears, in his death agonies, he is helpless and
frenzied. He feels no concern for his family; his regret about his
wife's death is that he wanted to inflict it on her himself. Of the two
traditional facets of Heracles, aspiring energy and social consciousness, Sophocles' hero shows only the former. But no one in the play
criticises him; his heroic prowess is accepted as setting him apart
from ordinary humanity and its standards of behaviour.

Both Sophocles' audience and the classically versed eighteenth-
century reader knew the rest of the story: Heracles' glorious public
role, his labours for mankind and his apotheosis. Broughton, himself
a classicist, may have been able to accept the play as a comment on
or complement to the myth, but his alterations show that he found
Sophocles' design, particularly the part concerning Heracles,
intolerable as a drama for public consumption. He eliminated
Heracles' habitual adultery (*Trachiniae* ll. 459–60), his destruction of
Oechalia as a route to Iole (ll. 475–8), his abduction of Iole and
intended 'double marriage' (ll. 356–8, 539–40, 544–5), his murder of
Lichas (ll. 772–82), his rage against Deianira (ll. 1066–9, 1109–11),
his threats to Hyllos (ll. 1199–1202, 1239–40), his insistence on
Hyllos' marriage to Iole (ll. 1221–9), his indifference to human
feeling, and the manner of his death. All that remains of Sophocles'
plot in Broughton's version is that Dejanira sends Hercules the robe
of Nessus, not knowing it to be poisoned, and it eats his flesh.
Hercules is innocent of any but polite feelings for Iole, so Dejanira
has no reason to send him a supposed love-charm, but Broughton
gives her a motive which Sophocles does not: jealousy. Whereas in
Sophocles' play this would be justified, in Broughton's it is
groundless, and thus a moral failing. Suicide would be an apter end
for Broughton's Dejanira than it is for Sophocles', but too shocking
for an eighteenth-century audience; instead Broughton restores her
peace of mind with a happy ending – the apotheosis of Hercules
familiar in myth. Eliminating Heracles' liaison with Iole also
removes the outrageousness from the divine command that she
marry Hyllus, and this in turn opens the way for a sustained love
interest between the young couple, which adds decorum: Broughton
secures it by bringing forward the news of Hercules' safety, so Hyllus
does not go in search of him, and is at hand to develop a relationship

with Iole when she arrives. Dejanira is attractively but dangerously volatile, prone to rash indulgence of emotion; Hercules is an affable retired general, exchanging heroic for domestic benevolence; Iole (mute in Sophocles) is the pattern of a crown princess, uttering right principles on every occasion.

Sophocles' chorus is a group of girls, friends of Deianira. At the outset it comments on what Deianira says, but with stock pieties only: life is uncertain, all humans have to bear pain as well as pleasure, nothing is permanent. Thereafter it shows no greater insight than the other characters, and makes no judgements, except to exonerate Deianira from blame for Heracles' death. Broughton's chorus of (male and female) Trachinians, irrelevant to the domestic melodrama he has constructed, has a major role: it provides moral commentary. It generalises each situation into a moral lesson, praising 'filial Piety' when Hyllus looks forward to the adventures he will have while looking for his father, advising Dejanira against depair ('Relief may come'), denouncing jealousy as a 'Tyrant of the human Breast'. So determined is Broughton to make the proper reaction explicit at all points of the drama that when the choric Lichas is acting as herald (Act III scene 1) he invents a '1 Trachinian' to fill the gap, and he transforms Hyllus into a sympathising bystander during Hercules' agony ('How is the Heroe fall'n!').

MORAL ALLEGORY

Broughton's libretto is a child of its time. Perhaps we should not be altogether surprised that a modern cultural historian refers to it as 'one of Handel's scriptural libretti'.[26] More or less obviously, the urge to teach a moral lesson likewise informs all the other English librettos which Handel set, and except in *Acis and Galatea* moral decorum and poetic justice generally rule. Where a character suffers finally (as distinct from temporarily) it is most often on account of a moral fault, and this, rather than blind or evil-eyed destiny, is the cause of disaster. The moral fault is always obvious and all the characters are uncomplicated: they are virtuous, virtuous except for one flaw, or wicked. The issues in which they are concerned are also uncomplicated. An action is either right or wrong (to this end Israelite warfare is bleached of its dubious political elements), and when a real dilemma arises (as it does for Jephtha), a deus ex machina intervenes. Except in *Acis* and, to a lesser extent, *Semele*, the righteous are rewarded and the wicked suffer. When the source proposes otherwise the librettist twists it as far round as possible (as in Iphis' reprieve and Hercules' apotheosis). The situations of the individual characters are constantly generalised by choric comments, uttered by the chorus itself but also by individual characters, to show that their experiences have lessons for us all.

The moralising impulse shapes the librettos to such an extent that some are generalised to the point of having no individual characters at all, or characters who are abstractions. *L'allegro*, *The Choice of Hercules* and *The Triumph of Time and Truth* are documents of eighteenth-century moral psychology, defining and discriminating between differing states of mind and emotion and forms of behaviour in order to assist listeners to the propitious ordering of their own lives. Hence the addition of *Il moderato*, enjoining pursuit of the middle road, to Milton's pictures of more extreme states of being, and it is interesting evidence of Handel's participation in the moral-aesthetic principles of his day that this seems to have been his idea: the librettist, Charles Jennens, writing to his friend Edward Holdsworth, refers to 'A little piece I wrote at Mr Handel's request to be subjoyn'd to Milton's Allegro & Penseroso, to which He gave the Name of Il Moderato, & which united those two independent Poems in one Moral Design'.[27] Setting moral philosophy to music would not have seemed odd to eighteenth-century connoisseurs, who were accustomed to hearing preachers justify the use of music to convey great truths because of its ability, surpassing that of philosophy and poetry, to lodge ideas in our minds and hearts (see chapter 3). Nor would the use of allegorical characters have seemed a lifeless contrivance. As we will constantly notice in this study, eighteenth-century readers and listeners had a particular readiness to understand (or make) allegorical interpretations which for them were vivid and engaging.[28]

A good idea of the enthusiasm which we should imagine Handel's moral odes evoking in their own time is suggested by the account of one of his operas in the full-page lead article in the *Universal Spectator* of 5 July 1735. Arguing that music is no hindrance to the stage's duty to teach virtue, the writer goes so far as to claim that 'If . . . an Opera, or a poem, set to good Musick, gives us in some pleasing Allegory, a Lesson of Morality, I can't but think it preferable to either the Comick Vein or the Tragick Stile'. He is prompted to this reflection by a young wit whom he has heard remarking of Handel's

Alcina that 'he cou'd find no Allegory in the whole Piece ... and nothing of a Moral'. We may be surprised that a young wit should be looking for either allegory or moral, but this does not in itself elicit direct comment from the author. He argues that, on the contrary, *Alcina* 'affords us a beautiful and instructive Allegory' on the 'short Duration of all sublunary Enjoyments', by showing the tendency of 'the giddy head-strong Youth' to chase after 'imaginary or fleeting Pleasures, which infallibly lead them to cruel Reflections and to too late Repentance'. The article fills one of its three columns with analysis of the 'agreeable Allegory'. Emotional involvement makes us stop thinking rationally, ignore advice, and block out the evidence of experience; it results in disillusion, regret and loss of self-esteem, and especially afflicts young people; pleasure never lasts long and often perishes by being achieved, either because we quickly tire of it or because it fails to answer our expectations; we continually have to struggle to thwart our worst inclinations and the more we give in to them the harder they are to resist; pursuing self-gratification leads to our losing any concern for self-respect and the respect of others – this paraphrases about half of the analysis of *Alcina*'s allegorical teaching. The twentieth-century reader is bound to be struck by the assumption that music dramas should furnish moral lessons, by the animation with which these lessons are decoded, and by the way in which the quest for instruction, far from resulting in a pat formula, is impelled and complicated by pleasure in exploring the psychology of human behaviour.[29]

REVIVING THE CHORUS

The moral and religious worth of Athenian tragedy was one of the main factors in the movement to revive the use of the chorus on the modern stage, a topic on which, according to one literary historian, debate 'raged throughout the eighteenth century'. Edward Niles Hooker stresses the weight of opinion against the use of the chorus to endorse his view that 'By the end of the century the idea was dying a natural death.'[30] However, by the end of the century the idea was flourishing in a related medium. Admittedly the chorus made little impression on the eighteenth-century spoken drama, but Handel and his librettists made the chorus a major constitutent of oratorio, distinguishing Handelian oratorio from other contemporary literary and musical forms. Handel has been credited with restoring the chorus to its Aeschylean status and hence providing the only drama of the period of heroic proportions according to the Greek model.[31] The use of a chorus in his oratorios may be partly a response to current opinions; it certainly reflects them.

André Dacier's standard commentary on Aristotle, which Hill clearly knew, pronounced of the Greek tragedians:

> Their Theatre was a School, where Virtue was generally better Taught, than in the Schools of their Philosophers, and at this very Day, the reading their Pieces will inspire an Hatred to Vice, and a Love to Virtue. To imitate them profitably, we should re-establish the *Chorus*, which establishing the *veri-similitude* of the *Tragedy*, gives an Opportunity to set forth to the People, those particular Sentiments, you would inspire them with, and to let them know, what is Vicious or Laudable, in the Characters which are introduced.[32]

In England Dacier's appreciation of the chorus had been anticipated by several distinguished authors. They included Davenant, who envisaged it reinforcing the moral principles arising from the action during scene changes, and Dryden, who was interested in reviving it as part of theatre architecture.[33] Dacier was echoed by numerous translators and propagators of Greek tragedy, for instance George Adams: 'The Way ... to make our Theatre as instructive as the *Athenian* was, is to restore the *Chorus*, and for ever to banish from the Stage such Stuff with which it is daily pestered.'[34] The Attic chorus was valued as the voice of moral and religious instruction. This identity was wholeheartedly taken over into oratorio by Handel's librettists.

Many comments indicate that advocates of the chorus intended to reintroduce not just the character, but its singing role. Moral improvement apart, the major benefit expected from the return of the chorus was an increase in variety of texture; the major disadvantage, dramatic irrelevance. If it was to be introduced, it must be 'always with regard to the *Scene*; for by no means must it be made a business independent of that; In particular our [mixed sung and spoken English] *Operas* are highly criminal, the Musick in 'em is for the most part an absurd Impertinence'.[35] Nevertheless, the anonymous author of a translation of Sophocles' *Electra* published by Watts in 1714, taking up Dacier's commendation of Greek tragedy as a school of virtue, advocates restoring the chorus because its *music* can contribute to the moral sense of serious drama:

> if we had a mind now usefully to follow their Steps, there would be need to re-establish the Use of their Chorus; whereby an occasion is given to instil, by the Charms of Musick, into the Minds of the Hearers those Sentiments

of Virtue and Goodness from the several Characters which are introduc'd
in the Play. Thus, instead of those idle Songs brought in often, without any
Coherence with the Action, to patch up our Plays; the intermediate Chorus
would serve both as an Ease and Diversion, and as a Moral to the Fable of
the foregoing Act. Thus Musick, that most delightful and soothing Art,
instead of cloying our Ears, crowding our Theatres and shutting out good
Sense, would no longer be abus'd, but be improv'd in carrying on the main
design of the Tragedy, which is to take the Soul as well as tickle the Ears,
and to please the Understanding and Judgment, as well as the Fancy. Then
Musick would have the same Effect upon us as *Polybius* relates it had upon
the *Arcadians*, who by it were civiliz'd, and were taught Humanity, Sweetness, and Respect for Religion. (preface, p. iii)

Here the practical use of music in the theatre as a charming diversion is linked with the tradition of music as a morally elevating
influence (see chapter 3). And it was in these terms that serious-
minded devotees appreciated Handel's oratorio choruses, praising
the religious elevation afforded by the stirring sentiments and
music.[36] Literary critics traced the origins of the Attic chorus to the
hymns of religious festivals, and the high status of hymns in
eighteenth-century England must have bolstered the claims of the
chorus.[37]

A less reverential assessment of the chorus' musico-dramatic possi-
bilities, the most extended one in known contemporary writing,
occupies part of the book formerly attributed to James Ralph, *The
Touch-stone: or, Historical, Critical, Political, Philosophical and Theo-
logical Essays on the Reigning Diversions of the Town. Design'd for the
Improvement of all Authors, Spectators, and Actors of Operas, Plays, and
Masquerades. In which Every Thing Antique, or Modern, relating to Musick,
Poetry, Dancing, Pantomimes, Chorusses, Cat-Calls, Audiences, Judges,
Criticks, Balls, Ridottos, Assemblies, New Oratory, Circus, Bear-Garden,
Gladiators, Prize-Fighters, Italian Strolers, Mountebank Stages, Cock-Pits,
Puppet-Shews, Fairs, and Publick Auctions, is occasionally Handled. By a
Person of some Taste and some Quality. With a Preface, giving an Account of
the Author and the Work* (1728).[38] It is not easy now to tell exactly
what the author of this fascinating 237-page work himself thinks,
because of his uneven tone. Apparently unironic recommendations,
which in fact anticipate oratorio, such as reintroducing the chorus,
or using scriptural stories, are purportedly bolstered by burlesque
examples: Dick Whittington as a sample of traditional British
history (previously used by Addison in one of his squibs on Italian
opera); a knockabout comedy version of the sacrifice of Isaac,
reminiscent of fair-booth drolls; an opera 'laid in Holland, or Hell'

to have an apt chorus of frogs (shades of Aristophanes). Some of this
reflects the author's immense contempt for Dutch music and drama
in particular, an ambivalent attitude to foreign art and artists
generally, and scorn for large sectors of the public – puritanical
religious zealots, people who enjoy crude slapstick, and mindless
opera goers. He 'sells' his ideas for 'improvements' of drama for these
sectors with the (assumed?) obliviousness of a Dunce; this casts
doubt on the sincerity of his recommendations, many of which seem
not at all bizarre, including a plea for a full chorus in heroic opera.
But, at the end of his twenty-page chapter 'Of Chorusses, Antique
and Modern; in great Esteem with the Antients; neglected by the
present Age. Of their Use and Beauty in all Stage-Entertainments',
he states that diverting spectacle is necessary to persuade the child-
ish and depraved majority to take instruction and have their
manners reformed. His flippant tone and recommendations would
seem to be part of a perfectly serious aim to get as many people into
the theatre as possible by broadening its appeal.

The Touch-stone's author displays his knowledge of the Attic
drama, makes the (conventional) point that modern opera derives
from the Greek chorus, and argues that though the Restoration
operas were not sung throughout, being in the French rather than
the Italian style, they had the merit of resembling '*Grecian* Tragedy
and Chorus'. But now the 'Grand Chorus, as practis'd by the
Antients' is 'entirely banish'd the *Play-House*, and only the Name
preserv'd in the *Opera*. This shall not deter me from introducing it
amongst our publick Diversions.' In Greek tragedy it was both
'beneficial and diverting', providing dramatic coherence, spectacle
(a stage full of dancing figures), music and moral instruction. It
'gave the Spectators the most exquisite Delight; and added an Air of
Magnificence and Surprize to the *Stage* and *Audience*'. It is this
Gesamtkunstwerk chorus that the author wants reintroduced. He
realises there is no hope for it on the spoken stage, and 'I would be
content, it should resign all Pretensions to an Interest in the *Play-
house*; was it but judiciously introduc'd in our OPERAS'. However, he
then makes a staged, acting and dancing, chorus sound rather silly
and, recognising this, issues what any composer as ambitious as
Handel could only read as a challenge:

A superior Genius ought to preside in the Conduct of these Affairs, lest we
be mistaken in the End propos'd, and have our Performances turn'd into
Ridicule, when we expect they should be admir'd ... In Fine, a CHORUS
rightly introduc'd in an OPERA, must give the WORLD the *NE PLUS ULTRA*

of Musick; and, I think it manifest, that by the wilful and careless Omission of it on the present *Italian Stage*, we lose the Perfection of *Harmony*; and never allow our Composers an Opportunity of exerting their highest Talents, and displaying the Greatness of a Genius, by shewing what Force of Musick can produce.

We may have an Idea of this from some Parts of our Church-Musick; which though generally very bad, yet demonstrates, that those full Parts of Musick, either in Church or Theatre, shew the Quintessence of Art in the Composer, and must give equal Delight to an Audience. (pp. 124–7)

Here the author even proposes (four years before the first public hearing of *Esther*) that the chorus should take its cue from church music in being elaborate, massive (sung by several voices to a part) and astonishing. If Handel read this, he would have had every encouragement to write choruses in what his contemporaries called his most 'artificial' (studied) style for the theatre, and make them a prominent part of his compositions. He may well have taken an interest in the book, because it mentions his compositional skills more than once in its discussion of opera.

Handel may also have been made aware of ideas for a dramatic chorus, and the musical form it ought to take, from another source. Thomas McGeary has persuasively suggested that 'My Lord Your Fathers Letter relating to Musick', referred to in a letter by Handel to the fourth Earl of Shaftesbury in 1736, is the letter from the third earl to the writer Pierre Coste prompted by Raguenet's treatise on the superiority of Italian to French opera (1702).[39] Shaftesbury makes three aesthetic recommendations for modern music theatre: less elaborate scenery; restoration of the chorus; and simpler recitative, nearer to normal speech. 'Machines and Decorations' are 'vulgar, miserable, barbarous'; they were directly responsible for the decline of the Roman theatre, hastening the decay of Roman liberty through the corruption of public taste, and they abet the decay of liberty wherever they are allowed to dominate the theatre at the expense of thought-provoking, instructive drama – wherever the appeal is to the eye rather than the ear. From this line of argument, which was current among literary-political reformers by the 1730s, Handel could gain confidence that unstaged music drama might be acceptable to the cultivated public he was aiming to please. Secondly, Shaftesbury speaks of the opportunity which the Italians have, in opera, for 'restoring the antient Tragedy (the true Opera) with its Chorus, and all the Charms depending on that antient Plan and Method'; as a result 'the Opera will every day gain upon the other Theater, and our best Tragedy at last melt into Opera, which Union will be a kind of reviving the antient Tragedy in all its noble Orders of Musick and continu'd Harmony'. Here again the prospect is held out of a version of opera as *Gesamtkunstwerk* that will displace even tragedy as *the* dramatic form. Finally, all action should be communicated in recitative, to avoid absurdity; song (that is, non-recitative setting) should be used only for soliloquies and for 'the real parts of the Chorus', which should be 'reserv'd for the great Art of the Musician, and attended by Symphonys'. Here again Handel had a directive to concentrate his most complex and massive effects in choruses. He received it at a crucial time for oratorio, in 1736, during the five-year gap between his first spell of oratorio productions and his second, which was to continue for the rest of his composing life. His positive, even enthusiastic, response, in his letter to the fourth earl, heralds his future output: 'I am extremly obliged to Your Lordship for sending me that Part of My Lord Your Fathers Letter relating to Musick. His notions are very just. I am highly delighted with them, and cannot enough admire 'em.'[40]

Two of Handel's oratorio librettists themselves made the link between the chorus in Greek tragedy and the modern musical stage. In his *Harlequin Horace*, James Miller, in the assumed role of Dunce, satirically applauds the modern stage from which

> The antient *Chorus* justly's laid aside,
> And all its Office by a *Song* supply'd:
> *Song* – when to the Purpose something's lack't,
> Relieves us in the middle of an Act . . .[41]

The chorus, used in the ancient manner, would guarantee good sense *and* dramatic appropriateness in the musical interludes which theatre patrons required. Morell, in his preface to his translation of Euripides' *Hecuba*, reiterated the arguments for the dramatic credibility and variety which the chorus could confer, like Shaftesbury and the author of *The Touch-stone* envisaging a superior kind of *Gesamtkunstwerk*: 'I cannot but think that were some of these ancient Plays judiciously translated and the Choric-songs reduced to proper Measure, and masterly set and perform'd, a more engaging and rational Entertainment could not be desired by the most polite Audience' (pp. xi–xii). His opinion was presumably strengthened by his active participation in the composition of choric songs at this time: his *Hecuba* came out in 1749, the year of his libretto of *Theodora* for Handel.

As has often been pointed out, the chorus entered English oratorio via Racine's choric religious dramas, *Esther* and *Athalie*, the sources of two of Handel's first three oratorios. Racine's use of the chorus was universally praised by literary critics in the first half of the eighteenth century, and was referred to whenever discussion about a possible revival of the chorus turned to its potential benefits for religion and morality.[42] One of the works in which it naturally receives particular praise is a translation of *Esther* by Thomas Brereton, published in 1715 and used by the author(s) of Handel's original libretto for Cannons. In his preface Brereton expresses the hope that his translation will recommend itself to 'chearfully virtuous Families',

> the rather, because here are interwrought throughout, after the Manner of the antient *Greek Chorus's* (long since commended to our Imitation by the late Critick Mr *Rhymer*) diverse Psalms or Hymns; which to such as are especially inclin'd to Musick, will have all the good Effects of the Modern *Opera*, without any of its Absurdities. (sig. A6r-v)

Brereton's whole preface is a model of the theatre reformers' arguments, related to music theatre. Brereton says he wrote his translation 'to the sole Intent of expelling Licence and Libertinism ... from their long Usurpation of our Stage' by providing 'a better Example', and to refute the belief that audiences could only be pleased with sex and violence ('Adulteries, Murders, and other Abominations of the *Pagan* World'). Tragedy could, 'next to *Preaching*, be of all Ways the most conducive to Morality; Nay ... I dare yet further affirm, with the Concurrence of the *Divine* [George] *Herbert* ...

> A Verse may find Him who a Sermon flies,
> And turn Delight into a Sacrifice'

(from Herbert's 'Church-Porch', the opening poem of *The Temple*, which Brereton also used as an epigraph). Indeed it would have even better results than preaching among 'the Young and High-bred ... I've been long of Opinion that this is a very feasible Reformation.' But being conscious of the novelty of his product, he is glad to be able 'to Back my Endeavour with the Authority of the great Name of *Racine*'.[43]

Racine's choric religious plays were accepted even by severe critics of the drama (Jeremy Collier and Isaac Watts, for example) because of their moral and religious didacticism. Brereton was not alone in adopting them as a means of reform. William Duncombe, brother-in-law and editor of another of Handel's early librettists, John Hughes (himself an ardent moralist, as his works and his friends attest), similarly commends Racine's *Athalie* in his preface to his translation of it because of its moral in this case moral-political – usefulness:

The Original ... was written by one of the finest Authors of the *French* Nation, who thought it no Disparagement to let his Wit and Learning be subservient to the Cause of Religion and Virtue ... he discovers in it a hearty Detestation of Tyranny, and the most generous Love of Legal Freedom, and did not design meerly to amuse and delight, but to instruct and improve his Auditors and Readers ... it abounds with noble and sublime Sentiments of Piety and Virtue. He was not contented to move the Passions, unless at the same time he likewise improved the Will, and mended the Heart.[44]

* * *

According to Thomson the stage was no less than 'the School which forms the Manners of the Age'.[45] The drama, private and public religion and morality, and national political integrity were all connected, as the author of *An Epistle to Charles Fleetwood esq* entitled *Of the Use and Improvement of the Stage* warned in 1737:

Then *Britain* learn what *Rome*'s sad Annals tell;
Taste, Morals, Liberty, together fell:
There trace her Rise, there see her Ruin shown;
Mark well the Cause, and thence presage thy own ...
By Vice we fell, by Virtue we must rise:
Diseases must be cured by Contraries.
Here be each *Greek* and *Roman* Worthy shown,
Till their transported Virtues shine our own.
Let God-like *Cato* gen'rous Warmth impart,
And wake the Patriot in each *British* Heart ...
Spread social Love, and heal our Party strife.
(ll. 177–80, 185–90, 195)

There was a moral void in the theatre, and the nation's health urgently required it to be filled. Some looked hopefully to music-and-words, or even music alone, and to the one composer sufficiently able to galvanise his audience. Repeatedly throughout his English career, Handel's admirers expressed their conviction that his music had the morally elevating power required of great art, and that through it he could achieve the reform of private and public morals and manners, and unite the nation harmoniously.[46]

When they turned their attention to the secular musical scene the campaigners for artistic reform found 'unnaturalness' of various kinds, but chiefly the unnaturalness and affront to good sense and good taste of two forms of music theatre, pantomime (mimed acrobatics and transformations) and Italian opera. Objections to the mindless and grotesque elements of pantomime are easily understood, but the twentieth-century audience which has learnt to pack theatres for revivals of Handel's Italian operas may need to be reminded why a man like Hill, who had hailed Italian opera's arrival in England as the dawn of new glory for British art (in the libretto to *Rinaldo*), was inveighing against it twenty years later in his journalism, dedications and correspondence, and imploring Handel to abandon it.

Much of the huge literature of adverse criticism of Italian opera in England (of which only a representative sample can be canvassed here) was generated by people with a professional reason for objecting to it: authors whose products and even livelihood were endangered by the fashionable world's opera addiction. They included leading dramatists and critics, Dennis, Addison and Steele among them.[47] Their objections should not be disregarded because of their self-interest or because their own work in fact failed to eradicate the rival form. For many (such as Pope), concern for their own success was united with concern for the integrity of art – the former was vested in the latter. On account of their interest, their criticism is often detailed and precise, giving us a full view of what native artists thought the artistic public merited. What they said against Italian opera, and in favour of native words set to music having native qualities and national flavour, concerns us both as the critical hinterland of English oratorio and as a blueprint for it which was largely realised.

As we have seen, critical orthodoxy required art to be morally instructive. As we have also seen, in the view of such cultivated admirers as the writer in the *Universal Spectator*, Italian opera could

achieve this. It is certainly arguable that the Italian operas produced in London by Handel and his rivals afforded lessons in how
(and how not) to behave,[48] but many Britons instead noticed
elements which they considered deplorable. Dr Johnson famously
described Italian opera as an irrational and exotic entertainment.[49]
By this he meant, simply, that it had no rational content for its
English auditors, most of whom did not understand the words; and
that it was foreign in origin and nature. His phrase sums up the
charges made against Italian opera by Handel's contemporaries. In
more detail, these were as follows. Italian opera is mindless, because
incomprehensible, and therefore degrading to an intelligent person.
As the words have no meaning for the audience the appeal is entirely
by the music to the senses; and music on its own can have insidiously
unmanning effects on the passions. The music of Italian opera is
especially subversive, being foreign and effete, and the performers
are likewise – sirens and eunuchs. Italian opera strikes at British
national identity and saps the nation's strength by persuading 'our
Princes, our Nobles, and the chief of our *Israel*' to prefer nonsense to
sense, the Italian language to English, foreign authors, composers
and performers to native ones, Italian music to national song, and
Italian half-men to Britons; by encouraging decadence, effeminacy,
faithlessness and family strife; and by draining the national
economy.[50]

Henry Carey is most familiar to music historians as the author of
one of the jolliest burlesques of Italian opera, *The Dragon of Wantley*
(1737), which Handel is known to have relished, and which in its
final lines encouraged him to write more oratorios.[51] In its preface
Carey recalled the pains (and pleasure) which he and his composer,
John Lampe, had taken in 'chopping and changing, lopping, eking
out, and coining of Words, Syllables, and Jingle, to display in
English the Beauty of Nonsense, so prevailing in the *Italian Operas*'.
He was not so lighthearted in his *Poems on Several Occasions*, which
includes a 'Satyr on the Luxury and Effeminacy of the Age'.[52] This
far less tolerant attack on Italian opera brings together all the stock
complaints against it:

> BRITONS! for shame, give all these follies o'er,
> Your antient Native Nobleness restore;
> Learn to be Manly, learn to be sincere,
> And let the World a BRITON's Name revere ...
> Curse on this damn'd, *Italian* Pathic Mode ...

> I hate this Singing in an unknown Tongue,
> It does our Reason and our Senses wrong ...
> I curse the unintelligible Ass,
> Who may, for ought I know, be singing Mass ...
> Can then our *British* Syrens charm no more,
> That we import these foreign Minstrels oe'r,
> At such Expence, from the *Italian* Shore?

During the first half of the eighteenth century music was a major metaphor for politics (see chapter 9). Italian opera was a useful focus for anyone wanting to exploit the prevalent xenophobia, since it threatened Englishmen at extremely sensitive points – sex and money. The castrati excited jealousy because women became infatuated with them, yet they were not even real *men*, and (it was alleged) they damagingly encouraged effeminacy among their British male admirers (to realise the distaste and fascination they equally aroused it may help to think of the effect of modern male pop stars with girlish features and suspect lifestyles). As Thomas McGeary points out, opera is an apt harbinger for the reign of Dulness in the *Dunciad* because it was felt to induce chaos, blurring distinctions which are essential to ordered society.[53] And yet the castrati persuaded men and women to part with huge amounts of money which they then took out of the country. Not only did they command enormous fees, they were a trade deficit. James Miller, later one of Handel's oratorio librettists, protested in the dedication of his play *The Man of Taste* (1735): 'When Husbands are ruin'd, Children robb'd, and Tradesmen starv'd, in order to give Estates to a French Harlequin, and Italian Eunuch, for a Shrug or a Song; shall not fair and fearless Satire oppose this Outrage upon all Reason and Discretion?'. His text, like many of his plays and poems, contains such satire: the gentlemen excitedly inform the ladies,

We are in treaty with all the Princes of Europe, to furnish us with Performers of every Country – in twenty unknown Languages at least, so that we shall have Performers of every Nation in *Europe* – but our own.

And all this too, Ladies, at the most trifling Expence imaginable – as we have contriv'd it.

Not above Fifty Thousand a Year at most – and suppose every Penny of it should be carried out of the Kingdom, what's that to a wealthy trading Nation, you know?[54]

The singers aroused religious as well as purely political xenophobia, being from a Catholic country. Carey's suspicion that they might, for all the audience knew, be singing Mass while pretending to sing operas, first voiced by Steele in the epilogue to *The Tender Husband* (1705), was more or less playfully deployed in numerous other broadsides (see chapter 9). The author of *The Touch-stone*, a friend to Italian operas, sardonically notes that 'their being perform'd in a foreign Tongue disgusts many of my Countrymen, who (tho' great *Philharmonicks*) yet being *True Britons*, and staunch *Protestants*, to shew their Love to their Country, and their Zeal for their Religion, are prepossess'd against Singing as well as Praying in an unknown Dialect'.[55] The sinister link of opera with a Catholic country had been stressed at the beginning of the century by Dennis, in his *Essay on the Opera's after the Italian Manner, which are about to be Establish'd on the English Stage: with some Reflections on the Damage which they May Bring to the Publick*, and he issued further warnings in four more publications to 1726.[56] His nationalism fuelled by the War of Spanish Succession, he pronounced that 'wherever Operas have been a constant Entertainment, they have been attended with Slavery', meaning the absolutist government of Catholic states. By the time the Royal Academy was founded to produce Italian operas, Italy was additionally *non grata* as the home of the Pretender.[57] Recent studies of eighteenth-century British nationalism have stressed France as the focus of xenophobia, including cultural xenophobia,[58] but in comments on music in the first half of the century it is Italy that is seen as the major cultural-moral threat. With our eye on oratorio it is worth noting, however, that the objection to opera as Italian seems to have been to the singers and the words, not the form. Similarly there do not seem to have been objections to oratorio as an Italian form. This may be because, though it had an Italian name, it was distinctively associated at its inception with English church music and English royal music.[59]

Clearly the answer to the insidiously fashionable Italian opera was to have English words set to English music: words that would convey rational meaning and native music sung by homegrown performers. 'Would it not be a glorious thing', asked Defoe persuasively, 'to have an *Opera* in our own, in our own most noble Tongue, in which the Composer, Singers, and Orchestra, should be of our own Growth?'[60] Language, then as now, was regarded as a prime index of national identity: Nahum Tate's prefatory poem to the *Grammar of the English Tongue* edited by Steele and others (fifth edition 1728), calling for the worldwide dissemination of English culture, exhorts readers

> To cultivate that long-neglected Soil
> Our *English* Language (stor'd with all the Seeds
> Of Eloquence, but Choak'd with Foreign Weeds).

In Pope's 'Epistle to Bolingbroke', Italian opera, derided as the acme of empty and tasteless fashion, is ranged with 'new Court jargon' and 'The modern language of corrupted Peers' against 'what was spoke at [the great victories of] Cressy and Poitiers' and 'the good old song'.[61] Dennis suggests that 'the Decay of Dramatick Poetry' is attributable to successive influxes of foreigners (at the Revolution of 1689, the Act of Union in 1701 and 'the *Hanover Succession*'), 'who not understanding our Language, have been very instrumental in introducing [mere] Sound and Show', Italian opera being the prime example.[62] Several of the journals advertising Handel's first public performances of his *Esther* billed it prominently as an 'ORATORIO IN ENGLISH', in capital letters of a size matched only by the title of the work itself. The demand for English word-setting had not escaped the notice of the market-conscious composer, and he made the English text the chief selling-point of his new venture.

The essence of the English language, as of the English character it expressed, was held to be 'manliness' – the antithesis of Italian's slithery softness (whose very aptness for musical setting was conducive to mindless babble). The same obtained for British music, and several librettists who campaigned for English word-setting prescribe for the music as well, notably Miller:

> In Days of Old when *Englishmen* were – *Men*,
> Their *Musick*, like themselves, was grave, and plain;
> The manly Trumpet, and the simple Reed,
> Alike with *Citizen*, and *Swain* agreed,
> Whose Songs in lofty Sense, and humble Verse,
> Their Loves, and Wars alternately rehearse ...
> Since *Masquerades* and *Opera's* made their Entry,
> And *Heydegger* and *Handell* rul'd our Gentry;
> A hundred different Instruments combine,
> And foreign *Songsters* in the Concert join ...
> All league, melodious Nonsense to dispense,
> And give us *Sound*, and *Show*, instead of *Sense*;
> In unknown Tongues mysterious Dullness chant,
> Make Love in *Tune*, or thro' the Gamut rant.[63]

Here Miller identifies sense with simplicity and a better past, variety with confusion and a disordered present. Carey likewise wanted traditional modes re-established:

A false Politeness has possess'd the Isle,
And ev'ry Thing that's *English* is Old Stile:
Ev'n Heav'n-born PURCELL now is held in Scorn,
PURCELL! who did a brighter Age adorn.
That Nobleness of Soul, that Martial Fire,
Which did our BRITISH ORPHEUS once inspire
To rouze us all to Arms, is quite forgot;
We aim at something – but we know not what:
Effeminate in Dress, in Manners grown,
We now despise whatever is our Own.
So *Rome*, when famous once for Arts and Arms,
(Betray'd by Luxury's enfeebling Charms)
Sunk into Softness, and its Empire lost.[64]

Miller and Carey were both echoing Hill, who had been calling
since the early 1720s for art that invigorates, and demanding opera
with music like Purcell's, 'in which the Dignity of *Reason* was not
sacrific'd, as it is now, to the Dissoluteness of *Sound*; but the Force of
Words and *Meaning*, was increas'd by *Musick*, and *Decoration*, and
impress'd upon the Soul'. Given this union of sound with sense,

our emasculating present Taste, of the *Italian* Luxury, and *Wantonness* of
Musick, will give way to a more *Passionate*, and animated Kind of *Opera*,
where not only the *Eye* and *Ear* may expect to be *charm'd*, but the *Heart* to be
touch'd and transported ... the Martial Spirit of our Nation, is effemi-
nated, and gradually relax'd, by the Influence of this softening *Syren*.[65]

Writing on music here joins the great body of eighteenth-century
English literature which connects a perceived decline of the arts
with corruption in private and public life, and loss of national
power. Ballad opera answered the call for native words and tunes –
hence its immense popularity – but did not meet the need for revival
of 'publick spirit': being satirical, it showed up all that was wrong in
British political life, but it presented no model to emulate. This high
ground was aimed at by English operas, with accounts of great
events of recent and remote national history, but they were only
fitfully successful in the absence, after the death of Purcell, of a
composer capable of providing music of matching grandeur.[66] Nor
did ballad opera educate the public to discriminate between 'good'
and 'bad' entertainment, a goal dear to those who saw themselves as
providers of the former and held Italian opera to account for the
prevalence of depraved taste: 'a People accustom'd for so many
Years to that, are as ill-prepar'd to judge of a good Tragedy, as
Children that are eating Sugar-plumbs are to taste *Champaign* and
Burgundy'.[67]

In looking for remedies for the national malaise, Miller, Carey and Hill specify what were to become elements of Handel's oratorios: words-and-music with 'lofty Sense, and humble Verse', dealing with love and war (as for example in *Joshua*), strongly moving the hearer and rousing positive emotions and patriotic pride.[68] The passage by Miller quoted above is from the edition of *Harlequin Horace* published in February 1735. By the time of the next edition, later in the same year, Miller had revised his opinion of Handel: '*Heydegger* and *Handell* rul'd our Gentry' now reads '*Heydegger* reign'd *Guardian* of our Gentry', Handel no longer being damagingly associated with 'melodious nonsense'. Miller may have been influenced by hearing the revivals of *Esther*, *Deborah* and *Athalia* performed by Handel during March at Covent Garden.[69] Certainly from this date he did not criticise Handel in print, and by 1739 in *The Art of Life* he was according him the highest praise, linking him with Pope, devoting thirteen admiring lines to an enthusiastic description of *Saul*, and commending his oratorios in a couplet that claims the composer as an ally in his own reforming intentions: 'When such Delights your leisure Moments know, / Virtue and Wisdom from Amusement flow.'[70] With oratorio, Handel had produced the exact contrary of the pantomime against which Miller had contended in *Harlequin Horace*: unstaged, unacted drama, requiring and repaying sustained attention, and more essentially verbal than any other form of English-language theatre (at no other did the patrons actually have the words in front of them during the performance).

Miller objected to a confusion of sound but wanted vigorous instrumentation, and at a later date Pope famously made Handel one of the very few recipients of praise in the fourth book of the *Dunciad*, for supplying just this in his oratorios. The lines already quoted (above, p. 45) from the *Dunciad*, spoken by Opera, are framed by these:

> 'Joy to great Chaos! let Division reign:
> Chromatic tortures soon shall drive them hence,
> Break all their nerves, and fritter all their sense . . .
> But soon, ah soon, Rebellion will commence,
> If Music meanly borrows aid from Sense.
> Strong in new Arms, lo! Giant HANDEL stands,
> Like bold Briareus, with a hundred hands;
> To stir, to rouze, to shake the Soul he comes,

And Jove's own Thunders follow Mars's Drums.
Arrest him, Empress; or you sleep no more—'
She heard, and drove him to th'Hibernian shore.[71]

Pope's and Warburton's note to 'let Division reign' explains: 'Mr *Handel* had introduced a great number of Hands [performers], and more variety of Instruments into the Orchestra, and employed even Drums and Cannon to make a fuller Chorus; which prov'd so much too manly for the fine Gentlemen of his age, that he was obliged to remove his Music into *Ireland*.' ('Cannon' presumably means the extra-deep kettledrums of the artillery train which Handel borrowed from the Tower of London for *Saul*.[72] Briareus averted chaos on Olympus, as Pope depicts Handel threatening to avert the reign of Chaos in England: jealous fellow deities fettered Zeus with a hundred bonds, but Briareus prevented anarchy by releasing him with the strength of his hundred hands.)

Pope is just one of many writers who registered Handel's oratorios as having exceptional volume of sound and hence being uniquely invigorating, and the representative recommendations of Hill, Miller and Carey show that in this respect too Handel was responding to a demand.[73] The demand was not simply for generally rousing but for *national* music, vigorous music being thought to be the kind that best expressed, as well as being best *for*, the British character. The author of an article in *Common Sense* about Handel's *Alexander's Feast* believes that each nation has and responds to a national style of music, or particular instrument, or tune. The Swiss, 'who are not a People of the quickest Sensations', are reported to be so responsive to a particular tune played on their national instrument that when they hear it 'they run Home as fast as they can', so the tune is strictly forbidden while they are on foreign service. The author wishes that a British composer could invent a tune that compelled such patriotic devotion; it could be played to advantage at the opening of Parliamentary debates, prayers having proved so ineffectual. Were it not for Handel's German birth, which would probably make him unable to provide the purely British idiom that is needed, he would be the ideal choice, for, as *Alexander's Feast* has shown, he 'certainly excels in the *Ortios*, or *Warlike Measures*' (the 'Ortios', or orthios, literally meaning physically upright, was one of Terpander's seven compositional forms, a stirring martial strain).[74] The fact that the writer turns instinctively to Handel to provide 'British' music *although* he is a foreigner is symptomatic of the

public's response to his music (see chapter 7). (Handel later took
up the challenge at its face value by producing a 'Song for the
Gentlemen Volunteers of the City of London' during the 1745
Rebellion.)

Pope's scenario of the dejected Muses lorded over by the insid-
iously weak harlot form of Italian opera had been anticipated by
Hill. In his *The Tears of the Muses*, Germanicus (Frederick Prince of
Wales) is petitioned by the weeping Muses as they prepare to leave
England, exiled by political faction and mindless opera, to restore
them (that is, good art) to their patrimony. Terpsichore laments:

> NEAR *opera*'s fribling *fugues*, what muse can stay?
> Where wordless warblings winnow *thought*, away!
> Music, when *purpose* points her not the road,
> Charms, to betray, and softens, to *corrode*.
> Empty of sense, the soul-seducing art
> Thrills a slow poison to the sick'ning heart ...
> HENCE, to the realms of *fame*, ye muses, fly;
> There, to the drum's big beat, the heart leaps high.
> There, sighing flutes but temp'ring martial heat,
> Teach distant pity and revenge to *meet*.
> The manly pipe, there, scorns th'expanded *shakes*,
> That wind wav'd nothings, till attention *akes*.
> There *now*, concurring keys and chords increase
> The heart's soft social tyes, and cherish *peace*.
> *Then*, trumpets, answ'ring trumpets, shrill, and far,
> Swell to the sounding wind th'inspiring *war*.
> There, the rous'd soul, in exercise, grows strong;
> Nor *pools* to puddly foulness, stopp'd, too long.
> Strength'ning and strengthned, by the poet's fire,
> There, music's meaning voice *exalts* desire.
> There, harmony not drowns, but quickens, thought;
> And fools, unfeeling words, by notes are *caught*.[75]

Here again is the demand for rousing 'manly' music, and in detail
unusually specific for his period Hill requests music which rouses
positive emotions: courage in battle, affection, exalted desire, love of
peace, even martial ardour offset by pity – all of which were to
feature prominently in Handel's oratorios. Hill makes a contrast, of
interest to Handelians, between harmony that quickens thought and
'expanded *shakes*, / That wind wav'd nothings, till attention *akes*'.
The over-extended melisma that seems to lose its way harmonically
and proportionately is often used by Handel in his English works to
suggest mental deficiency, whether the giant Polyphemus' simple-

mindedness as he woos Galatea ('O ruddier than the cherry'), Semele's infatuation with her own reflection ('Myself I shall adore') or Nitocris' criticism of her son Belshazzar's 'giddy Dissipation' ('The leafy Honours of the Field').

The lobby for English-language opera included several other writers close to Handel. Among these was John Hughes, who has the distinction of providing what are thought to be the first words of English which Handel set, the cantata *Venus and Adonis*.[76] This was the beginning of what can be interpreted as a series of attempts by English writers to make Handel into a composer of English opera, the most notably successful being *Acis and Galatea*, in which Hughes was also involved. In 1732, when Handel had shown a willingness to produce English music dramas for public consumption by revising and putting on *Esther*, another of his librettists gave him, not an English text, but a plea to change the course of his career. Hill wrote to him in December of that year:

I cannot forbear to tell you the earnestness of my wishes, that, as you have made such considerable steps towards it, already, you would let us owe to your inimitable genius, the establishment of *musick*, upon a foundation of good poetry; where the excellence of the *sound* should be no longer dishonour'd, by the poorness of the *sense* it is chain'd to.

My meaning is, that you would be resolute enough, to deliver us from our *Italian bondage*; and demonstrate, that *English* is soft enough for Opera, when compos'd by poets, who know how to distinguish the *sweetness* of our tongue, from the *strength* of it, where the last is less necessary.

I am of opinion, that male and female voices may be found in this kingdom, capable of every thing, that is requisite; and, I am sure, a species of dramatic Opera might be invented, that, by reconciling reason and dignity, with musick and fine machinery, would charm the *ear*, and hold fast the *heart*, together.

Such an improvement must, at once, be lasting, and profitable, to a very great degree; and would, infallibly, attract an universal regard, and encouragement.[77]

As instigator of Handel's first Italian opera for London Hill had hoped that this foreign form, so full of promise as a morally elevating *Gesamtkunstwerk*, would be naturalised. His dedication of the libretto of *Rinaldo* to Queen Anne stresses that it is 'born your Subject', being created in 'your Majesty's Dominions', and constitutes the beginning of 'my endeavour, to see the *English* OPERA more splendid then her MOTHER, the *Italian*.'[78] Twenty years on, English opera had been eclipsed for most of two decades by the strengths of Italian

opera instead of annexing them, was briefly showing signs of real
life, but was on the verge of lapsing again (see Introduction). As his
career in England progressed, Handel was identified with increasing
frequency as the composer who wrote 'manly' and 'nervous' (strong,
bold, substantial, astonishing) music, which touched the heart and
roused the soul.[79] He was the obvious rescuer of vitiated musical
taste and the frail native tradition of music drama. In fact Handel
the great Italian opera composer did not become Handel the great
English opera composer, but he did, from the year of Hill's letter,
publicly perform works in English, most of which had morally
improving texts and many of which had patriotic themes (see Part
II). The government sponsorship of the arts for which Hill campaigned took two centuries to materialise, but the royal encouragement he hoped for was given to Handel's initial oratorios, and had
Gibson not intervened they might have been fully staged. The
reformers' aims were almost realised, through Handel, whom they
had marked out as their best hope. Half way through his twenty-
year period of writing English theatre works he was reported as
succeeding with the public *because* he was setting English texts for
English singers, and in the year of his last oratorio he was praised for
having 'so bravely withstood the repeated Efforts of *Italian Forces*'.[80]
When his oratorio season of 1745 failed and he produced a public
apologia for his English word-setting (see above, pp. 37–8), he
phrased it in the terms of Hill, Miller and other members of the
lobby for moral art and English word-setting, appealing to canons
of words-and-music which he knew to be prevalent among his
supporters and which he had been praised for realising in his
oratorios.[81]

CHAPTER 3

Music, morals and religion

For those who wanted art to appeal to man's higher, rational, nature and engage the mind, music raised a constant problem: where it was not closely associated with comprehensible words it could smother rather than inform the understanding. The statement most frequently made about music in eighteenth-century England is that it is dangerous, because of its power over the emotions. Instrumental music, and music only loosely allied with words (as in extended melismas), is considered especially subversive because it stirs up emotions which drive out objective thought, and often, because of the indeterminate effect of instrumental music, the listener is confused even about what emotions it is evoking. The distress caused by such disturbance is perceptible in the literature of music, especially in comments on Italian opera:

> Music, when *purpose* points her not the road,
> Charms, to betray, and softens, to *corrode*.
> Empty of sense, the soul-seducing art
> Thrills a slow poison to the sick'ning heart.[1]

For Hill, as for others, certain instruments, when used singly, beneficially stir up useful emotions (for example, the drum and trumpet inspire courage, see the passage quoted above, p. 78); but the ability of concerted instrumental music to infuse and overcome us with 'unmanning' emotions renders it deeply suspect.[2] Professional musicians, and music lovers inclined to view human nature optimistically, might commend music without qualification, but they were a minority, and even they felt the need to justify music morally, as a civilising social influence.[3] The luscious scoring of Italian opera gave the moral reformers of art many uncomfortable *frissons*. Dennis, who declared himself highly susceptible to music ('There is no Man living who is more convinc'd than my self of the Power of

81

Harmony, or more penetrated by the Charms of Musick'), put their case: music can be 'profitable as well as delightful' when it is 'subservient to Reason'; but if it 'presumes to set up for it self, and to grow independent, as it does in our late Operas, it becomes a mere sensual Delight, utterly incapable of informing our Understanding ... soft and delicious Musick, by soothing the Senses ... by emasculating and dissolving the Mind ... shakes the very Foundation of Fortitude'.[4]

Whether we respect this reaction as a recognition that there is no such thing as 'purely aesthetic' experience or deride it as 'the Philistine fallacy behind most eighteenth-century music criticism, that the word is morally superior to the note',[5] the fact that it *was* a fundamental response to music must be taken into account when mapping the hinterland of the oratorios. It is based on the univerally accepted proposition that music's power over the emotions is a moral issue because it can affect behaviour.[6] Handel himself made this subject the theme of an entire evening's entertainment: *Alexander's Feast*. Timotheus' emotive playing reduces the 'hero' Alexander to a puppet and leads him to an orgy of drunken destruction (the burning of Persepolis). In both Dryden's poem and Hamilton's libretto (which makes no substantive alterations to the poem), Timotheus conspicuously lacks the motivation for good which eighteenth-century writers demanded in composers and performers. He is contrasted with the pious St Cecilia, whose music, wholly beneficial, attracts the attention of heaven itself. In the article about this work in *Common Sense* for 14 October 1738, the author is as serious and approving as his bantering tone will allow in relating the edict of the Lacedemonians against Timotheus for extending the compass of his lyre and hence its dangerously expressive powers. Art can affect the condition of the nation; the state is right to exert control over it. The two lyre-players of antiquity called Timotheus, the Milesian who overthrew tradition and the performer at Alexander's Feast, tended to be fused in the eighteenth-century mind, and the dangerous radical is implied in Dryden's poem and perhaps in Handel's setting. He was a potent symbol of subversive art in eighteenth-century English criticism (the topical mention in *Common Sense* had several precedents, among them an article in Aaron Hill's *The Plain Dealer*) and Handel was, as so often, tapping contemporary concerns, with the use of shared references, in *Alexander's Feast*.[7]

Fear of music's subversive power was especially strong in one of music's main arenas, the Church. The twentieth-century student needs to be reminded that the Church's views counted in eighteenth-century England for far more than they do now, and that sermons, biblical commentaries and works on religion formed a major, possibly the largest, part of the nation's reading-matter.[8] The comments of churchmen form the bulk of contemporary music criticism, reaching a much wider audience than the writings of professional musicians, and they were not confined to church music; they assessed the effects of all kinds of music.[9]

In their sermons and other writings on music churchmen express deep anxiety about secular music, but even their arguments in favour of church music, especially instrumental music, are defensive. The ideological battleground comprehended more than music and morals: supporters of the established Church were contesting Puritan polemic. The continuing fervour of the Puritan attack on church, especially the more complex cathedral, music long after the Restoration is evident in painstaking Anglican rebuttals of its arguments well into the 1740s.[10] The basis of the defence is that 'Musick, when rightly order'd, cannot be prefer'd too much', because it 'composes the Passions, affords a strong Pleasure, and excites a Nobleness of Thought', and 'Religious Harmony' is able 'to warm the best Blood within us, and take hold of the finest part of the Affections: To transport us with the *Beauty of Holiness*'.[11] In his charge to his clergy in 1741 Archbishop Secker encouraged choral praise of the Creator in terms which chime with contemporary descriptions of Handel's oratorio choruses on the same theme:

All persons indeed who are by nature qualified, ought to learn, and constantly join to glorify Him that made them, in psalms and spiritual songs ... the improvements made by a few ... will seldom equal the harmony of a general chorus, in which any lesser dissonances are quite lost; and it is something inexpressibly elevating, to hear the voice of a great multitude, as the voice of many waters and of mighty thunders, to speak in the words of Scripture, making a joyful noise to the God of their salvation, and singing His praises with understanding.[12]

But the traditional distinction of divine music, which praises God, and mundane music, which entertains men, is reinforced by anxiety arising from the incursion of modern 'light and airy' compositional styles into the music of worship, displacing 'the Solemnity and Gravity of what may properly be called the *Church-Style*'.[13] While some preachers turn a blind eye to music's ambivalent effects in their support for the cathedral style, many admit that

Music is a *two-edged Sword*; capable, as of *quelling* the *rebel passions*, so of giving a *mortal* wound to *virtue* and *religion*: and therefore should always be in a *sober* hand . . . What ought to *kindle* a *devout* affection, may *blow up* every *evil* desire into a *flame*; may be the *fuel* and *incentive* of *vice*.[14]

If this is the case for devotional music, music associated with secular pursuits is considered even more hazardous, and usually fatal. The central preoccupation of all the sermons concerning music is most succinctly and suggestively phrased by William Dingley: 'Musick is almost as Dangerous as 'tis Useful, *it has the Force of Gunpowder, and should be as carefully look'd after, that no unhallow'd Fire give it the power of Destroying*.'[15] Dingley took his gunpowder image from Jeremy Collier's *A Short View of the Immorality and Profaneness of the English Stage* (1698), in which, enlarging on his essay 'Of Musick', he suggests that censorship of music should be introduced: 'Musick is almost as dangerous as Gunpowder; And it may be requires looking after no less than the *Press* or the *Mint*. 'Tis possible a publick Regulation might not be amiss.'[16] Collier's *Short View* reached its fifth edition in 1730, his *Essays*, including 'Of Musick', were reissued seven times up to 1731, and in 1737 censorship was indeed introduced for musical among other stage performances.[17]

INSTRUMENTAL MUSIC

Elizabethan legislation for church services had allowed for non-liturgical music – 'an hymn, or such like song, to the praise of Almighty God, in the best sort of melody and music that may be conveniently devised', on condition 'that the sentence of the hymn may be understood and perceived'.[18] Insistence on the supremacy of the Word in worship fuelled continuing Puritan animosity to instrumental music, and sermons inaugurating organs in churches or celebrating the feast of St Cecilia ('inventress of the vocal frame') labour to defend it:

'Tis true, the Harp and the Organ were an Invention of one of the Sons of *Cain*, an unsanctified, ungodly Race: but yet God consecrated them to a Religious Use, and made them Instruments of much Honour to his Church, and much Devotion in his People; and if we are not affected with those lofty Strains of Harmony which they produce, it is not a Sign that our Religion is too high to stand in need of such Helps; but that our Affections are too low to be capable of such Improvements. Doubtless if our Souls were as pious as *David*'s, they would be as melodious too.[19]

Like the would-be reformers of secular music described in the previous chapter, this St Cecilia preacher, Charles Hickman (in common with many other preachers), values music for its unequalled ability to reach the mind and soul through the emotions. Worship itself is no cold act of reason but 'the workings of an exalted Love; the out-goings of an inflam'd Desire; the breathings of a pious Soul, in the extasies of his Joy and Admiration', arising from 'Tendernesses of our Nature, that lie not in the Head, but the Heart of Man; and there lie too deep to be reached, and too fine to be wrought upon by so gross a Faculty as Reason is'. But where philosophers and moralists fail music triumphs, penetrating our sensibilities

to the very quick: There is such a Charm in well compos'd, well animated Sounds, as musters up all our Passions, and commands all our Affections to pay Homage to it; and no sensible Soul can withstand the Summons ... Nay, this is a Charm, that Works not only upon our Affections, but upon our Understanding too; enlivens the Head, as well as the Heart, of Man, and opens our Ears, and our Eyes at once. When our Thoughts are involv'd in the dreggs of Matter, and our Minds are obscur'd with drowsiness, and heaviness of Sense; Musick rouses up our Soul, and puts our Thoughts in Motion; our very Reason *awakens with the Lute and Harp*; and the Song, like some Divine Inspiration, calls up all our brighter Faculties to discharge their Office.

Here the charge that music swamps our rational powers is countered by the assertion that the *right kind of music* galvanises them; even without words, it liberates and stimulates our 'brighter Faculties'. Hickman's claims that the best religious music is refined, refining, and exalting are endorsed in many of the comments by Handel's contemporaries on his compositions for church and oratorio.[20] But equally the preachers of music sermons who prescribe what church music composers should provide are sensitive to the danger of instrumental music 'being too affecting, lest it should too much dissolve the Mind, and destroy the Attention to the Matter, by the Delicateness of the Melody in which it is conveyed'.[21]

THE INSTRUMENT OF GOD

With respect to the use Handel made of his fame as a virtuoso organist, in particular as part of his oratorio career, it is interesting to note the considerable literature within the mass of early-eighteenth-century writing on instrumental music in church which focuses on contemporary, modernistic styles of composition for, and performance on, the organ. Conservative churchmen complain that though the organ is the special instrument of divine worship, organists are turning it into a vehicle of musical worldliness and exhibitionism, and using voluntaries during services to show off technical skill in unsuitably irreverent styles.

For Thomas Macro, preaching at the installation of an organ at Tiverton in 1734, instrumental music is a means by which 'the *Solemnity* of Religion may be advanced, and the People edified'. For this the most effective instrument is the organ, 'the most comprehensive of all other, for which Reason it has been appropriated to the Service of the *Sanctuary*, and made the *Instrument* of *God* in his own House'. Since it is so sanctified, 'Let not the Harmony of its Sounds be frisking, airy, or ludicrous, which tends to dissipate the Thoughts, and break the Attention of the Mind.' It should always be 'accommodated to the pure and heavenly Matter, and to the sublime and majestic Style of those *Psalms and Hymns* that are appointed to be sung to it, so shall it serve to raise and inflame the best Affections of our Nature'.[22] The Nonjuring writer on music and morals Arthur Bedford, who campaigned energetically to preserve the historical purity of worship, is characteristically vehement about modern church organ playing:

I know not any sober Person, who can understand any thing in it, except a *Jargon* of *Confusion*, without *Head* or *Tail*, including all the *Keys* of the *Gamut* in a promiscuous Manner, without any *Cadence* or Connexion, intermix'd sometimes with a wanton airy Fancy, and at others with a heavy sordid Performance ... and the Musick in the House of *God*, is exactly like the *Dithyrambick Verses*, composed by the *Heathens* in Honour of *Bacchus*, and sung at their drunken *Revels*.[23]

Such concern was not confined to the clergy. Technical bravura in church voluntaries was equally unsettling to the lay congregation: 'some to *Church* repair, / Not for the *Doctrine*, but the *Musick* there'.[24] Mastery of this most masterful of instruments was far more spellbinding than we readily appreciate in an age of amplified and

synthetic sound. Even professional musicians were critical. Charles
Avison deplores 'that foolish Pride of Expression in our Voluntaries,
which disgusts every rational Hearer, and dissipates, instead of
heightning true Devotion'. In a long footnote, he requires the
organist to be sensitive to poetry, so that he will respond appropriately to the rhetoric of the service; instructs him to listen atten-
tively to the psalm preceding his voluntary, 'pronounced in an awful
and pathetic Strain'; and 'then he must join *his* Part, and with some
solemn Air, relieve, with religious Chearfulness, the calm and well-
disposed Heart'. He must even be devout himself: 'if he feels not this
divine Energy in his own Breast, it will prove but a fruitless Attempt
to raise it in that of others'.[25]

Handel made his skill as an organist literally a central feature of
his oratorio performances from 1735 until the end of his active life,
by performing his own organ concertos between the acts. If we wish
to consider the nature of Handelian oratorio as Handel devised it
and his own audiences heard it, we should not neglect this vital
component. As Dean points out, 'The concertos helped to supply
that element of technical virtuosity which had been provided in
opera by the castrati and other great singers, and sometimes they
seem to have been more of a draw than the oratorios themselves.
They are very prominent in the advertisements, especially of a
flagging oratorio ... A great feature of the organ concertos was
Handel's improvisation of the solo part ... varied at each performance.'[26] Here is a splendid example of Handel's shrewdness as an
entrepreneur. English music lovers wanted to hear bravura organ
playing but many had qualms about hearing it in church, so he
transplanted it to the theatre, where no one could complain that it
interrupted devotion. But he limited the qualms that the devout
might feel about the propriety of an organ in a theatrical setting by
associating it with his least secular performances – oratorios.

Contemporary records indicate that Handel's reputation among
the music-loving English public was established by his organ playing
even more than his opera writing. The first of the many known
poems to him is *An Ode to Mr Handel, on His Playing the Organ* (1722)
by Daniel Prat, a former chaplain of the king.[27] This substantial
celebration (160 lines), foreshadowing not only the major varieties
of appreciative response to Handel's music by his public but also the
topics of several of his English works, describes Handel rousing,
directing and controlling the hearer's emotions with his playing,

inducing just the effect required by so many writers on music and cited by them as the achievement of the best religious music: exalted, transcendant rapture in which

> Each restless Passion's softly lulled to Peace
> And silent Thought seems only not to cease.

The organ is *the* instrument of the divine art of music and, in a witty twist of the stock comparison of Handel with Orpheus, Prat likens its opponents – still a force to be reckoned with – to 'they that tore the Thracian Bard'. As 'A Choir of Instruments in One' the organ provides a 'Blest Emblem of Seraphic Joys', an earthly representation – like the praisegiving chorus in the oratorio itself – of the heavenly choir of praise we hope to join; and Handel's 'volant Touch' on it can rectify not only individual passion but the disorders of the entire nation (see also chapter 9).

CATHEDRAL MUSIC AS TEMPLE MUSIC

Defenders of the more complex and sophisticated forms of church music, 'cathedral music', were obliged to defend accompanied vocal music as well as the use of instruments. The sermons preached regularly at the Three Choirs festival were not simply celebrations of the musician's art, they were apologetics and prescriptions for its employment in worship. They share the arguments of their predecessors, the sermons of St Cecilia festivals of the previous three decades. We can take the sermon which Thomas Bisse, Chancellor of Hereford Cathedral, gave at the first Three Choirs festival in 1720 as a stock example of constantly repeated ideas. The principal element of Christian worship, says Bisse, is praise; the best method of expression is words-and-music; being susceptible to music is not a weakness but a gift of God; music in worship on earth is a foretaste of music in heaven (Revelation V.14); music can refine the passions, evoke devotion, and make converts to religion (St Augustine); St Basil gave permission to use music to win men to virtue; instruments can be used to support the voice; both musicians and congregation must concentrate devoutly on the spiritual purpose of the music; singers must utter the words distinctly; and the music should be appropriately solemn and majestic.[28] Sermon after sermon repeated these formulas, preserving an Anglican canon of views on the setting of religious words to music – principally that it was a worthy endeavour and that the result should have a distinctively 'old-fashioned' church idiom. Handel's settings of religious words in his oratorio choruses in what contemporaries recognised as a church style were to fulfil this prescription. And it was a prescription: the need to defend church music created a literature *recommending* the production of religious words-and-music.

This in itself was an encouraging context from which oratorio might grow, but some of the sermons provided even clearer pointers, in the sanctions for religious music which they drew from biblical precedent. In the year before the first performance of *Israel in Egypt* the Three Choirs sermon was given by Thomas Payne, who dwelt enthusiastically on the stock Old Testament proofs of God's approbation of music in worship, particularly evident in 'its appointment for the more magnificent celebration of his praises under the *Jewish* Dispensation'. Notably, 'When all the children of *Israel* sang the Song of *Moses*, upon the overthrow of *Pharaoh* and his host, then *Miriam* the Prophetess, with her Choir of women, answer'd them, *with Timbrels in their hands*, sing ye to the Lord for he hath triumph'd gloriously' (a footnote refers to Exodus XV.20, 21). To this commonly cited instance Payne adds the equally common ones of David and Solomon before turning more specifically to the defence of instrumental music: 'Did not the Children of *Israel* make use of *Musick, Instrumental* as well as *Vocal*, in their holy Offices, both in the Wilderness, and in the Land of *Canaan*?' Moses must have learned music along with other Egyptian arts, and

we find that God had no sooner exalted Him to be a Ruler over his people *Israel*, and by his hand wrought a mighty redemption of them out of the house of bondage, but they were able to join with their deliverer in that noble *Song of Praise* which he composed upon the joyful occasion; and which (as we have before seen) they sang alternately in *two Choirs*, assisted with *Musical instruments*, to the God of their Salvation. And did *Moses*, (as well as *Miriam*, and the whole Congregation) He who was so signally magnified of God, – on whom he had so lately instamp'd his own Image and Character, – by whom he had just wrought such wonders and signs in the Land of *Egypt* and in the Red Sea; – did He likewise err in his judgment, and instead of offering up a suitable sacrifice of praise and thanksgiving, commit a gross abomination in suffering, and communicating in an unacceptable, carnal, mechanical way of Worship? It had not then surely been pass'd over without an instant token of the divine displeasure; nor he alone of all mankind so soon after had the special honour of a free converse with God, and of the Lord's speaking to him face to face, as a man speaketh to his friend.[29]

In the light of this passage, the Song of Moses which forms the concluding part of *Israel in Egypt* acquires a new *raison d'être*, worth setting not only as the prime example of the religious sublime in poetry (see chapter 4), but as the incontrovertible Ur-example of God's ratification of vocal and instrumental music in divine worship as practised in Anglican cathedrals (Payne deliberately describes the Song as an exact harbinger of cathedral usage, performed by an accompanied, antiphonal double choir). Major characters of the librettos and their roles in them are foreshadowed in this sermon tradition: Moses at the Red Sea (the last part of *Israel*), David the singer of psalms (portrayed as such while soothing the king in *Saul*) and Solomon the instigator of temple worship (the first part of *Solomon*).

For the congregation conversant with sectarian controversy as it affected church music, there was more to these examples than a simple proof of God's ratification of their practices. In fact to cite them as ratification was polemical. According to some Dissenters, they were null and void because they pertained to the old dispensation superseded by the teachings of Christ. They should be interpreted, Dissenters argued, metaphorically: music is to be made in the soul and heart, not materially. Instrumental music, in particular, was a merely ceremonial accretion to Jewish worship that never sullied the early Church, and Dissenters cited its presence in the medieval Church as evidence of corruption, not sanctified continuity. Rebuttal of this line is a standard feature of the music sermons defending Anglican practice, again generating copious arguments in support of cathedral music. Bisse, for example, typically argues that church music was 'never a *shadow* or *Type* of anything, unless of the harmony in the praises of the Church Triumphant', in which case it should be continued; and that ordinances for music in the temple were never instanced by writers of the New Testament as a part of the Jewish law to be abrogated.[30]

One group of churchmen had a particular interest in identifying cathedral practice with temple worship. The Nonjurors championed a return to pure, 'primitive' Church structures, including those of worship.[31] To this end they traced the origins of cathedral practice, especially double-choir psalmody, to pre-Babylonian Jewish temple psalmody, which, they pointed out, had instrumental accompaniment. In 1706 Arthur Bedford produced his scholarly apologia for cathedral music: *The Temple Musick: or, an Essay concerning the Method of singing the Psalms of David, in the Temple, before the Babylonish Captivity. Wherein, the Musick of our Cathedrals is Vindicated, and Supposed to be Conformable, not only to that of the Primitive Christians, but also to the Practice of the Church in all Preceding Ages.* Bedford naturally endorses the argument that this inheritance from the early Church is not part of the Jewish ritual which was to be set aside at the coming of Christ, but he goes further, identifying the Jewish dispensation as the summit of ancient musical practice and the forerunner of the best of modern practice. This is not mere anti-quarianism. Retaining practices which recognisably had their origins in the temple was thought to be a means of hastening the conversion of the Jews, which was expected to start in England – a seriously held belief, especially among Nonjurors.[32] Bedford is sure that, whatever the exact nature of the temple music under Solomon, it was the best in the world at the time; maybe, he suggests (perhaps providing a cue for the masque in Part III of *Solomon*), 'one Motive which brought the *Queen of Sheba* from her Country might be to satisfy her Curiosity in this particular, and to hear the *Musick*, as well as to see the *Temple*'.

While admitting with disarming candour that he cannot prove all his points, Bedford (like many other defenders of church music but in much more detail) justifies modern cathedral psalmody on the grounds that it corresponds to ancient liturgical practice, both Jewish and Christian. His focus on the Psalms is extended, intense and forward-looking: nearly half a century before Robert Lowth laid what is regarded as the basis of popular literary appreciation of the Old Testament, Bedford devoted over thirty pages to analysing the Psalms' rhetoric, metre and versification.[33] As we shall see in the next chapter, literary critics before Lowth also brought the Psalms into the scope of critical appreciation. In drawing so heavily on the Psalms for the texts of their choruses, the oratorio librettists were not (as would be the case now) exhuming unfamiliar material but sharing the matter not only of Anglican worship but of current critical interest. Nor was Bedford alone in his claims for music in the Jewish temple. In 1724 the historian Nicholas Tindal published *Antiquities Sacred and Profane: or, A Collection of Curious and Critical Dissertations on the Old and New Testament* (mainly translated from the work of the Benedictine Dom Augustin Calmet), which includes 'A Dissertation concerning the Musick of the Antients, particularly of the Hebrews' arguing that the music of the temple was not inferior to modern music, indeed was more affecting. Admiration did not stop at theorising. Chapter IX of Bedford's *Temple Musick*, on the kinds of music which individual psalms suggest, includes thirty-nine actual musical examples, his own conjectural reconstructions of temple psalmody. (In his subsequent *The Great Abuse of Musick*, which argued for the renovation of music, and hence morals and manners, through a revival of earlier composers and styles, and which also discussed temple music, Bedford advocated psalm singing outside the church, hoping, like the churchmen of the Reformation before him, that it might replace the '*impious, lewd,* and *blasphemous* Songs' which were corrupting society.)[34]

Bedford and other Anglican apologists combined the prevailing belief in divine music's efficacy with a desire to emulate the practice of ancient Jewish and early Christian worship in order, as Shapiro has pointed out, 'to achieve the communion with God that the biblical peoples had experienced ... By praising God in the sublime tradition of the ancient Israelites, the English hoped to come closer to the Christian God of salvation.'[35] The defence of current church music practice strongly associated it with the musical worship in the ancient Jewish temple, and in watching and hearing the oratorio Israelites hymning their God in elaborate choruses (often in two choirs), Handel's audiences were being reminded of the validity of their own forms of worship, and reaffirmed in their identification of themselves as God's chosen people in the modern world. In this respect as in many others (discussed in Part II), the oratorio Israelites were of real interest to them as images of themselves. The apologists for Anglican music also stressed that the singing of the prototypes of anthems – hymns, psalms and spiritual songs – was a feature of the primitive Church in times of persecution.[36] By a kind of back-formation, this gave the use of anthems in oratorios showing the Israelites endangered by persecution (such as *Esther*) a peculiar appropriateness, and a double appropriateness for the audience which identified the embattled Jewish Church with the embattled Church of England (see chapter 6).

THE ANTHEM AND THE ORATORIO LIBRETTO

Though Bedford bases his defence of cathedral music on ancient precedent, he takes a liberal view of certain elements in modern music which he regards as not only innovations, but improvements.

Repetitions and melismas 'may justly be reckoned some of the *Graces* of our *present Musick*', and 'the *Harmony* of a *Consort* or several Parts at the same time . . . is the real Glory of all *Musick*'. Indeed, one of the strengths of cathedral music is the scope it gives a composer, in the anthem, 'to use the utmost Strains which either Art or Fancy can invent' and, by providing the best music available, thwart the temptation to seek it in less proper contexts, 'that such who are delighted with *Musick* . . . may at once have an Opportunity both to *please* their *Ears*, and *edify* their *Souls*', cathedrals being 'the only places in *England*, which have *gathered up the Fragments of Antiquity* (in relation to Church musick) *that nothing might be lost*, and at the same time hath left a skilful Artist wholly at liberty to make the utmost improvements which the Age is capable of'.[37] The cathedral anthem, in other words, has for the listener the double merit of inducing spiritual experience and being the pinnacle of artistic achievement. The anthem has been identified as a major influence on the shaping of Handel's oratorios and as a constituent element of them,[38] so it is appropriate to give some consideration to the relation between the librettos and eighteenth-century anthem texts.

Anglican anthems are forerunners of Handelian oratorio in that they are musical settings for soloists and choir of texts from the Old Testament, and occasionally the Apocrypha and New Testament. In size, complexity of text and music, and demand for forces, the anthems that correspond most nearly to oratorio are the 'full' anthems (that is, for soloists and choir) written for the royal establishments (Chapel Royal, Westminster Abbey and St George's, Windsor), the cathedrals with choral foundations (twenty-two in England, two in Wales, four or five in Ireland), five colleges in Oxford and Cambridge, and one private establishment – that of the Duke of Chandos, for whom Handel composed his eleven Chandos Anthems. Anthems constitute the bulk of Handel's English word-setting before and besides oratorio. By the time of his first public performance of an oratorio, he had composed twenty-one anthems (some of them reworkings), as well as four settings of the Te Deum and two of the Jubilate. Some of his oratorios to varying degrees incorporated music, and sometimes words, of his anthems: two of his Coronation Anthems appeared in his public version of *Esther*, two Coronation Anthems and four Chandos Anthems in *Deborah* and a Chandos Anthem in *Athalia*; the first act of *Israel in Egypt* took over the funeral anthem for Queen Caroline, after this had been con-

sidered and rejected as the elegy for *Saul*; *Belshazzar* used two
Chandos Anthems (see the correspondence between Handel and
Jennens quoted in the Introduction) and the *Occasional Oratorio* a
Coronation Anthem.[39] Other anthems were incorporated for re-
vivals.[40] Artistic considerations aside, Handel had excellent market-
ing reasons for absorbing his anthems and his anthem style into his
oratorios: the public loved them. The Coronation Anthems and
Handel's other anthems for great state ceremonies were the *Pomp and
Circumstance* of their day, musically matching the communal exal-
tation the occasions generated and raising it to an even higher level.
Mrs Delany voiced common sentiments after hearing the Dettingen
Te Deum: 'It is excessively fine, I was all rapture . . . everybody says
it is the finest of his compositions'.[41]

The musical structures of Handel's anthems and of those of his
English predecessors and contemporaries, which have to be considered in any assessment of the musical origins of oratorio, are less
our concern here than their verbal composition.[42] In performance
the music was in any case often more ideal than real, because
choristers' attendance was so infrequent that the congregation did
not necessarily hear what the composer had written. But the *texts* of
the anthems intended for services at the establishments with choral
foundations could be relished by all with money to buy the collections of them which were published at three points during Handel's
English oratorio career, in 1724, 1736 and 1749, under the title *A
Collection of Anthems, as the same are now Performed in His Majesty's
Chapels Royal, &c*, with 'An Appendix: Being a Collection of Several
Select Anthems used at the Cathedral Church of St Paul, London,
St Peter's Church, Westminster, and at the rest of the Cathedral and
Collegiate Churches of England and Ireland'.[43] These make fascinating study in themselves, as pattern-books of the art of anthem-
text compilation in the Anglican Church of the sixteenth, seventeenth and eighteenth centuries (the composers represented run
from Tallis to Boyce). But they also point up the textual links
between anthems and oratorio. In particular, they indicate that the
existing modes of handling scriptural texts for setting as anthems
provided precedents for the oratorio librettists.[44]

The anthem texts are overwhelmingly drawn from the Old Testament, especially the Psalms in their King James Bible and Book of
Common Prayer translations (see Table 1), making the material of
the oratorios – the history and feelings of the Israelites – familiar

Table 1. *Use of source texts in anthem collections, 1724–49*

	1724	1736	1749
Number of texts	183	247	270
	%	%	%
Texts from Old Testament/Apocrypha	97	97.5	95
Texts from Psalms	91	92	90
Single segment of text	34.5	31	33.5
Verbatim use of text	34	31.5	32.5
Verbatim text + final 'Hallelujah'	10	7	7.5
Reordered or 'collage' texts	30	32	32.5

subjects of musical settings to anyone who attended choral services. The ingredients drawn from the Psalms into the anthem texts are those of numerous oratorio choruses: the awesome power of God, His marvellous works of nature, His rescue of His people from their godless enemies, His continuing goodness to them, their unworthiness, fear and hope, their appeals to Him, their gratitude to Him and their duty to praise Him. Most importantly, the anthems use the Scriptures with a close attention to content, and even more strikingly with a freedom, which anticipate the librettists' habits of selecting, adapting and interleaving parts of the Bible (see chapter 10). Despite the respect for the integrity of the sacred text inherited from the Reformation settlement, which prescribed clarity and absence of repetition ('a modest distinct song ... as plainly understood, as if it were read without singing'), anthems which simply set a single section of the Bible or of the Prayer Book Psalms verbatim are in the minority, as Table 1 shows.

Fewer than half the anthems set the biblical or Prayer Book text unaltered, even if one allows for the addition of a final 'Hallelujah' (the practice of concluding an anthem with a 'Hallelujah' is probably the origin of the frequent 'Hallelujah' choruses in Handel's oratorios – they occur in twelve out of eighteeen, sometimes completing choruses that are designated 'Anthem'). There are distinct varieties of adaptation. In order of increasing complexity and freedom they are:

(1) Alteration of tense or person: e.g. future to past tense, second to third person.
(2) Omission: e.g. only the first or second half of one or more verses is used.

(3) Condensation: a 'gluing together' of parts of two verses, e.g. uniting the first half of one with the second half of another.

(4) Selection: disjunct verses are selected from a single psalm or chapter, but used sequentially.

(5) Selection and rearrangement: verses from a single psalm or chapter are selected and reordered.

(6) 'Collage' texts: a selection of verses, verbatim, from any number of psalms and/or books of the Bible.

(7) Same as (6) with repetition of one or more verses.

(1)–(3) also occur in (4)–(7).

Some examples are given in Table 2, which shows that these devices were practised both by Handel's English predecessors and by his English contemporaries.

The rhetorical results can be striking. A change of tense can turn God's promise into accomplished fact. Omission can remove the particular occasion, generalising the event so that it can be taken as referring to the present congregation (see Table 2.2, which omits the references to the Israelites' march through the desert and experiences at Sinai). This accords with the widely respected recommendations of Isaac Watts, that psalms used for singing should be made more lifelike for modern worshippers by having local Israelite colour removed (see chapter 9). Editing out the most colourful similes also generalises, in a way which the twentieth-century reader probably regrets, but which would have seemed essential to the dignity of divine worship. Examples are the excision of the morning, the shepherd's tent, the weaver's cloth, and the chattering crane and swallow in Table 2.1, and the comparisons of God to a man of war, the earth's inhabitants to grasshoppers, the heavens to a tent and the race of Jacob to a worm in Table 2.5 – which also affords examples of changes of person and tense, and of condensation. A collage of texts from Matthew, Mark and Luke can demonstrate the harmony of the gospels (Table 2.3). Repetition of scriptural text, a liberty still disputed at this period by some Dissenters, can make one idea dominate, besides imposing musical shape. It was a favourite device of the compilers, and was absorbed into the structure of the oratorio librettos. To choose randomly from the first two dozen texts in the 1724 and 1736 collections, Pelham Humphreys sets Psalm XXIII.1, 2, 1, 3, 1, 4; Wise sets Psalm LVII.9, 10, 9, 11, 9, 12. In a more elaborate form, more than one verse is repeated, as in Table 2.6, where parts of verses 5, 11 and 16 are all repeated, 5 twice and 11 and 16 three times (and not in the order in which they occur in the

Table 2. *Anthem texts and sources compared*

KJB: King James Bible   BCP: Book of Common Prayer
+ : condensed text
capitalisation and spelling modernised for ease of verbal comparison

2.1: John Blow (1649–1708)

Biblical verse	KJB	Anthem
Job VII.20	I have sinned; what shall I do unto thee, O thou preserver of men? why hast thou set me as a mark against thee, so that I am a burden to myself?	O Lord I have sinned, what shall I do unto thee, thou preserver of men? O why hast thou set me up as a mark against thee, so that I am a burden to my self?
Job VII.21	And why dost thou not pardon my transgression, and take away mine iniquity? for now I shall sleep in the dust; and thou shalt seek me in the morning, but I shall not be.	O pardon my transgressions, and take away my sin.
Isaiah XXXVIII.12	Mine age is departed, and removed from me as a shepherd's tent: I have cut off like a weaver my life: he will cut me off with pining sickness: from day even to night wilt thou make an end of me.	Mine age is departed and removed from me, thou wilt cut me off with pining sickness.
Isaiah XXXVIII.14	Like a crane or a swallow, so did I chatter: I did mourn as a dove: mine eyes fail with looking upward: O Lord, I am oppressed; undertake for me.	Mine eyes fail with looking upwards: I did mourn as a dove; O Lord, I am oppressed, undertake for me, O Lord my God.
Job III.20	Wherefore is light given to him that is in misery, and life unto the bitter in soul;	O wherefore is light given to him that is in misery, or life to the bitter in soul?
Job III.21	Which long for death, but it cometh not; and dig for it more than for hid treasures;	Which long for death, but it cometh not;
Job III.22	Which rejoice exceedingly, and are glad, when they can find the grave?	And rejoice exceedingly, when they can find the grave?
Job III.23	Why is light given to a man whose way is hid, and whom God hath hedged in?	
Job III.24	For my sighing cometh before I eat, and my roarings are poured out like the waters.	For my sighing cometh before I eat, and my roarings are poured out like water.

Table 2 *continued*

2.2: *Maurice Greene (1696–1755)*

BCP verse	BCP	Anthem
Psalm LXVIII.1	Let God arise, and let his enemies be scattered: let them also that hate him flee before him.	Let God arise, and let his enemies be scattered.
Psalm LXVIII.2	Like as the smoke vanisheth, so shalt thou drive them away; and like as wax melteth at the fire, so let the ungodly perish at the presence of God.	Like as smoke vanisheth, as wax melteth at the fire, so let them perish and be driven away.
Psalm LXVIII.7	O God, when thou wentest forth before the people: when thou wentest through the wilderness;	O God! when thou wentest forth,
Psalm LXVIII.8	The earth shook, and the heavens dropped at the presence of God: even as Sinai also was moved at the presence of God, who is the God of Israel.	The earth shook, and the heavens dropped at the presence of God, even the God of *Israel*.
Psalm LXVIII.32	Sing unto God, O ye kingdoms of the earth; O sing praises unto the Lord;	Sing unto God, ye kingdoms of the earth: O sing praises unto the Lord.
Psalm LXVIII.20	He is our God, even the God of whom cometh salvation: God is the Lord by whom we escape death.	Sing praises unto him who is God of our salvation.
Psalm LXVIII.5	He is a father of the fatherless, and defendeth the cause of the widows: even God in his holy habitation.	He is a father of the fatherless:
Psalm LXVIII.6	He is the God that maketh men to be of one mind in an house, and bringeth the prisoners out of captivity: but letteth the runagates continue in scarceness.	He bringeth the prisoners out of captivity.
Psalm LXVIII.35	O God, wonderful art thou in thy holy places: even the God of Israel, he will give strength and power unto his people; blessed be God.	Blessed be God. Hallelujah.

Table 2 *continued*

2.3: Orlando Gibbons (1583–1625)

Biblical verse	KJB	Anthem
Matthew XXI.9	And the multitudes that went before, and that followed, cried, saying, Hosanna to the Son of David: Blessed is he that cometh in the name of the Lord; Hosanna in the highest.	Hosanna to the Son of *David*: blessed is he that cometh in the name of the Lord.
Mark XI.10	Blessed be the kingdom of our father David, that cometh in the name of the Lord: Hosanna in the highest.	Blessed be the King of *Israel*, blessed be the kingdom that cometh in the Name of the Lord.
Luke XIX.38	Saying, Blessed be the King that cometh in the name of the Lord: peace in heaven, and glory in the highest.	Peace in heaven, and glory in the highest places; Hosanna in the highest heavens.

2.4: George Holmes (d. 1721) Anthem for the Union of England and Scotland (part)

Biblical verse	KJB	Anthem
Ezekiel XXXVII.22 + 24	And I will make them one nation in the land upon the mountains of Israel; and one king shall be king to them all: and they shall be no more two nations, neither shall they be divided into two kingdoms any more at all; . . . And my servant David shall be king over them; and they shall all have one shepherd: they shall also walk in my judgments, and observe my statutes, and do them.	For the Lord will make them one nation in the land upon the mountains of *Israel*, and they shall have one shepherd: and my servant *David* shall be their king for ever.

2.5: Maurice Greene

Biblical verse	KJB	Anthem
Isaiah XLII.10	Sing unto the Lord a new song, and his praise from the end of the earth, ye that go down to the sea, and all that is therein; the isles, and the inhabitants thereof.	Sing unto the Lord a new song, ye that go down to the sea: the isles, and the inhabitants thereof.

Table 2 *continued*

Isaiah XLII.12	Let them give glory unto the Lord, and declare his praise in the islands.	Let them give glory unto the Lord, and declare his praise.
Isaiah XLII.13	The Lord shall go forth as a mighty man, he shall stir up jealousy like a man of war: he shall cry, yea, roar; he shall prevail against his enemies.	The Lord shall go forth in his might; he shall prevail against his enemies:
Isaiah XLIII.16 [not indicated in printed text]	Thus saith the Lord, which maketh a way in the sea, and a path in the mighty waters;	the Lord, who maketh a way in the sea, and a path in the mighty waters.
Isaiah XL.22	It is he that sitteth upon the circle of the earth, and the inhabitants thereof are as grasshoppers; that stretcheth out the heavens as a curtain, and spreadeth them out as a tent to dwell in:	He sitteth upon the circle of the earth; he stretcheth out the heavens as a curtain;
Matthew VIII.27 [and Mark IV.41]	But the men marvelled, saying, what manner of man is this, that even the winds and the sea obey him!	He speaketh the word, and the winds and sea obey his voice.
Isaiah XLI.10	Fear thou not; for I am with thee: be not dismayed; for I am thy God:I will strengthen thee; yea, I will help thee; yea, I will uphold thee with the right hand of my righteousness.	The Lord shall strengthen us with his arm: and uphold us with his right hand.
Isaiah XLI.14	Fear not, thou worm Jacob, and ye men of Israel; I will help thee, saith the Lord, and thy redeemer, the Holy One of Israel.	The Lord our God is with us; he is our Redeemer, even the holy One of *Israel*.

2.6: Michael Wise (1647–87)

Biblical verse	KJB	Anthem
Lam. I.4	The ways of Zion do mourn, because none come to the solemn feasts; all her gates are desolate: her priests sigh, her virgins are afflicted, and she is in bitterness.	The ways of Zion do mourn, because none come to her solemn feasts; all her gates are desolate: her priests sigh, her virgins are afflicted, and she is in bitterness.

Table 2 *continued*

Lam. I.16	For these things I weep; mine eye, mine eye runneth down with water, because the comforter that should relieve my soul is far from me: my children are desolate, because the enemy has prevailed.	For these things I weep; mine eye runneth down with water.
Lam. I.5	Her adversaries are the chief, her enemies prosper: for the Lord hath afflicted her for the multitude of her transgressions: her children are gone into captivity before the enemy.	Her adversaries are the chief, her enemies prosper: for the Lord hath afflicted her.
Lam. I.16	For these things I weep; mine eye, mine eye runneth down with water, because the comforter that should relieve my soul is far from me: my children are desolate, because the enemy has prevailed.	For these things I weep; mine eye runneth down with water.
Lam. I.5	Her adversaries are the chief, her enemies prosper: for the Lord hath afflicted her for the multitude of her transgressions: her children are gone into captivity before the enemy.	For the multitude of her transgressions; the Lord hath afflicted her.
Lam. I.11	All her people sigh, they seek bread; they have given their pleasant things for meat to relieve the soul: see, O Lord, and consider; for I am become vile.	See, O Lord, and consider: for I am become vile.
Lam. I.12	Is it nothing to you, all ye that pass by? behold, and see if there be any sorrow like unto my sorrow, which is done unto me, wherewith the Lord hath afflicted me in the day of his fierce anger.	Is it nothing to you, all ye that pass by? behold and see, if there be any sorrow like my sorrow.

Table 2 *continued*

Lam. I.15	The Lord hath trodden under foot all my mighty men in the midst of me: he hath called an assembly against me to crush my young men: the Lord hath trodden the virgin, the daughter of Judah, as in a winepress.	The Lord hath trodden under foot all my mighty men in the midst of me: he hath called an assembly against me, to crush my young men: the Lord hath trodden under foot the virgin, the daughter of *Zion*.
Lam. I.16	For these things I weep; mine eye, mine eye runneth down with water, because the comforter that should relieve my soul is far from me: my children are desolate, because the enemy has prevailed.	For these things I weep; mine eye, runneth down with water: because the Comforter that should relieve my soul is far from me.
Lam. I.11	All her people sigh, they seek bread; they have given their pleasant things for meat to relieve the soul: see, O Lord, and consider; for I am become vile.	See, O Lord, and consider: for I am become vile.

Bible). The most inventive style, what I have called 'collage' texts, is often used for special occasions, to focus appropriately on the event. Thus Benjamin Lamb of Eton, selecting texts for 29 May (the anniversary of Charles II's restoration), chose Psalms CXI.1 + CXVIII.24; CXI.2–4; LXXI.17–18; CXXXVI.23 + 25; CXXXVI.26; CXXXVIII.4, 5; CXXXVI.26 (+ = condensation), telling successively of God's greatness, His marvellous works, His rescue of His people from adversity and His continuing goodness to them, and their duty to praise Him – like so many anthems, the common material of many oratorio choruses.

The selection is sometimes so sophisticated as to seem perverse to the modern reader. Gibbons' paralleling of Mark XXI.9, Matthew XI.10 and Luke XIX.38 (Table 2.3) is surely intended to demonstrate the consistency of the gospel accounts of Christ's life, yet the anthem verses are not a copy but a sort of kaleidoscope of the biblical texts – the first phrase of the second verse is actually from the first phrase of Luke XIX.38, the last phrase of the third verse is the last phrase of Matthew XXI.9, and so on. In all the rearrangement, the one phrase that *is* common to all three texts, presumably prompting their selection in the first place, fails to get its three occurrences in the anthem ('Blessed . . . that cometh in the name of the Lord' occurs only in the first two verses of the anthem). Yet perhaps this is part of the point, and the pleasure, of mosaic work of this intensity: everyone involved knows perfectly well what the biblical texts say, so the anthem compiler descants on them, drawing new attention to their content by rearranging and adapting it. That could be the explanation for the curious form of Holmes' anthem for the Union of England and Scotland (Table 2.4), which omits the most relevant part of its biblical text, 'they shall be no more two nations, neither shall they be divided into two kingdoms any more at all'. The text can be assumed to be known – an assumption which the oratorio librettists also felt free to make (see chapter 10) – and the anthem writer, in this instance, can afford to concentrate on elevating the congregation to the status of the chosen people.

The 'collage' anthem method anticipates the oratorios which use biblical texts, even providing precedents for *Messiah*'s interleaving of Old and New Testament texts (for example, Table 2.5). The greatest collage anthem of Handel's time was of course by Handel himself, the Funeral Anthem for Queen Caroline. It is characteristic of him that he experimented with most of the types of text variation listed above, in his Chandos and Coronation Anthems (and added to them by drawing on two translations in Chandos II): for example, Chandos X takes the form Psalm XXVII.1, 3, 4, 7; Psalm XVIII.31, 7 (minus last four words), 14 + 13; Psalm XX.8 (minus last three words); Psalm XXXIV.3; Psalm XXVIII.8; Psalm XXIX.4 + 9; Psalm XXX.4; Psalm XLV.18 (+ = condensation). The text of the Funeral Anthem was compiled by the sub-dean of Westminster Abbey, Edward Willes (see Table 3).

It is easy to understand how readily Jennens (if he was the librettist of *Israel in Egypt*) would have welcomed this text into his oratorio, for it shares the delight in scriptural selection, comparison and compilation that he later brought to *Messiah*, like *Messiah* drawing on both Testaments and the Prayer Book (but ranging even further, drawing on the Apocrypha as well). He might even have been dubious about its boldness; respect for the integrity of the Scriptures could hardly be stretched further. Individual words, tenses and persons are changed; individual verses are plucked out of their context (verses occur in their proper sequence no more than two at a time); and of many verses only fragments are used. Repetition is used in an especially complex fashion: the 'refrain', taking its cue from the triple iteration of 'How are the mighty fallen' in 2 Samuel, unites this phrase with half a verse from Lamentations, transmuting its meaning (from the City of Jerusalem to the dead Queen – similarly the alteration of the text from Philippians claims that the Queen accomplished what the biblical verse commends). Like much in the oratorio librettos, the Funeral Anthem text celebrates the richness and versatility of Scripture with the freedom of intimate familiarity.[45]

Table 3. *Funeral Anthem for Queen Caroline and sources compared*

Verse	KJB/BCP	Anthem
Lam. I.4	The ways of Zion do mourn, because none come to the solemn feasts: all her gates are desolate: her priests sigh, her virgins are afflicted, and she is in bitterness.	The ways of Zion do mourn, and she is in bitterness;
Lam. I.11	All her people sigh, they seek bread; they have given their pleasant things for meat to relieve the soul: see, O Lord, and consider; for I am become vile.	all her people sigh,
Lam. II.10	The elders of the daughter of Zion sit upon the ground, and keep silence: they have cast up dust upon their heads; they have girded themselves with sackcloth: the virgins of Jerusalem hang down their heads to the ground.	and hang down their heads to the ground.
2 Sam. I.19	The beauty of Israel is slain upon the high places: how are the mighty fallen!	How are the mighty fall'n! –
2 Sam. I.25	How are the mighty fallen in the midst of the battle! O Jonathan, thou wast slain in thine high places.	
2 Sam. I.27	How are the mighty fallen, and the weapons of war perished!	

Table 3 *continued*

Lam. I.1	How doth the city sit solitary, that was full of people! how is she become as a widow! she that was great among the nations, and princess among the provinces, how is she become tributary!	she that was great among the nations, and princess of the provinces!
2 Sam. I.19	The beauty of Israel is slain upon the high places: how are the mighty fallen!	How are the mighty fall'n! –
2 Sam. I.25	How are the mighty fallen in the midst of the battle! O Jonathan, thou wast slain in thine high places.	
2 Sam. I.27	How are the mighty fallen, and the weapons of war perished!	
Job XXIX.14	I put on righteousness, and it clothed me: my judgment was as a robe and a diadem.	She put on righteousness, and it cloathed her; her judgment was a robe and a diadem.
Job XXIX.11	When the ear heard me, then it blessed me, and when the eye saw me, it gave witness to me;	When the ear heard her, then it blessed her, and when the eye saw her, it gave witness of her.
2 Sam. I.19	The beauty of Israel is slain upon the high places: how are the mighty fallen!	How are the mighty fall'n! –
2 Sam. I.25	How are the mighty fallen in the midst of the battle! O Jonathan, thou wast slain in thine high places.	
2 Sam. I.27	How are the mighty fallen, and the weapons of war perished!	
Lam. I.1	How doth the city sit solitary, that was full of people! how is she become as a widow! she that was great among the nations, and princess among the provinces, how is she become tributary!	she that was great among the nations, and princess of the provinces!

Table 3 *continued*

Job XXIX.12	Because I delivered the poor that cried, and the fatherless, and him that had none to help him.	She deliver'd the poor that cried, the fatherless, and him that had none to help him.
Ecclus. XXXVI. 23	If there be kindness, meekness, and comfort, in her tongue, then is not her husband like other men.	Kindness, meekness and comfort were in her tongue;
Philipp. IV.8	Finally, brethren, whatsoever things are true, whatsoever things are just, whatsoever things are pure, whatsoever things are lovely, whatsoever things are of good report; if there be any virtue, and if there be any praise, think on these things.	if there was any virtue, and if there was any praise, she thought on those things.
2 Sam. I.19	The beauty of Israel is slain upon the high places: how are the mighty fallen!	How are the mighty fall'n! –
2 Sam. I.25	How are the mighty fallen in the midst of the battle! O Jonathan, thou wast slain in thine high places.	
2 Sam. I.27	How are the mighty fallen, and the weapons of war perished!	
Lam. I.1	How doth the city sit solitary, that was full of people! how is she become as a widow! she that was great among the nations, and princess among the provinces, how is she become tributary!	she that was great among the nations, and princess of the provinces!
Psalm CXII.6	For he shall never be moved: and the righteous shall be had in everlasting remembrance.	The righteous shall be had in everlasting remembrance,
Daniel XII.3	And they that be wise shall shine as the brightness of the firmament; and they that turn many to righteousness as the stars for ever and ever.	and the wise will shine as the brightness of the firmament.
Ecclus. XLIV.14	Their bodies are buried in peace; but their name liveth for evermore.	Their bodies are buried in peace: but their name liveth for evermore.

Table 3 *continued*

Ecclus. XLIV.15	The people will tell of their wisdom, and the congregation will shew forth their praise.	The people will tell of their wisdom, and the congregation will shew forth their praise;
Wisdom V.15	But the righteous live for evermore; their reward also is with the Lord, and the care of them is with the most high.	their reward also is with the Lord, and the care of them is with the most high.
Wisdom V.16	Therefore shall they receive a glorious kingdom, and a beautiful crown from the Lord's hand; for with his right hand shall he cover them, and with his arm shall he protect them.	They shall receive a glorious kingdom and a beautiful crown from the Lord's hand.
Psalm CIII.17	But the merciful goodness of the Lord endureth for ever and ever upon them that fear him, and his righteousness upon children's children.	The merciful goodness of the Lord endureth for ever on them that fear him, and his righteousness on children's children.

CHAPTER 4

The biblical sublime

The anthem compilers' appreciation of the textual detail of Scripture and their confident handling of their biblical material comes as no surprise to the literary historian. There is an enormous amount of writing from the eighteenth century both recommending the use of the Bible for modern literary composition and actually using it; here I shall refer principally to publications from the period of the oratorios and only to the main topics in the discussion that have particular relevance to the librettos.[1]

Traditional esteem of the Bible as the whole, sufficient, truth for Protestant believers and of the Old Testament as matchless verse and prose was reinforced in the eighteenth century by the first-century treatise on rhetoric, *On the Sublime* (attributed at the time to Longinus though actually predating him), which received several translations from the late seventeenth to the mid eighteenth century and profoundly influenced English literature and criticism.[2] As defined by Longinus, the chief distinguishing features of the sublime style and effect are 'Boldness and Grandeur in the Thoughts'; 'the Pathetic, or the Power of raising the Passions to a violent and even enthusiastic degree'; 'a skilful Application of Figures, which are two-fold, of Sentiment and Language'; 'a noble and graceful manner of Expression ... not only to chuse out significant and elegant Words, but also to adorn and embellish the Stile, by the Assistance of Tropes'; and 'the Structure and Composition of all the Periods, in all possible Dignity and Grandeur'. Bold disregard for conventional correctness, strong emotional effect and an immediate and overwhelming impact are central features of the Longinian sublime: 'the Sublime not only persuades, but even throws an Audience into a Transport'.[3] The widespread influence of *On the Sublime* is familiar to Handelians from the frequent praise of Handel in his own time as master of the sublime style, with reference (for example in Mainwaring's biography) to Longinus as the authority for its nature and value.[4]

In England the eighteenth century is far more the age of the sublime than the age of reason. Sublimity was constantly sought and admired in art, and the religious sublime was considered the highest form of it.[5] According to Longinus 'the Mind is naturally elevated by the true Sublime', and 'the Sublime makes near Approaches to the Height of God'. Religious verse is one of the most fertile grounds for the true sublime, and for an exemplary expression of the power of God Longinus, to the joy of his eighteenth-century readers, approvingly referred to 'the Jewish Legislator, no ordinary Person' (Moses), quoting Genesis I.3, 'Let there be light'. Longinus provided critical sanction for literary appreciation of the Old Testament, endorsing traditional claims for the superiority of Judaeo-Christian poetry over heathen writing and, as Margaret Anne Doody notes, 'his treatise offered a particularly exciting example of the possibilities of blending the Judaeo-Christian and the Hellenic traditions'.[6] The notes to the translation by William Smith (1739, frequently reprinted) extend the connection by adding copious biblical examples to the classical ones of the text, and these, like the examples of the Longinian sublime culled from the Bible by dozens of other eighteenth-century critics, include several passages used by Handel's librettists.[7]

Longinus provided the critical, aesthetic basis for esteem of emotional religious verse and for admiration of biblical, specifically Old Testament, style. He was even invoked in biblical commentaries, for example that of Handel's collaborator Samuel Humphreys, to ratify appreciation of the Bible itself.[8] His authority was much valued by the literary reformers, who advocated the writing of religious verse as a means to improve modern poetry. As in other areas of their campaign, John Dennis led the way, claiming Longinus as the source for his argument 'that the greatest Sublimity is to be deriv'd from Religious Ideas'. (The character of Sir Tremendous Longinus in the farce *Three Hours after Marriage* (1717) was meant for Dennis.) In *The Advancement and Reformation of Modern Poetry* (1701), and again in *The Grounds of Criticism in Poetry* (1704), both reprinted several times during the next three decades and echoed throughout the oratorio years, Dennis points out that the most affecting poetry is that which treats subjects in which we have the greatest concern, chief of which is religion, and so poetry should employ subjects drawn from religion. Revelation, prophecies and miracles are the most striking elements of religion, so the Bible is the most fecund source.[9] Students of Handel will be reminded here of the emphasis on prophecy and miracles in the oratorios, and of Bishop Synge's opinion that the first reason for the artistic success of *Messiah* 'is the Subject, which is the greatest & most interesting'.[10] Dennis lays down 'Rules for employing Religion in Poetry', encouraging would-be practitioners to give rein to both 'the Violence of the Enthusiastick Passions' and 'the Violence of the ordinary Passions', in all their 'Change and Variety', and reassuring them that any 'divine and human Persons' depicted 'may have Inclinations and Affections' – paving the way for the combination of human drama and religious enthusiasm in the oratorios. Jennens had the 1718 edition of Dennis' works in his library.[11] This was not a symptom of eccentric tastes: among serious writers and critics Dennis spoke for his own generation and the next in advocating religious verse and in regarding the poetry of the Bible as far superior to most modern verse (*The Censor* judged even Shakespeare an inferior poet to David).[12]

Some of the advocates (and writers) of religious verse who followed Dennis were collaborators of Handel: Aaron Hill, John Hughes and Thomas Morell. Hughes' contributions to the religious sublime included an *Ode to the Creator of the World. Occasion'd by the Fragments of Orpheus*, another ode, *The Ecstasy*, and 'On Divine Poetry'. In this latter poem he embellishes with biblical references the common theme that prelapsarian poetry was praise of God taught to man by the divine muse, and that though vice frightened the muse back to heaven and 'In vain the Heathen Nine her Absence wou'd supply',

> Yet to some Few, whose dazzling Virtues shone
> In Ages past, her heav'nly Charms were known.
> Hence learn'd the Bard, in lofty Strains to tell
> How patient Virtue triumph'd over Hell;
> And hence the Chief, who led the chosen Race
> Thro' parting Seas, deriv'd his Songs of Praise;
> She gave the rapt'rous Ode, whose ardent Lay
> Sings Female Force, and vanquish'd SISERA;
> She tun'd to pious Notes the Psalmist's Lyre
> And fill'd ISAIAH's Breast with more than PINDAR's Fire![13]

The oratorio enthusiast will notice that Hughes refers in the space of six lines to four of the librettists' sources: Isaiah, the Psalms, and the songs of Moses and of Deborah. Repeatedly the point is made, in this so-called 'neo-classical' period, that the poetry of Judaism and Christianity is vastly superior to that of pagan religion, having the benefit of the essential Longinian elements of sublimity – great ideas and emotional power: it will affect us because it is about *our* religion and it is *true*.[14] 'For many eighteenth-century poets, the road to Parnassus runs through Jerusalem.'[15]

Morell, in the 'Prefatory Copy of Verses on Divine Poesy' prefixed to his *Poems on Divine Subjects* of 1732 (reissued 1736), commends the defence of religion through literature and praises the contributions of Watts (*Horae Lyricae*), Cowley (*Davideis*), Wesley (the *Life of Christ*), Blackmore (*The Creation*), Norris ('Sitting in an Arbour'), Prior (*Solomon* and the Paraphrase on 1 Corinthians XIII), Broome (*Epistle to Pope*), Waller (his divine verse), Pope (*Messiah*), Young (*Poem on the Last Day*) and Milton (*Paradise Lost*) – a list of interest both in identifying a perceived great tradition of religious verse of the previous hundred years and as indicating the nature of Morell's reading. These authors, says Morell, had the satisfaction of settling men's minds in the secure basis of religion:

> Thrice happy Bards, whose Song is not in vain,
> When Mortals relish the instructive Strain,
> And seek, sincere in Heart, to know the Pow'r
> Of Pow'rs Supreme, *and seek to know no more*;
> The *Sceptic* hence his anxious Doubts resigns.[16]

But what the future librettist of *Theodora* admires even more than the poets' power to teach is the wonder and rapture they evoke in the reader, kindling a desire for union with God by giving a foretaste of its joy. Through Young's verse, 'ravish'd now with Wonder and Delight, / We taste th'ecstatic Joys that crown the Right', and in *Paradise Lost* the reader

> joins the Triumph of the SON,
> As joyful *Seraphs* wait Him to the Throne,
> And num'rous Hosts thro' all the starry Plains
> Salute their *Saviour-God* with solemn Strains,
> Which none can sing but the Celestial Choir,
> And none repeat, unblest with *Milton*'s Fire.
> All hail, ye sacred Bards, whose Merits claim
> In the Poetic World a deathless Name;
> If to instruct the Mind, and please the Ear
> With Sounds, that Angels stoop from Heav'n to hear,
> Be *Poesy*'s noblest Aim; the Way, which *God*

First dictated, and godlike *Prophets* trod.
"*Oh! may some Spark of your celestial Fire
Spread through my Soul, and fill its large Desire,
That I at humble Distance may pursue,
And keep my Duty, and my *God* in view.
To teach vain Man a Lesson little known,
T'adore Superior Pow'r, and doubt his own."
 * Pope's *Essay on Criticism*[17]

Morell modestly enrols himself in the tradition of 'sacred Bards' as
an apprentice of his illustrious English predecessors. Other writers in
the reforming circle traced their poetic descent from God directly
through the Hebraic Bible. James Sambrook points out that in the
preface to the second edition of *Winter* Thomson acknowledged
Virgil as a model 'but implied that his own poem had even closer
links with a devotional literary tradition which included the Pentateuch, the Book of Job, and *Paradise Lost*'.[18] Thomson's friend Aaron
Hill, approvingly citing the common belief that God gave the gift of
poetry to Moses after the crossing of the Red Sea, makes the Bible
the source of all poetry: 'God then taught Poetry first to the
Hebrews, and the Hebrews to Mankind in general'.[19] In effect,
aesthetic and moral directives to write religious verse and to draw on
the Bible in doing so – cues to oratorio – were commonplaces of
literary criticism.[20]

'What', asked the Oxford professor of poetry, 'can be more suitable to the Dignity of a Poem, than to celebrate the Works of the
great Creator?'.[21] His premise was given poetic realisation with
Thomson's *Seasons*: the greatest lyric poem of the period was a
devotional work, an embodiment of the religious sublime. The 1730
edition concluded with a hymn on the immanence of God in nature
– one of hundreds of hymns on this subject published in the first half
of the century. The reformers' call was answered: religious verse
flowed from the presses. Religion was, in fact, the major publishing
category of the mid eighteenth century.[22] To take just one publication as an example: the *Gentleman's Magazine* ran a religious verse
competition each year during the three years 1735–7, publishing the
entries. The subjects were favourite topics of religious writings of the
period – Life, Death, Judgement, Heaven and Hell (1735), the
Christian Hero (1736) and the Divine Attributes (1737) – and the
first competition yielded a forty-page extra number of the magazine.
From 1733 religious verse appeared regularly in its poetry section,

the very first contribution being Hill's poem on Handel's Utrecht Te Deum.[23] Hymns to God as creator of the universe are the most frequent form of religious verse in the *Gentleman's Magazine*, appearing on average twice a year during the 1740s. 'They who would join *Poetry* to their *Devotion*, can do it no way more sublimely, and properly than by falling into the ancient Way of *Hymns*: it is to this kind of Poetry that we owe most Part of those *great*, and *sublime* Passages with which the *Scripture* so abounds', wrote Hildebrand Jacob.[24] The hymn acquired the status of a respected literary (and musical) genre in the eighteenth century, and it is one of the seedbeds of the oratorio chorus.[25] Doody describes the eighteenth-century hymn as a highly personal utterance about the individual's spiritual experience; but the examples she quotes are from the Dissenting tradition.[26] Oratorio drew on and supplied a less individualised Anglican congregational hymn, in which 'I' was submerged in corporate praise or appeal and in which the literary hymn acquired a musical voice.

SCRIPTURE TOPICS

Many writers of distinction recommended and attempted not just religious but biblical, and not just biblical but Old Testament, subjects for modern treatment. On the question of whether scriptural subjects could with propriety be used for drama, it had already been established in the seventeenth century, when under the terms of the Blasphemy Act (1605) staged biblical drama became illegal, that unstaged religious drama for private, 'closet', reading was permissible, providing the holy narrative was not altered, the characters were simple, exalted and edifying, and the language respected the style of the original.[27] *Samson Agonistes* is the prime example of a closet religious drama. Dramas intended for private reading naturally contained stage directions, to enable the reader to imagine the events more vividly; this is the rationale of stage directions in Handel's oratorio librettos, which the audience had in front of them during the performance (see above, p. 23). Biblical verse was more often recommended than biblical drama; many writers concurred with Charles de Saint Evremond's opinion that 'The Theatre loses all its agreeableness when it pretends to represent sacred things; and sacred things lose a great deal of the religious opinion that is due to them, by being represented upon the Theatre'. But Saint Evremond himself acknowledged that 'the Histories of the Old Testament are infinitely better suited to our Stage, MOSES, SAMPSON, and JOSHUAH, wou'd meet with much better success, than POLIEUCTES and NEARCHUS', specifying the passage through the Red Sea, Joshua's prayer stopping the sun in its course and Samson's feats with the jawbone of an ass.[28] Isaac Watts, of all people, thought that 'The Book of the *Revelation* seems to be a Prophecy in the Form of an *Opera*, or a Dramatic Poem.'[29] The author of *The Touch-stone*, invoking the authority of the Athenian stage for religious drama as well as the example of Milton and Dryden, recommends that 'our Poets would judiciously choose from out the Old T----nt or Ap----ha the finest Historical Parts', pointing out that 'of Consequence, our THEATRES would be crowded with Audiences as religious as polite ... no body daring to entertain an Objection to the *Play-house*'.[30] As he knew, he was in a minority in his advocacy of staged biblical drama, but admiration for the dramatic, especially the emotive, qualities of the Old Testament was commonplace.

It is remarkable how constantly the topics suggested for literary treatment in the first half of the eighteenth century are those of the librettos, and how thoroughly the methods suggested for handling them anticipate the librettists' methods. Dennis refers to Milton and Cowley as notable exponents of religious verse. In the preface to his epic poem *Davideis* (1656), which was one of Jennens' sources for *Saul*, Cowley suggested as suitable topics the stories of Samson and of Jephtha's daughter, the wars of David and of Joshua, the friendship of David and Jonathan, the passage of Moses and the Israelites into the Holy Land and the prophecies of Christ and his miracles – all subsequently adopted by the librettists. Cowley's achievement and his programme for the reform of poetry were recalled regularly, and always with respect, during the century following *Davideis*. His views are echoed by two other influential writers on biblical themes, Isaac Watts, in his much-reprinted *Horae Lyricae*, and Sir Richard Blackmore, in the preface to his *A Paraphrase on the Book of Job: As Likewise on the Songs of Moses, Deborah, David, on Six Select Psalms and some Chapters of Isaiah, and the Third Chapter of Habakkuk* (1700, second edition 1716) – many of which are also textual sources of librettos. Robert Boyle also praised *Davideis*, and argued for the appeal of religious verse written by 'Secular Persons of Quality', whose graceful style, reputation, and freedom from the suspicion of careerism (which might attach to clerical versifiers) makes them 'generally

more successfuller in Writing of Religion, (to Gentlemen especially)
than Scholasticks or Men in Orders'.[31] Boyle was vindicated in his
claim that such works by such authors attracted notice; his brother's
play about Saul and his own novel about Theodora were used by
Handel's oratorio librettists when both writers had been dead for
over fifty years.[32]

Boyle felt obliged to justify the fact that he had 'mentioned
Theodora's beauty more often and advantageously, and represented
her lover's passion more pathetically, than the subject of the story
exacted', but the 'fashionable stile' was necessary to hold the attention of 'youthful persons of quality' to this didactic work; 'unfortunate virtue' on its own would not be interesting enough for the
audience most in need of improving literature. The librettists evidently concurred, choosing sources which provided an attractive
heroine and a devoted admirer or husband, or grafting these into
their source material (*Esther, Deborah, Athalia, Saul, Samson* (a formerly devoted husband), *Joseph, Alexander Balus, Joshua, Solomon,
Susanna* and *Jephtha* as well as *Theodora*). For some, the literary
potential of biblical heroines was sufficiently developed by the
biblical text. 'Where', asked the author of *The Touch-stone*, 'do the
Triumphs of Virtue, or the just Rewards of Lust, appear more
conspicuous, than in *Susanna* and the two Elders? – Where can true
Fortitude, or invincible Piety, shine brighter, than in Heroick
Judith's Conquest over *Holofernes*? – or Captivating Modesty, than in
Esther's over *Ahasuerus*?'[33] Lord Shaftesbury's objections to the idea
of using the Bible as subject-matter for modern verse are germane
here; they likewise anticipate (and point out to us) what the librettists did to the Bible in making use of it. Admittedly, writes Shaftesbury, there are Old Testament heroes 'no-way behind the chief of
those so much celebrated by the Antients', but it would 'be hard to
give many of 'em that grateful Air, which is necessary to render 'em
naturally pleasing to Mankind, according to the Idea Men are
universally found to have of *Heroism*, and *Generosity*'. Try as we may
to side with the chosen people against the heathen, 'there will be still
found such a Partiality remaining in us, towards Creatures of the
same Make and Figure with our-selves', that we will be repelled by
the punishments inflicted on the infidels by these godly heroes.
Poetry invites us to relax our sterner faculties, and 'In such a
Situation of Mind, we can hardly endure to see *Heathen* treated as
Heathen, and *the Faithful* made the Executioners of the Divine Wrath

... The Wit of the best Poet is not sufficient to reconcile us to the Campaign of a JOSHUA, or the Retreat of a MOSES, by the assistance of an EGYPTIAN *Loan*.'[34] In their editorialising of the Scriptures the librettists displayed, and accommodated, precisely these ethical and moral scruples of the eighteenth-century man of feeling (see chapter 10).

The ethical humanist Shaftesbury was in the minority in his objection that biblical subjects offend civilised taste with their lack of refined feeling, which was rebutted over and over again. John Husbands commends the tender sentiments and dramatically heightened emotion of David's lament for Jonathan, Jacob's love for his sons and the whole story of Joseph, providing a cue for the climax of Jennens' *Saul* and for Miller's sentimental drama of *Joseph and his Brethren*. In common with biblical commentators, Husbands responds to the Joseph story as a finely wrought drama: 'Surely never was any Story, from the beginning to the End, contriv'd more artfully, never was any Plot for the Stage work'd up more justly, never any unfolded itself more naturally, than this of *Joseph*.'[35] Charles Rollin comes even nearer to providing a blueprint for the libretto's scenario, indicating to us how successfully Miller catered to the cultivated public's taste for tender sentiments choked with tearful emotion. Rollin's account of Joseph's reconciliation with his brothers would equally serve to describe Miller's dramatisation of it, except that Miller increases the pathos by drawing out the action, multiplying the emotional silences and making Joseph weep more often:

Nothing can be more affecting than the admirable story of Joseph; and one can scarce refrain from tears, when we see him obliged to turn aside in order to dry his own, because his bowels yearn'd at the presence of Benjamin; or when after having discovered himself, he throws himself about the neck of his dear brother; and folding him in the strictest embrace, mingles his tears with those of Benjamin, and discovers the same affectionate tenderness for the rest of his brethren, over each of whom it is said he wept. At that instant not one of them spoke, and this silence is infinitely more eloquent than any expressions he could have employed. Surprize, grief, the remembrance of what was past, joy, gratitude, stifle their words: their heart can express itself no otherwise than by tears, which would, but cannot sufficiently express their thoughts.[36]

Admiration for the scriptural account of Joseph's discovery of himself to his brothers was even voiced by Pope, who considered it superior to Odysseus' discovery to Telemachus.[37] Husbands also admires the Song of Solomon as 'a very regular dramatic poem', ignoring the traditional allegorical interpretation as completely as Handel's librettist did. Prior prefaced his *Solomon* (1708), on the other hand, by recommending for modern transcription the wisdom demonstrated in Solomon's 'works' (and celebrated in the central act of Handel's oratorio).[38]

Repeatedly we find the most admired scriptural passages incorporated in the librettos. The Songs of Moses, Miriam and Deborah, cited by Sir Philip Sidney as instances of the world's first poetry, became favourite eighteenth-century examples of the sublime, as did much of Isaiah (used in *Messiah*) and the Psalms (especially Milton's versions, which Hamilton used for the *Occasional Oratorio*) – the four *loci classici* noticed above in Hughes' lines on divine poetry. The crossing of the Red Sea forms the major part of *Israel in Egypt*, and the literary fashionableness of the Songs of Moses and Miriam sheds light on the fact that Handel set the part of the text containing them first, and as a self-sufficient unit. The Red Sea crossing is also referred to in the *Occasional Oratorio* (a reuse of part of *Israel in Egypt*), by analogy in *Joshua* (it is paralleled in the crossing of the River Jordan, which forms the subject of Part I) and in *Jephtha*, in the chorus 'When his loud voice in thunder spoke' – a reference that must be impenetrable to many twentieth-century listeners but would have been instantly recognised by contemporaries as a favourite figure for God's transcendant power. The 1735 religious verse competition number of the *Gentleman's Magazine* was prefaced by John Hulse's poem 'On the Dignity of Divine Poetry', which likewise singled out the Songs of Moses and Deborah for special admiration, as well as the Book of Job, Joshua's halting of the sun and David's Psalms. Charles Rollin devoted eighteen pages of appreciative analysis to the Song of Moses.[39] Again and again it is the Songs of Moses and Deborah and the Psalms that receive special praise. They recur in many of the Three Choirs sermons, cited as justification for church music. The Song of Moses is particularly sanctified by being sung in heaven, as Taswell (among many others) points out:

We find then this Art [sacred music] call'd in to the Assistance of Religion by the great Jewish Law-giver, who himself commun'd with God, and promulgated a Religion immediately from its Divine Author. Two of his sacred Songs are yet extant, in their Style and Manner peculiarly ennobled and elevated – and what may here deserve our particular Attention is – the last of these is recorded by the Author of Revelation as the Subject Matter of the Praise and Adoration of the Bless'd above, who are said to sing continually the Song of Moses. (Revelation XV.3)

Taswell's admiration for the song of Deborah readily explains why a librettist might choose to dramatise the story of Barak, Jael and Sisera which it celebrates, to modern minds so unedifying:

The Song of *Deborah* and *Barak* is the Height itself of Sublime, and under all the Disadvantages of Translation from a Language to whose Idiom it is so peculiarly adapted, whether we consider it for its Majesty of Style, or its Beauty and Simplicity of Sentiment, it must be acknowledg'd as the just Reproach of the most elevated *Human* Compositions that have ever since appear'd upon a Comparison.[40]

Similarly the librettist of Handel's *Deborah*, Samuel Humphreys, praised the Song of Deborah in his commentary on the Bible as far surpassing any classical attempts at sublime and affective poetry (his admiration fills four and a half folio pages, a lot even by the standards of eighteenth-century biblical commentary).[41]

All agreed that in the Old Testament 'Eloquence sits beside the Throne of Truth', giving us 'not only a Religion, but a Language from Heaven', in an awe-inspiring combination of simplicity and 'strange Movingness' which can 'set the Heart on fire, and at once surprize, improve, transport, the Reader'.[42] We can see the path prepared for Jennens' use of Isaiah in *Messiah* in contemporary admiration for the energy and pathos of the very passages which he chose. Charles Rollin (whose work Jennens possessed) points out that 'The prophets describe Christ's sufferings in a lively, affecting and pathetic manner, and abound with sentiments and reflections', whereas, less compellingly, 'the evangelists relate them with simplicity, without emotion, or reflections'. Rollin devotes one and a half pages to 'For unto us a child is born ... prince of peace', especially praising 'the government shall be upon his shoulder' as 'a wonderful image' which has 'a peculiar energy when considered with due attention'.[43] As Robert Manson Myers pointed out, Jennens' theme was not an original choice as a topic for artistic expression: Pope's *Messiah. A Sacred Eclogue, Compos'd of several Passages of Isaiah the Prophet. Written in imitation of Virgil's Pollio* (1712) was one of the earliest and most popular poems on the 'Messiah' theme but not at all a singular expression of it (for non-literary reasons for the prevalence of the topic and its association with Old Testament prophecy see chapter 6).[44] Like Jennens' libretto, many of these poems are highly allusive, assuming a thorough knowledge of the Bible. For example, in Thomas Harris' *An Hymn on Christ's Nativity, and Man's Redemption* (1722) the raising of Lazarus is described without naming him.

THE STYLE OF THE SCRIPTURES

Admiration for the Old Testament's content was matched by admiration for its style, not just in general praise of the kind already instanced, but in detailed comment on every rhetorical device employed by 'the sacred penman'. The greatest eighteenth-century critical analysis of the Old Testament as literature, Robert Lowth's *De sacra poesi hebraeorum praelectiones*, appeared just a year after Handel's last biblical oratorio and was not published in translation until 1787, but its predecessors during the oratorio years were legion.[45]

The Pentateuch's strength of diction was especially admired. Approaching the Bible as literature, even as theatrical drama, Husbands describes the texts attributed to Moses as

Strong and Masculine ... Tho' their Poetry was less artificial [elaborated], 'twas more nervous, lively, and expressive than ours ... The style of Moses is concise, nervous, simple, emphatical. The Diction of his Prose is natural and unstudied; of his poetry strong and bold ... All there is Action and Dialogue; the Historian retires out of Sight as much as possible, and the Persons themselves are introduced upon the Stage.[46]

Students of Handel will respond here also to the word 'nervous' (meaning sinewy, muscular, energetic, vigorous); after 'sublime' this was the word of praise most often applied to Handel's style in his own century.[47] What more obvious and exciting enterprise than to bring together the most sublime and nervous words ever written with the music of the master of the sublime and nervous style of composition?

Many of the rhetorical devices most keenly valued in the Scriptures also appear in the librettos: repetition; the use of abstract terms for concrete; the attribution of sense and action to inanimate objects; adjectives followed by a noun in the genitive; exclamation; interrogation; personification; apostrophe; exhortation; command; 'forms of admiration'; and that 'lofty impenetrability' which at best com-

bines the ambiguity, density, obscurity and surprise which denotes
the true sublime and even at worst imparts a sense of higher
mysteries to the receptive reader.[48] Critics' close focus on details of
biblical style, down to combinations of substantives and adjectives,
provided an anatomy of the sacred text which made it accessible to
the practising author in search of a model and broke it into convenient pieces for the author seeking authentically sublime phrases
for his libretto. For example, Humphreys does not actually transcribe or directly paraphrase the Song of Deborah at the appropriate point in his recounting of the drama. It would be too much at
variance with his own style: he himself noted in his biblical commentary that 'It is evident to all, that this hymn is expressed in another
kind of language, than the historical part of this book'. But he plants
phrases from it in his text as a kind of sublime leaven (including,
with a nice sense of irony, the words at the opening of Part II of
Sisera himself, whose demise the Song of Deborah will later celebrate).[49]

The Scriptures' richness of simile and allusion was admired for its
profusion, variety and boldness. 'All is figurative', with frequent and
sudden changes of both speakers and figures adding to the awed
astonishment imparted to the reader, amounting to a sense of
'heav'nly Magick'.[50] Instancing the Song of Deborah, Watts comments that 'the Figures are stronger, and the Metaphors bolder, and
the Images more surprizing and strange than ever I read in any
profane Writer'.[51] Again, this attribute is minutely demonstrated,
for example in Abbot Fleury's verse-by-verse analysis of Psalm XCI,
which reveals the 'Variety of beautiful Tropes and Figures' common
to the Psalms.[52] Admiration is tempered with reservations about the
success of some of the flights of boldness: Addison, for example,
cannot allow Solomon's likening of his beloved's nose to a tower of
Lebanon to pass without regret that he neglected to consider 'the
Decency of the Comparison'.[53] There is a parallel in the contemporary reaction to Handel's 'boldness' and power to astonish his
hearers by his daring and colourful neglect of conventional rules.[54]

For a generation which delighted to hymn God as the Newtonian
creator of the universe and published volume upon volume of
sermons celebrating His works of nature, the delineation of natural
life in the Old Testament was endlessly attractive; the favourite
psalm of the period was CIV. The Scriptures' vivid pictorialism was
constantly anatomised and praised, their poetry being 'more florid,

more enlivened, more expressive, more proper to paint and display the Images of Things before our Eyes, than the common Forms of Speech'.[55] Rollin enlarges on his observation that the Scriptures 'make those objects sensible which are the most remote from the senses, by lively and natural images of them' in an eighteen-page analysis of the Song of Moses which should be studied by anyone interested in the antecedents of *Israel in Egypt*.[56] This appreciative response to verbal pictorialism also has a corollary in the opportunities which the librettists gave Handel for word-painting and his (in the opinion of some contemporaries excessive) realisation of them.[57]

PARAPHRASE

Detailed analysis and appreciation of Old Testament style was fed by, and in turn nourished, the art of biblical paraphrase. Biblical paraphrase was a major and respected literary form, a test of sensitive expression.[58] It was also a useful means of concealing the limits of one's talents, to judge from Dennis' comment that even a mediocre poet writes better when paraphrasing Scripture, although the source is itself a translation (he gives examples).[59] In his campaign for religious verse Dennis buttresses his statement that it is positively our *duty* to make harmonious verse paraphrases of the prophetic parts of the Old Testament with arguments that should interest oratorio students. For Christians, says Dennis, the prophecies are the most important part of the Old Testament, 'because without them we could never be satisfy'd that *Jesus* is the Messiah'; the prophets expressed themselves in verse, because poetic utterance was one of their professional functions; the prophets also had the task of 'Praising God with Songs of the Prophets composing, accompany'd with the Harp and other Instrumental Musick'; Jesus, in his capacity as a prophet, 'prais'd God with spiritual Songs'; and 'the Method of his Instruction was intirely Poetical'. Dennis begins by using 'harmony' to mean only verbal euphony, but his references to music provide a clear pointer to the musical setting of passages taken or paraphrased from the Scriptures.[60]

Like the topics suggested for modern literary treatment, the passages selected for paraphrase or for its near cousin, versification, coincide with several of the librettos. For example, during the years 1733–52 the thirty-nine paraphrases published in the poetry columns of the *Gentleman's Magazine* included versions of the Songs of

Moses and Deborah, of the story of David and Goliath and of
David's lament for Saul and Jonathan, and of a chapter of Isaiah
and of three of the psalms used by Jennens in *Messiah* (all predating
the libretto's composition, and one of them headed 'The Sufferings
and Victory of Christ'). Despite the wide-ranging content and
general readership of the magazine, several of the contributors
address their task with scholarly seriousness. The versification
(in couplets) of one of the *Messiah* psalms (LXVIII) has footnotes
on parallel Old Testament texts and on the geography, history,
language and culture of ancient Israel, while a version of Psalm
CXXIX, claiming to reproduce the Hebraic metre, is part of an
ongoing essay-debate on the accuracy of biblical translation, giving
rise in the next issue to two rival translations of Psalms I and II with
the Hebrew text (partly in Hebrew characters, partly transliterated)
printed alongside.[61]

The first biblical paraphrase ever printed in the *Gentleman's Maga-
zine*, in 1733, was by one of the most enthusiastic practitioners,
Handel's friend Aaron Hill. It was an 'Abstract from Psalm CXIV'
recounting the Israelites' passages through the Red Sea and the
River Jordan, later the subjects of the final part of *Israel in Egypt* and
Act I of *Joshua*:

> When, from proude *Egypt*'s hard and cruel hand,
> High-summon'd *Israel* sought the promis'd land,
> The opening *sea* divided, at her *call*,
> And refluent *Jordan* rose, a *wat'ry wall!*

Hill's other paraphrases of passages later used as sources for the
librettos include the Song of Moses, David's lament, and two versions of Psalm CIV.[62] No. 87 of his journal *The Plain Dealer* carried a
discussion of the value of the Bible as a source of inspiration (possibly
by Edward Young) which concluded with Hill's metrical version of
a favourite passage for paraphrase, from Habakkuk III, which also
has resonances for oratorio students as it declares the Jews to be the
chosen people and invokes and celebrates God's exertion of His
miraculous power on their behalf:

> God of my fathers! stretch thy oft-try'd hand,
> And yet, once more, redeem thy chosen land:
> Once more, by *wonders*, make the *glories* known,
> And, 'midst thy *anger*, be thy *mercy* shown!
> ... Thus did my *God* (to save th'endanger'd land)
> March forth, indignant, with vindictive hand.[63]

Hill gave characteristically committed consideration to the art of biblical paraphrase and versification in his 'Preface to Mr Pope concerning the Sublimity of the Ancient Hebrew Poetry', prefixed to *The Creation. A Pindaric Illustration of a Poem originally Written by Moses on that Subject* (1720, later printed with the more explanatory subtitle *A Paraphrase upon the First Chapter of Genesis*). In this he examines attempts on the same text by Milton, Cowley and Blackmore in order to show how insensitive versification degrades the original:

There is, apparently, a divine Spirit, glowing forcibly in the Hebrew Poetry, a kind of terrible Simplicity! a magnificent Plainness! which is commonly lost, in Paraphrase, by our mistaken Endeavours after heightening the Sentiments, by a figurative Expression; This is very ill judg'd: The little Ornaments of Rhetorick might serve, fortunately enough, to swell out the Leanness of some modern compositions; but to shadow over the Lustre of a divine Hebrew Thought, by an Affectation of enliv'ning it, is to paint upon a Diamond, and call it an Ornament.

Hill finds that Blackmore's inapt metaphors distort the sense, whereas Milton provides 'Words so finely chosen, and so justly ranged, that they call up before a Reader the Spirit of their Sense'. The real extent of Hill's attention can be conveyed only by quoting at length a *part* of his criticism of Joseph Trapp's paraphrase of Psalm CIV:

The Hebrew Poet describing God, says, ' ... He Maketh the Clouds his Chariots, and walketh on the Wings of the Wind.' Making the 'Clouds his Chariots,' is a strong and lively Thought; But That of 'walking on the Wings of the Wind,' is a Sublimity, that frightens, astonishes, and ravishes the Mind of a Reader, who conceives it, as he shou'd do. The Judgement of the Poet in this Place, is discernable in three different Particulars; The Thought is in itself highly noble, and elevated; To move at all upon the Wind, carries with it an Image of much Majesty and Terror; But this natural Grandeur he first encreas'd by the Word 'Wings,' which represents the Motion, as not only on the Winds, but on the Winds in their utmost Violence, and Rapidity of Agitation. But then at last, comes that finishing Sublimity, which attends the Word 'walks'! The Poet is not even satisfied to represent God, as riding on the Winds; nor even as riding on them in a Tempest; He therefore tells us, that He walks on their Wings; that so our Idea might be heighten'd to the utmost, by reflecting on this calm, and easy Motion of the Deity, upon a Violence, so rapid, so furious, and ungovernable, to our human Conception. Yet as nothing can be more sublime, so nothing can be more simple, and plain, than this noble Imagination. But

Mr. Trapp, not contented to express, attempts unhappily to adorn this inimitable Beauty, in the following Manner.

> Who, borne in Triumph o'er the Heavenly Plains,
> Rides on the Clouds, and holds a Storm in Reins,
> Flies on the Wings of the sonorous Wind, &c.

Here his imperfect, and diminishing Metaphor, of the 'Reins', has quite ruin'd the Image; What rational, much less noble Idea, can any Man conceive of a Wind in a Bridle? The unlucky word 'Plains' too, is a downright Contradiction to the Meaning of the Passage. What wider Difference in Nature, than between driving a Chariot over a Plain, and moving enthron'd, amidst That rolling, and terrible Perplexity of Motions, which we figure to our Imagination, from a 'Chariot of Clouds'? But the mistaken Embellishment of the Word 'flies', in the last Verse, is an Error almost unpardonable; Instead of improving the Conception, it has made it trifling, and contemptible, and utterly destroy'd the very Soul of its Energy! 'flies' on the Wind! What an Image is that, to express the Majesty of God? To 'walk' on the Wind, is astonishing, and horrible; But to 'fly' on the Wind, is the Employment of a Bat, of an Owl, of a Feather! Mr. Trapp is, I believe, a Gentleman of so much Candour, and so true a Friend to the Interest of the Art he professes, that there will be no Occasion to ask his Pardon, for dragging a Criminal Metaphor, or two, out of the Immunity of his Protection.[64]

Hill's dismissal of 'little Ornaments of Rhetorick' as unbecoming to such sublime material has its corollary in the offence which contemporary music critics took at Handel's use of musical wit and ornament, of (as Hill says) 'mistaken Embellishments', detailed word painting and 'divisions', in his settings of texts drawn from this same sublime source.[65] Nor was Hill alone in expressing reservations about some of the products of the passion for biblical paraphrase. Others condemned the whole enterprise. Henry Felton observed in 1713 that 'the sublime Majesty, and royal Magnificence of the Scripture Poems, are above the Reach, and beyond the Power of all mortal Wit ... those who have presumed to heighten the Expressions by a Poetical Translation or Paraphrase, have sunk in the Attempt ... the Prose of Scripture cannot be improved by Verse'. Similarly Charles Gildon found the unmediated text of the King James Bible infinitely preferable to 'poetic' paraphrases because this attempt at close translation came nearer to the force of the original: 'I never found my soul touch'd by the best of these performances (even *Cowley* himself down to this day) though it has been scarce able to support the violent emotions, and excessive transports raised by the common translation.'[66]

These criticisms that versification and paraphrase insulted the status and power of the Scriptures might prompt an aspiring oratorio librettist to use the biblical text itself. *Israel in Egypt* and *Messiah* consist entirely of Scripture verses or their Prayer Book versions; *Esther* and *Belshazzar* quote the Old Testament verbatim. We are reminded again of Bishop Synge's list of reasons for *Messiah*'s excellence: the second he gives is that the words 'are all Sublime, or affecting in the greatest degree' (see above, p. 34). Patrons of the first performances of *Israel* responded similarly. One wrote that 'as the Words are taken from the Bible, they are perhaps some of the most sublime parts of it', and another voiced sentiments that would be heard repeatedly from Handel's audiences during his lifetime as well as afterwards:

The Whole of the *first* Part [of *Israel in Egypt*], is entirely Devotional; and tho' the *second* Part be but *Historical*, yet as it relates the great Acts of the Power of God, the Sense and the Musick have a reciprocal Influence on each other ... The Theatre, on this occasion, ought to be enter'd with more Solemnity than a Church; inasmuch, as the Entertainment you go to is really in itself the noblest Adoration and Homage paid to the Deity that ever was in one. So sublime an Act of Devotion as this *Representation* carries in it, to a Heart and Ear duly tuned for it, would consecrate even Hell itself.[67]

*   *   *

Several points relating to the oratorios emerge from early-eighteenth-century comments about the religious sublime. The one that perhaps strikes the modern reader most forcibly is the whole-hearted absorption of the principle of the Longinian sublime which the period made most its own: that verse of the stature of the Old Testament seizes and shakes the reader with almost unbearably strong emotion. The response of Handel's contemporaries to the source material of his librettos was not emotionally tepid. There is a sense that here, with relief and abandon, men of letters who were morally idealistic as well as linguistically sensitive at last found the arena, truly heaven sent, for emotional release. The same enthusiastic emotion, expressed in identical words, was evoked in the audiences of the oratorios: Handel's music, they testified, had the divine power of the true sublime, rousing the mind, piercing the soul, and sweeping the listener into an apprehension of heavenly joy. Handel fulfilled the hopes of Dennis and his followers. To cite one example of dozens documented by the invaluable Deutsch: Lawrence Whyte, experiencing the first performance of *Messiah*, found that

Handel's Art
Transports the Ear, and ravishes the Heart;
To all the nobler *Passions* we are mov'd . . .[68]

The next point to strike us is the prevalence of comments on the
Old Testament and hence the frequency with which specific texts
are mentioned – and how many of these texts became libretto
material. The literate audience of an oratorio was accustomed not
only to meeting the source texts in domestic and church reading of
the Bible, but to seeing them regularly descanted on in popular
magazines. We are also bound to be struck by the minute, exhaustive detail with which the Old Testament was analysed and appreciated as literature. Finally, cultivation of the art of biblical paraphrase in a context of acute critical attention led to heightened
respect for the integrity of the original text, and defence of it from
the abuses of lesser poetasters. In chapter 6 we shall see that the
defence of Scripture was not confined to the literary world.

CHAPTER 5

The survival of epic

In the opinion of eighteenth-century writers the most fitting vehicle of the religious sublime was the epic, established since Homer and ratified by Milton as the noblest literary form, and defined by Dryden as 'the greatest work that the soul of man is capable to perform', a definition kept alive by eighteenth-century literary authorities.[1] Religious nationalism is a prominent feature of the oratorios, and for many twentieth-century audiences a tiresome one. Eighteenth-century prescriptions for epic form a critical context which makes the librettos' insistent religious nationalism seem more conventional than we might suppose but also less superficial. 'National song' was a morally and idealistically loaded endeavour. Despite or perhaps because of the aspirations of its advocates, it was a lost cause in Augustan literature. But, point for point, contemporary prescriptions for epic can be matched in the librettos, finding in Handel's oratorios the realisation they never achieved in poetry.

The epic for which writers campaigned was moral, didactic, elevating and Christian.[2] The purpose of epic, according to Sir Richard Blackmore (one of its most prolific eighteenth-century practitioners), is to teach virtue and glorify the nation, so it must exhibit and respect the national religion. His own *Alfred* (1723), dedicated with educational intent to Frederick Prince of Wales, 'is contrived and finished upon the system of the Christian Institution, the established Religion of my Country, and which I my self sincerely believe'. Similarly the Oxford professor of poetry, Joseph Trapp, taught in the first decades of the century that 'An Epic Poem, properly so call'd, is, and always must be written in Honour of the Country, or Religion of the Author, between which, and the Hero, there is a near Relation; and therefore he ought to come off in Triumph at last.'[3] He could have been writing a blueprint for Handelian oratorio. The epic poet's purpose, 'the Advancement of

Heroick Virtue and the Glory of his Country', can only be accomplished, says Blackmore, if he observes 'thro' his whole Work a becoming Reverence to the sacred Rites and established Modes of Publick Worship'. This reminds us of the frequent scenes of worship in the oratorios. Blackmore rebuts the objections of Boileau, Watts and Dennis to the 'engaging of invisible Powers in the Action'. Not only does it add greatly to 'the Embellishment of the Poem ... making it sublime and admirable', but angels are credible and miracles still happen: 'The Angels especially are Attendants on Assemblies, congregated for Divine Worship, and are vigilant and active in protecting the Christian church', and 'Miracles are not totally ceased'. Divine power continues to operate in human life as it has always done, and should be shown to do so in epic.[4] It is certainly shown to do so, complete with miracles and angelic appearances, in the epic Israelite oratorios such as *Joshua*.

Manifestations of God's power, it was agreed, are the most fertile sources of sublime description. While the concrete evidence of His power in nature provides scope for the delights of imitative description, His miracles give rise to the awe and terror of the unknown. The Old Testament contains both. So, we observe, do the Israelite librettos. The combination – natural terrors striking from a supernatural source – was unbeatable: 'There is no grander or more awful subject, than that of the Deity executing his justice, publicly and sensibly, upon his offending creatures', wrote Thomas Leland, incidentally describing an essential element of the librettos.[5] Blackmore's thoughts about God's influence on the behaviour of nations and individuals and its relation to their own responsibility are likewise prophetic of the make-up of the Israelite oratorio libretto:

Besides the Physical Necessity of the Concurrence of the Supream Being to enable his Creatures to act, all Men, who have a just Idea of him, will allow that he does actually interest himself in the Government of Humane Affairs, and by his Providence disposes Things in such a manner, that those events, which he designs, shall certainly come to pass; that he brings about the Rise and Fall of Empires, promotes or disappoints the Schemes of Statesmen, and as Lord of Armies, bestows Victory on which Leader he pleases; that he inspires the Heart of his favour'd General with Courage and Wisdom, shields his Head in the Day of Battle, animates his Troops, and disheartens and confounds the enemy. Nor is the Hero's Valour or Prudence the less his own, because inspir'd and given by Heaven; nor is his Honour diminish'd by the Intervention of Providence, that dispos'd Circumstances in his Favour; for our Faculties and Powers are freely, and without Constraint, exerted in all our Operations; and the Concurrence of Divine Aid does not suspend, much less destroy, the Liberty and Self-determining Power of the Will; and therefore how much soever we are assisted by the Supream Being, as an universal Cause, our Actions are as much our own as it is possible that a Creature's should be.[6]

Blackmore feels that epic must show men acting of their own will, since blind destiny (a concept resisted as fervently here as in discussions of Greek tragedy) would make a mockery of the human virtue that it is intended to teach. Epic, states Blackmore in the preface to *Alfred*, anticipating the plots of *Deborah*, *Samson*, *Judas Macchabæus* and *Joshua*, 'contains the Pursuit of some important End to be attained by vertuous and heroick Deeds, by Patience, Perseverance, Supplication, and Reliance on divine Aids, for which the Heroe is at last honoured with Success; but this is all an idle and insignificant Business if fatal Necessity governs the Universe', as it does in '*Pagan theology*'.[7] The deities of classical epic offend Blackmore as much as his idea of the classical idea of fate. His condemnation shows that the attitude to heathens and paganism in the librettos (see chapter 10) was not unusual for its time, and the examples in his critique happen to provide an instructive gloss on two of the librettos: 'a Medley of Debauch and Divinity, where the convened Deities equal the Lewdness of *Alexander*'s and *Belshazzar*'s Feasts'.[8] Critics likewise eschewed the classical epic's concept of continuing endurance and uncertainty, and required a happy ending for the virtuous. Addison's demand that the conclusion leave the reader in 'a state of Tranquillity and Satisfaction'[9] is satisfied by the librettists, for instance in the final choruses of *Saul* and *Samson*, which are not dramatically prepared for or appropriate to the tragic climax, but which make a final resounding assertion that God cares for His people.

The human virtues and emotions which qualify for the epithet 'sublime' and which, according to its eighteenth-century proponents, epic should portray, are also portrayed in the librettos: heroism; desire for conquest; contempt of death, danger and rank; aspirations to fame and immortality; patriotism; justice; universal benevolence; and love of God.[10] Heroic virtue had been famously defined by Sir William Temple, in a much-reprinted essay. With a plangency which must have appealed to many of his high-minded eighteenth-century readers he hailed 'that antique shrine of heroic virtue, which, however forgotten, or unknown in latter ages, must yet be allowed to have produced in the world the advantages most valued among men'. The true hero had, not mere physical courage, but 'some great and native excellency of temper or genius tran- scending the common race of mankind in wisdom, goodness, and fortitude'. Heroism consists of patriotism, imperialism, aiding the oppressed, and serving 'the general good of mankind' by estab- lishing good government through 'the institutions of such laws, orders, or governments, as were of most ease, safety and advantage to civil society'. The ancient heroes' time was employed in 'defend- ing their own countries from the violence of ill men at home, or enemies abroad; in reducing their barbarous neighbours to the same forms and orders of civil lives and institutions'. They 'made great and famous conquests, and left them under good constitutions of laws and government', they 'instituted excellent and lasting orders and frames of any political state', and they were 'obeyed as princes or lawgivers in their own times'.[11] Again, all this is remarkably like a blueprint for the political content of the Old Testament librettos (see Part II). But Temple (unlike the librettists) comes down heavily in favour of civic order rather than conquest as the crucial distinc- tion of heroism:

After all that has been said of conquerors or conquests, this must be confessed to hold but the second rank in the pretensions to heroic virtue, and that the first has been allowed to the wise institution of just orders and laws, which frame safe and happy governments in the world. The designs and effects of conquests are but the slaughter and ruin of mankind.

So, continues Temple, 'the institutions of Moses leave him a diviner character than the victories of Joshua'.[12] The status of the Song of Moses as divine ratification of sacred song was one good reason for writing *Israel in Egypt*; its position as the epitome of the biblical sublime was another; Moses' accepted role as Ur-lawgiver offered a third. And the librettist of *Joshua* corrects Temple's slur on his hero by making him, too, a great lawgiver (see chapter 10, 'Covenant'). The librettists are inhibited by their source material from making Temple's distinction between right and might, but they share his respect for lawgivers: besides Joshua, the librettos depict great leaders who are also great lawgivers in the figures of Joseph, Solomon and Cyrus. Temple's ideas were kept current in the early eighteenth century by reprints of his essay and by their repetition by other writers; for example, Thomas Blackwell, in *An Enquiry into the Life and Writings of Homer*, defines heroism as 'a disinterested Love of

Mankind and our Country; unawed by Dangers, and unwearied by Toils'.[13]

Blackmore adds two qualifications to the view that the hero should be virtuous. A flawed hero can be sublime and is therefore admissible (we note that most of the libretto heroes are not perfect); and the hero should be passive as well as, or rather than, active:

All the essential Properties of an Epick Writing may be attain'd, tho the chief Person should be an eminent Sufferer, and no Battle should be fought through all the Poem ... As much divine Instruction relating to Providence, to the Encouragements and rewards of Virtue, and the terrible Consequences of Irreligion and Vice; as great and illustrious Examples of Piety, Fortitude, and Heroick Firmness of Mind; as noble and useful Morals, and as sublime Sentiments, all fit to inspire the Reader ... may be found in such a Poem, as well as in that which is full of Action and martial Atchievements.[14]

The penchant for passive suffering, reflecting current dramatic taste, is also evident in the librettos and again links them with contemporary literature. Milton's Samson, a figure of suffering and tempted virtue, is drawn largely from Job, one of Blackmore's prime examples of the instructive passive hero, and Blackmore anticipates the use Hamilton made of Milton in his libretto of *Samson*. For whereas Milton's Job–Samson is physically passive but spiritually and intellectually combative, Blackmore seems to propose, and Hamilton was to portray, a wholly subjective, responsive, but scarcely fighting hero. Less passive but still heroically suffering oratorio protagonists include Susanna, Theodora and Didymus.

Critics assured would-be practitioners that epic did not have to be all action and no dialogue, narration, comment or description. The epic convention of episodes, more or less loosely connected to the main narrative, satisfied the prevailing desire for inclusiveness and variety (see chapter 1). Blackmore encourages 'moral and political Discourses and Soliloquies, as well as Devotions and Thanksgivings, growing naturally from the Subject and apt to produce great and exalted Idea's and worthy Resolutions, if they are pertinent and spiritful, and not too long nor too frequent', and demonstrates from the Book of Job that 'divine and moral Sentiments ... may be intermixt in a due Proportion in the [epic] Poem with great Advantage'.[15] These requirements were fulfilled in, for example, Jennens' libretto of *Belshazzar*, as Handel himself appreciatively acknowledged (see above, p. 26).

Blackmore's suggestion for the contents of an epic provide sanction for many passages in the librettos that, like Jennens' in *Belshazzar*, may seem to the modern audience irrelevant or unrelated to the
heightening of character or emotion. Aaron Hill's unfinished epic,
on an Old Testament subject, *Gideon: or, The Patriot*, includes an
episode which his executors thought worth publishing as an extract
in his posthumous *Works*.[16] In a pastoral setting, rich with divinely
bestowed natural abundance, a pair of fugitive lovers experience a
series of occurrences quite unrelated to the military campaign of the
main action. These include the false accusation of a virtuous old
father, escape from prison engineered by change of clothes, three
last-minute escapes from death and one from rape, and love repulsed and then reciprocated – all which provide food for moral
reflection (and which can be paralleled with events in the librettos).
Hugh Blair's praise of the 'agreeable diversity' in James Macpherson's supposed ancient Celtic epics by Ossian (1760–3), his
admiration for their mixture of 'war and heroism, with love and
friendship, of martial, with tender scenes',[17] like Hill's similar
mixture, gives us a context of appreciation for librettos constructed
to such a pattern, for example *Joshua*. All the variety of rhetoric is
also encouraged, to open the mind to moral instruction by pleas-
uring the imagination. Blackmore allows 'lively Descriptions, Allusions, and beautiful Similitudes expressed in the finest Words and
elevated Diction' to be 'admirable Embellishments' even for the
high ground of epic.[18] This critical attitude would be sympathetic to
oratorio's mediation of moral instruction through pleasure by the
addition of music to the often chastening events and thoughts of the
librettos.

In these discussions of the nature of epic the nation is taken to be
the central concern, the individual hero existing principally as the
barometer of national strength. Trapp thought Virgil superior to
Homer because 'the Moral of the *Aeneis*, properly so called' is that a
virtuous nation which obeys God has the reward of being
'flourishing and happy'.[19] It is equally the moral of the Israelite
oratorios. Notwithstanding the proposed Christian basis, the action
was to be centred in this world – as is the action of the Israelite
oratorios. The real thrill of epic was that it told the story of the
reader's own history. (On the eighteenth-century's absorption with
this subject and its appearance in the librettos, see chapter 10,
'Continuity'.) Not only that, it gave the reader's past an un-

ashamedly heroic complexion. This was inspiring or (according to the reader's turn of mind) confirmed the gloomier view of modern human potential, already noted in Temple's projection of true heroism firmly and terminally into the past. (On the reflection of this view in the librettos see further chapter 10, 'Corruption'.) Here was a dilemma for the poet of Augustan England. On the one hand, to glorify the nation's past was didactic and patriotic, and epic was the summit of human endeavour; on the other hand, given the condition of modern man and the record of recent history, the project was impossible, unless one went as far back as Alfred, and even then the terrain was a minefield of bathetic traps. Small wonder that it was strewn with incomplete attempts (even Cowley did not finish *Davideis*). The task – to recount the nation's whole history to the present time – was too huge, and the call for a national song went almost unanswered, although it was heard and heeded by the nation's best poets.[20]

In laying out the problems of epic conventions in a Christian epic Dryden anticipates a quandary of the oratorio librettist: a machinery of angels under God's command would be uninteresting because God was bound to win. In any case, God (or the poet) could dispense with angels and just give the Christians greater courage or numbers, in the process, however, removing any dramatic tension. Dryden's own original solution, which is inspired by a passage in the Book of Daniel and of which he is very proud, but which evidently did not seem workable to the librettists, is to use national (Jewish, Persian, Grecian) guardian angels, each fighting on behalf of their own country and not certain of God's will.[21] The absurdity of grafting elements of the marvellous from classical epic into a modern poem is famously pointed out in Pope's parodic 'Receipt to Make an Epic Poem' (in his warning against the false sublime, *Peri Bathous*), which advises the author to pillage Homer and Virgil for ingredients and combine them indiscriminately, in the cheerful confidence that 'Epick Poems may be made *without a Genius*, nay without Learning or much Reading'.[22]

Yet Pope begins his 'Receipt' with completely straight assent to the time-honoured view that 'An Epic Poem is the greatest Work Human Nature is capable of'. But he is oppressed by the thought: 'They [the critics] have already laid down many mechanical Rules for Compositions of this Sort, but at the same time they cut off almost all Undertakers from the Possibility of ever performing them;

for the first Qualification they unanimously require in a Poet, is a *Genius*.' He might well feel haunted by the notion of this species of poetry, for a group of his friends and admirers, identified by Christine Gerrard as the Patriot poets and including some of the most zealous campaigners for artistic reform, ceaselessly reminded him that it was his duty to write his long-projected epic, *Brutus*. This doomed effort never got beyond the sketch stage, but its outlines are reminiscent both of Blackmore's prescriptions and of the elements of Israelite oratorio. Pope told Spence that the poem was to treat man 'in his Social, Political, and Religious Capacity', and the plot turned 'wholly on civil and ecclesiastical government ... The hero is a prince who establishes an empire ... the religion introduced by him is the belief in one God ... Brutus is supposed to have travelled into Egypt, and there to have learned the unity of the Deity' (as Moses was held to have done while in Egypt). According to Warburton, Brutus' 'Ruling Passion' was to be benevolence, prompting 'a strong desire to redeem the remains of his countrymen, then captives amongst the Greeks, from slavery and misery, and to establish their freedom and felicity on a just form of Civil Government. He had seen how false Policy, and Superstitions and Vices proceeding from it, had caused the ruin of Troy.' The oratorio librettists also treated these themes of slavery, redemption from slavery, establishment of monotheism, and establishment of justice (see Part II). Pope even seems to have been prepared to adopt (as some of the oratorio librettists did) the machinery of intervention by divine spirits, citing the Book of Daniel as authority.[23]

The more committedly Patriot poets were similarly exercised by the grail of epic. Thomson reported in 1730 that he felt he *ought* to write an epic, but 'My heart both trembles with diffidence and burns with ardor at the thought'; it would be 'the work of years'.[24] Aaron Hill, whose own epic, *Gideon: or, The Patriot*, was the work of over twenty years,[25] was especially energetic in the epic cause. An article in *The Prompter*, which internal evidence shows to be by Hill, assures potential authors that the difficulty of writing epic has been overstated, and provides a plain poet's guide (repeated in the notes to *Gideon*) in which the central point is consistent with the campaign to reform art: 'An *Epic Poem* is some noble and particular *Instruction in Morality* ... the Poet is never to have other View before him, but to strengthen, by the Persuasion and Authority of EXAMPLE, *That one Moral Lesson*, which he is desirous to imprint on the Mind of his

Readers'.[26] In the view of the Patriot poets, especially Hill himself, the production of British epic was vital because of the connection between the verse and the power of a nation, epic being the most nationalist form of poetry. France, Hill argued, had gained national strength because its government encouraged national poetry, which inspired the leaders of society with civic pride and the desire to set an example of patriotic confidence.[27]

In despairing of modern epic Pope was assuming that the ingredients would be second-hand classical. As Doody comments, Pope clearly thinks that 'the epic is, as a venture, passé. The author will be an imitator, not an original; he can assume specious originality only by trying to sound more ancient (i.e. out of date) than his predecessors. And as for all the properties of epic – its actions, its heroes, its gods, its scenes – we know them before they come up.' Likewise the popular journal *Common Sense* wondered in 1739, a few days before the first performance of *Israel in Egypt*, whether a modern writer could, 'in the Spirit of the Ancients, and without taking their Thoughts, produce another *Original Epick Poem*'.[28] But oratorio solves this problem. The persons and events of antiquity that it presents *are* peculiar to British epic, being drawn from ancient Israel, not ancient Greece, and the antique setting is itself significant, not merely ornamental, being the cradle of the British religion.

The greatest story that could ever be told in epic, the story of our creation and redemption, had of course been appropriated by Milton, and admiration for his scaling of this pinnacle of the sublime gathered momentum throughout the first half of the eighteenth century. Handel's contemporaries urged him to equal the achievement with what would surely be the greatest music ever written, a setting of *Paradise Lost*; two admirers are known to have worked on librettos of it for him (Handel is not known to have shown any interest, though two other composers capitalised on its fashionableness).[29] Discussing Milton's legacy, Doody comments that 'Even while he uses epic allusions and devices, Milton reminds us that such stories and such devices are only "feign'd", poor shady ineffectual ornament or weak fables substituted for the grand reality which only he can convey and which can only be told once and for all [in *Paradise Lost*]. After that, the epic had better shut up shop and keep quiet.'[30] But oratorio deals with parts of this same grand reality, God's plan for mankind; it meets the Miltonic challenge on a level as exalted as Milton's. Again, Doody remarks that

The poets needed to invent forms of narrative that were not epic; they had to contrive something suited to their particular purposes. New epic was just not possible. Milton, the one successful modern epic poet, had at the same time done the genre in ... The route to all traditional set genres was, like the road to epic, visibly signed 'No Entry'. Modern poets would have to manage on their own. If that meant doing without the familiar genial comforts of genre, it also meant poets could feel they were escaping from restrictions into liberty[31]

– for example, we could go on, by inventing the combination of drama, epic and music that was Israelite oratorio.

Hill, as befitted a keen champion of epic, dared to take his own theme, as Milton had done, from the Bible. His intention had more in common with *Samson Agonistes* than with *Paradise Lost*. *Gideon: or, The Patriot* had the subtitle 'In honour of the Two Chief Virtues of a People; Intrepidity in Foreign War: and Spirit of Domestic Liberty', and the introduction to the three books published in 1749 explained that it also advocated limited, constitutional monarchy. As we shall see constitutional historians of the period doing, Hill takes the Jewish state as a model. The possible objection that ancient Israelite history is not the history of Britain, and is therefore unsuitable for an English epic, is countered with an assertion of the analogy between the two nations – a fundamental concept of English religious and political thought (which is more fully explored in Part II). For Hill as for others of his time, the connection is not only analogical: 'there arise great Probabilities, toward finding in the first establish'd *Hebrew Model*, the Original of all the manly *Celtic Forms* [of government]: and, in particular, of That, which constitutes the *present System in Great Britain*'. Israelite history *is* British history because our constitution, as well as our religion, derives from theirs (this idea was commonplace). In addition, says Hill, the miracles which uniquely distinguish their history are excellent material for epic poetry, and they themselves were great poets (Moses, Miriam, Deborah, David and Solomon are of course instanced). Epic should in any case be a parable or allegory, conveying moral instruction by means of a story, so the real test is the chosen narrative's potential to teach us about modern politics, society and religion. As already mentioned, Hill's narrative has several elements that will be familiar to oratorio audiences, and there are further resemblances.

Like so many oratorio librettos, *Gideon* shows the Israelites oppressed by their enemies, having lapsed into idolatry, from which double nadir the hero, commissioned by an angel, redeems them. In his introduction and notes Hill points out the political morals, engaging with current debates. In opposition to the influential arguments of James Harrington, the seventeenth-century political writer who had most fully exploited the polemical potential of the model of the ancient Israelite constitution (see chapter 9), Hill holds that the Mosaic state was not a popular republic but a hereditary monarchy, with the sovereign power, that of God, vested in the person of the high priest. According to his reading of pre-exilic Israelite history, the division of territory under Joshua among the tribes fatally weakened national unity, military power was crippled by being decentralised, and when public spirit gave way to private self-interest (expressed by the scriptural desire that every man be able to sit under his own fig tree), greed, lawlessness and factious in-fighting quickly followed and inevitably resulted in loss of freedom through conquest by hostile nations. In applying all this to modern Britain, Hill's declared moral is that to be strong the nation must be united, and once a nation has fallen through faction into 'enslavement' by domestic or foreign governments, a 'Restorer of their Laws and Freedom' is needed to lead a band of patriots who will rouse the rest of the population. Britain, Hill concedes, is not at present (1749) at war, but its recent history amply justifies such a lesson.[32] Historians will recognise this as a transcript of Lord Bolingbroke's *The Idea of a Patriot King*, written in 1738 and finally published in the same year as *Gideon*. Hill in fact opens the 1749 version of his epic with an ardent tribute to Bolingbroke, whom he knew. In later chapters we will find much in the librettos that, like Hill's epic, reminds us of Bolingbroke's epitome of Patriot ideology.

Richard Savage, who saw a version of *Gideon* in the early 1720s, responded with an admiring poem. In it he praises Hill for portraying a patriot defender of his country's liberties in verse clearly inspired by Moses, David and Pindar which reaches to heaven and 'sweetly strikes th'Almighty's Ear' (in much the way that oratorio enthusiasts were to imagine Handel's music transcending earthly bounds).[33] In so far as *Gideon* is noticed at all in histories of English literature it is regarded as a sport, but it would not have seemed odd to its contemporary readers, for it was rooted in the thought and polemical practice of its time, and it should have a distinct place in music history as a remarkable forerunner of the oratorio librettos, like them (as we shall see in Part II) using pre-monarchical Israelite history to teach religious and moral-political lessons about the condition of modern Britain. Many of the individual biblical events and issues which Hill uses to point his morals also appear in the librettos: the crossing of the Red Sea (*Israel in Egypt*), the division of territory (*Joshua*), the role of the Amalekites (*Saul*), Saul's monarchical absolutism (*Saul*), the dire effects of self-interested greed (*Belshazzar*), the rallying of the nation by a patriot leader (*Jephtha*, among numerous instances), and Israelite apostasy (numerous instances, see chapter 10). It is worth reminding ourselves that Hill was a friend of Handel.

Blackwell had objected that since civil disorder and war are the fittest subjects for epic, and since Britain is happily free of these, we cannot write epic about ourselves: 'a People's Felicity clips the Wings of their Verse; It affords few Materials for Admiration or Pity . . . I am persuaded . . . That we may never be a proper Subject of an Heroic Poem.' But for ten of the twenty years during which the oratorios were first performed Britain was at war. Moreover, using allegorical epic solves Blackwell's dilemma. It also overcomes his objection that modern 'state Intrigues' will not 'receive the Stamp of *Simplicity* and *Heroism*' that is so necessary to epic – and that is so characteristic of the Israelite oratorios, which evade all modern pettiness.[34]

Allegorical epic was a well understood form. John Hughes explained that there are two sorts of allegory, one using fiction and one

in which the Story is fram'd of real or historical Persons, and probable or possible Actions; by which however some other Persons and Actions are typif'd or represented. In this sense the whole *Æneis* of Virgil may be said to be an Allegory, if we consider *Æneis* as representing *Augustus Caesar* . . . yet he has avoided the making it plain and particular, and has thrown it off in so many Instances from a direct Application, that his Poem is perfect without it . . . the Morals which may be drawn from the *Æneis* are equally noble and instructive, whether we suppose the real Hero to be *Æneis* or *Augustus Caesar*.[35]

The eighteenth-century audience had a natural tendency to seek and find allegory in art, as we saw in the article on the allegory of *Alcina* (above, p. 62). Such ready appreciation as Hughes demonstrates of the potential ambiguities of allegory in the epic should be borne in mind when we come to consider the allegorical meanings of the librettos (Part II).

Historically the singer of epic is a bard. One of the literary manifestations of the esteem accorded to the past which we have noticed throughout this survey of artistic principles is the cult of primitivism, which developed in the middle years of the century. It informs admiration of the 'oriental', archetypal, Old Testament writers. Central to the myth of the 'primitive' past is the figure of the bard, a visionary moral-political poet who seeks to put society back on the moral rails which lead to real national glory. He was modelled on (amongst other sources) the Old Testament prophets and patriarchs. His near relations in British literature, also manifestations of the interest in primitivism, especially in the origin of religions, are druids. These awesome priests and national leaders, whose religion was held by some to share a common origin with that of Moses, frequently had the role of prophesying a return to national glory after a period of decline, by means of a national regeneration of good intentions and energetic patriotism. In poetry of the 1730s and 1740s the two figures were sometimes conflated.[36] Oratorio made itself attractive to an eighteenth-century audience by providing a figure who likewise combines elements of the Old Testament prophet and the Old Testament priest with overtones of the bard and the druid. Vatic characters, many of them awe-inspiring, most of them agents of national regeneration, and all of them authoritative, include Deborah, Jehoida (in *Athalia*), Samuel (in *Saul*), Joseph, Daniel (in *Belshazzar*), Zadok (in *Solomon*) and Simon (in *Judas Macchabæus*). Here again the librettos connect with their literary context. Moreover, as mediated by the librettists, the primitive characters of the Old Testament also have all the advantages of modern sensibility, and their bardic spiritual leaders are heeded, with happy results (see further chapter 10). The writing of 'Ossian' has a hitherto unacknowledged family resemblance to the oratorios, and looks less revolutionary than it was considered to be by its first admirers when viewed alongside its libretto predecessors.

* * *

According to Christopher Hill, 'Milton is the last great writer of Biblical epic: the Augustan age lost interest in the tribal society of ancient Israel'.[37] Hill is refuted by the existence of Handel's oratorios. David B. Morris states that, despite critical interest, not only the religious epic but the whole genre of the religious sublime was defunct in eighteenth-century England.[38] But this is to ignore Handelian oratorio, which conforms to all the contemporary prescriptions and is the only form to achieve them. According to H. T. Swedenborg, during the oratorio period the agreed characteristics of epic were didacticism, verse, allegory, the sublime, narrative, and fiction, or mixed history and fiction.[39] All these are leading characteristics of the Israelite librettos. In his *Observations on Poetry, especially the Epic*, published the year before the première of *Israel in Egypt*, Henry Pemberton commented prophetically 'That pomp of sound has force to aid the sublime by giving additional energy to the expression, the powerful effects of music abundantly prove'.[40] The energy of Handel's music gave religious epic the 'pomp of sound' which ensured its survival.[41] As Doody remarks, a new genre was needed in which to locate the high moral ground that had been epic's domain. A similar need was being expressed in the realm of visual art, where painters and critics were calling for a British school of the visual form of epic – history painting.[42] The most successful response came not from literature or from painting but from music: Handel's oratorios fitted the need so well that they survived long after the eighteenth-century call for ennobling national song had ceased to sound.

CHAPTER 6

The defence of Christianity

Can ye, ye deists, the Apostle hear
With thankless Ear?

Thomas Morell, *The Christian's Epinikion* (1743)

THE SPREAD OF SCEPTICISM

Eighteenth-century Anglican teaching stressed good works more
than faith. Ethical social benevolence is the road to salvation in
countless sermons of the period by the latitudinarian Archbishop
Tillotson, his clergy and their followers. In this neglect of the
concept of original sin and emphasis on humanity's potential to fulfil
the requirements of divine precepts in this life, Christianity relaxed
its doctrine of redemption by grace further than in any previous
period of English history. Some versions of religion, most influen-
tially that of the third Earl of Shaftesbury, secularised ethics to the
extent of suggesting that men and women did not need God to teach
them perfection.[1] At the same time, in France, Richard Simon
initiated scholarly criticism of the text of the Bible, and a translation
of his work (*Critical History of the Old Testament*, 1682) devastatingly
undermined English Protestant faith in the integrity, inspiration
and authority of Scripture. These were the intellectual seedbeds of
the freethinking deist movement in England.[2]

The greatest importance of the English deist controversy to the
history of religion is that it gave rise to the major Anglican apologetics of the eighteenth century.[3] Its importance to students of
Handel's oratorios is that it helps to explain the librettos' content
and gives us a further sense of the strength of their engagement with
major concerns of their time. The 'father' of English deism, Lord
Herbert of Cherbury, published his *De veritate* in 1624, but the most
vigorous phase of the controversy dates from the last years of the

141

seventeenth century, when publication of John Toland's *Christianity not Mysterious* (1696) amply confirmed to churchmen the necessity for the annual Boyle Lectures (sermons) 'proving the Christian Religion against notorious Infidels'. The last major flurry came with the posthumous publication of Lord Bolingbroke's works in 1752. The years of the oratorios' first performances, 1732–52, are also the years of the major Anglican rebuttals of deism. Once we locate the librettos against this background of energetic debate – in which many participants felt that the bases of Christianity were being threatened – they appear more polemical, more committed and more complex than we had realised. When they are read alongside the topics of the debate and the arguments of the orthodox defence they are seen to bear so close a relation to that defence as to seem part of the response to contemporary freethinking.

The deist attack was on the concept of the Trinity, specifically on the personal nature of the Father and the divine nature of the Son; and on the Bible as divine revelation. The Bible enjoyed enormous status in eighteenth-century English Protestantism as the only source of truth and salvation, in favour of which Papal authority, the claims of tradition and the solitary revelation of 'inner light' were all to be rejected. As divine revelation it was justified by its account of miracles and the fulfilment of its prophecies. The dawn of Biblical criticism in the early eighteenth century brought the authority traditionally accorded to the Scriptures, on the grounds of their being directly inspired by God, under concerted *rational* attack. Since orthodox believers held that the Bible contained nothing contrary to reason, they were obliged to defend their doctrine on rational grounds. 'Since Divinity has been made a Science', lamented the Reverend Arthur Ashley Sykes, 'and Systematical Opinions have been received, and embraced, in such a manner that it has not been safe to contradict them, the Burden of vindicating Christianity has been very much increased.'[4] The result is that books of Christian apologetics have chapters entitled 'Prophetick Stile Enigmatical, but strictly Rational' and 'That it is not unreasonable to believe, that a Mediatour should be appointed between God and Man'.[5] The dispute could not be conclusive, since both sides assumed a rational stance to discuss matters which, in the absence at this date of sufficient historical knowledge, could be questions only of faith and doubt. (It is still not concluded, and looks set to run for ever. In March 1993 the British press carried reports about Professor

Thomas Thompson, who had been dismissed from Marquette (Jesuit) University, Milwaukee, for having published a study of *The Early History of the Israelite People* arguing that the first ten books of the Old Testament and their leading figures, Abraham, Jacob, Moses, David and Solomon, are fictional. Jewish leaders were reported as unruffled, commenting that the Bible does not require empirical supports; but the Reverend Clive Calver, general director of the Evangelical Alliance (1.2 million supporters), combatively described the book as beginning a new phase in attacks on the authenticity of Scripture.[6])

One of quickest and most revealing ways of understanding why deism hurt is to turn to the contents pages of a few of the hundreds of publications which the controversy generated. For example, the initial chapter headings of Part I of Anthony Collins' *A Discourse of the Grounds and Reasons of the Christian Religion* can still, with a small effort of historical imagination, shock even non-believers today, and help them to realise the horror of Collins' Christian readers in 1724, a horror which must have deepened when they grappled with his equally deadpan, sardonically *faux-naïf* text:

1 That Christianity is founded on Judaism, or the New Testament on the Old
2 That the Apostles [and Christ] ground and prove Christianity from the Old Testament
3 That the Old Testament is the Canon of Christians [and that the New Testament has no apostolic authority]
4 That it is a common and necessary method for new Revelations to be built and grounded on precedent Revelations
5 That the chief Proofs of Christianity from the Old Testament are urg'd by the Apostles in the New Testament
6 That if those Proofs are valid, Christianity is invincibly establish'd on its true foundation
7 That if those Proofs are invalid, then is Christianity false

Collins then goes on to insinuate that 'these Proofs' of Christianity *are* invalid, by arguing that Old Testament prophecies can be applied to Jesus only allegorically, and that this is no proof. Further, he contends that the whole of Christian revelation is contained in the Old Testament, and not in the New; that the Old Testament text became corrupted in transmission and is therefore unreliable; that the Septuagint translators were incompetent; and that the two testaments are irreconcilable.

It is easy to understand from this scheme of argument why defenders of Christian revelation became drawn into reiterated assertions of the validity of Mosaic Law and Old Testament prophecy, which is where the deist debate becomes most interesting for oratorio students. The debate had many strands, involving writers with agendas which were very varied and serious in varying degrees. Most deists were not anti-Christian and did not deny revelation, but their redefinition of revelation as allegory, as a 'republication' of the laws of nature, and even more, of course, the extreme provocations of such as Collins, brought out the defenders of traditional Christianity in force. The main points for us to register about the debate are that it bulked immensely large in the reading public's view; that it focused attention on the Old Testament; and that it is reflected in the librettos.

John Leland's *A Short View of the Principal Deistical Writers that have Appeared in England in the Last and Present Century* (1754, third edition 1757) testifies that this was no mere theological side-issue. The late-twentieth-century equivalent, in terms of the familiarity and alarm of the topic, would perhaps be global warming or the resurgence of fascism. Collins boasted that there had been thirty-five rebuttals of his *Grounds* in three years. The *Monthly Chronicle*'s Register of Books for August 1728 lists nineteen books published in the preceding seven months relating to just one deist tract; of twenty-three theological works listed for November 1729, eleven concern a single aspect of the debate. The issues were slugged out not only in specialist tracts and tomes but in the popular monthlies. For example, the problem of God's allowing the sacrifice of Jephtha's daughter – a topic taken on by two oratorio librettists, one of them for Handel (see chapter 14) – was canvassed in the *Gentleman's Magazine* for April 1734 (p. 615), while *Mist's Weekly Journal* took issue with *The Independent Whig* on the mysteries of Christianity and the interpretation of the Scriptures.[7] Countless sermons brought the debate to the attention even of the illiterate. The great series of Boyle Lectures, founded in 1691 by Robert Boyle and preached and published throughout the first half of the eighteenth century, required the annual lecturer to give eight sermons 'proving the Christian Religion against notorious Infidels, viz. Atheists, Deists, Jews and Mahometans', and by 1737 an abridged version of them filled four volumes.[8]

Two of Handel's oratorio librettists – Miller and Morell – were clergymen, one – Jennens – was a scholarly evangelising Christian, and another – Humphreys – wrote a massive three-volume biblical commentary with an introduction defending the Bible against charges of forgery and spuriousness. But even without such affiliations it was impossible to be a member of the reading public in the middle decades of the eighteenth century, the period of most intense and voluminous argument concerning the Old Testament, and be unaware of the debate, which itself became absorbed into a more general, and insistently broadcast, concern about the spread of irreligion. Handel himself could not have avoided knowing about these concerns, from his writers or simply from the discussion around him. He could have heard about them in detail from one of his close friends. His admirer Mrs Pendarves' husband-to-be, Dr Patrick Delany, was a major contributor to the defence of religion. An account he published in 1732 of *The Present State of Learning, Religion, and Infidelity in Great-Britain. Wherein the Causes of the Present Degeneracy of Taste, and Increase of Infidelity, Are Inquir'd into, and Accounted for* blamed lay indifference to religion on rationalist analyses of Scripture, which had popularly reduced the Bible to a collection of texts that could be treated objectively like any others. In 1740–2 he published a large two-volume study of the reign of David which was central to the controversy about the king's moral-political standing (it covers David's relations with Saul and Jonathan, the material of Jennens' libretto of 1739).[9] It is interesting that Dr Delany's regret about the rise of irreligion in Britain is marked above all with a desire that religious truths should be movingly conveyed – like the reformers of art, he wants discourse to be animated, in his case with 'the warmth of piety, the ardour of benevolence, and the zeal of *Christian* charity', in persuasive, pathetic and sublime rhetoric.[10] No wonder he and Mrs Delany were such devotees of Handel's oratorios.

THE DEIST DEBATE AND THE LIBRETTOS

The debate trained a spotlight on the Bible, especially the Old Testament, especially the details of its text. Champions of Christianity defending their sacred book, and their opponents seeking to discredit it, produced volumes of biblical criticism. Both sides, for their own purposes, stressed the lifelike emotions of the Old Testament's personages, the drama of its narrative, and the power of its rhetoric. Delany recounts the story of David, Saul and Jonathan as emotionally and dramatically as Jennens and Handel do, inferring feelings appropriate to every event recorded in his biblical sources. On the other side Thomas Morgan, intending to relegate the Old Testament firmly to the world of fiction, lauds its 'poetick Beauties, and dramatick Representations', drawing a parallel with the national mythologising of Homer: 'The History of the *Exodus*, and Conquest of *Canaan*, relates to Things done about six hundred Years before *Homer*'s Time, and is written in much the same oratorial and dramatick Way.'[11] By close attention and by libertarian criticism, the Scriptures were made available for treatment as drama.

In an attempt to represent Christianity as only one of the world's religions and so to limit its power to compel obedience, deists emphasised its origin in a 'merely' national religion – Old Testament Judaism. The effect of this was to highlight the Covenant of God with Israel, which in turn became a central theme of the librettos (see chapter 10). On theological grounds, also as part of the attempt to dispense with the essential doctrines of the Trinity and of Redemption, deists pointed out that Christ's teaching was based on Mosaic Law, showing the correspondences between them. Again one effect was to emphasise, for devout and sceptical alike, the closeness of the connection between Judaism and Christianity and to draw attention to the Old Testament.

In questioning (and attempting to undermine) the concept of the Trinity, which entailed questioning the claims for Jesus as Messiah, deism attacked one of the bases of these claims, the miracles reported in the Bible. Generally avoiding the scandal of questioning the miracles of Jesus himself, deists sought to undermine belief in them by giving rational explanations of miracles performed by Old Testament figures traditionally regarded as 'types' (forerunners) of Christ. Particular favourites of the polemicists which are also material of the librettos include Moses' miracles in Egypt and the parting of the Red Sea (*Israel in Egypt*), the crossing of the River Jordan and the stopping of the sun and moon (*Joshua*) and the amazing feats of Samson (*Samson*) (see further chapter 9).

Contemporary biblical commentaries by orthodox believers reflect the difficulties inherent in the rationalist position in their attempt to present miraculous events as both mysterious and explicable. Similarly the librettists of the Israelite oratorios try to have it both ways, giving a rational explanation (or 'second cause') while claiming divine intervention. Only *Israel in Egypt* insists on repeated, wholly miraculous manifestations of divine aid (the plagues in Egypt, the opening of the Red Sea, the drowning of the Egyptians) unassisted by any human contribution. In this connection it is again relevant that the story of the Exodus was interpreted as a type of the Redemption; hence the Book of Common Prayer prescribes Exodus XIV, the leading out of the Israelites from Egypt by Moses, as a reading for Easter Sunday. As Donald Burrows points out, all four of the performances Handel gave of *Israel in Egypt* took place in the weeks leading up to Easter.[12] (This strengthens the case for Jennens' authorship of the libretto of *Israel in Egypt*, by reference to the similar circumstances of *Messiah*: both draw on the connection traditionally made between Old Testament texts and salvation by Christ, both draw on biblical text that is also part of the liturgy, and both are written for Passiontide performance.)

But other librettos, like many contemporary apologetics, hedge their bets. Cyrus conquers Babylon with intelligent strategy as well as the aid of a God-sent dream; Jephtha has the skills of an outstanding general as well as the support of cherubim and seraphim; Joshua's men have courage as well as the help of a stationary sun – despite the admonition of Judas in Part II of Morell's *Judas Maccabæus*:

> To Heav'n let Glory, and all Praise be giv'n;
>   To Heav'n give your Applause,
>   Nor add *the second Cause*,
> As once your Fathers did in *Midian*,
> Saying, *The Sword of God and Gideon*.
> It is the Lord, who for his *Israel* fought,
> And this our wonderful Salvation wrought.

This clear directive to subscribe to orthodox belief in the matter of miracles is eloquent of the discomfort involved in fighting rationalists on their own ground, and it is interesting to find it in a libretto. Morell was well aware of the issues at stake, and had himself contributed more directly to the orthodox defence of the evidence of miracles, in his *Poems on Divine Subjects, Original, and Translated from the Latin of Marcus Hieronymus Vida, Bishop of Alba (and M. A. Flaminius)* (1732, second edition 1736). In 'The First Hymn of Vida. To God the Father', lines 961–70 recount the crossing of the Red Sea and the engulfing of the Egyptian army, and Morell's extensive footnotes argue (with numerous supporting references) that the division of the sea *was* a miracle and that through the Israelites' safe transit God was proving His power, His justice 'and his Mercy and Faithfulness to his People'. Lines 971–9 describe the fall of Jericho with even more extensive footnotes, exhorting respect for God's power; lines 980–5 cover the provision of food and water to the Israelites in the desert, and the notes give cross-references to other similar Old Testament miracles. Lines 986–95 concern the sun standing still for Joshua, and Morell's note on this event (two-thirds of a page) likewise declares its miraculous status: 'we cannot doubt of it, unless we renounce all human Faith, and the Evidence of our Senses'. In all this, and in his provision of a 'second cause' in his *Jephtha*, he is in the mainstream of anti-deist writing. For example, David Collyer's *The Sacred Interpreter: or, A Practical Introduction towards a Beneficial Reading, and a thorough Understanding, of the Holy Bible* provides a frontispiece map of 'The travels of the children of Israel out of Ægypt, through the Red Sea, and the wilderness, into Canaan or the Holy Land', which shows a passage through the Red Sea of about seventeen miles, and deduces from Joshua's history that the fall of Jericho was miraculous,

to manifest God's omnipotent Power, and to encourage the People; yet God was pleased they should take the rest by warlike Stratagems and Fighting ... thereby instructing us, that he who hath ordained the End, hath for the most Part designed the Means for attaining that End; and therefore we should not in general presume on the End, without asking the lawful and proper Means.[13]

Morell's commitment to the defence of Christianity is rather endearingly indicated by his commentary on Locke's *Essay concerning Human Understanding*; more than half of his bibliography consists of publications about religion, not philosophy, and the largest proportion pertains to debates stimulated by deism (see also the epigraph to this chapter).[14]

The deists also tried to kick away the other traditional plank of 'proof' by discrediting the application to Jesus of the Old Testament prophecies of the Messiah and of the miracles he would accomplish. The effect was again to focus attention on the Old Testament, and to prompt renewed efforts to validate Christian revelation and its concurrence with the gospels. The traces of this part of the debate in the librettos are particularly striking.

Messiah is the most obvious instance of a librettist taking up the cause of biblical prophecy. The voluminous, minutely detailed discussion of the biblical texts traditionally taken to refer to Jesus as the Messiah was the means to an end, that of 'proving' or 'disproving' that Jesus *was* the Messiah. The libretto of *Israel in Egypt* (conjecturally by Jennens) having restated the evidence afforded by the miracles in Egypt and at the Red Sea of the divine commission of Moses, Jennens boldly went to the heart of the matter with *Messiah* – but was given his groundplot by countless contemporary publications. On both sides it was accepted that accomplished prophecies are the most significant proofs of the Messiah. Arthur Ashley Sykes begins his *Essay upon the Truth of the Christian Religion*: 'The Christian Religion having its Origin from JESUS of *Nazareth*, and being manifestly founded upon the Scriptures of the *Old Testament*, there cannot be a more natural Method of examining its Truth, than to compare what was *foretold* with the Consequences and following *Events*.' This is what Jennens does, producing his own selection from contemporary tables which showed the parallels of Old Testament prophecy and New Testament fulfilment and 'the harmony of the gospels' with each other, and the actual verbal correspondences between Old and New Testament texts. Deists had pointed out that citations of the Old Testament in the New do not always correspond to the Old Testament text as we have it. As Joseph Hallet jnr reported,

The observation of this has made the inconsiderate adversaries of our holy religion triumph, as if these differences between the *two Testaments* would utterly destroy the credit of both, or, at least, the *New*. To abate their triumphs on this head, and to vindicate our Blessed Saviour and his Disciples in their citing the *Old Testament* in the manner they have done, the learned and ingenious Mr. *Whiston*, in his excellent *Essay toward restoring the true Text of the Old Testament*, has fully shewn, that the passages in the *New Testament*, which are cited from the *Old*, were originally in the *Old Testament* express'd in the same words, as are cited in the *New*.

Hallet goes on to describe the plan of a work which would show 'that among almost three hundred citations the far greatest part are exact', while only 'about twenty differ'.[15] At least seventeen, and possibly as many as fifty-one, of the eighty biblical verses in Jennens' libretto are either conscious quotations, or echoes, of the Old Testament in the New (for example, Isaiah XL.3, heard in the opening recitative, is quoted in Matthew III.3, Mark I.3, Luke III.4 and John I.23). Jennens was daringly original in his self-appointed task of bringing the evidences of Christianity into the theatre, but he was fully prompted in his choice of material.

Of course the libretto also has less contentious sources. Nearly all of Jennens' texts can also be found in the Book of Common Prayer.[16] And Jennens may have heard from Handel about the tradition, which flourished in Rome during Handel's stay there and terminated in the year before work started on *Messiah*, of performing Nativity cantatas with tableaux at the Papal court. As Carolyn Gianturco has shown in an article which students of *Messiah* should not overlook, these sometimes included the Old Testament prophecies of Christ. For example, the cantata for 1705 (two years before Handel's arrival in Rome), with a text by Silvio Stampiglia (a founder member of the Arcadia society, for whom Handel wrote) and music by Alessandro Scarlatti (who, like Handel subsequently, worked for Cardinal Ottoboni), had as its characters Abraham, Daniel, Ezekiel, Jeremiah and Isaiah.[17] (Jennens himself subsequently acquired manuscript Old Testament cantatas by Scarlatti and other Roman composers.) Old Testament types of Christian redemption were also made the subject of these Christmas cantatas, to judge from one reported by Gianturco, apparently concerning the passage through the Red Sea ('Di questo fatal fiume', 1736), in which the characters are Moses' parents, Miriam and Pharaoh's daughter. Finally, as is well known, Jennens' theme was not an original topic of literary composition even in England (see chapter 4). His method, however, owes little to literary models and nearly everything to contemporary religious debate.

For some of the texts in his collage of Old and New Testament verses Jennens needed to go no further than an annotated Bible giving marginal indications of parallel texts. But the texts he used were also the bases of attack and defence in scores of contemporary publications about the nature and mission of Christ. He was a scholarly reader of biblical criticism and his extensive library was particularly well stocked with recent and contemporary works on theology.[18] For example, it contained *A Demonstration of the Messias. In which the Truth of the Christian Religion is Proved*, by Richard Kidder, Bishop of Bath and Wells (second edition 1726), a key work in the debate and one whose list of contents reads like a blueprint for the libretto of *Messiah*. Kidder cites forty-one of the eighty verses that make up Jennens' libretto. The extent to which Jennens selected *the* texts about the Messiah is evident in other major anti-deist publications. John Entick, in *The Evidence of Christianity* (1729), devotes ninety-six of his 247 pages to a double-column parallel (with commentary) 'of the Old and New Testaments, in all that refers to the

Messiah', the Old Testament column headed 'prophesy'd' and the New Testament one headed 'accomplish'd': he cites thirty-eight of *Messiah*'s verses. William Harris, in his *Practical Discourses on the Principal Representations of the Messiah throughout the Old Testament* (1724), cites thirty; Thomas Stackhouse, in *A Complete Body of Speculative and Practical Divinity* (1729, second edition 1734), cites thirty-five; Samuel Parvish, in *An Inquiry into the Jewish and Christian Revelation, wherein all the Prophecies relating to the Jewish Messiah are Considered, and Compared with the Person and Character of Jesus Christ, and the Times of the Gospel; the Authority of the Canon of Scripture; the Nature and Use of Miracles, etc.* (1739), cites twenty-eight. Conversely, Anthony Collins devotes a substantial portion of *The Scheme of Literal Prophecy Considered* (1727: pp. 39–64) to deriding the Church's attempt to read Messianic expectations into Greek and Roman literature, specifically Virgil's Fourth Eclogue, the text from which Jennens took one of his epigraphs. Even Jennens' title is rooted in the debate, which revolves round and constantly asks, in so many words, 'Was Jesus the Messiah?'; and his epigraph from 1 Timothy and his text boldly announce, just at the time when the orthodox defence was beginning to relax its attempt to hold a strictly rationalist position, that the mysteries of Christianity *are* mysterious, in defiance of the first major deist salvo, Toland's *Christianity not Mysterious*. Toland had quoted this text from 1 Timothy as the culmination of a list of passages he cited to take the mystery *out* of Christianity by claiming that in the New Testament '*Mystery* is read for [nothing more than] the *Gospel* or Christianity'.[19] Jennens subscribed to a more literal reading of 'mystery'; as he said in a letter to Holdsworth, complaining of obscurities in Virgil and Pope, 'our Fellow Creatures ought to speak to us so as that we may understand them, & that with ease'; but 'the Bible is not affected by the same objections; it stands upon a better Authority. Our Maker has a right to speak to us in what Language he pleases, & to humble our Pride with things above our Understandings.'[20] Thoroughly in tune with the evangelising anti-rationalists of his time, Jennens here almost quotes the *Weekly Miscellany* (1732–41), a periodical entirely dedicated to combating the prevailing contempt for religion.[21]

Much of the text of *Messiah* is indeed 'mysterious' and 'above our understandings' in that it consists of prophetic utterances, and (as has frequently been pointed out) the life and achievement of Christ are presented almost entirely through *allusion*. His name, Jesus, appears only once, near the end of the whole work – a striking rhetorical way of expressing faith that Jesus *was* the Messiah. Of the eighty Scripture verses that make up the libretto, only ten are to be found only in the gospels, and of these only six are narrative, and they relate a pronouncement by an angelic host. So, for example, Christ's Passion is not described; but the whole scheme of redemption is invoked in the words 'and with his stripes we are healed'. Jennens does not confine himself to the evidence of prophecy, referring to the miraculous in the life of Jesus as well: Christ's incarnation and resurrection, his healing, conversion and redemption of mankind are all included. But with the confidence of faith Jennens avoids the trap of trying to define or explain the concept of the Trinity, at which the most serious deist objections aimed most successfully, instead letting the 'evidence' speak for the doctrine – more effectively and more lastingly than any of his fellow Christians did.

Another libretto by Jennens, *Belshazzar*, contains an even more explicit defence of Old Testament prophecies. Yet they are prophecies that relate not to the coming of the Messiah but to the liberation of the Jews and the rebuilding of the temple, which did take place, as the libretto makes plain. In this way Jennens apparently restricts orthodox claims for scriptural authenticity while at the same time implying that prophecy so triumphantly fulfilled in one instance can be trusted everywhere. This argument is strengthened by the central role in the libretto of the prophet who correctly interprets the prophetic texts in question: Daniel, who has a particular association with the foretelling of Christ. The prophecies of the Messiah attributed to Daniel had been the subject of intense theological discussion for centuries and were vital to the orthodox defence of Christianity. Over a dozen books were published on his prophecies between 1700 and 1760, most famously Newton's *Observations*.[22] Throughout Jennens' drama the sacred text appears as a dominant character in its own right and in association with Daniel, from the opening of Act I scene 3 ('Daniel, with the Prophecies of Isaiah and Jeremiah open before him. Other Jews. *Daniel:* "Oh sacred oracles of Truth!"') to the climax, in which Daniel shows the conquering Cyrus the prophecies in Isaiah which have just been fulfilled in his victory, and Cyrus is so impressed by their validity that he worships the Jewish God and undertakes to fulfil the remainder of the prophetic text, liberating the Jews and rebuilding Jerusalem.[23]

Jennens' theme of the endorsement of biblical prophecy in the career of Cyrus may not strike the modern listener very forcibly. But it had been argued in numerous anti-deistical writings; for the audience of his own time he only needed to allude to it. He would have found it expounded in what he clearly used as a major, immediate source for *Belshazzar*, Charles Rollin's *Ancient History* of (among other peoples) the Persians (second edition 1738–40). This standard work, still being reprinted in the nineteenth century, was in his library, and combines elements from Daniel, Isaiah, Jeremiah, Xenophon and Herodotus to make a dramatic narrative. Jennens makes his libretto out of the same elements from the same sources. Rollin's Book IV chapter 1 article 2 concerns 'The History of the Besieging and Taking of Babylon by Cyrus', of which Section 1, 'Predictions of the Principal Circumstances relating to the Siege and Taking of Babylon, as they are set down in Different Places of the Holy Scripture' includes this: 'Cyrus, whom the divine providence was to make use of, as an instrument for the executing of his designs of goodness and mercy towards his people, was mentioned in the scripture by his name, above two hundred years before he was born ... God was pleased to declare, in very lofty and remarkable terms, that he himself would be his guide; and that in all his expeditions he would lead him by the hand, and would subdue all the princes of the earth before him. "Thus saith the Lord to his anointed, to Cyrus"' – here Rollin cites the first four verses of Isaiah XLIV.1–6, the passage which Jennens gives Daniel as a recitative in Act I scene 3 of *Belshazzar* (with a marginal reference to the source). In his correspondence Jennens – not given to bestowing praise lightly – comments that Rollin's writings 'show him to be a man of Sense, Learning, & Virtue'.[24]

After discrediting Old Testament prophecy the next step, for the radical deist, was to undermine Christian dogma by discrediting Old Testament Judaism – by portraying the Israelites, their actions and the God who chose and directed them as morally despicable. This chimed with the idea of God fostered by the scientific discoveries of Newton. Newton had made God essential to the universe by determining that matter was dead and that only God could move it: the entire natural world depended on Him. Newton and his many followers in the Church were able to reconcile their new science with belief in scriptural revelation: the God who ordered the universe could also destroy it at the second coming. Newtonianism did not rule out providential intervention, and as already indicated, Newton himself devoted much energy to proving Christianity by bringing his mathematical skills to bear on questions of biblical prophecy and chronology and calculations concerning the end of the world.[25] But the very universality of Newton's discoveries rebounded on the Church when they were applied by deists to the idea of the God of the Old Testament.

How could a benign cosmic creator, keeping the planets in their orbits, be identified with a vengeful, petty, national deity favouring a rabble of ex-slaves in a remote corner of a single world? On this point freethinking embraced many writers of the best humanitarian intentions: the intolerant, imperialist Israelites served for lessons in religious and political tolerance and ethical aspiration as well as to attack Christian doctrine. The effect was, once more, to elicit statements contending for Israelite history as morally legitimate and exonerating the partisan deity from ethical impropriety. Key biblical passages at issue here are of interest to oratorio students. They included warfare against the Amalekites (*Saul*), the destruction of the Canaanites (*Joshua*), the massacre of the native population brought about by Esther, Jael's murder of Sisera prompted by Deborah, the unmerited suffering of Jephtha's daughter, and the moral and religious questionableness of the careers of Joseph, David and Solomon – all material of the librettos (discussed further in Part II). Moreover, in answering the deist criticisms of the Old Testament Jews – that they were wild, brutish, ungovernable, drenched in their own and other nations' blood (these are Thomas Morgan's words, but 'How odd / Of God / To choose / The Jews' was a deist theme tune) – defenders portrayed the Mosaic law as containing all the guidance for enlightened benevolence that a refined sensibility could require. Francis Webber, for example, preaching to the University of Oxford in 1737, pointed out (with scriptural references) that the Old Testament taught 'principles of benevolence, charity, and every social virtue ... Hospitality to strangers, bounty and goodness to the poor, generosity to an enemy, and friendly dispositions to all their neighbours ... all evidently calculated to promote peace, and harmony, and brotherly love'.[26] Here is the foundation for the portrait of the Israelites in the librettos as a nation with which the audience can be pleased to identify (see further chapter 10).

Newton's ideas were not used only to discredit revelation; on the contrary, they inspired many of the Boyle Lectures founded to defend it.[27] Those given by Richard Bentley and Samuel Clarke (1692, 1704–5) were written under Newton's influence and demonstrate the existence of an interventionist God by *a priori* argument. Later lecturers, however, tended to base their claims on the evidence of experience, specifically the natural world, and sermon after sermon traces the God of revelation in His ordering of creation, and reconciles the Bible and natural history. To judge from the number of editions, they had a huge readership; for example, William Derham's series of 1711 and 1712, *Physico-Theology, or a Demonstration of the Being and Attributes of God from his Works of Creation*, had reached its eleventh edition by 1745. The Boyle lecturers' celebration of God as the creator of a marvellous universe was readily taken up by poets. Addison's hymn, 'The spacious firmament on high', is a frequently cited instance. Less often noticed in this context, the oratorio choruses praising God in just the same terms reflect the same intellectual premises and the same theological intention. Additionally they serve this intention by countering freethinkers' attacks on Christianity's Old Testament forbears as small-minded nationalists. In such choruses as 'By that adorable Decree, / That Chaos cloath'd with Symmetry' (*Deborah*, Part I scene 1), 'The rising World Jehovah crown'd' and 'The mighty Power in whom we trust' (*Athalia*, I.1, II.1) and 'Jehovah, Lord, who from thy Mercy-Seat' (*Joseph and his Brethren*, final chorus), which echo contemporary demonstrations of the existence of a beneficent deity from the evidence of His harmoniously ordered creation, the God of Israel becomes the God of the whole world.

The Mosaic dispensation was also challenged on account of its pedigree. Deists argued that it (and so by implication Christian doctrine) lacked divine authority because it was Egyptian in origin and content. This charge was largely anticlerical in aim: Jewish priesthood was shown to be derived from the (corrupt) Egyptian model, in order to blacken the Christian clergy. The orthodox response was to reassert the God-given nature of Jewish law, again endorsing the Old Testament record. In an extension of this part of the debate, the probity of the Mosaic priesthood was questioned, again with anticlerical intention, as a not very covert demand for reform of the modern Church hierarchy. Again the response validated the Old Testament, by ratifying the priesthood described in it. (The librettos' part in the defence of the priesthood is discussed in chapter 13.)

Christian revelation was assumed to have routed its attackers, on rational grounds, after the publication of Butler's *The Analogy of Religion, Natural and Revealed* in 1736. But the defenders were called out again by Thomas Morgan's three-volume *The Moral Philosopher* (1737–40), and it is possible to adduce direct contradictions of Morgan's charges in the librettos (most of the charges had been heard before but Morgan restated them with particular vehemence). The librettos' obsession with the persecution of the Israelites by aggressors inverts Morgan's insistence on the Israelites' unprovoked belligerence and cruelty to other nations. The librettos' insistence, in their triumphant conclusions and in much of the effort to reach those conclusions, on the restoration of religious and political liberty, rebuts Morgan's stress on the Israelites' enslaved and enslaving character. The librettos' moral ground – the Israelites are favoured by God only so long as they observe eighteenth-century ethical standards – counters Morgan's picture of a morally blind race taking divine favour for granted and unwarrantably receiving it. The librettos' constant theme of Israelite victories achieved with God's help counters Morgan's insistence that events disproved Israel's claim to be in the peculiar care of God. The oratorio Israelites' direct appeals to God short-circuit Morgan's argument that a corrupt priesthood came between people and God; their many hymns to God as creator and ruler of the universe rebut Morgan's stress on the Israelites' conception of their God as a local tutelar deity; and the disciplined complexity of the chorus's utterances refutes his view of the Israelite populace as a brutish, ignorant, superstitious mob.

The tally could continue (some specific instances are discussed further in Part II). The impact of the debate is not felt only in the Israelite, or even the biblical, librettos. Morgan demanded that 'Revelation be brought down to our Understandings'; *Messiah* takes up and meets this challenge. Morell places an account of one of Christ's miracles at the centre of *Theodora* ('He saw the lovely Youth'), and its seemingly slight relevance to the action gains weight from knowledge of the controversy about miracles as proof of Christ's divinity. In short, the connections between the matter of the oratorios and arguments of the freethinkers are so strong that we can confidently assign the librettos as contributions to the defence of Christianity, and recognise that many of their individual topics, including several which may initially elude or perplex the modern listener, were vital issues for the authors and for their audiences.

CHAPTER 7

Towards oratorio

'Diversion here, is to Devotion join'd'

The Post Angel, March 1701/2

In the first half of the eighteenth century the assumption that the best art teaches religion is as firmly entrenched in musical as in literary circles, perhaps even more so. As we saw in chapter 3, music was felt to have irresistible power over the emotions and mind, such that it could do dreadful damage; but in alliance with a moral or religious message it was a wonderful force for good. John Blow's preface to his *Amphion Anglicus* is indicative. This introduction to a (very) secular song collection stresses music's religious pedigree and its ability to civilise, to reform 'and, above all, to inflame the Pious and Devout'. Still bound by the Protestant tradition that views lay singing of anything but psalm settings with suspicion,[1] Blow makes the case for merely social music almost apologetically, and he ends his preface with an assurance that the present volume will shortly be followed by one 'incomparably better: I mean my Church-Services, and Divine Compositions'.[2] The opinion of Humphrey Wanley, librarian to Robert and Edward Harley, Earls of Oxford, is evidence of the assumption among disinterested connoisseurs that sacred music is superior to secular because it is more improving:

A young man may make a better *Minuet* or *Jigg*; but the elder a more sound Service or *Anthem*. The music of the former (with other accomplishments) may go a great way towards enticing a foolish girl to love; but that of the latter excites the Devotion, moves the Affections, and raises the Passions of those truly religious Souls, who take pleasure in singing Praises to the Honour and Glory of His Name, who lives for ever.[3]

Matthew Prior's compliment 'to the Countess of Exeter playing on the Lute' makes elegant use of the well-worn idea that sublime music, even in a secular context, can give a foretaste of heaven and redeem sinners:

When to your Native Heav'n you shall repair,
And with your Presence crown the Blessings there;
Your Lute may wind its Strings but little higher,
To tune their Notes to that immortal Quire.
Your Art is perfect here, your Numbers do
More than our Books, make the rude Atheist know,
That there's a Heav'n, by what he hears below.[4]

As we have seen, Anglican churchmen encouraged the composition of emotionally compelling and spiritually uplifting religious music. They did not limit themselves to recommendations for liturgical music. Arthur Bedford, in a sermon on *The Excellency of Divine Musick*, urged domestic psalm singing on Sunday evenings and appended to the published version of his text 'A Proposal for promoting divine musick and benefactions for parochial libraries'. This was a recommendation by members of religious societies in the City to print and sell monthly hymn sheets on the same lines as ballads, with three or four hymns to a penny sheet; any profits were to go to establishing and stocking parochial libraries in especially needy parishes. Bedford provides some suggestions for both words and music in a thirty-page 'Appendix. A Specimen of Hymns for Divine Musick', including two carols, two hymns by Campion and three settings of his own.[5]

Many other examples could be cited, both of the belief that music can inspire devotion and of the conviction that, since it can, we are duty bound to write and participate in religious music.[6] The most famous summary of these ideas is Addison's, worth quoting at length because it also summarises virtually every idea which I have so far identified as a harbinger of Handel's oratorios (the emphases are mine):

I could heartily wish there was the same Application and Endeavours to cultivate and improve our Church-Musick, as have been lately bestowed on that of the Stage. Our Composers have one very great Incitement to it: they are sure to meet with Excellent Words, and, at the same time, a wonderful Variety of them. *There is no Passion that is not finely expressed in those parts of the Inspired Writing, which are proper for Divine Songs and Anthems* ...
Since we have therefore such a Treasury of Words, so beautiful in themselves, and *so proper for the Airs of Musick*, I cannot but wonder that Persons of Distinction should give so little Attention and Encouragement to *that kind of Musick, which would have its Foundation in Reason, and which would improve our Virtue in proportion as it raised our Delight.* The Passions that are excited by ordinary Compositions, generally flow from such silly and

absurd Occasions, that a Man is ashamed to reflect upon them seriously; but the Fear, the Love, the Sorrow, the Indignation that are awakened in the Mind by *Hymns and Anthems, make the Heart better*, and proceed from such Causes as are altogether reasonable and praise-worthy. Pleasure and Duty go hand in hand, and the greater our Satisfaction is, the greater is our Religion.

Musick among those who are stiled the chosen People was a Religious Art. The Songs of Sion, which we have reason to believe were in high repute among the Courts of the Eastern Monarchs, *were nothing else but Psalms and Pieces of Poetry that adored or celebrated the Supreme Being*. The greatest Conqueror in this Holy Nation [David], after the manner of the old *Grecian* Lyricks, did not only compose the Words of his Divine Odes, but generally set them to Musick himself: After which, *his Works, tho' they were consecrated to the Tabernacle, became the National Entertainment, as well as the Devotion of his People*.

The first Original of the *Drama was a Religious Worship consisting only of a Chorus, which was nothing else but an Hymn to a Deity*. As Luxury and Voluptuousness prevailed over Innnocence and Religion, this form of Worship degenerated into Tragedies; in which however *the Chorus so far remembered its first Office, as to brand every thing that was vicious, and recommend every thing that was laudable*, to intercede with Heaven for the Innocent, and to implore its Vengeance on the Criminal.

Homer and *Hesiod* intimate to us how this Art should be applied, when they represent the Muses as surrounding *Jupiter*, and warbling their Hymns about his Throne. I might shew, from innumerable Passages in Ancient Writers, not only that Vocal and Instrumental Musick were made use of in their Religious Worship, but that their most favourite Diversions were filled with Songs and Hymns to their respective Deities. *Had we frequent Entertainments of this Nature among us, they wou'd not a little purifie and exalt our Passions, give our Thoughts a proper Turn, and cherish those Divine Impulses in the Soul*, which every one feels that has not stifled them by sensual and immoderate Pleasures.

Musick, when thus applied, raises noble Hints in the Mind of the Hearer, and fills it with great Conceptions. It strengthens Devotion, and advances Praise into Rapture. It lengthens out every Act of Worship, and produces more lasting and permanent Impressions in the Mind, than those which accompany any transient Form of Words that are uttered in the ordinary Method of Religious Worship.[7]

From the evidence presented in previous chapters it will be clear that Addison is, as usual in the *Spectator*, making an elegant synthesis of current ideas; he is original here only in being the first to draw them all together and in the comprehensiveness of his survey. The need to cultivate church music; the Bible as a rich source of emotional expression, apt for musical setting; the use of music in ancient Jewish worship; the precedents in antiquity for the use of religious music in secular contexts; the national-religious purpose of David's Psalms; the improving effect of emotionally compelling religious words-and-music; the religious origin of drama and of the Greek tragic chorus; the chorus' moral didacticism; the need for spiritual musical entertainments – these are all familiar topics. Bringing them together like this, however, yields a startlingly prophetic prescription for Handelian oratorio.

But Addison was not original in this synthesis either, for many of the ingredients of Handel's oratorios had been anticipated in spiritual entertainments of which Addison himself must have been aware. Against the critical background outlined in the preceding pages, Cavendish Weedon's monthly musico-poetical productions, which have until recently been overlooked or regarded as oddities, seem on the contrary to be just what might be expected to emerge from the existing seedbed of ideas if an attempt were made to unite the aims of the literary reformers with the skills of church composers. In fact they coincide with some of the earliest literary formulations, being mounted in 1702. As precursors of oratorio, and as fascinating expressions of contemporary social and artistic idealism, they deserve attention here.[8]

Weedon was a lawyer in Lincoln's Inn, where his devotion to the established Church manifested itself in plans for improved choral services and for a new chapel in which to celebrate them, to be designed by Wren.[9] His 'Entertainments of Divine Musick' seem to have taken place from January to May 1701/2; the earliest surviving advertisement announces the first for 6 January, and the last dates from mid-May.[10] The location, originally intended to be St Bride's (the venue for the sermon during the St Cecilia celebrations), was switched just before the first occasion to Stationers Hall (where the musical part of the St Cecilia celebrations took place).[11] Weedon's intention, no less ambitious than his plans for Lincoln's Inn, was to have two performances in the first week of each month, each consisting of an 'oration' and poems (he invited his public to send contributions), to be spoken 'by Persons in Holy Orders, or Gentlemen of the University' – in other words, practised public speakers – and two anthems. These were all to expound the subjects of the performance, which during the first month were to be 'the Praise of God, and setting forth his Mightiness' on Tuesdays, and on Saturdays 'against all sorts of Irreligion, Vice and Immorality, without Reflections on Persons or Parties'.[12] Weedon's declared goal was threefold: moral reform through religious awareness; the rescue of music from sordid applications and its recovery for religious and moral purposes; and charity:

an endeavour to reduce Musick (which is so charming to the Ears and Hearts of most People) back to its nobleness and chiefest end the praise of our great Creator, the Author and Fountain of all harmony, and to begin the Year and succeeding Months with the Celebration of his Praises ... for the better Encouraging of Piety and Morality, and discouragement of Vice ... For the benefit of decay'd Gentry, and the Maintenance of a School for the Education of Children in Religion, Musick and Accounts.[13]

Spiritual music in a charitable cause is a concept familiar to students of Handel: it was through regular performances for charitable purposes that *Messiah* gained its place in British consciousness. (The first performance, in Dublin, was given in aid of three charitable causes, and annual performances at the Foundling Hospital began in 1750.) To attract sponsorship of the right kind Weedon assured his public that 'there shall be convenient places for to prevent all Crowding, the great inconvenience of such meetings [as the managers of Handel's charitable oratorio performances in Dublin were to find], as also places shall be kept distinct for Nobility'.[14]

Three surviving quasi-librettos published after the performances, with additional commendatory addresses, show that Weedon realised his plan for the content of his entertainments, an interleaving of anthems with poems and an oration (which he had stipulated should not last longer than 'a Quarter of an Hour's speaking').[15] The composers were Turner (Psalm XIX, for countertenor, bass and chorus; Psalm XXI, for countertenor, tenor and chorus) and Blow (Psalm XCVI, for soloists, chorus and orchestra; Queen Anne Coronation Anthem, Psalm LXXXIV; Te Deum). The spoken contributions were by equally 'establishment' figures, all with an interest in the cause of religion: the reforming Nonjuror Jeremy Collier; the poet laureate, Nahum Tate; his fellow psalm versifier Nicholas Brady; and a future prebendary of Lichfield, Edward Welchman. Their contributions adhere to Weedon's prescription, celebrating God as creator of the universe (Collier provides a Newtonian mini-Boyle sermon) and urging 'that so Divine a Gift, as Musick is, may no longer like a Prodigal, wander from its true Parent, and become an Ornament to Trifles, but may recover its Station, and be received into the Protection of its Guardian Divinity'.

This was the topic of Tate's 'Poem for Mr Weedon's First Entertainment of Religious Musick', ninety-two lines (despite the sixty-line limit set in the advertisements for contributions) in pentameter couplets. The speaker is a 'Suppliant Envoy' from Music, herself a penitent prodigal who

> (of Heav'nly Birth)
> Was consecrated first to Sacred Mirth;
> And, Only to the Altar's Service bound,
> Anthems and Hallelujah's did resound . . .
> Devotion then did Harmony inspire
> And Harmony Sublim'd Devotion's Fire.

But she began to wander, first to innocent pastoral ('Not Prostituted yet to loose Desire'), then to court, where she was first pampered but soon neglected, and finally as a hired minion

> To Serenades, Masques, Banquets, Rev'ling Rage;
> Buffoon'ry, Farce; those Witch-Crafts of the Stage,
> And dire Diversions of a Graceless Age.

Disgusted at being set to witless words, Music 'forsook the Town', and is now a desolate Magdalen. At this point the audience was enjoined to hear her mournful melody, and a stage direction reads: 'Pauze here; a Mournful Symphony play'd soft and faint, as at a Distance'. The narrator announces that 'These tuneful Sighs charm down th'Angelick Quires', who readmit Music to heaven, whence she now descends, bringing to the listeners an apprehension of its divine joys:

> She Comes . . . Now Listen Earth to her blest Hymns of Praise
> That bring Heav'n down to Thee, And Thee to Heav'n will raise.

Turner's setting of Psalm XIX followed. Besides taking on a wide-ranging set of moral aims, Weedon was making artistic experiments, not only bringing sacred music, descriptive music, poetry, preaching and polemic together in a public performance in a secular setting but combining them. He was on the way to creating unstaged music drama.

The entertainment for 31 January embraced another regular element of English music drama, politics. A special performance 'For the Entertainment of the Lords Spiritual and Temporal and the honourable House of Commons', in the second of two poems by Tate it addresses 'This Glorious Galaxy' as 'The CONSTELLATION on

whose Influence wait / Distress'd EUROPIA's Fortune and her Fate'
(in the War of Spanish Succession). Anticipating the kind of nationalism we will find in oratorio, Tate depicts music as encouraging
'*Brittain*'s PEERS and PATRIOTS' to rebut 'th'Insults of Lawless
GALLICK POW'R, / Th'Insatiate Dragon that would ALL Devour'
and become the saviours of Europe:

> And lo, how soon, by your Kind Aspects drawn
> From Dark Despair, to Hope's reviving Dawn,
> The World's Black Scene is chang'd – in threatn'd Pow'rs
> Fresh Courage Springs – the Threatning Dragon Cow'rs!

Music, Tate goes on, again anticipating Handel's oratorios, would
happily dedicate herself to praise of Britain's heroic potential as
exemplified in her heroic past, defining '*Brittain*'s Fame' as the
capacity 'To Humble Tyrants, and Relieve Mankind.' 'Or', continues Tate, echoing countless Renaissance celebrations of music
and anticipating the themes of Handel's 1739 St Cecilia Ode and of
several of his oratorio choruses,

> Nature's SELF, whose Self is Harmony,
> The Wond'rous Subject of our Song might be.
> How Infant *Matter*, Swath'd in Darkness slept;
> And formless *Chaos* into Order leapt.
>   Then with Sublimer Glories to Surprize,
> To Upper Worlds the tow'ring Song might Rise;
> Traverse the Stars, and, to your ravish'd Ears,
> Bring down the Musick of the Rowling Spheres.
>   But Higher YET Our Harmony must Climb,
> And Treat SUCH GUESTS with Musick more *Sublime*,
> Soar, above Nature, to Celestial Layes,
> And Charm You with her Great CREATOR's Praise.
> While Angels a Performance so Divine
> Are Proud t'assist, and in the Consort Joyn.
>   O SACRED PRAISE! how shalt thou be defin'd?
> The Noblest Task of an exalted Mind ...

The surviving text for May continues the patriotic theme with an
expression of the concern for native art familiar from the writings of
the campaigners for English words-and-music. A prefatory 'Letter
to Cavendish Weedon' from a supporter of his aims declares that
'The Compositions and Performance of your Entertainment, are
Demonstrations that we have as able Masters of *Musick* as any in the
World; and shall our own Artists want that Encouragement, which

at this very Time, is so Liberally dispensed to Foreigners?' The writer's sense of the urgent need for national moral as well as artistic reform is echoed by Edward Welchman's four-stanza poem to Weedon which follows, and which compares Weedon to Moses liberating the Israelites:

> When under *Pharoah's* [sic] Tyranny,
>> *Israel* the chosen Nation lay,
> Oppress'd with sordid Slavery:
>> It drudg'd in smoaky Kilns, condemn'd to Mire and Clay:
> But the same People, when once freed
>> By God-like *Moses* mighty Hand,
> From *Egypt* and from Bondage led,
> Built up the Ark of God and won the promis'd Land.
>
> How long, alas! hath Musick's Art Divine,
>> In worse than *Egypt*'s Bondage been?
> She hath been Damn'd to Lust and Wine,
>> Defil'd with all th'Impurities of Sin:
> But You the great Deliverer are,
>> You have her from her wretched Thraldom led,
> And We, by your Auspicious Care,
>> (The Flesh-pots left behind) are now with Manna Fed . . .
>
> Now then, that Musick and Devotion join,
>> The way to *Canaan* Pleasant is,
> We travel on with Songs Divine,
>> Ravish'd with sacred Extasies:
>>> No longer do we pass,
>>> Thro' a dry barren Wilderness;
> But thro a Land where Milk and Honey flow,
> The Path to Heav'n above, leads thro a Heav'n below.

Here again is an anticipation of Handel's oratorios, in this case *Israel in Egypt*, and not only in the use of the Exodus story, but in the allegorical use of it. Tate's concluding poem 'in Praise of Virtue' continues the allusion, referring to the pillar of cloud, the pillar of fire, the provision of manna and the fountain from the rock, endorsing Welchman's likening of Weedon's venture on behalf of his stricken fellow Britons to the moral and spiritual redemption achieved by Moses for the Israelites.

The response of Weedon's public attests to the existence of like-minded spirits and to the readiness we have found elsewhere to be fervently affected by the principles and impact of such a performance. *The Post Angel* of March 1701/2, 'containing a New Athenian

Mercury, resolving the most nice and curious questions propos'd by
the ingenious of either sex', having been asked 'What Methods does
Mr. *Weedon* take with his Musical entertainment, and what Transport does his Performance yield to the Audience?', replies:

We are now convinc'd by Experience (says an Ingenious *Remarker* upon
this Undertaking) that Musick never exerts her Charms so Sovereignly, as
in Religious Compositions; and, Altho' she's agreeable in (almost) any
Dress, Angelical only in Hymns and Anthems. This Design therefore of
Mr. *Weedon*'s of getting that noble Faculty restor'd to her Primitive and
Sacred Employment, must be acceptable to all Lovers of Harmony or
Piety. Moreover, by the addition of ingenious Oratory and Poetry, we
have (in great Measure) the Diversion of the Theatre; and, by their being
upon *Divine and Moral Subjects*, the Instruction of the Pulpit. Young
Persons, and especially of Quality and Gentry, must and will have Diversions; and, if no better are provided for 'em, they will take to those that
are vicious and Destructive. Could therefore possibly be invented a more
useful Recreation than this of Religious *Musick*, *Oratory*, and *Poetry*?

The writer makes exactly the point that the Bishop of Elphin was to
make in connection with *Messiah* (see above, pp. 34–5): the offspring
of the more leisured classes want pastimes, and will pursue vicious
ones if they are not given attractive alternatives. (As Thomas
Brereton was to do in the preface to his translation of *Esther*, the
'Letter to Cavendish Weedon' prefacing the surviving entertainment
text for May quotes Herbert's 'Church-Porch', 'A Verse may find
Him who a Sermon flies, / And turn Delight into a Sacrifice'.) The
phrase 'we have (in great Measure) the Diversion of the Theatre;
and ... the Instruction of the Pulpit' marks the entertainments as a
realisation of some of the literary reformers' principal goals and as
an anticipation of oratorio's combination of scriptural texts and
church music style with theatrical elements but without stage
action. The Oration of the first entertainment had hoped that 'if we
join our Hearts to our Voices, they will perhaps afford us a faint
Tast and Antepast of more lasting Joys', anticipating oratorio choruses with the opinion that 'the Sublimest and Divinest Exercise' of
worship is to sing 'the *Praises* of our *Creator*'. According to *The Post
Angel* the audience responded as ardently as Weedon and his fellow
reformers could have wished, with 'Transport', to the 'Angelical'
charm of religious music; and the paper concluded its report with a
poem urging the director to '*Weed-on* and pull up every Root of
Vice':

Your Sacred Anthems, Pious Hymns and Psalms
Stir up to Spiritual Zeal, not to Carnal Flames,
Like the Lascivious Airs of those Loose Times,
Set to the words of more Lascivious Rhymes;
To those vain Places of the Box and Pit
Where *Phillis* is Addresst with Song and Wit,
Let's bid adieu, and at your Consort sit;
With Beauty, Love, and Wit, be Charm'd no more,
But the Creator of those Gifts adore;
Diversion here, is to Devotion join'd,
In one sweet Exercise, they're both Combin'd.
Musick Divine that with its Harmony,
Provokes to Heavenly Love and Charity . . .

I have described Weedon's entertainments at length (though not exhaustively) because copies of them are rare and they are not described elsewhere, because they are a remarkable early fulfilment of the proposals for sublime religious art propounded by Dennis, and because, like so much described in the preceding chapters, they anticipate elements of Handel's oratorios. But they were not alone in this; they form a link in a tradition of thought about the use of words-and-music to instruct the public while entertaining it which reaches well back into the previous century. In the 1650s Davenant planned to take the masque out of its elitist sphere and turn it into a *Gesamtkunstwerk* whose primary purpose was didactic, reforming both art and citizens in the process. Many of the ideas of the reformers described in the preceding chapters and many of the elements of oratorio appear in Davenant's proposals, in *The Preface to Gondibert*, *A Proposition for Advancement of Moralitie* and *The First Dayes Entertainment*, for a new type of multimedia show (including music). This was to be a government initiative, a principal aim being to ensure a law-abiding populace. Davenant is at one with churchmen, moralists and politicians of the eighteenth century in identifying music theatre as a force so affective that it should be under state control, and like Dennis and Hill he envisages its being useful to the state. As Handel's oratorios were to do, his proposed productions would deal with recent national history in elevated, heroic, epic terms, they would teach moral behaviour and civic virtue, and they would have a chorus to reinforce their moral lessons.[16]

Like oratorio, Weedon's entertainments defy the boundaries of genre and the conventions of location assumed to be normative by

English contemporaries, indicating 'how undefined were the borders between devotion and entertainment in early-eighteenth-century London',[17] and showing us that oratorio was not original in blurring them and in gaining public acceptance despite, or perhaps even because of, doing so.[18] But oratorios were themselves not original in this respect. Sacred music was common fare in public and semi-public concert rooms (for example, to take an instance familiar to Handel, Thomas Britton's) and among music clubs meeting in hired rooms in taverns (the context of the first London airing of *Esther*).[19] Weedon's ideas did not die with him. In 1728 Defoe was urging the institution of a regular Sunday 'entertainment' of appropriately serious music with 'Sacred Poesy and Rhetorick ... suitable to a Christian and Polite Audience; and indeed, we seem to want some such commendable Employment for the better Sort' to deflect them from 'Drinking, Gaming, or profane Discourse'. As Brian Trowell has pointed out, Defoe had referred approvingly to 'Esq; *Weedon's* Divine Consort' in his *Review* for 11 November 1704.[20] Handel's first biography, published in the year after his death, suggests that in his lifetime the performance of scriptural material in places of entertainment 'seemed to be a dangerous innovation' in 'forming a sort of alliance between things usually considered in a state of natural opposition, the church and theatre', and whereas now (1760) enlightened tolerance admits of this, earlier times 'when narrow notions were more in vogue' would not have countenanced oratorio.[21] The facts suggest that had Handel performed in a concert room rather than a theatre, oratorio would have been acceptable at any time in the eighteenth century, and that in any case it was not quite so original as some of his contemporaries and subsequent admirers imagined.

The greatest artistic innovation which Handel and his librettists brought to the arena of the religious sublime was, as the music historian Sir John Hawkins recorded, to give the words and music narrative coherence (of the sort which Davenant had proposed): 'for he was used to say, that, to an English audience, music joined to poetry was not an entertainment for an evening, and that something that had the appearance of a plot or fable was necessary to keep their attention awake'.[22] But the plots are not the focus of admiration in the comments of Handel's contemporaries: their praise is chiefly for his mastery of the religious sublime. Again and again, in the early part of his English career, contemporaries hail him as a composer – the only composer – who can realise the full sensory, spiritual and moral potential of music. Aaron Hill identified him as the artist who could realise the reformers' goals:

> Ah! give thy *Passport* to the Nation's Prayer,
>   Ne'er did Religion's languid Fire
>   Burn fainter – never more require
> The Aid of such a fam'd Enliv'ner's Care:
> Thy Pow'r can *force* the stubborn Heart to feel,
> And rouze the Lucke-warm Doubter into *Zeal*.[23]

Fourteen years before he produced his ode about an instrumentalist evoking and controlling human passions, Handel was being written about as such:

> Thou our Spirits do'st command,
> Which rise and fall by just Degrees,
> Each Soul obsequious to thy Hand.[24]

Throughout his career admiring publications acknowledged his ability to stimulate and direct his hearers' emotions, both as performer and composer, with works of unprecedented power in respect of volume, scale and strength of composition. Even the caustic Lord Hervey, no Handel enthusiast, described him as 'having more sense, more skill, more judgement, and more expression in music than anybody'.[25] Well before he began writing oratorios for the English public he was identified as a master of the sublime, never more impressive than when giving his listeners an apprehension of heavenly bliss. His oratorios were greeted – by listeners of widely differing characters – as unprecedented, unequalled expressions of the religious sublime, which filled them with the spiritual ardour for which they longed and which made them better:

though the Words [of *Joshua*] were not quite so elegant, nor so well as I could have wished adapted to the Music, I was transported into the most divine Extasy. – I closed my Eyes, and imagined myself amidst the angelic Choir in the bright Regions of everlasting Day, chanting the Praises of my great Creator, and his ineffable *Messiah*. – I seemed, methought, to have nothing of this gross Earth about me, but was all Soul! – all Spirit!

I cannot help thinking, but that Entertainments of this Nature frequently exhibited, would have an Effect over the most obdurate Minds, and go a great Way in reforming an Age, which seems to be degenerating equally into an Irreverence for the Deity, and a Brutality of Behavior to each other; but as this Depravity of Taste, of Principles, and Manners, has spread itself from *London* even to the remotest Parts of this Island, I should be glad there were *Oratorios* established in every City and great Town throughout the Kingdom; but even then, to be of general Service, they ought to be given *gratis*, and all Degrees of People allowed to partake of them.[26]

Eliza Haywood is writing in the persona of a lady to a bishop, but the warmth of her response is not peculiar to her sex; copious examples could be cited of the same sentiments in Handel's 'manly' audience. The theatre manager Benjamin Victor, for example, declaring himself willing to ride forty miles in the wind and rain to be present at a performance of *Messiah* directed by Handel, urges his correspondent to

get a book [libretto] of the oratorio some days before, that you may well digest the subject, there you will hear *glad tidings* and truly divine rejoicings at the birth of *Christ*, and feel real sorrows for his sufferings – but oh! when those sufferings are over, what a transporting full chorus! where all the instruments, and three sets of voices are employed to express the following passage, which I must quote –

> Lift up your heads, O ye gates! and be ye lift up ye
> Everlasting doors, and the king of glory shall come in.
> Who is the king of glory? The Lord strong and mighty,
> *He* is the king of glory!
> And he shall reign for ever, King of Kings, Lord of Lords.

How truly poetical is the diction of the Oriental writers ... O how magnificent the full chorusses.[27]

The construction of the oratorios as drama or narrative elicits scant comment in surviving contemporary critiques, but the words themselves, especially those taken directly from the Bible, are regarded as crucial to the sublime effect. Like Victor, the writer praising *Israel in Egypt* in the *London Daily Post* in April 1739 urges readers to take the libretto along to the performance, 'For tho' the Harmony be so unspeakably great of itself, it is in an unmeasurable Proportion more so, when seen to what Words it is adapted; especially, if every one who could take with them the Book, would do their best to carry a Heart for the Sense, as well as an Ear for the Sound'. But as he warms to his subject of the music's aptness to the text the author feels that following the libretto during the performance is not enough, it must be studied in advance: 'if People, before they went to hear it, would but retire a Moment, and read by themselves, the Words of the Sacred Drama, it would tend very much to raise their Delight when at the Representation'. The author has heard a rumour that the Words were selected out of the Sacred Writings by the Great Composer himself. If so, the Judiciousness of his Choice in this Respect, and his suiting so happily the Magnificence of the Sounds in so exalted a Manner to the Grandeur of the Subject, shew which Way his natural Genius, had he but Encouragement, would incline him.[28]

* * *

The groundplot for Handel's oratorios had been laid out in advance. They met the calls, charted in the preceding pages, for morally ennobling, spiritually uplifting religious art, for scriptural drama, for native, national, Protestant words-and-music, and for the revival of an instructive singing chorus in dramatic works – all of which must be emotionally affecting and which could be allegorical. They built on the intense attention being devoted to the Old Testament in its several eighteenth-century roles – as the basis of Christianity needing defence from freethinkers, as the peerless repository and source of sublime writing, as the record of the origins of our best music, and (a topic to be explored in Part II) as an image of the history of Britain. The depiction of history was the noblest form of painting; epic was the highest form of literature; the Old Testament was the greatest repository of the sublime; religious music was music at its best; and the 'grand chorus's' which concluded large sacred choral compositions were 'the most noble pieces human nature is capable of'.[29] Oratorio, which combined all these, was waiting to happen.

PART II

The Patriot libretto from the Excise Bill to the Jew Bill: Israelite oratorios and English politics

Shew me the man that dares and sings
Great *David*'s verse to *British* strings:
Sublime attempt!

Isaac Watts, 'The Hebrew Poet', in *Reliquiae Juveniles: Miscellaneous
Thoughts in Prose and Verse, on Natural, Moral, and Divine Subjects,
Written chiefly in Younger Years* (1734)

It is no doubt, as worthy of Praise in an *Englishman* to fight in
Defence of his Religion, whenever it is necessary in order to
preserve our Church, as it was heretofore in the *Jews* to take up
Arms in Defence of theirs: And, to speak Truth, our Nation is in
point of Religion, in Circumstances that pretty much resemble
the *Jewish*; for, let our Enemies come from what Quarter they
will, who can say that our Religion is so out of Danger, that a
prudent Lover of it will have no Cause to be afraid of its being
hurt?

*A Dissertation on Patriotism: Shewing, the Use of those Two Great
Qualifications of a Patriot, Integrity and Courage* (1735)[1]

CHAPTER 8

Political events and political thought

While there is much in the oratorios that does not have to do with politics, there is much that does – more than has hitherto been recognised. Few musicians are conversant with the details of mid-eighteenth-century political ideas and events; most historians are unaware of the detail of the librettos. Hence political references in the oratorios have been neglected, though there have been several notable studies of political references in other literature of the 1730s and 1740s, including music theatre, and the accounts by John Loftis, Bertrand Goldgar and Christine Gerrard have provided stepping stones for the present study.[2] Mid-eighteenth-century Britons were obsessively political in their outlook; our interpretations of one of the major artistic genres of the period should acknowledge this fact, and add Handel's oratorios to our evidence for it. The second part of this book suggests connections between the political concerns of the day and the Israelite librettos, those based on the Old Testament or Apocrypha, in which the Israelite nation is the society which the action concerns. Political themes, including some identified in these chapters, could be (and are beginning to be) elucidated in Handel's secular librettos, as in his operas;[3] but the Israelite librettos take precedence among his works, and among all eighteenth-century English music theatre works, as a distinct group of compositions portraying the life of a nation.

What were the political events and thoughts of the oratorio years which the librettists could have absorbed into their texts? The first public performances of the Israelite oratorios, from *Esther* in 1732 to *Jephtha* twenty years later, span the period from the beginning of the Excise crisis to the beginning of the Jew Bill crisis. Oratorio authors, so far as we know, had no access to deliberations of crown and ministers; if we want to gauge their political knowledge, we need to look at the London press and contemporary comments on public opinion, not diplomatic dispatches, bearing in mind both that public knowledge included information about Parliamentary debates and detailed accounts of overseas events and that the press and public opinion could misrepresent and misinterpret events.[4] Contemporaries did not have the benefit of hindsight vouchsafed to historians, so, for example, the fact that the 1745 Rebellion was eventually suppressed is irrelevant to an attempt to define the relationship of the libretto of the *Occasional Oratorio* to the mood of the time when it was written – when the outcome of the Rebellion was in doubt. For the benefit of readers who are not historians of the period, a brief account follows of political events within the public domain.[5]

The oratorio years were decades of wars and the rumours of war. Relations with other European powers were deteriorating throughout the 1730s. In 1731 there was a French invasion scare, serious enough for the British fleet to be deployed in the Channel. In 1733 Britain's ally Austria was attacked by the Bourbon powers (War of Polish Succession, 1733–5). Government and public opinion were divided on Britain's obligations, and George II's chief minister, Robert Walpole, was able, in the face of royal opposition, to maintain his peace policy. Not so with regard to the trade war against Spain in the West Indies. Aggressive measures, principally over the Spanish right to search British merchant ships, were being urged throughout the late 1730s in Parliament and the press by various opposition groups, briefly united, until the government unwillingly acceded and the so-called War of Jenkins' Ear began in 1739.[6] Britain was subsequently at war until 1748.

In 1740 George II's hated European rival, his nephew Frederick II of Prussia, precipitated the War of Austrian Succession by invading the Austrian territory of Silesia, and a combination of factors, chiefly the obligation to support Austria, George II's position as Elector of Hanover, and fear of the traditional enemy, France, involved Britain in this major European conflict, at first financially and then militarily.[7] Naval success at Porto Bello in 1739 was followed by disaster at Cartagena, failure at Santiago da Cuba and aborted attempts at Panama and on the Venezuelan coast in 1741–2, and failure to contain the Spanish and French fleets in the

Mediterranean in 1744. The *Gentleman's Magazine* regularly printed depressing lists of 'Ships taken by the Spaniards', which frequently outnumbered those taken by the British. Similarly on land, there was only one resounding victory, at Dettingen in 1743, to set against an inconclusive battle at Toulon in 1744, defeat at Fontenoy in 1745, at Rocoux in 1746 and at Laffeldt in 1747, and, throughout 1746–8, the fall of a series of towns in the Low Countries regarded as vital to Britain's defence against France. A French invasion attempt in 1744 reached the Channel and was repulsed by bad weather, not the British navy. During the last years of the war colonial hopes revived with the capture in 1745 of Louisbourg (Cape Breton), which in the following two years was accorded immense value by press and public opinion as a door to North American trade. Naval victories at Cape Finisterre and Belle Ile in 1747 led to divided opinion on whether or not to continue the war, optimists believing that it offered a chance of major colonial gains. In the event, Louisbourg was relinquished in exchange for Madras, which had been lost to the French in 1746, and as the price of French withdrawal from Flanders. It can be argued that the war was a success in terms of containment of conflicting powers' interests; but this was no satisfaction to the public which wanted such a protracted, expensive engagement to yield at least a boost to national pride. The Peace of Aix-la-Chapelle (1748) was widely recognised as only a temporary respite. Attempts in the following years to influence the Imperial elections came to nothing.

After the first flush of enthusiasm for the war against Spain there was a signal lack of unified, national 'war spirit'. There was lack of consensus, within the administration and among the politically interested public, on how far Britain should be involved in the European war. The struggle was characterised by an absence of victories of the kind that would give the nation confidence and its leaders popular support, and by a kaleidoscopic array of alliances. Britain was seen as being dangerously threatened by the possible combination of Spain and France and by France's sweeping success in the Low Countries; as being in need of strong allies and hamstrung by dubious ones. Austria, for example, was not a natural ally, being a Catholic power given to suppressing its Protestant subjects. George II's abiding preoccupation with the security of Hanover was a constant source of trouble to his British ministers and resentment among his British subjects, and it bedevilled the conduct of the war, since British and Hanoverian interests were frequently divergent. On the whole question of foreign policy, political opinion divided on the issue of 'blue-water' versus 'continental' strategies: whether to put resources into the navy and colonial and commercial expansion, or into the army (and the armies of others) and engage in alliances with European powers in order to influence events on the Continent.[8] Any newspaper-reading member of the oratorio audience would have been aware of these issues; foreign affairs were the subject of major debates in Parliament and were extensively reported by the press.[9]

At home, war of another kind was waged, during the first of the oratorio decades, by a vociferous opposition against the chief minister. Walpole had held leadership of the government since 1721; since 1725 the *Craftsman*, the newspaper managed and largely written by the leading dissident Whig, William Pulteney, and the leading Tory (and intermittent Jacobite), Lord Bolingbroke, had been a thorn in his administration's side, giving the opposition an apparently unified voice. It made the most of the Excise crisis, which riveted political attention in 1732–3 and (as chapter 9 recounts) affected Handel's oratorio career. Walpole remained in the saddle, but he had to give up his Excise plans to do so.[10] From 1735 the opposition found a focus in Frederick Prince of Wales, thus gaining the respectability of Hanoverian association and stronger Whig definition, 'an irrefragible answer to the reproach of Jacobitism' as Lord Chancellor Hardwicke ruefully observed.[11] The longstanding open hostility between the heir to the throne and his parents deepened to a more or less permanent rift in 1737, when Frederick was dismissed from the court. The prince had considerable popular appeal, and his gift for public relations highlighted his father's signal lack of common touch and common courtesy.[12]

Walpole's fall in 1742 was expected by supporters of the opposition to produce a new era in political life but in fact led to more of the same, the chief opposition spokesmen being brought into the administration (Pulteney in 1742 and other leaders in 1744), but failing even to attempt promised reforms. Lack of unity, always a problem for the opposition during the Walpole years, now affected government and opposition alike and was compounded with political disillusion.[13] Jacobite plots were hatched, exploded or investigated in 1730–2, 1743–4 and 1750–2 (to take only the oratorio years).[14] The Young Pretender landed in Scotland in July 1745, two months later was victorious at Prestonpans, and in December reached Derby. The Jacobites were defeated at Culloden the following April and Scotland was bloodily repressed. In England the Rebellion defused the anti-Hanoverian feeling that had marked public political opinion in the previous two years, but antagonism within the ruling family continued. The Prince of Wales was again active in creating a distinct opposition, sufficiently threatening to prompt the administration to bring the septennial general election forward a year (to 1747) as a spoiling measure. But there was no strong leadership until William Pitt came to power in 1756. Many individuals enjoyed prosperity and stability, justifying the government's claims that (in the words of a later prime minister) they had never had it so good; but the political scene, and public comment on it, gave ample grounds for all shades of disquiet from apprehension to despair.

This picture of home and foreign affairs does not match the common modern interpretation of the political mood of the oratorios. According to the drama historian Murray Roston, 'Handel succeeded in glorifying in Biblical terms the confident patriotism of the English people as they rose on the wave of imperial expansion, convinced that they were carrying the true word of God to the pagan corners of the world. The heroic, martial splendour of *Deborah*, of *Judas Maccabeus*, and of *Joshua* was adopted enthusiastically as symbolic of English integrity and courage.'[15] The political historian Linda Colley, despite her perception that 'Britons reminded themselves of their embattled Protestantism in what often seems a wearingly repetitive fashion precisely because they had good cause to feel uncertain about its security and about their own', thinks Handel's oratorios characterised by 'sublime confidence'. Ignoring the existence of the librettists, she believes that 'The moral Handel wanted his listeners to draw was an obvious one ... a violent and uncertain past was to be redeemed by the new and stoutly Protestant Hanoverian dynasty, resulting in an age of unparalleled abundance.'[16] The following chapters question the common view that as political reflectors the oratorios chiefly express unqualified national confidence, and align them more nearly with the events and mood of their time. They will also be shown to be rooted in, and to express, their contemporary ideologies.

POLITICAL IDEOLOGIES OF THE ORATORIO YEARS

The appropriate names for the political groupings which existed in the 1730s and 1740s and the dates at which they can be said to have existed and at which they did or did not uphold particular views have been matters of energetic and increasingly detailed debate among modern historians of the period. The two main party labels, inherited from the previous century, 'Whig' and 'Tory', could (and can) scarcely be used without qualification, and debate over whether they still had any meaning formed part of political self-definition. (Put very simply, the traditional essentials of Tory and Whig identity were: Tory: High Church/established Church, monarchical, landed; Whig: Low Church/Dissenting, parliamentarian, mercantile.) Court Whigs, supporters of the administration, were distinguished from Patriot or opposition Whigs, their critics who, while loyal to the Hanoverian succession, were critical of the policies of its ministers; Tories, likewise opposed to the administration, might be covert Jacobites or loyally Hanoverian. Modern historiography reflects the diversity and complexity of mid-century opposition politics. Linda Colley has described a surviving, coherent Tory party, Jonathan Clark an *ancien régime* lasting until 1832 and Eveline Cruickshanks and Paul Monod the survival of Jacobite identity. Christine Gerrard has given renewed emphasis to the Whig component of opposition to Walpole, while Robert Harris has characterised opposition in the 1740s as subsuming Tory within Patriot principles.[17]

The picture was blurred at the time by the fact that party organisation in the modern sense did not exist, and political events, as distinct from theory, could cut through or across all ideological and traditional standpoints. For example, anti-Hanoverian feeling which had been rife in the two years up to 1745 was swept aside by the Rebellion, while calls for constitutional reform, civil liberty and the purging of faction, of the kind traditionally associated with radical Whiggism, were promulgated by Charles Edward Stuart in his Rebellion manifestos.[18] At the beginning of our period, the opposition Whigs agreed with the king and his two Secretaries of State that Austria should be supported in the War of Polish Succession, while Tories, wary of continental engagement, found themselves in agreement with the object of their detestation, the king's chief minister, that it should not;[19] and at the end of our period, as chapter 15 explains, the Jewish Naturalisation Bill brought together men of Tory principles and City Whigs, who had very different interests, against the administration. The picture is further complicated for oratorio students by the fact that an individual's adherence to an ideology does not necessarily match his actions or lack of them. For example, Jennens was an ideological Jacobite inasmuch as he was a Nonjuror (that is, he refused to abjure the deposed Stuarts and swear allegiance to the Hanoverian dynasty), yet his correspondence indicates that he did nothing to further the Jacobite Rebellion when it happened.[20] Jennens was consistent in his ideology; others moved their ideological as well as their active allegiance pragmatically, so that it becomes impossible to define even an individual or a group politically for longer than a specific moment. Some of the period's major ideological statements were themselves highly eclectic, in their effort to appeal to the widest possible audience; to take the leading example, in *The Idea of a Patriot King* Bolingbroke fused Old Whig republican principles of liberty with a high Tory vision of quasi-Messianic kingship to produce a manifesto for a Patriot party to end parties. The fluctuating identity, aims, strength and influence of the groups within the basic division of opposition/administration over twenty years of animated politicking are topics too extensive and complex to be detailed here.[21] Instead, it will be useful to pick out and – at the risk of over-simplification – sketch the import of some of the more keenly debated key concepts which had special senses in contemporary political thinking, as a prelude to showing how they are reflected in the librettos.

The 1688 Revolution, which ousted the Stuart royal family and ushered in the Hanoverians, had necessitated a complete revaluation of the rationale of English politics, and fifty and sixty years later this omphaloscopy was still in progress. Administration and opposition professed support of many of the same principles – such as preservation of the constitution, expansion of trade, loyalty to Protestantism – but defined them differently, and not only their implementation but their definitions were intensely contested. The debated terms of the period were central to political life, or, to put it the other way, debate about who should have power and how it should be used centred to an unusual degree on the meaning of individual words. This was a period (in this respect perhaps unparalleled in British politics) in which political theories were signalled in simple terms, even single words, many of which were used by writers and speakers of every political shade. Even when these were reduced to simplistic emotional triggers (as many complained they too often were) they were charged with the possibility of complex meaning.

This had several advantages for literature. The fact that dense meanings were signalled by individual words meant that the words could be used in rhetorical discourse without dragging its flow into the boggy complexities of explanation. Their apparent simplicity meant that they could be used without embarrassment in relatively uncomplicated literary scenarios, such as those of the librettos, while their freight of potential implication meant that their use in such settings did not necessarily trivialise. And the fact that the same individual words had value for people of widely varying opinions, and conveyed meaning of different levels of complexity according to the political attunement of listener as well as author, meant that unspecific rhetoric employing them could appeal to very large audiences; for example, as Dean notes, 'Tis Liberty' and 'Come, ever-smiling Liberty' in *Judas Macchabæus* gained instant and immense popularity.[22] The concepts outlined below are all central to the Israelite librettos.

Patriot

'Patriot' could denote either a political group with an agenda, or the principles which it professed to uphold, or a more general, non-party nationalism. At its most basic 'Patriotism' was a rallying cry on which everyone could agree, meaning love of country and devotion to its interests. In the 1755 edition of his dictionary Dr Johnson described a patriot as 'One whose ruling passion is the love of his country'. But the term was malleable as well as inclusive, and since in the mid century it was used to mean a good citizen, it also came to carry diverging senses of what a good citizen was. For a critic of the government a true patriot was one who engaged in public affairs at least to the extent of taking a critical view of the administration's handling of them; false patriots were the executive and their pensioners, destroying citizens' rights and undermining national probity. For the administration a true patriot was one who let wiser heads rule, kept his own house in order, and acknowledged that the country had every reason to be proud of itself thanks to the government; false patriots were the opposition, hypocritical in their abuse of the term. Dr Johnson's additional definitions of patriotism as 'the last refuge of a scoundrel' and of a patriot as 'sometimes used for a factious disturber of the government' were anticipated by, amongst others, one of Handel's oratorio librettists, the unillusioned James Miller, in a note to a line in his updated version of Horace:

Patriotism, an *antient* Word with a *modern* Signification: For whereas in Days of Yore it denoted a *Generous* Disposition in a Man towards *Serving* the *Publick*, now, these *Times* of *Reversing* are come; it importeth a more *provident* One towards *Serving Himself*; and is indiscriminately made use of by each Party when *out* of Power (which Party is always presum'd to be in the Right) in order to consecrate their Opposition to that which is *in*.[23]

The Patriot opposition of the first oratorio decade, which originated in the co-operation of Pulteney and Bolingbroke, aimed to remove Walpole, with the declared intention of initiating a programme of national political reform and moral regeneration. In the 1730s it allied itself with mercantile interests in urging aggressive action against Spain, and from 1735 to 1742, as described above, it had the Prince of Wales as its figurehead. A major plank of its platform was national unity transcending party and self-interest, as promulgated in Bolingbroke's *The Idea of a Patriot King*. The overthrow of Walpole's government, they declared, would put an end to political parties and religious differences: there would be no more need for them because there would be national accord.[24] But the Patriots were not themselves a unified group,[25] nor did they achieve the much-desired national unity. They lost credit with Pulteney's 'betrayal' in 1742, when he joined the administration without changing it, and with the accommodation of their other leaders to prevailing home and foreign policies in the 'Broad Bottom' administration formed in 1744. But after the Rebellion the Prince of Wales made moves to continue a Patriot opposition; this phase, anticipating the comprehension achieved at the accession of George III, might now appear more prominently had the prince's sudden death in 1751 not deprived it of its focus. According to Robert Harris, in the 1740s, when the main political division was patriot/ministerial, all elements of opposition opinion sought to identify themselves with the Patriot cause, yet as a political force it declined, for the reasons outlined above.[26]

The resilience of Patriot philosophy, as distinct from Patriot political power, is another matter; its two most recent historians, Gerrard and Harris, see it as the major strand of opposition theory in the 1730s and 1740s. By the 1740s Patriotism was dominating the ideological terrain by virtue of bringing together strong traditions of English political principle, derived most immediately from Whig and Country party thought, which emphasised the civil and religious rights of the subject (see below, 'Liberty'), civic humanist thinking encouraging the participation of the citizen in public life, and the promotion of national interests in the form of trade and empire (which had come to imply strong measures against foreign rivals).[27] The language given to these goals by Patriot writers also had wide appeal, being idealistic and moral rather than political and mundane. Throughout the oratorio period, when used adjectivally by the opposition the word 'patriot' itself contained strong moral pressure. It implied criticism and self-criticism and an acknowledgement of the individual's responsibility to foster corporate integrity. It referred to a programme of national renovation which would restore high standards of integrity to public life as well as securing national prosperity and international respect. When used by the more thoughtful government writers, even though its emotional charge was more complacent and its aim was weighted more towards prosperity than renovation, it was still firmly linked to the cultivation of virtue.[28]

It is not surprising that in this sense 'patriotism' was the most popular literary theme of the 1730s and early 1740s. How far into the 1740s its ideals survived as significant literary ingredients is debatable, but in the following chapters I suggest that in the oratorio librettos they are detectable until the death of their princely patron and for as long as Handel was writing oratorios about a nation.

Walpole was uninterested in literary patronage beyond hack journalism, and the Patriot opposition attracted many of the best writers of the time as spokesmen; by the 1730s the demand for encouragement of native art (and for boycotts of foreign artists) was one of its main themes. The emphasis of Patriot philosophy on moral principles was eminently transferable to rhetorical literature – whether poems, dramas, epics, or opera and oratorio librettos. (The librettos of the Opera of the Nobility await examination for ideological content.[29]) Though government measures such as the Licensing Act curbed topical satirical drama, the Prince of Wales' alliance with the opposition invigorated the production (begun in the early 1730s) of another line of patently political plays and verses. These were elevated rather than comic, hortatory rather than satirical, analogical rather than specifically allusive, concerning history and national myth rather than current events (though in their recurrent themes of monarchy misled by an evil chief minister and the renewal of national strength the analogies were not hard to decipher). As will emerge in subsequent chapters, there are several points of correspondence between the Patriot opposition dramas and poems and the Israelite oratorios. Christine Gerrard describes the former:

These works share certain features. They are all governed by historic or heroic themes. A nation threatened by domestic corruption or foreign oppression is saved by a 'deliverer of his country' – Frederick by name or by implication. Their language is elevated, their ethos romantically patriotic; and their concluding vision, like that of Bolingbroke's *Patriot King*, optimistically pictures the conquest of faction and corruption and a new golden age of peace and national prosperity through trade and foreign commerce.[30]

This description of Patriot literature strikingly matches the Israelite librettos. However, it lacks one major element of the librettos: religion. Historians have linked the mid-century idea of 'patriotism' in the sense of service of one's country to the tradition of civic humanism derived from Roman republicanism,[31] but the librettos link it to a different traditional source for British thinking about the individual's virtue and the virtuous society: the Bible. Though recent historians have emphasised religion as still a powerful influence on thought and life in the eighteenth century, Scripture itself has not featured largely in their discussions, and the following chapters suggest how much it was still a vital ingredient of political ideology and, in the librettos, of one of the main strands of political philosophy, patriotism.

Liberty

Throughout the Walpole years in particular, 'liberty' was the banner under which the opposition assailed the administration's handling of government. Whether or not the nation had it, and if so, when it acquired it, and if not, when it lost it, and how to preserve or regain it, were themselves major topics of debate.[32] 'Orators and journalists', writes one modern historian, 'found drama and urgency in what was potentially the most compelling issue of all – the future of liberty.'[33] The government claimed that the nation had been virtually enslaved under the Stuarts and could date its present proper degree of liberty (which the current administration wisely safeguarded) from the Glorious Revolution; the opposition claimed that the liberty fostered by Elizabeth I and her successors was now threatened by government moves to enslave the nation. In the contemporary political arena during the first oratorio decade 'liberty' was also used as a slogan by the Patriot opposition in the arena of foreign affairs to heighten popular demands in the conflict with Spain: the Spanish coastguards were described as oppressing and enslaving British seamen (see further chapters 10 and 12).

Constitution

All agreed that the safeguard of the liberties of her citizens, and her greatest glory, was Britain's balanced constitution, which prevented monarchical absolutism, guaranteed the independence of Parliament from crown influence and checked popular power. From Commonwealth, Old Whig thought via the Country party of the 1690s the Patriot opposition derived a central concern for the 'balanced constitution' and fear for its security, claiming that, far from preserving liberties established at the Revolution, the government was destroying a fabric which dated from Saxon times. Much political debate in the eighteenth century invoked previous history and this is especially true of the debate about the constitution. Its charged exploration of Britain's historical myths was readily transferable into literature (see further chapter 10).

Standing army

The allegation that the government was threatening the liberties of the citizens drew on the debate, dating from before the Revolution, about the desirability of a militia as opposed to a standing army. (Britain actually had the smallest professional army of the major European powers, but this was seldom acknowledged by opposition writers.) The argument that weapons and property should be in the hands of the same men to ensure that the interests of the warriors were those of the nation, to foster patriotism, to limit the drain on the public purse, and to prevent any possibility of the ruling powers – monarch or executive – turning the army on the nation was a cardinal point of Whig doctrine, adopted and expounded in the oratorio period by the Patriot opposition. After 1745, when the ease of the Jacobites' progress to Derby showed the existing militia organisation to be hopelessly ineffectual, arguments in favour of a strong militia included the need to protect the crown, and therefore accommodated a wide range of political opinion.[34]

Corruption

In opposition terms and with regard to public life, this meant the absence or the betrayal of moral-political principle, for instance the attacks on the constitution allegedly made by the government. It loomed large in civic humanist opposition writing and was a catch-all term used to brand the government as the destroyer of citizens' liberty by means of 'bribery' with places (public appointments) and pensions, the extension of bureaucratic power, attempts to increase taxation, measures to muffle the stage and the press, rigged elections and long parliaments. Writers for the administration responded by acknowledging the existence of 'corruption' but defining it less reprehensibly as self-interest, and aimed to defuse the moralising tone of the opposition's charge and to divert it from public into private life. Always pragmatic, they calmly took 'corruption' as an inevitable and unexceptionable condition of private and public life, argued that it made government and society function productively, and stressed material well-being as a worthy goal of government.[35] Patriot opposition writing, particularly in the late 1730s and early 1740s, frequently depicts a nation at its last gasp of moral-political integrity, blighted by its own apathy, and desperately in need of regeneration (see further chapter 10).

Luxury

In opposition terms this was an emanation of corruption in both private and public life. During the 1730s 'luxury' was closely associated by the opposition with the financial revolution – the rising power of the Bank of England, the growing National Debt, the increase of stockjobbers and foreign stock ownership, the growth of monopolies, financial disasters and scandals (such as the South Sea Bubble and the Charitable Corporation swindle), and a transfer of wealth and hence power from landed estates to the City.[36] The activities of the Societies for the Reformation of Manners (*c*. 1690–

1738), which brought prosecutions against individual citizens for immoral behaviour, reflected concern that the supposed increase of vice in private life harmed the state.[37] During the 1740s and into the 1750s moral-political commentators continued to warn of an imminent disintegration of social order, brought about by an unprecedented level of materialist self-interest and neglect of religion.[38]

According to opposition writers the government encouraged 'luxury' in this sense to render the nation more malleable, and they used the term almost interchangeably with 'tyranny' or 'slavery' as the antithesis to 'liberty'. Decadent consumerism and uncaring greed were identified as prime causes of social and spiritual rot: 'the continual Tide of Riches, pour'd in upon this Nation by Commerce, have been lost again in a Gulph of ungraceful, inelegant, inglorious Luxury'.[39] The virtuous strength of a simple, frugal society, located firmly in the past, is a theme of much literary opposition writing.[40] The administration argued that the availability of commodities was in itself a benefit of prudent government, and that private frugality and industry in the present, not a turning back of the economic clock, would adjust any personal and civic imbalance. Bernard Mandeville disturbed his contemporaries of all political complexions by inverting this position so far as to argue that selfishness and greed were politically beneficial because they encouraged commerce, and that the problem of 'luxury', purely political, would be managed by proper control of the balance of imports and exports.[41]

Divisions

Faction was agreed to be a cancer of modern political life. National unity was equally agreed to be desirable. Political division – even the existence of parties with differing agendas – was considered by many to be damaging.[42] But the opposition, with its vision of an ideal Patriot King who would resolve all political difference of interest and opinion, put much more emphasis on unity as a political lodestar than the administration which, as so often on questions of political philosophy, made a point of dealing in realities. Writers for the administration – which maintained the proscription of Tories from positions in the army, the Civil Service, the legislature and the Church[43] – insisted that the continuing existence of parties and party distinctions was a fact of political life, and used the allegation of 'faction' to decry opposition.[44] It was easy to point to divisions in political life. The most obvious included the rift in the ruling family, between the king and his heir; the conflicts of interest in the roles of George as King of England and Elector of Hanover, which caused perpetual difficulties in the conduct of foreign affairs and, at home, meant the uninspiring experience of a monarch who was not British and was frequently absent; difference of opinion about 'blue-water' versus 'continental' foreign policy (see above, p. 176); a lack of consensus among crown and ministers about foreign policy during the War of Austrian Succession, and a lack of consensus about when to make peace. The call for national unity was one of the most consistent and persistent sounds in political rhetoric of the oratorio years.

THE ORATORIOS' AUDIENCES AS POLITICAL LISTENERS AND THEIR AUTHORS AS POLITICAL COMMENTATORS

Intended political references – references to contemporary or recent political events, or ideology, or both – in a collaborative, public, literary or literary-musical work can be intended by both authors, or intended by one author and perceived and accepted by the other, or intended by one author and unperceived by the other. They can have a single meaning or they can have two or more, aimed at different sectors of the audience, possibly one generally acceptable and overt, the other a minority view, 'coded' and disownable. Intended meaning(s) can be understood, or missed, by all, or part(s) of the audience; and all or part(s) of the audience (at the time of first performance and subsequently) can 'read in' meanings not intended by the author(s). My main interest is meaning intended by the librettists; but we have to consider Handel's likely attitudes, and the attitudes of the audience naturally have a bearing too, as its capacities to read political meanings and its expectation of them relates to the authors' use of them. Political references can be made with an intention to influence attitudes alone, or attitudes and, consequently, events, or without any such intention – for example, simply for a financial return – or from a mixture of these motives. They can comment on the past, present or future, or all three; they can be celebratory or critical in their judgement of the past or present; they can be more or less optimistic in prescribing for the present or the future.[45]

How can we judge whether it is reasonable to look for political references in the oratorio librettos? We need the answers to several questions. Is it usual at this date to put political references into these kinds of works? Are the materials used in these works (for example, Scripture) commonly used at this date to convey political meaning? Are the authors given to making political references in anything else they write for public consumption? What do we know of the place of politics in the authors' lives? Let us take these in order.

In the first half of the century the 'political nation' – that is, the politically aware – included a larger proportion of the population than perhaps at any time before or since.[46] The pervasive presence of political allusion in literature, especially drama, is well documented. The tradition of political reference was equally strong in native and imported music theatre. In the sixteenth and seventeenth centuries English masques and operas customarily honoured ruling monarchs and aristocrats and marked specific occasions. Early-eighteenth-century Italian opera in England was a regular vehicle for political allusion, and the struggling English opera, itself a declaration of national identity, made specific reference to national events.[47] From John Loftis' study it emerges (though he does not himself make the point) that *music* drama was the period's pre-eminent theatrical vehicle for critical or subversive political innuendo, and Curtis Price has identified such innuendo in late-seventeenth and early-eighteenth-century English opera.[48] Among ballad operas (the form most given to open political satire) Gay's *The Beggar's Opera* (1728) is now the best known but was not the most blatant; in *The Welsh Opera* (1731), for example, Fielding not only attacked Walpole and the evils perceived to result from his administration, as Gay had done, but mockingly and unmistakably pilloried the king, queen and Prince of Wales.[49] Not that music theatre was now held to be capable only of oppositionist messages: Christine Gerrard has pointed out the efforts made to transform Dryden's covertly Jacobite masque-opera *King Arthur* into *Merlin* (1735–6), a loyally Hanoverian celebration of national unity.[50]

Students of this period do not need to find contemporary testimony in order to be justified in accepting that a specific work was capable of political interpretation. Intended and perceived political reference was habitual. In a culture which was always ready to interpret a text politically, the oratorio audience would have been alive to potential political allusions. But we do have some examples of such testimony in the case of some of the oratorios, from authors and audience. In 1733 Samuel Humphreys, dedicating his wordbook of *Deborah* to Queen Caroline, invited his audience to make a connection between the events of the oratorio and contemporary happenings: even the most polished portrait of his Jewish heroine, he loyally allowed, would be bound to be eclipsed by '*BRITANNIA's QUEEN*'. *Israel in Egypt*, as chapter 9 describes, was given a tendentious political interpretation by a partisan newspaper. So closely was Newburgh Hamilton's *Occasional Oratorio* related to current events – the 1745 Rebellion – that, according to one contemporary, who considered the scriptural words 'expressive of the rebels' flight and our pursuit of them', it was wholly dependent on them for its public performance: 'Had not the Duke [of Cumberland] carried his point triumphantly, this Oratorio could not have been brought on'.[51] Thomas Morell recalled of his *Judas Macchabæus* that 'The plan was designed as a compliment to the Duke of Cumberland, upon his returning victorious from [quelling the Rebellion in] Scotland. I had introduced several incidents more apropos, but it was thought [by Handel, presumably] they would make it too long, and were therefore omitted. The Duke however made me a handsome present.'[52] Oratorio librettos could refer, and were understood to refer, to contemporary political events.

The second question, about the material used by the oratorios' authors, is addressed in chapter 9. This brings us to the questions about the authors themselves, which have already begun to be answered for three of them in the previous paragraph. What we do know, or what can we surmise, of their political interests? The librettists of three of the Israelite oratorios are unknown (*Joshua, Solomon, Susanna*). Those of two others are uncertain: the librettist(s) of the Cannons *Esther* are conjectural (see chapter 11), and there is strong but only circumstantial evidence that *Israel in Egypt* is by Jennens (see chapter 12). We know varying amounts about the political affiliations of the identified librettists, and almost nothing about Handel's politics. The last part of this chapter discusses the librettists in the order in which they first wrote oratorio texts for Handel, and finally Handel himself.

Samuel Humphreys (c. 1698–1738)

Humphreys is still a very shadowy figure. The *Gentleman's Magazine* for September 1743 refers to him as 'known for his well received translations and poems', but his most substantial work was the vast biblical commentary he produced towards the end of his life, *The Sacred Books of the Old and New Testament, Recited at Large,* in three folio volumes each of over a thousand pages. This shows a strong interest in the political elements of Israelite history and their lessons for modern times.

Humphreys had a connection with Handel's patron for whom the original *Esther* was written: in 1728 he published (also in folio) *Cannons. A Poem. Inscrib'd to his Grace the Duke of Chandos,* for which Chandos gave him £20 on 13 June. Alexander Shapiro points out that besides providing Handel with translations for his Italian opera librettos Humphreys also wrote the libretto for J. C. Smith jnr's *Ulysses* (1733), which contains lines open to Jacobite reading; and that he edited the posthumous *Poems on Several Occasions* of Matthew Prior, a Tory 'martyr'. Humphreys' prefatory Life of Prior, expanded in the third edition (1733), details Prior's employment in foreign affairs and is at pains to rehabilitate him, on the grounds that he revised his view of the wisdom of the Treaty of Utrecht. Humphreys included in this collection 'Malpasia', an elegy for Walpole's daughter which hailed Walpole as the true Patriot, his country's saviour.[53] As already mentioned, Humphreys dedicated *Deborah* to Queen Caroline. Humphreys is an excellent instance of an eighteenth-century author whose writings transmit apparently contradictory political signals.

Charles Jennens (1700–73)[54]

Jennens came of a rich and well-connected Warwickshire gentry family. His activities as squire, connoisseur, patron, author and friend were underpinned by two deeply held allegiances, religious and political: to Protestant Christianity and to the deposed house of Stuart. He was one of many English squires forced by the Roman Catholicism of James II and his heirs into a genuinely agonising conflict, between loyalty to the family which had the hereditary (and, many believed, divine) right to rule, and an obligation to protect the English constitution and the Church of England. Refusing – because James II was still alive, and had heirs – to swear allegiance to William and Mary and, once the Protestant succession had been established in 1701, refusing to take the oath abjuring loyalty to the Stuarts, Nonjurors excluded themselves from all political and ecclesiastical office. Had he not been a Nonjuror,

Jennens would certainly have been a magistrate, and he might have followed the family tradition of studying at Middle Temple.

Nonjurors' political activity had to be either symbolic and polemical, or treasonable. Jennens steered an honourable course between subversion and passivity. No suspicion of treasonable involvement attaches to him. But he was an assiduous reader of opposition propaganda, and helped to circulate it; and within the bounds of legality, he declared his loyalty to the old regime. His seal portrayed the head of Charles I, and he collected, and displayed, a remarkable number of portraits of the Stuarts and their deposed descendants. Eighteenth-century collections of non-family portraits were assembled to represent the collector's idea of the truly great and good, his pantheon of 'worthies'; contemporaries recognised this part of Jennens' collection as a statement of loyal adherence. He even had a piece of Charles II's oak, so called, built into the communion table in his chapel at Gopsall, and he crossed the names of the Hanoverian royal family out of the prayer books that he used there.

Jennens was the leading patron of Nonjurors of his generation, and some of the recipients of his kindness were not only Nonjurors but probably Jacobites. His close friend Edward Holdsworth was suspected of being an agent of the Pretender, and his correspondence with Jennens was regularly opened by British government spies. Jennens was among the first subscribers to the history of England by the Jacobite historian Thomas Carte and (judging from the presence of all four volumes in his library) did not (unlike others) cancel his subscription after the appearance of the first volume with its inflammatory account of touching for the King's Evil. He patronised the Jacobite bookseller William Russel. However he was also involved in helping a circle of Nonjurors who, like him, took no active part in politics.

Many Nonjurors had wide circles of friends of diverse political and religious complexions, and Jennens' friendship with Handel – an employee of the Hanoverian court – is no sign of confused loyalties. Nor did being a Nonjuror necessarily mean cutting oneself off from the established Church. On the contrary, as we have already seen in the case of Arthur Bedford (chapter 3), many Nonjurors were devout Anglicans and made a great contribution to English religious life of the time. Jennens himself remained part of the established Church, indeed he was the patron of two livings,

Nether Whitacre and Gotham. As should be clear by now, he was not, as several sources describe him, a Nonconformist, in the sense of being a Dissenter. In common with High-Church believers of his day, Jennens was if anything opposed to Dissenters, as both his correspondence and the contents of his library attest. The evangelising doctrinal Protestantism of his *Messiah* has already been discussed (chapter 6).

Newburgh Hamilton (fl. *1712–59*)

Hamilton's politics are not known, but he associated himself with people of distinct political leanings. His St Cecilia Ode (1720) was 'most humbly inscribed, by his lordship's most obliged, and most obedient servant' to Peregrine Marquess of Carmarthen, a Tory whose father, the second Duke of Leeds, was from 1716 to 1723 admiral and commander-in-chief of the Pretender's fleet. Most of Hamilton's working life (1725–54, perhaps longer) was spent as steward to the third Earl of Strafford, his widow, and their son. The third earl was created Duke of Strafford in the Jacobite peerage in 1722 and named as commander-in-chief of the Pretender's forces north of the Humber and one of the Lords Regent in the Pretender's absence; he was a leading conspirator in both the Atterbury Plot (1720–2) and the Cornbury Plot (1731–5) to restore the Stuarts, and was also involved in negotiations on behalf of the Stuart cause in 1725.[55] As Strafford's trusted factotum Hamilton was presumably aware of his master's consistently Jacobite allegiance. His choice of Dryden's *Alexander's Feast* for Handel to set in 1736 is interesting in this connection, since it contains a Jacobite subtext.[56] However, his libretto for the *Occasional Oratorio* is a prayer for the defeat of the 1745 Rebellion. He had dedicated his libretto of *Samson* to the Prince of Wales at the height of Frederick's opposition campaign.

James Miller (*1704–44*)

Miller was a clergyman, a playwright and a satirist, and in all three roles he attacked the follies and vices of the age. His life and works have been admirably studied by Paula O'Brien (I follow her definition of the canon), and here I mention only the main features of his moral-political writing.[57] His satires recall those of Pope, and in fact Pope drew on several of them.[58] Like Pope and like the Patriot poets, Miller made the connection between the decline of art and the decline of the nation, for example in *Harlequin Horace: or, the Art of Modern Poetry* (see chapter 2). Like Pope, Miller was recognised in his own time as a leading opposition writer.[59] In 1734 the anonymous *The Dramatick Sessions; or, The Stage Contest* aligned him with Fielding, Thomson, and Aaron Hill, all current or incipient opposition playwrights.[60]

Some of Miller's scorn is directed straight at Walpole, whose expedient style of government was seen by moralists as pre-eminently encouraging and contributing to national corruption. His *Seasonable Reproof, or, A Satire in the Manner of Horace* (1735) begins with a contemptuous reference to Walpole and his failed tax, coupled with denigration of the fashion for Italian opera singers,

> For whose sweet Pipe the City's so forsaken,
> That, by *Excisemen*, it might now be taken,
> And great Sir *Bob* ride thro', and save his Bacon.[61]

In *An Hospital for Fools: A Dramatic Fable* (1739) Miller portrays a (generic) statesman glorying in his abuse of power and in the sycophancy of the deluded public:

How we are follow'd, courted and ador'd! What Mountains of Wealth do we heap up for our selves and Families! And how are we flatter'd and cring'd to by all Mankind! Away with Wit and Learning out of the World, they are good for nothing but to make People impertinent and seditious. (p. 21)

The theme of peculation here connects with Miller's libretto of *Joseph and his Brethren* for Handel (see chapter 13), but more generally this passage is interesting for its association of the spread of vice with the decay and repression of educated, discriminating, free thought and expression – a major theme of the leading opposition writers. Miller explores this theme again, with reference to moral and religious decay, in his Fast sermon of 1740, *The Cause of Britain's being become a Reproach to her Neighbours* (Daniel IX.16). Here he castigates vice, irreligion, selfishness and corruption in oppositionist terms, decrying foreign influences, lamenting the decline of national strength, and deploring the collapse of public integrity:

The Question is not, whether we shall have Popery or Protestantism? whether we shall be Slaves, or a free People? But how we, each of us, shall *fill the Basket* – Who shall have this Place, or that Pension in the State, who this Dignity, or that *Sine-Cure* in the Church, or who this Monopoly, or fraudulent Advantage in Traffick. (p. 15)

Miller's severity deepened as the Patriot opposition to Walpole gathered strength. His most incisive shaft is one of the most swingeing of all the attacks on Walpole, the anonymous *Are These Things So?* (1740; he also probably wrote one of its nine sequels, *The Great Man's Answer*).[62] It adopts the persona of Pope himself to expose the first minister, in an open letter from 'an Englishman in his Grotto' to 'a Great Man at Court'. Typically Patriot criticisms of Walpole's policies and abuses of power end with suggestions for his replacement, fictitious in the first edition but in the second (six weeks later) a roll-call of opposition worthies. In 1741 Miller dedicated his *Miscellaneous Works* to the Patriot opposition's figurehead, the Prince of Wales. The subscription list, which includes a strong opposition presence, also includes Handel. *The Year Forty-One: Carmen Seculare* was dedicated to another opposition patron, the Dowager Duchess of Marlborough. Rich in tropes dear to the Patriots, it invokes their favourite British monarch, Shakespeare's Henry V; laments the banishment of liberty; and (in biblical phraseology) demands the dismissal of the king's evil ministers.[63] *The H[anove]r Heroes*, written between the completion of the libretto of *Joseph* and its first performance, similarly voices current opposition grievances, in this case the pro-Hanoverian stance of Walpole's successor, Carteret, and the treatment of British troops at Dettingen.[64]

Miller's identity as a Patriot opposition writer is unquestionable, and the consistency of his allegiance is remarkable, as his early biographers attest. Despite his penury,

His integrity ... in these principles was so firm, that he had resolution enough to withstand the temptation of a very large offer made him by the agents of the ministry in the time of general opposition ... He, indeed, frequently acknowledged, that this was the severest trial his constancy ever endured ... thus far he was willing to have temporized, that though he would not eat the bread purchased by writing in vindication of principles that he disapproved, yet he would have stipulated with the ministry, on the same terms, never to have drawn his pen against them. But this proposal was rejected on the other side, and so terminated their negotiations. Thus did Mr Miller's wit and honesty stand for many years the most powerful bars to his fortune.[65]

Thomas Morell (1703–84)

Morell's comment on his dedication of *Judas Macchabæus* to the Duke of Cumberland (quoted above, p. 189) illuminates the potentially ambiguous nature of dedications. The author might admire the dedicatee, with or without qualification, or might hope that the dedicatee would be guided by the accompanying work to change some aspect of his or her behaviour,[66] or might hope for money, or all three. Morell acknowledges the last motive; this dedication may not tell us much about his politics. It is certainly the case that he was always chronically hard up, particularly in 1746, when he had just lost a main, though inadequate, source of income, and a dedication was an investment for which a cash return could be expected.[67]

In about 1729 Morell had been appointed sub-curate of the Chapel of St Anne, Kew Green (later Kew Church), where from 1733 he served as acting curate but with no extra financial recognition. Having asked for an increased stipend, he was relieved of his duties by the vicar in 1745.[68] We do not know enough about Morell to be able to determine whether he was indeed a convinced court Whig, or just desperate for money, when he took up libretto writing in 1746. But we do have evidence that in the 1730s he identified himself, by contrast, with the Patriot opposition cause, and that in the early 1740s he was a satellite of Prince Frederick's opposition circle.

Morell's public and private attachment to the opposition cause is evident in some of his poems (which have not previously received attention).[69] In 1731 the *Gentleman's Magazine* published his 'The Lord and the 'Squire. A Ballad', one of many comments on the almost bloodless duel between the dissident Whig leader William Pulteney and the court Whig Lord Hervey, which originated in a particularly savage pamphlet duel in the larger campaign between the government and its chief hornet, Bolingbroke's and Pulteney's *Craftsman*.[70] Morell's humorous account is more favourable to Pulteney than the facts warranted and, in applauding Pulteney (the ''Squire'), he supports his cause:

> Great Favourites both, they are or have been;
> But they say, one is *out*, and the other is *in*;
> Tho better twoud be, there's no one can doubt,
> If the one he was *in*, and the other was *out*.

Mentioning that the duellists risked arrest gives Morell the opportunity for a characteristically oppositionist thrust, against the
government's corruption of the executive by patronage (Pulteney
had resisted such inducements):

> How then had They triumph'd, who *Walpole* espouse,
> To have had the great Squire debar'd from the *House*;
> But his *Lordship*'s Confinement They valued not much,
> When in Pay, and full Pension They had 300 such.[71]

In 'The Patriot' (1732, thirty lines of pentameter couplets; MS fols.
26–7) Morell eulogises Pulteney in even more deliberately partisan
terms, and in the language associated with his poem's title, as one
'Who dares oppose Corruption, Pensions, Bribes . . . freely good, and
obstinately just'. Again in standard Patriot opposition mode, he
depicts Britain as a 'suff'ring Land' which Pulteney defends,
Perseus-like, from the government's 'vile Measures'. One of these
measures, the Excise, prompted 'A new ballad' (MS fols. 22–3),
which Morell interestingly annotates 'Gilliver, the Bookseller,
offer'd me handsomely for this Ballad; but, as I scribbled, merely for
my own Diversion, and my Friend's, I refused his Money.' (Gilliver's anti-Walpole publications at the time of the Excise included
Swift's 'Epistle to a Lady' (1732), for which he was arrested.[72])
Addressing 'my Countrymen', Morell again reads them current
Patriot doctrines:

> In vain of your old English Freedom you boast,
> The Freedom, which many a year has been lost;
> E'er since Quart'ring, and Pensions, and Bribes came in Fashion,
> And a d—d Standing Army, to eat up the Nation.

Now the nation is to be impoverished still further by 'Sir Noble'
(Walpole),

> For a Scheme he has laid with his politic crew,
> To excise your Tobacco, your Sugar, Wines too;
> And so on; to excise all exciseable Ware,
> Til' nothing be free, but the pure vital Air.

In line with the countless other protests the Excise prompted,
Morell raises the spectre of privacy invaded by an excise officer ('He
pops in your Warehouse, your Cellar, your Shop') and, by extension, civil rights destroyed: 'here, *Magna Charta* is not worth a
groat'.[73] He also includes another strand of opposition doctrine, that

the current peace is peace without honour ('a Peace we have got; / Whether fought for, or paid for, it signifies not'). He heads the ballad with references to the *Gentleman's Magazine* which explain the political context: reprints of articles from the *Craftsman* about the evils of a threatened excise (1731) and standing armies and excises (1732); Wyndham's reply to Walpole's salt tax proposal in the 1732 session; and a ballad reprinted from the other major opposition paper, the *Grub Street Journal*, 'The Constitution Clapp'd, an Excise' (1733).[74] These references, evidently added for the benefit of his wife, who was reading the poem long after it was written, show the strength of Morell's concern – years after the event – to have his alignment with the opposition appreciated.

There are several indications that Morell was still within the opposition orbit during the late 1730s and the 1740s. In 1737, after his expulsion from court, the prince moved into Morell's neighbourhood, and Kew House was thenceforth Frederick's family home.[75] Morell dedicated his edition of modern versions of Chaucer's *Canterbury Tales* (1737) to Frederick as a wedding present, and he is said to have tried to secure financial support through the agency of the prince's dancing-master, Denoyer.[76] His poem 'The Widow'd Swan' depicts him strolling in the grounds of Cliveden, another of the prince's country homes, and includes, as part of the dying swan's song, lines in praise of Frederick,

> The Sacred Guard of Innocence,
> On whom the Graces all attend,
> Fortitude's Mirrour, Virtue's Friend;
> Gen'rous, humane, benign, and free,
> The Joy of Life and Liberty.   (MS fol. 137)

His poems include 'To my Friend Mr Thomson, on his unfinished Plan of a Poem, called The Castle of Indolence. – in Imitation of Spenser. – ' (MS fols. 63–5), four aptly Spenserian stanzas dating from 1742, when Thomson was one of the Prince of Wales' chief writers. The poem which Morell was urging Thomson to complete has itself been interpreted as a Patriot opposition work, in which 'indolence' means political lethargy, the pursuit of private pleasure to the neglect of public duty (akin to Pope's 'dulness') – a clash of interests which Morell himself was to explore in his librettos.[77]

There is also evidence that Morell had contact of a kind with another opposition writer, the greatest of them all, Pope. His volume of poems contains 'Mr Pope's Epistle to the E. of Burlington. –

versified', a verse rendition of Pope's letter to Burlington about his ride to Oxford in the company of Lintot. Only one other copy of this versification is known, preserved in a group of Burlington family manuscripts, and that copy too is in Morell's hand. (Morell probably became acquainted with the Burlingtons through his socially superior wife, Anne Barker, whose parental home adjoined the Burlingtons' Chiswick property.) The question of the author of this display of wit remains open, but on the evidence of his poems, librettos and other writings it cannot be Morell. However, as James Osborn remarks in discussing the Burlington copy, 'the preservation of the manuscript with a packet of Burlington-connected papers suggests that the verses were an ingroup joke, intended for the Burlington circle instead of for wide circulation', which in turn suggests that Morell was connected to that circle.[78] In the light of the prince's continuing encouragement of artistic endeavour buttressing his opposition campaign after the Rebellion,[79] Morell's report that Handel approached him for a libretto with 'the honour of a recommendation from Prince Frederic' is particularly suggestive: was Frederick hoping for something in his support to result from the combination of Morell's record as an opposition writer with Handel's genius and fame?[80]

But Morell also derived an income from the members of the Hanoverian family whom the Patriots and the prince opposed. He dedicated *Judas*, the first fruit of his partnership with Handel, not to Frederick but to Cumberland (who had no truck with the opposition and whose conduct in Scotland Frederick deplored), and earlier he had been curate of Queen Caroline's chapel at Kew and was commissioned by her to provide a commentary on Locke's *Essay on Human Understanding*.[81] His bitterness at losing the queen's favour to the 'thresher poet' Stephen Duck, whom he had encouraged, is documented in his manuscript of poems in a touching aside to his wife and 'to those in whose hands they may have heretofore fallen, or may hereafter fall' (fols. 65–7); he was sufficiently vehement for the incident to be recalled years later in an anonymous squib, *The Curatical Battle for Q. Chappel: Address to the Reverend Parsons, D--k and M----l* (1746).[82]

The author of the (doubtfully attributed) *Letters of Lord [Thomas] Lyttelton*, writing sympathetically (in Letter 36) of 'your very learned friend Morell', considered 'that the acute critic and profound grammarian seems to be impelled rather by the love of science, than the desire of gain, – is generally in the habit of frugal contentment, and hides himself in that shade of retirement, where the learned few alone can find him'.[83] But in his thirties and forties Morell moved in political circles, put political allusions into his works – not always for pecuniary gain, according to his statement about turning down Gilliver's offer – and was apparently willing to write in support of people in different and differing political camps. In one very strong sense he was a servant of the state, in that he was a beneficed clergyman of the Church of England (his defence of religion was discussed in chapter 4 and of orthodox Christian belief in chapter 6).

Handel

The jury is still out on the question of Handel's politics. We have no verbal clue from him. His one recorded party-political action is voting Whig in the 1749 Westminster by-election.[84] His biography does not confirm any political allegiance for motives beyond the furtherance of his career, in the sense of taking opportunities to write the music he wanted to write and get paid for it. From the moment that he first arrived in England, he was involved in producing music for national events, most of which were also royal: the Peace of Utrecht, Queen Anne's birthday, the coronation of George II and Caroline, the weddings of Princess Anne and Prince Frederick, Caroline's funeral, the Dettingen victory, the Peace of Aix-la-Chapelle. He sought and obtained naturalisation as a British citizen in 1727. He was a crown servant, receiving from Queen Anne a royal pension which was continued by George I and George II; appointed music master to the Hanoverian princesses; commissioned to provide music for Hanoverian royal occasions; and granted royal copyright privileges.[85] On the other hand, his two chief aristocratic patrons at the beginning of his English career, Burlington and Chandos, are now thought by some to have been not only opposed to the court but associated with the Jacobite cause, and during his main oratorio years he was supported by the Prince of Wales, who was then in opposition to his father the king, Handel's ostensible master (Newburgh Hamilton, among others, describes Handel as a bone of contention within the royal family).[86]

Handel may or may not have been interested in politics, but no one of average intelligence in London at this date could have been unaware of the events outlined at the start of this chapter, and there is no reason to suppose him to have been politically naive. His own circumstances, as an employee of the monarchy and aristocracy, and as a competitor in the market-place, involved him personally in the political currents of his time. His Utrecht Te Deum celebrated a treaty which was anathema to his then master, George the Elector of Hanover, and Donald Burrows has concluded that it was directly responsible for his dismissal from his Electoral post.[87] In England his career was affected by national politics both positively, with commissions and opportunities for works marking national occasions, and adversely, as when the 1715 Rebellion aborted the 1715–16 opera season[88] and (as described in the next chapter) the Excise crisis impacted on his oratorio career. The operas of the German courts habitually glorified the reigning monarch with plots drawn from national or local history; in Italy Handel had set at least one unambiguously political opera libretto,[89] and in England he encountered a strong tradition of political allusion in music theatre works (see above, p. 188).

The librettists' possible reasons for writing for Handel were discussed in the Introduction, and only in Jennens' opaque remark about making use of Handel do we come anywhere near a statement of deliberate intention to convey a message to the public; but the absence of such statements of course does not preclude such an intention. Jennens and Miller had strong political-ideological commitment; Humphreys, Miller and Morell put political allusions in their other works; Hamilton's employer was involved in politically subversive activity. I think that all the permutations mentioned in the first paragraph of this section *could* apply to the oratorios, though it is most likely that any deliberate political references usually originated with the librettist and that Handel did or did not recognise them and, where he did recognise them, did not object to them. Whether the librettists who incorporated political comment intended to effect change in public affairs seems doubtful, but possible in the case of Jennens and Miller. In relation to his oratorios (and for that matter his operas) political implications seem to have come a long way down Handel's list of priorities. The wrangle with Jennens over the proposed Hallelujah chorus at the end of *Saul* and its outcome (see chapter 13) supports this view, and so far as I am aware it is the only record we have of discussion between Handel and one of his librettists about a politically meaningful element in a libretto. Handel's alterations to his librettists' words in his autograph scores might usefully be looked at again with this in mind. From the present state of knowledge we cannot deduce that an apparent political meaning in a libretto reflects Handel's political interest; nor can we assume, from Handel's court employment, that interpretations of the librettos which discern 'messages' contrary to the political orthodoxy of court and administration are implausible.

CHAPTER 9

Allegorical politics

Besides being often didactic, the politically imbued verse, drama
and music theatre of the first half of the eighteenth century is often
allusive and cryptic. Many of its 'lessons' were so familiar to readers
that only a phrase was needed to bring whole ideologies to mind.
This makes comprehension a challenging business for the twentieth-
century reader. Understanding – even noticing – the coded references needs the basic equipment of acquaintance with not only the
topics which interested eighteenth-century writers and readers, but
their methods of referring to them. Without such knowledge we see
these works, which include the oratorio librettos, through a fog, and
are in danger of thinking there is nothing there. This chapter offers
some signposts to the allusive practices of three areas occupied by
oratorio: the theatre, the interpretation of Scripture, and the writing
of history. But it begins with political journalism, and the verbal
involvement of Handel and his music in day-to-day political life.

MUSIC AS POLITICAL METAPHOR

The previous chapter noted the importance of music theatre as a
vehicle for political messages. Music and musicians also served as a
prime analogy for the state and statesmen. This had a direct impact
on the history of oratorio. On 7 April 1733, at the height of the
Excise crisis, the *Craftsman* devoted a whole issue to attacking
Walpole through a lampoon of Handel. It took its cue from 'a little
Epigram, lately handed about Town', which represented the composer as the prime minister's alter ego, not only using Walpole's
methods but in league with him:

> Quoth *W*[alpol]*e* to *H*[ande]*l*, shall We Two agree,
> And exise the whole Nation?
>   *H*[andel]. *si, Caro, si.*

In the *Craftsman*'s extended play with this idea, Handel's opera management stood for Walpole's management of the state, and his new form of entertainment, oratorio, for Walpole's Excise. The allegory was completely transparent (and still is to historians), in that substantial parts of its narrative repeat well-rehearsed critical versions of Walpole's conduct, even using his own words, and are quite inapplicable to Handel. But the slight pretence is gleefully ornamented with detailed ramifications:

Notwithstanding all these and many more Objections, Mr. *H----l*, by and with the Advice of *his Brother*, at last produces his *Project*; resolves to cram it down the Throats of the Town; prostitutes *great* and *aweful Names*, as the Patrons of it; and even does not scruple to insinuate that they are to be Sharers of the Profit. His *Scheme* set forth in Substance, that the late decay of *Opera*'s was owing to their *Cheapness*, and to the great *Frauds* committed by the *Doorkeepers*; that the *annual Subscribers* were a Parcel of *Rogues*, and made an ill Use of their Tickets, by often *running* two into the Gallery, that to obviate these Abuses he had contrived a Thing, that was better than an *Opera*, call'd an *Oratorio*; to which none should be admitted, but by *printed Permits*, or Tickets of one Guinea each, which should be distributed out of *Warehouses of his own*, and by *Officers of his own naming*.[1]

After this Handel did not risk launching a new oratorio in London for nearly six years.

The *Craftsman*'s immediate reason for picking on Handel as a vehicle for tilting at Walpole was that coincidentally with the Excise Bill furore Handel had introduced his new oratorio, *Deborah*, at double the normal ticket prices and as a non-subscription performance, so that his seasonal opera subscribers could not claim their usual free seats.[2] Walpole's tax, his detractors complained, would make life more expensive; it was financially maladroit; it was an insult to the public; it was an infringement of civil rights. Similar charges were made against Handel's procedures with *Deborah* and in the Royal Academy opera company. The language of the *Craftsman*'s attack ('project', 'scheme') plays on the fact of the Royal Academy's having been a joint-stock venture (like the South Sea Company) to arraign what it considered to be the morally bankrupt and bankrupting world of finance in Walpole's Britain. But readers would have seen other parallels. Both men were servants of George II: Walpole was his chief politician, Handel was his favourite musician. Walpole, in serving the king, was securing the Hanoverian dynasty, whose foreignness was a cause of distress, and even resentment, to many of his British subjects; Handel provided music to celebrate the Hanoverian dynasty, and he was German too. The king was supportive of Walpole, in opposition to many of the nobility (and others) who resented what they saw as his high-handed style of political management, dangerously threatening constitutional balance by a combination of royal favour and manipulation of Parliament. The king was also conspicuously supportive of Handel's musical ventures, in opposition to many of his nobility, who were forming an opera company in direct competition to Handel's and partly out of resentment at what they considered his unwarrantably high-handed style of musical management (which was the main ostensible target of the *Craftsman*'s attack).[3] The paying public saw the mishandling of *Deborah* as an occasion of such brashness, and of its successful repression: 'The subscribers being refused unless they would pay a guinea, they, insisting upon the right of their silver tickets, forced into the House, and carried their point.'[4]

The author of the *Craftsman* article was not the only political writer to draw on the capital of *Deborah*. On the previous day, 6 April, Henry Fielding had produced, as an afterpiece to *The Miser*, a ballad opera called *Deborah: or, a Wife for You All*. Previously advertised simply as *A Wife for You All*, this *Deborah* lasted only for a single performance; it was not published and the text is lost. Given Fielding's opposition allegiance at this date and his recent entry to the patronage of the Duke of Richmond, who was about to become a director of the Opera of the Nobility, Martin Battestin persuasively conjectures that the piece was suppressed, because of its mockery of the king's favourite composer and its satirical association of Walpole's and Handel's projects.[5]

The *Craftsman* disregarded *Deborah*'s content along with other facts about Handel's compositions and performances, but it could have invoked both libretto and music to support its argument, for they both allude flatteringly to the Hanoverian regime. As already mentioned, the librettist, Samuel Humphreys, dedicated his text to Queen Caroline (Walpole's most powerful and most supportive ally – and a German), and for the music Handel reused two of his anthems for the coronation of George II and Queen Caroline.[6] He had reused the other two anthems in *Esther*, which he had first publicly performed the previous year, at royal command. The *Craftsman*'s (and maybe Fielding's) connection of Handel's oratorios' and the ruling powers at this date is not fantastic.[7]

The Excise crisis was the major domestic political upheaval of the two decades 1721–42, generating hundreds of pamphlets, articles, ballads, prints and petitions to Parliament. The *Craftsman* was the most prominent opposition organ of mid-eighteenth-century England, and this piece bears the monogram 'O' common to many of the articles written by Bolingbroke, Walpole's major opponent. Handelian oratorio was being prominently, publicly, involved, satirically but with deadly serious intent, in a political event of the highest significance. Historians are aware that the *Craftsman* occasionally used music as an allegory for politics; but they have tended to pass over the fact that such commentary invoked the musical world in remarkably copious detail.

As was indicated in chapter 2, art, including music, was regarded as an index of national well-being. Close attention to musical life on the part of political writers is not confined to the *Deborah*/Excise parallel, and sometimes they leave the metaphorical arena for a straightforward connection of the politics of music with the politics of the state. James Miller's political criticism in his satirical song about the castrato Farinelli in his play *The Coffee House* was sufficiently blatant to be censored,[8] and other squibs made a link between Farinelli's 'capture' by the Spanish court (to which he retired from the London stage) and the Spanish capture of British merchant ships.[9] *The Devil to Pay at St James's*, published at the height of the opera mania of the 1720s, claimed that 'it is not now, as formerly, *i.e.* are you High Church or Low, Whig or Tory; are you for Court or Country; King *George* or the Pretender; but are you for *Faustina* or *Cuzzoni* [rival sopranos in the Royal Academy Opera], *Handel* or *Bononcini*, there's the Question'. Not only does the opera rouse emotions that used to be more properly devoted to critical national issues, but it probably exists to subvert the twin establishment pillars of Church and state. The author guys the laborious putting of two and two together by self-appointed public watchdogs, perhaps with a glance at Walpole's zealous espionage networks:

I cannot but think there is more in this Matter than People are aware of; who knows but they [opera singers] are sent here to raise Dissensions among true Protestants! There are too many shrewd Causes of Suspicion.
1. They come from *Rome*;
2. The Pope lives at *Rome*;
3. So does the Pretender.
4. The Pope is a notorious Papist;

5. So is the Pretender;
6. So is Madam *Faustina*,
7. And so is Madam *Cuzzoni*.
8. King *George* (God bless him) is a Protestant;
9. The Papists hate the Protestants;
10. The Pope hates King *George*;
11. The Pretender can't abide him.
12. But Madam *Cuzzoni* and Madam *Faustina* love the Pope, and in all probability the Pretender.
Ergo,
****
****
From whence I infer, that it is not safe to have Popish singers tolerated here, in *England* . . .[10]

The suspicion that opera personnel, being Italian, might be spies for the Pope or the Pretender recurs in numerous more or less sardonic pieces. To take one example on the lighthearted side: in the *Craftsman* for 12 August 1732 Bolingbroke presents in great detail a ludicrous anecdote in which an overzealous Whig makes out that a newspaper advertisement by the husband of Strada, Handel's operatic soprano, is a coded message from the Pretender.[11] On the other hand *Do You Know What You Are About? Or, A Protestant Alarm to Great Britain; Proving our Late Theatric Squabble, a Type of the Present Contest for the Crown of Poland; and that the Division between Handel and Senesino has more in it than we Imagine. Also that the Latter is no Eunuch, but a Jesuit in Disguise; with other Particulars of the greatest Importance* (1733), a twenty-nine-page pamphlet bearing the epigraph 'God save his Church, our King, and Realm, / And send us Peace, and Trade, Amen', begins with an exhortation to the nobility and gentry that 'before they subscribe, or at least pay any of their Money to *H--d-l*, or *S--n----o*, they take especial care to be satisfied, that the Singers are true Protestants, and well affected to the present Government'.[12] Any that are not should be made to comply with the Act of Conformity (Anglican observance) and swear loyalty to the crown. In common with other attacks on Italian opera (see chapter 2) this pamphlet alleges that opera singers are actually singing the Mass, but adds the unusually inventive proof of a translation of 'V'adoro, pupille' (Cleopatra's seduction of the hero in Handel's *Giulio Cesare*) as a hymn to the Virgin and an elaborately fanciful description of the staging of the accompanying scene, in which a chorus of priests intones the Mass under cover of the orchestra. The author deplores the music of the operas ('Harmony perverted'), and the unedifying spectacle of Senesino and Handel 'playing at Dog and Bear, exactly like the Two Kings of *Poland*', but his real concern is that, as 'any one may see with half an Eye, Religion is more their Business than Musick'. Senesino is a disguised Jesuit sent by the Pope, the proof – most interestingly, for oratorio students – being his 'implacable hatred to *Handel*, for making him sing in the English Oratorio's, whereby he incurr'd the Pope's Displeasure'. Most foreign artists are likely to be spies, castrati especially so, and any rewards for their singing go straight into 'the Building and Support of Mass Houses and Monasteries abroad'. Everyone connected with Italian music is suspect, even the concert-giving amateur Thomas Britton.[13] In these publications music is no longer only a metaphor for politics, it is a part of a major political issue, fear of foreign Catholic powers.

The *Craftsman*, being given to 'the allegorical way of writing', affords particularly numerous instances of music as political metaphor, but did not monopolise the analogy, which was widespread, repeatedly used, and apt. John Dennis enumerated the divisions inflicted by politics: Whig/Tory, Whig/Whig, Tory/Tory, father/son, husband/wife, and, among the clergy, both Whig/Tory and, among the Tory clergy, Juror/Nonjuror: 'the People of *Great Britain* were never so divided as they are at present'.[14] Like political life, English musical life was riven with conflicts: between the opera and the playhouse, between Italian opera companies, between Handel and his singers, between the English and the Italian opera, between the leading opera singers and their supporters, and between the supporters of Bononcini and of Handel (divisions instanced in several of the publications linking music and the state). Lord Lyttelton, the Prince of Wales' secretary and leader of his circle of Patriot opposition writers in the late 1730s, makes the analogy the opening gambit of his critical account of English manners in the *Persian Letters*. The innocent Persian visitor overhears a member of the opera audience dismiss the music and singing as detestable:

You must not mind him, said my Friend, he is of the *other Party*, and comes here only as *a Spy*.

How, said I, have you Parties in Musick? Yes, reply'd he, it is a Rule with us to judge of nothing by our Senses or Understanding, but to hear, and see, and think, only as we chance to be differently engaged.

I hope, said I, that a Stranger may be neutral in these Divisions.[15]

Lyttelton neatly combines a tilt at the inferred mindlessness of the sort of people who go to the Italian opera with a reference to the senseless disputes within musical life, a pun on 'Divisions' (melismas) and, most seriously, a protest against the damage done to political life through irrational adherence to factions (the fragmented nature of the opposition was its greatest problem, and the abolition of opposing parties was one of its most fervently expressed aims).

In responding to such connections of music and politics, modern commentators have concentrated on the link between the critique of Italian opera and contemporary English nationalism. For students of oratorio and of political history there are other points of interest. Such sophisticated treatments as Lyttelton's, such detailed treatments as the *Craftsman*'s, suggest ways in which some members at least of the audience of a musical theatre event such as oratorio came ready tuned to the reception of political messages, and confirm that for them, in a way that is unfamiliar to us, serious as well as satirical music drama readily suggested political connotations, notably the political management of the country. Furthermore, in the most elaborate instance of the parallel that has come down to us, at a time of national turmoil and governmental crisis Handel was made to stand for the prime minister. The identification must have affected not only the composer himself but the perceptions of his audience. And the composition on which the identification was based was an oratorio; from very early in its history, irrespective of the intention of librettist or composer, or the perception of the audience at the actual performance, Handelian oratorio was brought into the arena of political debate.[16] In the same year, in *Do You Know What You Are About?*, Handel's *English* oratorios were taken to be capable of standing for, and indeed as consciously being, defiantly national expressions of British identity (see above). Nor was the *Craftsman* unique in comparing Handel and a leading politician. In a letter of 1735, Lord Hervey compares Handel's career with that of Walpole's chief opponent, Lord Bolingbroke: as Bolingbroke tried for power in both courts (Stuart and Hanoverian), shone and then failed, so Handel in the two theatres.[17] That so political an animal as Hervey, at the centre of court life, should think of Handel in these terms is an indication both of Handel's perceived stature in the musical world as extraordinary, and of the naturalness of the musical trope for the politically minded.

Representing the divided state with the figure of musical divisions is an inversion of the time-honoured emblem of harmonious music representing the harmonious state. Hervey's connection of Handel to contemporary politics suggests that the composer had so powerful an effect as to destabilise the context in which he operated. A different, more positive – indeed idealising – connection between Handel and national politics had been made in print only a month before the *Deborah* débacle, when his friend Aaron Hill appealed to him (in the pages of William Webster's *Weekly Miscellany* and the *Gentleman's Magazine*) to resolve the nation's discords with his harmonies:

> Teach us, undying Charmer, to compose
> Our inbred Storms, and 'scape impending Woes ...
> And, since thy Notes, can ne'er, in vain implore!
> Bid 'em becalm unresting Faction o'er;
> Inspire Content, and Peace, in each proud Breast,
> Bid th'unwilling Land be blest ...[18]

Here is a suggestion, in an ode commemorating a religious event, that through his spiritual compositions Handel could achieve for the country what all its political managers had failed to bring about: contentment, tranquillity, success and, above all, unity. Again, the idea was not idiosyncratic: other admirers of Handel's music had voiced it during the previous ten years. Daniel Prat's *Ode to Mr Handel, on his Playing the Organ* (1722) claimed as much in its concluding section. When Handel plays,

> See! Discord of her Rage disarm'd,
> Relenting, calm, and bland as Peace;
> Ev'n restless noisy Faction charm'd ...[19]

Listening to the 'Proportions low and high' of Handel's 'wond'rous fugue' prompts in Prat the idea that the traditional power of music to cure disorders of the mind should be brought to bear on the subversive and treasonous elements in British life, to whom Handel's harmonies will restore the light of reason:

> Oh then that they whose Rage and Hate
> A Brood of deadly Mischiefs nurse,
> Who secret All our Ills create,
> And then their own dire Off-spring curse,
>   That All in one Assembly join'd,
> Cou'd hear thy healing soothing Strain!
> Soon shou'dst thou calm their troubled Mind,
> And Reason shou'd her Seat regain.

Handel's music will then be no less than the catalyst of national unity, as the author proclaims in his concluding couplet. The same idea is stated in an anonymous *Epistle to Mr Handel, upon his Operas of Flavius and Julius Caesar* (1724):

> What Pow'r on Earth, but Harmony like Thine,
> Cou'd *Britain*'s jarring Sons e'er hope to join?[20]

Music uses divisions, the musical world is a mass of divisions, but through his music Handel can heal the nation of its disabling political divisions. The idea that great political leaders – especially of the heroic past – could resolve state discords, as great composers resolved aural clashes into an ordered whole, was commonplace. Pope conceded that it might still be possible for an exceptional 'Poet or Patriot' to restore natural unison,

> 'Till jarring int'rests, of themselves create
> Th'according music of a well-mix'd State.[21]

But the idea that a man of the present day, and not a philosopher or statesman but a composer, could actually make the state harmonious is very striking indeed, and, if it is as unfanciful as the other uses of the music/politics connection, extraordinary testimony to Handel's public significance. Did contemporaries really think he could influence political activity through his music, and to the extent of achieving the goals of the Patriot King? If so, deliberate political allusions in the librettos might – unlikely as it seems – be not just judgemental and intended to affect attitudes, but prescriptive and intended to prompt action. I do not intend to press this possibility in discussing the librettos in the rest of this book, but it should be borne in mind in any detailed examination of an oratorio.

LITERARY POLITICAL ALLUSION

The *Craftsman*'s use of satirical allegory to convey a serious polemical message should not in itself surprise us. The mode was habitual to eighteenth-century writers and readers, as their major literary works attest – to instance only some of the best known, *Gulliver's Travels*, *The Dunciad* and *Rasselas*. These and other works of the time employing allegory are parables, intended to *instruct*; but their allegories are often opaque or equivocal, capable of double (if not multiple) meanings in addition to the literal one. *Mist's Weekly Journal*

observed that 'Things seem to appear more lively to the Understanding, and to make a stronger Impression upon the Mind, when
they are insinuated under the Cover of some Symbol or Allegory,
especially where the Moral is good, and the Application obvious and
easy',[22] a precept which opposition journalists of the period evidently lived by. But the application did not have to be 'obvious and
easy'; often symbols were used flexibly and read variously.[23] As
discussed in Part I of this book, audiences of Handel's time were
highly skilled in the art of interpreting allegory in all forms of art
and letters. His friend Aaron Hill, in pointing out (in *The Progress of
Wit: A Caveat*) allegory's anarchic capacity to deliver different
meanings to different readers, not only anticipates deconstruction-
ism but revels in displaying the workings of the very techniques and
responses he purports to deplore.[24] To understand allegory in the
oratorios we need to be aware of the varieties of allegory with which
eighteenth-century theatre audiences were familiar.

In discussing political drama of the 1730s Robert Hume distinguishes between 'topical allusion' plays, mainly comedies, referring
openly to current events, and 'application' plays, mainly tragedies,
inviting the audience to draw parallels between the historical or
legendary events of the drama and contemporary affairs.[25] By these
lights, the *Craftsman*'s piece about Handel is topical allusion, as was
most ballad opera, whereas semi-opera, resembling much Patriot
writing in taking its material largely from national history and
myth, favours application.

Characters in works for the serious spoken and musical theatre
can allude to actual people, or abstractions. Henry in Addison's
Rosamond represents the Duke of Marlborough; Emmeline in
Dryden's and Purcell's *King Arthur* is best understood as Britain.
Sometimes both modes co-exist in the same work. A favourite theme
of Jacobite literature represents the Pretender contesting William
III or a Hanoverian king for possession of a heroine who is to be
understood as Britain. The 'message' can be simple and single; for
example (to stay in the realm of music theatre), in Dryden's *Albion
and Albanius* Albion stands for Charles II, Albanius for James Duke
of York, and the message is celebration of the security of the throne
and the legitimate succession. Or the allegory can be double, even
contradictory, allowing the author to adopt an air of injured innocence if challenged on the more provocative reading: *King Arthur* can
be understood as ostensibly welcoming, or obliquely deploring, the

Glorious Revolution, while *Rosamond* can be taken to congratulate or denigrate Marlborough.[26] Thus an author can address his elite fellow thinkers with a minority view on which they agree, while dispensing (in elite eyes hollow, but) generally accepted views to the unwitting mass, adding the pleasure of privately shared understanding to the satisfaction of decoding.

The identities of the characters as understood by the audience can vary according to the interpretation a member of the audience chooses to recognise. As Price writes of Handel's *Rinaldo*, 'Depending on one's loyalties or one's degree of cynicism, or both, Goffredo could represent either the Old Pretender or the Elector of Hanover. Jacobites could sympathise with the repossession of the Holy City, while would-be Hanoverians could reflect on a righteous usurpation.' One may not agree with Price's deduction that 'Hill and perhaps Handel were keeping their options open' but his observation that the ambivalence of the implications is a defining characteristic of the English semi-opera tradition provides a valuable guideline for readers of oratorio librettos.[27] Conveying and understanding dual allegory did not require great ability in the writer or great acumen in the audience.[28] But frequently the (or one) intended message was clearly stated in a prologue (as in Henry Brooke's *Gustavus Vasa*) or epilogue (as in Granville's revised *British Enchanters*) or final tableau (as in *Merlin*, Giffard's pro-Hanoverian version of Dryden's *King Arthur*, and in Thomson's and Mallet's *Alfred*).[29]

Audiences felt free to make interpretations which the writer may not have intended. This was obviously likely to be the case when the work dated from long ago, for example a history play by Shakespeare, but was also possible with more recent works. A famous instance was Addison's *Cato*, which both Whigs and Tories claimed to be promulgating their cause when it was first performed in 1713, and which both supporters and opponents of the administration likewise claimed when it was put on in 1737 as a Patriot play in the presence of the Prince of Wales.[30] An old text could be revised to give it a new meaning for the new times, as Hill did for Shakespeare's *Henry V* (see chapter 14). Not that the story had to be altered for the audience's interpretation(s) to change, which was likely to happen in accordance with the altered circumstances of different times. This common fact of theatrical life is familiar from twentieth-century political interpretations of Handel's oratorios. In Germany in the late 1920s the hero of *Judas Macchabæus* became an exemplar of Teutonic military superiority, while in England in 1938 Alan Bush and Randall Swingler staged *Belshazzar* (with some textual adjustment) as a protest 'against the iniquities of rampant imperialism'.[31] Eighteenth-century audiences were also ready to accept a message superseded by events subsequent to the time of composition. *Judas Macchabæus* celebrated Cumberland as the recent victor over rebel troops at home but was first performed on 1 April 1747, by which time he was back on the continent as commander of forces abroad, fighting foreign troops and doing rather badly. They were also willing to accept allegories based on very inexact correspondences; for example, in *Judas Macchabæus* the English *quelling* an insurrection are represented by the Israelites *instituting* an insurrection. The situation being commented on could be past history, the intention being to set the record straight (for example about the Glorious Revolution), with implications for the present state of affairs. It is a feature of patriotic poetry, plays and semi-operas that though their material is often a mythical version of national history they look to the future in their allegorical application, imagining an end to present fear and oppression in reconciliation, unity, revival, trade and empire acquired without strife and peace gained with honour.[32] In reading the librettos we should always remember that flexibility and multiplicity are the hallmarks of literary interpretation in the oratorio era.

BRITISH ISRAEL

On 18 April 1739 the *London Daily Post* carried a letter about the previous evening's performance of *Israel in Egypt*. The first part of this oratorio is 'The Israelites' Lamentation for the Death of Joseph', their threnody for their national leader; the second part describes the plagues which God, in response to their prayers, visits on the Egyptians who are cruelly oppressing them; and the third part celebrates their salvation, brought about by divine annihilation of the Egyptian forces in the Red Sea. The author of the letter, 'R. W.', congratulates the audience on its cultivated appreciation of this work, hoping that on other similar occasions 'numerous and splendid Assemblies shall enter into the true Spirit of such an Entertainment, "Praising their Creator, for the Care he takes of the Righteous" (see Oratorio [that is, the libretto], p. 6)'. He then pregnantly remarks: 'Did such a Taste prevail universally in a

People, that People might expect on a like Occasion, if such Occasion should ever happen to them, the same *Deliverance* as those Praises celebrate; and Protestant, free, virtuous, united, Christian England need little fear, at any time hereafter, the whole Force of slavish, bigotted, united unChristian popery, risen up against her, should such a Conjuncture ever hereafter happen.'[33]

When this letter first appeared the country was in the grip of war fever. The popular prints, the opposition journals and petitions to Parliament demanding tough action against Spain were full of representations and accounts of English sailors 'enslaved' by the Spanish who had captured them: compare the oratorio's account of the Israelites enslaved by the Egyptians. The demand was for a naval war, in the confidence of a rapidly successful outcome because of Britain's supposed control of the sea: compare the engulfing of the Egyptians' land forces in the divinely controlled Red Sea during Part III of the oratorio, framed by the words: 'The horse and his rider has he thrown into the sea'.

R. W.'s jingoistic contrasts of united Christian Britain and menacing Papist forces and his heavy disingenuous irony about 'should such a conjuncture ever hereafter happen' present *Israel in Egypt* to *Daily Post* readers as war propaganda. A year later, the war being now an unpleasant reality, his letter was reprinted, reputedly by popular request, to coincide with the revival of the oratorio on 1 April; its political message for the current times was pointed out in an introduction.[34] R. W.'s analogy of the oratorio Israelites and the modern audience was, apparently, readily understood, and this should not surprise us; not only did it draw on the language and ideas of current polemic on the same topic, but it belonged to a tradition of English writing at least two centuries old and still going strong.

The analogy of the biblical Israelite to the present-day Briton, which is commonplace in sixteenth- and seventeenth-century religious and political writing, continued to flourish in the eighteenth century.[35] It is present in poetry, fiction and drama; in the liturgy, in biblical paraphrases, in sermons and tracts; and even in political theory. Its continuing importance has been recognised by Linda Colley, but her conclusion that to detail its occurrences 'would be superfluous as well as wearisome' cannot apply to a discussion of one of its major vehicles, and certainly the longest lasting, Handelian oratorio.[36] Because its occurrences have been little noticed and because the librettos are a prime example, the major part of this chapter explores its varied and lively implementation.

The analogy of ancient Israel to modern Britain was not confined to pulpit oratory and theological tracts. Its use in major monuments of seventeenth-century secular literature, such as Dryden's *Absolom and Achitophel* and Milton's *Samson Agonistes* (the basis for Newburgh Hamilton's libretto for Handel's *Samson*), was readily accepted in the eighteenth century. Indeed, during the oratorio decades *Samson Agonistes* was read principally as a political tract for its times, for example by John Upton, prebendary of Rochester:

Sampson imprison'd and blind, and the captive state of Israel, lively represents our blind poet with the republican party after the restoration, afflicted and persecuted ... How would it have rejoiced the heart of the blind seer, had he lived to have seen, with his mind's eye, the accomplishment of his prophetic predictions? when a deliverer [William III] came and rescued us from the Philistine oppressors.[37]

The analogy also obtained during the sixteenth and seventeenth centuries in a genre close to oratorio, biblical drama. According to Murray Roston, in Bale's *King John*, English kings mirror the actions of Moses and Joshua in leading their people from bondage into a land of milk and honey; the anonymous *Godly Queene Hester* can be read as attacking Wolsey under the figure of Haman; Udall's *Ezechias* compares Hezekiah and Henry VIII; and Greene's and Lodge's *A Looking Glasse for London and England* compares the vices of London with the ungodliness of Nineveh – all applications which have resonances in the oratorios.[38] The analogy is also assimilated in eighteenth-century patriotic verse and drama. In Ambrose Philips' tragedy *The Briton* (1722) the ancient Britons (like the ancient Israelites of the oratorios) are resisting foreign aggression, in this case the Roman invasion. The patriot Prince Varnoc describes his island home as 'set apart, / Seated amidst the Waves': clearly 'indulgent Nature' meant the Britons to be 'A chosen People, a distinguish'd Race' (Act I scene 7).

The analogy was central to the literature of religion. It was enshrined in the liturgy which Anglicans heard (or sang) every day. The responses at Evening Prayer in the 1662 Prayer Book equate the Israelite chosen people with the people of present-day Britain in what amounts to a blueprint for the plots of several of the simpler oratorios:

O Lord, save the King. And mercifully hear us when we call upon thee. Endue thy ministers with righteousness. And make thy chosen people joyful. O Lord, save thy people. And bless thine inheritance. Give peace in our time, O Lord. Because there is none other that fighteth for us, but only thou, O God.

The analogy likewise permeated biblical paraphrases of the time (and many Israelite librettos, we recall, are a form of biblical paraphrase). It was probably most familiar from Isaac Watts' Christianised versions of the Psalms for congregational singing, in which, to make the texts more meaningful for latter-day worshippers and to make their songs to God more expressive of their own feelings and experiences, Watts frequently substituted Britain for Israel:

> O *Britain*, trust the Lord: Thy foes in vain
> Attempt thy ruin, and oppose his reign;
> Had they prevail'd, darkness had clos'd our days,
> And death and silence had forbid his praise:
> But we are sav'd, and live: Let songs arise,
> And *Britain* bless the God that built the skies.

The points of connection are the same as in many of the sermons and many of the Israelite oratorios – God's salvation of His chosen people from threatened extinction and their grateful worship of Him. Of all the books of the Bible the Psalms provide the fullest and most frequent expressions of these themes, and hence also their use as the basis of many oratorio choruses. Watts' title in this particular instance makes explicit the normal analogical reading. Britain's foes are specifically the Roman Catholic nations and the reign they oppose comprehends the English monarchy's as well as God's: 'Psalm CXV ... Popish idolatry reproved. A psalm for the 5th of November.'[39] Watts allowed himself still more specific religious-political application when he was making hymns out of pagan poetry, as in his version of the last lines of Horace's *Odes* III.29:

> Let *Spain's* proud traders, when the mast
> Bends groning to the stormy blast,
> Run to their beads with wretched plaints,
> And vow and bargain with their saints ...[40]

Other paraphrasers of the Psalms were even more liberal in their application of the same analogy. In Thomas Brereton's *Protestant*

Version of the Second Psalm (1716, twenty-seven six-line stanzas), the raging heathens are the Catholic promoters of the 1715 Rebellion, the bands they propose to sunder are those of the Hanoverian Succession, and God's son, who will break his domestic foes 'like Potter's Ware', to whom Louis XIV will submit, and by whom 'the Papist's Reign' will be curtailed, is George I. (This Brereton was the same as the loyal subject whose translation of Racine's *Esther* was an intermediary source for the libretto set by Handel; Psalm II was used in both *Messiah* and the *Occasional Oratorio*, in the Prayer Book translation in the former and (mainly) in Milton's in the latter.)[41]

The pervasiveness of the analogy in religious literature is un-surprising, given the centrality of the typological tradition to English interpretation of the Old Testament. Biblical typology (the practice, dating from apostolic times, of arguing for the coherence of the Old and New Testaments and for the latter's authority, by identifying Old Testament persons and events as types, or fore-shadowings, of persons and events in the New) provided a precedent for the paralleling, within a theological framework, of two sets of circumstances separated by time, whereby one enhanced the value of the other. Typological reading of the Scriptures was still a commonplace of theological exposition in the oratorio period. Para-doxically, typology in the strict sense gained an extended lease of life from attempts by rationalist critics of the Scriptures to discredit it. As described in chapter 6, deists attacked the claims for Christ's divinity by attacking the dependence of the New Testament's auth-ority on the prophecies of the Old Testament. The Church's response, asserting that the Old Testament prophecies were indeed literally meant of Christ and were literally fulfilled by him, included a reaffirmation of the identity of many Old Testament figures as foreshadowings of Christ; and notable among these were the ora-torio figures Joseph, Moses, Joshua, Samson, David, Daniel and even Susanna.[42] For example, in the year before the composition of Handel's *Joseph and his Brethren*, the fourth edition appeared of a much-read translation of Charles Rollin's educational guide, *The Method of Teaching and Studying the Belles Lettres*; in its twenty-page account (with commentary) of Joseph's story, two pages are filled with a double-column list of twenty 'Particulars of agreement between Jesus Christ and Joseph', such as:

Joseph	Christ
He is sent by his father to his brethren at a distance	He is sent by God his Father to the lost sheep of the house of Israel
His brethren conspire against his life	He is delivered up to the Romans by the Jews
Placed between two criminals, he foretels the advancement of one, and the approaching death of the other	Placed between two thieves, he foretels the one, that he should go into paradise, and lets the other die impenitent
He lies three years in prison	He lies three days in the grave
He was called the Saviour of the world	His name of JESUS signifies a Saviour, and is indeed the only one by whom we can be saved
Joseph's brethren come to him, own him, fall down before him, and are fixed in Egypt	The Jews will one day return to Jesus Christ, own him, worship him, and enter into the church

To which Rollin adds:

In all these applications, and I could add several others, is there anything forced or constrained? Could pure chance have possibly thrown together so many resembling circumstances, so different, and at the same time so natural? 'Tis plain, that an intelligent hand did purposely contrive and apply all these colours to make a perfect picture, and that the design of God in joining together so many singular circumstances in the life of Joseph, was to describe the principal lines, in that of his son.[43]

Rollin's was only one of several educational works to give a typological reading of Joseph's story.[44]

The mid-eighteenth-century audience had been taught to regard the scriptural protagonists whom oratorios portrayed not just as figures from the semi-mythological history of a remote race and culture but, in a tradition dating from early Christian times, as reminders of their own redeemer, connected with their own individual lives. As the Bishop of Exeter instructed them: 'we are not to read the *Old Testament* as a bare relation of matters of fact, of the exploits of *Moses* and *Joshua*, and of the Kings of *Israel* and *Judah*; things at a great distance, and not concerning ourselves: but as a faithful repository of *future* truths'.[45] The Dissenting tradition, coupling desire for a sense of individual salvation with enthusiasm for personal interpretation of Scripture, contributed to this symbolical version of typology, whereby scriptural events become allegories of the progress of the soul (and fictional narratives are composed as such, for example *The Pilgrim's Progress* and *Robinson Crusoe*[46]). To take traditional instances which also form part of the oratorio plots: the Israelites' deliverance from Egypt prefigures our deliverance from the bondage of sin, while their transit of the River Jordan (*Joshua*) prefigures our baptism and, as in Watts' hymn 'A Prospect of Heav'n Makes Death Easy', our passage to eternal life:

> Sweet Fields beyond the swelling Flood
> Stand drest in living Green:
> So to the *Jews* Old *Canaan* stood,
> While *Jordan* roll'd between.[47]

In fact the whole history of the Old Testament chosen people was intended by God as 'the type and figure of what was afterwards to happen to the church'.[48]

A large part of the huge debate on 'evidence' for the 'truth' of Christianity focused on allegorical interpretation of Scripture, and had political implications, in that dual literal and allegorical reading of the prophecies (Patristic in origin) was favoured by the conservative elements in the Church of England.[49] How intently the focus was trained on the typological question can be gauged from a single example, the table in Daniel Waterland's *Scripture Vindicated* (1731–2) which distinguishes twenty-two sub-sub-varieties of 'figurative' and 'mystical' (as opposed to 'literal') interpretations of Scripture.[50] At the same time, under the pressure of rationalist readings of the Bible, typology had broadened to include analogical interpretation, a search for correspondence of traits (as in the case of Watts' hymn cited above) rather than an assertion of direct prophecy of New Testament events in the Old Testament.[51] Making a connection with eighteenth-century literature's penchant for character *types*, Thomas Preston observes that 'the hermeneutic practice of exemplary reading, reinforced by the redefinition of type by the Christian apologists, transformed the Bible and its received interpretation into a repertoire of timeless patterns applicable to past and present human situations' – for example, we might add, the situation of the oppressed nation struggling for liberty, both in *Israel in Egypt* and in the Spanish War pamphlets, according to the pattern to be found in the Book of Exodus.[52]

As has already been stressed, any consideration of received thought in Handel's England needs to take account of the sermon literature, and students of oratorio librettos cannot fail to notice both that the preachers habitually identify modern Britain with ancient Israel and that they make recurrent specific parallels which bear on the subjects of the librettos. The following comparisons are commonplace:

The Stuart family	Saul and his descendants
George II	David or Solomon
The Glorious Revolution and Hanoverian succession	The crown of Israel passing from Saul and his family to David and his family
Catholic Europe	The Philistines
The threat of Popery	'Egyptian bondage' or heathen rites
Irreligion	Israelite idolatry
Licentiousness	Israelite neglect of God's laws

All the figures and circumstances in the right-hand column are subjects of one or more of the Israelite librettos.

The preachers acknowledge that God is God of all the world, but they rejoice that 'our Israel', as Britain is repeatedly called, is especially favoured. As Thomas Amory notes in his Fast sermon at Taunton during the 1745 Rebellion, unconsciously delineating the groundplot of the Israelite oratorio, 'We can, like the Jews, reckon up many remarkable deliverances, and discoveries of the kind interposition of heaven'. Naturally the parallel was especially invoked on national occasions, such as coronations, royal anniversaries (for example, accession day), victories, and fasts to solicit divine aid in times of emergency. As might be expected from the specific analogies I have instanced, the lessons extrapolated are frequently those of the oratorios (described more fully in later chapters).[53] Two of the surviving sermons for 9 January 1739/40 (a Fast day for the Spanish War) which use the analogy are actually by oratorio librettists, James Miller and Thomas Morell. Morell subscribes to the view that the 'Jewish Constitution' is a type of the Christian Church and comments: 'there are some Instances in which our present condition so nearly resembles the ancient State of Israel, that I doubt not, but while I was reciting the foregoing passages from the History of that Nation, your Minds were fixed at home'.[54]

The librettos correspond especially closely with Fast and Thanksgiving sermons, which put a spiritual yardstick on the nation's political condition. The parallels are remarkably numerous. The sermons comment on military setbacks and failures, and celebrate victories. They posit a moral world order in which divine intervention punishes human failings, interpreting 'acts of God' as warnings to the nation (comparable to those visited on the Israelites) to eradicate blasphemy, pride, luxury and greed. They assume that Britain is (like ancient Israel) under God's particular care, receiving His miraculous assistance, so long as it honours its Covenant with Him by worshipping Him and obeying His commandments. They express apprehension about the nation's ultimate political stability. They warn against internal schism and faction. They urge moral and religious reform, without which God will cast off Britain (as He cast off the Israelites). They give encouragement and endorsement to foreign wars, especially against Catholic nations, while continuing to warn that the nation's sinfulness may prevent success. They attribute lack of success in war to continued vice rather than military incompetence or an unjust cause. They regard a successful outcome to war as depending entirely on God's aid, which must be implored, and they interpret such success as ratification of God's special relationship with Britain, a signal aspect of which is His bestowal on it of the best Constitution in the world.[55] The librettos correspond point for point.

Belief in divine intervention in human affairs underpins this world view. It was widely held, and united the simplest churchgoer with the most intellectually free-ranging authors. In the latter category, Alexander Pope writes to Francis Atterbury, in connection with the South Sea Bubble, that England's proud avarice has brought down a dramatic rebuke from God (a common interpretation of this financial disaster); George (later Bishop) Berkeley, in *An Essay towards preventing the Ruin of Great Britain*, argues that God has visited punishment on England to make it repent of its corrupt social and economic practices.[56] The religious frame of reference was not confined to preachers and moralists. Christian belief still informed, indeed formed, political life and thought. The librettos' basis in an assumption that God responds to and intervenes in men's affairs would have seemed normal to a far larger proportion of the original audience than of most modern ones. (Most, not all: one in five Americans reportedly believed that the Mississippi floods of 1993 were God's punishment of an ungodly nation.[57]) As Frank McLynn states, mid-eighteenth-century society was still 'a context where it was assumed that all political forms and all political authority came from God'.[58] Hence the rhetoric of divine responsiveness to individual and national human behaviour was freely invoked even by politicians, especially opposition politicians. Sir William Wynd-ham's peroration in the debate on the Convention of El Pardo in 1739 contained a prayer which makes the same assumptions of divine partisanship as the oratorios: 'May . . . that power, which has so often, and so visibly, interposed in behalf of the rights and liberties of this nation, continue its care over us at this worst and most dangerous juncture; whilst the insolence of enemies without, and the influence of corruption within, threaten the ruin of her constitution.' Lord Carteret, addressing the House of Lords on the European situation in 1741, like the librettists and their sources sees the nation thwarting the special favour extended to it by God: 'my Lords, we neglected the best opportunity that could have offered, for establishing the system of affairs in Europe, upon that footing which is the most happy for this nation: but providence atoned for this neglect, and would have done it for us, if we had not . . . counter-acted this new interposition of providence'.[59] Neglect of political self-interest is seen as wilful neglect of the terms on which God provides for His nation. Conversely, material success is still attributed to divine favour, and not only in official church celebra-tions. In his report of the recent narrowly successful attack on San Luis during the Caribbean campaign, Admiral Vernon, like the authors of Thanksgiving sermons and like the librettists, draws on the Psalms to express his relief: 'one can't but say with the Psalmist, it is the Lord's doing, and seems marvellous to our Eyes'.[60] When the government seemed likely to give up the war's most popular gain, Louisbourg (Cape Breton), during the peace negotiations of 1748, the *Gentleman's Magazine* ran two lengthy accounts of a sermon on the same text preached at Boston, which demonstrated from the individual occurrences of the assault that 'the taking *Cape Breton* has all the marks of being eminently the work of God' – a view which the author of the articles fully supports, as the most powerful argument that can be mustered for retaining the prize.[61] The earthquakes in London and Westminster in 1750 (and a prediction of more to come) elicited a spate of pamphlets making the same inference of divine interventionism as the Fast sermons, enumerating the crimes which Britain was being warned to eradicate and, again, pointing the lesson with the Israelite parallel:

What is there that should skreen Us from the divine Wrath, or give us a Title to the privilege of Exemption? Shall we plead for ourselves, in the Style of the *Jews* of old; *The Temple of the Lord, The Temple of the Lord*; The

Protestant Religion, The *Protestant Religion*? ... where are the *Noahs*, the *Daniels*, and the *Jobs*, God's eminent Saints and Servants, the Choice Favourites of Heaven, who should turn away God's Fury from such a Land and People?[62]

Modern commentators on eighteenth-century biblical critics stress that in moralising the Scriptures they rationalised them, but the librettists do not wholly rationalise God, nor did contemporary preachers, nor did the majority of the British population. For them He was a consistent parent, not an objective watchmaker. For some, belief in divine interventionism was still sustained by the belief that the saving of the righteous and the destruction of the wicked was imminent. The millennium continued to be expected, though actual predictions and specific timetables were issued mainly by Dissenters and others outside the Anglican Church, those within it being very cautious about dates (Newton's work on Daniel's apocalyptic prophecy, mentioned in chapter 6, is symptomatic).[63] But even to think it possible that the world as we know it *may* end in our own lifetime can have considerable influence on political as well as religious thought.

God could intervene in the life of the British nation as He had done in the life of the Israelites. The analogy was routine. Its application was not necessarily straightforward. As Patrick Collinson points out, it raised questions of definition: who exactly was the modern chosen nation? Who were its enemies? Who would feel God's wrath?[64] By the mid eighteenth century there was enough religious unity for Israel to represent the entire Protestant nation, Anglican and Dissenter alike, if a preacher so chose, and there is nothing in the librettos to prevent a similarly comprehensive interpretation, though equally any sectarian listeners could choose to identify the oratorio Israelites exclusively with their own sect. Preachers and librettists alike assume, on the evidence of 'natural' disasters, that until the apocalypse itself the innocent will be engulfed with the guilty if and when divine patience is tried too far. For the less fundamentalist believer this was an unpalatable proposition. As chapter 6 described, the oratorio period was one of animated debate about God's sense of justice as demonstrated in the Old Testament record of His dealings with His chosen people and their neighbours. (The reflection of this debate in the librettos is discussed in later chapters.)

The analogy raised questions for theologians and Christian

humanists, but for moral-political polemicists it had the benefit of kaleidoscopic mutability. Sheep and goats could be variously identified according to circumstances. The heathen was the foreign aggressor in time of war, or the rebels in 1745, or freethinkers, or depraved members of the community enticing others to vice. Likewise there was no cut-and-dried application to individuals. Depending on one's point of view (just as with literary allegory), in the Exodus story Moses stood for William III and Pharaoh for James II, or Moses stood for James III and Pharaoh for George I; to Hanoverians David could represent the Protestant succession, while Jacobites saw in his experience of defeat and hiding from Absalom a symbol of Charles II. As recent writers have pointed out for the literary-political sphere, the symbols were themselves part of the contested political terrain, being claimed, counter-claimed and reclaimed through the use made of them. To identify a British ruler with an Old Testament leader, especially a royal one, was in itself a polemical statement. Even more than in political allusion in the theatre, because of the stature, familiarity and long history of the symbols, the choice of the symbol was itself a focus of interest. Like typology, this gave Old Testament figures life outside their scriptural context. Identification with the Israelites has of course proved an enduring political metaphor in Bible-centred cultures, especially in times of repression, exile and release. More recent uses may help us to sense the force it could have had for the original audiences of *Israel*, *Joshua* and *Belshazzar*: in Negro spiritual, in spirituals in Tippett's *A Child of our Time* ('Go down Moses'), in Joe Slovo's comment in 1990, 'We've been in the wilderness and we don't see the promised land yet',[65] and in the explanation of his prayers by the Rev. Alfred Dlamini on the occasion of his people's return from township to patrimony in 1993: 'the Almighty had a hand in the return of my people ... I was saying to the people that we were like the Israelites who were removed to Babylon and only after many years returned to Jerusalem. I prayed for ... intercession for the people coming to build their houses.'[66]

A surprisingly extensive use of the Israel–Britain analogy occurs in the field of political theory. Ancient Israel being a theocracy, we would hardly expect to find it seriously used as an exemplar for the government of the modern British state beyond the time of the Protectorate. But we have already encountered it being deployed as such, without any sense that it might be considered odd, by Aaron

Hill in his epic, *Gideon* (chapter 5). While the habitual reference point is ancient Rome, the comparison with ancient Israel is quite common, and is invoked with a degree of detail and at a length that now seem astonishing in the works of two writers in particular, James Harrington and Moses Lowman, of whom the former is now famous among historians as a progenitor of opposition Whig ideology.[67]

Harrington's political writings – *The Commonwealth of Oceana* (that is, a model Britain) and works defending and amplifying its arguments – date from the period 1656–60, but they were reprinted several times during the first half of the eighteenth century: the major works in Toland's edition (1700, 1737, 1738), and virtually the whole canon in Birch's (1737, 1747). The index to Pocock's edition (1977) shows how thoroughly Harrington drew on Old Testament exemplars: there are 185 entries under 'Old Testament', 19 for Joshua, 50 for Moses, 65 for Israel (more than for Athens or Greece; Rome has 86). Harrington had an immediate precedent for his analogy in Hobbes' *Leviathan*, to which he was responding, but whereas Hobbes had used Israel as a model of monarchy, Harrington used it as a model of a republic.[68] However, both writers, having an anticlerical agenda, argued from the position that Israel was a civil (rather than a religious) society, thus secularising their source and hence keeping the political analogy viable for a later generation which took a more secular view of political principles than had its seventeenth-century predecessors.

The extent to which Harrington integrated his arguments for republican government with the Israelite analogy is suggested by the subtitles alone of some of his works, for example that of *The Prerogative of Popular Government* (a defence of *Oceana* against Matthew Wren's *Considerations* on it): 'A political discourse in two books . . . in which two books is contained the whole commonwealth of the Hebrews, or of Israel, senate, people and magistracy, both as it stood in the institution by Moses, and as it came to be formed after the captivity . . . '. His chapter headings can startle the modern reader into appreciation of the blatantly anachronistic and pragmatic nature of some of the readings of the Scriptures engineered by, and for the sake of, the analogy in this period: 'Whether the Ten Commandments, proposed by God or Moses, were voted by the people of Israel?'; 'Whether the temptations of advancing did sway more with the many in the commonwealth, than with the few under the monarchies of the Hebrews, that is, under the kings of Judah, Israel, or the high priests when they came to be princes?' In Harrington's case, some of his readings went too far for his contemporaries, and *Pian Piano*, from which the latter of these headings comes, is mainly concerned with justifying his interpretation of Scripture. But, we should note, it is his specific applications, rather than use of the analogy itself, that required defence, and the defence itself would have drawn contemporary readers' attention to the continuing potential of the analogy.

Moses Lowman (1680–1751), as his footnotes acknowledge, had absorbed Harrington's work, but his purposes in *A Dissertation on the Civil Government of the Hebrews. In which the True Designs, and Nature of their Government are explained* (1740, second edition 1745) are very different from Harrington's, and his use of the analogy, while at least as remarkable, is both more thoroughgoing and more straightforward. As his subtitle reveals, his main purpose is that of dozens of contemporary works, the defence of orthodox Christianity: 'The *Justice, Wisdom* and *Goodness* of the Mosaical Constitutions, are vindicated: in particular, from some late, unfair and false representations of them in the Moral Philosopher' (the deist Thomas Morgan). He counters the deists' attacks on the Old Testament dispensation with arguments designed to show that the *original* Israelite constitution, that established by Moses and Joshua, was not (as the deists claimed) obscure, absurd and inhumane, but wise, a bulwark against corruption and, moreover, an exemplary safeguard of liberty and landed property.[69]

In his opening pages Lowman confidently proclaims the aptness of the analogy: 'The *Hebrew* Commonwealth is, without question, one of the most ancient of the World, and justly looked upon as a Model of Government of divine Original; it will deserve our Attention, as much sure, as any of the Forms of Government in the ancient times'. As Christians we should pay it particular attention, since its foundation and laws derive from our own God, and we can expect it to provide 'a wise and excellent Model'. Like Harrington, he compares the Israelite constitution with that of other ancient civilisations and some other modern ones. But his focus is the parallel of ancient Israel with modern Britain: the Hebrew 'assembly' is a model of parliament, the Hebrew 'senate' of the Privy Council, the Hebrew judge of the modern king, the Hebrew oracular consultation of the parliamentary process, Hebrew idolatry of Popery.

Lowman welds the analogy in place by using modern British terms for the Israelite customs he is describing: 'here were the *Princes* and all the *Congregation*, which shews the Authority of the Commons of *Israel*, in a plain Instance of Matters judiciary, brought before the States-General of the united Tribes ... So that the *Commons* of *Israel*, as distinguish'd from the Princes and the Judge, will make one of the States then assembled in full Parliament'. The thoroughness of his parallclism may appear bizarre now, but there was nothing frivolous about (for example) his attempts to disprove Morgan's claims that the tithe system unfairly favoured the priesthood (see chapter 13).[70] In one passage he relinquishes his stance that the Mosaic consti-tution *would* make a good model for the British constitution to support the view, not uncommon (he cites Bacon as one of its exponents), that it really *was* the model, for the government of King Alfred (for Alfred as hero of Whig constitutionalism see chapter 12).[71]

Over and over again, in his discussion of Israelite political systems, Lowman describes parts of the Old Testament which also form the plots of Handel's oratorios, in terms which give us a precedent for reading eighteenth-century political meaning in the librettos. In this he is not unique: the same use of the identical material recurs in numerous sermons. But the modernity of his terminology is striking. For example, he argues for the legality of Solomon's kingship as

confirm'd by a Parliamentary Sanction ... The same Assembly, at the same Time that they anointed him, or appointed by their Resolution *Solomon* to be anointed unto the Lord to be Chief Governor, appointed *Zadok* to be Priest ... so that this Assembly confirmed as by Authority of Parliament, or as the Representatives of the People, two of the highest Acts of Government, the Settlement of the Crown, and of the High-Priesthood.[72]

This linguistic clinching of the analogy is especially striking in Lowman's discussion of a perennial bugbear, God's destruction of Saul in reprisal for his sparing of the Amalekite booty (1 Samuel XV), an easy target for deist objections to the moral tone of the Old Testament (see further chapter 13). Lowman invokes both the orthodox rebuttals, that Israel was under a permanent mandate from God to eradicate the Amalekites and that Saul had no business to question, let alone disobey, God's law; but in making the conventional analogy with James II's absolutism he produces a fascinating back-formation. Not only was Saul

assuming to himself a dispensing Power, but it was a direct Violation of the Original Laws of *Jehovah* ... Now to assume and exercise a Power of dispensing with and suspending of Laws, was justly understood by our Legislature, as a principal Evidence, that the Late King *James* II. did endeavour to subvert and extirpate the Laws and Liberties of the Kingdom.

'Laws' is footnoted 'Stat.I.William and Mary, Sess.ii.c.2'.[73] The application of the analogy in reverse, the modern half being used to ratify the ancient one, shows just how easily the eighteenth-century mind slipped between the Israelite exemplar and its modern parallels. (On *Solomon* and *Saul* see further chapter 13.)

Peculiar as Harrington's and Lowman's readiness to draw lessons in modern constitutional government from the Old Testament may seem to us, it would have seemed quite normal to their contemporaries, who prolifically, even obsessively, identified models (positive, negative or both) for their own society in most of the previous societies known to them, especially archaic ones. In his widely read and much reprinted essay 'Of Heroic Virtue' (1692), Sir William Temple even extended the frame of reference to include China, Peru and the Islamic world;[74] by comparison the Mosaic political dispensation, subject to exhaustive scrutiny in the oratorio period by deists seeking to discredit its status as forerunner of the New Dispensation and by apologists responding, and familiar from regular Bible reading, was actually one of the more obvious models available. As Manuel Schonhorn has shown, Defoe repeatedly turned to the record of Old Testament leaders for his model of ideal kingship.[75] The constitutional historian Samuel Squire cited Lowman extensively and respectfully to bolster his claims for the virtues of the Saxon original of the English constitution.[76] Harrington and Lowman were unusual only in the detail of their demonstration, not in their recourse to the model itself or their individual applications of it.[77]

Nor was the comparison of the modern nation with ancient Israel idiosyncratic to British thought, or even to Protestant thought, and Handel could have encountered it before he came to England. In Venice it figured in both painting and music. Giambattista Tiepolo's painting of the crossing of the Red Sea, *Farone sommerso*, caused a sensation when it was exhibited in August 1716 because, it has been convincingly suggested, besides accepting the subject as a type of baptism and redemption in a tradition begun in early Christian art, Venetians took this depiction of the just-in-time drowning of a pagan enemy through God's aid as a hopeful prediction concerning their own national emergency: Corfu was enduring a siege by the Turkish navy which lasted forty-two days.[78] Before news arrived that the Turks had been repulsed the analogy with Israel was spelt out in the libretto of Vivaldi's oratorio *Juditha Triumphans, Sacrum Militare Oratorium*, which parallels the story of Judith with the Venetians' recent victory over the Turks at Petrovaradin. The Venetians evidently had the same flexible attitude to allegory as their English contemporaries: Judith is Venice and her handmaid is Faith, while Holofernes is the Ottoman sultan, and his servant is the Turkish commander.[79]

ALLEGORICAL HISTORY

In their return to the past the librettos joined other major public utterances of their time, political, sermonic and poetical, in adopting a practice of previous generations – reading historical events analogically, as lessons for present and future behaviour. One of the the chief proponents of the classical humanist view that history's function is to make men better and wiser through the study of moral examples was Lord Bolingbroke. In his *Remarks on the History of England* (1743, a republication of articles written for the *Craftsman* in 1730–1) and in his *Letters on the Study and Use of History* (written 1730s, published 1752), Bolingbroke kept alive the traditional civic humanist belief that the retelling of history can have a practical, improving influence on the actions of men in the present and future, training them in private and public virtue, especially the virtue of patriotism.[80]

The chief message which Bolingbroke placed in the vehicle of historical narrative was the opposition interpretation of the idea of the ancient constitution: past liberty contrasted with present slavery. His *Craftsman* historical articles imbued the narration of ancient and recent history with blatantly topical, partisan messages – so blatant that they drew government replies which, perforce, treated the same historical material (for example, something apparently so remote from the political here-and-now as the character and administration of Pericles). Again, as in other forms of allegorical

political debate, each side responded to attack by staking a claim to
the rhetorical ground which the other had marked out as its own.
The oratorio librettist had only to open his paper to find a model for
an analogy between ancient history and current events which was,
moreover, a vehicle for partisan political propaganda. This retelling
of history was not mere intellectual display, it was political action
and recognised as such. The *Craftsman*'s printer (the paper proudly
noted) was arrested for publishing Bolingbroke's accounts of the
reigns of Edward III and Richard II.[81]

Enthusiasm for the application of history was not confined to
partisan utterances in newspapers. G. B. Hertz refers to 'the appeal
to history which runs through every manifesto of the war party' in
the years 1738–42, for example in Johnson's *London*. Bonamy Dobrée
notices the emotional charge of historical reference in not only
Patriot but patriotic verse. Jeremy Black (amongst others) points
out Parliament's 'marked preference for discussing past policies and
treaties' and its 'obsession with the past conduct of foreign affairs'
during the oratorio decades.[82] It is no surprise to find (as the next
chapter describes) a sense of past history woven into the oratorios.

Political theorists could invoke the government of ancient Israel
as a practical model, and could mention it alongside Athens and
Rome, because they and their readers shared an understanding that
the Old Testament record was historically true. This was still
accepted by orthodox Christians, among whom we can number the
librettists. The long-established practice of using Old Testament
events to work out a chronology of world history was still the
innocuous pastime of hundreds of antiquarians, among them
Thomas Morell.[83]

But freethinking biblical scholarship was undermining the Old
Testament's authority as reliable history writing (see chapter 6),
and hence as useful material for teaching good government. Bolingbroke's *Letters on the Study and Use of History* raised a storm by
specifically discounting the value of the Old Testament as history.
Following the new sceptical biblical criticism, Bolingbroke argued
that the only history worth studying is a complete, reliable record,
that the early 'fanciful' history of a nation is worthless, and that the
Old Testament is a broken, confused narrative by multiple anonymous authors. Therefore, as history and, by inference from his view
of history, as moral example, it is worthless. The revival of deist
arguments thought to have been laid to rest, and by a man of

Bolingbroke's status and powers of expression, was deeply shocking, and thirteen rebuttals were published in the three years after the *Letters'* publication. This response indicates the value still put on the Old Testament as history, and its authority, *as* history, to teach modern generations, around the time of the last of Handel's Old Testament oratorios.

The readiness of eighteenth-century Britons to identify their national history with Old Testament history is nicely captured in an elegy on Handel written in the year after his death by the Rev. John Langhorne, which mentions several of the oratorios admiringly (and describes their action vividly: no sense here that lack of staging is a disadvantage), but gives most space to *Judas*:

> I see the brave Youth lead his little Band,
> With Toil and Hunger faint; yet from his Arm
> The rapid Syrian flies. Thus HENRY once,
> The British HENRY, with his way-worn Troop,
> Subdued the Pride of France – now louder blows
> The martial Clangor, lo NICANOR's Host!
> With threat'ning Turrets crown'd, slowly advance
> The ponderous Elephants . . .[84]

Besides commemorating Cumberland, Judas calls up for Langhorne a great military hero of Britain's past. The modern British hero apotheosed by one of the nation's great artists through comparison with the Israelite hero recalls the apotheosis of the earlier British hero by another of the nation's great artists – for the Henry recalled is of course the Henry V of Shakespeare, history improved into example by authorship (and a favourite mid-eighteenth-century model of the Patriot King).

* * *

According to the government voice in the *London Journal* for 17 February 1732/3, allusive writing of the kinds described in this chapter was a distinctly opposition strategy. The opposition author

pretends indeed, to give you a short Account of the Revolution in *Portugal*; but, you know, that these Weekly Journals are not wrote *merely to Retail old History*; no; the Weapons of their Warfare are *Allegories, Fables, Parables, Hieroglyphicks*, and *parallel History*; and *this History* is now sent Abroad on purpose to tell you, 'That a few Gentlemen of *Courage*, and *Publick Spirit*, are able to rescue their Country from Slavery.'

But in reading possible political allusions in the Israelite oratorios we should probably keep a very open mind. The intended allusion

could be single or double. The characters could represent real
individuals (is Solomon meant to stand for George II?) or ideal ones
(is Jephtha an embodiment of the Patriot King?). The story could be
celebratory and/or critical (if Solomon *is* meant to represent
George, which aspect of Solomon is being invoked, his pious wise
government or his concubinage and apostasy or both?). It could
refer to past, present or future. Interpretations different from the
one(s) originally intended by the authors and/or received by the
audience could be afforded by changed circumstances (see below,
pp. 296–9). Fully to fathom the possible, and most likely, meanings
of the librettist and interpretations of the audience, we need to know
about the librettist at the time of writing, about political circumstances (material and ideological) at the time of writing and the time
of performance (so we need to be clear about which performance we
are considering), about the nature of the audience on that occasion,
about the state of the text for the performance in question (since
Handel customarily altered his oratorios for each season's revivals),
and about other contemporary treatments of the librettist's material. We are unlikely ever to be certain of all these for any of the
oratorios, but we can establish enough to make valid suggestions of
what the librettos meant for their authors and their first audiences.
This is undertaken in the following chapters.

CHAPTER 10

Moral politics

To the modern audience of Handel's Israelite oratorios the narratives of the librettos and their common themes are unremarkable and usually unremarked. But if we look at their biblical sources, we notice that the librettists made choices – what to take, what to leave, what to emphasise – and used their minds more than they admitted in their genteel disclaimers of the value of their librettos. Compilers of anthem texts had established a precedent for bold selection, rearrangement and adaptation of holy writ for musical setting (see chapter 3), on which the librettists built. Some common elements, and some common emphases, in their manipulation of the Scriptures become apparent when we compare their texts with their sources. In general, we can say of the librettists that

- they used the partisan focus on the Jewish people but not the division into factious tribes
- they emphasised the conflict with other nations and greatly reduced the proportion of internecine strife
- they used divinely aided Israelite victories but proportionately far fewer Israelite disasters
- they used the priestly caste but not its dominance
- they used the heroes' virtues but proportionately fewer of their human weaknesses
- they used the concept of the Covenant and extended it (for example, there is no mention of God in the biblical Book of Esther)

Comparison of an individual libretto with its source fills out this picture. *Joshua*, a libretto which has few advocates among Handelians, provides particularly clear instances of the ways in which the librettists manipulated their sources, and this chapter takes it as the starting point for a survey of the librettos' reflection of current moral-political concerns (see Table 4).

The major divergences of the libretto of *Joshua* from the version of the story in the Old Testament show how selectively the librettists read the Scriptures and how, in adapting them, they sought to raise the moral, ethical and emotional tone.[1] The alterations are typical of the Israelite librettos and of their time. As we might expect from the long-established habit of likening the modern British to the ancient Israelites, in the librettos both God and His chosen people are far more admirable than their biblical originals. Even the least sophisticated librettos are remote from the Old Testament world of a partisan, intolerant, vengeful deity promoting a disobedient, complaining rabble of in-fighting tribal colonists entirely in His own interests and often apparently at their expense.[2] This was the God and the people which so offended the deists, and the librettos – more lastingly than any of the dozens of volumes published by contemporaries in defence of established Christianity – take on, answer and use the criticisms of the humanist freethinkers. The third Earl of Shaftesbury, an early and influential English deist, had established the moral ground for later, more direct, attacks on the Old Testament basis of Christianity by suggesting that

If there be a Religion which teaches the Adoration and Love of a GOD, whose Character it is to be captious, and of high resentment, subject to Wrath and Anger, furious, revengeful; and revenging himself, when offended, on others than those who gave the Offence: and if there be added to the Character of this GOD, a fraudulent Disposition, encouraging Deceit and Treachery amongst Men; favourable to a few, tho for slight causes, and cruel to the rest: 'tis evident that such a Religion as this being strongly enforc'd, must of necessity raise even an Approbation and Respect towards the Vices of this kind, and breed a suitable Disposition, a capricious, partial, revengeful, and deceitful Temper.[3]

Jehovah, in other words, is the worst possible kind of father-figure, and Jews are chips off the old block. But the God of the oratorio librettos is the protective, corrective God of the Old Testament enhanced by the ethics of eighteenth-century Anglican Christianity, not Shaftesbury's Jehovah but the just ruler of all mankind. And the oratorio Israelites are not a debased rabble but a nation conscious of a natural right to freedom, and endowed with all the sensibilities of the eighteenth-century man of feeling as well as with the heroic courage and epic potential of a noble past.

In the librettos the most obvious and consistent instance of the tendency to elevate biblical characters is the introduction or amplification of virtuous romantic love, which in *Joshua* is also neatly used

Table 4. *Joshua*: libretto and biblical source compared

Old Testament	Libretto
4.1 *Israelites' conquest of Canaan* Deut. IX.1–6: God gives new land to Israel 'not ... for thy righteousness' but as a punitive example to the wicked heathen	I.1: Moral of Jordan crossing and entry to promised land: obeying God (unlike the previous, apostasising, generation) yields 'vast Rewards'
4.2 *Destruction of Jericho* Josh. VI.2–5: God gives Joshua precise instructions for taking Jericho, but no reason	I.2: God's angel says Joshua will destroy Jericho, but not how; and gives reason – Jericho's 'Tyrant King' and 'Heathen Train'
4.3 *Sparing of Rahab* Josh. II, VI.17, 22–5: Rahab, a harlot, spared because of services rendered as betrayer of Jericho	II.1: Rahab spared, no reason given; described as 'hospitable', otherwise unidentified
4.4 *God's Covenant with Israel* Josh. V.2–9: Circumcision re-established (its significance not explained here) V.11: Passing reference to Passover	II.2: Feast of Passover instituted to commemorate annually, in future ages, Israel's deliverance and protection by God
4.5 *Aftermath of defeat by Ai* Josh. VII.6–10: Joshua despairs; God rouses him	II.3: Israelites despair; Joshua rouses them
4.6 *Reason for defeat by Ai* Josh. VII.1, 11–12, 20–1: Sin of one man, Achan	II.3: Israelite pride
4.7 *Reasons for defeat of Ai* Josh. VII.16–26: Achan purged; strategy; extra troops	II.3: Trust in God; courage; extra troops
4.8 *Battle of Gibeon* Josh. X.8–14 (a) God assures Joshua of total victory before battle (b) God kills Israel's fleeing enemy with hailstones (c) Sun and moon halted during battle, affording victory (d) 'The Lord discomfited them before Israel, and slew them'	II.7 (a) Outcome not certain before battle (b) No hailstones (c) Sun and moon halted after victory, affording vengeance (d) Israel wins by courage supplemented with divine aid
4.9 *Giving of Achsah in marriage* Josh. XV.15–17: Achsah offered as prize to conqueror of Debir; acquired by Othniel; no mention of love motive; no previous mention of either character (and Debir previously conquered by Joshua, XIV.38–9)	III.1–2: Achsah offered as prize to conqueror of Debir, as yet unvanquished; Othniel conquers Debir, gains Achsah; they have been in love throughout (I.3, II.4–6)

to improve the logic of events (Table 4.9). In *Esther, Athalia, Saul,
Joseph, Solomon* and *Susanna* romantic love is likewise introduced or
much expanded from the biblical source. The most blatant instance
in *Joshua* of ethical enhancement is the whitewashing of the prostitute secret agent as, *tout court*, 'the hospitable Rahab' (Table 4.3);
behind this bland phrase lie pages of deist attack and establishment
apologetics relating to her role and the biblical writers' acceptance
of it (Stackhouse's defence, for example, takes up four folio columns).[4] The libretto's most conspicuous instance of moral
heightening is the alteration in Joshua's role after the defeat by the
men of Ai (Table 4.5). Other librettos offer similar instances of
moral improvement. In *Esther* there is no retributive massacre of the
Persians. In Humphreys' *Deborah*, as Dean points out,[5] Jael's
husband is not, as he is in the Bible, Sisera's ally, so Jael's despatch of
Sisera has no taint of treachery (in his biblical commentary Humphreys shows himself much exercised by this alliance, excusing the
murder only on the grounds of its divine commission).[6] In *Athalia*
Humphreys confines mention of the participants' family relationships to the wordbook's list of characters, presumably to limit the
shock caused by the enmity between Athalia and Joas (she is his
grandmother). In pulpit oratory the British are compared with the
Old Testament Israelites; the librettos congenially offer a comparison of the British with a much 'improved' version of the Israelites. Intermediary sources are likewise purged. In *Samson* Hamilton
does not retain from *Samson Agonistes* the conflict between Samson
and his fellow Israelites or their failure to support him, which
Milton retained from the Book of Judges. In *Athalia*, Racine's many
allusions to Israel's past and future bloody internecine strife and
present vacillation are all suppressed.

These ameliorations are consonant with contemporary defence
and interpretation of Scripture. The direct riposte to Shaftesbury
and subsequent deists was that the Old Testament God is consistent
with the New Testament one. He is merciful, forgiving and patient,
and His laws for His chosen people, as promulgated by Moses,
'breathe the utmost Humanity', inculcating 'mutual Benevolence,
Charity, and Good-will ... these Laws prescribe a humane, benign,
social Conduct towards one another'. The injunction to love one's
neighbour, Leland reminded the deists, first appears in Leviticus,
and comprehended 'even the *Strangers* that were *Sojourners among
them*'. So fervently do the defenders of Christianity recommend Old

Testament ethical and moral codes that there seems little left for Christianity to add.[7]

The same tendency to moralise God and elevate man characterises eighteenth-century biblical commentaries. Matthew Henry's, perhaps the most widely read, had ten editions in the eighteenth century.[8] Henry's warm imagination invests biblical personages with sympathetic emotions which make them recognisably 'like us'. Furthermore, his desire to justify God to man leads him – in common with the majority of contemporary commentators – to rationalise biblical events. He cuts the Old Testament down both literally and figuratively to convenient proportions and into psychologically bite-sized pieces (again, a common practice), from which a potential librettist would readily have been able to reassemble it into an evening's entertainment in adapted *opera seria* form. His commentary on each part of the text draws out its lesson for the reader's moral and spiritual life; to take one of his more extreme efforts, the establishment of the memorial during the crossing of the Jordan (Joshua IV.1–9, corresponding to the first scene of *Joshua*) reminds us, especially those of us who are heads of families encumbered with responsibilities, never to let our business commitments take precedence over punctual religious observance. He would have approved the librettist's moralising of the entry to Canaan in the same scene (Table 4.1), to the effect that the promised land was withheld from the previous generation of Israelites because they had disobeyed God (a lesson which the librettist had to cull from another part of the Old Testament).

The same approach shapes contemporary biblical paraphrase. Very similar techniques to Henry's are applied by Samuel Wesley in his versifications of the Bible in rhymed pentameter couplets.[9] The text is broken down into potential 'scenes', cleaned up (Rahab is not a prostitute), and punctuated with moral comments (the fall of Jericho is delayed by seventeen lines on human frailty). Wesley provides two further bridges from Scripture to libretto. Like the librettists, he invents incidents: guards on the walls of Jericho see the Jordan divide and are awestruck; Joshua tries to destroy Jericho with military equipment before learning better from the angel. He also employs the diction of the stage – and of the librettist: for example, Rahab tells the spies, 'A Panic Fear does every Breast invade, / We faint, we melt, of Israel's Arms afraid'. In their adaptation of the Scriptures as in so many other respects, the librettists use the ideas and language of their time.

COMMUNITY

The flattering reconciliation of Israelite and British character naturally makes for a readier association (by librettists and audience) of
situation, and this too is adjusted to strengthen the parallel and
make it morally more gratifying to the audience. Though the oratorio Israelites are a chosen people, they receive no more (but no
less) special favour than the eighteenth-century Englishman
expected from God; and they operate under a much more moral and
humanitarian (though ultimately unfathomable) divine dispensation than their biblical counterparts. God helps those that help
themselves, more consistently in the librettos than in their Old
Testament sources. Whereas the biblical Israelites are often given a
foolproof battle-plan, the libretto Israelites have to be self-reliant as
well as faithful. In the libretto Joshua is told he will conquer Jericho,
but not, as in the Bible, how (Table 4.2); similarly, the outcome of
the battle of Gibeon is not known in advance, and though it is won
with God's help, the Israelite contribution is greater than in the
Bible (Table 4.8, also an example of 'improving' the deity).

The Israelites' typically beleaguered situation typically evokes a
strong military response, rather than the frequent disarray of their
biblical counterparts. Calls for strong military action occur in
Deborah, Saul, Samson, Belshazzar, the *Occasional Oratorio, Judas
Macchabæus* and *Jephtha* as well as *Joshua*. Military action is not an
automatic response: it is sometimes preceded by tough diplomatic
representation, as in *Deborah* (Part I scene 4 – Part II scene 1, a
parley which has no biblical counterpart), sometimes by strenuous
efforts to secure an honourable peace, as in *Jephtha* (I.7–II.1, a
simplified and ethically pointed version of Judges XI.12–28). The
frequent leaderlessness of the biblical Israelites is often echoed in the
librettos by the initial lack of a strong leader in the face of oppression, as in *Deborah, Athalia, Israel in Egypt, Samson, Joshua* and *Jephtha*,
but the librettos always provide a hero – in the case of *Joshua*, in the
form of Othniel (Table 4.9).

The librettists amend their sources, and the resulting picture of
national unity also improves on the perceived *status quo* of British
Israel. Time and again the librettos touch a raw nerve of British
national pride and soothe it with fantasy. The lack of a leader in
several of the librettos echoes the Bible but it also reflects a contemporary sense of need. The persistent cry for an individual,

personal leader 'to call up all our ancient virtue and restore so great
a people to themselves', as John Trenchard had put it in 1720, was
sounded throughout the oratorio years.[10] After the brief period in
the early war years of Admiral Vernon's triumphs abroad, after
Walpole's departure from the political scene at home, and ruled by a
foreign king whose overriding concern for his other realm was
perceived to thwart or even endanger their own, many Britons
acutely felt the lack of a native, patriot, leader such as the librettos
depict.[11] It was this need which Bolingbroke was addressing in his
description of the unself-interested ruler whose devotion to the
national interest would end all disunity. *The Idea of a Patriot King*
(written 1738, fully published 1749) provided a romantic epitome of
the many current prescriptions for a good leader, as do several of the
librettos. The martial Old Testament leaders had served as a model
of British kingship for Defoe, and (as mentioned at the end of the
previous chapter) their oratorio embodiments were readily seen as
reminders of famous British warrior kings – of the past.

Their chosenness gives the libretto Israelites a unity of identity
and purpose which, by comparison with mid-eighteenth-century
Britain, was also wishful thinking. To be Jewish, in the oratorios, is
to be Israelite: religious adherence confers citizenship, religion *is*
nationality, whereas in Britain Christianity was various, and differentiated full citizens from the partially excluded. As described in
chapter 8, political division raised for many the spectre of faction,
the cancer of modern political life, while the promise of unity with
which the Patriot opposition appealed to the nation remained
unfulfilled. But the Israelites *are* united. Unlike the British nation,
they harbour no opposition party, no rebellious factions, no seditious
mobs, no traitors, no groups negotiating with foreign governments
and giving rise to invasion scares.[12] This unity is imposed on the
scriptural source material. By virtue of some of the librettists'
more blatantly selective readings of the Old Testament, the oratorio
Israelites are generally innocent of internecine strife, or have purged
it (as at the beginning of *Jephtha*), or have purged it by the time they
reach the concluding chorus (*Athalia* and *Saul*). When we see it in its
contemporary context such wishful enhancement looks poignant
rather than complacent.

Joshua has an example of this kind of amelioration, the deviant
Achan being replaced with another reason for defeat (Table 4.6–7).
Here is an instance of an emendation of the biblical source which a

modern audience is unlikely to notice but which was highly charged for its first audience. Achan was a recognised type of internal disunity. Henry's comment on his crime (keeping for himself some of the heathen booty which should have been entirely devoted to God, Joshua VII) is that 'treacherous Israelites are more to be dreaded than malicious Canaanites'. As the symbol of sinful weakness within the state, and as the figurative focus of the debate as to where responsibility for that weakness lay, Achan had played a large part in the aftermath of Cromwell's unsuccessful 'western design' against Spain in the Caribbean (1654–6); and as David Armitage points out, much of the polemic of that debate, including reference to Achan, was reprinted in the build-up to war with Spain in the Caribbean in the late 1730s and during the war itself. As it applied to Cromwell's campaign, 'None could be sure whether the sin of Achan lodged in the nation as a whole, its governors, or the army in the West Indies.'[13] The librettist of *Joshua* relocates the sin un-ambiguously, retaining the defeat which Achan causes (suppressing so familiar and significant a part of the narrative would strain wishful thinking beyond credibility), but commuting the greed of one man to something apparently worse: moral failure on a national scale. This suggests just how strong the need for, and lack of, unity was felt to be (of course in the libretto the failure is only temporary). In 1747, when *Joshua* was written, the Prince of Wales was con-cerned at the decline of popular patriotism and was campaigning for its revival: perhaps this libretto, like *Samson*, reflects his influence.[14]

The wishfully unified picture obtains with respect to foreign as well as domestic affairs. Whereas British policy was bedevilled by the tie to Hanover, the monarch and his British ministers in effect having different priorities,[15] and British opinion was divided on the question of whether to pursue a 'blue-water' or 'continental' policy (see chapter 8), the libretto Israelites are at one in their defence of national security.[16] Politics are simpler for them. Whereas the War of Austrian Succession was a stop–start affair which involved the British in such uncertainties as fighting the army of a nation with whom they were not officially at war (the French at Dettingen), in the oratorios battle-lines are clear-cut. The Israelites are able to concentrate their efforts on one crucial battle in one place at a time; the arena of war in which Britain was involved spanned half the globe, including the Americas and India as well as the length and breadth of Europe. The Israelites' wars, like the British wars of the

decade 1739–48, encompass defeats as well as victories, but they
entail fewer defeats, failures and frustrations than the British suffered, and more, and much more conclusive, victories.[17] Cecil
Moore's comment on Whig panegyric fits the Israelite librettos: 'At
times the discrepancy between the theoretic perfection described by
the poet and the actual conditions is painfully great.'[18] This is
especially true of *Joshua*, which shows successes on land at a time
when the only real British successes were being won at sea, and
which was written during the most disastrous eighteen months of the
war, while the French ravaged the vital Low Countries defences.
The siege of Jericho, which falls instantly to the Israelites, was
counterpointed in real life by the siege of the great fortress of Bergen
op Zoom, begun in July 1747 (when Handel began to set *Joshua*),
lasting three months, arousing intense public interest in London,
and ending in allied defeat.[19] The hard facts of the crippling expense
of war and the humiliating burden of peacetime subsidies to foreign
governments to safeguard Hanover's European position are side-
stepped in the oratorios, which depict (except in *Solomon*, see chapter
13) a premonetary society – war is won by strength of faith and arm,
not cash and land resources. Pocock cites Charles Davenant, writing
at the beginning of the century:

> war is quite changed from what it was in the time of our forefathers; when
> in a hasty expedition, and a pitched field, the matter was decided by
> courage; but now the whole art of war is in a manner reduced to money;
> and now-a-days, that prince, who can best find money to feed, cloath, and
> pay his army, not he that has the most valiant troops, is surest of success and
> conquest.[20]

Davenant (a text-book source for opposition theorists of the 1730s
and 1740s)[21] would have felt more at home in the world of *Joshua*.
Defoe, taking as model rulers the warrior leaders of the Old Testament, specifically admires their personal military engagement. As
Schonhorn comments, 'The sword-bearing sovereign was made
necessary by England's variegated society.'[22]
   Whereas the British people smarted under the expense and dishonour of having to finance Hanoverian and Hessian troops,[23] the
oratorio army is a militia raised from the community and united by
common ties, not a professional army, almost never the army of
allies or dependants and absolutely not mercenaries. Part I scene 3
and Part II scene 5 of *Joshua* show Othniel, a potential hero but not
a professional soldier, being summoned to battle from his betrothed

and (his?) fields and flocks, in the second instance with an echo from
Shakespeare's *Henry V*, 'Now all the Youth of *Israel* are in Arms',
which stresses the occasional nature of the call-up. It is wicked
usurping despots who maintain a standing army – for example
Athalia, and she also shows a tendency to use it against her dissenting subjects. The contemporary audience would unhesitatingly have
related the clear delineation in *Joshua* of a national militia (a rare
instance in the librettos of unmediated transcription from the Old
Testament) to the ongoing debate, dating from before the Revolution, on the desirability of a militia and the danger of a standing
army. The oratorio militia has a hinterland of argument stretching
back half a century and involving vital issues of civil rights, liberty
and government (see chapter 8). It exemplifies the argument that
weapons and property should be in the hands of the same men to
ensure the preservation of liberty in home as well as foreign affairs.
David Hume's account of the condition of a state that fields a militia
rather than a professional army is both a succinct version of many
similar statements and a good match with the libretto Israelite
nation: free, young, small, egalitarian; constantly needing to defend
itself; its citizens frugal, unacquisitive, and filled with patriotic
public spirit.[24] For the first oratorio audiences this was not mere
theorising; they could refer to a live British example. The new
colony of Georgia, founded in 1732, allotted land to its population in
return for military service. But at home the militia was shown by the
1745 Rebellion to be inadequate, and overseas the professional army
had only one clear victory (when Handel began *Joshua* its command
had just bungled the battle of Laffeldt).

CONQUEST

The use of the militia in the oratorios is exemplary: the Israelite wars
reflect contemporary ideas of what justifies armed conflict. War was
thought to be unquestionably justified by the aggression of a foreign
power, especially a Catholic one. A pre-emptive strike against such a
power was also justifiable, if that power threatened British interests
(which missionary Catholicism was held to do). Religion, the
traditional justification for war in English apologetics, was still
offered as grounds for aggression in contemporary sermons as well as
in political rhetoric, and the 'holy war' groundwork of the oratorios
would have been familiar to the eighteenth-century audience, not

least in that the traditional evidences for just war were culled from the Old Testament. Two developments in just-war theory in the seventeenth century, described by J. T. Johnson, show oratorio to be a particularly apt paradigm of virtuous conflict: the introduction of a concept of divinely 'commanded' rather than merely permitted war, and almost exclusive reliance on Old Testament precedent rather than New Testament teachings.[25] There were some dissenting voices, in literature as well as in politics. When the villainess of George Lillo's hugely popular morality play, *The London Merchant* (1731), arraigns religion as the chief destroyer of the human race, the exemplary Thorowgood assents: 'Truth is truth, tho' from an enemy and spoken in malice. You bloody, blind and superstitious Bigots, how will you answer this?' (Act IV scene 18). By 'superstitious Bigots' Lillo means missionary Catholics, just as in Robinson Crusoe's excited condemnation of massacres of innocent populations 'Christians' turns out to mean Spanish Catholic zealots in South America ('I See the Shore spread with Bones'). But contemporary freethinking produced dramas such as Aaron Hill's version of Voltaire's *Zaïre* (*Zara*, 1736) and James Thomson's *Edward and Eleonora* (1739), which contrast enlightened, humane Islam with fanatical, destructive Christianity, deploring all military crusades and all forms of religious aggression. The prominence in these plays of the debate on the justice of wars of religion suggests that it was a live topic of concern, and that while the religious battles of the oratorios may seem rebarbative or tedious to modern commentators, they had thought-provoking connotations for their original audiences.

But to claim the librettos as expressions of 'the confident patriotism of the English people as they rose on the wave of imperial expansion, convinced that they were carrying the true word of God to the pagan corners of the world'[26] is to impose anachronistic ideas of both missionary endeavour and empire. The oratorios predate the beginnings of British imperialism in its modern sense by at least a decade. Missionary activity in foreign parts by the Anglican establishment, directed by the Society for the Propagation of the Gospel, was not primarily concerned with conversion of the heathen. The society's charter (1701) chiefly aims to rescue British Christian colonists in danger of lapsing into atheism or being converted by Jesuits, and though some attempts were made to Christianise natives, chiefly in North America, they met with such opposition from settlers that success was limited to isolated pockets of a few dozen baptisms at a time – frequently with subsequent lapses. During the oratorio years, despite intermittent expressions of concern among the Anglican hierarchy for the plight of the heathen, there was no SPG activity at all in the West Indies, South America, Africa or Australasia.[27] So in showing more interest in the retrieval of apostates than in conversion of the heathen the Israelite librettos reflect current concerns. They are scarcely missionary in the nineteenth-century sense. At most, obstinate idolators are to be forced by demonstrations of divine power to recognise that Jehovah is the only God, but on the whole the heathen is eliminated rather than converted (a faithful rendition of Old Testament rather than New Testament means of spreading monotheism). The analogy for the contemporary audience would seem to be with evil Papists rather than innocent savages.

At this date British imperialist endeavour was likewise unconcerned with religious uniformity; local populations enjoyed religious tolerance. 'Empire' was a commercial concept, possessions being seen as trading posts, and there was no British administration in the later colonial sense.[28] However, territorial expansion for the sake of commercial prosperity was a problematic issue for political theorists during the oratorio years. Trade was an unquestionable good, but it was likely to mean war, which was not. Trenchard, Gordon and Hume were some of the more widely read of the many political authors who pointed to ancient Rome and modern Spain as admonitory examples of imperial overreach leading to national decay: 'Conquest, or Fighting for Territory, is, for the most part, the most shameless thing in the World'[29] (see further below, 'Continuity'). One polemical solution was to suggest that trade could be an alternative to territorial expansion, or even – as in Thomson's *Britannia*, Lillo's *The London Merchant* and, most famously and idealistically, Pope's *Windsor Forest* – a means to international harmony. It is typical of the librettos that the only one to take on the subject of trade (see chapter 13) sidesteps its possibly unsavoury corollaries: conveniently, the biblical Solomon had a trade agreement with a fellow monarch, and in the oratorio commerce and peace flourish together without territorial expansion.[30]

In the oratorios the militia's normal and irreproachable task is the defence of national security, which, this being a theocracy, encompasses the national religion. Time and again the Israelites are (as in

Richard Glover's Patriot epic *Leonidas*) 'facing the world's whole multitude in arms', defending themselves against, or subject to, a hostile, foreign, heathen power. The xenophobia and religious antagonism that go hand in hand in eighteenth-century political rhetoric are conveniently fused in the oratorios. The Israelites are exiled, embattled or persecuted in all the librettos except *Solomon* and *Joseph* (and Joseph is himself forcibly located in an alien society). They are in immediate danger in *Esther, Deborah, Athalia, Saul, Samson, Judas Macchabæus, Joshua* and *Jephtha*. In *Joshua* the defensive posture is exemplified first in the encounter with the men of Ai (Part II scene 3), and then in the need to help the Gibeonites against the king of Jerusalem (II.6). The latter episode – the Israelites have been tricked into the compact and have to honour it at great risk to themselves – makes a sour comment on the demands of alliances with weak nations, which the British unwillingly experienced during the European war.[31] The libretto Israelites' political isolation, their only temporary and always hazardous alliances with other nations, accurately transcribes the Old Testament Israelites' political conduct, itself an expression of their national character. The chosen people are distinguished by their separateness from other nations. This chimes with 'blue-water' as against 'continental' policy. Until the 1745 Rebellion resistance to commitments to continental powers was associated most strongly with the opposition. The opposition briefly urged continuing involvement in Europe when it seemed that commercial gains might result but, according to Robert Harris, a major consequence of the apparent failure of the continental strategy pursued in the war was to reinforce the convictions of the isolationists. In this light the librettos' transcription of Israelite independence, proclaimed by the militia-chorus, has a perceptibly oppositionist hue.[32]

Whatever the immediate cause for conflict, the principles prompting Israelite action are those professed by the British nation. 'If to fall', sings the chorus of Morell's *Judas Macchabæus* going into battle, 'for Laws, Religion, Liberty, we fall', echoing, in common with other librettos, a catch-phrase of contemporary patriotism heard in contexts as varied as the sentimental drama and the House of Lords. In the opening lines of Lillo's *The London Merchant* (still drawing capacity audiences while Morell was writing *Judas*), the exemplary master merchant expresses relief that the 'religion, liberty and laws' of England are safe from the Spanish threat.[33] The same unifying concepts were invoked in the House of Lords' loyal address to the king following the declaration of hostilities with France: 'we look upon the defence and support of your majesty, and of the Protestant succession in your illustrious house, as the only security (under God) of our *religion, laws, and liberties* ... in this national and glorious cause, all true Britons and Protestants will zealously unite' (my italics).[34] (The use of identical language highlights the differences between the fiction of the librettos and the reality of the political scene: the last phrase quoted from the Lords' address admits to a *dis*unity either not reflected, or purged, in the Israelite librettos.) *Joshua* apart, the oratorio Israelites are chiefly fighting not for territory but for liberty, and even in *Joshua* it is as a saviour of 'his Country's Liberty, and Laws' that the rising hero Othniel is praised. They struggle not so much, as in the Bible, to assert God's omnipotence, but to gain freedom from the oppressor in order to worship God freely – an up-to-date rendition of the Old Testament equivalence of religious with political identity. The rallying cry of 'liberty' would have had more than religious and wartime resonances for the oratorio audience (see chapter 8), but the oppression under which the oratorio Israelites labour is simpler and more capable of solution (and hence more suited to an evening's entertainment) than that allegedly suffered at the hands of the government at home, being externalised to the field of foreign policy.

The librettos take the step of transcribing the Old Testament's lessons about liberty into verse, but for this too there was at least one precedent. Thomas Rowe's 'Ode on Liberty', published in the year of *Israel in Egypt*, provides a pattern for the librettos in showing the Israelites achieving liberty. Stanza VI records the salvation of the Israelites at the Red Sea; stanza VII traces first Moses' leadership of the Israelites out of slavery through the desert, then their renewed slavery in Babylon followed by release from captivity and return from exile (the subjects of *Israel in Egypt* and *Belshazzar*, the former probably and the latter definitely by Jennens). Succeeding stanzas describe individual bringers of liberty to the Israelites, including the oratorio figures Deborah, Jephtha and Samson (the ode is incomplete and stops at Hannibal). We should note that the Israelites' attainment of liberty is offered not as an analogue of modern society but as an inspiring example for the present from the past.[35]

Explicit Israelite territorial conquest is almost wholly absent from the oratorios. Where it does happen it has, of course, the incontestable justification of divine ordinance. But this sanction is not arbitrary: it fits human behaviour, as for example in the libretto which shows two imperial nations, neither of them Israelite, at war. In Jennens' *Belshazzar* Belshazzar and his court are wicked and the Babylonian conquests are condemned by God, while Cyrus and his army are virtuous and the Persian conquest is sanctioned, indeed ordained, by God. Not that *Belshazzar* commends imperialism; on the contrary, Cyrus conquers only to liberate, restoring the virtuous Nitocris to her wicked son's throne and redeeming the captive Israelites: 'To Tyrants only I'm a Foe, / To Virtue, and her Friends, a Friend' (Act III scene 3).

Joshua is interesting in coming nearer than any other libretto to what may look like Israelite territorial imperialist conquest, but to the eighteenth-century audience, which knew its Old Testament, the Israelites crossing the Jordan into Canaan were not simply invading a neighbour. They were repossessing the land which God had given to them as part of the Covenant with Abraham which determined the whole course of human existence, down to the individual redemption of the members of the audience themselves. Their action was thus not only justified but (in common with the entire history of the Israelites) a ratification of God's promises of a Messiah and mankind's salvation, which His pledge to Abraham (Genesis XII.2–3) and all subsequent biblical references to the Covenant were taken to imply.[36] The headings of Joseph Hallet's 'Discourse' on 'The Scripture-Doctrine of Circumcision and Baptism' include: 'The covenant made with *Abraham* and his seed ... is the covenant of *grace*'; 'The covenant made with *Abraham*, and with his seed, *includes*, and was *design'd* to extend to, all believers'; 'The covenant made with *Abraham*, and with his seed, is still *in force*'; and so '*believers* now belong to the very *same covenant* and *church*, as *Abraham* did of old'.[37] (This highlights the inappropriateness of an approach to the librettos which treats them exclusively as drama in the modern sense, expecting them to be self-sufficient and self-enclosed. No part of the Bible is like that to its attentive readers, certainly not to those of the eighteenth century, who delighted in its interconnectedness: 'everything in Scripture is connected, and this coherence is the most great and wonderful thing to be seen in the sacred writings'.[38]) A further biblical justification for the Canaanites' extirpation is their descent from Ham, the deservedly cursed son of Noah (Genesis IX.20–7, which also entitles the Israelites to enslave them).[39]

These arguments, however, held no weight for the rationalists attacking the Old Testament basis of Christianity during the first half of the eighteenth century. From Matthew Tindal's *Christianity as Old as the Creation* (third edition published in the year of the first public performance of *Esther*) to Bolingbroke's *Letters on the Study and Use of History* (published in the year of the first performance of *Jephtha*), God's directive to the Israelites to invade Canaan and destroy the Canaanites and their efforts to obey Him were repeatedly held up as appalling instances of the Old Testament's tendency to cite morally reprehensible behaviour as exemplary and to promote an idea of the deity irreconcilable with an ethical 'supreme Being'. The topic was crucial because this was the Israelites' first military action as a nation, a precedent (good or ill according to the biblical reader's attitude) for all subsequent Israelite defences of their terrain and for all aggression in the name of religion – including the wars and conquests of eighteenth-century European powers. Tindal directly asked whether the Spaniards would have murdered so many millions in the West Indies if they had not had the example of Canaanite destruction to follow.[40] (Leland's answer to Tindal on this point is that 'had there been no such thing ever done, as the Extirpation of the *Canaanites* by the *Israelites*, the *Spaniards* would have done what they did, which was evidently owing to their own Ambition, Avarice, and Cruelty'; typically of his contemporaries, he responds in kind to an argument over modern politics based on biblical example rather than questioning the relevance of the example.[41]) The biblical writer, Bolingbroke deduces, was providing the Israelites with an authorised genealogy and aiming thereby 'to establish their claim to the land of Canaan, and to justify all the cruelties committed by Joshua in the conquest of Canaan'. His indignant rebuttal of the grounds for the Canaanite conquest is his most extended critique of a single instance of Old Testament narrative and reflects his abhorrence of religious wars.[42]

The pressure on Christian apologists to deal with this challenge to Old Testament ethics is evident in the response of one who was also, incidentally, a librettist for Handel (though not of an Israelite oratorio but of a drama which he was careful to transform morally): Thomas Broughton, author of *Hercules*. His answer to Tindal, *Christianity Distinct from the Religion of Nature* (1732), reaches for every possible justification. The Canaanites were wicked and deserved what they got; the conquest led to the Gospel; in a national disaster the innocent must expect to be destroyed along with the wicked; the innocent were rewarded in the afterlife; children were spared being taught idolatry by their parents; the Israelites were only instruments of deserved divine vengeance; and the whole event was an eternally useful lesson against idolatry.[43] All these arguments were standard, and had to be repeated with renewed vigour after Thomas Morgan published *The Moral Philosopher* (1737–40), in which he disputed both the claim to Canaan (on the grounds that God's Covenant with Abraham was conditional on continuous worship of God, which the Hebrews did not maintain) and the credibility of divine support for a brutal massacre of peaceable people.[44] As already mentioned, Morgan was the catalyst of Lowman's *Dissertation*, which provides the most extended justification of the possession of Canaan published during the oratorio years, and which moreover takes on and makes a virtue of the central importance accorded to this part of Bible history by deists. According to Lowman, 'The Protection of the *Hebrew* Nation, and the Favour of God to them as a peculiar People, was a visible and standing Confutation of Idolatry.' The Hebrew constitution is worth study and emulation because it was designed (by God) to quash 'idolatry' (for which read immorality, irreligion, deism and, probably, Catholicism – Lowman is especially hard on images, intercessory spirits and guardian angels), and the prime instance of its implementation is the elimination of the Can-aanites. These practitioners of child sacrifice to idol gods and 'many other abominable Immoralities ... did well deserve an exemplary Punishment from the righteous Judge of the Earth', a punishment which demonstrated both the falsity of idols ('a perpetual Source of innumerable Vices and Immoralities') and the existence of the one true God. Lowman's statement of the Israelite claim to Canaan is a blueprint for both *Israel in Egypt* and *Joshua*:

The common Rights of Nations, and any personal Claim of the *Hebrews*, are altogether out of this Question; the History plainly shews, they made no personal or national Claim at all to the Land of *Canaan*; but that God cast out the People before them, for all their Abominations; that it was not their own Power, but the Hand of God, which brought them out of the Land of *Egypt*, and into the promised Land. So that the whole is considered as the immediate Act of God himself, for the Proof of which the History gives a long Series of Miracles, in *Egypt*, at the Red-Sea, for many Years in the Wilderness, at the taking of *Jericho*, and settling the *Hebrew* Nation in the Possession of the promised Land.

The Israelites 'set up not Title to the Land of *Canaan*, either civil or religious, in their own Right'; the commission to destroy came from God, and to question this is to question the validity of Scripture, an issue which Lowman can thankfully set aside as already answered by abler pens.[45] Likewise in *Joshua* (Part I scene 2), the Canaanites deserve destruction because they are persisting in a false religion (understand Catholicism) and their king is a tyrant (understand absolutist foreign Catholic monarchs). The Israelites do not take the initiative, they act only on the specific instruction of God's angel (Table 4.2), and the divine origin of these instructions is confirmed, as for Lowman and others, in miracles – the fall of Jericho and the halting of the sun and moon. The oratorio is yet another, but an unprecedentedly dramatic, restatement of familiar apologetics, with contemporary overtones, on a central issue in one of the major debates of the century. Needless to say, the libretto makes no mention of the fact that the Israelites habitually enslaved the surviving Canaanites and the remnants of other nations they conquered, nor does *Solomon* mention that the temple and Solomon's other lauded public constructions were built with the forced labour of non-Israelite slaves (1 Kings IX.15, 20–2). In real life, the trade which Britain was meanwhile fighting to secure in the war against Spain included the trade in slaves. But *Israel in Egypt*, associated in the press with that trade war, mentions slavery only as what is being done *to* the Israelites, by the Egyptians (Spain).

In Part III of *Joshua* there does seem to be a definite reflection of the infant colonialism of Georgia and an anticipation of the territorial expansionism of the later 1750s, as the Israelites prepare to 'lot among the Tribes the conquer'd Land'. Joshua's fellow hero Caleb recalls their joint exploration of Canaan in Moses' time, their confident assessment of Israelite chances for invasion, their return to base with samples of local produce, and the conflicting report of the 'tim'rous Spies'. In response, Joshua recalls Caleb's resolution in the face of their compatriots' hostility (in the Bible he and Joshua were threatened with stoning), and God's consequent promise that Caleb will possess Hebron. This recension of Numbers XIII and XIV, as we might expect, minimises the Israelites' supineness and rebellion – the last of the many occasions in Moses' career when they stretch his and God's tolerance to its limits – and omits God's adverse decree, that none of those now living except the truly faithful Joshua and Caleb will enter the promised land (this however has been alluded to in the opening scene). It may be that this very deliberate passage of retrospection recalls the extended debate about the importance and feasibility of forcibly acquiring Spanish trading possessions during the late 1730s and early 1740s, a debate which was about to be revived in the press. It certainly seems to reflect the debate being conducted in government and press at the time of *Joshua*'s composition, on whether or not the purpose which had become the chief aim of the war, that of making commercial and colonial gains from France, was best served by prolonging armed conflict or making peace.[46] Both in the late 1730s and in the two years before the peace, those advocating the pursuit of colonial and commercial gains through aggression rather than diplomacy were chiefly writers opposed to government policy. Again, there is a large gap between libretto and reality. Whereas the dramatic point of this exchange between Joshua and Caleb is to celebrate acquisition of the promised land, and whereas writers urging continuation of the war claimed that colonial prizes were within easy reach, in fact the enemy was sweeping through the Low Countries while the libretto was being written, and the only substantial colonial gain of the war, Cape Breton – which if properly developed would, it was thought, prove 'of more value than the mines of *Peru* and *Mexico*, or than any other Possession or Property that can be had in any part of the World' – was restored to France in the peace treaty being prepared during *Joshua*'s composition.[47]

The libretto's account of the division of land amongst the tribes has further resonances. It springs into new focus and carries a great deal of meaning if we conjecture that the librettist was a reader of Harrington (a perfectly possible circumstance – as we have seen, Aaron Hill engages with Harrington in *his* biblical epic). The partition of Canaan was for Harrington the origin of the Israelite 'agrarian', the ordering of society based on land ownership which in his view formed the foundation of right government:

This kind of law fixing the balance in lands is called agrarian, and was first introduced by God himself, who divided the land of Canaan unto his people by lots, and is of such virtue that, wherever it hath held, that government hath not altered, except by consent; as in that unparalleled example of the people of Israel, when being in liberty they would needs choose a king. But without an agrarian, government, whether monarchical, aristocratical or popular, hath no long lease.[48]

In other words, the division of Canaan by Joshua under God's direction was the birth of the Israelite nation, and since the division was based on principles of land ownership essential to the prosperity

and stability of any society, it was or should be the pattern of all
societies – including, for the audience of *Joshua*, their own. According to Harrington their agrarian law was the key factor which
saved the Israelites from falling into typical eastern servility; and
though himself a republican, he applies his theory to other forms of
society (as in the passage quoted above) and elaborates it
throughout his works, computing the amount of land allotted per
person, drawing further examples from the Old Testament, and
setting these against detailed parallels with English government.[49]
Both Harrington and Lowman – who also computes the amount of
land per individual in the partition of Canaan and cites Harrington
extensively on this issue – make a connection between the landed
property of the Israelites and their military force. They both
identify this force as a militia, and Lowman commends it in Old
Whig terms as

a numerous Soldiery ... of Men bred up neither in a servile nor indigent
Condition, but in a free and sufficiently plentiful Condition; not of Persons
who had nothing of their own to lose, but of Persons who had both a valuable Property and Liberty to defend ... the whole Nation was as a standing Army ... This military Service, by which the *Hebrews* held their Land,
is of such Consequence to the right Understanding of the Constitution,
that it will deserve a particular Attention.[50]

Where deists deplored the 'artificial' aid supplied to this fighting
force by the deity (often taking particular exception to the halting
of the sun for Joshua), defenders of the sacred text praised the
Hebrews' valorous exploits. Calmet opens his 'Dissertation concerning the Art of War among the Hebrews':

The *Jews*, as *contemptible* as they appear at present, were once the most
warlike People in the World. Few Nations have acquired more Glory by
their Arms ... *Israel* has produced such Prodigies of Strength, such
Instances of Courage, Conduct and Wisdom, as deserve as well or better
to be held in Remembrance, than *those* of any other Nation whatever. And
the History of their warlike Exploits ... is no *idle Romance* of *Fabulous*
Heroes. It treats not of those Conquering Ravagers of Cities and
Provinces, that without any Reason, carry War and Destruction into the
Territories of their Neighbours; but, for the most part, of wise and valiant
Generals, who were rais'd up by God, to execute the Vengeance of the
Lord, to punish the Wicked, and protect the Innocent. Such were the
Joshuas, the *Calebs*, the *Gideons*, the *Jephthas*, the *Samsons*, the *Davids*, the
Maccabees, and many others, whose illustrious Names will be had in ever-
lasting remembrance.[51]

The Israelite librettos enact this admiration, choosing the same individual heroes to celebrate (Calmet's list is commonplace). So thoroughly did the eighteenth century take these Old Testament figures to its heart that Joshua, son of Nun, and Caleb became pen-names denoting patriotism, claimed and counter-claimed like other trigger-words as a badge of *true* patriotism. To take only two of numerous instances: an article in the *Flying Post* of 22 April 1731 saluting the Second Treaty of Vienna (which averted the threat of a union of Catholic powers against Britain) as a great patriotic achievement was signed by 'Joshua Nun'; on the other side, the fictitious editor-author of the *Craftsman* was called Caleb.[52]

COVENANT

The librettos and British political utterances both link 'religion' and 'liberty' with 'laws'. British liberty was located in the law of the land, written and unwritten – the constitution. As described in chapter 8, a major area of dispute between administration and opposition concerned the constitution, each claiming to have its inviolable preservation most at heart. For both, the bedrock of the constitution was the law; it was the supremacy of the known law over kings and subjects which the Revolution had irreversibly established, and to embody the rule of law was the constitution's 'ultimate political and social purpose'.[53] The Israelites too have their constitutional 'laws', in both the Bible and the librettos – the Law of Moses, the embodied proof of their special identity as God's chosen people, of His Covenant with them dating from the time of Abraham. Like the British with their monarch, the Israelites are bound with God in a mutually beneficial contract. Unlike the British, however, the Israelites have the benefit of a visible constitution, the Ark containing the written Law.[54] This concreteness of the Jewish constitution enables it to be introduced as a potent image of nationhood in an Israelite libretto, and the librettist of *Joshua* selects biblical episodes in which it can be invested with the status of a leading character. In the first scene the Israelites set up memorial stones recording, 'to long Posterity', the point at which the Ark was carried into the Jordan, causing the waters to part and enabling the Israelites to cross into the promised land (Joshua III–IV, illustrated on the jacket of this book). In the first scene of Part II the Ark causes the fall of Jericho: the *mise-en-scène* includes 'The Priests bearing the

Ark of the Covenant' and Joshua's instructions are followed with 'A solemn March during the Circumvection of the Ark' round the walls of Jericho, which thereupon collapse.

A connection between the Old Testament Covenant and the British constitution was made by at least one major political theorist. In his 'First Vision of Camilick', a political allegory using Old Testament language and, with the heading 'In hoc signo vinces', invoking Christianity triumphant, Bolingbroke refers to Magna Carta, British prototype of the balanced constitution, as 'the Sacred Covenant'. In a letter to his nephew in 1735 he writes of the endangered constitution in language of particular resonance for oratorio students: 'The Victim [the constitution] may be saved, even tho' the same butcherly Priests should continue to administer our political Rites, or who knows? a zealous high priest may arise, and these priests of Baal may be hewed to pieces.' In *The Idea of a Patriot King* he writes that the ideal king will consider the constitution 'as one law, consisting of two tables, containing the rule of his government, and the measure of his subjects' obedience' – a reference to the two tables (tablets) of the Law granted to Moses for the Israelites on Mount Sinai. And in *Remarks on the History of England*, analysing modern political life, he invokes the scriptural account of the Ark of the Covenant and its relation to political and religious turbulence in Israel to illustrate the fragility of constitutional government.[55]

Bolingbroke's invocation of the Hebrew Covenant is largely a matter of rhetorical heightening, but it is not solipsistic. Other political writers of the first half of the century made the same parallel with similarly forthright partisan intention.[56] The Covenant as a metaphor for good government, and hence for the uncorrupted British constitution, lies at the heart of Lowman's *Dissertation*. In his opening pages he describes the terms of the Covenant with a pure Whig gloss: 'The *Hebrew* Government appears ... designed to serve the common and general Ends of all good Government: to protect the Property, Liberty, Safety, and Peace of the several Members of the Community, in which the true Happiness and Prosperity of National Societies will always consist'. Here and elsewhere, with even more markedly Old Whig terminology, he calls 'this solemn Transaction between God and the *Hebrew* Nation ... the *original Contract* of the *Hebrew* Government'. Contemporary believers in the holy grail of a British constitution which somehow retained its integrity despite the corruption of the executive would have responded positively to Lowman's arguments that the Israelites' survival was due to the excellence of their Covenant-based constitution *in its original form* and that their rescinding the contract – through irreligion, immorality and the demand for a secular king – did not destroy it. Again, his language makes the link with modern life:

Was it ever a Maxim of Law or Equity, that the unlawful Rebellion of a People, could extinguish the lawful Powers or Authority of their Prince? or that when a Compact between two Parties was agreed to, and perfected, it remained still in the Will of either Party singly, to annul it, without the Consent of the other. The *Israelites* in renouncing *Jehovah* as their King, could not annul his Authority, or his Right by the original Compact.[57]

If we relate the Covenant to the constitution in Lowman's terms, the building of the temple by the great lawgiving king, Solomon, to house the Ark takes on new significance: it represents not only the king's piety but his virtuously non-absolutist respect for the supremacy of law. The epigraph of *Joshua* likewise comes to life and reveals its bearing on the rest of the libretto. The librettist quotes from the concluding lines of Virgil's *Georgics*, 'Victorque volentes / Per Populos dat Jura, viamque affectat Olympo' ('and the conqueror [Augustus] gives laws to willing nations and pursues a route to heaven'), directing our attention to the oratorio's account of the institution of the Law for the willing nation in the conquering Joshua's care. Possibly the librettist had seen one of the early copies of *The Idea of a Patriot King* and was taking his cue from Bolingbroke's use of the same tag in the glowing peroration to that work. We can infer that, like Defoe, he admired Joshua as the archetypal Patriot King.[58] (The indirect reference to Augustus should not, I think, be taken as encouragement to read Joshua as equivalent to George II; given the contemporary critiques of Augustus as an absolutist prince who perverted the laws he pretended to safeguard, the analogy was at best ambivalent. As Howard Weinbrot documents, writers of the English 'Augustan' age recognised Virgil's praise of Augustus as a grateful courtier's compliments (or worse) rather than sincere admiration.[59])

The connection of constitution and Covenant gives the numerous recalls of the Covenant in the librettos the vitality of political relevance and may even explain some points of Handel's settings. In *Joseph* the deracinated hero, weary with administering an alien people, longs for his home, his father and

his sacred Lessons
Of God's Creation, of Man's fatal Fall,
Of the deep Waters covering all the Earth,
The Race-preserving Ark, the Heaven-hung Bow,
Jehovah's divine Promise to our Fathers,
The glorious Hope of *Abraham* and his Seed

To unadjusted modern ears this passage probably sounds like mere pious padding, and in fact the authors wavered about its inclusion, for it is not printed in its entirety in the libretto and is marked as unset; but the autograph score shows that Handel did set it, perhaps because he appreciated its reference to current thought. Lowman had likewise pointed to the Covenant, basis of the Hebrew constitution, as the blessing which set the Israelites off from other nations – a metaphor for the Old Whig reverence for the British constitution.[60] Further implications suggest themselves (and would have suggested themselves more readily to eighteenth-century audiences than to modern ones) if we consider other versions of 'covenants' current at the time. One could say that in place of the 'artificial' and defective human 'covenants' posited by Hobbes and the 'compact' described by Locke, modified to a 'contract' by his successors and still 'the fashionable system' when it was subjected to Hume's reductive analysis,[61] oratorio reminds its audience of *the* Covenant, not based on human frailty but guaranteed by divine sanction.

In considering the analogy of the Covenant with the constitution we should notice further that the Covenant, both in the librettos and in their Old Testament sources, is *ancient*: it dates back to the time of Abraham. Lowman repeatedly describes the Hebrew constitution as perfect in its *original* form, identifying the time of Joshua, the birth of the nation, as its purest moment. Samuel Squire combines contemporary enthusiasm for tracing the British constitution back to Anglo Saxon times with respect for the Old Testament's antiquity when he argues (at length) that the Hebrew Covenant is *the* archetypal constitution and the Saxon original of the British constitution resembles it.[62] To this extent the librettos are Patriot/Country as distinct from governmental in their view of the constitution; they depict the Ur-example of the uncorrupted constitution and its upholders, predating even Athens and Sparta. This historic dimension could be dismissed as an inevitable consequence of drawing a text from the Old Testament, whose narrative is located in the past. More cogently, it could be pointed out that the Old Testament authors stress national history as a lesson for the present and future (constantly recalling the promise to Abraham and the salvation from the Egyptians and in the desert), and that the librettists *chose* to transcribe this aspect of their source, apparently with deliberate emphasis. The Covenant is only one of many instances throughout the Israelite librettos of reference to past events which provide inspiration down the ages, a feature discussed in the next section.

CONTINUITY

Reading the history of one's own country is pleasurable, says Samuel Squire, but reading its constitutional history is positively a duty:

the history of the civil constitution cannot be too carefully studied, or too carefully enquired into, especially in such a country as ours is, divided into parties, and where each party confidently appeals to the ancient constitution of the kingdom for the opinions it maintains, and pretends to make that the measure of its political principles, by which alone it is ready to stand or fall.

Englishmen neglect this study to the hazard of public safety, as when 'mistakes' were made about the constitution during the reigns of the later Stuarts, 'to say nothing', adds Squire darkly, 'of more modern times'.[63] As Quentin Skinner has pointed out, using the study of exemplary history to understand how liberty is lost and how it should be preserved had been a central theme of late-seventeenth- and early-eighteenth-century Whig philosophy.[64] What has been less noticed is that three major exponents of Whig principles of liberty and property – Harrington, Lowman and Squire – use early Israelite history as their point of reference to discuss the nature of good government.

Exemplary history of the kind that civic humanists such as Bolingbroke commended to the study of rulers and citizens is secular: it roots rewards and punishments in this life, substituting posthumous reputation for the divine rewards and punishments of the Christian dispensation. However, it shares Christianity's moral goals, the promotion of virtue and the discouragement of vice.[65] Similarly, Israelite oratorio is located in a pre-Christian dispensation where success and failure are temporal. However, these successes and failures are shown to relate to a moral scheme of divine rewards and punishments. Israelite oratorio is a synthesis drawing on the strengths of both exemplary history and Christian teaching.

In fact in two major respects the librettos' use of history is closer to that of moral humanist historians than to that of their Old Testament source. Firstly, whereas the Old Testament refers to past events to teach that God saves Israel, the librettos, while attributing the salvation of Israel which they dramatise to the hand of God, as often assign to historical record, or recall from the past, the conduct of their *human* leaders. Just as Bolingbroke and earlier humanist historians advised, they examine the actions of exemplary individuals: time and again the hero's or heroine's achievements are not just celebrated, they are marked out as examples for posterity – and so (as in humanist history) are adverse examples, such as Samson. A typical instance of such straightforward recall is Judas' address to his troops in his new role as their leader:

> 'Tis well, my Friends; with Transport I behold
> The Spirit of our Fathers, fam'd of old,
> For their Exploits in War. – Oh may *their* Fire
> With active Courage *you* their Sons inspire;
>   As when the mighty *Joshua* fought,
>   And those amazing Wonders wrought;
> Stood still, obedient to his Voice, the Sun,
> 'Till Kings he had destroy'd, and Kingdoms won.

(The reference to Joshua anticipates a later libretto; the halting of the sun in its course was one of the period's favourite examples of the miraculous.)[66]

The second respect in which the librettos echo mid-century humanist historiography is their use of what I would call the future perfect (for which there seems to be no biblical pattern): the rhetorical trick of designating the present marvellous action as the inspiring historical record of the future. The example of patriot kings 'as mighty Patterns stand / To Princes yet unborn' (*Solomon* II.1); Solomon is 'Thrice happy King, to have atchiev'd / What scarce will henceforth be believ'd', providing 'endless Themes for future Praise' (*Solomon* III.1); Othniel likewise has achieved 'What scarce, in future Times will be believ'd' (*Joshua* III.2); the institution of the feast of Passover (Table 4.4) will set an example to 'Ages unborn'; and the passage of the Ark of the Covenant through the Jordan is marked to teach future generations about the sense of special identity which they should derive from their past:

> JOSHUA   bear twelve Stones from the divided Flood,
>   Where the Priests Feet, and holy *Cov'nant* stood;

> In *Gilgal* place them: hence twelve more provide,
> And fix them in the Bosom of the Tide:
> These when our Sons shall view with curious Eye,
> Thus the historic Columns shall reply.
> CHORUS   To long Posterity we here record
> The wond'rous Passage, and the Land restored ...

Joshua is especially permeated by the sense of history. Joshua's first recitative recalls the fate of the previous generation (who 'in the Desart, met an early Grave' because they disobeyed God's Law); Achsah's first recitative and air recall the Egyptian slavery and deliverance from it by 'the first Lawgiver' (Moses); then follows the sequence just cited, concluding 'So long the Memory shall last / Of all the tender Mercies past'. In the second scene, the angel's prediction of the fall of Jericho ends with attention to the historical record, from which the city will be expunged, 'The Place, the Name, and all Remembrance lost'. In Part II scene 2 the Passover, besides being an example to 'Ages unborn', provides occasion (as it does in real-life celebration) for a recital of the deliverance from Egypt, succour in the desert, and giving of the Law at Sinai. In the following scene Joshua rallies his failing troops with 'Remember *Jericho*!'. In II.6 the Chorus, commending the decision to honour the treaty with Gibeon, shows its sense of exemplary history: 'Nations, who, in future Story, / Wou'd recorded be with Glory ... ', and at the beginning of Part III it promises Joshua that 'Our Children's Children shall rehearse / Thy Deeds in never-dying Verse'. The recollection by Caleb and Joshua of their return from the exploration of Canaan follows, and the next scene contains the praise of Othniel already cited. It will be noted how many of these passages give history the heightening of the 'future perfect' mode, and how many of them connect a sense of continuity from past to future with the bedrock of Jewish (British) identity, the Law (constitution).

The librettos' sense of history stretching forward as well as backward could have been culled from many earlier literary sources: Greek tragedy, classical epic, Shakespeare's history plays (most pertinently, *Henry V*, which unsurprisingly enjoyed a revival – in both Shakespeare's and Aaron Hill's versions – during the late 1730s and the 1740s[67]). But it could be found in writing contemporary with the librettos, in Patriot treatments of history. The imagined reception of the present by 'Ages unborn' or 'generations yet unborn' makes frequent appearances in Bolingbroke's rhetorical armoury as he recounts past history with a view to effecting present change, and he shows himself aware of the emotional appeal of the forward and backward vista.[68] Likewise James Thomson not only dwells on past national history (notably in *Liberty*, 1735), but brings past and future together in his plays at moments of especial intensity. Coriolanus' mother, pleading with him to spare his city, reminds him that

> thy ever-sacred country ... consists
> Not of coeval citizens alone:
> It knows no bounds: it has a retrospect
> To ages past; it looks on those to come ...[69]

More expansively, the whole climax of Thomson's and Mallet's masque, *Alfred* (Act II scene 3), the vision of great English monarchs who will succeed the Saxon king, plays on the sense of past and future, envisaging a time when the 'present' will be the actual past and locating the actual present and recent past in the 'future':

> O ALFRED! should thy fate, long ages hence,
> In meaning scenes recall'd, exalt the joy
> Of some glad festal day, before a *prince*
> Sprung from that king belov'd ...

This reference within the historical time-scale of the masque to the 'festal day' of its first performance invests the actual immediate future (Frederick's accession) with an aura of ardent anticipation, and conveys a sense of a special privilege to be bestowed on the longing nation.[70]

It seems to me that the librettos derive a similar emotional charge from their use of history, especially from their use of the 'future perfect' mode, and that this charge would have registered strongly with the contemporary audience and still has the power to affect a modern one. The emotions are those of epic rather than tragedy. We contemplate examples which inspire, yet cannot be equalled. Our ancestors' past glories were wonderfully achieved, against the odds. They give us confidence; but they also burden us with a sense of our own inadequacy and of the uncertainty of the future which no assurance of divine protection can completely dispel. The telescoping of past and future compels us to view humanity *sub specie aeternitatis* and recognise that we are insignificant – yet responsible for fulfilling our God-given capacity to be latter-day heroes. We are poignantly made aware at the same moment of continuity and mortality.

The humanist historian viewed the evanescence of individual endeavour as part of political mutability, of the cyclical course of national destiny and the inevitable decay of empire. One libretto opens with a resounding restatement of this theme. The whole opening scene of Jennens' *Belshazzar* – the monologue of Belshazzar's mother, Nitocris, and her conversation with Daniel about the condition of Babylon – is a transcription of the theory of political mutability: all nation states are in constant flux, tending towards extinction. Jennens could have taken this theme straight from Polybius and Machiavelli (whose works were in his library),[71] but he could equally have read it in numerous more modern works. The cyclical growth and decay of empire, especially that of Rome, was a topic that particularly attracted and moved eighteenth-century writers as they contemplated their instructive ancient models for modern life. From Thomas Gordon's *Discourses* on Tacitus (1728) to John Dyer's *The Fleece* (1757), to take only the period of the oratorios, a series of works pointed to the warning offered by Rome, a model of government in the late Republic, which disintegrated politically, morally and artistically with the increase of empire, materialism and self-interest and the loss of civic liberty. John Dennis, whose works were in Jennens' library, not only included Israel among his admonitory examples of extinct empires but provided a hint for *Belshazzar* with a connection between empire and prophecy (the libretto's other major theme): 'the Governments that have been most renown'd upon Earth, flourish'd with their respective Revelations, and with them decay'd, as the *Israelites* did with their Prophets, the *Grecians* with their Oracles, and the *Romans* with their Divinations'.[72] Jennens begins *Belshazzar*:

> Vain fluctuating State of Human Empire!
> First small and weak it scarcely rears its Head
> 　　　　. . . Anon it strives
> For Pow'r and Wealth, and spurns at Opposition.
> Arriv'd to full Maturity it grasps
> At all within its Reach, o'erleaps all Bounds,
> Robs, ravages and wastes the frighted World.

At length grown old, and swell'd to Bulk enormous,
The Monster in its proper Bowels feeds
Pride, Luxury, Corruption, Perfidy,
Contention, fell Diseases of a State,
That prey upon her Vitals. Of her Weakness
Some other rising Power advantage takes,
(Unequal Match!) plies with repeated Strokes
Her infirm aged Trunk: She nods – she totters –
She falls – alas! never to rise again ...
  Thou, God most high, and Thou alone
  Unchang'd for ever dost remain ...

Belshazzar predates the official publication but not the writing of *The Idea of a Patriot King*, and the two works share a similar treatment of this common-stock theme. Bolingbroke writes, in a now famous passage:

Absolute stability is not to be expected in anything human; for that which exists immutably exists alone necessarily, and this attribute of the Supreme Being, can neither belong to man, nor to the works of man. The best instituted governments, like the best constituted animal bodies, carry in them the seeds of their destruction: and, though they grow and improve for a time, they will soon tend visibly to their dissolution. Every hour they live is an hour less that they have to live.[73]

Jennens could have read this before writing the libretto; but the immediate source for his lines was possibly a work to which he subscribed and which he had in his library, Conyers Middleton's widely admired *History of the Life of Marcus Tullius Cicero* (1741; further editions 1741, 1742). Of Octavius' birth, in which, as an upholder of Old Whig principles, he foresees the doom of Rome, Middleton writes:

If *Rome* could have been saved by human counsil, it would have been saved by the skill of Cicero; but it's destiny was now approaching: for Governments, like natural bodies, have, with the principles of their preservation, the seeds of ruin also essentially mixt in their constitution, which after a certain period begin to operate and exert themselves to the dissolution of the vital frame. These seeds had long been fermenting in the bowels of the Republic; when Octavius came, peculiarly formed by nature and instructed by art, to quicken their operation and exalt them to their maturity.[74]

The shared ideas, images and even vocabulary of these three passages indicate, once more, the extent to which the librettists – even so pronounced an individualist as Jennens – drew on a common stock of themes and expression. The elements of Jennens' eclecticism are themselves not idiosyncratic or unprecedented: Bolingbroke himself was drawing on Old Whig thought and fusing it with royalism in *The Idea of a Patriot King*. The sequence of ideas and images retained its currency during the eighteenth century: nowadays its best-known expression is probably Goldsmith's, in the penultimate paragraph of *The Deserted Village*. By giving it a non-secular, dramatic context Jennens is doing what was characteristic of artistic procedures of his time (and what he himself regretted Handel's doing) – drawing on the striking ideas of others to create something new.[75]

All three texts view the state as permanently unstable and tending to decay. Jennens and Bolingbroke contrast this condition with divine immutability; they also suggest that the decline can, after all, be halted, along the lines suggested by Machiavelli – with a restoration of national integrity through purgation and return to first principles brought about by human intervention. In his other writings, Bolingbroke held out no hope for such recovery, but in the *Patriot King* he envisages an individual ruler who will save the state by these means, which will be no less than 'a standing miracle'. Likewise Jennens envisages a human redeemer, Cyrus, the image of a Patriot King and in this case explicitly 'a standing miracle' in that he is directed by God's command to bring liberty to an oppressed people, inaugurate an era of universal harmony and build the New Jerusalem.[76]

For many of the commentators on Rome's corruption, its decline began with the depredations by Julius Caesar, Augustus and their successors on the liberties of its citizens. Roman imperial rule was lawless, tyrannical, and an image of modern absolutist (Catholic) European states. Conversely, ancient societies in the early stages of their development, including Rome, were lauded for their establishment of civil liberty. Dyer's paean to liberty at the centre of *The Ruins of Rome* (1740), praying for its continuance in Britain, is based on the common proposition that in virtuous early societies, where liberty guaranteed property rights, equitable land ownership promoted modestly prosperous agriculture and the land-based populace was contentedly frugal. In his own version of early Rome, this is consonant with (justified) warfare:

> From the plough
> Rose her dictators; fought, o'ercame, return'd;

> Yes, to the plough return'd, and hail'd their peers;
> For them no private pomp, no household state,
> The public only swell'd the gen'rous breast . . .   (ll. 425–9)

As Lawrence Goldstein notes, 'Like James Thomson [in *Britannia*],
Dyer is loyal to irreconcilable myths: that of the pastoral Golden
Age and that of the progress of empire'.[77] Dyer here (unlike
Thomson) chooses not to recognise that national wars mean individual hardship. The next generation, in the person of Hume,
suffering nostalgia fatigue ('To declaim against present times, and
magnify the virtue of remote ancestors, is a propensity almost
inherent in human nature'), disputed the notion of an ideal primitive frugal society: early societies were not in fact egalitarian, they
consisted of proprietors and vassals or tenants.[78] But the oratorios
show the virtuously pastoral Israelites acquiring new territory by
conquest, for example in *Joshua*. Dyer names the 'majestic daughters'
by whom liberty was 'nobly hail'd of old': Rome comes some way
down the list of ancient societies, which is headed by 'Judah fair'.
While republican Rome is the usual model of virtuously vigorous
agrarian frugality, Dyer's treatment invites the reader to see ancient
Israel as the Ur-example.

  Once the identification of the healthy society as recently founded,
unsophisticated, egalitarian, industrious and essentially *agrarian* is
appreciated as a point of view in the eighteenth-century political
debate, not only do key texts of the period, such as the *Georgics* and
The Seasons, gain in significance for us, but the image of Israelite
society in many of the oratorios – pastoral, simple and newly
asserting its independence – acquires a new moral dimension. Lewis
Crusius' explanation of the *Georgics* to the readership of the 1730s
makes an interesting gloss on the warrior-herdsman Israelites presented to the oratorio audience:

You may see the plan of a well regulated government . . . Industry and
sobriety, the love of one's country, and a religious frame of mind, are every
where inculcated . . . The design . . . seems to have been . . . no less than
settling the Commonwealth, that had been long harrassed with civil wars,
in a habit of peaceful industry; and to join the soldiery and common people
in one, and the same interest, the improvement of their lands, and the
increase of their fortunes . . . Having complimented them upon their
warlike spirit, he urges to their imitation the example of their frugal
ancestors, shewing they were all trained up in the country life; and this he
inforces from the happy simplicity of *Saturn*'s reign, and the golden age.[79]

Industry, sobriety, patriotism and religion are likewise taught by example in the oratorios, which similarly compliment the nation on its warlike spirit and show its frugal ancestors pursuing a country life. The agrarian ordering of early Israelite society was the basis of Harrington's recommendation of it as a model, and Lowman followed him with the difference that in his *Dissertation* the Law which justifies Israel's settlement of Canaan is unequivocally divine in origin. The Covenant between God and Israel is described as the gift of *land* in return for monotheism and the suppression of worship of other gods:

Jehovah promises them a pleasant Land to inhabit, he brings them into that promised land, and settles them in it; they hold it of *Jehovah*, as his Gift; he drives out the *Canaanites* before them for their abominable Wickedness, the Fruits in great measure of their Idolatry; he blesses this Nation in the Land he gave them with Liberty, Plenty, Peace and Prosperity, as they keep his Covenant; but when they break it, he permits their Enemies to afflict and oppress them.[80]

Besides providing a blueprint for *Joshua*, Lowman here links land tenure (property rights) with religious obedience, affording an even better model for modern virtue than his contemporaries who took their image of admirable early society from (pagan) ancient Rome. As his contemporaries described the virtues of Roman agrarian life, so Lowman describes the beneficial property rights of the early Israelites:

this equal and moderate Provision for every Person, wisely cut off the Means of Luxury, with the Temptations to it, from Example. It almost necessarily put the whole *Hebrew* Nation upon Industry and Frugality, and yet gave to every one such a Property, with such an easy State of Liberty, that they had sufficient Reason to esteem and value them, and endeavour to preserve and maintain them.[81]

Lowman's thesis, as already mentioned, is that the original constitution of Israel is a model for our times, and here he reinforces the parallel with a reference to Bacon's praise for the wisdom of similar legislation under Henry VII. Again following Harrington, he spells out that Israel as originally constituted had none of the sophistications of modern economy and government that lead via self-interest to corruption:

No *Israelite* could increase his Estate by the Constitution, in virtue of the universal and perpetual *Agrarian Law*; and no Man could make a great Estate any other way, in a Country where there was no foreign Trade, and where Interest of Money, if any one could be supposed to have much, was strictly prohibited by Law; and when, finally, he could not, on any Pretence whatsoever, raise Money by a Tax on the People.[82]

For Lowman, as for the commentators on Rome's decline, social disintegration begins when prosperity produces excessive 'luxury', in the sense of both surplus possessions and enfeebling decadence. Materialism feeds self-interest and breeds the 'corruption' described by Jennens' Nitocris. Of all the elements of the political vocabulary to which the mid eighteenth century gave special meanings, 'corruption' was the most highly charged and most intensively laboured. Gunn goes so far as to speak of 'the interminable debate about the causes, extent, and meaning of corruption – a debate that produced very nearly the whole substance of British political argument in the forty years after 1723', while according to Hammond 'It was quite impossible by 1735 to use the term *corruption* without its being understood as part of a specifically political register'.[83] It had two main political meanings. There was alleged (and proven) 'corruption' of forms of government which entailed abuse of the governed by the administration (see chapter 8). This formed the basis of the opposition's charge against the administration and was its own reason for existing. The other sense of 'corruption', also oppositionist and linked to the first, was a conviction that the whole nation was in a desperate condition of moral decay. Corruption spread from government to the entire populace, but it was a two-way process: the degenerate nation allowed itself to be imposed on by a corrupt government, and in turn the government stripped away the liberties proper to a self-respecting nation.

The stress by contemporary writers on luxury as a cause and symptom of national corruption (see chapter 8) enables us to recognise the wanton riot of Belshazzar's court as politically all of a piece with Nitocris' monologue on the death of empire, Daniel's explanation to his students of the relevance of Isaiah's and Jeremiah's prophecies to the Babylonian period, and Cyrus' emergence as Patriot King. The parallels which contemporary moral historians constantly made with the terminal decadence of Rome also clarify an oratorio outside the Israelite canon, *Theodora* – a story of sober Christian virtue pitted against the machinery of the decadent state and society of imperial Rome. Contemporaries' juxtapositions of luxury and irreligion with frugality and virtue should adjust our view of all the oratorios' hedonistic heathens. To modern listeners

Handel's beguiling music for them seldom suggests criticism, indeed it has encouraged the idea that Handel was a humanist with pagan tendencies, sympathising with the revelling idolators he portrays. To draw this inference from (dramatic) music and to go on to deduce that the composer's approach was that of 'a dramatist, without moral preconceptions' is to make the old confusion of the portrayal with the author; but in the case of the words such confusion cannot arise, for the librettists make heathen vice only minimally attractive.[84] Jennens' comment on Handel's reported remorse for such seductive settings is of interest here: 'being a little delirious with a Fever, he said he should be damn'd for preferring Dagon (a Gentleman he was very complacent to in the oratorio of Samson) before the Messiah'.[85] Jennens was repeating something heard second-hand which gratified him (he resented Handel's having, to his mind, taken greater pains over Hamilton's *Samson* than over his own *Messiah*) and the report may be fictitious, but, if true, it refutes the idea of Handel pursuing 'purely aesthetic' ideals, unconcerned with moral import, in his oratorios; and even if fictitious, it shows that at least one contemporary took the ungodly forces in the oratorios seriously, as a genuine opposition of evil to good, and felt concerned by ambiguity in Handel's representations of them – correctly anticipating, we could say, that such ambiguity would prove subversive and liable to misinterpretation.

Corruption is not confined to the heathens in the oratorios. In most of the librettos the Israelites suffer a setback, and it is traced to their moral or religious failure. Contemporary writers' constant complaints of religious decline are mirrored in Israelite apostasy and doubt of divine support. Just as in contemporary jeremiads, so in the librettos spinelessness and presumption are identified as the causes of national disaster, and in their portrayal of the embattled Israelites the librettists dramatise the imminence of disaster apprehended by contemporary pulpit and political writers.[86] Faintheartedness before battle, 'pride' (usually taking victory too much for granted) and religious backsliding are the specific vices. *Joshua* contains instances of the first two of these (Table 4.5–6), for which the librettist adapts his source. In the Bible the Israelites are defeated because one man among them disobeys God's veto on the taking of booty from Jericho; in the libretto they are vanquished because they are 'Elate with Pride, deluded by Success' and underestimated their enemies. And whereas in the Bible it is Joshua, alone, who is shown despairing at this setback, the libretto, like contemporaneous moral-political analysis, widens the application to include the whole nation (which enables Joshua himself to remain the hero and rally his forces: 'Whence this Dejection? rouze your coward Hearts'). In analysing the reasons for the demise of the Societies for the Reformation of Manners (*c.* 1690–1738), which brought 101,683 public prosecutions against private individuals for crimes such as blasphemy and drunkenness, Shelley Burtt focuses on the Societies' rationale that such crimes harmed the state by creating a degenerate populace and inviting God's wrath (in just the way posited by the preachers and by oratorio), whereas private virtue would bring temporal rewards. She argues that the cause of religion was actually damaged by this secular, political, materialist justification for personal virtue and piety.[87] The librettos continue the Societies' teaching that religious obedience and observance are essential to national well-being, but avoid the Societies' error of sitting in judgement on individuals. Achan's crime of personal greed is transmuted to a corporate failing in respect to God.

'Idol worship' by Israelites in the librettos (for example *Jephtha*) would readily have been understood not only as a synonym for irreligion but more generally as a metaphor for vice. In Patriot writing the phrase seems to have enjoyed a vogue as a catch-all for a range of moral-political failings. Pope and Bolingbroke use it as an image of government corruption and national slavish compliance. For Thomson it serves as an image of self-interest: in 'that vast Temple of *Corruption*, under which this Generation, more than any other that ever boasted Freedom, worships the dirty, low-minded Idol of Self-interest ... to this Idol is every public Work, which we have the Soul to attempt, made an immediate Sacrifice'. Aaron Hill deploys it as an image of the surrender of artistic integrity to patronage: 'What a shameful idolatry is that, which hath bepagan'd the apostate sons of the Muses! degenerate worshippers, not in the *groves*, I confess, but, in far less inviting HIGH PLACES! *Bowers of the knee before* BAALS, of the same lumpish quality with the *Calf*, in the wilderness, and composed of the same damning metal!'. Handel's librettist James Miller uses it, like Thomson, to signify corrupt self-interest, represented in this instance by Walpole's parade of the garter he was so pleased to acquire:

> *Ribbands* must rank Corruption straight impart,
> And the *gilt Star* betray a grov'ling Heart;

The *garter'd knee* must needs to *Baal* bend,
And who *in Place* can be his Country's Friend?[88]

Lowman, whose readers are to understand the Hebrew commonwealth as a model for the modern state, bases his work on the idea
that Israel was founded to combat 'idolatry', that is, both irreligion
and vice. The Israelite possession of Canaan was a far better rebuke
of Canaanite irreligion than (for example) a plague would have
been, since it entailed an obligation on the Israelites themselves to
refrain from idolatry, and hence was

a publick Condemnation of Idolatry and a standing Confutation of it, in
maintaining and supporting the *Hebrews* in possession of this Grant, by the
superior Power of the one *true* God, in Opposition to the Power of all the
Idol Gods, their neighbouring heathen Nations worshipped ... this particular Providence to the *Hebrews*, is no ways contrary to any general good
Design to the whole World, but manifestly in Aid of one good Design, to
prevent the universal Corruption of the World, by the Prevalency of
Idolatry.[89]

In Lowman's reading of Israelite history, the Hebrew state disintegrated when it neglected the fight against this idolatry; his
identification of the administration of Moses and Joshua as the
apogee of Israelite virtue and success provides a further gloss on the
librettist's choice of Joshua as an oratorio subject and emphasis on
the Covenant (constitution). Lowman's diagnosis of the reasons for
the Israelites' defeat by enemy nations – their tolerance of 'idolatry',
their self-interested neglect of corporate responsibilities (as their
husbandry prospered they became 'intent on their own private
affairs' and 'greatly neglected many of the Constitutions for the
Publick Good') and their 'Corruption of the original Constitution of
their Government and Religion'[90] – draws together the themes of
personal and governmental corruption in the context of Israelite
history as a lesson for the modern audience. It is a very short step
from here to the Fast sermons and to oratorio librettos.

As already mentioned (chapter 8), the 'modern' Whigs, the
administration and its supporters, took a very different view of both
governmental and personal 'corruption'. They interpreted 'Luxury'
simply as living beyond one's private means. Individual citizens
may be vulnerable to political bribery; if so, the answer is not that
they should engage in public life in order to safeguard their political
integrity, but that they should ensure their financial independence

by industry, sobriety and good housekeeping. This, not governmental or corporate reform, will be sufficient to save the nation from decline. But in any case, the nation is not in decline, and is nowhere near the brink of disaster, it is patently flourishing under an enlightened, freedom-guaranteeing government. Personal corruption is no concern of government, self-interest is ineradicable, and national reform or renewal of virtue is not the remit of (any) government. The government is 'corrupt' only in the sense that men are paid to do jobs which are in the public interest, to make government work. The system is working admirably, achieving the ends of national order and prosperity, and so the means are justified.[91] These arguments from expediency and materialism are strikingly secular for an age still so committed to religious belief, and they make the basis of political ethics in the librettos, obedience to God and civic responsibility, look suddenly curiously old-fashioned – and remote from the tenets of the court Whigs.

For those unable to accept what they regarded as the evils of modern life, the opposition of bucolic frugality to luxurious decadence was extended to suggest a solution: the retreat from the city to the garden. According to Thomson in *The Seasons*,

> The happiest he! who far from public rage
> Deep in the vale, with a choice few retired,
> Drinks the pure pleasures of the rural life.
>
> (*Autumn*, ll. 1236–8)

Thomson's theme was so central to mid-century thought that it has provided material for an entire (and excellent) book.[92] Again the ideal had an ancient model, in the writings of Horace in particular. Again (to continue with Thomson's version), the association of the ideal with a primitive and godly society makes for a ready transcription to oratorio:

> This is the life which those who fret in guilt
> And guilty cities never knew – the life
> Led by primeval ages uncorrupt
> When angels dwelt, and God himself, with man.
>
> (*Autumn*, ll. 1348–51)

Industrious, contemplative, in harmony with nature, innocent of the corruption unavoidable in wordly life, these high-minded spirits (unlike Dyer's unsophisticated Roman agriculturalists) are unmoved by 'the rage of nations', but both what they have escaped from, and the fact that it is an escape, are always present. Thomson gives as much detail, in this episode, to the corrupt ways of life being spurned as to the innocent style of life being preferred. Invoking the garden serves to define and emphasise the evils of the city. Elsewhere he presents the country retreat as part of an irretrievable 'Patriarchal or Golden Age'.[93]

In the librettos we can perhaps discern the same sense that perfected retreat is impossible. Othniel is wrenched from a pastoral idyll with his beloved Achsah to go to battle (*Joshua*, Part I scene 3); the seclusion of Susanna's garden is invaded and her innocent enjoyment of it betrayed (II.3); Solomon's retreat into a bower of bliss (created by the imagery of the Song of Songs) is only an episode (I.2). The contrast of the urban and country life informs some of the secular librettos even more noticeably. It is a major element of *L'allegro ed il penseroso*; in *Acis and Galatea* the swains of the opening chorus are 'honest' and 'free' as well as 'happy' and 'gay'; in *Semele* the denizens of Arcadia, unlike those of Thebes, 'taste the Sweets of Love without its Pains' (II.3); and in *Hercules* Princess Iole contrasts the burden of public greatness with the happiness of peasant obscurity (II.1, 'How blest the maid'). Scholars have noted that Handel responded with particular warmth to the idea of rural life. Dean found 'a nostalgia of overpowering beauty' in Joseph's 'The peasant tastes the sweets of life' (II.3), while R. A. Streatfeild observed a 'wonderful suggestion of the far-away patriarchal life of the Old Testament' in Caleb's 'Shall I in Mamre's fertile plain' (*Joshua*, III.1);[94] it should further be noted that both airs in their context juxtapose rural retirement with the pressures of public life. Handel and his librettists seem to be at one in endorsing this particular strand of current thought.

CORRECTION

As in contemporary sermons, so in the librettos, the setbacks which result from national corruption are interpreted as divine retribution. The preachers reminded their hearers that though the sins of individuals will be punished hereafter, national crimes can be dealt with only in the lifetime of the nation, hence war, earthquake, plague and similar acts of God.[95] (As Patrick Collinson points out, Old Testament prophecy by its nature gave the Israel–Britain parallel a judgemental cast, being mainly castigatory, seldom congratulatory,

'anything but triumphalist', and threatening the entire nation.[96])
When the Israelites complain of their Babylonian captivity in
Susanna (Part I scene 1) the virtuous Joacim has the analogous
answer: 'Our Crimes, repeated, have provok'd his Rage, / And now
He scourges a degenerate Age.' Similarly the oppression by the
Ammonites at the beginning of *Jephtha* is interpreted as God's
reproof of recent Israelite apostasy. The Israelites' dilemma is likewise interpreted as divine correction of their individual or corporate
failings in *Esther, Saul, Samson, Joseph, Belshazzar* and *Judas Macchabæus*.

When in Part II of *Judas Macchabæus* Antiochus' army threatens
'To root out *Israel*'s Strength, and to erase / Ev'ry Memorial of the
Sacred Place' and the Chorus despairs, its spiritual leader Simon
explains:

> Be comforted – Nor think these Plagues are sent
> For your Destruction, but for Chastisement.
> Heav'n oft in Mercy punisheth; that Sin
> May feel its own Demerits ... Turn to God,
> And draw a Blessing from his Iron Rod.

National failure is visited with divine retribution, but neither contemporary moralists nor librettists go on to imagine the worst
scenario, final destruction of the species: the idea that God might
abandon His creation forever is not seriously entertained.[97] For
present or impending disaster the antidote, in both contemporary
writing and librettos, is purgation. These lines from *Judas* can be
paralleled in contemporary sermons, in moral-political polemic and
even, most tellingly, in private correspondence, such as Bolingbroke's letter to Swift about Pope's campaign against corruption:
'A real reformation ... requires ... punishments as well as lessons:
National corruption must be purged by national calamities.'[98] The
high drama of Bolingbroke's language in *The Idea of a Patriot King*
seems especially close to the tone as well as the content of the
librettos:

to save or redeem a nation, under such circumstances [of corruption], from
perdition, nothing less is necessary than some great, some extraordinary,
conjuncture of ill fortune, or of good, which may purge, yet so as by fire.
Distress from abroad, bankruptcy at home, and other circumstances of like
nature and tendency, may beget universal confusion. Out of confusion
order may arise ...

but, Bolingbroke now argues, it may be the order of repression rather than enlightened government, which can be guaranteed only by a Patriot King.[99]

In these prognoses purgation by disaster is itself a cure, an apocalyptic view given reality by such memorable recent catastrophes as the bursting of the South Sea Bubble. But more positive remedies are also adduced, subscribed to by preachers, moralists, moral politicians and librettists alike. To secure God's favour once more the nation must repent and reform. The call for reform is made again and again in mid-century writing, by churchmen and moralists (as we saw in chapter 6), by the opposition, and in the librettos (but less frequently by writers supporting the administration, which held that men's morals and religion were not the concern of public interest). It is of two main kinds, both constituting a return to pure first principles.

The first is religious and moral: obey God, renounce vice, fulfil religious observance, and live frugally and industriously.[100] The second has more to do with political reform and aims at national strength through national unity. Epistle III of Pope's *Essay on Man*, Bolingbroke in his *Craftsman* articles and in the *Patriot King*, Berkeley in his *Essay*, Ralph in *The Remembrancer*, Horace Walpole in his *Letters to the Whigs*, Brown in his *Estimate* and the preachers all urge the end of faction in unity, the surrender of personal ambition to the common good which is true patriotism, the renewal of pride in national endeavour and the fostering of 'public spirit'.[101] These reforms may be effected by blows from outside, corruption being too far advanced for the nation to heal itself (as for example Berkeley believes), or they may be achieved from within through the emergence of a great leader (as in Brown's final pages and in Bolingbroke's final vision of national unity under a Patriot King, whose 'great object' is 'the union of his people').[102] In Bolingbroke's writing particularly, the idea of the Patriot leader and the salvation which he will bring to society, the suddenly transforming restoration of virtue and national revival which he will effect, has pronounced Christian (as well as utopian) resonance even for modern commentators.[103] A return to the pure tenets of the original constitution is crucial to the corporate reform proposed by Bolingbroke and other writers drawing on Old Whig doctrine. Lowman sets this theory in an Old Testament context, thus bringing it close to the material of the oratorios: the Israelites lapsed into self-interest which caused the nation to fragment and the covenanted constitution to decay, and the only remedy would have been 'reviving it in some form or other'.[104] Lowman focuses his discussion of this point on the time of the judges and early kings, the period of many of the oratorios.

The librettos correspond to these analyses and correctives at every point. National renewal is shown resulting from a blow from outside (such as the Ammonite aggression in *Jephtha*) and the emergence of a heroic leader (as in *Jephtha*). The same solutions to national ills are offered. All the Israelite librettos depict a nation filled or rekindled with the religious zeal which contemporary writers found lacking in the modern nation, and several dramatise the required reformation with a rejection of false gods. Israelite acquiescence in idolatry is purged in *Deborah*, *Athalia*, *Belshazzar*, *Judas Macchabæus* and *Jephtha*. The renewed pledge of loyalty to God, a renewal of faith to the Covenant, takes the form of devout religious observance (as recommended by contemporary preachers and moralists). This bulks extremely large in the librettos. Besides the devotion to God manifested in every Israelite libretto, the major Old Testament religious festivals are marked. Chanuka is celebrated in *Judas Macchabæus*, Passover in *Joshua* and Tabernacles in *Athalia*, while the story of Esther is itself the text of Purim (such events of course provide perfect pretexts for anthem-type setting of the text).[105]

The librettists are more optimistic than the gloomier moralists such as Berkeley. Firstly, in the librettos reform can be instant and total, expressed in worship which is natural and delightful. (For this the librettists are obliged to depart from their Old Testament narrative sources, drawing instead on the Psalms.) God is inscrutable but ethical; He can be engaged by direct appeal, and the chorus never needs to undertake sustained spiritual trial or development in order to be vouchsafed access to Him. Secondly, national success is the prompt reward of renewed virtue. Corruption has never gone too far to admit salvation, and the national oppressor is vanquished. With their hymns of thanksgiving and praise, however, the librettos break the bonds of nationalism. These passages of worship, especially their celebration of God as creator, echo contemporary demonstrations of the existence of a beneficent deity from the evidence of His harmoniously ordered creation (see chapter 6). In them the God of Israel becomes the God of the whole world. But with the eighteenth century's customary flexibility of viewpoint, He is equally capable of turning back into a partisan deity in the next breath.

The librettos dramatise the required sinking of individual self-seeking in espousal of the common cause, showing the nation united *contra mundum*. The importance attributed to national as against individual survival is especially clear in those librettos where a difference of interests among the characters fractures the dramatic coherence of the narrative. For example, in *Saul*, the king persecutes the most virtuous members of the community, on whom the survival of the community depends, so the chorus lamenting his death is, illogically, a threnody for the enemy of the people, while the final chorus turns its back on the tragedy of the central character of the work. The duty of the individual to serve the country has already been instanced in connection with Othniel's summons to battle in *Joshua* – one of numerous possible examples.[106] In relation to his society, the libretto hero is at the furthest possible remove from the self-realising Romantic type, for example the meteoric figures of Dryden's early heroic dramas, who pursue their goal independently, intransigently and intractably. In Shakespearian terms, he is Henry V, not Coriolanus. Like the Patriot King, he is the willing, co-operative agent of new national unity, virtue and strength.

CHAPTER II

'Esther' to 'Athalia'

Elucidating the possible political implications of an oratorio libretto, it will by now be agreed, is unlikely to be plain sailing. This is abundantly illustrated by *Esther*, which not only demands attention as Handel's first English oratorio but has the most complicated textual history. Trying to 'unpack' its meaning demonstrates the delicacy of the operation and the often unexpectedly rich nature of its results.

The story begins in France. The first performances of Racine's *Esther*, in January and February 1689, by the protégées of Mme de Maintenon's school of St Cyr, were given to a highly select court audience. At the third performance, 5 February, this included the recently deposed James II of England and his queen, Mary of Modena. The cast included Mlle Marie-Claire Decamps de Marcilly, who so enchanted the Marquis de Villette in her role of Zarès that he subsequently married her (thus causing a rift with Mme de Maintenon, who was also the Marquis' aunt).[1] The possible importance to Handel's *Esther* of both Marie-Claire's participation and its outcome will appear presently.

In England there was no performance of Racine's *Esther* on the public stage in the early eighteenth century, but the play was known in French – Swift had Racine in his library, as did Handel's friend John Arbuthnot, a member of the Burlington House and Cannons circles which generated the first *Esther* libretto.[2] From 1715 it was available in English in a translation by Thomas Brereton of Chester as *Esther, or Faith Triumphant. A Sacred Tragedy.* In other parts of his life, and indeed in his death, Brereton was involved in politics (see *Dictionary of National Biography*), but he appears to have had no political axe to grind with his translation of *Esther*. He makes nothing political of the play's favour in the French court, nor does he mention the modern British political connotations of the Esther story. He proffered his text as a specimen of reformed drama (see chapter 2). Politically the most interesting aspect of his translation is its dedication to Archbishop William Dawes, who had been Bishop of Chester. Dawes' most famous sermon had referred to the Esther story. He had given it on 5 November 1696. The Esther story, relating one of the 'miraculous' deliverances of the chosen people from persecution, was a popular source for texts for sermons on 5 November, a patriotic red-letter day in the English Church calendar so signal that it was marked by a Thanksgiving service in the 1662 Prayer Book (the only other days so celebrated being the sovereign's accession and the 1660 Restoration): the Gunpowder Plot had been discovered on 5 November 1605, affording a parallel with the Jews' last-minute preservation from an impending holocaust. The feast day took on additional meaning when William of Orange landed at Torbay on 5 November 1688, affording a parallel with the Jews' deliverance from religious tyranny.

Handel's *Esther* in its original version dates from 1717/18, when he was working for the then Earl of Carnarvon, James Brydges, later Duke of Chandos, at Cannons.[3] The unknown author(s) of the libretto used Brereton's translation, but Brereton is not known to have had any connection with the Chandos circle.[4] When the work reached London fourteen years later, the libretto was attributed to Pope. Viscount Perceval (a Handel enthusiast) was at the Philarmonic Society's first performance at the Crown and Anchor (see above, p. 14), and recorded in his diary: 'From dinner I went to the Music Club, where the King's Chapel boys acted the *History of Hester*, writ by Pope, and composed by Hendel'.[5] Chandos had recently been admitted as a member of this same club.[6] We do not know if he was at any of the club performances of *Esther*, nor who told Perceval that the words were by Pope, nor who provided Gates with the score. But it is possible that Percival had his information about the authorship of the text direct from Chandos. Supposing this to be the case, it is also possible that Chandos misinformed him. Chandos was still smarting from the adverse publicity he had received as a result of Pope's *Epistle to Burlington*, and could have been promoting the idea of *Esther*'s being by Pope to prove that the slur that Pope was criticising his taste in the *Epistle* was false and that, on the contrary, Pope had previously endorsed his taste to the extent of providing for his entertainment. Pope was certainly party to the other drama which Handel composed for Chandos, *Acis and*

Galatea.[7] The first public performance of *Esther*, on 20 April 1732 at York Buildings, advertised the work as 'compos'd originally for the most noble James Duke of Chandos, the Words by Mr. *Pope*, and the Musick by Mr. *Handel*'.[8] This was the first public attribution of the libretto to Pope. Pope had publicly contested the public's inference that he had referred to Chandos in his *Epistle to Burlington*; he made no public reference to or refutation of this public linking of their names, only two months later, so presumably he was satisfied to have the authorship of *Esther* ascribed to him. Perhaps *Esther* was brought out of mothballs at this particular moment in part to smooth the troubled Burlington–Pope–Chandos relationship with proof of happy collaboration.[9] It was after the York Buildings production that Handel brought out his own much altered and amplified first London version of the work, performed at the King's Theatre.

Modern critics have considered the possibility of Pope's author-ship, and it is accepted in the Twickenham edition of his works, on the grounds of verbal echoes (rightly queried as valid grounds by Dean).[10] So far as I am aware, no one has considered why Pope and his friends might have taken an interest in Racine's play. Pope himself has left no reference to *Esther*. But one of his closest friends had a curiously strong connection with it. In 1716 Lord Bol-ingbroke, in exile in France, took as his mistress Marie-Claire Decamps de Marcilly, who (as already mentioned) had not only acted Zarès in the first court performances (and incidentally had been commended by Louis himself for her acting), but as a result had married the Marquis de Villette. One of these performances, as mentioned above, had been in the presence of James II, the man on whose account Bolingbroke was in exile and whose son he served. The liaison with Marie-Claire was not a transient one: the couple was still together when the Cannons *Esther* was completed, and they married the year after, in 1719.[11] Pope could have heard about the play and its early performances from Bolingbroke, who (given its consequences for her) would surely have heard about it from Marie-Claire; so could Brydges, with whom Bolingbroke was in correspondence.[12] There is also a connection, this time a striking verbal one, between the heroine of Racine's play and the women most important to another of Pope's closest friends, Swift: in reality Stella's first name was Esther, and Vanessa's (and her mother's) was Hester. Another thread connecting the circle of the oratorio's birth with its content concerns Chandos himself and Arbuthnot. Their correspondence includes letters showing that, like most well-read men of their time, they kept abreast of publications opposing atheism, and suggesting that (unlike Pope) Chandos had no truck with modern rationalism. The story of Esther would have suited a believer in divine interventionism.[13]

For Pope, a Catholic and a Jacobite sympathiser, James II's attendance at the play soon after the start of his exile would have added to its stature, and Bolingbroke's connection with it would have brought it even closer home. The same applies to the libretto's other putative author, their mutual friend Arbuthnot, whose brother fought on the Jacobite side in the 1715 Rebellion.[14] The actual story of Esther in the Bible and Apocrypha (itself fictional wishful thinking), and as transmitted by Racine and/or Brereton, would also have had great personal meaning for Pope. The Jews in Persia, an exiled minority, of a different religion from their over-lords, are nevertheless loyal to the regime. One of them, Esther, is King Ahasuerus' wife, but is not assured of royal favour. The Jews' safety depends on the king's being persuaded of their loyalty. The king's evil first minister, Haman, represents them as seditious to the king in an attempt to destroy them which rebounds on him through the brave action of Esther and through the king's recollection that Esther's cousin and guardian, Mordecai, once saved his life. Jewish probity is rewarded and irreligion punished – in the Bible by the massacre of 75,000 Persians as well as the execution of Haman. The feast of Purim marks this event. There is no mention of God in the biblical account (though there is in the Apocryphal elaboration, which Handel's librettists fully exploited), but in the dramatic reworkings under consideration here the Jews interpret their threat-ened persecution as a merited punishment from God for their religious inadequacy (as it often is elsewhere in the Old Testament). This chimes with the moral tone of remarks by Pope's own circle, and by Pope himself, about the ethical and religious decline of Britain.[15]

In relating both Racine's *Esther* and his *Athalie* to political events in England, Olivier Lutaud points out that contemporaries referred to James II as Ahasuerus and Mary of Modena as Esther, interced-ing with her husband for the international Catholic cause as repre-sented by the British minority (an allegory which would have added meaning to James' and Mary's presence at one of the first perform-ances of *Esther*). He also notes the recurrent use of the Esther story in

English Catholic (Jesuit) plays in the sixteenth and seventeenth centuries to represent God's care of His true followers.[16] Even without these connections the story has obvious potential, in the years immediately after the 1715 Rebellion, as an allegorised plea for justice for loyal Catholics indiscriminately victimised by punitive taxation as well as continued exclusion from public office. For Pope, and for any Catholic, this interpretation would have had the additional satisfaction of an allegorical takeover: the text used each year by Protestants to congratulate themselves publicly on victories over 'evil' Catholic forces was now used to represent Catholics in the role of the chosen people saved from misfortune.

The Cannons libretto favours the chosen people, adjusting the biblical and Racinian accounts to strengthen sympathy for the endangered Jews. In the Bible, Haman is activated by resentment of Mordecai's lack of deference to him; this motivation is almost totally absent from the libretto, so Haman appears more simply as a prototype paranoid dictator. The king is remote from his people, enabling Haman to work on him. The libretto's first line presents a colleague recommending tolerance to Haman: ''Tis greater far to spare than to destroy'. Haman responds that the king has vested all power in him and the Jews are to be wiped out and their temples destroyed: 'Pluck root and branch out of the land ... Shall we the God of *Israel* fear?' There is no ethically repellent massacre of the native majority in the libretto and, most significantly, all Racine's references to, and condemnations of, the irreligion of gentiles (who would be British Protestants in a Catholic reading of the story) are suppressed. Finally, Esther's status as heroine is enhanced, the Jews' salvation being more entirely her achievement. In the Bible, the king independently recollects her uncle Mordecai's service, which prompts him to reverse the decree against the Jews; in the libretto, he is reminded by Esther.

It is easy to read the Cannons libretto of *Esther* as produced by a circle sympathetic to Jacobitism and containing an unexceptionable plea for tolerance of minority views and the repeal of anti-Catholic legislation.[17] There is no reason to suppose that such a subtext would have been inimical to Handel who, as I have argued, seems always to have measured commissions principally according to their scope for his compositional power. But this is an instance where a coded message could have escaped the notice of the composer. The allegory was sufficiently flexible to stand for any national-religious group spared from persecution, hence its use in connection with the Torbay landing. So it could have seemed politically unexceptionable in 1732 as well, when *Esther* was first heard outside the Cannons circle, first at the Philarmonic Society and then at York Buildings. At this date it could also have acquired a new topicality: there had been a serious French invasion scare the previous year, and once more the story could aptly be enlisted to celebrate 'danger averted'.[18]

The potential or intended 'Catholic' reading could have been unrecognised by the majority. Yet the public linking of the libretto with Pope, known to be Catholic and suspected of being Jacobite, could have signalled an interpretation unacceptable to the crown and government. Perhaps this was one reason for some of the circumstances of the revised *Esther*: for the reported wish of Princess Anne for its public presentation, for the alterations to the text, for the royal family's conspicuous patronage of the work in its revised, 'Hanoverianised', form, and for the fact that the author of the libretto was not mentioned in Handel's advertisements, nor any reference made to Chandos (or anyone else) as the person for whom it was originally composed.[19] If so, this text, which may already have constituted an allegorical takeover, was now retaken. Tussles for ideological 'possession' of both biblical texts and historical record have already been noted. *Esther* may be a prime example of the similar tussles for historical myths and symbols which took place in the field of music theatre.[20] As so often, the ground had been prepared. Racine's *Esther* had already been given a Hanoverian association (*contra* its connection with James and Mary) by Pierre Coste, who in 1723 brought out the first English edition of Racine's works, including *Esther* and *Athalie*. His prefatory dedication, to Frederick Duke of Gloucester (the future Prince of Wales), is an early instance of efforts to teach Frederick the duties of a Patriot King.

The 'Hanoverianising' of *Esther* may have emanated from the Church as well as the crown. As is well known, according to Burney, Edmund Gibson, Bishop of London, took an active interest in Handel's first public performance of the oratorio, affecting the whole subsequent history of oratorio performance by prohibiting stage action.[21] Gibson at this period was doing his utmost to maintain the Church–state alliance which he had forged with Walpole and which he considered essential to the security of British Protestantism. This entailed enmity to latitudinarianism, Catholicism, and any political opposition to the Whig administration, which Gibson tended to see as Jacobitism in disguise.[22] Gibson's position weakened during the years 1727–36, as both Queen Caroline and Parliament opposed his policy. In 1731 his visitation charge included special exhortations to loyalty, as laymen and clergy showed signs of coming under Pulteney's spell, and in the same year he investigated a disturbing report of a sermon preached at St George's, Hanover Square (Handel's parish church), which was said to have promulgated opposition views and was on a text from the Book of Esther (V.13).[23] So Esther had come to Gibson's notice, and as a potentially seditious text, before Handel's performance. With his propensity for seeing Jacobites lurking under every Tory cloak, Gibson would surely have been aware of the possibility of reading Jacobite propaganda in *Esther*, whose libretto was publicly said to be by a Tory Papist. But the basic story of the libretto would certainly have appealed to him, since it enacts the goal he always had in view, the preservation of the true religion through the alliance of religion and state, and he might well have thought a Hanoverian version worth encouraging.

The new *Esther* received an unmistakable and prominent Hanoverian stamp in the form of two of the 1727 Coronation Anthems. The first, written for the part of the service during which the queen was anointed, was placed at the end of a new first scene of the Jews at prayer, voicing their hope that through Esther's power over the king

> Again shall Salem, to the Skies,
> From all her Woes triumphant rise,
> And our avenging God, with Speed,
> Captivity shall captive lead.

The second was placed at the end of Esther's audience with Ahasuerus. Choruses from the 1718 version, praising Esther's 'Virtue, truth and innocence' and anticipating God's deliverance of the Jews and His vengeance on their foes, are dwarfed in 1732 by an interpolated anthem, of which the second line of text comes from 'Zadok the Priest', but the first does not:

God is our Hope, and he will cause the King to shew Mercy to Jacob's Race.

God save the king! Long live the king! May the king live for ever! Amen. Hallelujah.

What are we to make of this reference to 'Jacob's Race' and a hope for royal indulgence to it, cast in Old Testament language and grafted onto an expression of loyalty to the regime by a nonconformist minority, set to music of the Hanoverian coronation? Or to the idea in the first scene that the queen will intercede for her persecuted co-religionists with the king, likewise associated with the music of the coronation? Conversely, from the final Israelite chorus of the 1718 version the 1732 version omits the claim that God 'plucks the mighty from his seat and cuts off half his days', which could be read as insulting to the crown and government, and the promises that 'The Lord his people shall restore / And we in Salem shall adore', which could be read as a subversive hope for a Stuart restoration. On the other hand again, the 1732 version enlarges the villainy of the king's first minister and deepens his fall. Act I scene 2, which is only in the 1732 version, shows the devoted minister informing his trusting master the king that

> The vassal *Jews*, through all thy Realms, disdain
> A due Subjection to thy gracious Reign;
> They boast, their God will plead their Cause,
> Restore their Temple, and their Laws.

In his opinion, 'Captivity's too mild to quell' their 'pernicious pride' and 'impious ardour'. The king naturally gives him a mandate to 'Avenge thy monarch on his foes ... Pursue their pride ... purge Rebellion from the tainted land'. But the Jews are not rebelling. The first minister is misrepresenting the peaceful oppressed minority to the ruler, who consequently orders repression. Here is a favourite theme of Patriot opposition drama, majesty misled by an evil minister. Appropriately the denouement is the rewarding of the true patriot, and to Ahasuerus' command in the 1718 libretto to execute Haman and honour Mordecai, the 1732 libretto adds an extended air for Ahasuerus more specifically replacing Haman with Mordecai: 'Through the nation he shall be / Next in dignity to me'. In opposition writing of the time Haman was one of the figures for Walpole.[24]

Apparently the royal family not only received this work equably, they conspicuously supported it. If they did not see it as allegory, what did they make of the prominence in it of their Coronation Anthems, the story which was so often used to refer to national events, and the familiar Patriot opposition theme? If they did, how could they read it to suit themselves, and how could any government supporter? The use of the anthems suggests that Ahasuerus represents George II and Esther Queen Caroline, and that we should view them favourably. This reading, however, fails to account for Ahasuerus' and Esther's different nationalities and religions (George and Caroline shared theirs), the extreme villainy and punishment of Haman (no one writing for rather than against the royal family would blacken Walpole so thoroughly), the need for Esther's plea to the king, the fact that the Jews are a nonconformist minority (the English are not), and the decree against them. A reading which mixes people and personifications, whereby Ahasuerus is George and Haman is Walpole but Esther is Britannia, guardian of British constitutional liberties, is warranted by other allegorical music theatre works, possibly including Humphreys' *Ulysses* (reading Ulysses as the Stuart king, the suitors as the Hanoverians and Penelope as Britain). This would please the Patriot opposition, who could see themselves as the Jews, but would not gratify the king, queen, minister or bishop. A Gibsonian version is possible, in which all the characters are personifications: the king is the state, Esther is the Church, enlisting the state's defence of true Protestant religion, and Haman is Catholicism. Even an anti-Gibson version is also possible, in which Esther (Caroline) intercedes with the king (George) in favour of the Tory and latitudinarian clergy, whom Caroline favoured in opposition to Gibson (Haman): this would be plausible in that Caroline's opposition brought Gibson close to resigning his bishopric.[25]

Other readings are probably available. But none I can think of fits neatly, and the lack of correspondence strongly suggests a hasty attempt at allegorical takeover. Like other attempts to stamp an alternative ideological impression on an existing work, *Esther* shows the joins in the scissors-and-paste treatment. For example, in *Merlin* (1735), reclaimed from Dryden's *King Arthur* for Hanoverian glorification, the centrepiece of Act I shows the German invaders of Britain sacrificing white horses; but this is highly inappropriate, since the white horse was Hanover's emblem. It would seem that some aspects of the revised *Esther*, and royal patronage of it, embody a Hanoverian attempt to annex a potentially subversive text when it became public and showed signs of becoming popular.

Though we have no decisive factual evidence of Humphreys' politics, we can find a very clear political interpretation of the

Esther story in his three-volume biblical commentary, *The Sacred Books of the Old and New Testament, Recited at Large*, which, Humphreys' title informs us, is 'illustrated with critical and explanatory annotations, carefully compiled from the commentaries and other writings of Grotius, Lightfoot, Pool, Calmet, Patrick, Le Clerc, Lock, Burkit, Sir Isaac Newton, Pearse, and a variety of other authors, ancient and modern'. He does not indicate the individual sources of his comments, but it is obvious what he himself thinks about the story of Esther. He has two main points to make: that the salvation of the Jews is miraculous (notwithstanding apparent 'second causes'), and that it warns kings not to neglect their responsibilities. His comments are an outspoken version of the Patriots' 'majesty misled' theme:

She then laid before him the wickedness of Haman then present, who by his fraudful lies had surprised the king, and insolently made use of his royal name and authority, to prescribe [proscribe?] and destroy the whole nation of the Jews. Ahasuerus, who was a prince naturally inclined to justice and mercy, was astonished, when he considered, to what an excess his own credulity, and the inhuman disposition of his favourite, had like to have carried him ... It is evident from this history, that the heart of kings is in the hand of God, who by this book teaches them, that they must bear the burden of the crown themselves, and see with their own eyes; lest leaving their authority to others, they should meet with those who abuse it, like Haman, in the gratification of their own passions and corrupt interests, to the prejudice of justice, and of their prince's credit and reputation.[26]

Given the opposition's appropriation of this theme, it is difficult to avoid a partisan, or at least tendentious, reading of Humphreys' gloss. But his subsequent librettos for Handel do not suggest a consistent political intention. As already mentioned, he dedicated *Deborah* to Queen Caroline, expressing the utmost 'Loyalty and Veneration' and acknowledging that he was quite unable to represent his heroine, 'acting for the Happiness of her People, with half the Lustre that diffuses itself around Your Majesty's Conduct'. As for *Esther*, the music of *Deborah* underscores this loyalty, by recycling the Coronation Anthems.[27] But Deborah's first action in the libretto is to select a leader for the Israelites, who desperately need to find a new one who will rescue them from heathen oppression. In the early 1730s the lack of a strong national leader to redeem the population from tyrannical rule was a favourite theme of Patriot opposition writing (see chapter 10), whereas Caroline was Walpole's most powerful supporter, so clearly the analogy of heroine and queen cannot be pushed very far in the political direction.

More surprising, if we take Humphreys' protestations of loyalty to be genuine, is his authorship of the libretto of *Athalia*. This dramatises a part of the Old Testament which was a crucial debating point in the discussion of the validity of the 1688 Revolution and a favourite Nonjuror and Jacobite parallel: the story of the restoration of the true heir to the throne and the despatch of the usurping queen.[28] The story had a strong tradition of interpretation as an example of Whig principles of law and liberty triumphing over tyrannical despotism and religious persecution. Previous exponents of it in this guise included the author of the anti-Cromwellian *Killing No Murder* (1657, frequently reprinted in the mid eighteenth century), who used as epigraph 2 Chronicles XXV.27, 'And all the People of the land rejoyced, and the City was quiet, after that they had slain *Athaliah* with the sword',[29] and William Duncombe, in the prefatory dedication of his translation of Racine's play (1722, 1726, 1746).[30] Humphreys himself, in his biblical commentary, described how 'Athaliah tyrannised over Judah without controul, filling Jerusalem with blood, and destroying the servants of the true God, that she might the more effectively establish the worship of Baal throughout the kingdom.'[31] But since the Revolution, when the Nonjurors established a strong claim to it, this was one of the ideological tropes which had most firmly resisted dual possession.

Athalia was written for the English stronghold of Toryism and Jacobitism, Oxford,[32] where three months before its first performance toasts had been drunk to the Pretender for three nights in succession to celebrate the defeat of the Excise Bill.[33] As already mentioned, the Athalia of the libretto has the characteristics of a despot as well as a usurper, and the priesthood (whose power was a constant Whig bugbear) is a more powerful force for radical, just, beneficial political change than in any other libretto. It is conceivable that Athalia represents James II and Joad the brave bishops who opposed him, but such a reading leaves the discovery and restoration of the true king, devoted upholder and future reformer of the true religion, unaccounted for. That discovery has exactly the effect that Jacobite writers depicted for the Pretender: instant recognition and acceptance as the indubitably rightful monarch.[34] Philip Brett and George Haggerty suggest that the coronation scene was intended to inspire the disaffected elements in the Oxford audience with loyalty to the ruling monarchy, but the line they cite in support of this idea, 'Bless the true Church and save the king', is capable of being taken either way: it expresses Nonjuring as well as Hanoverian sentiments, as Dean realised.[35]

If this libretto constitutes a Hanoverian allegorical takeover it is peculiarly inept, it is unsupported by musical references (there are no Coronation Anthems, or any other music associated with the crown, in *Athalia*), and its ideological ambition is foolhardy: one could hardly find a more challenging part of the Bible to reclaim or a more hostile venue for the first performance. As Shapiro points out, the first London performance of the music was for a royal event, the marriage of the Princess Royal, but the words were changed, to a whole new story (*Parnasso in festa*).[36]

*   *   *

From their inception, Handel's oratorios concerned themselves with scriptural events that had strong, and strongly contested, applications to contemporary political life for the mid-eighteenth-century audience, at least its educated members. They well illustrate how closely religion and politics were bonded in eighteenth-century English thought. The ambiguity of political meaning in these first three librettos is, we shall see in subsequent chapters, characteristic, and perhaps deliberate on the part of composer as well as librettist. The more numerous the possible interpretations, the wider the appeal, and Handel would be the first to appreciate the benefit this would bring to box-office takings.

CHAPTER 12

In time of war

ISRAEL IN EGYPT

As described in chapter 9, on 18 April 1739 the *London Daily Post* carried a letter, by 'R. W.', about a performance of *Israel in Egypt*. This is a remarkable instance both of how much political weight a single artistic text could be made to carry in mid-eighteenth-century England, and of the assured dexterity with which allusion could be wielded. The writer particularly mentions the presence in the audience of the Prince and Princess of Wales, rejoicing that these leading lights of the British people were 'able to be so highly delighted' with the oratorio: 'what a glorious Spectacle! to see a crowded Audience of the first Quality of a Nation, headed by the Heir apparent of their Sovereign's Crown and Virtues, with his lovely and beloved Royal Consort by his Side'.[1] The three performances of *Israel* coincided with the conclusion of Bolingbroke's stay in England (July 1738 to April 1739) to co-ordinate the attempt to bring down Walpole's government, and this 'review' is a single shot in the concerted assault. The performance attended by the prince and princess had not been part of Handel's programme for his season; the second was publicised as the last, and this extra one was announced as being mounted 'at the Desire of several Persons of Distinction'.[2]

The reviewer deploys the analogy of Britain with Israel to present the idea of a unified nation as natural, desirable, and, in the face of foreign aggression, essential, and Prince Frederick is presented in all his current Patriot opposition roles: as a popular leader of that united people (at one with his subjects in attending and enjoying the oratorio); as the figurehead of the opposition demands for war against Spain; and as a discerning patron of the arts.[3] Once again Handel's music was claimed as the focus for hopes of national unity

288

and strength, and served as a vehicle for political polemic. And in his conviction that if the whole population came together at times of national crisis to listen to Handel's oratorios about the chosen people's deliverance from foreign foes, it 'might expect ... the same *Deliverance* as those Praises celebrate', the writer aims to annex the idea that Handel's music can not only allude to, but actually create, national harmony and strength.[4]

This weight of interpretation rests on the Britain–Israel analogy and specifically on the word 'slavery', the opposition's rallying cry. The oratorio's account of the Israelites enslaved by the Egyptians matched the popular prints which urged strong measures against Spain. For example, a design of 1738 entitled 'Slavery' and used at least twice shows a Spaniard driving four Englishmen in a plough; Walpole, walking behind, compels the British lion to follow at sword-point, while a Spaniard cuts off Jenkins' ear and at sea a Spanish ship fires on an English one which does not return fire, the caption being a quotation from John of Gaunt's dying speech in *Richard II*. The frontispiece to the poem *The Voice of Liberty* (1738) shows a subterranean prison in which British sailors lie manacled, chained to the floor, exhibited by their gaoler to a Spaniard and a fat friar, the legend reading 'And dare they, dare the vanquish'd sons of Spain / Enslave a Briton?' – a quotation from Mark Akenside's 'A British Philippic' (*Gentleman's Magazine*, August 1738), which also describes this scene.[5] In February 1738 the *Craftsman* reported English sailors 'enslaved' in Spanish prison labour gangs; on 22 February 1739 the petition of the London merchants to the House of Lords protesting against the Convention of El Pardo which had been agreed with Spain referred to Spaniards' 'barbarous and inhuman treatment of the British sailors on the taking of their ships, and their carrying them afterwards into slavery in Old Spain'.[6]

R. W. was not the only writer of his day to detect a partisan message in *Israel in Egypt*. The *Daily Post*'s equally oppositionist sister paper, the *London Evening Post*, also claimed the oratorio as topical political polemic, reporting, the day after the first performance, that future performances might be banned because of its political content: 'the Patrons and Lovers of Musick were in great Pain for the fate of the new oratorio at the Haymarket; some persons apprehending, with a good deal of reason, that the title of *Israel in Egypt* was, to the full, as obnoxious as that of *The Deliverer of his Country*'.[7]

But this report gives a different twist to the political inference. *The*

Deliverer of his Country was the inflammatory sub-title of Henry Brooke's Patriot opposition play *Gustavus Vasa*, which was considered so subversive by the government that it was suppressed – the first victim of the Licensing (stage censorship) Act of 1737. Like other plays forbidden the stage, it was published. 'Such a prohibition alone, as people are now inclined', wrote Thomas Edwards of Lincoln's Inn about it to the Virgil scholar Lewis Crusius, 'is enough to raise their curiosity and pique them into a subscription.'[8] Possibly this mention of the oratorio's threatened cancellation was invented as a means of increasing the subscription.[9] The Patriot opposition paper directed by Lord Chesterfield, *Common Sense*, reprinted the play's very explicit prologue three days after *Israel in Egypt*'s première (7 April). One reason for the play's suppression may have been that it could be read not just as being heavily imbued with Patriot opposition themes (a king misled by an evil chief minister, a national hero saving his country from corruption and oppression, the restoration of national integrity) but as propagating Jacobitism: as proposing not only reform of the government but a change of monarchy. The king from whom Gustavus delivers his country, Sweden, is a usurping Dane, while Gustavus himself belongs to the old, native, ousted royal family. 'Obnoxious' had the strong sense of 'reprehensible' in the eighteenth century, and must have been an entirely appropriate description of the government's view of the play.[10]

Is the *Evening Post*'s linking of the play and the oratorio more than opportunist advertising; does it mean that *Israel in Egypt* was seen to be capable of bearing a Jacobite interpretation? The allegory, as so often in eighteenth-century writing, is there if one wants to see it. The Israelites, first dispossessed by a new, hostile regime in Egypt and then led by a native hero (brought up in a foreign court) to reclaim the land (Canaan) given them by divine will, can be read as standing for the exiled Jacobites, supplanted by the Hanoverians, led by the Pretender (likewise brought up in a foreign court and in Jacobite eyes king by divine right) to the restoration of the legitimate succession (and of their own rights). There is textual and biographical support for this reading.

Moses' redemption of the Israelites and their passage to the promised land through the Red Sea, like many national myths in the eighteenth century, had a history as contested ground, but in this case the terrain was mainly occupied by the opposition. It had been invoked as an image of the Stuart Restoration, for example by Abraham Cowley in his *Ode upon His Majesties Restoration and Return* and by Thomas Rawlins on his medals representing Charles II as Moses rescuing the Israelites from Egyptian slavery.[11] William III subsequently made a bid for it: in Shadwell's Birthday Ode for Queen Mary in 1689, William was the 'great Moses' who freed the English people from 'the most abject slavery'.[12] More recently another Stuart sympathiser, the poet Richard Savage, had harnessed the image to modern Jacobitism with a wish, in 'Britannia's Miseries', that the sea had 'to the Usurper's Cost / Renew'd the Scene of Pharoah and his Host' during George I's crossing to Hanover in July 1716.[13] In his study of Jacobite songs Murray Pittock notes parallels being made between great Jacobite families in England and the Israelites in Egyptian bondage.[14] *Israel in Egypt* joins *Athalia* (see chapter 11) as an oratorio susceptible of Jacobite interpretation.

Such an interpretation may have been intended by one of the authors. The libretto is very probably by Charles Jennens, a Non-juring Jacobite sympathiser (and one of the anti-governmentalists who subscribed to the publication of *Gustavus Vasa*). He referred to his compilation of *Messiah* as 'another Scripture Collection I have made for him [Handel]',[15] and the only Handel oratorio before *Messiah* which could be so described is *Israel*. Moreover, Jennens' friend the Jacobite Edward Holdsworth, who was interested in Handel only insofar as Jennens was involved, recalled offence taken by a Church dignitary at 'Exodus' (that is, *Israel*), when discussing with Jennens 'the clamours rais'd against Messiah' reported 'to arise from the B^Ps' (bishops).[16] Whether the clergy's objection was pro-voked by the use of Scripture in the theatre or by Jacobite impli-cations (or both) is not known. As in *Messiah*, the words of *Israel* are taken unaltered from the Bible, except for the passages from the Psalms, which use the Book of Common Prayer version. (*Esther* had used verbatim biblical text; but this was before the Licensing Act caused librettos to be inspected.) A further hint that Jennens com-piled *Israel* is the fact that Handel performed both *Israel* and *Messiah*, alone among his oratorios, in Passiontide, the season for which Jennens stated he specifically intended the latter.[17] This timing incidentally suggests that the authors of *Israel* were subscribing to the typological interpretation of the Israelite salvation at the Red Sea as an image of Christian salvation.

But the form of political opposition decoded from the libretto need not have been so extreme as Jacobitism. In contemporary usage, 'slavery' was a potent antithesis for 'liberty' not just in the context of conflict with Spain but in relation to home affairs, referring to the alleged oppression of the populace by the administration (see chapter 8) – a staple of Patriot rhetoric which would have come naturally to the *Craftsman*-reading Jennens, and which should be borne in mind whenever 'slavery' is resisted in the librettos. The oratorio could be taken as suggesting the hoped-for release of traders from Spanish 'oppression', of Stuart loyalists from Hanoverian 'usurpation', and of citizens from the administration's 'oppression'. In *Israel in Egypt*'s language and reception we have a further striking instance of the ability of texts to carry, and their eighteenth-century readers to elicit, topical and varying political messages.

SAMSON, ALFRED AND THE PRINCE OF WALES

In its basic plot of the renewal and exertion of national strength against the heathen oppressor, Newburgh Hamilton's libretto of *Samson*, written in its initial form by autumn 1741 and dedicated in the wordbook to the Prince of Wales, again reflects the prince's support of the war with Spain for which the Patriots had clamoured.[18] The oratorio's 'story' is that of its source, Milton's *Samson Agonistes*. As already described (chapters 9 and 10), in the eighteenth century *Samson Agonistes* was read as a political document, and Hamilton served his dedicatee's role at the head of a party whose chief tenet was national unity by excising all references to the conflict between Samson and his fellow Israelites and their failure to support him, which Milton had retained from the Book of Judges.[19] The political weight of *Samson* itself was buttressed by several extra-textual supports. The libretto was not an isolated instance of harnessing the reputation of Milton the radical to current opposition propaganda. On the contrary, it was written precisely during the years (1738–42) when his works (genuine and attributed) were reprinted to uphold the liberty of the press against the Licensing Act (*Areopagitica*) and to support opposition demands for robust behaviour towards Spain (the *Manifesto of the Lord Protector*, justifying Cromwell's war with Spain). Like Milton, the latter-day Patriots regarded a free press as a cornerstone of civil liberty, and *Areopagitica*, we recall, contains the unforgettable comparison of regenerate England with Samson triumphant – 'Methinks I see in my mind a noble and puissant Nation rousing herself like a strong man after sleep, and shaking her invincible locks.' Andrew Millar's edition of 1738 was announced in the *Craftsman*, and the *Manifesto* was given an epigraph from Thomson's *Britannia*, a key Patriot poem. Dustin Griffin has drawn attention to further invocations of Milton by opposition writers to sanction their polemic; clearly Milton was something of a Patriot opposition figurehead at the time of *Samson*.[20]

But there may be a secondary source for the libretto, which would also connect it with the prince's political interests. I believe it has not previously been noticed that the first part of *Samson* is strikingly similar to the corresponding part of David Mallet's, James Thomson's and Thomas Arne's masque *Alfred*, also written for the prince and first performed in 1740, the year before Handel began *Samson*.[21] *Alfred* begins with the hero collapsed on the ground, isolated and dispossessed, being discussed (unknown to him – he is too prostrated to notice) by his sympathising fellow-countrymen, who, like him, are being oppressed by a foreign, viciously heathen, foe. So does *Samson*. And in both works, by the mid-point of the action, if such it can be called, the hero has *done* nothing, except grieve (his first utterance is a sustained cry of despair), be pitied, receive advice, and encounter his wife – although every speaker identifies him as the beleaguered nation's only hope of salvation. Of course this is also the groundwork, stripped of its argumentativeness, of *Samson Agonistes*, Hamilton's primary source, which raises the question whether that poem was also a source for *Alfred* – especially given that Thomson was a devoted reader of Milton. It was he who wrote the preface to the 1738 edition of *Areopagitica*, enlisting Milton on behalf of the opposition's fight for civic liberties. (Part of his preface illuminates *Israel in Egypt*, which was written in the year of its publication, and indeed other Israelite librettos in which the nation is enslaved, captive or oppressed: 'We are told in History, of a People [the Cappadocians] that after they had been inured to Slavery, were in a panick Fear, when their Liberty was offered to them. And this *terrible* Effect of Slavery ought to make every Lover of Mankind tremble at the Thoughts of any Steps or Approaches towards the Diminution of Liberty.' Willing submission to enslavement is common to the Israelites of Exodus and of *Samson Agonistes*, but conspicuously uncharacteristic of the oratorio Israelites.)

Thomson's masque was not the first literary work about King Alfred to be dedicated to the prince; Sir Richard Blackmore had inscribed his epic poem *Alfred* to the sixteen-year-old Frederick, with the same purpose of teaching him good kingship and with a similarly passive hero – indeed, Blackmore, to whose prescriptions for morally inspiring creativity his literary successors frequently referred, defended at length this unorthodoxly inactive kind of hero, with examples from Scripture. His claims for the power of an epic with a passive hero make an instructive gloss on *Samson*, suggesting to us the warmth with which the eighteenth-century audience could respond to a treatment which some modern commentators find tedious (see chapter 5).[22]

For the Patriot opposition, the historical King Alfred was more than an ideal ruler; he represented the purity of the 'gothic' (Saxon) constitution, from which, according to Old Whig and mid-century Patriot opposition thinking, descended the present constitution – the glory of England and safeguard of her people's interest, which the government was threatening to destroy by multiple instruments of 'corruption'. One of the greatest opposition poems, Johnson's *London* (1738), includes the myth of 'Alfred's golden reign' among its stock ideological references; likewise in the 'Epistle to Augustus' (1737) Pope's pantheon of British rulers who subdued enemies, secured property, humbled ambition 'Or Laws establish'd, and the World reform'd' comprises Edward III, Henry V, and 'a more sacred name', Alfred. With this application in view Frederick had invested heavily in the Alfred topos, for example by erecting a statue of him in the garden of his London house bearing, as the *Craftsman* pointedly reported, 'a Latin Inscription; in which it is particularly said, that this Prince was the Founder of the Liberties and Commonwealth of England'. (To refer to Alfred in one's garden architecture was itself a fashionable opposition gesture, also made by Lord Bathurst at Cirencester and Lord Cobham at Stowe.) In the best traditions of English masque, *Alfred* is highly charged with the ideology of its patron. There is no question now, and there was none in 1740, about its political import: it famously includes 'Rule Britannia' and has for its principal theme not simply the triumph of British defences of British independence but Britain's capacity for supreme political, civic, artistic, commercial, naval and military strength, to be realised through national revival brought about by virtuous government under a Patriot King. The bulk of the masque teaches good kingship, and after a sequence of visions of glorious British monarchs (also a feature of two earlier patriotic English operas, Addison's *Rosamond* and Aaron Hill's unrealised *Hengist and Horsa, or The Origin of England*)[23] Frederick is instructed to model himself on Alfred in order to become the climax of that sequence. In doing so, he would not have been a sectarian prince, for though Alfred and the Saxon state were especially admired in Patriot circles, like so many touchstones of political worth they were also claimed by the administration.[24] Nevertheless, *Alfred* was received by the discerning as an undoubtedly opposition work, to judge from the comment of the young Elizabeth Robinson (later Montagu), who compared it with a paradigm of an opposition play: 'I think the plot seems not unlike *Gustavus Vasa*, a hero in distress whose je ne scai quoi heroical fashion, in taking a walk, or sitting down on a bank, betray an air of majesty that you know may be a compliment to our countrymen, to show how sagacious they are; or that, like lions, they can smell the blood royal.' Here is a striking example of shared tropes, for the sudden recognition of the disguised but unmistakably rightful king by his loyal subjects was a favourite Jacobite topic.[25]

The common theme, common dramatisation, common date, common dedicatee and possibly common source of *Alfred* and *Samson* are powerful arguments for bringing the oratorio libretto into the canon of Patriot dramas. But where *Alfred* gets down to the business of Frederick's moral-political education it leaves *Samson* behind. Hamilton's libretto is – by comparison with *Alfred* and with its Miltonic source – conspicuously unencumbered with political discussion: debate is distilled to religious-political confrontation. The two texts were of course written for very different audiences, *Samson* for a paying public of varying political interests, *Alfred* for a private patron with a distinct political agenda (*Alfred* was itself filleted of its political theory for its public performances in 1745 and 1751).[26] Unlike the masque, the oratorio does not refer explicitly to the condition of Britain, and to that extent it is not tied to a specific (or indeed any) allegorical interpretation. But if we accept it as implying the Israel–Britain analogy, on the basis of contemporary reading of Milton's text and the currency of the parallel, the libretto is topical in a way the masque is not, in that it does not look beyond the present conflict (whereas *Alfred* anticipates an era of peaceful, virtuous splendour); its action is bounded by the struggle against the enemy. However, within this general situation it is unspecific: the audience can associate the Israelite–Philistine confrontation with any hostilities, and if the original audiences associated it with current hostilities, they could make connections with any phase of them. Focusing on the political contexts in which *Samson*'s early performances were heard both suggests ways in which the oratorio may have been interpreted and reminds us of the fluctuations of interpretation caused by changing circumstance.

Even when an oratorio was new, its libretto was old. There was usually at least a ten-month gap between the day on which Handel began to set a text (which might of course have been finished earlier) and the first performance of the resulting work. During the gap of seventeen months between Handel's start on *Samson* and its first performance the political scene changed considerably. While Hamilton was writing his libretto the press was reporting the parliamentary 'motion' to remove Walpole and commenting on an opposition pamphlet criticising British foreign policy since 1725 with regard to the conflict in Europe, attacking the conduct of the war in the West Indies, and arraigning corrupt government at home.[27] Samson could well symbolise this Britain – native strength shackled by maladministration. He might also represent an actual national hero, for Hamilton was writing at the height of the national adulation of Admiral Vernon, who was popularly regarded as having achieved the few triumphs of the Spanish war in the teeth of the obstruction and incapacitating dilatoriness of a hostile government. Vernon was a trenchant critic of that government as Member of Parliament for Penrhyn, and after his victories he was adopted as an opposition totem. It is easy to believe that Hamilton's image of his thwarted hero, forced to suffer the insults of his enemies and critical of his compatriots, would have struck a very topical chord with its audience if the oratorio had been performed soon after completion of its libretto.[28] But it was not, and at its actual first performance (18 February 1743) the image of the defeated hero may have made the audience wince in a way Hamilton could not have anticipated, for the final actions of the West Indies campaign had been the disastrous attack on Cartagena and the abortive expeditions to Cuba and Panama – perceived at home as the culmination of government mismanagement, causing disunity in British high command, national humiliation, and the beginning of the end of the Spanish war – while Britain's involvement in the European war had so far been conspicuously ineffectual.

It is just possible that in addition to being a potential symbol of (according to one's inclination) Britain, the British naval forces, and Vernon, Samson could symbolise the unfortunate Brigadier-General Thomas Wentworth, commander of land forces, whose reputation had to wait nearly two and a half centuries to be cleared from the misrepresentations of his opposite number, Vernon. The public image of Wentworth being successfully projected by Vernon during 1743 was one of inept passivity; in fact it appears that he was constantly thwarted and frustrated by Vernon. Either way, Samson's inactivity in the face of the enemy is an apt enough parallel, and Wentworth may well have been in Hamilton's mind even more clearly than he was in the public's, because he was a kinsman of Hamilton's late master the Earl of Strafford.[29]

Britain's role in Europe – by 1743 of greater public concern than the war with Spain – was also seen by the opposition to be stymied by government malingering. The press made much of that perennial thorn in the side of British desires for national unity, the influence of Hanover on British foreign policy. This resentment had been hugely exacerbated in 1741–2 by a Hanoverian treaty of neutrality with France of which Parliament was informed only after the event.[30] Parliament had voted subsidies for Hessian and Danish troops to rescue Britain's ally Austria and thereby avert the threat of French domination, but these troops were first immobilised in Hanover and then put into winter quarters, and Austria collapsed.[31] The 16,000 Hanoverian troops taken into British pay in August 1742 were not deployed and British troops sent to the Low Countries appeared ineffectual. The issue of the Hanoverian troops was the major popular grievance of the months immediately leading up to *Samson*'s first performance and provoked the suggestion (not new to the royal family) that the union with Hanover be dissolved and the electorate ceded to one of the princes.[32] But during the latter part of 1742, after Prussia made peace with Austria, the war went against France and there was talk of carving up her territory. The press even spoke of conquest.[33] In early 1743 Samson's initial incapacity and eventual triumph over the Philistines must have seemed a plausible as well as apt image of British fortunes in the war. While the opposition's usual attitude to European conflict was that Britain should not become involved, in 1743 Frederick was coming under the spell of Carteret's policy of full engagement, so *Samson*'s dedication to him was still appropriate, even though the focus of public interest and the war which the prince was encouraging had changed since the libretto was written.[34]

A later revival of *Samson*, in 1744, again coincided with national events to which the libretto's plot must have seemed peculiarly relevant. Allied victory against the French at Dettingen the previous summer had not been followed through with further action, and lack of unity at home was mirrored by discord in the army, preferential treatment of the Hanoverian troops at the expense of British forces provoking the resignation of the veteran commander, Lord Stair. Press reports during winter 1743–4 presented Dettingen as a lucky fluke and brought xenophobia in general and anti-Hanoverian feeling in particular to an unprecedented pitch. Then the mood was switched to one of loyal unanimity. Two days before the performance of *Samson* on 24 February 1744 a French fleet, having sailed unopposed up the Channel, anchored off Dungeness, where it remained until the night of the performance itself when, as the *Gentleman's Magazine* reported, it was deflected by the weather rather than the British navy.[35] The navies of Spain and France (now dangerously allied) had evaded the British Mediterranean fleet's attempts to contain them, and the Pretender's eldest son had been seen at Calais on the point of embarking for an invasion of Britain supported by France.

The helpless Samson must have seemed all too vivid an image of the threatened British nation; and, as handled by Hamilton, the hero's revival offered the interested audience a very singular form of reassurance. This is an instance where the librettist differs significantly from his source. By the time of his refusal to perform at the Philistine feast the Samson of Milton's poem has regained all his former heroic stature and reassumed complete confidence in his powers; across a vast spiritual distance, he reassures his countrymen. But Hamilton's Samson inspires no confidence in his compatriots at this juncture; on the contrary:

MICAH
> How thou wilt here come off surmounts my Reach;
> 'Tis Heav'n alone can save both us and thee.

CHORUS OF ISRAELITES
> With thunder arm'd, great God, arise;

> Help, Lord, or Isr'el's champion dies:
> To thy protection this thy servant take,
> And save, O save us, for thy servant's sake.   (Act III scene 1)

Alfred/Frederick is galvanised by instructive human examples; Samson and the Israelites, no longer hero and inferiors but, at the crisis, equally powerless, wait upon God's aid, and there is no certainty that it will materialise. Hamilton echoes the contemporary preachers' presentation of the survival of the nation as entirely dependent on divine compassion; he has turned *Samson Agonistes* into a Fast sermon. In this case the appeal is answered, and Samson is inspired to pull the heathen temple down on the Philistines, but (as in Milton) he destroys himself too. The nation's setbacks, its oppression by an alien race, the only partly heroic career of its hero, its absolute dependence on divine favour which cannot be claimed to be merited, and its recognition of divine agency in every success – all these aspects of this oratorio, which recur throughout the librettos about the Israelites, even when taken with the many expressions of faith, strength and confidence which also recur, do not add up to triumphalism.

Hamilton, Handel and *Alfred* were to coincide once more, in another plea for divine aid at a time of national emergency: the air 'Prophetic visions strike my eye' in the *Occasional Oratorio*, hoping for victory, peace and an end to war, appropriately quotes the music of the prophetic vision of national prosperity at the end of *Alfred*, 'Rule Britannia'.[36]

THE PAIN OF WAR: *JUDAS MACCHABÆUS* AND *ALEXANDER BALUS*

Morell's *Judas Macchabæus* has more shadows in it than modern critics' comments suggest. The music may convey 'external glitter and violent asseveration',[37] but the libretto is fraught with anxiety. Of the fifty-nine numbers twenty-five are about oppression, or the recovery of freedom, or both (deploying the prime emotive political trigger-word of the period, 'liberty'); nine refer to, call for, or are prayers for aid; eleven concern rededication to the service of God, as the only real basis of security. Taking their cue from the congratulatory preface to the Duke of Cumberland, modern critics have read the libretto simply as celebrating the satisfactory quelling of the Rebellion, but it was written soon after the official declaration of war with France, to which there was no satisfactory outcome in sight. The libretto's anxiety reflects the devastating French inroads on the crucial defences in the Low Countries, where the Barrier fortresses were 'going down like ninepins' during 1746–7.[38] The opening scene of lamentation and fear was apt:

> From this dread Scene, these adverse Pow'rs,
>   Ah! whither shall we fly?
> O *Solyma*, thy boasted Tow'rs
>   In smoky Ruins lie.
> Ah whither shall we fly?

Handel began composition in July 1746, and by the time of the first performance (1 April 1747) the French had also seized Madras from Britain, while hopes for success in Italy, kindled in 1746, had been extinguished. The final air hymns the blessings of 'lovely Peace', and the prayer at the most exalted moment of the libretto – not a victory but an act of worship, the celebration of Chanuka – expresses unequivocally the suffering caused by the double trauma of rebellion at home and war abroad:

> O grant it, Heav'n, that our long Woes may cease,
> And *Judah*'s Daughters taste the Calm of Peace;
> Sons, Brothers, Husbands to bewail no more,
> Tortur'd at Home, or havock'd in the War.[39]

There is a literary parallel in William Collins' odes to peace and to liberty, probably also written in 1746, which invoke the return of peace and concord to 'Britain's ravaged shore'.[40] Among librettists Morell is particularly aware that the Israelite army consists of *people*. It is likely, given his interest in the militia debate, as shown in his Excise ballad (see chapter 8), that the prominence of the citizen army in his librettos reflects the contemporary desire for militia reform. But in 1746–7 to wish for peace was not necessarily just a simple humane desire; it could be a polemical declaration. Fuelled by the capture of Louisbourg (see chapter 10), enthusiasm was widespread for continuing the land war in order to make commercial gains from France, while James Ralph's paper *The Remembrancer* maintained the opposition orthodoxy of 'blue-water' policy – only the defence of Britain (in the form of attempts to halt the overthrow of the Barrier towns) justified continuing the war on land. *The Remembrancer* was sponsored by the prince, and in view of Morell's connection with Frederick it is interesting that the desire expressed

in *Judas* for a war to end war accords with *The Remembrancer*'s policy
rather than reflecting the populist desire for further engagement.[41]

Morell's *Alexander Balus* (libretto 1747) has had a particularly bad
press. Winton Dean summarises the plot in his most reductive vein,
commenting that 'The material in *Maccabees* ... was not promising,
and Morell's fumbling treatment has not improved it.'[42] His main
criticisms of the libretto are that personal motives and relationships
are underdeveloped or obscure, that the two apparent themes, 'a
glorification of Jewish patriotism and religion and a pathetic love
story', are not fused, and that the end is 'ethically repulsive' in that
'Alexander is destroyed, not by the consequence of his own acts or
defects of character, but by his father-in-law's treachery', and his
ally does not mourn him but attributes all that has happened to the
just will of God. This is to criticise the libretto for not being like a
Shakespearian tragedy, which may damn it for a modern listener;
but Morell's text would have suited the eighteenth-century play-
goer. Steele's prescriptions for tragedy, for example, propose just
this sort of ending, in which the catastrophe is not the 'fault' of its
victim.[43] Perhaps a closely knit tragedy concerning the characters
and emotions of individuals, was not Morell's aim. Alexander's
death is like life, not art, and the libretto makes more sense as a
consideration of the hazards of international *Realpolitik* in which
personal feelings go for nothing and individual virtue is unre-
warded.

The action opens with the victory parade of Alexander, who has
wrested the Syrian throne from its occupant and who may or may
not be its rightful heir – a provocative *donnée* at this date, less than
two years after the most successful post-Revolution Jacobite
attempt to regain the British throne. Two alliances are rapidly
formulated and another is mentioned as being recently concluded:
Syria–Israel (Jonathan), Israel–Rome, Syria–Egypt (Ptolemy). In
contrast to these public affairs, Ptolemy's daughter Cleopatra and
Alexander fall in love, Alexander being completely overpowered by
his emotion. Ptolemy turns out to have been using Cleopatra as a
pawn to win Alexander's trust, which he then abuses by seizing
control of Syria and abducting her. The end is desolate. Alexander,
vanquished by Ptolemy, is murdered by an ally from whom he seeks
help; Ptolemy is killed in battle; Cleopatra, racked with grief,
withdraws from the world. The messages are bleak, and they are
culled from recent political experience: trans-national dynastic

marriages are fraught with danger, and international alliances are at best high-risk enterprises.

But Morell (unsurprisingly for his time and for his calling as a clergyman) distinguishes throughout his libretto between the heathen and the Jewish characters (in contemporary terms, Papist and Protestant) and some of his additional messages are more encouraging to the Protestant cause in the ongoing war against France. Heathens are prone to treachery, but in the end this will harm them more than it harms believers in the true God. God's ways are mysterious but 'always true and just' and include the preservation of His chosen people. In the message (distasteful to modern humanists) that heathens are unlikely to succeed, simply because they are heathen, there may be a reference to the chief block to readmission of the Stuarts to the throne, their religion. Morell shows that Alexander is morally unimpeachable (this is the point of the scene in which he scorns the attempt of 'a sycophant courtier' to calumniate Jonathan), but doomed nevertheless, because of his false religion. When he goes to fight (Part III), Jonathan fears for his safety, since 'The Creature-Gods he trusteth, cannot help. – / They are no Gods, but mere Delusion all'.

The libretto's connection of correct piety to temporal success (and the reverse) and its attribution to God of an appropriate conclusion to human hostilities may reflect another of Morell's professional interests, besides his clerical calling. In the year after the first performances of *Alexander Balus* he published a two-volume edition of Euripides for Eton (where he had been a pupil himself before taking up a scholarship at King's College, Cambridge), and in the following year he brought out a translation of Euripides' *Hecuba*.[44] In the works of Euripides he would have found dramatisations of man's relation to the controlling powers of his life on this earth which reach very similar conclusions to those of his libretto. His account of *Hecuba* in the preface to his translation provides a gloss for the conclusion of *Alexander Balus*: the 'chief Moral ... is the Frailty and Uncertainty of all human Grandeur, wherein Mortals cannot put their Trust, and are therefore led to an humble Resignation in all Things to divine Providence'.[45]

More instances could be cited from *Alexander Balus* of Morell's moral-political consciousness, for example his encapsulation of Patriot watchwords in the phrase 'Liberty, that Life of Life itself, / And Soul of Property' (Part I). The most interesting seems to me to be his focus (intensified by his combination of stories which are separate in the Apocrypha) on the frailty of those tools of human grandeur, alliances. During his lifetime Britain had moved from an isolationist peace to involvement in an intercontinental war, an increased amount of secret diplomacy, and multiple, fluctuating alliances whose net result (in 1747) was severe disenchantment with allies, notably the Dutch. The opposition press consistently criticised government policy for excessive attempts to negotiate and sustain alliances that were largely for Hanover's benefit and did nothing for the British interest, and its views were not confined to opposition sympathisers. The war itself was read as resulting directly from the fragility of complicated alliances, many based on family relationships, which concerned Britain only through Hanover, and it prompted pained comment on the treacherous opportunism of most of the powers embroiled in it.[46] Whether there are specific references in *Alexander Balus* to recent events (for instance to Britain's alliance with a Catholic power (Austria) in the Israel–Syria alliance) I leave to historians of this highly complex period of foreign diplomacy to determine; certainly Morell's gloomy account of foreign entanglements is consistent with his opposition track record.[47] The contemporary political context lends the libretto more vitality and coherence than do the canons of mid-twentieth-century literary criticism hitherto used to condemn it. To adopt Pocock's grand sentence, which could be applied equally to other texts considered in this chapter, 'What to one investigator looks like the generation of linguistic muddles and misunderstandings may look to another like the generation of rhetoric, literature, and the history of discourse.'[48]

CHAPTER 13

Images of government

THE PRIME MINISTER

James Miller's libretto of *Joseph and his Brethren*, which begins with its hero's entry to the service of Pharaoh, portrays in the character of Joseph a perfect chief minister. It was written after the fall of Robert Walpole, the most powerful chief minister since Wolsey (to whom Walpole was often compared by his detractors). Polemic against Walpole continued well into 1743; government critics demanded that the minister who had been forced to resign should be called to account. Almost nothing came of this, and disillusion with government was deepened among Patriots committed to reform by the apostasy of their leader William Pulteney (see chapter 8). While Miller's libretto was being set by Handel, the king's chief minister was Lord Carteret, whose pro-Hanoverian mind-set enraged patriots of every hue. The long-desired changes of political management altered none of the defects in government and public life of which moral-political writers like Miller complained.

Much of Miller's description of his hero recalls contemporary writing about the desired qualities of a head of government:

> PHANOR   He's *Egypt*'s common Parent, gives her Bread;
> He's *Egypt*'s only Safety, only Hope;
> Whilst *Egypt*'s Welfare is his only Care.
> CHORUS   Blest be the Man by Pow'r unstain'd,
> Virtue there itself rewarding!
> Blest be the Man to Wealth unchain'd,
> Treasure for the Publick hoarding!
> ASENATH   *Phanor*, we mention not his highest Glory,
> Mark midst his Grandeur what Humility,
> The Gift of that great God whom he adores.   (Part II scene 1)

These are the phrases, this is the language used both by government hacks defending Walpole and by the Patriot opposition prescribing the longed-for saviour who would redeem the nation from the depredations of Walpole's government. Joseph had been familiar as a figure for Walpole since at least 1733, when during the Excise crisis Sir Robert was baited in Parliament with a damaging comparison between himself and Joseph:

Sir Robert continues to be every day affronted and exposed in the Parliament House ... The other day Mr Oglethorpe run a parallel between Sir Robert and Joseph; said how oppressive Joseph was to the Egyptians – contrived to get both their land and children after reducing 'em to the hard condition of selling 'em for bread, while he fed his own family with the fat of the land; but Pharaoh at last died, and then there arose a king that knew not Joseph, and his posterity was forced to make bricks without straw.[1]

Here and elsewhere in mid-century opinion Joseph is the image of the *evil* prime minister, an epitome of arbitrary government. But he also figured as an ideal governor. The flurry of publications during the late 1730s and early 1740s for and against Joseph's character and career reflects the debate about Walpole, which concerned not only his behaviour in the role of chief minister but the propriety of the role itself.[2] Like so much mid-century allegory, the figure of Joseph was capable of more than one interpretation.

Dean comments that Handel's setting of 'Blest be the man' 'might have come from a Coronation Anthem; the opening words are asseverated with the same rhythmic emphasis as "God save the King" in *Zadok the Priest*', which suggests a readiness on Handel's as well as Miller's part to connect biblical and modern rulers. Handel also cemented the Britain–Israel analogy in the last chorus, by drawing for it on his recent Dettingen Te Deum, which celebrated national success against the forces of Catholic absolutism.[3] Some interesting alterations which he made to Miller's text in the process of setting it may, moreover, indicate an an awareness of Joseph as a potentially ambiguous and inflammatory symbol. Miller's Pharaoh describes Joseph as 'godlike', which Handel cancelled, substituting 'worthy'. Pharaoh also, in both Bible and libretto, gives Joseph a name which Miller in a footnote (correctly) says means 'saviour of the world'; Handel altered this to 'father of the country'.[4] Miller's terms briefly remind us that Joseph was one of the major types of Christ in the traditional Christian interpretation of the Old Testament (see chapter 9); they also invoke the Patriot opposition's ideal of the virtuous ruler, a messianic figure. Handel's toning down of Joseph's status here may reflect a consciousness of the implied issues

and an unwillingness to implicate himself in the ideas of the opposition. 'Father of the country' was an adroit substitution in that it
could offend none of the audience, being used both by Patriots to
describe the ideal king and by supporters of the administration to
describe the actual king and prime minister.

Miller chose to follow what Duncan Chisholm has identified as his
intermediary source, Apostolo Zeno's *Giuseppe*,[5] rather than the Old
Testament, in making Joseph's responsibilities as Egypt's first
minister the reverse of the ones he has in the Bible. In the libretto
Joseph categorically states that 'Pharaoh made me not / Dispenser,
only Keeper of his Treasure', whereas in Genesis XLI.55–6 Pharaoh
gives Joseph sole responsibility for selling corn during the famine.
This change enabled Miller to continue Joseph's speech:

> Nor should Corruption cleave unto these Hands,
> Or would I touch what's sacred to the Publick,
> To save myself and Race from instant Ruin.
>
> (Part III scene 2)

There is no suggestion in the Genesis story that Joseph is liable to
charges of corruption in his execution of Pharaoh's decrees, but
peculation was precisely one of the forms of corruption of which
Walpole was most consistently accused. Another of the vices for
which oppositionists insistently upbraided him was ingratitude,
which Miller makes a major topic of his text – exemplified in
characters *other* than Joseph. Carteret was popularly seen as sacrificing his patriotism to his king, serving George's German interests
in high-level diplomacy and becoming altogether too European (he
spoke excellent German). Joseph too serves his monarch loyally, but
much is made of his unshakeable faith to his native customs and
interests. The evidence of Miller's other writings suggests overwhelmingly that his Joseph was meant as a pattern of what a good
statesman *should* be – *unlike* the modern chief ministers. As already
described, he wrote incisively against both Walpole and Carteret
(see chapter 8).

Joseph is a complement to the many current descriptions of the
Patriot King: a delineation of the ideal prime minister. Were it not
for Miller's known commitment to the opposition cause, we could
not be certain whether the modern parallel was perceived by the
author as a model or a reverse model, and the libretto's opacity may
have been deliberate. A supporter of the administration could have

accepted it as a grateful valediction to Walpole, while Miller's
co-oppositionists would have welcomed it as an addition to the
Patriot canon. *Joseph* has been derided by modern critics but, not
surprisingly given its combination of political topicality and sentimental drama, it was popular in Handel's day, and the composer
revived it frequently.[6] Consistent with his expressed principles,
Miller satirised Handel when he was a German composer of Italian
operas, but increasingly praised him when he turned to setting
English words – until he had entirely given up Italian opera,
whereupon Miller wrote him the text of *Joseph*, one of his final
meditations on the qualities required of a political leader.[7]

THE KING, THE STATE, THE CHURCH AND THE LAW

Handel's oratorios all had their first public performances during the
reign of George II. The exception in George's dismal record as a
patron of the arts was his love of music; he famously maintained his
favour to Handel even when the composer was at his least fashionable. Yet none of the librettos is dedicated to George, and only one
of the fifteen narrative oratorios portrays a successful Israelite king.
In seven there is no king at all, and in seven the ruling king (or
queen) is deeply flawed, or not the king of Israel, or both.[8] Only
Solomon seems to continue the English masque and court ode tradition of allegorically celebrating the monarch in words-and-music.
This is unlikely to be because the time-honoured analogy of the
British monarchy to the Old Testament kings was now thought
obsolescent. As Manuel Schonhorn notes, Defoe, in many respects a
modernist, returns to it constantly, and not as mere decoration: his
ideal of kingship *is* the Old Testament warrior king.[9]

But monarchy does not appear as a happy institution in the
librettos. There is no problem-free dynasty. In *Esther* the king is led
astray by Haman, his first minister; Athalia and Saul are, or
become, despots and are deposed; Pharaoh (in *Joseph*) has a defective legal system and worse religion; *Belshazzar* and *Alexander Balus*
recount the overthrow of monarchies; and Solomon has arrived at
his throne by executing his elder half-brother. Contemporary
polemic draws parallels between the biblical originals of some of
these flawed libretto figures and similarly unsatisfactory modern
counterparts. Haman is paralleled with Walpole in opposition
literature; the destructive absolutism of Saul is paralleled with that

of Charles I and James II in sermons and political theory; and the deposition of the usurping Athalia through the restoration of Joash is a trope for the possible restoration of the Stuarts in Nonjuror and Jacobite writing.[10] Moreover, we can find little resemblance to George II among the victorious oratorio heroes, in that they are mostly native and not royal, and indeed some of the strongest are women (and in some of the librettos the 'hero' is the nation). The use of women leaders is more likely to recall Queen Elizabeth, heroine of the Patriot opposition.[11] Comparison with words-and-music which officially celebrate the monarchy, the court odes, shows how far the oratorios are from glorifying the Hanoverian dynasty in the parallels they make with former rulers.[12]

One reason for the absence of allegorical glorified kingship in the librettos is suggested by the public identification of Handel's English oratorios as *English*. George was painfully evidently not English. Unlike his elder son Frederick, he appeared personally far more concerned about Hanover than Britain (to Britain's detriment), making excessively long and frequent visits there, and he made no effort, again unlike Frederick, to be ingratiating, or even polite, to his British subjects. But he was the last British monarch to lead his troops in battle, which he did with much valour at Dettingen. In 1743 he was, momentarily, more the living image of the Old Testament warrior king than any British monarch since Henry V. Yet no oratorio, opera or masque emerged to enshrine this personal triumph in national mythology (the lasting musical memorial was Handel's Dettingen Te Deum). The occasion cried out for such mythologising, not least in order to mitigate the public resentment that welled up when it was learned that George had worn the yellow sash of Hanover on the battlefield and had apparently shown undue favouritism to his Hanoverian troops; but it was not forthcoming. Britons longed for a personal, royal, native leader, but George was not he, and there is no oratorio about King David, in eighteenth-century eyes the best of the Israelite kings (*Saul* concerns his life only before his kingship).[13] In sermons of the time George does figure as King David. Possibly no oratorio exploited the analogy because David had been made a figure of very questionable virtue by the sceptical encyclopaedist Pierre Bayle, and his failings were used in mid-century polemic to cast aspersions on the king of Britain.[14] Worse, from the Hanoverian angle, was the Jacobite adoption of the figure of David in his flight from Absalom as an image of the beleaguered Pretender.[15] David was certainly not a wholly positive parallel. In fact the whole question of Israelite kingship was politically very boggy ground, churned up by a host of commentators intent on finding ratification for their views on divine right, elective kingship and hereditary succession in the stories of Saul, David, and Solomon. Unsurprisingly, the librettos that concern these monarchs are not simple to unpack.

The librettist of *Solomon* is not known, nor do we know of any contemporary comments on the oratorio's meaning. Most modern commentators have assumed that Solomon is to be favourably identified with George II.[16] The authors and the first audiences of *Solomon* very probably connected the king and nation of the libretto with their own king and nation. They were familiar with this parallel from its use in sermons, and Bishop Potter's sermon at the coronation of George II and Caroline, on 2 Chronicles IX.8, was based on it. The high priest of the oratorio, Zadok, is the 'Zadok the priest' of Handel's anthem for the coronation. Needless to say, Potter's use of the parallel is entirely favourable to Solomon, George and the nation.[17] But what was meant and/or understood by it in the oratorio? Politically inclined members of the audience could see *Solomon* as a celebration of George II, if they took it as meaning 'Solomon is great and George II is his equivalent', or as a criticism of him, if they took it as meaning 'Solomon was flawed and so is George II' or indeed as meaning 'Solomon was great – how unlike the home life of our own dear king.' Similarly, the condition of the nation depicted could imply, or could be read as, a favourable or a critical comparison with the state of Britain: as meaning either 'this is what Britain is like' or 'this is what Britain should be like – but is not'.

There were precedents for the use of Solomon as a hostile allegory for George II and his government. On 28 January 1734/5 Aaron Hill's *Prompter* (no. 23) included a spoof advertisement for a play called *Court and Country* to be performed by 'the Norfolk Company of artificial Comedians, at Robin's great Theatrical Booth in Palace-Yard' (Norfolk was Walpole's county and Robin the diminutive of his name used by his detractors), 'in which will be revived the entertaining Scene of Two Blundering Brothers, with the Cheats of Rabbi Robin, Prime Minister of King Solomon'. In his diary Lord Egmont describes this playbill actually being handed to the king at a masquerade, and comments drily, 'Those who know the times know the satire of this.'[18] Maynard Mack additionally notes various reiterated hostile formulas employed by the opposition which 'were certain to intend the King, especially if accompanied by allusions to King Solomon'.[19]

More than any other Handel oratorio, however, *Solomon* seems to promote court Whig doctrine: it exalts peace and trade, proclaims national prosperity, shows Church and crown endorsing each other's interests to the benefit of society, and at its centre depicts the monarch – no arbitrary, absolute ruler – dispensing true justice. No other Handel libretto so signally advocates the benefits of peace, which was being brokered by the government while the oratorio was being written: 'No more shall armed Bands our Hopes destroy, / Peace waves her wing and pours forth ev'ry Joy' (Part II scene 3).[20] Despite the reference to 'armed Bands', there is – exceptionally among the Israelite librettos – no trace of conflict with another nation, no enemy overcome. In broad outline, the first part of the libretto presents the king's investment of funds in the promotion of national religion and major building programmes (the temple and palace) and his securing of the dynasty in a satisfactory marriage; the second establishes his claim to the throne and demonstrates his wisdom (the judgement of Solomon); and the third shows the king and nation, rich, cultivated, virtuous, powerful and at peace, receiving the admiring tribute of the foreign world (the visit of the Queen of Sheba). The final scenes recall the peroration of *The Idea of a Patriot King*, published in the year of *Solomon*'s first performance, in which Bolingbroke envisages the glorious united nation:

Concord will appear, brooding peace and prosperity on the happy land; joy sitting in every face, content in every heart; a people unoppressed, undisturbed, unalarmed; busy to improve their private property and the public stock; fleets covering the ocean, bringing home wealth by the returns of industry . . .[21]

Solomon comes nearer than any other libretto to showing an interest in the national economy, and is quite clear about what benefits it: home manufacture and agriculture nourished by foreign trade.

> A Palace shall erect its Head,
> Of Cedar built, with Gold bespread:
> Methinks the Work is now begun,
> The Ax resounds on *Lebanon*:
> And see, bedeck'd with Canvas Wings,
> The dancing Vessel lightly springs,

While *Ophir*'s Mines, well-pleas'd, disclose
The Wealth that in their Entrails glows.

Thus Solomon to his Queen in Part I; by Part III the palace is built
and

Gold now is common on our happy Shore,
And Cedars frequent are as Sycamore ...
Fair Plenty does her Treasure raise ...
How green our fertile Pastures look!
How fair our Olive Groves!

These lines can be paralleled in the many patriotic 'Whig panegyric' poems celebrating maritime trade as the major artery of
English success, for example Edward Young's *Imperium Pelagi*
(1729), which includes a glowing account of Solomon's temple as
grounded in trade (Strain IV stanza 9).[22] Trade was second only to
patriotism among the favourite themes of contemporary secular
writing, persistently invoked as a major element of any patriotic
agenda, and voluminously discussed by political commentators. For
Solomon's audience these passages in the libretto would have been
rich in references to traditional and current political theory. Trade
is specified as being maritime (rather than overland); trade (not
conquest) is the source of raw materials; and home manufacture and
agriculture (not the provision of services or the manipulation of
capital) are the generators of prosperity. These were all major
threads of contemporary political discourse, and the themes of
extensive debate. For example, the libretto's presentation of trade as
directed by the king rather than by private enterprise reflects not
only Solomon's traditional role as the great trading king, but the
discussion, ongoing during the whole century, on the place of trade
in state policy.[23] There would have been topical interest here for all
listeners, and nothing for an adherent of any party to cavil at.

But listeners who knew their Old Testament might have noticed
what the libretto left out. Solomon's temple and palace were built
by slave labour. They were also built with foreign imports. This the
libretto does record, raising a contentious matter. At the time of
the oratorio's composition the Prince of Wales was reviving a concern
of his Tory preceptors by promoting a protectionist 'buy British'
policy, and in the biblical account the result of Solomon's foreign
trade was punitive: he had to pay for his imports with territory,
giving twenty cities to his trading partner.[24] The libretto suggests

that peace fosters trade, whereas the experience of its first audiences was that trade provoked war. It is silent on the much-canvassed issue of the need for empire (implying conquest) to provide markets and materials, despite ascribing 'imperial State' to Solomon.[25]

Solomon is the only libretto to take on the contemporary concern about the damaging relationship of trade (good) to luxury (bad). According to one major strand of contemporary moral-political theory, members of a subsistence society are likely to be virtuously frugal and mutually supportive, whereas trade, especially in peace-time, generates wealth surplus to necessity and encourages 'luxury': self-interest, materialism, greed and decadence.[26] (As contemporaries recognised, the question was of course more complicated than this: for example, trade provoked war (bad) but also created jobs (good).[27]) The pastoral and agrarian early Israelites both in the Old Testament and in most of the oratorios clearly belong in the virtuously frugal category (see chapter 10); *Solomon* is different, despite its references to olive groves and rustic swains. However, Solomon's rich court finds an answer to the problem of peacetime surplus, one which the cultivated oratorio audience must have approved: wealth and leisure remaining after reinvestment in religion and productivity are dedicated to the arts. The concert which entertains the Queen of Sheba gives the composer scope for display and gives the audience (within the text and outside it) scope for cultivated moral-aesthetic appreciation. It also expresses Solomon's moral-political, as well as musical, magnificence.

Spending money on the arts, specifically music, is just what Handel would have wanted his king to do, and this feature of court life in *Solomon* could have been received as a graceful acknowledgement of his own encouragement by the Hanoverians. But at a more political level, artistic patronage is a responsible civic act. The charges against Walpole's government had included, prominently, the complaint that it did not foster the arts, a complaint which opposition writers loaded with all the moral fervour they could draw from the common assumption that good art (the only kind deserving the name) is the vehicle of truth and hallmark of a free people. State patronage was itself a subject of large discussion, based – characteristically for this period – on a historical exemplar: Augustus, whose record as a patron was closely examined and frequently presented as an awful warning.[28] The libretto shows *its* example from ancient history to be an entirely admirable patron of the arts, both economically and politically. Handel himself may have given Solomon's artistic interest its public, civic emphasis: Dean has pointed out that the masque was originally intended to entertain the queen in Act I.[29] He may well have been conscious of the debate about patronage, because one of the most trenchant contributions to it, Pope's *Epistle to Burlington*, was dedicated to one of his early aristocratic patrons and caused a furore by seeming to criticise the other (see chapter 11). As the centrepiece of the official reception of a foreign monarch, the masque amounts to a state pronouncement, and the message it conveys is that in Solomon's court and realm, culture is encouraged and arises from native productivity and peaceful trade.

In this respect the libretto anticipates the themes and some of the arguments for a sophisticated consumer society in Hume's essay 'Of Luxury'.[30] It also echoes an earlier verse discussion of the growth of industry, arts and luxury and their connection with just government which is positive but not glibly upbeat about highly developed societies, in one of the major works of the period, James Thomson's *Seasons*.[31] In fact Thomson's account of newly civilised man digging up minerals, taking the axe to the 'tall ancient forest', chipping wood and hewing stone 'Till by degrees the finished fabric rose' (*Autumn* ll. 78–83) has a parallel in the librettist's description of Solomon's building works quoted above. A friend of the current administration could see in the librettist's picture of Solomon's court a pleasing reflection of his own world; an adherent to Patriot ideals would catch a glimpse of a past, irrecoverable civilisation, or a condition to be aspired to and being fostered by the Prince of Wales in *his* encouragement of British arts, so much more committed and extensive than his father's.[32] A reader of the Old Testament might in addition have pointed out that the opulence of Solomon's court did not result entirely from surplus wealth: each of the twelve provinces had to supply his provisions for a month, and oppressive taxation was a major reason for rebellion and the division of the kingdom after his death.[33]

Many listeners in 1749 could have found a modern parallel for the transient nature of Solomon's glory in the Peace of Aix-la-Chapelle which the oratorio celebrates and which was widely regarded, even by government politicians, as badly timed, humiliating, expensive and only temporary. As peace negotiations got under way, the opposition press fuelled the idea, born of recent successes, that

French power was on the verge of being decisively broken. But the opportunity (in opposition eyes) was thrown away, and Britain was made to bow to France in a peculiarly hateful way by sending noble hostages as guarantors for the return of the much-prized Louisbourg. Among other defects of the peace, one that would have raised wry comparisons with the facts omitted from *Solomon*, and with its picture of prosperity, was a failure to deliver the financial gains from Spain for which Britain had gone to war in the first place.[34] In the year of *Solomon*'s composition there was no shortage of publications by anti-government writers of varying political complexions deploring the conduct and outcome of the war. 'I always thought myself a Whig, but now I am quite ashamed of the Character', wrote one, because 'we are now forty Millions poorer, than when we began the War, and have lost our Reputation by the present Treaty'; in fact 'we are ... brought to the Brink of Destruction.'[35] Other publications similarly describe Britain's condition as 'lamentable', 'melancholy', 'abject', 'wretched': the Patriots incited the war but the government has mismanaged it, overspent on it, negotiated a humiliating end to it and given away Britain's position of strength in Europe and 'all her former Glories'.[36]

During the Queen of Sheba's audience, Zadok comments to Solomon:

> The Temple rose to mark thy Days
> With endless Themes for future Praise.
> Our pious *David* wish'd, in vain,
> By this great Act to bless his Reign;
> But Heav'n the Monarch's Hopes withstood,
> For ah! his Hands were stain'd with Blood.   (Part III scene 1)

Here is a blot on Solomon's reputation that the librettist has chosen not to suppress. It is an astonishingly tactless reference to the events leading up to Solomon's birth, which involved his father's arranged assassination of his mother's first husband (2 Samuel XI–XII). And not only Solomon's father's hands, but his own, have blood on them – the blood of three members of his court. For this the king thanks God, who

> led me, abject, to imperial State ...
> Then impious *Joab* at the Altar bled;
> The Death he oft deserv'd, stern *Shimei* found;
> And *Adonijah* sunk beneath the Wound;

> Forc'd by his Crimes, I spoke a Brother's Doom,
> Ah may his Vices perish in his Tomb!   (Part II scene 1)

This is a reference, again astonishing, to the fact that, though he was not the royal first-born, and therefore was not the conventionally legitimate inheritor of the throne, Solomon was selected as David's successor by divine will and on gaining the throne ruthlessly purged the trouble-makers of the previous reign (1 Kings I–II), including his older half-brother Adonijah. The suggestion that the librettist mentioned these aspects of Solomon's career out of respect for sacred history 'as if not quite daring' to omit them does not convince;[37] as we have seen, the librettists generally, and this one no less freely, picked and chose from amongst the Scriptures, amending as they transcribed. The librettist of *Solomon* compiled his text from both Kings and Chronicles, and the alternative account in 1 Chronicles, which omits these episodes and presents an uncontested succession from David to Solomon, could have been used instead. The indirect succession of Solomon was a familiar validation of the Hanoverian settlement (it showed the interposition of divine will – Potter had used it to this end in his Coronation sermon), but the question remains why the two instances of bloodletting are referred to, and presented so starkly. Is this only an incompetent author bungling his use of a piece of loyalist mythology, or is it a subversive author casting a shadow over Solomon's glory in order to darken George?[38]

Solomon recalls his executions while dedicating himself to God, at which a choric Levite comments:

> Great Prince, thy Resolution's just,
> He never fails, in Heav'n who puts his Trust;
> True Worth consists not in the Pride of State;
> 'Tis Virtue only makes a Monarch great.
>   Thrice bless'd that wise discerning King,
>   Who can each Passion tame,
>   And mount on Virtue's Eagle Wing
>   To everlasting Fame:
>   Such shall as mighty Patterns stand
>   To Princes yet unborn;
>   To Honour prompt each distant Land,
>   And future Times adorn.   (Part II scene 1)

This is a remarkably clear transcription of contemporary rhetoric prescribing the qualities of the Patriot King: virtue, modesty, wisdom, discernment, controlled emotion and an altogether exemplary nature. There are two points to notice about this application of the theme. Solomon is being praised not for *being* an exemplary monarch, but for *trying to be* one; and such monarchs, not Solomon himself, are being described as patterns for future rulers. To analogise, a clear distinction is being made between George II and the ideal king;[39] the text does not seem to support a reading whereby George II is a realisation of the 'mighty Pattern'. To put *Solomon* into perspective with a thoroughgoing music theatre celebration of George II it is instructive as well as diverting to turn to Thomas Lediard's and John Frederick Lampe's masque *Britannia* (1732), whose 'Prefatory Argument' declares an intention 'to display the Glory and Happiness of *Great Britain*' through characters which are 'all *Ideal* or *Allegorical*'. Despite a disclaimer of reference 'to any particular Persons, Things or Circumstances, now, or at any Time heretofore, really existing', the centrepiece of the fantastically elaborate set (which takes five pages to describe) is an equestrian statue of George II crowned by Fame and flanked by Victory and Valour, while the action includes the descent of a machine containing a bust of the king inscribed 'He restores the Golden Age'.[40] Like the court odes but unlike *Solomon*, *Britannia* ensures the safe passage of its laudatory analogy by carefully avoiding equivocal detail.

The most conspicuous omissions of the facts of Solomon's career from the libretto concern his relations with women. In his standard commentary on the Old Testament, Thomas Stackhouse rebuts the deists' objections to Solomon's execution of his brother, his marriage to a queen from idolatrous Egypt, his opulence, and his temple's opulence. But he has to yield on the matter of the biblical record of Solomon's concubinage, which led to idolatry: 'the later Actions of his Life do sadly tarnish and disgrace his Character ... so unbounded was his Lust, that he had seven hundred Wives, and three hundred Concubines, who conspir'd ... to ... seduce him ... to the Worship of their several *Idols* ... in the very *Maturity* of his Age, he discover'd a strong inclination to Idolatry, which could not but make a bad Impression on the Minds of his *Subjects*'[41] – this from a defender of the Bible as a repository of good precepts and examples. In the biblical narrative Solomon's moral and religious decline sets in immediately after the Queen of Sheba's visit, the point at which the libretto tactfully ends, thus avoiding the major blots on the king's character. But contemporary publications had drawn attention to these blots, not only in religious polemic but in political prints which connected them to the Hanoverians. *Solomon in his Glory* showed the king embracing his mistress Lady Walmoden, ignoring the portrait on the wall behind them of George's recently deceased queen, Caroline. *Solomon's Glory, or the Rival Mistresses*, lampooning the Duke of Cumberland, was issued (and prosecuted) in the year of the oratorio's first performance.[42] According to the biblical account, while the human cause for the troubles that befell Solomon's dynasty after his death was his fiscal policy, their principal source was divine resentment at his whoring after strange women and other gods.[43] In the latter part of his reign Solomon was decidedly not a Patriot King.

The monarch who most closely embodies the Patriot King in Handel's oratorio canon is not Israelite, but Persian: Cyrus in Jennens' *Belshazzar*. This is hardly surprising, for Xenophon's Prince Cyrus was a favourite eighteenth-century model of good kingship.[44] The mission statement of Jennens' hero to Gobrias (whose son Belshazzar has murdered), during the siege of Babylon, is a text-book pattern. Cyrus intends

> At once a Tyrant's Reign to end,
> Avenge thy Wrongs, my injur'd Friend,
> Restore a People long opprest,
> From Exile to their native Land,
> And execute Divine Command! (Act I scene 2)

Cyrus will stand by his friend, fulfilling the claims of personal attachments; he will purge the world of a tyrannical ruler; he will disinterestedly liberate an oppressed people; and he is justified by God's instruction. God has sent him an enlightening dream, which he heeds, though he is not yet a believer, and which begins his conversion. In his preparation for battle he shows the humility and scrupulousness required of the Patriot King:

> Great God! who yet but darkly known,
> Thus far hast deign'd my Arms to bring;
> Support me still, while I pull down
> *Assyria*'s proud injurious King.
> So shall this Hand thy Altars raise,
> This Tongue for ever sing thy Praise;
> And all thy Will, when clearly shown,
> By thy glad Servant shall be done.
> My friends ... not unjustly
> We have attack'd, but being first attack'd

> We have pursu'd th'Aggressor. Add to this,
> That I proceed in nothing with Neglect
> Of Pow'r divine . . .   (Act I scene 2)

To this last statement Jennens adds a footnote reference to Xenophon, for he is concerned to demonstrate historical evidence of the
power of God working through Cyrus, historically a very secular
conquering hero (see chapter 6). Xenophon is not entirely helpful.
In his account of the taking of Babylon Cyrus gives orders to kill
anyone found out of doors, even after Belshazzar's death. But in the
libretto, as his troops enter the city Cyrus declares:

> I seek no Enemy except the Tyrant;
> When he is slain our Task is at an end.
> My worthy Friends, let us not stain our Swords
> With *needless* Slaughter: I begin already
> To count this People mine, myself their Shepherd,
> Whose Office is to feed and protect them,
> Not to destroy.   (Act II scene 3)

Jennens has found the perfect Old Testament embodiment of the
Messianic father-figure of Bolingbroke's manifesto.

An intermediary source for both Bolingbroke's Patriot King and
Jennens' Prince Cyrus was presumably the Chevalier Ramsay's
Travels of Cyrus, an anti-sceptical educational romance published in
1727 and widely read for the rest of the century.[45] Bolingbroke and
Ramsay were both in Paris at the same time, were both in the service
of the Pretender, and belonged to the same literary club, L'Entre-
sol.[46] Ramsay was writing for a potential latter-day Cyrus, his pupil,
the Young Pretender. Bolingbroke was careful to make his text,
written in the late 1730s, applicable to either of the two possible
future kings, the Young Pretender or Frederick Prince of Wales; and
the Prince of Wales openly identified himself with it, taking it as his
manifesto. 'I shall be that patriot King', he is said to have told Lord
Lichfield.[47] Frederick owned an early copy of *Belshazzar*.[48] It is
likely that Jennens was aware of the prince's order for copies of
Handel's works, and we can hazard that this was what he had in
mind when he spoke of 'making use of' Handel in connection with
Belshazzar (see above, p. 27) – that he was 'making use' of this
channel to convey his ideas to the future ruler.

If this is the case, *Belshazzar* has a place among the Patriot
opposition works associated with the Prince of Wales. Like them it is
idealistic, ideological and prescriptive, rather than programmatic or

representative of real circumstances. On the eve of the 1745 Rebellion, Jennens envisages the peaceful overthrow of a vicious (but rightful) ruler by a divinely guided invading foreigner, who swiftly restores order, declares a general amnesty, returns the (chastened) exiles safely to their homeland, converts to the true religion, inaugurates an era of universal harmony and undertakes to build the New Jerusalem:

> The God of *Israel* – (he alone is God)
> Hath charg'd me to rebuild his House and City,
> And let his exil'd captive People go.
> With Transport I obey. Be free, ye Captives,
> And to your native Land in Peace return.
> Thou, O *Jerusalem*, shall be rebuilt;
> O Temple, thy Foundation shall be laid.
> No Thanks to me! – To God return your Thanks,
> As I do mine ...   (Act III scene 3)

Jennens' *Belshazzar* matches the major part of opposition propaganda, a mixture of prescription and wishful thinking. Murray Pittock has identified exile as a consciously Jacobite trope in this period: 'Perhaps the reality [of continuing Hanoverian rule] led to a subgenre of the Jacobite voice concerning itself more intensely with the Aenean experience of exile, rather than homecoming or success'.[49] The Israelites are an exiled people in *Susanna* (author unknown), *Esther*, of which one putative author (Pope) was a Jacobite sympathiser, and *Belshazzar* (by a Jacobite sympathiser); and in *Israel in Egypt* (also probably by Jennens) they are in an alien land until their exodus. But as usual, the possible analogy is not insisted on by the text, and can be perceived by those inclined to it, while being accepted by other members of the audience as merely narrative.

The advice to Solomon to be a Patriot King comes from a Levite, a member of the priestly caste of which Zadok is the high priest. To the modern audience these priestly figures – especially in unstaged performances, without visible and outward signs of grandeur – probably seem no more than masters of ceremonies or even mere courtiers. But the eighteenth-century audience would have noticed that through them the librettist shows the established Church both supporting and advising the monarch, and the monarch supporting and letting himself be guided by the Church. Lowman had drawn the contemporary parallel in his *Dissertation*, singling out the succes-

sion of Solomon to the throne of Israel as a model of Church–state
relations, when the Israelite equivalent of Parliament 'confirmed . . .
the Settlement of the Crown, and of the High-Priesthood'.[50] In the
libretto it is Zadok who confirms God's approval of Solomon:

> Imperial *Solomon*, thy Pray'rs are heard,
>   See! from the op'ning Skies
> Descending Flames involve the Sacrifice . . .   (Part I scene 1)

and his outspoken reference to David's murky record is far beyond
the province of a court stooge. But though the priests give Solomon
advice, their contributions as the libretto progresses are increasingly
exclamations of unqualified praise. The complete picture is of a
Church–crown relationship of mutually reliant powers of which the
crown is the greater – a Whiggish account which would have had
more than immediate interest for its audience.

During the oratorio years the whole topic of the priesthood, and
more generally of organised, public, state-sponsored religion, was
brought into a prominence it had not had since the Commonwealth
by two very different critiques. In 1717 Benjamin Hoadly, Bishop of
Bangor, preached, on the text 'my kingdom is not of this world', a
sermon undermining the value of the Church visible and hence the
whole framework of national organised religion. The statement by a
bishop of the established Church that only Christ had authority over
Christians in matters of belief, that 'He hath, in those Points, left
behind Him, no visible, humane Authority . . . no Judges over the
Consciences or Religion of his People' and that 'No One . . . more
than Another, hath *Authority*, either to make New Laws for Christ's
Subjects; or to impose a sence upon the Old Ones . . . or to Judge,
Censure, or Punish the Servants of *Another Master*, in matters relating purely to *Conscience*, or Salvation', called in question the entire
hierarchy of Church government and its secular supports (and this
at a time when only communicants of the established Church could
hold public office). It raised a storm ('the Bangorian controversy')
which continued to reverberate in Church circles throughout the
oratorio years.[51]

At the same time the priesthood was the subject of a major strand
of deistical writing. According to Matthew Tindal (1730) and
Thomas Morgan (1737–40) in particular, priests deceive the people,
fostering public religion to serve their own interests – wealth and
political power – and they are supported by the state to keep the

people subservient. These are the usual complaints of any period against a priesthood, and in their eighteenth-century context form part of a larger attack by radicals (political as well as religious) on Church government.[52] For oratorio students the especial interest of many of the deists' restatements is that they attacked the priesthood not directly, with open criticism of (for example) the tithe system or the political appointments by the crown to the bench of bishops in the House of Lords, but under the disguise of critiques of the Mosaic dispensation which originally established and authorised priests, under God's mandate, as recounted in the Old Testament. To take an example from the middle of the oratorio period, Morgan pointed to Joseph as instituting the first recorded instance of an independent priesthood and giving it inalienable lands and income and an excessive hereditary tithe; he asserted that the supposed oracle of God was actually an imposture of the high priest; and he alleged that the Mosaic Law was 'a blinding, enslaving, tyrannical Consti-tution, with regard especially to its Sacrifices and Priesthood'. These latter were 'founded upon the same Principles of human bad Policy with the Laws and Priesthood of Egypt': Morgan makes particular play with the familiar freethinker's strategy, derived from Strabo, of tracing the origins and elements of Mosaic Law in Egyptian 'super-stition' as a means of discrediting Judaism's, and thus Christianity's, claims to uniqueness and divine sanction (hence his location of the origin of the priesthood in the Egyptian sojourn of Joseph).[53] Con-temporaries recognised that to attack the grounds of Christian doctrine and suggest public freedom of religion, as the deists did, was to attack the state, because 'Our Religion is incorporated into our Civil Constitution and become a legal Part of our Property', a cornerstone of 'the Revolution and the happy Settlement con-sequent to it'; and that to attack the priesthood, the chief link between the state and the national religion, was to court anarchy and raise the spectre of the Great Rebellion.[54]

Orthodox responses to these attacks met the deist authors on their chosen ground, and included copious defence of the Mosaic laws concerning the priesthood. The most extensive is Lowman's, his *Dissertation* being prompted by Morgan's diatribe. 'Some', as he remarks in his opening pages, with a footnote to Morgan, 'have fallen with uncommon Severity both on the religious and political Constitution of *Moses* ... These Constitutions are said to be "a Refinement of the Superstition of *Egypt*"'. He rebuts all Morgan's anticlerical points at great length (over 80 of his 365 pages), minutely calculating, for example, the Levites' real income from tithes with detailed arithmetical demonstrations that it was not fourteen shillings in the pound as Morgan had asserted but 'no more of the whole Produce than £3 6s 8d *per Cent*'. The Levites' role was to teach religion and justice, and to undertake the service of God on behalf of the people, hence they were scattered through the other tribes, neither owning property nor belonging to the militia (in other words, they had no temporal power), and receiving tithes for public services rendered, not as a birthright (Morgan, Lowman pointed out, had wilfully confused tithes with other, unexception-able, state taxes partly used to support the national religion, which the Levites had to pay like everyone else). What makes the original Mosaic constitution so ideal a model, in Lowman's eyes, is that it both promotes religion and virtue, which the priests are to teach, and avoids the very priestcraft of which Morgan and other deists had accused it, by restricting the political power of the clergy. Their potential to cabal and their sphere of influence were circumscribed by their landlessness and diffusion and by Moses' careful exclusion of his descendants from the high priesthood: 'I cannot but look upon it as a wise Intention and an original Design in the Constitution, appointed with great political Skill, to cut off all possible Abuse of such Power and Influence, as their Character might give them.'

None of these defences of the Mosaic priesthood is original to Lowman, nor is his view of it through the filter of modern politics, but he pushes further than his contemporaries in the direction of modern political polemic. Throughout, he encodes Whiggish constit-utionalism in his biblical apologetics, and this is especially clear in both the content and the language of his comments on the checks and balances operating between Church and state. On the one hand 'this Constitution has taken the utmost Care, and with all the Marks of political Wisdom, that the Judge should not have it in his Power to stretch his Authority beyond its legal Bounds; for his Authority was temper'd by the *Oracle*'; on the other, 'the Constitution has taken the wisest Care that it should not be in the Power of any one Part of the Nation, least of all in the Power of the Priests, either to invade the Property or oppress the Liberties of any Part of the Nation'.[55] Lowman is in part answering Harrington, to whom he makes frequent marginal references. Harrington, who seems to have coined the word *priestcraft*, anticipated deist anticlericalism by transmitting to the eighteenth-century reader in a just-palatably allegorical guise the message that priests are the potential enemy of the state, and that their power must be limited by the civil authorities, whose servants they must be. This warning to the flawed modern state is drawn from the Israelite model in its corrupted monarchical form; both Harrington and Lowman hold that in the original, uncorrupted Hebrew commonwealth, under Joshua, the whole people participated, themselves or through their representatives, in civil and religious decisions, and the Levites were simply teachers and masters of ceremonies.[56]

This is largely the picture of state–Church relations presented in the oratorios. The entire oratorio community of Israelites (when it is not in its frequent posture of backsliding) is holy. However, this does not make it either a throwback to the Puritan Commonwealth or an anticipation of Methodist congregations. Mid-century complaints against 'enthusiasm' in religion included warnings such as the one by John Dupont against 'men who make themselves priests from the lowest of the people, and are not of the tribe of Levi'.[57] One of the many respects in which the librettos are not early expressions of Methodism is that they entirely lack 'inspired' utterances by ordinary individual Israelites (see further Appendix 2). Prophecies and other messages of divine origin are almost without exception transmitted through, and voiced by, God's prophets (Deborah in *Deborah*, Daniel in *Belshazzar* and *Susanna*), God's priests (Joad in *Athalia*, Zadok and the Levite in *Solomon*), and God's elected leaders of His people (Joseph in *Joseph and His Brethren*, Simon in *Judas Macchabæus*): they are the preserve of the religious elite. Two church historians have commented that 'Hoadleian theology seemed to leave little room for the role of the priesthood as mediators between God and Man', but it has that role in the oratorios.[58] The religious community of the librettos also evades the political problem raised by Hoadly, for it is not under the thumb of the state: on the contrary, the Israelite oratorios, including *Solomon*, present a world in which the Church creates the state. There are two ways of reading this through the eyes of the eighteenth-century audience. It could be seen as reinforcing ultra-Tory, High-Church views on the need to preserve the power of the Church of England. But it could also be seen as more Whiggish and Low Church. The confessional state is an inescapable *donnée* of Old Testament stories; the significant element is what is done by the librettists to the biblical originals with respect to the religious hierarchy. It is demystified: worship is unritualistic, and though messages *from* God to His people need mediation, they need no intermediary for their appeals *to* Him. The priesthood has only limited power. Hebrew priests (as distinct from prophets) appear in only six of the fifteen Israelite librettos (*Deborah*, *Athalia*, *Solomon*, *Judas Macchabæus*, *Joshua* and *Jephtha*), and of these they are silent in one and in two others they do not merit a mention in the list of characters. Nevertheless, the contemporary debate about the priesthood can be seen to affect the librettos.

The freethinkers' association of the Mosaic code, especially the priesthood, with unsavoury Egyptian superstitions illuminates two of the oratorios. The contents of Parts II and III of *Israel in Egypt* – the plagues inflicted on Egypt by God on the Hebrews' behalf, the Israelites' escape from Egypt, God's destruction of the pursuing Egyptians at the Red Sea and Moses' song of triumph at their overthrow – all emphasise the separateness of the Egyptians and the Israelites. We deduce, *contra* the deists, that Jewish identity begins with a rejection, not an assimilation, of Egyptian culture. Likewise in *Joseph and his Brethren* Miller stresses the distinctions between the Hebrew and the Egyptian religions, minimising the importance of the latter. The Egyptian high priest appears in two early scenes (Part I scenes 4, 8) but utters only in one, and then only for two lines, to marry Joseph and Asenath. Joseph's Egyptian steward Phanor is made to remark that Joseph's melancholy may be a yearning for 'his native Land, / Whose God and Laws are the *Reverse of Egypt's*' (II.1; my italics). Joseph recalls, at length, the essential, never-to-be-forgotten Jewish doctrine he learned from Jacob *before* he came to Egypt (II.3). At the crisis of the action Joseph, in conversation with his Egyptian wife, censures Egyptian idolatry, which he contrasts with the truths of monotheism; whereupon Asenath likewise dismisses '*Egypt's* visionary Gods', and her confession of the true faith is immediately rewarded with a conviction of their future happiness (III.2). Handel omitted the couple's further twelve lines condemning Egyptian religion, but they were printed in the libretto. Miller was a clergyman, and he defended his calling from Morgan's slurs on its purity by reclaiming the story of Joseph which Morgan had used as evidence.

Interestingly and predictably, the one oratorio in which the clergy plays a crucial role, indeed in which it is a priest who makes most of the action happen, is the one written for the most Tory,

High-Church audience in Britain, the University of Oxford. In *Athalia* the high priest, Joad, makes himself responsible for the deposition of Athalia and the restoration of the true king Joash, whom he has hidden and brought up in the tenets of the true religion from which Athalia apostasised. The biblical Joash went on to reform the state religion and strengthen the priesthood, and the libretto appropriately has Athalia dream of him as 'A Youth ... in shining Robes array'd, / Such as the Priests of *Judah* wear' (Part I scene 4). By comparison with the priests of the other librettos Joad is a dominant and dominating character. But by comparison with his Racinian original even he shows a conscious intention on the librettist's part to reduce his power. Racine's Joïada refuses to tolerate any human frailty: he rejoices in violence as an attribute of his God, and reflects it in his own bullying of everyone in the play. Humphreys' Joad has all the warmth of the protective father, husband and lover; the oratorio even ends with a love duet for him and his wife.[59]

In *Athalia* the priesthood overthrows the regime. In *Solomon* it supports the *status quo*, but it gives instruction too. The priestly admonition to Solomon to be a good king is immediately followed by his exercise of his kingly responsibilities, the scene in which he judges the case of the two mothers and the contested baby, itself the centre of the libretto and one of only two occasions in the Israelite oratorios when we see the law in action (the other is in *Susanna*, see below). The celebration of impartial justice in this scene echoes the high regard for the excellence and integrity of British justice voiced by commentators of all political shades (for example, it is the only aspect of British life unreservedly praised by Lyttelton in the *Persian Letters*[60]). Here was a cornerstone of the constitution, that system of checks and balances guaranteeing individual liberty, which was still laudably untainted by corruption (except that of exploitative advocates).[61] How different from the government of Catholic countries, which was seen to be based on absurd superstitions and cruelly repressive absolutism. The analogy with the Israelites – with their God-given, reasonable, feasible Law as against the disgusting perversions of their hostile neighbours – is particularly easy to make here.

However, the way in which Solomon reaches and makes his judgement, though hailed within the text as wise and just, may perturb the reader who refers to the very extensive debate on the question of the king's relation to the law, which was at the heart of the 1688 Revolution and was still crucial to political thinking in 1749. In the libretto Solomon is cross-examiner, judge and jury, and he does not refer to the law of the land, he makes it up. This may be the result simply of the librettist's faith to the source, and the emphasis on impartial justice and the king's collaboration with it may be more significant than any apparent critique of Solomon. Nevertheless, if one wants to push the analogy, by Whig canons justice should be administered in this fashion only in the lower courts (by a magistrate), and this is not how the law should be made, nor is it how – vital issue – the king should behave in relation to the law. In his sermon on the anniversary of Queen Anne's accession Bishop Fleetwood celebrated Solomon's rule, and by analogy that of post-Revolution British rulers. Wandering somewhat from his text, he located the freedom of Solomon's people from tyranny and capricious absolutism in the king's rule of and by, precisely, *known laws*: the phrase becomes a hammered-out refrain:

after all the fine Discourses that may be made on either Side there is nothing certain but this, that a Prince can never be happy in his People, without their Submission and Obedience to the KNOWN LAWS, nor a People happy in their Prince unless he governs by those KNOWN LAWS ... That is the Difference betwixt an *Arbitrary Prince*, and one that governs by *Known Laws* ... the Arbitrary Prince does what he pleases with his Subjects Lives, Estates, and Liberties; whereas the Prince who governs by Known Laws, knows he can no more injure his Subject, than he can suffer one Subject to injure another. He rules in Justice and the Fear of God, and is therefore restrain'd himself from doing Evil.[62]

Fleetwood's analogy was so conventional that he did not need to spell out even its detail, for example the implied references to James II's absolutism: Solomon here is the stock sermonic model of the king operating within the law of the land. In secular contexts the governmental style of another great prince of antiquity, Augustus, was exhaustively dissected with a view to its implications for modern Britain. The librettist of *Solomon* would have found in appraisals of Augustus' rule a precedent for a critical, admonitory picture of a monarch whose reign was glorious, whose people were prosperous and apparently free, and under whom trade and arts flourished, but who dispensed with the framework of established law (to the eventual ruin of the state).[63]

The librettist certainly intended the judgement scene as a *judge-*

ment scene rather than an informal arbitration. Showing the self-abnegation required of the Patriot King, Solomon initiates the hearing with the weighty comment that 'when we mount a Throne, / Our Hours are all the People's, not our own' (Part II scene 2), and before giving his verdict he announces that 'Justice holds the lifted Scale' (II.3). It would have been perfectly possible for the librettist to insert at least some reference by Solomon to the known (Mosaic) Law as guiding him in his judgement. Far from seeming anachronistic to a contemporary audience, the idea of a king ruling according to biblical precept would have appeared positively modern. At William and Mary's accession the coronation service was remodelled to include a prominent role for the English Bible, which was handed to them 'To put you in mind of this rule and that you may follow it', an innovation retained in subsequent coronations.[64] There are several possible interpretations of the fact that, instead, Solomon is shown improvising the law. Is he being the Ur-lawmaker, and (in that these events are actually past) does his action mirror Old Whig respect for the idea of the Ancient Constitution; or (inasmuch as these events are an allegory for the present) is his lack of reference to ancient (Mosaic) Law being used *either* to endorse modern Whig belief in the superiority of modern to ancient civil liberty *or* to represent opposition claims that the king's government was eroding civil rights? The supporting cast universally approve Solomon's handling of the case ('thou art first of mortal Kings, / And wisest of the Wise', II.3), but the text affords scope for an adverse response. The very last words in the whole work addressed to Solomon chillingly suggest the possibility of oppression and corruption by the crown: 'May thy People sound thy Praise, / Praise unbought by Price or Fear' (III.1). Though this libretto seems to claim the Solomon story as support for the crown and its administration, it has enough ambiguities (by design or by inadvertence) to gain a hearing from critics of the regime.

Whether or not the librettist of *Solomon* intended to raise questions about the king's relation to the law, his text gives a central place to a central contemporary issue. But this was not the first time a libretto had dealt with the relation of the king to both the national religion and the law of the land. In *Saul* (1738 or earlier) Charles Jennens dramatised the conflict of principle which Englishmen faced when the anointed king, James II, threatened his people's liberty through his absolutism and Roman Catholicism. Jennens too was developing a conventional analogy. The story of Saul's downfall was widely used in contemporary rhetoric justifying the Glorious Revolution, drawing a parallel between Saul and James II.[65] However it was also used in sermons for the Feast of King Charles the Martyr, drawing a parallel between Saul and Charles I to condemn the execution of the king (and, for those who wished to make the connection, the deposition of his son James II).[66] The biblical narrative is admirably convenient to both purposes, because on the one hand (Hanoverian) God Himself has willed the succession away from Saul's family to David, who, no less than Saul, is God's anointed; on the other hand (Stuart) the killing of Saul is regarded as an appalling crime. While the successors of James II were still alive and still claiming the throne (whose incumbent they showed to be fifty-eighth in legitimate line of succession[67]) the story of Saul remained one of the most intensely debated texts of the century. Manuel Schonhorn has shown how prominently it figured in political thought and how variously it could be mined.[68] Jennens' libretto does not concern itself with the debate about Saul's accession (the text was used to prove either that God chooses kings or that the people elect them): his story is Saul's decline and death. He did not put his name to his libretto, but knowledge of his sympathy for the Stuart cause and his position as one of the leading Nonjurors of his generation alerts us to its implications. Here is an instance where we can assign meaning to a libretto on the basis of knowledge of its author.

The preface to Jennens' chief non-biblical source for *Saul*, the Earl of Orrery's tragedy on the same subject, passionately condemns acquiescence in the regicide; his was one of dozens of texts in Jennens' library concerning the Great Rebellion and, especially, the Royal Martyr.[69] It is surely no coincidence that the final scenes of the libretto, recounting Saul's death, the killing of the Amalekite, and David's lament for Saul and Jonathan, are a transcription of the text of the first lesson of the morning service for the Feast of King Charles the Martyr, 2 Samuel I.[70] Charles Wheatly, in his much-reprinted *The Church of England Man's Companion*, comments:

The *first Lesson* for the *Morning* is 2 *Sam* I. There is no Parallel for this inhumane Murder of a good and innocent King by his own Subjects in all the *O. Testament*, and therefore the Church is content to read the History of *David's* Justice upon the Infidel who kill'd *Saul*, and his Mourning for him, who had been his Sovereign, though he was his Mortal Enemy, and had apostatiz'd from God, and was forsaken by Heaven. How much more reason then had our State to punish those barbarous *Rebels*, who murther'd the *Best of Kings*, for adhering to the Best of Religions? and also to set apart a Day of *Humiliation* for *Fasting* and *Prayer*, and to draw up a mournful Office after the Example of *David* in the *Lesson*.

Wheatly says of the first psalm for the day, Psalm IX, that it 'was writ upon *Goliah*'s Death, and was design'd for *David*'s Victory over the *Philistines*'; so the service contained the beginning, as well as the end, of Jennens' libretto.[71]

Among Jacobite sympathisers in particular, lapse of time and absence of individual guilt were considered no mitigation of the crime. Nathaniel Mist, in one of his weekly essays, scourged 'the Folly of those Persons who imagine themselves exempted from the Observation of the Anniversary Fast, for the barbarous Murther of that glorious Saint and bless'd Martyr King *Charles* the First, because their Ancestors were unconcerned in the unparalelled [sic] Villainy of that Day'. God may still have punishment in store: 'Are these Gentlemen sure that sacred Blood is so fully attoned for, that it will never more be requir'd of us or our Posterity?'[72] Against this ideological background, Jennens' strenuous resistance to Handel's inclination to end the oratorio with a Hallelujah, a chorus of rejoicing, acquires new point.[73] His efforts to convey Nonjuring principles did not stop here. Anthony Hicks has drawn attention to Jennens' striking alteration to Handel's setting at the point where the killing of Saul is announced – bringing the voice of horror-struck reaction in straight away instead of after the ritornello.[74] Knowing of his Stuart adherence, we can infer why Jennens would seize on this moment of the score, and why he proposed to amend it as he did. The strongest possible sense of outrage at the regicide was to be expressed by David and implanted in the audience.

Jennens was not the only librettist to transcribe the text for the feast of the Royal Martyr as an oratorio. John Lockman drew on the same source for his *David's Lamentation over Saul and Jonathan* for William Boyce (1736), which may have preceded Jennens' composition of *Saul*.[75] In Lockman's libretto the episodes of the slaying of the Amalekite and David's lament bulk even larger, indeed they constitute the entire oratorio. Previous commentators have dismissed his text as 'a clumsy, ill-balanced affair more concerned with the encounter between David and the captured Amalekite than with the lamentation of the title',[76] even while noticing that it was

also set by another composer, Handel's assistant, the elder John
Christopher Smith (1738): evidently contemporaries found its
content worth attention. One word leaps off the page and provides
the clue. Lockman was Secretary to the royally chartered British
Herring Fishery, of which the Prince of Wales was Governor, but he
calls the completion of Saul's suicide by the Amalekite 'Regicide'.[77]
It was not only Stuart loyalists who still felt driven to exorcise the
corporate guilt of king-killing, a century after the event.

The Amalekite incident is in fact rich in meanings which would
have been clear to the eighteenth-century audience, but which need
explanation now. The individual Amalekite's *coup de grâce* was
scarcely regicide by comparison with the execution of Charles I:
Saul was already half dead by his own hand, *and* was finished off by
the Amalekite at his own request, *and* was not the Amalekite's ruler.
Both Lockman and Jennens are using the Amalekite as a scapegoat,
transferring the nation's guilt to a member of another race:

> Then *David* the *Amalekite* survey'd;
> Look'd pensive round, and to a young Man said,
> Advance: unsheathe thy Sword. – The Man obey'd.
> Plunge, plunge it deep, cry'd *David*, in his Side: –
> He smote the Regicide, he fell: he died: –
> The Chieftain then: – Thy Blood be on thy Head,
> For Thou a Monarch's sacred Blood hast shed;
> As thine own Lips now testify'd too plain,
> Saying, the Lord's Anointed I have slain.   (Lockman)

> DAVID   Whence art thou?
> AMAL.   I am an *Amalekite*.
> DAVID   Impious Wretch, of Race accurst!
>   And of all that Race the worst!
>   How hast thou dar'd to lift thy Sword
>   Against th'Anointed of the Lord?
> [To one of   Fall on him – smite him – let him die;
> his Attendants, On thy own Head thy Blood will lie;
> who kills the   Since thy own Mouth has testify'd,
> *Amalekite*]   By Thee the Lord's Anointed dy'd.
>   (Jennens, Act III scene 4)

The biblical account also involves two interconnected historic
crimes. Saul's fate is pure poetic justice. He loses the battle of Gilboa
against the Amalekites and dies because God has forsaken him on
account of his disobedience in an earlier encounter with the Amalekite forces. God ordered all that remained of the Amalekites on that

occasion to be sacrificed to Him, but Saul flouted His commands
(2 Samuel XV). Thereafter God persecutes him, as Jennens shows in
his libretto, with madness, with the loss of his son's affection, with
the loss of his people's support, and with the transfer of the throne to
another family. This was a major crux in the deist controversy,
because liberal humanists, then as now, were repelled by the idea of
a God who demanded a holocaust and punished so ferociously a
man who spared his enemy. The orthodox response was twofold.
God's law is Law, and not to be disobeyed; and the individual
incident relates to a deeper and wider issue, the place of the Amalekites in Israel's history. They were the very first people to oppose
the progress of the Hebrew ex-slaves, the first to make war on them,
unprovoked; the first enemies of monotheism, and hence the
especial, eternal enemies of God, who put His people, the Israelites,
under a permanent obligation to eradicate them (Exodus
XVII.8–16; this too was naturally repellent to those wishing to
believe in God as the father of all mankind).[78] Lockman mentions
none of this, but Jennens, characteristically, is more inclusive. The
effect of God's persecution of Saul forms the drama of his libretto,
and the reason for it underpins his tragic climax, the scene at Endor
(Act III scene 3), when the ghost of Samuel, far from providing the
comfort and advice for which Saul longs, makes him understand the
connection between his unforgivable crime and his unavoidable
ruin:

> Hath God forsaken thee? And dost thou ask
> My Counsel? Did I not foretel thy Fate,
> When, madly disobedient, thou didst spare
> The curst *Amalekite*, and on the Spoil
> Didst fly rapacious? Therefore God this Day
> Hath verify'd my Words in thy Destruction;
> Hath rent the Kingdom from thee ...[79]

In other words, even God's anointed cannot escape the consequences of breaking God's Law. Jennens was himself enough of a
liberal humanist to present as moral *grounds* for Saul's destruction
what the biblical author would have seen as the moral *results* of his
God's desertion of him – anger, envy, tyranny and murderous
violence. For modern audiences the great chorus 'Envy, eldest born
of hell' perhaps overbalances the impact of his portrayal in this
direction. The effect might have been different had Handel completed a chorus which he began to set, at an early point in the

libretto, Act I scene 5, just after Saul throws his javelin at David. Its text survives in the autograph score in the British Library:

> What words can tell how happy they
> Who all their God's commands obey!
> Peace to their souls their God will speak,
> Nor storms without that peace can break.
> But justly doom'd the wicked mind . . .

Jennens fully subscribes to the view that Saul is justifiably deprived of his throne because he has tried to rule outside the known Law. At Endor Saul has indeed just compounded his original crime, breaking another divine ordinance by resorting to witchcraft, a form of apostasy which he had himself outlawed in the cause of monotheism. As one of the biblical authors baldly summarises:

So Saul died for his transgression which he committed against the Lord, even against the word of the Lord, which he kept not, and also for asking counsel of one that had a familiar spirit, to inquire of it; And inquired not of the Lord; therefore he slew him, and turned the kingdom unto David the son of Jesse. (1 Chronicles X.13–14)

This sheds light on another alteration that Jennens made to Handel's original setting, in the scene at Endor. Correcting the accentuation by raising Samuel's vocal line on 'and dost thou ask *my* counsel', Jennens also stresses the enormity of Saul's attempt to seek guidance through the false practices of apostate religion.[80] In contemporary terms, James II's Catholicism and lawbreaking autocracy justified his removal: the king must govern within the law of the land and support its religion. The audience of Jennens' unsigned libretto would not necessarily have deduced his political leanings from it, for David is faultless and God is clearly on his side, endorsing (in contemporary terms) the Hanoverian succession.

Another aspect of Jennens' portrayal of Saul deflects some of the horror of setting aside the Lord's anointed. The oratorio was written during the height of the opposition's campaign against Walpole, and one of the vices for which that first minister was particularly condemned, envy,[81] is also one of the moral elements of Saul's downfall. For a contemporary audience the Saul–Walpole parallel would have been unmistakable, and would have mitigated the connotations of the parallels with Charles I and James II. It is worth noting in this connection that according to opposition writers (especially in the *Craftsman*), David is not only Saul's righteous successor; being the chief poet of the Scriptures, he is the archetype of all virtuous (that is, opposition) writers.[82] It is of course *while he is singing and playing* that Saul tries to kill him, and this incident forms a central episode of the libretto.

The theme of justice recurs in the libretto which modern commentators think may share a common author with *Solomon*.[83] The Israelite society of *Susanna*, by contrast with that of *Solomon*, is deracinated, dispossessed, threatened and unconfident, oppressed by Babylonian exile (a circumstance given great prominence in the libretto but not even mentioned in the source); and the gravest symptom of its dislocation is the perversion of justice. God's perfect justice is contrasted throughout the oratorio with man's iniquity. In the very opening scene the Israelites (true to their biblical originals) complain of God's treatment of them, but Joacim points out its justice: 'Our Crimes repeated, have provok'd his Rage, / And now He scourges a degenerate Age' – an epitome of contemporary teaching on 'corruption' and one of many instances in this text of dramatic irony, in that 'degenerate Age' also describes the Elders (yet to appear). The Elders, 'the boasted Guardians of our Laws' who seem virtuous to all but the wholly virtuous Susanna, God and God's agent Daniel, act as prosecuting counsel, prosecution witnesses and judges and perjure themselves, yet convince the Chorus of their probity. The happy conclusion endorses the message, reiterated throughout the text, that because God sees through all human hypocrisy justice will eventually prevail, but the libretto's overriding preoccupation with the frailty of security is potently expressed in the narrowness of Susanna's escape from infamy and death.[84]

Winton Dean, taking his cue from the Arne-like cast to some of the music, calls *Susanna* a 'comic opera' and 'village idyll'.[85] But the central facts of the libretto are attempted rape, perjury and false conviction in an alien city, and two of its high points strikingly invoke the most solemn moment of human existence – not temporal but final judgement. When Susanna is left alone after her husband's departure on business, she has a sudden sense of an imminent strange event. She thinks it may be beneficent, but 'If bad, on me alone the Danger fall'. Instead of leaving the dramatic irony at that, the librettist gives Susanna a prayer of intense and exalted gravity:

> Bending to the Throne of Glory
>   This alone, great God, I crave;
> Let me innocent before you

> Rise from the devouring Grave.
> If thy Will is now requiring
>   That I die before my Time,
> All my longing Soul's desiring
>   Is to fall without a Crime.   (Part I scene 2)

This twists the dramatic irony further, anticipating Susanna's death
sentence; it affirms Susanna's purity and devoutness in the most
convincing way possible – soliloquy; but it also, unusually in the
Israelite librettos, brings forward the ideas of the afterlife, of the Last
Judgement, of the danger of eternal damnation, of the hope of
eternal salvation. They continue to reverberate in Susanna's subsequent rebuttal of her accusers and judges, with added overtones of
Christian sacrifice:

> If guiltless Blood be your Intent,
>   I here resign it all;
> Fearless of Death, as innocent,
>   I triumph in my Fall   (II.4)

> ... welcome Death! I meet you with Delight,
> And change this Earth for Realms of endless Light ...   (III.1)

The librettist has chosen not to suppress the potential Christian and
Christological interpretations of Susanna's story, presenting an
image of redemption under a plot of judicial deliverance.[86] As
already mentioned in connection with *Israel in Egypt*, *Joseph* and
Joshua, many of the scriptural events and figures selected by the
librettists – including Daniel, who saves Susanna from destruction –
had been interpreted for centuries as types (that is, foreshadowings)
of Christ, and a typological level of interpretation of Old Testament
events in the librettos would have been no innovation or anachron-
ism. Awareness of the allusions to the Christian scheme of judgement in *Susanna* intensifies the seriousness with which we register the
actors and events of the drama (*Clarissa* is the obvious literary
parallel). And it is possible that one level of allegorical significance
which the eighteenth-century audience garnered from the political
and military deliverances depicted in the other Israelite oratorios
pertained likewise to the redemption of the Christian soul.

CHAPTER 14

The conflict of public and private interests

In the discussion of good citizenship which political controversy kept alive throughout the mid-century, government writers presented personal and public life as easily reconcilable spheres in which variable behaviour was unobjectionable and moral consistency uncalled for; or they were still less idealistic, assuming self-interest to be the unexceptionable basis of any politician's activities.

To expect Men in Power and Office should *pursue the Good of the Publick*, without any Regard to *their own particular Interest*, is the most ridiculous Expectation in the World: 'tis contrary to *Reason* and *Justice*, and the *Good of the Community* too; 'tis a *Romantick Notion*, and meer *Visionary Virtue*.[1]

James Pitt is jeering at Patriot political ideals. These prescribe that rulers respond to political corruption with the moral rectitude which they exercise in their private lives; there are to be no double standards and no expediency. Only men of integrity can be trusted to serve their country. Walpole's greatest iniquity as chief minister, according to the Patriots, was 'the constant endeavour he has employed to corrupt the morals of men. I say thus generally, the morals; because he who abandons or betrays his country, will abandon or betray his friend.'[2] But to take this stand will involve a clash of interests, which itself becomes a touchstone of true patriotism. The real Patriot, the opposition journal *Common Sense* declared (7 October 1738), is 'one who pursues the Good of his Country, preferable to, and independent of, all private Considerations'. Separate, conflicting claims are assumed; sacrifice is anticipated; anguish is implied. It is easy to see how readily Patriot philosophy became Patriot literature.

The writers in Frederick's circle, notably Morell's friend Thomson in his plays and Bolingbroke in *The Idea of a Patriot King*, drawing on earlier Whig writings in the neo-Stoical, civic humanist

335

tradition, continually warned that the patriotic ruler must be prepared to yield his personal feelings to the good of his country. As a
literary theme the clash of rulers' public and private interests has of
course a very long history, going back to Homer. The specific theme
of private grief and loss which result from the rulers' duty to serve
the best interests of their country, so thoroughly explored in the
previous generation by Dryden, was reworked in simpler and more
didactic terms by exponents of Patriot principles.[3] The requirement
that the ideal ruler be prepared to sacrifice personal attachments to
the national interest is starkly conveyed in the final words of
Brooke's *Gustavus Vasa*, where the hero vows 'I will / Of private
passions all my soul divest, / And take my dearer country to my
breast' while suppressing his grief for the loss, during the play's
action, of sister, mother, friend and beloved. In an undated
commonplace book, Morell copied out from Burnet's *History of his
own Times*: 'There is nothing more evident than that the Prince is
made for the People, and not the People for them',[4] and his *Alexander
Balus* shows the perils that await a ruler who yields to personal
feelings (see chapter 12). In making the clash of private and public
interest in the lives of rulers a focus of two of his librettos, *Alexander
Balus* and *Jephtha*, Morell was keeping faith with his Patriot opposition past.

He could have found copious patterns in the dramas of his own
literary circle, most immediately his friend Thomson's *Sophonisba*
(Prince Masinissa, torn between alliance to Rome and love for the
Carthaginian queen, has to be the agent of her death), *Edward and
Eleonora* (Edward's deeply loved queen Eleonora offers her life as the
only means to save their country) and *Tancred and Sigismunda* (the
tragic consequences inherent in dynastic marriages). Thomson in
turn had been influenced by that ubiquitous background figure of
Handel's English theatre career, Aaron Hill, whose popular version
of Shakespeare's *Henry V* exemplifies the varieties of exquisite
emotional heightening of which the theme was capable.[5] Characteristically, the Patriot drama portrays high-minded figures in positions
of public responsibility whose pure, generous, legitimate love
for a worthy object is contrary to the interest of their country, for
which their love is equally pure and generous, thus forcing them to
make morally complicated choices. Mutual admiration tunes the
quality of mutual love to the highest pitch, which in turn raises the
moral level of conduct aimed at. Through relationships between

several of his characters in *Henry V* Hill explores individuals'
responses to the pressures of public life, and in their comments on the
dilemmas into which he puts them he helps to transmit the idea of
the Patriot King to the next generation of writers. Though his play is
only distantly indebted to Shakespeare's text, he retains an exceptional amount of Henry's meditation on the burdens of kingship
('Upon the king ... we must bear all' etc.), making it his central
moral-political theme. His emphasis on the ruler's need to sacrifice
himself brings the Patriot idea of the kingly role as 'godlike' to the
boundaries of sacrilege in Henry's prayer before Agincourt, not (as
in Shakespeare) a plea for absolution, but the self-surrender of a
secular Christ:

> Preserve my life, for all my people's safety!
> But, if my death can free my dear-lov'd country
> From any deep distress my life might cause her,
> Oh, then! accept me as my subjects sacrifice,
> And I have liv'd enough ...   (Act V scene 1)

The leading royal Patriot in *Henry V* is not, however, Henry but the
French princess, after the pattern of noble, warm, sensitive, generous heroines common to the Patriot drama and notably embodied in
the heroine of Morell's *Jephtha*.

The 'romantic' and 'visionary' quality (to use James Pitt's words)
of this doom-laden ideal of unself-interested leadership, as of opposition ideology in general, admirably fitted it for didactic literary
semi-fictions such as oratorio. It would be interesting to know why it
was not transferred to what we might expect to have been a natural
home, Handel's operas. Time after time the librettos of these works
had shown rulers coping with personal dilemmas, but hardly ever on
the terms of Patriot tragedy. In the early London and the Royal
Academy operas the clash is between personal desire and personal
honour: princes worthy of the title must behave honourably in
personal matters. Moral exhortations abound, but they have little to
do with the prince's obligations to his subjects, who literally have no
voice apart from four lines in *Sosarme*. (Elizabeth Gibson's comments
that in accordance with contemporary canons of art the Royal
Academy operas were 'intended to illuminate how the great should
behave', 'teach a moral lesson' and 'impart a theory of decorum',
and that they were mainly 'serious and exemplary' should be
explored in more detail.[6]) In most of Handel's operas kingdoms are
rightful or illegitimate acquisitions and marks of status, but not

responsibilities: their welfare is not a concern, and they are plunged into war and restored to peace as side effects of their rulers' volatile personal relationships. The exception, which shows that there was nothing about the genre which ruled out Patriot subject-matter, is *Muzio Scevola* (1721), with a libretto by Paulo Rolli about the preservation of liberty in republican Rome full of Patriot sentiments and situations (and worth study as such).[7] But this is an isolated example, although political dilemmas of other kinds abound, as do contemporary political trigger-words. Handel's opera librettos still await thorough explanation.

However, the Patriot theme of conflict between public and private interest is prominent in Handel's oratorios, and not only in his. The Prince of Wales' chaplain, John Hoadly, explored it to its full extent of sacrifice unto death in his libretto for Greene's oratorio *Jephtha* (1737), which casts interesting light on Morell's own libretto on the identical part of the Bible.[8] In dramatising Jephtha's tragic dilemma both librettists were choosing the biblical version of the classical story on this topic, which also concerns the offering up of a daughter for the sake of national success – Agamemnon's sacrifice of Iphigenia at Aulis, which would have been very familiar to Morell the classicist from Homer, Aeschylus and Euripides, and to Morell the clergyman from biblical commentaries.[9]

The Book of Judges seems to provide as harsh an example of the demands of leadership as does the Greek myth. The death of Jephtha's daughter is the price of his successful command of his people. This at any rate is Hoadly's interpretation, and he does not attempt to palliate the affront to the idea of a loving God which the narrative offers. Like several parts of the Old Testament that became oratorio texts, the story of Jephtha had drawn and was still drawing deist fire and orthodox counterblasts, some in the very year of Hoadly's publication.[10] In Hoadly's libretto as in the Bible, Jephtha vows that he will sacrifice to God the first thing he encounters on his return from battle (though in Hoadly's version the condition is safe return, not victory). His daughter comes to meet him; he is horrified; she accepts her fate (and in Hoadly's version prevents Jephtha from killing himself instead), asking only for a spell of solitude in which to prepare herself for death. Father and daughter part disconsolate, bound by submission to higher powers: 'Obey the Lord on high'. Hoadly simplifies the political issue by omitting the long account of Jephtha's dispute with the king of

Ammon on the relative merits of their people's conflicting territorial claims (Judges XI.12–28), and builds the opening part of his drama (more than a third of the whole) by combining two topics which are separate in Judges X.6–XI.11: the Israelites' idolatry, rejection by God and repentance, and the Gileadites' successful persuasion of the exiled Jephtha to return to lead his country in battle.

This is the part of the story that really interested Hoadly, and no doubt interested his master too; the libretto was written at the time of the prince's removal from his parents' court. Jephtha reproaches the elders of Gilead:

> Did ye not cast me out
> An Exile, tho' a Brother? Did ye not
> With hostile Treatment chase me from those Seats,
> Those pleasing, native Seats; to seek new Brethren,
> New Friends, new Lands, new Dwellings to inherit?
> And come ye now, cover'd with Guilt and Shame,
> With Fears dispirited, to ask my Aid
> 'Gainst *Ammonitish* Arms? Necessity,
> It seems, hath taught you Justice ...

This may sound like a reference to the Stuart exile, but Hoadly's employment makes an identification of Jephtha with the Hanoverian heir apparent far more plausible. Hoadly's hero in this first section is much more exemplary than his biblical counterpart (needless to say Jephtha's illegitimacy, Judges XI.1, is not mentioned). In the Bible Jephtha is sought as a leader simply on account of his valour. He shows no interest in the Israelites' spiritual condition, his grievance against them is entirely personal (their earlier repudiation of him), and he makes subsequent rule a condition of his leadership in battle. Hoadly's men of Gilead repeatedly identify Jephtha as 'the Hand of Heaven', the 'belov'd Deliverer' raised by God for the nation's salvation, godlike in his compassion for the nation's desperate plight. The condition which Hoadly's Jephtha makes is national purification – the rejection of idolatry and hypocrisy and renewed allegiance to God. He does not ask for the judgeship but is offered it, and replies:

> Pity soothing melts my Soul,
> And does each angry Thought controul:
> But Thou bear Witness, *Israel*'s God,
> 'Tis not Ambition's lofty Charms,
> Nor empty Fame my Rage disarms,
> But Pity to the General Good.

His concern for and accomplishment of national reform, his lack of personal ambition, his taming of his baser passions and his allowance of softer ones, all for the sake of the 'general good', are features common to the numerous portrayals of the Patriot King produced in the prince's circle and foreshadow their incorporation in Bolingbroke's *The Idea of a Patriot King* itself.

A further reason for the Prince of Wales' likely interest in the story of Jephtha's appointment to leadership can be traced in Lowman's analogy of the event in modern political practice:

Jephtha went to the Elders of *Gilead*, and the People made him Head and Captain over them. Here, as the Elders are plainly distinguish'd from the People, so it is plain to perceive a very near Resemblance to the known Form of Government by a Senate and Assembly of the People. The Choice of *Jephtha* was a just Act of the Senate and People of *Gilead*.[11]

Lowman consistently reads the Old Testament as endorsing wide franchise and representative government, and here he makes Scripture endorse the power of Parliament. Frederick's own dynasty had been established by Act of Parliament; here it was being ratified by Scripture.

With Hoadly's text in mind it is interesting to reconsider Morell's *Jephtha*, written shortly before the prince's sudden death (Handel began setting it on 21 January 1751; the prince died on 20 March). Verbal parallels indicate that Morell knew Hoadly's libretto.[12] Morell could have seen the text in the *Gentleman's Magazine*, which his poems show him to have been reading in the 1730s. His other source, apart from the Bible, was George Buchanan's Latin play *Jephthes, sive Votum* (1554). From this he took the characters and names of Jephtha's brother Zebul and his wife (Storgè, Greek for the love between parents and children) and the name of his daughter (Iphis, a reminiscence of the sacrificed Iphigenia). It also provided Storgè's nightmare and waking fears, a precedent for the use of a chorus, the allusion to the miraculous crossing of the Red Sea (scene 2), Iphis' lute and flute (scene 4) and, possibly, hints for 'How dark, O Lord' (scene 9), 'Open thy marble jaws' and 'Hide thou thy hated beams, O sun' (scene 10) and 'For joys so vast' (scene 12), among other verbal parallels.[13]

Like Hoadly, Morell drastically alters the proportions of his source, the embassy to the Ammonites being telescoped into two lines and the events between Jephtha's victorious return and the conclusion filling half the narrative instead of less than a sixth. He takes over Hoadly's combination of the penitent Israelites' religious renewal with their appeal to Jephtha to lead the nation, and his hero too is depicted (in the opening words) as the potential Patriot King recalled from unjust exile:

> True, we have slighted, scorn'd, expell'd him hence,
> As of a Stranger born; but well I know him;
> His generous Soul disdains a mean Revenge,
> When his distressful country calls his Aid –
> And, perhaps, God may favour our Request,
> If with repentant Hearts we sue for Mercy.   (Part I scene 1)

In response to the offer of power Morell's Jephtha too expresses the Patriot King's noble aspiration to a public life guided by moral principles (rather than political expediency): 'Virtue my Soul shall still embrace; / Goodness shall make me great'. This and the two following scenes show that Jephtha's entire family (all, except his daughter, invented by Morell) share his principles, to carefully graded degrees. We have already seen the patriotism, the religious scruples and the sensitive compunction of his brother, leader of the embassy to him. Jephtha's wife is a worthy consort, alert to the suffering condition of the country which, as repeatedly in Patriot opposition literature, is perceived to be at its last gasp:

> 'Twill be a painful Separation, *Jephtha*,
> To see Thee harness'd for the bloody Field.
> But ah! how trivial are a Wife's Concerns,
> When a whole Nation bleeds, and groveling lies,
> Panting for Liberty and Life.

This is in the second scene; in the third, Jephtha's daughter persuades her betrothed likewise to rise above personal interests and devote himself to the national cause. The whole exposition is a dramatised equivalent of the Patriot tenet which Morell had summarised in his poems:

> How godlike is it to be great!
> When Greatness, free from private ends,
> The Good of all Mankind intends![14]

It is also, as is the whole libretto, highly characteristic of Patriot drama in using predominantly family relationships, rather than those of lovers, as a source of trial, pain and tenderness. This has a peculiar and touching aptness. At the time of Hoadly's *Jephtha*,

Frederick was soon to become a father for the first time. His own childhood had been emotionally deprived, and his whole life was blighted by his parents' lack of parental feeling. But he reversed this family tendency, and became a tender, devoted, cherishing father, happiest when at home with his wife and children. Few stories could have engaged his emotions more nearly than that of Jephtha and Iphis. Morell may have been encouraged in his choice not only by Hoadly's precedent – to which he added an entire dimension, for Hoadly had no scenes of family life – but by a famous incident exemplifying the prince's respect for Patriot principles. Frederick keenly and affectionately supervised his children's education, and his choice of subject for their amateur theatricals (when the future George III was only eleven) was Addison's *Cato*, with a prologue identifying true patriotism as defence of the nation's liberty and laws – a love of country so generous that it does not flinch from supreme sacrifice.[15]

The exploration of family relationships has a pitfall, however. In chapter 2 we noted that the chorus of Trachinian citizens in *Hercules* was a dramatically inappropriate intrusion on a domestic tragedy. There is a similar fracture between family and nation in Morell's libretto. Jephtha's catastrophe occurs at the height of the national triumph he has brought about, *because* of that triumph – a triumph that is unaffected by his own disaster. The result is that a huge gap opens between the victorious nation and its broken leader. This contributes greatly to the poignancy of the climactic scenes, but needs an eighteenth-century flexibility to be accepted as dramatically viable. Morell wants the chorus to retain its role as commentator, but the Israelite army has no place in Jephtha's home (the setting for the confrontational quartet) or in his inmost meditation ('Deeper and deeper still'), at both of which it is present (Part II scenes 3–4); and, considered as a character, it retrenches inconsistently in moving from confident faith in God, recently ratified by experience, to Christian stoicism ('How dark, O Lord'). Jephtha is not a dynastic ruler, so his daughter's fate has no bearing on the nation's welfare, and in its national role the chorus has no reason to claim that God has turned 'our Triumphs into Mourning': *its* triumph is unimpaired.

Morell leaves us in no doubt that God ratifies Jephtha's 'bargain' with Him, for whereas the biblical text cryptically records of the Ammonites that 'the Lord delivered them into his hands' Morell takes up a hint from Buchanan and introduces the full epic machinery of divine aid:

> The thund'ring Heavens open'd, and pour'd forth
> Thousands of armed *Cherubim* ... (II.1)

and he strengthens the sense of God's approval with a set-piece chorus ('*Cherub* and *Seraphim*, unbodied Forms') whose final line, 'They ride on Whirlwinds, and direct the Storms', quotes Addison's famous poem *The Campaign*, which itself refers to God's protection of Britain–Israel. Morell's God intervenes in the most emphatic manner to cause Jephtha's victory, as the result, we infer, of his pledge. This unavoidably brings the vexed matter of the vow and its redemption into question. Whereas Hoadly retained the den-ouement of the biblical story, Morell mitigates the harshness of Iphis' fate from death to perpetual virginity, thus incurring the nearly universal derision of modern critics.[16] But Morell's interpret-ation of 'sacrifice' to God as meaning perpetual virginity was neither novel nor unacceptable in his day. On the contrary, it was given as self-evidently reasonable by numerous anti-deistical authors defending God from the charge of cruel and unethical demands. The most substantial case is laid out in three folio columns of his biblical commentary by Samuel Humphreys, who argues that human sacrifice was specifically outlawed by God, that in the crucial sentence, 'Whatsoever cometh forth of the doors of my house to meet me ... shall surely be the Lord's, and I will offer it up for a burnt offering', the Hebrew word translated 'whatsoever' is not gender-specific and the particle translated 'and' can also be trans-lated 'or', and that in the phrase suggesting bereavement, 'the daughters of Israel went yearly to lament the daughter of Jephthah', the word translated 'lament' can also mean 'condole with'. Thus, the sense of the vow is that Jephtha will sacrifice what first en-counters him, *or* devote it to God; and so his daughter is devoted to God, in the sense of perpetual virginity. This is still a tragedy – for Jephtha in that he has no other children so he will have no posterity, and for his daughter because every Jewish girl hoped that her child would be the Messiah; hence the yearly condolences of the Israelite maidens.[17] Hoadly ignored this possible let-out quite blatantly:

> what first shall meet my Eye,
> Of purest Virgin Blood,
> A Victim worthy God,
> Shall to Him devoted die.

But Morell adopts Humphreys' solution, to the letter:

> *What, or who-e'er* shall first salute mine Eyes,
> Shall be for ever thine, *or* fall a sacrifice.
>
> (Part I scene 4; my italics)

But he does not want to forego the pain of personal sacrifice. On the contrary, it inspires him to one of his most productive moments as Handel's librettist (the quartet, II.3), intensifying the conflict between private feelings and public duty by adding to Jephtha's torment the outrage and grief of his wife, his brother and his daughter's betrothed, for whom the demands of the divine will – as they understand it – are too great. So determined is Morell to evoke the classic Patriot anguish of personal versus private obligations that he leaves his plot open to accusations of inconsistency. Since Jephtha phrased his vow to allow for an alternative to human sacrifice, why does he not reassure his family that his daughter need not die? One answer supported by Morell's text (and by Simon Patrick's standard biblical commentary)[18] is that the vow was divinely inspired, uttered almost in a trance, and Jephtha subsequently failed to understand it fully. Again, the dilemma allows a display of Patriot virtue. Like the Patriot King and unlike arbitrary rulers, Jephtha abides by his compact: 'Alas! it was my Daughter, and she dies ... have I not vowed?' Morell's ending simultaneously corrects Hoadly and reassures the Patriot King in waiting: the royal family must be prepared to sacrifice their own feelings for individuals, but they will have the satisfaction of acting for their country's good, and need not fear to be stretched beyond their capacity. His ending is attuned to the rest of his audience as well. In full accordance with the tastes and practice of his time, Morell extorts all the painful emotions of tragic loss by making his characters and audience expect Iphis' death, yet avoids the shock of enacted brutality and provides the catharsis of relief.

* * *

According to Shelley Burtt, 'religious conceptions of political virtue lost their hold on the English political imagination by the middle of the eighteenth century, so too did the republican ideal of the good citizen as public-spirited patriot'. But both were preserved in oratorio librettos well beyond the mid-century. She elaborates: 'By 1740, the idea of a public virtue as crucial to the well-being of the state or excellence of the citizen simply did not figure prominently in either political argument or practice'.[19] But it figured prominently in Handel's oratorio librettos well beyond 1740. According to the evidence of her study, mid-century secular writing about political virtue shows uncertainty and lack of consensus about the relevance of God and religion, despite the prevailing acquiescence in a God-centred world view. Bolingbroke, she notes, rests his case for individual virtue on God's plan for mankind, and she considers him rather eccentric in holding that selfless dedication to the public good is the mainspring of patriotic virtue.[20] If she is right, then the linking of patriotism, public virtue, self-sacrifice and obedience to God in the oratorios strongly shows the influence and persistence of the thought of Bolingbroke. But Bolingbroke was not so out of step with his contemporaries as Burtt's account of his writings suggests, and the librettos in fact continue staple Patriot opposition ideas. And, like Bolingbroke, but much more decisively, the librettists widen the appeal of their version of what constitutes public virtue, far beyond the normal scope of Patriot drama, by invoking the sanction of God.

CHAPTER 15

Coda: the end of Handel's Israelite oratorios

Why did Handel produce no Israelite oratorio after *Jephtha*? The obvious answer is that he was growing blind and exhausted; yet this did not prevent the production, when his sight was completely extinguished, of a 'new' work. *The Triumph of Time and Truth* (1757) was a compilation (perhaps by a collaborator) of earlier compositions fitted to a text provided by Morell. The libretto and most of the music derived from Handel's *Il trionfo del tempo*, but for the public it was a new oratorio.[1] Why did Morell and Handel choose a non-biblical text at this juncture? Morell had to fit new words to the music, and though some were ready made (the translation by George Oldmixon in the 1737 libretto of *Il trionfo*), he could have found Old Testament ones to adapt that would have done as well. That he was not averse to making up more texts from the Old Testament is evident from his doing so after Handel's death: his *Nabal* (1764) and *Gideon* (1769) are characteristic Israelite librettos, which he fitted to existing music by Handel. The collaborators had had much more success with their Israelite oratorios up to 1753 than with their one full-length oratorio on another theme (*Theodora* was a box-office disaster). If Handel was the one who resisted another Israelite topic, one must ask why, his health being (in view of *The Triumph of Time and Truth*) an insufficient reason. It is plausible that the reason was the 1753 Jew Bill furore.

On 3 April 1753 Lord Halifax introduced to Parliament a Bill, supported by the government, 'to permit persons professing the Jewish religion to be naturalised by Parliament', which would make it possible for foreign Jews living in Britain to apply for naturalisation. It met with increasing opposition during its successive readings, but not enough to prevent its being enacted. However, vehement objections to it meanwhile developed outside Parliament, and by the third reading the opposition had seen it as a possible

346

means of unseating the government in the forthcoming election.[2] What had begun life as a very minor legislative means of increasing British revenue and commerce grew into a national rumpus which its historians describe as 'a violent politico-religious controversy', 'An agitation ... which has few parallels in English history', and 'Among the most remarkable popular movements in eighteenth-century England', in which 'England was thrown into paroxysms of excitement'.[3] The Jew Bill (as it was known to contemporaries, though during most of the upheaval it was already on the statute book) became the chief topic of political discussion for over six months. It generated over sixty pamphlets (mostly hostile to the measure) and twenty-five prints (all hostile), new editions of old tracts made relevant to the occasion, daily newspaper reports, comments and attacks, and copious constituency Instructions to Members of Parliament (Perry mentions over four closely printed pages of addresses and answers in the *Gentleman's Magazine* for November).[4] A casual reader of history thinking it was a storm in a teacup would be misinterpreting the mood of the time.[5]

The first organised opposition came from City merchants, and was based on their belief in a static economy and a finite amount of available wealth; they produced an image of bread being taken out of Englishmen's mouths. But they did more. Their petition, presented during the bill's third reading, shrewdly introduced the idea that it would 'tend greatly to the dishonour of the Christian religion [and] endanger our excellent Constitution' before advancing any economic objections, and the economic objections easily roused conservative fear of the growing power of financiers.[6] By the end of the same day opposition speeches had included such remarks as 'God have mercy upon such of the natives as shall continue Christian; for I am sure our rulers the Jews would have none', and by the following October Archbishop Herring was writing that 'faction, working upon the good old spirit of High Church, has made wild work in the nation'.

The administration, perhaps unaware of the Bill's reflection of Whig economic, political and religious latitudinarianism, had failed to anticipate that it could be used to rouse the hostility to these principles shared by (as it transpired) the majority of the nation, whether country Tories, landed Whigs, High Churchmen, City merchants, small traders, or the eighteenth-century equivalent of Little Englanders, once they felt their identity and self-interest was threatened. The opposition propagated wildly exaggerated versions of the Bill, alleging it proposed to naturalise all foreign Jews (in fact it only allowed them to seek naturalisation, a long and expensive process). The government had decided on repeal by the time Parliament reconvened, but by then the issue had assumed such importance that it prompted a remarkable debate in the House of Commons in which the events of the previous forty years were rehearsed, with opposing interpretations of their bearing on the present state of the nation. During the recess anxious politicians had referred to the Sacheverell case, when government resistance to public pressure had lost it the election, and the Excise crisis, when repeal averted election defeat – the latter precedent being followed, with similar results, in 1754.[7]

The nationwide opposition to the Jew Bill was to immigration and naturalisation as such, and expressions of antisemitism reflected or did duty for a wider and more ingrained xenophobia (there is only one recorded instance of an actual anti-Jewish demonstration).[8] But animosity to Jews was the trigger, Jews were the butt, and during 1753 'Jew' came to mean 'enemy of the Church and constitution', as in the slogans 'No Jews; Christianity and the Constitution' and 'No Jews; no Jacobites; New Interest and Christianity for ever'. The identification of Jews with *any* threat to Church and state is especially clear in the prints. *Vox Populi, Vox Dei* shows a 'mob of Jews and Deist's' led by Samson Gideon (a highly respected and utterly loyal London Jew) and the late Lord Bolingbroke (byword to his opponents for Jacobitism and treachery, and recently revealed as heretically sceptical of the validity of Scripture[9]), who threaten the cross, which is protected by 'the Eye of Providence'. Another print, *A Prospect of the New Jerusalem* (London), calls the Bill 'Some Popish Plot to bring in the Pretender'. The pamphlet *The Crisis, or, an Alarm to Britannia's True Protestant Sons* (1754) pointed out that 'Jew' and its equivalents had simply become a cant term for anything one disapproved of in politics:

In the mouth of a Jacobite, Judaism is another name for the revolution of 1688, a limited monarchy, the Hanover legacy, and the royal family . . . In the mouth of a pretended patriot and flaming bigot, Judaism is a Whiggish administration and House of Commons, a Protestant Bench of Bishops, liberty of conscience and an equitable toleration.[10]

The eighteenth-century British reader was perfectly well able to distinguish between Old Testament Israelites and contemporary

Jews (not least in that the former could not be accused of having killed Christ), but while this passage from *The Crisis* provides yet another instance of Jews (though in this case modern Jews) being used as a metaphor for the modern English, it also suggests that the figure of the Jew, of any period, was far too politically loaded in 1753–4 to be capable of a neutral or favourable implication or of a non-political meaning. The popular press disregarded historical distinctions in its zeal to blacken modern Jews and hence the government: Cranfield gives several instances of the *London Evening Post*'s references to alleged atrocities by Jews in the Middle Ages, rehearsed to 'demonstrate' the tribe's permanently evil character.[11]

Israelite oratorios may have been curbed because of hostility to Jews as both literal and metaphorical beings.[12] But the deterrents were more germane even than this. The Old Testament itself, it was suggested, should be purged of Israelite references. The letter from 'B. B.' in the *Gentleman's Magazine* for September 1753 now sounds like one of the more absurd of the many bizarre utterances of the crisis, but as the writer points out, what he recommends had the precedent of no less an authority than Isaac Watts (as we saw in chapter 9):

I have long observed the impropriety of a Christian congregation adopting the *Jewish* phrases in their worship of the Almighty. There is without doubt no composition in the world so full of strong and elevated expressions as the Psalms, so suitable to raise the mind to adore the divine being, and to render us truly sensible of his great goodness and mercy; his continual providence over them that keep his statutes, and his dreadful visitations on the wicked [quotes Psalm XXXII.11]. But as many passages are peculiar to the *Jews*, either by way of figure, or in plain words, it is wish'd, by those that reflect, that they were omitted, or so altered as to be fitted to the state of the Christian church. As some seasons are more favourable to reform than others, I am willing to hope that the present disposition of the people against the *Jews*, might be successfully laid hold of, that while we are opposing the favour that seems intended for them, we may not be praying for their establishment and prosperity, in the very words which they themselves use; and addressing the Almighty in such terms as can only be proper for a *Jewish* synagogue. These are so frequent in the Psalms that it is scarce necessary to give an instance: – [quotes a selection of verses, for example 'Stand up, O Lord God of Israel, to visit all the heathen' and 'O pray for the peace of Jerusalem, they shall prosper that love thee'].

Dr *Watts* long since purged and improved the singing psalms, so that they are all now Christian hymns, and may be used with great profit and delight; and, why may not the reading psalms be so improved and rendered Christian?[13]

The Psalms are used far more often than any other book of the Bible in the Israelite oratorios; if they were now to be censored or bowdlerised to exclude references to the nation and land of Israel, how could the librettists draw on them for choruses? Worse, if the success of the biblical Jews was anathema, how write an Israelite oratorio at all?

Modern commentators have deduced from Handel's remark about *Theodora* (that the Jews would not come to it because the story was Christian), and from the presence of some leading Jews among his subscribers, the supposition that a substantial part of his oratorio audience was Jewish.[14] If this is the case, it could help to explain why, despite the ferocity of anti-Jewish feeling, Handel's 1754 season (and subsequent seasons) included revivals of Israelite oratorios, though no new ones.[15] Some of Handel's post-1753 revisions of his Israelite oratorios were surprisingly drastic, apparently unmotivated by the usual practical considerations of cast, length and popularity, and have puzzled modern commentators.[16] A musicologist might like to examine them again to see whether they bear out the suggestion that, like the Excise Bill at the beginning of Handel's oratorio career, the Jew Bill had a decisive effect on his work.

Libretto authors and sources

HANDEL'S ENGLISH ORATORIOS

Title	Librettist	Chief sources of libretto (OT: Old Testament; Ap: Apocrypha; NT: New Testament)
Haman and Mordecai	? Alexander Pope, John Arbuthnot	OT: Esther II–X; Ap: Esther XII–XVI; Jean Racine: *Esther*, trans. Thomas Brereton
Esther	Samuel Humphreys	1718 libretto and sources
Deborah	Samuel Humphreys	OT: Judges IV–V
Athalia	Samuel Humphreys	OT: 2 Kings VIII–X; Racine, *Athalie*
Saul	Charles Jennens	OT: 1 Sam. XV–XX, XXVI, XXVIII, XXXI, 2 Sam. I, II; Abraham Cowley: *Davideis*; Roger Boyle: *The Tragedy of King Saul*
Israel in Egypt	? Charles Jennens	OT: Exod. I, II, VII, XV, 2 Sam. I, Pss CIII, CV, CVI, CXII, Job XXIX, Lam. I, II, Dan. XII; Ap: Wisd. of Sol. V, Ecclus. XXXVI, XLIV; NT: Phil. IV
Messiah	Charles Jennens	OT: Job XIX, Pss II, XVI, XXII, XXIV, LXVIII, LXIX, Isa. VII, IX, XXXV, XL, L, LIII, LX, Lam. I, Hag. II, Mal. III, Zech. IX; NT: Matt. I, XI, Luke II, John I, Rom. VIII, X, 1 Cor. XV, Heb. I, Rev. V, XI, XIX

Samson	Newburgh Hamilton	OT: Judges XIII–XVI; John Milton: *Samson Agonistes*, paraphrase of OT Pss VII, LXXX, LXXXI, LXXXIII, LXXXIV, LXXXVI, CXIV, CXXXVI, *The Passion, On Time, On the Morning of Christ's Nativity, An Epitaph on the Marchioness of Winchester, At a Solemn Music*
Joseph and his Brethren	James Miller	OT: Gen. XXXVIII–XLV; Charles-Claude Genest: *Joseph*; Apostolo Zeno: *Giuseppe*
Belshazzar	Charles Jennens	OT: 2 Kings XXIV, XXV, 2 Chron. XXXVI, Ezra I, II, V, VI, Isa. XVI, XLIV, XLV, Jer. XXVII–XXIX, XXXII, XXXIII, XXXIX, Dan. I, V; Herodotus: *Histories*; Xenophon: *Cyropædia*
Occasional Oratorio	Newburgh Hamilton	Milton: paraphrases of OT Pss II, II, V, LXXXI, CXXXVI; Edmund Spenser: *Faerie Queene, Hymn to Heavenly Beauty, Tears of the Muses*; libretto of *Israel in Egypt*
Judas Macchabæus	Thomas Morell	Ap: 1 Macc. II–VIII; Josephus: *Antiquities*
Alexander Balus	Thomas Morell	Ap: 1 Macc. IX–XII
Joshua	?	OT: Exod. XII, Lev. XXIII, Num. IX, XIII, XIV, Joshua I, III–XI, XIII–XV
Susanna	?	Ap: Susanna
Solomon	?	OT: 2 Sam. XVI, XIX, 1 Kings I–XI, 1 Chron. XXII, XXVIII, XXIX, 2 Chron. I–IX
Theodora	Thomas Morell	Robert Boyle: *The Martyrdom of Theodora and of Didymus*
Jephtha	Thomas Morell	OT: Judges X–XII; George Buchanan: *Jephthes, sive Votum*

HANDEL'S ENGLISH MASQUES, MUSIC DRAMAS, CANTATAS AND MORAL ODES

Title	Librettist	Chief sources of libretto
Acis and Galatea	John Gay, with John Hughes and probably Pope and Arbuthnot	Ovid: *Metamorphoses*, trans. John Dryden; Homer: *Iliad*, trans. Pope; Pope: *Autumn*
Alexander's Feast	Newburgh Hamilton	Dryden: *Alexander's Feast*
Ode for St Cecilia's Day		Dryden: *A Song for St Cecilia's Day*
L'allegro, il penseroso ed il moderato	Charles Jennens	Milton: *L'Allegro* and *Il Penseroso*
The Story of Semele	? Newburgh Hamilton	William Congreve: *Semele* and poems; Pope: *Summer*[1]
Hercules	Thomas Broughton	Sophocles: *Trachiniae*; Ovid: *Metamorphoses*
The Choice of Hercules	? Thomas Morell	Robert Lowth: *The Judgement of Hercules*
The Triumph of Time and Truth	? Thomas Morell	Benedetto Pamphili: *Il trionfo del Tempo e del Disinganno* (set by Handel 1708), trans. George Oldmixon (for performance in 1737 as *Il trionfo del Tempo, e della Verità*)

[1] See Brian Trowell, 'Congreve and the 1744 Semele Libretto', *MT* 111 (1970), 993–4.

The oratorios and Methodism

Some students of Handel's works, observing the connection in the late eighteenth century between the growth of Methodist choral societies and the popularity of Handel's oratorios, and their subsequent association, have projected backwards and linked the writing of the oratorios with the rise of Methodism.[1] There are two issues here. First, is there any concrete evidence that the principles of Methodism were carried into the texts of Handel's oratorios? Second, does there seem to be any similarity in the religious temper of the two expressions of religious faith? It is on the second that the link has been based; the first has not been considered.

The first can be answered with a simple negative; it is historically impossible. The 'conversion' of Whitefield and the Wesleys, from which the beginning of the Methodist movement can be dated, occurred in 1738. None of the oratorio librettists writing after 1738 whose religious position is known to us was a Methodist. Jennens was devoted to the cause of the Church of England and the acceptance of its doctrine. Miller was a clergyman and reputedly High Church. Morell, also a practising clergyman, campaigned, as his Three Choirs sermon attests, for the general adoption of choral services in parish churches (anathema to Wesley).[2] Nor is it possible that the audiences for whom the oratorios were written were Methodist. Historians of the movement agree that the real growth of the society began only in the 1750s. In 1741 there were only a thousand or so Methodists, and by 1750 only twelve preaching houses.[3]

The oratorio audience consisted chiefly of 'the Quality', but apart from a few titled women, early Methodism did not reach the upper classes or fashionable society;[4] and whereas oratorio, even after abolition of the subscription system, cost at least five shillings, Whitefield counted the collections taken at his open-air meetings in halfpennies.[5] While Handel was writing Wesley was still the controlling force of organised Methodism and he discouraged the indiscriminate expansion of the society: his aim was the establishment of small groups of intensive, mutually self-examining devotees of the spiritual life,[6] and it is hardly conceivable that these, the first real practising Methodists as distinct from the curious crowds, were the audiences of oratorio.

Besides, Wesley was a resolute opponent of the forms of church music in which oratorio had its ecclesiastical roots, the Anglican hymn and anthem.[7] Methodist hymns, unlike the libretto choruses, were 'songs of individual experience, marking the successive stages of penitence, conversion, justification, pardon, and sanctification in the life of the Christian pilgrim through this vale of sorrow to eternity'.[8] In its music as well as its words Methodist worship was remote from the oratorio concept. Like Watts, Wesley wanted hymn singing to be the spontaneous utterance of the heart, so the more complex the music was, the less suitable he found it. Organs and choral part-singing were discouraged. He detested anthems in the elaborate Anglican style, on the familiar Protestant grounds of abuse of the sacred text and degradation of human reason: 'The repeating the same word so often, (but especially while another repeats different words, the horrid abuse which runs through the modern church-music,) as it shocks all common sense, so it necessarily brings in dead formality, and has no more of religion in it than a Lancashire hornpipe'.[9]

There is little common ground between the doctrinal principles of Wesleyan Methodism of this period and the substance of the oratorio texts. A summary of the former shows the absence of any points of contact. Just as the experience of conversion, of the New Birth, was essentially personal and inward – something that could not be humanly taught or inculcated or even consciously prepared for – so faith meant faith in a very personally orientated scheme of redemption: a belief that Jesus died 'for *me*'.[10] The Methodist revival was a revival initially of Christian doctrine in its least latitudinarian interpretation: Wesley stressed original sin as total depravity, and accepted grace as 'a favour altogether undeserved'.[11] He displaced the importance of the Mosaic covenant with the idea of a pre-lapsarian Adamic covenant, and by the precept that fallen man is incapable of keeping the laws of God until he is visited by grace.[12] The contemporary claims made for conscience as the director of the virtuous life were excessive, for conscience could not of itself produce faith, hope, love of God or of one's neighbour: these were the gifts of grace.[13] Naturally in this scheme of belief the Eucharist was highly valued as the means of spiritual refreshment (by eighteenth-century standards Methodists communicated abnormally often), and for Wesley it was valuable as proof of the availability of grace to all (it was on this point that his doctrine diverged from that of the Calvinist Whitefield).[14] But while Wesley believed that all could be saved, and also established a democratic church without priests but with lay preachers, he also believed in gradations of piety, and that even after men had been reborn some, being more constant in their faith and habits than others, were more able to 'grow in grace' for the rest of their lives.[15] The rules of life demanded by Wesley's Christianity were severe by the standards of the contemporary established Church. 'According to Wesley it was of the essence of Methodism to stand as a rebuke to the natural human desire for security, praise, comfort, and the honour which comes from men' and he insisted on the perfect Christian love, including love of one's enemies.[16]

Obviously, these are not the doctrines of the oratorios. In the first place, any overt reference to Christian doctrine is excluded from the texts drawn from Old Testament narrative doctrinally based on the Mosaic covenant, and the distinction at the level of common man is not between man wholly depraved and man graciously redeemed, but between a group *naturally* born into the special favour of God, and other groups wilfully rejecting God's sovereignty. The latter are not redeemed but eliminated. The elect of the Old Testament in these works do not admit the availability of grace to all, nor do they love their enemies, since the survival of their God depends upon their enemies' death. The Old Testament vision of redemption, that of the prophets, is not (with the obvious exception of *Messiah*, discussed below) given expression; salvation is not only temporal, but national (extremely limited in comparison with, for example, Zechariah VIII.20–3 and XIV.9). There is no need for sacraments or spiritual redemption (except from temporary backsliding): the Israelites are already God's people, and the spiritual crisis of their lives centres on persecution, not conversion.

This last was probably a point of attraction for the Methodists who later responded to the oratorios. Though they could not find any doctrinal affinity, they could follow the tradition of English religious nonconformists in interpreting the history of the Israelites allegorically, as a pattern of their own peculiar fellowship with God and persecution by unbelievers. Even so, the Israelites' battles are communal, whereas Methodist doctrine emphasised the personal element in the commitment of each individual to belief. In the oratorios solitary wrestling with the devil is rare, and the fate only of those (Saul, for example) who have divorced themselves from the community and hence from God. Moreover, the Israelites in battle have none of the sustained assurance of God's support that new-born Methodists could expect for the rest of their lives. God's intervention is hoped for and trusted in, but its recurring manifestation is miraculous each time: experience teaches that God may, this time, temporarily abandon His people. And it need hardly be pointed out that the Old Testament does not discourage the cultivation of the benefits of this world, and that the librettists do not abjure them either. *Solomon* is the outstanding example of the glorification of material good, but in none of the oratorios is the renunciation of worldly enjoyment a necessary condition of virtue, as it was for the Methodists. Finally, the oratorios, unlike Methodism, retain and endorse the concept of a priesthood as the channel of divine inspiration and public representation of faith; and there is no sense of graded piety among believers, since the Israelites are born elect and can fulfil the conditions of the virtuous life by obedience to a known and not impossibly demanding law. The suggestions throughout the Old Testament (for example, Deuteronomy XII.30, Micah VI.8) that the duty of man to God is easily and happily fulfilled are repeated throughout the oratorio texts as throughout latitudinarian preaching of the eighteenth century.[17]

This is even true of *Messiah*, which asserts the mysteries of Christianity and the doctrine of redemption by grace. Jennens (as has often been observed) gives a latitudinarian rather than Calvinist reading of the doctrine. Salvation is general. Two signal elements in the theology of early Methodism are notably absent from *Messiah*: a sense of individual worthlessness or sin, and a concept of judgement in which the sinner is consigned to hell. At 'the day of his coming' the fire is refining, and the sons of Levi, that is, the chorus, that is, the audience, will be purified, not burnt eternally. Those to be 'dashed in pieces' are always 'them', and the audience is not, unlike the congregation of Bach's Passions, implicated in the denial of Christ. Jennens (in keeping with contemporary latitudinarian

preaching) does not contrast salvation in the life to come with pain
and nothingness of life on earth, but describes the benefits of God
and the ease of access to Him and pleasure in His service that can be
enjoyed here ('Every valley', 'He shall feed his flock', 'Then shall the
eyes', 'His yoke is easy'). There is no hint of the doctrine of predesti-
nation, nor any distinction drawn between the individual and the
community; above all there is no suggestion that baptism is not
enough and that we need to be born anew by conversion to attain
grace.

The question of a similarity of religious feeling and expression
remains. The test case must be *Theodora*, since none of the other
librettos encompasses both the doctrine and the dramatic context of
the new dispensation, whereas *Theodora* is the story of an early
Christian martyr, and was written late enough to show any influence of Methodist preaching creeping in under the guard of its
Anglican author. But its words do not express the intense personal
assertion characteristic of the Methodist new birth. Conversion is
not the result of an overpowering inward change, but is achieved by
precept (Didymus, Part II scene 5) and example (Septimius in the
omitted conclusion). Heaven is often mentioned as the life to come
but is to be attained not through the special intervention of Christ
for the individual – the connotations of theatre performance prevent
the second person of the Trinity from being mentioned by name –
but by virtuous behaviour based on faith in God as the omnipotent
creator. There is only one exception to this, the oblique 'He saw the
lovely youth' (II.6), and this has to be interpreted allegorically to be
made to refer to resurrection in the life to come. The contrast made
in Theodora's duet with Irene (III.1) between death in life and life
in death is not consistently maintained: the reward of martyrdom to
which Didymus and Theodora look forward is their union in heaven
not so much with Christ as with each other. The intensity of
individual witness which divides the new born from the
unredeemed, lacking here because of the absence of any conversion
of the Methodist kind, is also prevented by the presence of the
chorus which, as in all the oratorios, posits an attainable norm of
spiritual commitment and a corporate approach to and worship of
God. The expressions of religious feeling in *Theodora* are common to
all the 'sacred' oratorio librettos and are the normal elevated expressions of contemporary religious verse, conveying warm, generalised
religious excitement – a world apart from the personal, individual,

intensely dramatic terms of Charles Wesley's hymns. We may feel that Handel's music invests the words with an impression of deeply personal spiritual intensity; but this is not what they themselves dictate.

Notes

INTRODUCTION

1 'Neoclassical Criticism of the Ode for Music', *PMLA* 62 (1947), 399–421, at p. 412.

2 *Handel's Dramatic Oratorios and Masques* (1959), p. 333.

3 E.g. *Oratorios*, p. 282, recommends cuts in *Saul* 'where the tension of the story is relaxed', and likewise cuts on non-musical grounds in *Semele* (p. 373), *Susanna* (p. 541) and *Theodora* (p. 563).

4 Contrast the number of performances in Handel's lifetime of *Esther* and *Judas Macchabæus* (many) and of *Hercules* and *Belshazzar* (few), listed by Dean, *Oratorios*, pp. 631–7, with Dean's own evaluations of these works. For *Joseph* see Dean, *Oratorios*, p. 401, and Deutsch p. 586.

5 'Intellectual Contexts of Handel's English Oratorios', in *Music in Eighteenth-Century England: Essays in memory of Charles Cudworth*, ed. Christopher Hogwood and Richard Luckett (Cambridge, 1983), pp. 115–33.

6 Principally, in the first category, Friedrich Chrysander, *G. F. Händel* (Leipzig, 1858–67); Otto Erich Deutsch, *Handel: A Documentary Biography* (1955); Paul Henry Lang, *George Frideric Handel* (1967); Christopher Hogwood, *Handel* (1984); Jonathan Keates, *Handel: The Man and his Music* (1985); in the second, Jens Peter Larsen, *Handel's Messiah: Origins, Composition, Sources* (1957); Dean, *Oratorios*; Howard E. Smither, *A History of the Oratorio*, I and II, *The Oratorio in the Baroque Era* (Chapel Hill, NC, 1977); Winton Dean and J. Merrill Knapp, *Handel's Operas 1704–1726* (1987). The earliest book-length study of the composer, [John Mainwaring et al.,] *Memoirs of the Life of the Late George Frederic Handel* (1760), uses both approaches.

7 The 'historicist' approach very helpfully described and discussed by Robert D. Hume, 'Texts within Contexts: Notes toward a Historical Method', *PQ* 71 (1992), 69–100.

8 The only full-length study by a Handelian to attempt to understand Handel's oratorios through contemporary eyes is Lang's *Handel*, but he produces very little evidence for his assertions. Still more hypothetical are the assertions of Hamish Swanston, *Handel* (1990), which shoots itself in the foot, if not the head, by crediting Handel with ideas and

beliefs inferred from the librettos and by ignoring the contribution and identity of the librettists. Robert Manson Myers, *Handel's Messiah: A Touchstone of Taste* (New York, 1948), like much of Dean's chapter on the contemporary context ('The Oratorio and English Taste'), concerns the oratorios' public reception and later reputation (not always distinguishing these sufficiently), rather than the milieu from which they sprang. Percy Young recognised that Handel's oratorios 'become individual in form and expression because they reflect the feelings, emotions, and ideals of his contemporaries' but did not pursue the point in any depth (*The Oratorios of Handel* (1949), p. 44).

9 E.g. Linda Colley, *Britons: Forging the Nation 1707–1837* (New Haven, 1992), pp. 31–3. Dean himself, while calling attention to the librettists' contribution, often gives this impression, as on his first page: 'the English oratorio was Handel's own creation' (*Oratorios*, p. 3; see similarly e.g. pp. 4, 33, 36, 42). Similarly Lang: 'Like Shakespeare and other great dramatists, Handel took any known story and plot in which a usable idea was present, then proceeded to work it out for the theatre' (*Handel*, p. 362, discussing oratorio); 'The oratorio, or more precisely the English music drama, was an entirely personal creation of this naturalised Briton' ('The Composer' in *Man versus Society in Eighteenth-Century Britain*, ed. James L. Clifford (Cambridge, 1968), pp. 85–101, at p. 95).

In *Britannia's Issue: The Rise of British Literature from Dryden to Ossian* (Cambridge, 1993), published since I finished drafting this book, Howard D. Weinbrot considers *Israel in Egypt* in the context of contemporary attitudes to the Jews, the Old Testament and the Pindaric ode, as evidence of the strong influence of diverse but concordant native traditions on eighteenth-century British literature, historiography and political attitudes. He mentions many issues that are relevant to Handel's oratorios (I cover most of them in this book), but I find his presentation of them unhelpfully jumbled. Like the whole book, his section on Handel seems to me damaged by his aim to find 'synthetic compromise' in contemporary documents, by his treatment of the years 1660–1780 as a single span, and by his neglect of the context behind the context (the agendas of the commentators he cites: see for example p. 419). Politics, religious doctrine and literary appreciation are insufficiently differentiated. With reference to the Jew Bill Weinbrot asks, 'Why in 1753 refuse to allow a few native-born Jews to be naturalized, while also exploiting the spiritual values, poetic devices, and historical parallels of the Old Testament?' (p. 557). But eighteenth-century Britons, less inclined to 'synthesis' and more ready to interpret on multiple levels, did not see any reason to be nice to the Jews competing with them in the Stock Exchange because the Song of Moses was great literature. To bring together their enthusiasm for Old Testament style, respect for the origins of Christianity in Judaism, and desire to hasten the conversion of the Jews under the denomination of 'philosemitism', as Weinbrot does, is to confuse literature and life, self-interest and altruism.

Readers who are not Handelians should be warned: the libretto which Weinbrot prints on pp. 572–6 is not the original version; the idea of a 'final' or 'authorised' version of an oratorio (p. 435) is at odds with Handel's practice; Weinbrot has invented a work by Handel ('Lamentations of Saul', *recte* 'Lamentations of the Israelites for the Death of Joseph', p. 435 and index); he has not taken recent work on Jennens into account; and like so many commentators, he neglects the contributions of Handel's librettists, ignoring, in his discussion of *Israel in Egypt*, the prior existence of *Esther*, *Deborah* and *Athalia* in his claim that out of current admiration of the Pindaric ode and the Song of Moses 'Handel would virtually invent the British sacred choral oratorio' (p. 432).

10 J/H 4–8 February 1741/2.
11 Philip Brett and George Haggerty, 'Handel and the Sentimental: The Case of *Athalia*', *M&L* 68 (1987), 112–27. See also the ground-breaking article by A. H. Shapiro, '"Drama of an Infinitely Superior Nature": Handel's Early English Oratorios and the Religious Sublime', *M&L* 74 (1993), 215–45.
12 Julian Herbage, *Messiah* (1948), p. 14.
13 *Oratorios*, p. 402.
14 E.g. p. 139: 'the eighteenth-century attitude towards the whole province of aesthetics seems astonishingly naïve', vitiated by (p. 129) 'confusion between aesthetic and ethical values'.
15 *Oratorios*, p. 42; see similarly p. 279, 'the complacent and irrelevant moralizing so dear to the eighteenth-century poetaster and so wearisome in the librettos of Humphreys and Morell', and ch. 7, 'The Oratorio and English Taste'. But when the music of a moralising passage appeals to Dean, he praises words and music as dramatic; see his comments on 'O fatal consequence of rage' in *Saul*, p. 291, 'Jealousy' in *Hercules*, p. 419, and 'O calumny' in *Alexander Balus*, p. 487.
16 'Handel and the Sentimental'.
17 *A Handelian's Notebook* (1965), p. 98; see similarly review of Dean by J. A. Westrup, *M&L* 40 (1959), 366–9: 'A Greek chorus, whether one likes it or not, does express moral judgements.' Young paved the way for Dean's approach in looking primarily for the delineation of attractive and interesting *individuals* to the neglect of other dramatic or thematic elements; see e.g. Young, *Oratorios*, pp. 65, 73, 88, 123–6, 130, 144–5, 195.
18 'Land without Music?', *Times Literary Supplement*, 27 November 1992, p. 22.
19 Notably in Myers, *Messiah*, but also in Dean's ch. 7, which takes Myers as its starting-point. The oratorios' reception has been well described by Donald Burrows, *Handel: Messiah* (Cambridge, 1990); Richard Luckett, *Handel's Messiah: A Celebration* (1992); Shapiro, 'Drama'.

20 Steven N. Zwicker, *Dryden's Political Poetry: The Typology of King and Nation* (Providence, RI, 1972), p. 29.

21 For contemporary notice of Handel's plagiarism (of Alessandro Scarlatti) see J/H 17 February 1742/3; for modern comment, see John H. Roberts, 'Handel and Jennens' Italian Opera Manuscripts', in *Music and Theatre: Essays in honour of Winton Dean*, ed. Nigel Fortune (Cambridge, 1987), pp. 159–202; on Handel's assimilation of the musical models which he found on his arrival in England see Graydon Beeks, 'The *Chandos Anthems* of Haym, Handel and Pepusch', *GHB* 5 (1993), 161–93, at pp. 172–3.

22 Notably Larsen, *Handel's Messiah*, pp. 20–9. Larsen's whole description of Handel's oratorios is driven by a notion of a (very restricted) model, which no individual oratorio actually matches, and in which the role of the librettist is all but negated; later Larsen revoked the 'evolutionary', classifying approach, and declared the impossibility of defining Handel's oratorios as a genre ('Wandlungen der Auffassung von Händels "Messias"', *GHB* 1 (1984), 7–19).

23 It is not possible here to do justice to the recent surge of scholarly interest in religion in eighteenth-century Britain. On the primacy of religion in mid-eighteenth-century England see J. C. D. Clark, *English Society 1688–1832: Ideology, Social Structure and Political Practice during the Ancien Régime* (Cambridge, 1985); on providentialism see Jacob Viner, *The Role of Providence in the Social Order* (Philadelphia, 1972), pp. 19–20, 58–60, and Margaret C. Jacob, *The Newtonians and the English Revolution 1689–1720* (Hassocks, Sussex, 1976); on religious publishing see Thomas R. Preston, 'Biblical Criticism, Literature, and the Eighteenth-Century Reader', in *Books and their Readers in Eighteenth-Century England*, ed. I. Rivers (Leicester, 1982), pp. 97–126; on the attempt by religious societies to reform society see Shelley Burtt, *Virtue Transformed: Political Argument in England, 1688–1740* (Cambridge, 1992), ch. 3; on the prominence of religion in recent eighteenth-century historiography see W. A. Speck et al., '1688 and All That', *BJECS* 15 (1992), 131–49.

24 Jeremy Gregory, 'Anglicanism and the Arts: Religion, Culture and Politics in the Eighteenth Century', in *Culture, Politics and Society in Britain, 1660–1800*, ed. Jeremy Black and Jeremy Gregory (Manchester, 1991), pp. 82–109.

25 According to [Mainwaring,] *Life*, pp. 64–5, Handel resisted conversion to Catholicism while in Rome as a young man and (p. 113) in 1729 refused a pressing invitation from Cardinal Colonna in order to avoid meeting the Pretender; and see Sir John Hawkins on his 'very serious notions' about the importance of religion and his appreciation of the tolerance allowed by the British constitution, *A General History of the Science and Practice of Music* (1776, repr. New York, 1963), II, 911.

26 Quoted approvingly Dean, *Oratorios*, p. 40.

27 *Oratorios*, p. 40. This thesis has been adopted by other Handelians; see e.g. Lang, *Handel*, pp. 550–6; Hogwood, *Handel*, p. 168.

28 *Handel's Messiah*, p. 16.
29 *Oratorios*, p. 331–2.
30 Justin Champion, *The Pillars of Priestcraft Shaken: The Church of England and its Enemies, 1660–1730* (Cambridge, 1992), p. 6 (and introduction). Champion's study stops short of the oratorio years but the attitudes to religion and their relevance to politics which he identifies in the early eighteenth century apply equally to the mid century. Clark has gone furthest in defining England as a 'confessional' state (i.e. one in which religious loyalties shape politics): *English Society*, esp. pp. 9, 43, 48, 136, 277. For a recent considered assessment of the relationship between Church, state and people and overview of current research in this area see John Walsh and Stephen Taylor, 'Introduction: The Church and Anglicanism in the "Long" Eighteenth Century', in *The Church of England c. 1689 – c. 1833: From Toleration to Tractarianism*, ed. John Walsh, Colin Haydon and Stephen Taylor (Cambridge, 1993), pp. 1–66. These English historians were anticipated by Henning Graf Reventlow, trans. John Bowden, *The Authority of the Bible and the Rise of the Modern World* (1984), pp. 308, 319–31, 389.
31 *Britons*, p. 18 and ch. 1, esp. pp. 23–4, 43, 45–6, 53.
32 John Dennis, *Vice and Luxury Publick Mischiefs* (1724), pp. ix-xiii, xlv-xlvi, 81, 118. Dennis was more prone than many fellow Whigs to Jacobites-under-the-bed alarms, but his view of the mutual dependence of the state and the state religion was commonplace, as was his anti-Catholicism. For a later example see [Samuel Chandler,] *The Old Whig; or, The Consistent Protestant*, 1735–8, collected in two volumes (1738), esp. I, 5–6, 198–200.
33 F. de P. Castells, *English Freemasonry in its Period of Transition AD 1600–1700* (1931), pp. 81, 201; Leslie J. Biddle, 'The Principal Characters of the Royal Arch Story', *Ars Quatuor Coronatorum* 79 (1966), 283–9; Keith B. Jackson, *Beyond the Craft* (Shepperton, 2/1982), p. 12 (I owe these references to Jane Clark).
34 The suggestive articles of Jane Clark, notably 'Palladianism and the Divine Right of Kings', *Apollo* (April, 1992), 224–9, and ' "Lord Burlington Is Here": A View without Architecture', in *Lord Burlington: Architecture, Art and Life*, ed. Toby Barnard and Jane Clark (1995), have done most among recent studies of eighteenth-century English freemasonry to prompt the idea that Handelians should take account of it. It is intriguing that during the period of Handel's employment by the Duke of Chandos (for whom he wrote *Acis*, *Esther* and the Chandos Anthems), the duke's chaplain was John Desaguliers FRS, 'after 1717 the guiding force of British Freemasonry' and later chaplain to Frederick Prince of Wales (Margaret C. Jacob, *The Radical Enlightenment* (1981), pp. 122, 124).
35 Hence I refer to *Judas Macchabæus* (not as in current usage *Judas Maccabeus*), a spelling which Merlin Channon (personal communication) conjectures that Morell derived from the Vulgate.

36 Margaret Anne Doody, *The Daring Muse: Augustan Poetry Reconsidered* (Cambridge, 1985), p. 190.
37 The best-documented and most transforming instance known to us of a librettist's influence on a performance subsequent to the first is Jennens' effect on the first English performance of *Messiah* (1743): see Burrows, *Messiah*, ch. 3.
38 On provincial performances see further Dean, *Oratorios*, pp. 84–5.
39 Paul Langford, *A Polite and Commercial People: England, 1727–1783* (Oxford, 1989), p. 746.
40 *Britons*, p. 8.
41 The society was also known as the Philarmonic Club; the meeting was at the Crown and Anchor Tavern in the Strand. There is no record of any performance of *Esther* outside Cannons before this one, for which see Deutsch pp. 285–6. At Cannons the work was known as *Haman and Mordecai* and 'The Oratorium'. See Graydon Beeks, 'Handel and Music for the Earl of Carnarvon', in *Bach, Handel, Scarlatti: Tercentenary Essays*, ed. Peter Williams (Cambridge, 1985), pp. 1–20, at pp. 16–19.
42 It was billed by the *Daily Journal*, 19 April 1732, as 'Never Perform'd in Publick before' and given what at this date was an exceptionally well-informed description: 'an oratorio, or sacred drama' (Deutsch p. 288).
43 *See and Seem Blind; or a Critical Dissertation on the Publick Diversions, &c . . . in a Letter from . . . Lord B----- [Burlington?] to A--- H--- [Aaron Hill?] esq* (1732), quoted Deutsch pp. 300–1; Deutsch pp. 272–3, 290; Dean, *Oratorios*, pp. 171–2; Richard Platt, 'Theatre Music I', in *The Blackwell History of Music in Britain: The Eighteenth Century*, ed. H. Diack Johnstone and Roger Fiske (Oxford, 1990), pp. 96–158, at pp. 137–43.
44 Cited Dean, *Oratorios*, p. 205.
45 Deutsch pp. 288, 308.
46 On Humphreys and his texts for Handel see further chs. 8, 11. The fullest discussion of the music and early performances of *Esther* is Dean, *Oratorios*, ch. 9.
47 The cantata *Venus and Adonis*, probably also set in 1712. On Pepusch's and Galliard's masques see e.g. Platt, 'Theatre Music I', pp. 110–19, and Roger Fiske, 'Galliard, John Ernest', in *The New Grove Dictionary of Music and Musicians*, ed. Stanley Sadie (1980), VII, 107–9. On the relation of *Acis* to its immediate predecessors see Dean, *Oratorios*, pp. 153–9.
48 Patrick J. Smith, *The Tenth Muse: A Historical Study of the Opera Libretto* (1971), pp. 65–7; Brian Trowell, 'Libretto', in *The New Grove Dictionary of Opera*, ed. Stanley Sadie (1992), II, 1185–1252, at p. 1208.
49 Ruspoli also commissioned Handel's first oratorio, *La Resurrezione* – in terms of subject-matter, an antecedent of *Messiah* (for an account of this work see Anthony Hicks, 'Handel's "La Resurrezione"', *MT* 110 (1969), 145–8). For a succinct account of Handel's development as a composer of oratorio see Burrows, *Messiah*, pp. 1–7; for more detail of

the German and Italian antecedents of Handel's English oratorios see e.g. Dean, *Oratorios*, ch. 1; Smither, *Oratorio*, I, 4–15.

50 Dean, *Oratorios*, pp. 173–5, while deploring the outcome, fully appreciates Handel's entrepreneurial motives. See also Ellen T. Harris, *Handel and the Pastoral Tradition* (1980), pp. 212–23.

51 Dean, *Oratorios*, ch. 10, who denies Greene's work the description of oratorio (p. 226); but its libretto is a biblical verse paraphrase organised into recitative, air and chorus passages, and its movement between narrative and dramatisation has precedents in Italian oratorio.

52 In terms of duration, the setting of Dryden's poem comprised little more than half of the work Handel called *Alexander's Feast*, a point also made by Keates, *Handel*, p. 190, though our calculations differ: by my computation, the setting of Dryden (including the overture) comprises only 53 per cent of the total, not two-thirds.

53 For details see Deutsch pp. 423–36.

54 On burlesque operas (e.g. Carey and Lampe's *The Dragon of Wantley* (1737, reputedly enjoyed by Handel) and generally on the varieties of music theatre served up to the English public in the 1730s and 1740s, see Platt, 'Theatre Music I', pp. 132–58.

55 Jennens' probable authorship of *Israel in Egypt* is discussed in ch. 12.

56 The letter, from his amanuensis J. C. Smith to the fourth Earl of Shaftesbury, was published by Betty Matthews, 'Unpublished Letters concerning Handel', *M&L* 40 (1959), 261–8.

57 For fuller discussion of Handel's theatre activities 1738–45 see Carole Taylor, 'Handel's Disengagement from the Italian Opera', in *Handel Tercentenary Collection*, ed. Stanley Sadie and Anthony Hicks (1987), pp. 165–81, persuasively suggesting that they were by turns intended to fill gaps in the market, to eschew competition, or to beat the competition at its own game.

58 See (with the articles cited in it) Robert D. Hume, 'Handel and Opera Management in London in the 1730s', *M&L* 67 (1986), 347–62, which shows how little is known for certain.

59 For Handel's oratorio seasons, see Deutsch.

60 For details of his programmes, see Deutsch, and E. L. Avery, A. H. Scouten and G. Winchester Stone, jnr, eds., *The London Stage 1660–1800* II–IV (Carbondale, IL, 1960–2).

61 The process was gradual. In papers presented at the London Handel Institute Conference, 1993, Howard Serwer and Donald Burrows independently concluded that during the mid-1730s, while his company was a mixture of Italian and English singers, Handel's revivals of English works were probably mostly or always macaronic.

62 *London Stage*.

63 'A Proposal to Prevent the Expensive Importation of *Foreign Musicians*, &c. by forming an Academy of our Own', in *Augusta Triumphans* (1728), repr. in *Selected Poetry and Prose of Daniel Defoe*, ed. M. F. Shugrue (New York, 1968), pp. 315–19. On the differing demands of English and

Italian words and music and singers' capacities see Stoddard Lincoln, 'Handel's Music for Queen Anne', *Musical Quarterly* 45 (1959), 191–207, at pp. 196–202.

64 *Oratorios*, p. 107.

65 Larsen, *Handel's Messiah*, p. 71; Leopold, '"Israel in Egypt" – ein mißglückter Glücksfall', *GHB* 1 (1984), 35–50, at pp. 46–7.

66 E.g. the opening chorus of *Susanna*; see e.g. Dean, *Oratorios*, pp. 536–9.

67 See further ch. 7; on the variety of Handel's oratorio choruses see e.g. Larsen, *Handel's Messiah*, pp. 48–93; Dean, *Oratorios*, pp. 65–7.

68 [Mainwaring,] *Life*.

69 Dean, *Oratorios*, p. 392; see also e.g. pp. 349, 471 and Appendix I. Acceptance of unstaged drama supported by a detailed libretto is suggested by the performance of the masque of *Alfred* 'after the manner of an Oratorio' in 1745; see *Memoirs of Dr Charles Burney 1726–1769*, ed. Slava Klima, Garry Bowers and Kerry S. Grant (Lincoln, NE, 1988), p. 47.

70 On the printing of the librettos see Dean, *Oratorios*, pp. 95–101.

71 Burrows, *Messiah*, ch. 3; Merlin Channon, 'Handel's Early Performances of *Judas Maccabaeus*: Some New Evidence and Interpretations', *M&L* forthcoming.

72 For the Italian and German precursors of English oratorio see further e.g. Dean, *Oratorios*, pp. 7, 11, 12; Smither, *Oratorio*; Denis and Elsie Arnold, *The Oratorio in Venice*, Royal Musical Association Monographs 2 (1986); Carolyn Gianturco, '"Cantate spirituali e morali", with a Description of the Papal Sacred Cantata Tradition for Christmas 1676–1740', *M&L* 73 (1992), 1–31. For drolls see Sybil Rosenfeld, *The Theatre of the London Fairs in the Eighteenth Century* (1960). For mentions in poems to Handel of later oratorio subjects see e.g. Deutsch pp. 139–43, 306–7, 322, 533. See also John Lockman, *Rosalinda: A Musical Drama . . . to which is Prefixed, An Enquiry into the Rise and Progress of Operas and Oratorios. With some Reflections on Lyric Poetry and Music* (1740), xx–xxi.

73 J/H 3 March 1745/6.

74 Dean, *Oratorios*, p. 87.

75 For Mrs Delany as potential Handel librettist see Deutsch pp. 587–8; for Upton, Clive T. Probyn, *The Sociable Humanist: The Life and Works of James Harris 1709–1780* (Oxford, 1991), pp. 72–3.

76 This and the following letters from Handel are printed by Deutsch pp. 590–6.

77 Dean, *Oratorios*, p. 34.

78 See chs. 6 and 14 and my 'The Achievements of Charles Jennens (1700–1773)', *M&L* 70 (1989), 161–90, at pp. 183–6.

79 Deutsch p. 851.

80 Notably in connection with *Semele* and *Susanna*: *Oratorios*, pp. 366–70, 395–7, 547, 549–55.

81 Letter from Jennens to Lord Guernsey, 19 September 1738 (in the

possession of Lord Aylesford, and consulted by kind permission); printed with some minor inaccuracies, Deutsch pp. 465–6.

82 'Handel, Jennens and *Saul*: Aspects of a Collaboration', in *Music and Theatre: Essays in honour of Winton Dean*, ed. Nigel Fortune (Cambridge, 1987), pp. 203–27. See further ch. 13.

83 Hicks records the changes to the other autograph which Jennens annotated, that of *Belshazzar*, as few and insignificant, 'Handel, Jennens and *Saul*', p. 226.

84 John Dryden, preface to *Albion and Albanius* (1685).

85 [Charles Gildon,] *The Laws of Poetry ... Explained and Illustrated* (1721), pp. 83–4, commenting on the Duke of Buckingham's comments on song in his *Essay on Poetry*; but contrast the more positive comments on writing opera librettos by Handel's early collaborator John Hughes, *Calypso and Telemachus: An Opera* (1712), preface, p. vii.

86 For Morell's receipts from *Judas* see Deutsch p. 851. One indication of the librettists' financial situations is the first codicil of Handel's will (Deutsch p. 776). He left bequests to Hamilton and Morell. Humphreys and Miller predeceased him; Jennens was immensely rich.

87 'Handel's Early Performances of *Judas Maccabaeus*'.

88 J/H 21 February 1742/3.

89 *Oratorios*, p. 549.

90 King's College, Cambridge, Modern Archives, Coll.34.11, consulted with the kind assistance of the archivist, Jacky Cox.

91 Hamilton's enthusiasm for Handel's music is further attested in the letters of the Strafford children; see Ruth Loewenthal [= Smith], 'Handel and Newburgh Hamilton: New References in the Strafford Papers', *MT* 112 (1971), 1063–6.

92 J/H 10 July 1741, 2 December 1741.

93 Joseph Warton, *An Essay on the Genius and Writings of Pope* (1756), quoted Deutsch p. 780.

94 'The Achievements of Charles Jennens', pp. 175–89, and see chs. 6 and 14.

95 Transcribed by kind permission from the original in the collection of the late Gerald Coke. The bishop's comments are in the hand of Handel's assistant J.C. Smith. The text is printed in Walter and Margret Eisen eds., *Händel-Handbuch Band 4: Dokumente zu Leben und Schaffen auf der Grundlage von Otto Erich Deutsch, Handel, A Documentary Biography* (Kassel, 1985).

96 William C. Smith, *Concerning Handel* (1948), pp. 34, 146–7; *London Stage 1729–47*, Introduction, p. lxii; Deutsch p. 460. *Common Sense* being an opposition journal, it may be invoking Handel's association with the court in its 'us–them' stance.

97 Pat Rogers, 'Introduction: The Writer and Society', in *The Eighteenth Century*, ed. Rogers (1978), pp. 51–2.

98 *Concerning Handel*, p. 147.

99 *Covent-Garden Journal*, 31 March 1752, of one of the first performances (quoted Deutsch pp. 722–3).

100 Letter to Ann Granville, 28 March 1734, quoted Dean, *Oratorios*, p. 133. For a suggestion that even the most vapid members of the audience took notice of the libretto so long as it was in English, see *Common Sense*, 14 October 1738.

101 Letter dated 8 March, published 15 March 1743, printed Deutsch p. 562.

102 On his compositional procedures in the oratorios see Dean, *Oratorios*, pp. 86–95.

103 For a summary of the nature of and possible motives for these changes see Dean, *Oratorios*, pp. 91–3. ('The astounding thing about most of these changes is that they have no aesthetic motive.')

104 Dean, *Oratorios*, pp. 346–7.

CHAPTER 1

1 *See and Seem Blind; or a Critical Dissertation on the Publick Diversions, &c ... in a Letter from ... Lord B----- [Burlington?] to A--- H--- [Aaron Hill?] esq* (1732), quoted Deutsch pp. 300–1. On the circumstances of *Esther*'s first public performance, see above, p. 14.

2 *The Daring Muse: Augustan Poetry Reconsidered* (Cambridge, 1985), p. 61.

3 2 May 1732 (HMC Egmont MSS, Diary, I, 266, quoted Deutsch p. 290).

4 Letter to her cousin James Harris, 11 February 1748/9, quoted Deutsch p. 657.

5 *The Man of Taste. Occasion'd by an Epistle of Mr Pope's on that Subject* (1733), quoted Deutsch p. 338.

6 Letter to Elizabeth Carter, 13 April 1756, quoted Deutsch p. 773.

7 Notably Dean, *Oratorios*, p. 139.

8 For other complaints on these grounds see Deutsch pp. 317, 339, 493, 563–5, 568.

9 'R. W.' *London Daily Post*, 18 April 1739; 'A Gentleman', *Daily Advertiser*, 31 March 1743, quoted Deutsch pp. 482, 565–6.

10 John Lockman, *Rosalinda: A Musical Drama ... to which is Prefixed, An Enquiry into the Rise and Progress of Operas and Oratorios. With some Reflections on Lyric Poetry and Music* (1740), p. xxi. Charles de Saint Evremond, 'Of Antient and Modern Tragedy', *Works Made English from the French Original* (2/1728), II, 104.

11 Herbert M. Schueller, 'The Use and Decorum of Music as Described in British Literature, 1700 to 1780', *Journal of the History of Ideas* 13 (1952), 73–93, esp. pp. 87–91.

12 *The Dunciad*, IV, 57–60, ed. James Sutherland, *The Poems of Alexander Pope*, V (3/1963), p. 347.

13 Thomas Bisse, *Musick the Delight of the Sons of Men. A Sermon Preached at*

the Cathedral Church of Hereford, at the Anniversary Meeting ... September 7. 1726 (1726), p. 27.

14 Bisse, *Musick the Delight of the Sons of Men*, p. 26; William Sherlock, *A Sermon Preach'd at St Paul's Cathedral, November 22 1699 being the Anniversary Meeting of the Lovers of Musick* (1699), p. 20; Peter Senhouse, *The Right Use and Improvement of Sensitive Pleasures, and more particularly of Musick. A Sermon Preach'd in the Cathedral Church of Gloucester, at the Anniversary Meeting ... September 20, 1727* (1728), p. 24. For the survival of this view into the twentieth century see for example E. H. Fellowes, *English Cathedral Music* (1941), new edn rev. J. A. Westrup (1969), pp. 163–4, 184: 'The charge of theatricality [against late-seventeenth- and early-eighteenth-century church music] is not entirely to be set aside.' Music sermons are discussed in more detail in ch. 3.

15 *The Influence of Church-Music. A Sermon Preached in the Cathedral Church of Worcester, at the Anniversary Meeting ... September 8. 1725* (1725, 3/1753), pp. 11–15.

16 Richard Banner, *The Use and Antiquity of Musick in the Service of God. A Sermon Preach'd in the Cathedral-Church at Worcester, September 14 1737 at the Anniversary Meeting* (Oxford, 1737), pp. 1–2.

17 *The Great Abuse of Musick* (1711), p. 209.

18 See Percy Lovell, '"Ancient" Music in Eighteenth-Century England', *M&L* 60 (1979), 401–15. William Weber has argued that there was a connection within and beyond Church circles between musical and political conservatism during the first half of the century, *The Rise of Musical Classics in Eighteenth-Century England* (Oxford, 1992).

19 Christopher Hogwood, 'Thomas Tudway's History of Music', *Music in Eighteenth Century England: Essays in memory of Charles Cudworth*, ed. Christopher Hogwood and Richard Luckett (Cambridge, 1983), pp. 19–47, esp. pp. 19–20, 24–30, 42–4.

20 *Musical Dictionary*, under 'Style'.

21 H. Watkins Shaw, *Eighteenth Century Cathedral Music*, Church Music Society Occasional Paper 21 (Oxford [1952]), p. 6.

22 William Croft, *Musica Sacra: or, Select Anthems in Score* (1724, 1730), preface, p. 4 (on p. 2 he refers to 'The Solemnity, Gravity, and Excellency of Style, peculiarly proper to *Church-Musick*'). Schueller, 'Use and Decorum of Music', p. 87, shows that this doctrine survived to the end of the century.

23 *An Essay on Musical Expression* (1752), pp. 105–6.

24 [John Mainwaring et al.,] *Memoirs of the Life of the Late George Frederic Handel* (1760).

25 *Essay* (2/1753), p. 94n, cited with further discussion of Avison's detailed categorisation of kinds of musical expression by Roger B. Larsson, 'Charles Avison's "Stiles in Musical Expression"', *M&L* 63 (1982), 261–75.

26 Jens Peter Larsen, *Handel's Messiah: Origins, Composition, Sources* (1957), pp. 16–17; Dean, *Oratorios*, pp. 7–8.

27 Pier Francesco Tosi, *Opinioni de'cantori antichi e moderni, o sieno osservazioni sopra il canto figurato* (Bologna, 1723), trans. J. E. Galliard as *Observations on the Florid Song* (1742, 2/1743); see especially pp. 66–9.

28 On Handel's use of the ceremonial church music style in his oratorios see A. H. Shapiro, '"Drama of an Infinitely Superior Nature": Handel's Early English Oratorios and the Religious Sublime', *M&L* 74 (1993), 215–45.

29 Diary, 31 August 1731, quoted Deutsch p. 277.

30 Pp. 12, 17, 25, 40, 42.

31 *Literary Anecdotes of the Eighteenth Century* (2/1812–15), IX, 789.

32 Ed. Paul Fussell jnr, Augustan Reprint Society 55 (Los Angeles, 1956), pp. 99, 101, 102, 104, 110. Avison and other writers on music also subscribed to the principle of variety; see e.g. *Essay* (1752), pp. 95–6.

33 *Harlequin Horace* (3/1735), ll. 25, 27–8, 43–4, 84–8.

34 *A Critical Dissertation on the Poems of Ossian, Son of Fingal* (1763), pp. 27–8.

35 On which see e.g. Doody, *The Daring Muse*, pp. 28–9, 64–5.

CHAPTER 2

1 Collier, *A Short View of the Immorality and Profaneness of the English Stage* (1698, 5th corr. edn 1730); Law, *The Absolute Unlawfulness of the Stage-Entertainment Fully Demonstrated* (1726).

2 *Common Sense*, 14 October 1738.

3 James R. Jacob and Timothy Raylor, 'Opera and Obedience: Thomas Hobbes and *A Proposition for Advancement of Moralitie* by Sir William Davenant', *The Seventeenth Century* 6 (1991), 205–50 (I owe this reference to Jeremy Maule); Jeremy Gregory, 'Anglicanism and the Arts: Religion, Culture and Politics in the Eighteenth Century', in *Culture, Politics and Society in Britain, 1660–1800*, ed. Jeremy Black and Jeremy Gregory (Manchester, 1991), pp. 82–109, stressing the initiatives of the state (established Anglican) Church in the campaign.

4 'A Discourse on Epick Poetry', *The Collected and Miscellaneous Prose Works of John Dryden*, ed. Edmond Malone (1800), III, 425–6. See also his 'Defence of an Essay of Dramatick Poesy', *Prose Works*, I.ii, 170: 'poesy ... must be ethical'.

5 *The Advancement and Reformation of Modern Poetry* (1701) and *An Essay on the Opera's after the Italian Manner* (1706) in *The Critical Works of John Dennis*, ed. Edward Niles Hooker (Baltimore, 1939), I, 224, 386, 388. Hooker points out that Dennis' arguments were indebted to Milton.

6 On Dennis and the ideas of this circle see Christine Gerrard, 'The Patriot Opposition to Sir Robert Walpole: A Study of Politics and Poetry, 1725–1742', D.Phil. diss., University of Oxford (1986), and James Sambrook, *James Thomson, 1700–1748: A Life* (Oxford, 1991).

7 James Beattie to the Rev. Dr Laing, *The Letters ... from Sir William Forbes's Collection* (1819–21), II, 77–8, quoted Deutsch pp. 854–5.

8 On Hill's contribution to the literary reform movement and his identity

as a Patriot poet see Gerrard, 'Patriot Opposition', and her *The Patriot Opposition to Walpole: Politics, Poetry, and National Myth, 1725–1742* (Oxford, 1994), pp. 48–57; on his ideas for literary reform see also Robert Inglesfield, 'James Thomson, Aaron Hill and the Poetic "Sublime"', *BJECS* 13 (1990), 215–21; Dorothy Brewster, *Aaron Hill* (New York, 1913), prints a bibliography of his works, pp. 279–88. Christine Gerrard is writing a critical biography of Hill.

9 Winton Dean and J. Merrill Knapp, *Handel's Operas 1704–1726* (1987), p. 172. Hill's part in the libretto is detailed by Curtis Price, 'English Traditions in Handel's *Rinaldo*', in *Handel Tercentenary Collection*, ed. Stanley Sadie and Anthony Hicks (1987), pp. 120–37.

10 Prologue to *The Mother in Law or, The Doctor the Disease. A Comedy* (taken from several plays by Molière, London, 1734, and dedicated to the Countess of Hertford, as an exemplar of rectitude); see similarly the prefaces to *The Humours of Oxford. A Comedy* (1730), dedicated to Philip [Stanhope] Earl of Chesterfield, and *Art and Nature. A Comedy* (1738), dedicated to an unnamed lady, with the same intention of purging and improving the stage. On Miller's plays see Paula O'Brien, 'The Life and Works of James Miller', Ph.D. diss., University of London (1979). I am grateful to Tom McGeary for drawing my attention to this work.

11 'Preface to Mr Pope concerning the Sublimity of the Ancient Hebrew Poetry', prefixed to *The Creation. A Pindaric Illustration of a Poem originally Written by Moses on that Subject* (1720), ed. G. G. Pahl, Augustan Reprint Society ser. 4 no. 2 (Ann Arbor, 1949), pp. 5–6.

12 *Advice to the Poets: A Poem, to which is Prefix'd, an Epistle Dedicatory to the Few Great Spirits of Great Britain* (1731), pp. v, 23.

13 *Handel's Operas*, p. 172.

14 *The Grounds of Criticism in Poetry* (1704), on the use of religious themes in poetry, *Works*, ed. Hooker, I, 325. Hooker notes (I, 509) that part of this long essay was reprinted by Hill, *The Prompter* no. 171 (25 June 1736) and thence in the *London Magazine*, 5 (1736), 319–20, titled 'Poetry a Friend to Religion'.

15 Hill, *Advice to the Poets*, pp. viii, xii–xiii.

16 The preface and the conclusion of *Advice to the Poets* is one of the most direct of many contemporary appeals for crown and state sponsorship of high art, on the grounds that it fosters national strength. See Gerrard, 'Patriot Opposition', ch. 1.

17 John Brown, *A Dissertation on the Rise, Union, and Power, the Progressions, Separations, and Corruptions, of Poetry and Music* (1763).

18 [Charles Gildon,] *The Laws of Poetry ... Explained and Illustrated* (1721), p. 149; see also Thomas Rymer, *Monsieur Rapin's Reflections on Aristotle's Treatise of Poesie ... made English by Mr Rymer* (1694), pp. 12, 103–4; André Dacier, *Aristotle's Art of Poetry Translated from the Original Greek according to Mr Theodore Goulston's Edition. Together, with Mr D'Acier's Notes Translated from the French* (1705), pp. 78–80 (the standard com-

mentary on Aristotle); George Adams, *The Tragedies of Sophocles, Translated from the Greek, with Notes Historical, Moral, and Critical ... to which is Prefix'd, a Preface: containing I. A Defence of Tragic Poetry ... II. An Historical Account of its Rise and Progress. III. A Comparison of the Ancient Tragedies with each other* (1729); Pierre Brumoy, trans. Charlotte Lennox, 'Discourse upon the Theatre of the Greeks' in *The Greek Theatre of Father Brumoy* (1759), I.i (frequently referred to as authoritative by translators and commentators of the period).

19 Lewis Theobald, *The Censor*, no. 36 (2/1717), II, 40; [Gildon,] *Laws of Poetry*, p. 162; Collier, *Short View*, pp. 25–30, 87–94; Charles Johnson, prologue to *The Tragedy of Medaea* (1731).

20 Brown, *Dissertation*, p. 39.

21 *Prometheus in Chains, Translated from the Greek of Aeschylus* (1773), introduction.

22 Dennis, *The Usefulness of the Stage, to the Happiness of Mankind, to Government, and to Religion. Occasioned by a Late Book, Written by Jeremy Collier, MA* (1698, 2/1727), *Works*, ed. Hooker, I, 183; see similarly for Thomson, Sambrook, *James Thomson*, pp. 81–2, 150.

23 Charles de Saint Evremond, 'Of Antient and Modern Tragedy', *Works Made English from the French Original* (2/1728), II, 110–11.

24 The comparison has been made most emphatically by Dean, *Oratorios*, pp. 40, 41, 164, 251, 280, 281, 289, 332, 370, 416–19, 515, 539, 596, followed by Paul Henry Lang, *George Frideric Handel* (1967), pp. 371–3, and Howard E. Smither, *A History of the Oratorio*, II, *The Oratorio in the Baroque Era* (Chapel Hill, NC, 1977), pp. 190, 348, 352. See however J. A. Westrup, review of Dean, *Oratorios*, in *M&L* 40 (1959), 366–9, at p. 367. The morality and constructive intervention of the divine powers in Greek tragedy apparent to eighteenth-century readers have escaped most modern commentators but not all; see T. V. Buttrey, 'Tragedy as Form in Euripides', *Michigan Quarterly Review* 15.2 (Spring 1976), 155–72, at pp. 167–72.

25 E.g. *Christianity Distinct from the Religion of Nature* (1732).

26 Jonathan Barry, 'Cultural Patronage and the Anglican Crisis: Bristol *c* 1689–1775', in *The Church of England c. 1689 – c. 1833: From Toleration to Tractarianism*, ed. John Walsh, Colin Haydon and Stephen Taylor (Cambridge, 1993), pp. 191–208, at p. 198.

27 J/H 4–8 February 1741/2.

28 A point made by Donald Davie with reference to what Thomson could expect of his readers, *Purity of Diction in English Verse* (1952, New York, 1967), p. 40.

29 Cf. Dennis, *The Stage Defended* (1726), *Works*, ed. Hooker, II, 308: 'a Dramatick Fable is a Discourse invented to form the Manners by Instructions disguised under the Allegory of an Action'.

30 Dennis, *Works*, ed. Hooker, I, 437.

31 Handel's choruses are compared to those of Greek tragedy by e.g. Percy Young, *The Oratorios of Handel* (1949), p. 69; Dean, *Oratorios*, pp. 40,

284; Lang, *Handel*, pp. 283, 378, 425; Stanley Sadie, *Handel* (1962), pp. 102, 130.

32 Dacier, *Aristotle's Art of Poetry*, p. xx.

33 Jacob and Raylor, 'Opera and Obedience', p. 213; Dryden, 'A Parallel of Poetry and Painting', *Prose Works*, III, 334–6.

34 *Tragedies of Sophocles*, preface.

35 Charles Gildon (attrib.), *A Comparison between the Two Stages*, ed. S.B. Wells (Princeton, 1942), p. 30.

36 E.g. Deutsch pp. 481–2, 611, 616–17, 729. The musical chorus of tragedy is given a churchman's approval for being the voice of virtue by William Taswell MA, vicar of Wotton-under-Edge, *The Propriety and Usefulness of Sacred Music. A Sermon Preach'd in the Cathedral Church of Gloucester, at the Anniversary Meeting ... September 8, 1742* (Gloucester, n.d.), pp. 22–3.

37 On the hymn see ch. 4.

38 Irving Lowens, 'The *Touch-Stone* (1728): A Neglected View of London Opera', *Musical Quarterly* 45 (1959), 325–42, discusses the essay and questions the attribution; see now Lowell Lindgren, 'Another Critic Named Samber whose "Particular Historical Significance Has Gone Almost Entirely Unnoticed"', in *Festa Musicologica: Essays in honor of George Buelow* (forthcoming), who suggests Robert Samber as the author.

39 Thomas McGeary, 'Shaftesbury, Handel, and Italian Opera', *HJb* 32 (1986), 99–104 and (with extended discussion of Shaftesbury's ideas) 'Shaftesbury on Opera, Spectacle and Liberty', *M&L* 74 (1993), 530–41.

40 Deutsch p. 412. The observations about confining action to recitative and restricting arias to soliloquies were also made by Pier Francesco Tosi, *Opinioni de'cantori antichi e moderni, o sieno osservazioni sopra il canto figurato* (Bologna, 1723), trans. J. E. Galliard as *Observations on the Florid Song* (1742, 2/1743), p. 68.

41 *Harlequin Horace: or, The Art of Modern Poetry* (3/1735), ll. 327–30. In fact probably the second edition; see O'Brien, 'James Miller', pp. 25–6, 32, 89, 126–82.

42 E.g. Thomas Rymer, *A Short View of Tragedy* (1692); Dacier, *Aristotle's Art of Poetry*, preface; *Touch-stone*, p. 126.

43 *Esther, or Faith Triumphant: A Sacred Tragedy by Mr. Brereton of Brazen-Nose College, Oxford. With a Dedication to the Lord Archbishop of York* (1715).

44 William Duncombe, *Athaliah, A Tragedy Translated from the French of Monsieur Racine* (1722), preface, Sig A3r–A6r. Isaac Watts sent Duncombe a complimentary note on this translation shortly after it was published, wistfully remarking that 'dramatic poesy might have been useful to many happy purposes, had it always been kept within the bounds prescribed by virtue and religion, as Racine has done' (John Duncombe, ed., *Letters by Several Eminent Persons Deceased* (1773), II,

50–1); cf. Watts in his *Horae Lyricae* (1709, 9/1753), p. xvi, to the same effect. Collier: *Short View*, p. 124.

45 Letter to Aaron Hill, 23 August 1735, *James Thomson (1700–1748)*, *Letters and Documents*, ed. Alan D. McKillop (Lawrence, KS, 1958), p. 98.

46 For their belief in Handel's ability to achieve national reform and unity, see ch. 9.

47 For Dennis, see below. For Addison and Steele in the *Spectator* see e.g. nos. 5 (6 March 1711), 13 (15 March 1711), 14 (16 March 1711), 18 (21 March 1711), 29 (3 April 1711), ed. Donald F. Bond (Oxford, 1965), I, 22–7, 55–65, 78–82, 119–23. Addison was the librettist of the English opera *Rosamond*, unsuccessfully set by Clayton (1707) and better served by Arne after the librettist's death (1730). Steele also criticises Italian opera in his plays; see *The Conscious Lovers* (1723), II.1.

48 Elizabeth Gibson, 'The Royal Academy of Music and its Directors', in *Handel Tercentenary Collection*, ed. Stanley Sadie and Anthony Hicks (1987), pp. 138–64, at p. 149.

49 'Life of Hughes', *Lives of the English Poets*, ed. G. B. Hill (Oxford, 1905), II, 160: 'an exotick and irrational entertainment, which has been always combated and always has prevailed'. Johnson was preceded in describing Italian opera as 'exotic Entertainment' by John Lockman, *Rosalinda: A Musical Drama ... to which is Prefixed, An Enquiry into the Rise and Progress of Operas and Oratorios. With some Reflections on Lyric Poetry and Music* (1740), p. ii.

50 The most comprehensive survey is still K. G. Ruttkay's 'The Critical Reception of Italian Opera in England in the Early Eighteenth Century', *Angol és Amerikai Filológiai Tanulmányok / Studies in English and American Philology*, ed. L. Kéry and N.J. Szenczi, I (Budapest, 1971), 93–169; as it is not readily accessible, I cover some of the same ground here.

51 Richard Luckett, *Handel's Messiah: A Celebration* (1992), p. 38. For Handel's approbation see Deutsch p. 449.

52 *Poems on Several Occasions* (3/1729), pp. 28–37.

53 '"Warbling Eunuchs": Opera, Gender, and Sexuality on the London Stage, 1705–1742', *Restoration and Eighteenth-Century Theatre Research* 2nd ser. VII/1 (Summer, 1992), 1–22.

54 Dedication (to Lord Weymouth) and pp. 61–2. See similarly *The Coffee House* (1737), I.2.

55 *Touch-stone*, p. 21.

56 *Essay on the Opera's* (1706, reprinted in *Select Works*, 1718), *Works*, ed. Hooker, I, 382–93; *An Essay upon the Publick Spirit* (1711), *Works*, II, 394; *Reflections Critical and Satyrical, upon a Late Rhapsody, Call'd, An Essay upon Criticism* (1711), *Works*, I, 396–7; *Remarks upon Cato, a Tragedy* (1713), *Works*, II, 41–80; *The Stage Defended, from Scripture, Reason, Experience, and the Common Sense of Mankind for Two Thousand Years. Occasion'd by Mr. Law's Late Pamphlet against Stage-Entertainments* (1726), *Works*, I, 304.

57 The Pretender settled in Rome in 1719, the year the Royal Academy was founded; Dennis links Nonjurors' attacks on the English stage with Jacobite plotting on the Pretender's behalf, *The Stage Defended, Works*, ed. Hooker, I, 321.

58 Gerald Newman, *The Rise of British Nationalism 1740–1830: A Cultural History* (1987), pp. 37–9, 63, 74, 110–13; Linda Colley, *Britons: Forging the Nation 1707–1837* (New Haven, 1992), pp. 17, 24–5, 33–5, 86, 88–90. Newman's study is deeply flawed by his thesis that (p. 127) 'The English quest for National Identity began around 1750'.

59 On this aspect of Handel's early oratorios see A. H. Shapiro, '"Drama of an Infinitely Superior Nature": Handel's Early English Oratorios and the Religious Sublime', *M&L* 74 (1993), 215–45.

60 Daniel Defoe, 'Proposal to prevent the Expensive Importation of *Foreign Musicians*, &c. by forming an Academy of our own', *Augusta Triumphans* (1728), repr. in *Selected Poetry and Prose of Daniel Defoe*, ed. M. F. Shugrue (New York, 1968), pp. 315–19.

61 'The First Epistle of the First Book of Horace Imitated', *Imitations of Horace*, ed. John Butt, *The Poems of Alexander Pope*, IV (1939), p. 287 (ll. 97–104).

62 *The Stage Defended, Works*, ed. Hooker, II, 302.

63 Miller, *Harlequin Horace*, ll. 337–42, 353–6, 363–6.

64 'The Poet's Resentment', *Poems on Several Occasions*, pp. 75–8.

65 *The Plain Dealer* (2/1734), II, 309–11 (no. 94, 12 February 1724/5).

66 Oratorio's concern with national events (discussed in Part II) is anticipated in e.g. *Dido and Aeneas* (Tate and Purcell), *Albion and Albanius* (Dryden and Grabu), *King Arthur* (Dryden and Purcell), *The British Enchanters* (Granville and Eccles et al.) and *Rosamond* (Addison and Clayton); see Curtis Price, 'Political Allegory in Late-Seventeenth-Century English Opera', in *Music and Theatre: Essays in honour of Winton Dean*, ed. Nigel Fortune (1987), pp. 1–29 (the article also covers the early eighteenth century).

67 Dennis, *Remarks upon Cato, a Tragedy, Works*, ed. Hooker, II, 44.

68 For other examples see Thomas McGeary, 'Opera, Satire, and Politics in the Walpole Era', in *The Past as Prologue: Essays to Celebrate the Twenty-Fifth Anniversary of ASECS*, ed. Carla H. Hay with Syndy M. Conger (New York, 1994), pp. 347–72.

69 O'Brien, 'James Miller', p. 89.

70 James Miller, *The Art of Life, in imitation of Horace's Art of Poetry* (1739), p. 14.

71 *The Dunciad*, IV, 54–6, 63–70, ed. James Sutherland, *The Poems of Alexander Pope*, V (3/1963), pp. 346–8.

72 Cf. Deutsch pp. 472–3; Dean, *Oratorios*, p. 275.

73 For contemporary notice of exceptional numbers of performers and volume of sound in Handel's music see e.g. Deutsch pp. 140–2, 308 (12 March), 309 (27 March), 322, 424 (18 January), 640 (18 April), 715, 729, 758, 761; *Common Sense*, 14 October 1738.

74 *Common Sense*, 14 October 1738, an application of commonplace theories
   of affective music: see Dean Tolle Mace, 'The Doctrine of Sound and
   Sense in Augustan Poetic Theory', *Review of English Studies* new ser. 2
   (1951), 129–39.

75 *The Tears of the Muses: in a Conference between Prince Germanicus and a Male-
   content Party* (1737), repr. in *Works* (2/1754), IV, 163–88, at pp. 175–6.

76 In *Six Cantata's or Poems for Musick. After the Manner of the Italians* (1710),
   repr. in *Poems on Several Occasions* (1735), II, 64–5. In the preface
   Hughes tackles the question of whether English is (by comparison with
   Italian) mellifluous enough for satisfactory musical setting, to which he
   returned two years later in the preface to his *Calypso and Telemachus: An
   Opera* (1712), pp. v–vii. Handel's letter to Andreas Roner, a mutual
   friend, responds to one from Hughes which would seem to have been
   suggesting a collaboration: 'I shall take the liberty of writing to him at
   the earliest opportunity. If however he wishes to honour me with his
   commands and add thereto one of his charming poems in English, that
   will afford me the greatest possible pleasure' (Deutsch pp. 44–5).

77 *Works* (2/1754), I, 174–5, repr. Deutsch p. 299, and many others.

78 Deutsch p. 32.

79 See e.g. Deutsch pp. 159, 169, 231, 322, 349–50, 389, 396, 458, 469,
   476, 547, 618, 634–5, 640, 677 (Fielding), 695, 715, 733–4, 736, 761,
   842; Miller, *The Art of Life*, pp. 14–16; Bishop Synge's notes on *Messiah*
   (see Introduction); [John Mainwaring et al.,] *Memoirs of the Life of the
   Late George Frederic Handel* (1760), pp. 162–3, 167, 174–6, 201, 204.

80 Faulkner's *Dublin Journal*, 15 March 1743, quoted above, Introduction;
   [William Hayes,] *Remarks on Mr Avison's Essay on Musical Expression*
   (1753), p. 130. This is the first of the 'various Excellencies, which still
   remain unmentioned in *Handel* ... wherein he excels *all others* of his
   Profession' with which Hayes concludes his *Remarks*.

81 *Daily Advertiser*, 17 January 1745, repr. Deutsch p. 602. On the audience's appreciation of Handel's English settings see further above,
   Introduction.

CHAPTER 3

1 Aaron Hill, *The Tears of the Muses: A Poem* (1737), repr. *Works* (2/1754),
  IV, 163–88, at pp. 175–6.

2 A point also made in Hill's magazine *The Plain Dealer* (2/1734), II,
  309–16 (no. 94, 12 February 1724/5).

3 Alexander Malcolm, *A Treatise of Musick* (Edinburgh, 1721, London,
  1730), pp. 1, 480, 598; Hildebrand Jacob, 'Of the Sister Arts', *Works*
  (1735), pp. 383, 385; Charles Avison, *An Essay on Musical Expression*
  (1752), pp. 5–6.

4 *An Essay on the Opera's after the Italian Manner* (1706) in *The Critical Works
  of John Dennis*, ed. Edward Niles Hooker (Baltimore, 1939), I, 385, 389;
  see also *The Stage Defended*, in *Works*, II, 301.

5 Winton Dean and J. Merrill Knapp, *Handel's Operas 1704–1726* (1987), p. 147; cf. Herbert M. Schueller, 'The Use and Decorum of Music as Described in British Literature, 1700 to 1780', *Journal of the History of Ideas* 13 (1952), 73–93, at p. 84: 'Three factors were ever-present in eighteenth century theories about the effects and use of secular music ... First, there was the idea that art can, that indeed it must, instruct and improve human beings.'

6 See e.g. John Playford's preface to his *A Brief Introduction to the Skill of Musick*, which reached its eighteenth edition in 1724 and was still being quoted as an authority in 1726 (by Thomas Bisse, *Musick the Delight of the Sons of Men. A Sermon Preached at the Cathedral Church of Hereford, at the Anniversary Meeting ... September 7. 1726* (1726)); John Blow's preface to his *Amphion Anglicus* (1700); *Common Sense*, 14 October 1738; and the sources cited in n. 3 above.

7 See my 'The Argument and Contexts of Dryden's *Alexander's Feast*', *SEL: Studies in English Literature* 18 (1978), 465–90; *The Plain Dealer*, II, 310–11 (no. 94, 12 February 1724/5).

8 See Thomas R. Preston, 'Biblical Criticism, Literature, and the Eighteenth-Century Reader', in *Books and their Readers in Eighteenth-Century England*, ed. I. Rivers (Leicester, 1982), pp. 97–126.

9 See Bibliography, 'Sermons and tracts related to them'.

10 Although Percy Scholes, *The Puritans and Music* (1954), does all he can to exonerate the Puritans from the charge of enmity to music, he is obliged to report their destruction and removal of church organs (pp. 231–45). See also the eyewitness accounts of John Evelyn, *Diary*, ed. E. S. de Beer (Oxford, 1955), II, 109, 262, 265.

11 Jeremy Collier, 'Of Musick', *Essays upon Several Moral Subjects* (2/1697), II, 19, 25.

12 Charge II, in *Works*, V, 343–4, quoted Norman Sykes, *Church and State in England in the XVIIIth Century* (Cambridge, 1934), p. 16.

13 William Croft, *Musica Sacra: or, Select Anthems in Score* (1724, 1730), preface, p. 4.

14 George Lavington, *The Influence of Church-Music. A Sermon Preached in the Cathedral Church of Worcester, at the Anniversary Meeting ... September 8. 1725* (1725, 3/1753), p. 18.

15 William Dingley, *Cathedral Service Decent and Useful. A Sermon Preach'd before the University of Oxford at St Mary's on Cecilia's Day, 1713* (Oxford, 1713), p. 14.

16 5th corr. edn (1730), p. 279.

17 The previous Licensing Act had lapsed in 1695. On the Licensing Act of 1737 see John Loftis, *The Politics of Drama in Augustan England* (Oxford, 1963), pp. 128–30; L. W. Conolly, *The Censorship of English Drama 1737–1824* (San Marino, CA, 1976).

18 Royal injunction of 1559, quoted Nicholas Temperley, *The Music of the English Parish Church* (Cambridge, 1979), I, 39.

19 Charles Hickman, *A Sermon Preached at St Bride's Church on St Cecilia's Day*

November 22nd 1695 (1696), pp. 14–16. On the continuing controversy as to the rightness of organs in churches see e.g. Christopher Dearnley, *English Church Music 1650–1750* (1970), pp. 168–75; in connection with Handel's *Alexander's Feast*, my 'Argument and Contexts'.

20 See ch. 7; A. H. Shapiro, '"Drama of an Infinitely Superior Nature": Handel's Early English Oratorios and the Religious Sublime', *M&L* 74 (1993), 215–45, at pp. 224–7; Deutsch pp. 139–43, 159, 279, 306–7, 322, 476, 481–3, 577, 609, 657–8, 678, 695, 758, 761, 773, 822, 823, 832.

21 James Brooke, *The Duty and Advantage of Singing to the Lord. A Sermon Preach'd in the Cathedral Church of Worcester, at the Anniversary Meeting … Sept. 4. 1728* (n.d.), p. 16; see also Richard Banner, *The Use and Antiquity of Musick in the Service of God. A Sermon Preach'd in the Cathedral-Church at Worcester, September 14 1737 at the Anniversary Meeting* (Oxford, 1737), pp. 13–14.

22 *The Melody of the Heart. A Sermon Preach'd at the Opening of an Organ in St Nicholas's Church, in Great Yarmouth, December the 20th 1733* (1734), pp. 24, 31.

23 *The Great Abuse of Musick* (1711), pp. 209–11; see also pp. 182–4, and compare Collier, *Essays*, II, 25, and Macro, *Melody of the Heart*, p. 31. For other and similar appraisals of contemporary church music, see especially Evelyn, *Diary*, III, 347, and *Roger North on Music*, ed. J. Wilson (1959), pp. 125, 167–70. The objection to Italianate, 'airy' and theatrical organ voluntaries is also noted by Temperley, *Music of the English Parish Church*, I, 102–3, 136–7; Dearnley, *English Church Music*, p. 127.

24 Alexander Pope, *An Essay on Criticism*, ll. 342–3, *Pastoral Poetry and An Essay on Criticism*, ed. E. Audra and Aubrey Williams, *The Poems of Alexander Pope*, I (1961), p. 277; and see similarly his *Epistle to Burlington*, ll. 141–4.

25 Avison, *Essay* (1752), pp. 74–5, endorsed [William Hayes,] *Remarks on Mr Avison's Essay on Musical Expression* (1753), pp. 75–6.

26 *Oratorios*, p. 109.

27 Deutsch pp. 139–43. For other contemporary comments on Handel's organ playing see Deutsch pp. 323, 351, 383–4, 388, 390, 440, 485, 501, 708, 709, 734, 754, 758, 822.

28 Thomas Bisse, *A Rationale on Cathedral Worship or Choir-Service: A Sermon Preach'd in the Cathedral Church at Hereford, at the Anniversary Meeting … Sept. 7. 1720* (1720). See also my 'Argument and Contexts', and Shapiro, 'Drama', pp. 227–32.

29 *A Defence of Church Musick. A Sermon Preached in the Cathedral-Church of Hereford at the Meeting of the Three Choirs, September 6, 1738* (Oxford, 1738), pp. 7–8, 16–20.

30 Shapiro, 'Drama', pp. 227–32, citing James Peirce, *A Vindication of the Dissenters* (1717), III, 100; Bisse, *Rationale*.

31 On the Nonjurors' views on worship see J.H. Overton, *The Nonjurors* (1902); Henry Broxap, *The Later Non-Jurors* (Cambridge, 1924);

Gordon Rupp, *Religion in England 1688–1791* (Oxford, 1986), pp. 17–21; Richard Sharp, 'New Perspectives in the High Church Tradition: Historical Background 1730–1780', in *Tradition Renewed: The Oxford Movement Conference Papers*, ed. Geoffrey Rowell (1986), pp. 4–23.

32 Charles Leslie, *A Short and Easy Method with the Jews* (8/1737).

33 *Temple Musick*, pp. 29–34, 64–5, 93–210, 221, 229–36; on anticipations of Lowth see further ch. 4.

34 Bedford and *The Great Abuse* are discussed by William Weber, *The Rise of Musical Classics in Eighteenth-Century England* (Oxford, 1992), pp. 47–56. On the Reformation Church's advocacy of psalm singing see Patrick Collinson, *The Birthpangs of Protestant England: Religious and Cultural Change in the Sixteenth and Seventeenth Centuries* (1988, repr. 1991), p. 96.

35 'Drama', p. 230.

36 Blow, *Amphion Anglicus*, preface.

37 *Temple Musick*, pp. 52, 54, 61, 91–2, 220.

38 Notably by Jens Peter Larsen, *Handel's Messiah: Origins, Composition, Sources* (1957), pp. 25–9, 48–94.

39 For the anthems in the 'dramatic' oratorios see Dean, *Oratorios*, App. E, pp. 641–8. William Herrmann points out in his Schirmer edition of the Funeral Anthem (New York, 1976, p. ix) that a cancelled page of the autograph score of *Saul* directs the copyist to use the Sinfonie and nos. 1, 2, 3, 5 and 8 for the Elegy and new recitatives.

40 E.g. Chandos V and a Coronation Anthem in the 1756 revival of *Athalia* (Dean, *Oratorios*, p. 262).

41 Deutsch p. 573, from *Autobiography and Correspondence of Mary Granville, Mrs Delany* (1861–2), II, 222.

42 On the music of the anthems see Nicholas Temperley, 'Music in Church', in *The Blackwell History of Music in Britain: The Eighteenth Century*, ed. H. Diack Johnstone and Roger Fiske (Oxford, 1990), pp. 357–96, at pp. 358–74; for a description of Handel's church music see Basil Lam, 'The Church Music', in *Handel: A Symposium*, ed. Gerald Abraham (1954), pp. 156–78.

43 Compiled by Chapel Royal sub-deans Edward Aspinall, George Carleton and Anselm Bayley, respectively; respectively 136, 182, 214 pp. in extent.

44 They have been little studied. See however Graydon Beeks, 'The *Chandos Anthems* of Haym, Handel and Pepusch', *GHB* 5 (1993), 161–93, esp. p. 175. Pre-Restoration anthem texts are analysed by John Morehen, 'The English Anthem Text, 1549–1660', *Journal of the Royal Musical Association* 117 (1992), 62–85. While Alfred Mann was right, following Larsen, to point to similarities of text selection linking Handel's anthems and his oratorios ('*Messiah*: The Verbal Text', in *Festskrift Jens Peter Larsen*, ed. Nils Schiørring, Henrik Glahn and Carsten E. Hatting (Copenhagen, 1972), pp. 181–8), he and Howard Cox, 'The Text Selection Process in Handel's Chandos Anthems', *Bach*

24/2 (Spring–Summer 1993), 21–34, are wrong to imply that the structural principles of his anthem texts were novel.

45 The sources are identified by Herrmann in the Schirmer edition, pp. v–vi, from the *Gentleman's Magazine* 7 (1737), 763–4, and the *Old Whig*, 22 December 1737.

CHAPTER 4

1 The use of the Bible as the basis of epic composition is discussed in ch. 5. Some of the ground surveyed here has also been covered by David Norton's survey of responses to the King James Bible in the first half of the eighteenth century in *A History of the Bible as Literature* (Cambridge, 1993), II, 4–73, by Howard D. Weinbrot, *Britannia's Issue: The Rise of British Literature from Dryden to Ossian* (Cambridge, 1993), ch. 11, and by Alun David, 'Christopher Smart and the Hebrew Bible: Poetry and Biblical Criticism in England (1682–1771)', Ph.D. diss., University of Cambridge (1994).

2 'Longinus', *On the Sublime*, ed. D. A. Russell (Oxford, 1964), pp. xliv–xlv.

3 *Dionysius Longinus on the Sublime: Translated from the Greek, with Notes and Observations*, ed. and trans. William Smith (1739, 2/1743), pp. 3, 14, 16, 18, 22, 78–81, 86, 87. On eighteenth-century assimilation of Longinus see David, 'Christopher Smart', pp. 18–40.

4 A. H. Shapiro, ' "Drama of an Infinitely Superior Nature": Handel's Early English Oratorios and the Religious Sublime', *M&L* 74 (1993), 215–45; [John Mainwaring et al.,] *Memoirs of the Life of the Late George Frederic Handel* (1760), pp. 162–4, 167, 174–6, 190–1, 201–4; Peter Kivy, 'Mainwaring's *Handel*: Its Relation to English Aesthetics', *Journal of the American Musicological Society* 17 (1964), 170–8.

5 Samuel H. Monk, *The Sublime: A Study of Critical Theories in Eighteenth-Century England* (New York, 1935, repr. Ann Arbor, 1960); David B. Morris, *The Religious Sublime: Christian Poetry and Critical Tradition in Eighteenth-Century England* (Lexington, KY, 1972). Much of the material in this chapter derives from Morris' excellent study, and more remains to be extrapolated from it to illuminate the oratorios.

6 *The Daring Muse: Augustan Poetry Reconsidered* (Cambridge, 1985), p. 267.

7 In Smith's *Longinus*: David's lament for Saul and Jonathan (*Saul*); the Song of Deborah (*Deborah*); the end of Psalm XXIV, Matthew XI.28–30, Revelation XIX.11–17 (*Messiah*) and Job XXIX (*Israel in Egypt*). See also the Three Choirs sermons, e.g. William Taswell, *The Propriety and Usefulness of Sacred Music. A Sermon Preach'd in the Cathedral Church of Gloucester, at the Anniversary Meeting ... September 8, 1742* (Gloucester, n.d.), pp. 11, 13 (Songs of Moses and Miriam and of Deborah and Barak); Joseph Trapp, *Lectures on Poetry*, trans. W. Bowyer and W. Clarke (1742, first pubd in Latin, Oxford, 1711–19), pp. 97,

205; [Charles Gildon,] *The Laws of Poetry ... Explained and Illustrated* (1721), p. 115 (the 'Odes' of Moses, Deborah and David).

8 *The Sacred Books of the Old and New Testament, Recited at Large* (1735), I, 3 (on Genesis.I.3).

9 *The Advancement and Reformation of Modern Poetry* (2/1709, repr. in *Miscellaneous Tracts*, 1727), in *The Critical Works of John Dennis*, ed. E.N. Hooker (Baltimore, 1939), I, 197–278; *The Grounds of Criticism in Poetry*, partly repr. in *Selected Works* (2/1718), by Aaron Hill in *The Prompter* no. 171, 25 June 1736, and thence in the *London Magazine* for the same month under the title 'Poetry a Friend to Religion'. Hooker ed., *Works*, I, 508–9, my source for these details, lists six sources among Dennis' contemporaries expressing the same views.

10 See above, p. 34.

11 Messrs G. Trollope (London), *Gopsall, Leicestershire, Catalogue of ... the Extensive Library*, 14 October 1918 (copy in Victoria and Albert Museum Library).

12 Lewis Theobald, *The Censor*, no. 84 (1717), III, 156; see similarly e.g. Taswell, *Sacred Music*, p. 13.

13 *Poems on Several Occasions* (1735), I, 92–3.

14 E.g. Dennis, *The Advancement and Reformation of Modern Poetry*, *Works*, ed. Hooker, I, 251, 261–71; Alexander Pope, 'Advertisement' to his *Messiah* (first published in *Spectator* no. 378, 14 May 1712): 'the reader by comparing the several thoughts might see how far the images and descriptions of the Prophet are superior to those of the [pagan] poet', *Pastoral Poetry and An Essay on Criticism*, ed. E. Audra and Aubrey Williams, *The Poems of Alexander Pope*, I (1961), p. 111; *Spectator* nos. 453 (9 August 1712), 663 (15 December 1714), ed. Donald F. Bond (Oxford, 1965), IV, 94–5, V, 163–7; Sir Richard Blackmore, *A Paraphrase on the Book of Job: As Likewise on the Songs of Moses, Deborah, David, on Six Select Psalms and some Chapters of Isaiah, and the Third Chapter of Habakkuk* (2/1716), p. lxxxi; Anthony Blackwall, *A New Introduction to the Classics* (1718), p. 102; Thomas Stackhouse, *A Complete Body of Speculative and Practical Divinity* (1729, 2/1734), p. 60.

15 Morris, *Religious Sublime*, p. 92.

16 *Poems on Divine Subjects, Original, and Translated from the Latin of Marcus Hieronymus Vida, Bishop of Alba (and M. A. Flaminius)* (1732, 2/1736), pp. i–vi, forty-one couplets, with footnotes specifying the works referred to.

17 *Poems on Divine Subjects*, pp. 53, 65.

18 *The Seasons and The Castle of Indolence*, ed. James Sambrook (Oxford, 1972, rev. 1987), p. xiii.

19 'Preface to Mr Pope concerning the Sublimity of the Ancient Hebrew Poetry', prefixed to *The Creation. A Pindaric Illustration of a Poem originally Written by Moses on that Subject* (1720), ed. G. G. Pahl, Augustan Reprint Society ser. 4 no. 2 (Ann Arbor, 1949), p. 4.

20 For *opposition* to biblical verse in the first half of the century (some by

critics who themselves wrote biblical verse, such as Pope), see David, 'Christopher Smart', pp. 41–54.

21 Trapp, *Lectures on Poetry*, p. 190.

22 For evidence of 'an almost astonishing interest in religious works generally and biblical criticism specifically' see Thomas R. Preston, 'Biblical Criticism, Literature, and the Eighteenth-Century Reader', in *Books and their Readers in Eighteenth-Century England*, ed. I. Rivers (Leicester, 1982), pp. 97–126.

23 'An Ode, on the Occasion of Mr Handel's Great Te Deum, at the Feast of the Sons of the Clergy', quoted Deutsch pp. 306–7.

24 'Of the Sister Arts', *Works* (1735), p. 401.

25 On hymns and other sacred songs in this period see further Shapiro, 'Drama', pp. 217–18, 232–3, pointing out the close connection with Old Testament texts; Donald Davie, *The Eighteenth-Century Hymn in England* (Cambridge, 1993); Madeleine Forsell Marshall and Janet Todd, *English Congregational Hymns in the Eighteenth Century* (Lexington, KY, 1982). According to Morris, *Religious Sublime*, p. 79, over 7000 hymns were written during the eighteenth century.

26 *The Daring Muse*, p. 75.

27 On Protestant biblical drama before 1605 see Patrick Collinson, *The Birthpangs of Protestant England: Religious and Cultural Change in the Sixteenth and Seventeenth Centuries* (1988, repr. 1991), pp. 98–113, and (not always reliable, but stimulating to the oratorio student) Murray Roston, *Biblical Drama in England from the Middle Ages to the Present Day* (1968), chs. 2 and 3.

28 'Of Antient and Modern Tragedy', *Works Made English from the French Original* (2/1728), II, 104.

29 *Horae Lyricae* (1709, 9/1753), p. xvii.

30 *The Touch-stone* (1728), pp. 50–1. On this work's relevance to oratorio see ch. 2.

31 *Some Considerations touching the Style of the Holy Scriptures* (1661), Epistle Dedicatory to his brother, the Earl of Orrery.

32 Boyle's tragedy on the subject of Saul was Jennens' chief extra-biblical source for his libretto; see my 'The Achievements of Charles Jennens (1700–1773)', *M&L* 70 (1989), 161–90, at p. 187. On Cowley's work, and its themes of monarchical absolutism and divine right (close to Jennens' heart), see Doody, *The Daring Muse*, pp. 62–3. The characters and events of Morell's *Theodora* (1750) closely follow those of Boyle's *The Martyrdom of Theodora and of Didymus* (1687, repr. *Works* (1744), IV, 425–63).

33 *The Touch-stone*, p. 55.

34 *Characteristicks of Men, Manners, Opinions, Times* (6/1738), I, 356–8.

35 'Preface containing Some Remarks on the Beauties of the Holy Scriptures', *A Miscellany of Poems by Several Hands*, ed. John Husbands (Oxford, 1731).

36 *The Method of Teaching and Studying the Belles Lettres* (1734, 4/Dublin, 1742) II, 377.
37 Note to Odyssey XVI, cited Norton, *History of the Bible*, II, 30.
38 *Literary Works*, ed. H. Bunker Wright and Monroe K. Spears (Oxford, 2/1971), I, 306.
39 *Method of Teaching*, II, 392–409, derived from Rollin's teacher Marc-Antoine Hersan (as he notes, II, 385).
40 *Sacred Music*, pp. 11, 13.
41 *The Sacred Books of the Old and New Testament, Recited at Large* (1735), on Judges V.1–2.
42 Boyle, *Some Considerations*, pp. 242–3; Joseph Spence, *An Essay on Pope's Odyssey* (1726), II, 57–8, echoed verbatim by Husbands, *Miscellany of Poems*, preface, sig. b2r,v; Rollin, *Method of Teaching*, II, 349–55.
43 *Method of Teaching*, II, 349, 358–9.
44 Robert Manson Myers, *Handel's Messiah: A Touchstone of Taste* (New York, 1948), p. 58.
45 On Lowth see Norton, *History of the Bible*, II, 59–73; David, 'Christopher Smart', ch. 2.
46 Husbands, *Miscellany of Poems*, preface.
47 See above, p. 80
48 All but the last are commended variously by Sir Richard Blackmore, 'An Essay on the Nature and Constitution of Epick Poetry', *Essays upon Several Subjects* (1716), pp. 150–2; Abbot Claude Fleury, 'A Discourse concerning Poetry in General and concerning that of the Hebrews in Particular', in Dom Augustin Calmet, trans. Nicholas Tindal, *Antiquities Sacred and Prophane: or, A Collection of Curious and Critical Dissertations on the Old and New Testament* (1724, 2/1725), pp. 5–12; Husbands, *Miscellany of Poems*, preface; Rollin, *Method of Teaching*, II, 365–409. For the last see e.g. Thomas Sherlock, *The Use and Intent of Prophecy in the Several Ages of the World* (2/1726), p. 34; Stackhouse, *Complete Body*, p. 64 ('some Passages are obscure, in order to raise in Men a more sacred Awe and Veneration'); and Hugh Blair, *A Critical Dissertation on the Poems of Ossian, Son of Fingal* (1763), p. 18, where the figurative language of Ossian is compared to that of the Old Testament.
49 *Sacred Books*, on Judges V.2.
50 E.g. Fleury in Calmet trans. Tindal, *Antiquities*, pp. 4–5; Sherlock, *Use and Intent of Prophecy*, p. 34; Boyle, *Some Considerations*, pp. 242–3.
51 *Horae Lyricae*, p. viii.
52 In Calmet trans. Tindal, *Antiquities*, p. 12
53 *Spectator* no. 160, ed. Bond, II, 127.
54 William Hayes, *The Art of Composing Music by a Method Entirely New* (1751), pp. 8–10; Charles Avison, *A Reply to the Author of Remarks on the Essay on Musical Expression* (1753), p. 51; [Mainwaring,] *Life*, pp. 162–4.
55 Calmet trans. Tindal, 'A Dissertation concerning the Poetry of the Ancient Hebrews', *Antiquities*, p. 36.

56 By Marc-Antoine Hersan, in Rollin's *Method of Teaching*, II, 392–409.
57 See below, n. 65.
58 Monk points out, *The Sublime*, pp. 26, 93, that biblical paraphrase was encouraged by the fact that the language of the King James Bible was now beginning to seem remote from normal diction.
59 *Works*, ed. Hooker, I, 269.
60 *Works*, ed. Hooker, I, 370–2.
61 *Gentleman's Magazine* 6 (1736), 419–20, 610, 644–6. For examples of versifying (as distinct from paraphrasing) see e.g. Thomas Rowe, '*David*'s Lamentation over *Saul* and *Jonathan*', in *Original Poems and Translations by Mr Thomas Rowe* (1738), in *The Miscellaneous Works in Prose and Verse of Mrs Elizabeth Rowe* (1739), II, 272–6; Aaron Hill, 'Song of Thanksgiving, by Moses, on the Overthrow of Pharaoh, in the Red Sea', and 'Elegy by David: for the Death of Saul and Jonathan', in his *Gideon: or, The Patriot. An Epic Poem* (1749), pp. 445–7, 48–9.
62 These are only some of his total output of biblical paraphrase and versification, repr. in *Works* (2/1754), III, IV.
63 Repr. in *Works*, III, 24–6. According to Dorothy Brewster, *Aaron Hill* (New York, 1913), p. 164, Hill's literary friendship with Dennis may have been based on shared enthusiasm for scriptural paraphrase: Hill versified nearly all Dennis' favourite passages in the Old Testament.
64 Paraphrase repr. in *Works*, IV, 189–201; preface here cited from Augustan Reprint Society ser. 4 no. 2, ed. G. G. Pahl (Ann Arbor, 1949), pp. 4, 6–8, 12–14. On Hill and the religious sublime see also Robert Inglesfield, 'James Thomson, Aaron Hill and the Poetic "Sublime"', *BJECS* 13 (1990), 215–21.
65 As a general principle, John Lockman, *Rosalinda: A Musical Drama . . . to which is Prefix'd, an Enquiry into the Rise and Progress of Operas and Oratorios. With some Reflections on Lyric Poetry and Music* (1740), p. xvii; with reference to Handel, Charles Avison, *An Essay on Musical Expression* (2/1753), p. 74 (the sun standing still in *Joshua*, quoted Deutsch p. 730); [Mainwaring,] *Life*, pp. 184–7.
66 Henry Felton, *A Dissertation upon Reading the Classics and Forming a Just Style* (1713, 5/1753), pp. 93–5; [Gildon,] *Laws of Poetry*, p. 120.
67 *London Daily Post*, 13 April 1739, 18 April 1739, quoted Deutsch pp. 480, 482.
68 *The Dublin Journal*, 20 April 1742, quoted Deutsch p. 547. For other similar testimonies to the divine inspiration of Handel's music and the religious ecstasy induced by it see e.g. Deutsch pp. 139–43, 206, 251, 306, 322, 340, 388, 389, 543, 546, 565–6, 577, 589–90, 609, 657, 658, 678, 695, 729.

CHAPTER 5

1 'A Discourse on Epick Poetry', *The Collected and Miscellaneous Prose Works of John Dryden*, ed. Edmond Malone (1800), III, 425–6; Joseph

Trapp, *Lectures on Poetry*, trans. W. Bowyer and W. Clarke (1742, first pubd in Latin, Oxford, 1711–19), p. 10.

2 Sir Richard Blackmore, preface to *Prince Arthur, an Heroick Poem* (1695), 'An Essay on the Nature and Constitution of Epick Poetry', *Essays upon Several Subjects* (1716), preface to *Creation, a Philosophical Poem* (1722), and preface to *Alfred, an Epick Poem* (1723); Joseph Trapp, *The Aeneis of Virgil Translated into English Blank Verse* (1718); Thomas Blackwell, *An Enquiry into the Life and Writings of Homer* (2/1736); John Baillie, *An Essay on the Sublime* (1747); Hugh Blair, *A Critical Dissertation on the Poems of Ossian, Son of Fingal* (1763).

3 *Lectures on Poetry*, p. 377.

4 Preface to *Alfred*, pp. i, ii, x.

5 *A Dissertation on the Principles of Human Eloquence* (1764), quoted David B. Morris, *The Religious Sublime: Christian Poetry and Critical Tradition in Eighteenth-Century England* (Lexington, KY, 1972), p. 118.

6 'Essay on Epick Poetry', *Essays*, I, 66–7.

7 Preface to *Alfred*, pp. xix–xx.

8 Preface to *Alfred*, p. xiii.

9 *Spectator* nos. 297 (9 February 1712) and 369 (3 May 1712), ed. Donald F. Bond (Oxford, 1965), III, 59, 388.

10 Baillie, *Essay*, pp. 19–20.

11 'Of Heroic Virtue', in *Five Essays*, ed S. H. Monk (Ann Arbor, 1962) pp. 98–172, at 98–100.

12 'Heroic Virtue', p. 172.

13 *Enquiry*, p. 59.

14 'Essay on Epick Poetry', *Essays*, I, 49–52; see also his preface to *Alfred*, pp. xxxii–xxxiii, and preface to *A Paraphrase on the Book of Job: As Likewise on the Songs of Moses, Deborah, David, on Six Select Psalms and some Chapters of Isaiah, and the Third Chapter of Habbakuk* (2/1716), p. xxxiii.

15 Preface to *Alfred*, pp. xxxi–xxxiv.

16 *Works* (2/1754), IV, 243–62.

17 *Critical Dissertation*, pp. 27–8.

18 Preface to *Alfred*, p. xxxi.

19 *The Aeneis*, p. xxi.

20 On the obligation to write a British epic and the perceived difficulty or impossibility of doing so see variously Dustin Griffin, 'Milton and the Decline of Epic in the Eighteenth Century', *New Literary History* 14 (1982), 143–54; Margaret Anne Doody, *The Daring Muse: Augustan Poetry Reconsidered* (Cambridge, 1985), pp. 62–7; Christine Gerrard, 'The Patriot Opposition to Sir Robert Walpole: A Study of Politics and Poetry, 1725–1742', D.Phil. diss., University of Oxford (1986), pp. vi, x, 93–5, 117–25.

21 'A Discourse on the Original and Progress of Satire', *Prose Works*, III, 100–7; guardian angels do protect the British hero's national interests in Addison's opera *Rosamond* (1707), III.1.

22 *Peri Bathous*, 'The Art of Sinking in Modern Poetry', chapter XV

(*Selected Prose of Alexander Pope*, ed. Paul Hammond (Cambridge, 1987), pp. 206–8).

23 *Selected Prose*, ed. Hammond, App. A, pp. 290–6. On *Brutus* see also George Lyttelton, *An Epistle to Mr Pope, from a Young Gentleman at Rome, 1730*; *The Correspondence of Alexander Pope*, ed. G. Sherburn (Oxford, 1956), IV, 348–9 (13 June 1741); Donald T. Torchiana, 'Brutus: Pope's Last Hero', *Journal of English and Germanic Philology* 61 (1962), 853–67; Miriam Leranbaum, *Alexander Pope's 'Opus Magnum' 1729–1744* (Oxford, 1977), ch. VII; Valerie Rumbold, 'Pope and the Gothic Past', Ph.D. diss., University of Cambridge (1984), pp. 216–51; Gerrard, 'Patriot Opposition', pp. 117–25, and *The Patriot Opposition to Walpole: Politics, Poetry, and National Myth, 1725–1742* (Oxford, 1994), pp. 93–5.

24 Letter to Dodington, *James Thomson (1700–1748): Letters and Documents*, ed. Alan D. McKillop (Lawrence, KS, 1958), p. 74.

25 Dorothy Brewster, *Aaron Hill* (New York, 1913), p. 166. He published Books I–II and extracts from five more in 1720, and Books I–III (with copious notes to Book I) in 1749: D. F. Foxon, *English Verse 1701–1750: A Catalogue of Separately Printed Poems* (Cambridge, 1975), I, 346.

26 *The Prompter*, 18 July 1735.

27 *Advice to the Poets: A Poem, to which is Prefix'd, an Epistle Dedicatory to the Few Great Spirits of Great Britain* (1731), pp. vi–xi.

28 Doody, *The Daring Muse*, p. 66; Gerrard, 'Patriot Opposition', p. 93.

29 John Galliard, *The Hymn of Adam and Eve* (a cantata, 1728), and John Christopher Smith, *Paradise Lost* (an oratorio, libretto Benjamin Stillingfleet, 1757–8). For encouragement to Handel to treat this theme see above, p. 25, Deutsch p. 615, and John Lockman, *Rosalinda: A Musical Drama . . . to which is Prefixed, An Enquiry into the Rise and Progress of Operas and Oratorios. With some Reflections on Lyric Poetry and Music* (1740), pp. xx–xxi. One of Handel's opera librettists, Paolo Antonio Rolli, became famous for his fine translation of *Paradise Lost* into Italian (1736).

30 *The Daring Muse*, p. 64.

31 *The Daring Muse*, pp. 65, 67.

32 *Gideon: or, The Patriot* (1749), introduction, pp. 2–9, 40–4, 63–4, 66, 71–2.

33 'Verses, Occasioned by reading Mr *Aaron Hill's Poem*, call'd *Gideon*', *Miscellaneous Poems* (1726), repr. *Poetical Works*, ed. Clarence Tracy (Cambridge, 1962), pp. 60–3. For similar responses to oratorio see the conclusion of ch. 7.

34 Blackwell, *Enquiry*, pp. 26–8.

35 John Hughes, 'An Essay on Allegorical Poetry', prefixed to *The Works of Spenser*, ed. Hughes (1715, 2/1750), I, xxvi–xxvii.

36 Valerie Rumbold points out that the pious druids of Pope's sketches for *Brutus* belong to a tradition according to which druidism descended from Abraham, 'Pope and the Gothic Past', pp. 227–9; see also Torchiana, 'Brutus'; Leranbaum, *Pope's 'Opus Magnum'*, p. 169; Howard D. Weinbrot, *Britannia's Issue: The Rise of British Literature from*

Dryden to Ossian (Cambridge, 1993), pp. 396–8, 491–6; Gerrard, 'Patriot Opposition', pp. 14–15, 168–87 and *Patriot Opposition*, pp. 136–49.

37 *The English Bible and the Seventeenth-Century Revolution* (1993), p. 441.

38 Morris, *Religious Sublime*, p. 45.

39 H. T. Swedenborg jnr, *The Theory of the Epic in England 1650–1800* (Berkeley, 1944), pp. 155–6.

40 *Observations on Poetry, especially the Epic* (1738), p. 154.

41 On the call for a national music and appreciation of 'pomp of sound' in Handel's choral works see ch. 2.

42 History painting, like epic, presented great heroic national events of symbolic importance, often from the Old Testament. The genre also embraced all depictions of biblical scenes. Jennens owned four of Britain's earliest biblical history paintings, by Francis Hayman, including two on subjects of his own librettos, *The Cure of Saul* and *The Resurrection of Christ* (both lost: see Brian Allen, *Francis Hayman* (1987), pp. 61–2). The relationship between Handel's biblical oratorios, continental biblical history paintings known in England and English biblical history painting is virgin terrain, ripe for exploration.

CHAPTER 6

1 William E. Alderman, 'Shaftesbury and the Doctrine of Moral Sense', *PMLA* 46 (1931), 1087–94; Cecil A. Moore, 'Shaftesbury and the Ethical Poets in England', *PMLA* 31 (1916), 264–325. For a reminder that Tillotson's sermons, and the beliefs of like-minded eighteenth-century Christians, nevertheless had a firmly doctrinal base, see Roger L. Emerson, 'Latitudinarianism and the English Deists', in *Deism, Masonry and the Enlightenment: Essays honoring Alfred Owen Aldridge*, ed. J. A. Leo Lemay (Newark, NJ, 1987), pp. 19–48.

2 Roland N. Stromberg, *Religious Liberalism in Eighteenth-Century England* (1954); John Redwood, *Reason, Ridicule and Religion: The Age of Enlightenment in England* (1976). Gerard Reedy, *The Bible and Reason: Anglicans and Scripture in Late Seventeenth Century England* (Philadelphia, 1985), esp. pp. 10, 15–17, 36–9, 48–57, 66–8, 87–9, 103–5, 142–3, gives clear accounts of some of the major themes still being debated by the mid-eighteenth century. The most readable and entertaining account is still that of Leslie Stephen in *History of English Thought in the Eighteenth Century* (1876, 3/1902, and very sympathetic to the rationalists).

3 Most substantially represented by Joseph Butler's accommodating *The Analogy of Religion, Natural and Revealed, to the Constitution and Course of Nature* (1736).

4 *An Essay upon the Truth of the Christian Religion: wherein its Real Foundation upon the Old Testament Is Shewn. Occasioned by the Discourse* [by Anthony Collins] *of the Grounds and Reasons of the Christian Religion* (1725, 2/1755), preface, p. ix.

5 William Whiston, *The Accomplishment of Scripture Prophecies. Being Eight Sermons Preach'd ... at the Lecture founded by the hon. Robert Boyle esq.* (1706, 1708); Samuel Clarke, *A Discourse, concerning the Unchangeable Obligations of Natural Religion, and the Truth and Certainty of the Christian Religion* (1705). See also the list of contents in Richard Watson, *Collection of Theological Tracts* (Cambridge, 1785), V, iii–viii.

6 *Independent on Sunday*, 28 March 1993, p. 1.

7 Nathaniel Mist, *A Collection of Miscellany Letters Selected out of Mist's Weekly Journal*, II (1722), pp. 89–92, 113–15, 124–8.

8 Gilbert Burnet (of Coggeshall), *A Defence of Natural and Revealed Religion: being an Abridgement of the Sermons Preached at the Lecture Founded by the Honourable Robert Boyle Esq* (1737). The Lectures are identified in John Cooke, *The Preacher's Assistant* (Oxford, 1783).

9 Patrick Delany, *An Historical Account of the Life and Reign of David, King of Israel* (1740–2); see further ch. 13.

10 *Present State of Learning*, pp. 6, 10.

11 [Thomas Morgan,] *The Moral Philosopher* (1737–40), I, 250–1.

12 'Israel in Egypt', *Maryland Handel Festival Programme Booklet*, (Bethesda, 1987), p.35.

13 *The Sacred Interpreter: or, A Practical Introduction towards a Beneficial Reading, and a thorough Understanding, of the Holy Bible* (1732), I, frontispiece, 241–3.

14 *Notes and Annotations on Locke on the Human Understanding* (1794), MS notes (in Morell's hand) facing the title page (on the copies in the University Library, Cambridge and, Les Robarts informs me, the British Library). On this publication see further ch. 8, 'Morell'.

15 *A Free and Impartial Study of the Holy Scriptures Recommended* (1729–36), I, 89–91.

16 Some of this ground has been covered by Geoffrey Cuming, 'The Text of "Messiah"', *M&L* 31 (1950), 226–330.

17 '"Cantate spirituali e morali", with a Description of the Papal Sacred Cantata Tradition for Christmas 1676–1740', *M&L* 73 (1992), 1–31. This article also has much interest for students of what Gianturco aptly calls Handel's moral cantatas (the two St Cecilia odes, *L'allegro ed il penseroso*, *The Choice of Hercules* and *The Triumph of Time and Truth*).

18 E.g. Richard Simon's ground-breaking biblical criticism and the works of a noted defender of scriptural credibility, Edward Stillingfleet, Bishop of Worcester (see Reedy, *Bible and Reason*, pp. 39, 48–50, 103–5). On Jennens' library, and also on the connections of the libretto with his own life and beliefs, see further my 'The Achievements of Charles Jennens (1700–1773)', *M&L* 70 (1989), 161–90. For near-contemporary testimony of Jennens as 'a great student of Theology and there are many MSS. notes in Greek of his annotations of passages in Scripture at [his house,] Gopsall' see William C. Smith, 'The Text of "Messiah"', *M&L* 32 (1951), 386–7.

19 *Christianity not Mysterious: or, A Treatise shewing, that there is Nothing in the*

Gospel contrary to Reason, nor above it: and that no Doctrine can properly be Called a Mystery (1696, 1702), p. 98.

20 J/H 15 September 1743.

21 'Richard Hooker' (William Webster), *The Weekly Miscellany. Giving an Account of the Religion, Morality and Learning of the Present Times* (2/1738), I, xv–xvi, II, 36–53, 424–31.

22 Isaac Newton, *Observations upon the Prophecies of Daniel* (1733). An early example of the debate on the validity of Daniel's visions as prophecies of Christ is Jerome's Commentary (407), a rebuttal of the treatise by Porphyry (died 303) assailing such an interpretation.

23 Mark Goldie points out to me that while James II was seen to be, though a Papist, protective of Protestants, during the first half of his reign, he was praised as a new Cyrus (a gentile who protected the Jews). This is of interest in view of Jennens' sympathy with the Stuart royal family.

24 J/H 10 July 1741. For other anti-deistical accounts of the importance of Cyrus as a validator of prophecy, 'appointed by Name to be the Restorer of the State of *Israel*, above an hundred and fifty Years before he was born', see Stackhouse, *Complete Body*, p. 489, and, in seven dense folio columns on Isaiah XLIV.27 and XLV.1 and Ezra I.1, Handel's oratorio librettist Samuel Humphreys, *The Sacred Books of the Old and New Testament, Recited at Large* (1735).

25 On the absorption of Newton's ideas by the Church see Margaret C. Jacob, *The Newtonians and the English Revolution 1689–1720* (Hassocks, Sussex, 1976).

26 Francis Webber, *The Jewish Dispensation Consider'd and Vindicated, with a View to the Objections of Unbelievers, and particularly of a Late Author Call'd the Moral Philosopher* (Oxford, 1737, 2/1751), pp. 42–3.

27 See Jacob, *The Newtonians*, pp. 143–200. For a useful brief explanation of the Lectures' relationship to contemporary science and religion see James Sambrook, *The Eighteenth Century: The Intellectual and Cultural Context of English Literature, 1700–1789* (1986), pp. 29–30.

CHAPTER 7

1 Patrick Collinson, *The Birthpangs of Protestant England: Religious and Cultural Change in the Sixteenth and Seventeenth Centuries* (1988, repr. 1991), pp. 95–6.

2 John Blow, *Amphion Anglicus* (1700).

3 'Of the Age of MSS. Authors, Painters, Musicians, etc' in *The Philosophical Transactions (From the Year 1700 to the Year 1720) Abridg'd and Dispos'd under General Heads* (1749), V.ii.9, cited in John Hollander, *The Untuning of the Sky* (New York 1961, repr. 1970), p. 256 n. 28.

4 *Poems on Several Occasions ... to which is Prefixed the Life of Mr Prior, by Samuel Humphreys, esq;* (3/1733), I, 6, ll. 29–35.

5 *The Excellency of Divine Musick: or a Sermon Preach'd in the Parish-Church of*

St Michael's Crooked Lane, in the City of London, on Thursday the Fourth Day of October, and at Sir George Wheeler's Chapel, on Monday the Fifth of November ... 1733. Before Several Members of Such Societies who are Lovers of Psalmody. To which is Added, a Specimen of Easy, Grave Tunes, instead of those which are Used in our Profane and Wanton Ballads (n.d.). Nicholas Temperley, *The Music of the English Parish Church* (Cambridge, 1979), I, 126–7, conjectures that Bedford was the promoter of the quarterly periodical of psalms, hymns and carols, *Divine Recreations*, begun in 1736. On 'the pervasive presence of religious music in London's musical culture' in the first half of the eighteenth century see A. H. Shapiro, '"Drama of an Infinitely Superior Nature": Handel's Early English Oratorios and the Religious Sublime', *M&L* 74 (1993), 215–45, at pp. 216–21, 224–7.

6 For examples of actual publications of vocal religious music (psalms, hymns, anthems), including several by religious societies, see Temperley, *Music of the English Parish Church*, I, 126–7, 134, 142, 144, 146.

7 *Spectator* no. 405 (14 June 1712), ed. Donald F. Bond (Oxford, 1965), III, 514–16.

8 Errors of dating in Bruce Wood, 'Cavendish Weedon: Impresario Extraordinary', *The Consort* 33 (1977), 222–4, are corrected by Shapiro, 'Drama', p. 220, who also locates Weedon's innovation in its cultural reforming context. Wood is mistaken in his references to pamphlets, to mentions of St Cecilia in Tate's poems, and to Weedon's reforming purpose as a late add-on to his charitable one.

9 Wood, 'Cavendish Weedon', p. 222.

10 *The Post Man*, 13–16 December 1701; *The London Gazette*, 14–18 May 1702. See also *The Post Boy*, 25–7 December 1701, 1–3 January 1701/2; *The Post Angel*, March 1701/2; *The London Gazette*, 12–16 February 1701/2, 19–23 February 1701/2, 30 April–4 May 1702; *The Post Boy*, 5–7 May 1702.

11 *The Post Man*, 13–16 December 1701.

12 *The Post Boy*, 25–7 December 1701.

13 *The Post Boy*, 25–7 December 1701, 1–3 January 1701/2.

14 *The Post Man*, 13–16 December 1701. For other charitable musical events in the early years of the century see Shapiro, 'Drama', pp. 219–20. For the famous request that patrons of *Messiah* attend unencumbered with swords or hoops see Deutsch p. 545.

15 *The Oration and Poem at Mr Weedon's Entertainment of Divine Musick ... Perform'd at Stationers-Hall, on Tuesday the 6th of Jan. 1702* (1702); *Oration, Anthems and Poems, Spoken and Sung at the Performance of Divine Musick. For the Entertainment of the Lords Spiritual and Temporal and the honourable House of Commons at Stationers-Hall, January the 31st 1701* [old style] *Undertaken by Cavendish Weedon Esq* (1602 [recte 1702]); *The Oration, Anthems and Poems, Spoken and Sung at the Performance of Divine Musick, at Stationers-Hall, for the Month of May, 1702, Undertaken by Cavendish Weedon, Esq.* (1702).

16 James R. Jacob and Timothy Raylor, 'Opera and Obedience: Thomas

Hobbes and *A Proposition for Advancement of Moralitie* by Sir William Davenant', *The Seventeenth Century* 6 (1991), 205–50, at pp. 205, 208, 209, 211, 213–14, 226, 231–2, 243, 245–6 (I owe this reference to Jeremy Maule).

17 Shapiro, 'Drama', p. 216.

18 So far as Handel himself was concerned, there was nothing unusual about oratorio performance in a setting on the border of sacred and secular. In Italy as a young man he became familiar with oratorio in the chapels of the palaces of the nobility (see ch. 1).

19 Shapiro, 'Drama', pp. 218–19. Weedon himself was perhaps providing a gentrified, secularised version of the heartstring-pulling annual celebrations of the charity schools, which included a special sermon and specially composed hymns and anthems (Temperley, *Music of the English Parish Church*, I, 103–4).

20 The proposal is paragraphs 21–2 of his plan for a musical academy in *Augusta Triumphans*; Brian Trowell, 'Daniel Defoe's Plan for an Academy of Music at Christ's Hospital, with Some Notes on his Attitude to Music', in *Source Materials and the Interpretation of Music: A Memorial Volume to Thurston Dart*, ed. Ian Bent (1981), pp. 403–27, at pp. 410, 423, 426–7.

21 [John Mainwaring et al.,] *Memoirs of the Life of the Late George Frederic Handel* (1760), pp. 127–8.

22 Sir John Hawkins, *A General History of the Science and Practice of Music* (1776, repr. New York, 1963), II, 890.

23 'An Ode, on the Occasion of Mr Handel's Great Te Deum, at the Feast of the Sons of the Clergy' (1733), quoted Deutsch pp. 306–7.

24 Daniel Prat, *An Ode to Mr Handel, on his Playing on the Organ* (1722), quoted Deutsch pp. 139–43.

25 Quoted Deutsch p. 396.

26 Eliza Haywood, *Epistles for the Ladies* (1749), I, 79, quoted Robert Manson Myers, *Handel's Messiah: A Touchstone of Taste* (New York, 1948), pp. 125–6.

27 Benjamin Victor to the Rev. William Rothery, 27 December 1752, in *Original Letters, Dramatic Pieces, and Poems* (1776), I, 189–90, quoted Deutsch p. 729.

28 Deutsch pp. 481–3.

29 John Frederick Lampe, *The Art of Musick* (1740), p. 11, quoted Shapiro, 'Drama', p. 232.

CHAPTER 8

1 I am grateful to David Armitage for this reference.

2 John Loftis, *The Politics of Drama in Augustan England* (Oxford, 1963); Bertrand A. Goldgar, *Walpole and the Wits: The Relation of Politics to Literature 1722–1742* (Lincoln, NE, 1976); Christine Gerrard, 'The Patriot Opposition to Sir Robert Walpole: A Study of Politics and

Poetry, 1725–1742', D.Phil. diss., University of Oxford (1986), and *The Patriot Opposition to Walpole: Politics, Poetry, and National Myth, 1725–1742* (Oxford, 1994).

3 E.g. Wilfrid Mellers, review of *Semele*, *Times Literary Supplement*, 27 July 1991. Political readings of Handel's operas have been pioneered by Reinhard Strohm, 'Handel and his Italian Opera Texts', in *Essays on Handel and Italian Opera* (Cambridge, 1985), pp. 34–79, and Curtis Price, 'English Traditions in Handel's *Rinaldo*', in *Handel Tercentenary Collection*, ed. Stanley Sadie and Anthony Hicks (1988), pp. 120–37. See also Price, 'Political Allegory in Late-Seventeenth-Century English Opera', in *Music and Theatre: Essays in honour of Winton Dean*, ed. Nigel Fortune (1987), pp. 1–29. Thomas McGeary is preparing a study of politics and Handel's operas.

4 On the press see Jeremy Black, *The English Press in the Eighteenth Century* (1987); Michael Harris, *London Newspapers in the Age of Walpole: A Study in the Origins of the Modern English Press* (1987); Simon Targett, 'Sir Robert Walpole's Newspapers, 1722–42: Propaganda and Politics in the Age of Whig Supremacy', Ph.D. diss., University of Cambridge (1991); Robert Harris, *A Patriot Press: National Politics and the London Press in the 1740s* (Oxford, 1993).

5 A particularly helpful introduction to the politics of the period is Geoffrey Holmes and Daniel Szechi, *The Age of Oligarchy: Pre-Industrial Britain 1722–1783* (1993), especially the 'Framework of Events' and 'Compendium of Information' (pp. 3–11, 239–51, 341–408); see also, for home affairs, chs. 1–3, 5, 18, and for foreign affairs, chs. 4, 17, 18.

6 For the origins and development of the conflict with Spain, among many good accounts see particularly G. B. Hertz (Hurst), 'The War Fever of 1739', in *British Imperialism in the Eighteenth Century* (1908); Jeremy Black, *British Foreign Policy in the Age of Walpole* (Edinburgh, 1985), esp. pp. 7–22, 107–13, 168–9; Philip Woodfine, 'The Anglo-Spanish War of 1739', in *The Origins of War in Early Modern Europe*, ed. J. Black (Edinburgh 1987), pp. 185–209, and 'Ideas of Naval Power and the Conflict with Spain, 1737–42', in *The British Navy and the Use of Naval Power in the Eighteenth Century*, ed. J. Black and P. Woodfine (Atlantic Heights, NJ, 1989), pp. 71–90; Kathleen Wilson, 'Empire, Trade and Popular Politics in Mid-Hanoverian Britain: The Case of Admiral Vernon', *Past & Present* 121 (1988), 74–109; Gerald Jordan and Nicholas Rogers, 'Admirals as Heroes: Patriotism and Liberty in Hanoverian England', *Journal of British Studies* 28 (1989), 201–24. On the actual conduct of the war in the West Indies see now Richard Harding, *Amphibious Warfare in the Eighteenth Century: The British Expedition to the West Indies 1740–1742* (Woodbridge, Suffolk, 1991). On the view of Spain as an 'empire of evil' and 'the anti-Hispanic rhetoric suffusing the literature of the First British Empire' see David S. Shields, *Oracles of Empire: Poetry, Politics, and Commerce in British America, 1690–1750* (Chicago, 1990), pp. 175–94.

7 On the impact at home of the war in Europe see e.g. Harris, *Patriot Press*, esp. chs. 4–7; Paul Langford, *The Eighteenth Century, 1688–1815* (1976), pp. 115–32, and *A Polite and Commercial People: England, 1727–1783* (Oxford, 1989), pp. 189–94, 209–10, 219–20; Black, *British Foreign Policy*, pp. 20–1, 27–45, and *Natural and Necessary Enemies: Anglo-French Relations in the Eighteenth Century* (1986), pp. 36–51; Graham C. Gibbs, 'English Attitudes towards Hanover and the Hanoverian Succession in the First Half of the Eighteenth Century', in *England und Hannover / England and Hanover*, ed. Adolf M. Birke and Kurt Kluxen (Munich, 1986), pp. 33–51, esp. pp. 35, 43, 46–7.

8 See e.g. Jeremy Black, *A System of Ambition? British Foreign Policy 1660–1793* (1991), pp. 85–6.

9 In addition, foreign diplomats fed Members of Parliament and the press with confidential material at critical periods of decision-making: Black, *British Foreign Policy*, pp. 78–83, 160–72.

10 J. H. Plumb, *Sir Robert Walpole*, II, *The King's Minister* (1960, repr. 1972), pp. 239–83; Paul Langford, *The Excise Crisis: Society and Politics in the Age of Walpole* (Oxford, 1975), esp. pp. 1–3, 44–78, 101–6, and *A Polite and Commercial People*, pp. 28–33; Eveline Cruickshanks, 'The Political Management of Sir Robert Walpole, 1720–42', in *Britain in the Age of Walpole*, ed. J. Black (1984), pp. 23–43, at pp. 35–6.

11 George Harris, *The Life of Lord Chancellor Hardwicke* (1847), I, 378.

12 Averyl Edwards, *Frederick Louis, Prince of Wales 1707–1751* (1947); Betty Kemp, 'Frederick, Prince of Wales', in *Silver Renaissance: Essays in Eighteenth-Century English History*, ed. Alex Natan (1961), pp. 38–56.

13 Harris, *Patriot Press*, pp. 60–1, 70–1, 179, 219.

14 Holmes and Szechi, *The Age of Oligarchy*, p. 97.

15 *Biblical Drama in England from the Middle Ages to the Present Day* (1968), p. 185: two sentences in which every statement is open to question. See also, for the same view expressed in a general music history textbook, Donald J. Grout with Claude V. Palisca, *A History of Western Music* (3/1981), p. 443.

16 *Britons: Forging the Nation 1707–1837* (New Haven, 1992), pp. 23, 31–3.

17 Linda Colley, *In Defiance of Oligarchy: The Tory Party 1714–60* (Cambridge, 1982); J. C. D. Clark, 'A General Theory of Party, Opposition and Government, 1688–1832', *HJ* 23 (1980), 295–325, and *English Society 1688–1832: Ideology, Social Structure and Political Practice during the Ancien Régime* (Cambridge, 1985); Eveline Cruickshanks, *Political Untouchables: The Tories and the '45* (1979); Paul Monod, *Jacobitism and the English People, 1688–1788* (Cambridge, 1990); Gerrard, 'Patriot Opposition', and *Patriot Opposition*; Harris, *Patriot Press*.

18 Gerrard, *Patriot Opposition*, ch. 1; Cruickshanks, *Political Untouchables*, pp. 47–9.

19 Black, *System of Ambition*, p. 163.

20 See my 'The Achievements of Charles Jennens (1700–1773)', *M&L* 70 (1989), 161–90.

21 In addition to the studies already mentioned, non-historians could profitably start with (in alphabetical order): Herbert M. Atherton, _Political Prints in the Age of Hogarth: A Study of the Iconographic Representation of Politics_ (Oxford, 1974), esp. ch. 5; Jeremy Black, 'Introduction: An Age of Political Stability?' in _Britain in the Age of Walpole_, pp. 1–22; Reed Browning, _Political and Constitutional Ideas of the Court Whigs_ (Baton Rouge, LA, 1982), esp. pp. 10–34, 175–209; H. T. Dickinson, _Bolingbroke_ (1970), _Liberty and Property: Political Ideology in Eighteenth-Century Britain_ (1977), and 'Whiggism in the Eighteenth Century', in _The Whig Ascendancy_, ed. J. Cannon (1981), pp. 28–50; M. M. Goldsmith, 'Faction Detected: Ideological Consequences of Robert Walpole's Decline and Fall', _History_ 64 (1979), 1–19; J. A. W. Gunn, _Factions No More: Attitudes to Party and Government in Eighteenth-Century England_ (1973), and _Beyond Liberty and Property: The Process of Self-Recognition in Eighteenth-Century Political Thought_ (Kingston and Montreal, 1983); J. P. Kenyon, _Revolution Principles_ (Cambridge, 1977); Isaac Kramnick, _Bolingbroke and his Circle: The Politics of Nostalgia in the Age of Walpole_ (Cambridge, MA, 1968); Frank McLynn, 'The Ideology of Jacobitism [and the opposition more widely] on the Eve of the Rising of 1745', _History of European Ideas_ 6 (1985), 1–18, 173–88; J. G. A. Pocock, _The Machiavellian Moment_ (Princeton, 1975), and _Virtue, Commerce, and History: Essays on Political Thought and History, chiefly in the Eighteenth Century_ (Cambridge, 1985), pp. 230–53; W. A. Speck, _Stability and Strife: England 1714–60_ (1977); Simon Varey, 'Hanover, Stuart, and the _Patriot King_', _BJECS_ 6 (1983), 163–72.

22 _Oratorios_, p. 473.

23 _Harlequin Horace: or, The Art of Modern Poetry_ (3/1735), l. 509, n.

24 Bolingbroke's manifesto, written in 1738 and circulated and excerpted before full publication in 1749, gave provocative, romantic, rhetorical expression to widespread ideas about national unity and leadership, and represents a summation of idealised Patriot philosophy. Of many accounts of its meaning, influence and transmission into creative literature, particularly helpful for oratorio students are Giles Barber, 'Bolingbroke, Pope, and the _Patriot King_', _The Library_, 5th ser., 19 (1964), 67–89; Kramnick, _Bolingbroke_; Varey, 'Hanover, Stuart, and the _Patriot King_'; Brean Hammond, _Pope and Bolingbroke: A Study of Friendship and Influence_ (Columbia, MO, 1984); Gerrard, _Patriot Opposition_, esp. ch. 3.

25 Gerrard, _Patriot Opposition_, ch. 1; Harris, _Patriot Press_.

26 Harris, _Patriot Press_, pp. 23, 44, 48–9, 55–6, 77. For contemporary evidence of Patriot principles surviving into the 1740s see e.g. [James Ralph,] _The Remembrancer . . . the Twelve First Essays, from the Weekly Paper_ (1748), pp. 3–7, 10, 11, 13–15, 17, 72–9.

27 Harris, _Patriot Press_, pp. 5–6.

28 For example in Edward Young's _Imperium Pelagi_ (1729).

29 Deutsch pp. 303–4.

30 'Pope and the Patriots', in *Pope: New Contexts*, ed. David Fairer (Hemel Hempstead, 1990), pp. 25–43, at p. 30.

31 Isaac Kramnick ed., *Lord Bolingbroke: Historical Writings* (Chicago, 1972); Shelley Burtt, *Virtue Transformed: Political Argument in England, 1688–1740* (Cambridge, 1992); Gerrard, *Patriot Opposition*, ch. 1.

32 See e.g. H. T. Dickinson, 'The Eighteenth-Century Debate on the "Glorious Revolution"', *History* 61 (1976), 28–45, and *Liberty and Property*, pp. 140–2.

33 Gunn, *Beyond Liberty and Property*, p. 229. For a continuation into the late 1740s of criticism of government in this respect, of the kind more commonly associated with the Walpole era, see e.g. [Ralph,] *Remembrancer*, pp. 5, 8, 10–11, 75–9; [Horace Walpole,] *A Letter to the Whigs* (2/1748), pp. 2–6, 10–12.

34 Pocock, *Machiavellian Moment*, pp. 386, 410–16, 424, 428, 431–2, 435, 437–8, 470, 478; Dickinson, *Liberty and Property*, pp. 185–6; Browning, *Court Whigs*, pp. 189–90; Quentin Skinner, 'The Principles and Practice of Opposition: The Case of Bolingbroke versus Walpole', in *Historical Perspectives ... in honour of J. H. Plumb*, ed. N. McKendrick (1974), pp. 93–128, at pp. 96–7, 118–20, 123, 125; Gunn, *Beyond Liberty and Property*, pp. 53–5. J. R. Western, *The English Militia in the Eighteenth Century* (Toronto, 1965), pp. 90–5, 105–17, identifies 'an agitation for the reform of the militia, beginning in 1745, reaching a climax in 1756', which is discussed in more detail by Eliga H. Gould, 'To Strengthen the King's Hands: Dynastic Legitimacy, Militia Reform and Ideas of National Unity in England 1745–1760', *HJ* 34 (1991), 329–48. For a very clear instance of a contemporary writer linking the use of a militia with the fostering of patriotic unity see John Brown, *An Estimate of the Manners and Principles of the Times* (1757–8), II (1758), pp. 160–5.

35 Targett, 'Walpole's Newspapers', p. 324; Burtt, *Virtue Transformed*, pp. 113–27.

36 See e.g. Pocock, *Machiavellian Moment*.

37 T. C. Curtis and W. A. Speck, 'The Societies for Reformation of Manners: A Case Study in the Theory and Practice of Moral Reform', *Literature and History* 3 (1976), 45–64; Burtt, *Virtue Transformed*, pp. 22–4, 42–53.

38 E.g. Brown, *Estimate*, I (1757), 'Advertisement', pp. 12, 15, 18, 66–7, 72, 164–5, II (1758), pp. 238–9.

39 James Thomson to Aaron Hill, 11 May 1736, *James Thomson (1700–1748): Letters and Documents*, ed. Alan D. McKillop (Lawrence, KS, 1958), p. 105.

40 Maynard Mack, *The Garden and the City: Retirement and Politics in the Later Poetry of Pope 1731–43* (Toronto, 1969).

41 Burtt, *Virtue Transformed*, pp. 134–5; M. M. Goldsmith, *Private Vices, Public Benefits: Bernard Mandeville's Social and Political Thought* (Cambridge, 1985).

42 Terence Ball, 'Party', in *Political Innovation and Conceptual Change*, ed. Terence Ball, James Farr and Russell L. Hanson (Cambridge, 1989), pp. 155–76, at pp. 167–72.
43 Cruickshanks, *Political Untouchables*, pp. 3–6.
44 For the energetic and extensive discussion on whether faction and party were identical and whether either was politically healthy see examples cited in Gunn, *Factions No More*, and his analysis esp. pp. 6–11, 17, 21–5; Dickinson, *Liberty and Property*, pp. 175–81; Kramnick, *Bolingbroke*, pp. 153–9. On the opposition's lack of and attempts at unity see e.g. Speck, *Stability and Strife*, pp. 220, 222, 240; Hammond, *Pope and Bolingbroke*, pp. 94–5, 131–7.
45 For fuller and helpful discussion of these issues of reading and understanding see Robert D. Hume, 'Texts within Contexts: Notes toward a Historical Method', *PQ* 71 (1992), 69–100.
46 J. C. D. Clark, *The Dynamics of Change: The Crisis of the 1750s and English Party* (Cambridge, 1982), pp. 3–4; Pocock, *Virtue, Commerce and History*, p. 244.
47 See ch. 2, and Strohm, *Essays*; Price, 'English Traditions', and 'Political Allegory'.
48 Loftis, *Politics of Drama*; Price, 'English Traditions', pp. 130–3, and 'Political Allegory'.
49 John Loftis, 'Political and Social Thought in the Drama', in *The London Theatre World 1660–1800*, ed. Robert D. Hume (Carbondale, 1980), pp. 263–75; John Gay, *The Beggar's Opera*, ed. P. E. Lewis (Edinburgh, 1973), pp. 15–21. J. V. Guerinot and R. D. Jilg, *Contexts 1: The Beggar's Opera* (Hamden, CT, 1976), print contemporary documents illuminating the work's literary, underworld, political and musical-theatrical backgrounds and its early reception.
50 On Dryden's text, see Price, 'Political Allegory'; Gerrard, *Patriot Opposition*, pp. 119–20, 172–4.
51 The Rev. William Harris to Mrs Thomas Harris, 8 February 1746, quoted Deutsch pp. 629–30.
52 HMC 15th Report, App., Pt II, Hodgkin MSS, p. 92, quoted Deutsch p. 851.
53 Shapiro, '"Drama of an Infinitely Superior Nature": The Relationship of Handel's First English Oratorios to Early-Eighteenth-Century Sacred Music Theory and Practice', M.Litt. thesis, University of Cambridge (1988), pp. 121–2; Matthew Prior, *Poems on Several Occasions ... to which is Prefixed the Life of Mr Prior, by Samuel Humphreys, esq;* (3/1733), prefatory 'Memoirs of the Life of Prior' and III, 154–8.
54 For a fuller account of Jennens and for supporting references for the facts given here, see my 'The Achievements of Charles Jennens', pp. 162–3.
55 M. H. Massue, Marquis de Ruvigny et Raineval, *The Jacobite Peerage* (Edinburgh, 1904), pp. 244, 248, 170; G. V. Bennett, *The Tory Crisis in Church and State 1688–1730: The Career of Francis Atterbury, Bishop of*

Rochester (Oxford, 1975), pp. 234, 239, 254; Paul S. Fritz, *The English Ministers and Jacobitism between the Rebellions of 1715 and 1745* (Toronto, 1976), pp. 70, 73, 75, 77; Eveline Cruickshanks, *Lord Cornbury, Bolingbroke and a Plan to Restore the Stuarts 1731–5*, Royal Stuart Papers 27 (Huntingdon, 1986), pp. 3–4.

56 See my 'The Argument and Contexts of Dryden's *Alexander's Feast*', *SEL: Studies in English Literature* 18 (1978), 465–90.

57 'The Life and Works of James Miller', Ph.D. diss., University of London (1979). Any future work on Miller as librettist should take into account a squib on him full of references to music, 'Christopher Columbario', *The Pigeon-Pye, or, a King's Coronation, Proper Materials for forming an Oratorio, Opera or Play, according to the Modern Taste: to be Represented in Opposition to the Dragon of Wantley* (1738; BL 11775.c.26); O'Brien identifies its characters, 'James Miller', pp. 17–18.

58 Alexander Pope, *The Dunciad*, ed. J. Sutherland, *The Poems of Alexander Pope*, V (3/1963), pp. xlv, 342, 373, 396, 402, 405; O'Brien, 'James Miller', pp. 50–1, 313–18; and see *The Correspondence of Alexander Pope*, ed. George Sherburn (Oxford, 1956), III, 173, for Pope's praise of Miller's *Harlequin Horace*, and Peter Dixon, 'Pope and James Miller', *Notes & Queries* 215 (1970), 91–2, for his use of it in the *Essay on Man*.

59 On Pope as Patriot opposition writer see especially Maynard Mack, *The Garden and the City*; Hammond, *Pope and Bolingbroke*; Gerrard, 'Pope and the Patriots'; Howard Erskine-Hill, *The Social Milieu of Alexander Pope* (New Haven and London, 1975), and 'Alexander Pope: The Political Poet in his Time', *ECS* 15 (1981–2), 123–41; and H. T. Dickinson, 'The Politics of Pope', in *Alexander Pope: Essays for the Tercentenary*, ed. C. Nicholson (Aberdeen, 1988), pp. 1–21: 'Pope, at least in the 1730s, is best described as one of the most searching critics of the political vices of Walpolean Britain and as one of the most insistent voices raised in support of Country or Patriot principles' (p. 12).

60 Calhoun Winton, 'Benjamin Victor, James Miller, and the Authorship of *The Modish Couple*', *PQ* 64 (1985), 121–30, at p. 126.

61 See further Mack, *The Garden and the City*, pp. 190–1; O'Brien, 'James Miller', pp. 287–300.

62 *Are These Things So?* and *The Great Man's Answer*, ed. I. Gordon, Augustan Reprint Society 153 (Los Angeles, 1972); see also Mack's account of the author's political acumen, *The Garden and the City*, pp. 194–200.

63 O'Brien, 'James Miller', pp. 79, 340.

64 O'Brien, 'James Miller', pp. 93–5.

65 David Baker et al., *Biographia Dramatica* (3/1812), III, 512–15, probably drawing on the same account in [Robert Shiels] rev. Theophilus Cibber, 'The Life of the Revd. Mr. James Millar', in *The Lives of the Poets of Great-Britain and Ireland* (1753), V, 332–4.

66 Gerrard, 'Patriot Opposition', ch. 1.

67 Morell's penury and other biographical details are chronicled by John

Nichols (a not always reliable source), *Literary Anecdotes of the Eighteenth Century*, (1812–15, repr. New York, 1966), I, 651–6, III, 89–91, IV, 599–603, V, 251–2, 711–12, IX, 789.

68 The parishioners complained to the Bishop of Winchester about his removal and a resident curate was appointed in place of the nominal, absentee curate, a crony of the vicar, the Rev. William Comer; Comer was finally sued for malpractice and depredations in 1757. See G. E. Cassidy, *The Chapel of St Anne, Kew Green, 1710–1769*, Richmond Historical Society Paper no. 2 (Richmond, 1985), pp. 15, 18–20, 26–31, 36–45, 70 (I owe this reference to Merlin Channon).

69 A volume (pages numbered 1–155, no pp. 14–15, 96–7, 100–3, 128–33, 146–7) of poems in Morell's hand, many signed with his monogram, and with annotations addressed to his wife of which one is dated 1779 (five years before his death), is now in the Osborn Collection, Yale University Library, call mark Osborn Shelves c.395; see Stephen Parks, 'The Osborn Collection: A 4th Biennial Report', *Yale University Library Gazette* 50 (1975–6), 182. I am assuming that all the poems in the MS are by Morell, except those he attributes to another source; his monogram is applied inconsistently and cannot be taken as a guide. However it should be said that of the poems referred to here only 'The Lord and the 'Squire' is monogrammed.

70 *Gentleman's Magazine*, 1 (1731), 28; Dickinson, *Bolingbroke*, p. 218; Robert Halsband, *Lord Hervey: Eighteenth Century Courtier* (Oxford, 1974), pp. 107–20.

71 MS fols. 24–5. Halsband, *Lord Hervey*, pp. 117–20, surveys the literary aftermath of the duel, in which 'politics remained the dominant satiric theme'. For another, more ambitious, ballad which also speaks of 'A Youth that is *In*, and a Man that is *Out*', see Milton Percival, *Political Ballads illustrating the Administration of Sir Robert Walpole* (Oxford, 1916), pp. 46–8.

72 David Nokes, *Jonathan Swift: A Hypocrite Reversed* (Oxford, 1985), pp. 382–3.

73 On this view of the Excise as a symptom of governmental oppression see e.g. Dickinson, *Liberty and Property*, pp. 182–4, and *Bolingbroke*, pp. 230–7.

74 *Gentleman's Magazine*, 1 (1731), 115; 2 (1732), 1021, 1037–40; 3 (1733) 41 (not 42, as in Morell's MS). For other Excise ballads see Percival, *Political Ballads*, pp. 61–76.

75 Edwards, *Frederick Louis*, pp. 114–19.

76 Nichols, *Literary Anecdotes*, IX, 789.

77 See chs. 12, 14. On the poem to Thomson, which exists in several MSS, see *Thomson: Letters*, ed. McKillop, pp. 135–6. On *The Castle of Indolence* as a Patriot opposition work see further Christine Gerrard, '*The Castle of Indolence* and the Opposition to Walpole', *Review of English Studies* new ser. 41 (1990), 44–64.

78 James M. Osborn, 'Pope, the "Apollo of the Arts", and his Countess',

in *England in the Restoration and Eighteenth Century*, ed. H. T. Swedenborg, jnr (Berkeley and Los Angeles, 1972), pp. 101–43, prints the poem with the text of Pope's letter on facing pages and sets it in the context of Pope's friendship with Burlington. The identification of Morell as the scribe of both MSS of the poem was made by Parks, 'The Osborn Collection'. The traditional view of the political stance of Burlington has been questioned by Jane Clark, '"Lord Burlington Is Here": A View without Architecture', in *Lord Burlington: Architecture, Art and Life*, ed. Toby Barnard and Jane Clark (1995), suggesting that he was more of a Jacobite than an independent Whig.

79 Gerrard, *Patriot Opposition*, ch. 3; Stephen Jones, *Frederick, Prince of Wales and His Circle* (Sudbury, 1981).

80 Morell's statement is printed by Deutsch p. 851.

81 According to a leaf in his own hand, dated 1735, 'I was preparing these for the Cave [the Queen's grotto] by Order'. This appears opposite the title page of his *Notes and Annotations on Locke on the Human Understanding, Written by order of the Queen*, which was finally published in 1794 to elucidate an edition of Locke brought out the previous year. The copies in the British Library and Cambridge University Library both have this apparently inserted page.

82 I am grateful to Merlin Channon for drawing my attention to this squib (copy in Huntington Library, class mark 315993). Morell had provided commendatory prefatory verses 'To Stephen Duck: occasion'd by his Poem on Friendship' for Duck's *Verses on Several Occasions* (1736); he later rewrote the verses, branding Duck as a hypocrite friend (MS poems, fols. 68–70).

83 *Letters of the Late Lord Lyttelton* (2/1785), II, 29–32.

84 J. Simon ed., *Handel: A Celebration of his Life and Times* (1985), p. 178.

85 Christopher Hogwood, *Handel* (1984), pp. 68–9, 84; Deutsch pp. 105–6, 397, 415, 488–9. Handel's first biographer goes to great lengths to give honourable political reasons for his willingness to write the Utrecht Te Deum, [John Mainwaring et al.,] *Memoirs of the Life of the Late George Frederic Handel* (1760), pp. 86–7.

86 For Burlington see above, n. 78; for Brydges see Dickinson, *Bolingbroke*, p. 135, and G. Davies and M. Tinling, 'Letters from James Brydges, Created Duke of Chandos, to Henry St. John, Created Viscount Bolingbroke', *Huntington Library Bulletin* 9 (1936), 119–66, showing Brydges' sustained financial and political support of Bolingbroke during Bolingbroke's association with the Pretender, and Jane Clark, '"Lord Burlington Is Here"'; for the Prince of Wales see Carole Taylor, 'Handel and Frederick, Prince of Wales', *MT* 125 (1984), 89–92; for Hamilton's comments see Ruth Loewenthal [= Smith], 'Handel and Newburgh Hamilton: New References in the Strafford Papers', *MT* 112 (1971), 1063–6, at 1066. The dedicatees of the librettos of Handel's operas and oratorios seem to reflect this political duality of patronage – a topic worth investigating.

87 'Handel and Hanover', in *Bach, Handel, Scarlatti: Tercentenary Essays*, ed. Peter Williams (Cambridge, 1985), pp. 35–59, at pp. 39–46; on Handel's involvement with the concerns of the royal family see also Graydon Beeks, 'Handel and Music for the Earl of Carnarvon', in *Bach, Handel, Scarlatti*, pp. 1–20, at p. 2.

88 Colman's Opera Register, 31 October 1715, February 1715/16, quoted Walter and Margret Eisen, eds.: *Händel-Handbuch Band 4: Dokumente zu Leben und Schaffen auf der Grundlage von Otto Erich Deutsch, Handel, A Documentary Biography* (Kassel, 1985), pp. 68–9.

89 Strohm, *Essays*, pp. 40, 47 (*Agrippina*).

CHAPTER 9

1 This is only one eighth of the article, fully printed Deutsch pp. 310–13, with explanations of the parallels, and Christopher Hogwood, *Handel* (1984), pp. 104–6. Jeremy Black, 'Lord Bolingbroke's Operatic Allegory', *The Scriblerian* 16 (1984), 97–9, gives a contemporary source confirming most of the modern explanations. On the *Craftsman*'s circulation figures at this date see Michael Harris, *London Newspapers in the Age of Walpole: A Study in the Origins of the Modern English Press* (1987), pp. 189–90.

2 Dean, *Oratorios*, p. 236.

3 Lord Delawarr to Duke of Richmond, commenting on the formation of the Opera of the Nobility, quoted (and correctly dated) J. Simon ed., *Handel: A Celebration of His Life and Times* (1985), p. 146n: 'There is a Spirit got up against the Dominion of Mr. Handel'. Dean, *Oratorios*, p. 237, suggests that a secondary purpose of the *Craftsman*'s piece may have been to further the Opera of the Nobility's plan to capture the opera market. For contemporary views of the Opera of the Nobility and Handel's dominance see further Deutsch pp. 347–8, 351.

4 Lady Irwin to Lord Carlisle, 31 March 1733, HMC Carlisle 15th Report, App., Pt VI, p. 106, quoted Deutsch p. 310.

5 Martin C. Battestin with Ruthe R. Battestin, *Henry Fielding: A Life* (1989, repr. 1993), pp. 164–5.

6 The Coronation Anthems 'Let thy Hand be Strengthened' and 'The King shall Rejoice', among many other sources, including the Birthday Ode for Queen Anne; see Dean, *Oratorios*, p. 642.

7 Handel used 'Zadok the priest' again in the *Occasional Oratorio*. The question arises whether the audience recognised the music when it was set to new words in *Deborah*, having heard it at most twice before (the public rehearsal of the music and the coronation itself). In *Esther* the texts were largely unchanged. On the association of Handel's early oratorios with the royal family see A. H. Shapiro, '"Drama of an Infinitely Superior Nature": Handel's Early English Oratorios and the Religious Sublime', *M&L* 74 (1993), 215–45.

8 Paula O'Brien, 'The Life and Works of James Miller', Ph.D. diss., University of London (1979), p. 64.

9 Thomas McGeary, 'Opera, Satire, and Politics in the Walpole Era', in *The Past as Prologue: Essays to Celebrate the Twenty-Fifth Anniversary of ASECS*, ed. Carla H. Hay with Syndy M. Conger (New York, 1994), pp. 347–72.

10 *The Devil to Pay at St James's: or a Full and True Account of a Most Horrid and Bloody Battle between Madam Faustina and Madam Cuzzoni ... moreover, how Senesino has taken Snuff, and is going to Leave the Opera, and Sing Psalms at Henley's Oratory ...* (1727), repr. in John Arbuthnot, *Miscellaneous Works* (Edinburgh, 1751), I, 214–15.

11 *Lord Bolingbroke: Contributions to The 'Craftsman'*, ed. Simon Varey (Oxford, 1982), pp. 136–41. For further musical-political allegory in the *Craftsman* see also 27 February 1726/7, 10 June 1727, 15 July 1727 and 31 August 1728 (using the Royal Academy opera company as a trope for the state) and 17 February 1726/7 and 1 February 1728/9 (on *The Beggar's Opera* and its suppressed sequel *Polly*).

12 Partly repr. William C. Smith, *'Do You Know What You Are About?'*: A Rare Handelian Pamphlet', *Music Review*, May 1964, 114–19.

13 *Do You Know What You Are About?* (1733), preface, pp. 14–22.

14 *Vice and Luxury Publick Mischiefs* (1724), p. 24. For modern comment on this theme see e.g. Paul Langford, *Public Life and the Propertied Englishman 1689–1798* (Oxford, 1991), pp. 118–31.

15 [George, Lord Lyttelton,] *Letters from a Persian in England, to his Friend at Ispahan* (2/1735), repr. in *George Lyttelton's Political Tracts 1735–1748*, ed. Stephen Parks (New York, 1974), p. 4.

16 Thus fulfilling the criterion for seeing political allusions in theatre works of the 1730s – the affirmation of a political interpretation in contemporary sources – determined by Robert D. Hume, 'Henry Fielding and Politics at the Little Haymarket, 1728–1737', in *The Golden and the Brazen World: Papers in Literature and History, 1650–1800*, ed. J. M. Wallace (Berkeley, 1985), pp. 79–124, at pp. 96–7.

17 Quoted Deutsch pp. 395–6.

18 'An Ode, on Occasion of Mr Handel's Great Te Deum, at the Feast of the Sons of the Clergy', quoted Deutsch pp. 306–7.

19 Deutsch pp. 139–44.

20 Deutsch pp. 158–60.

21 *Essay on Man*, III, 293–4, ed. Maynard Mack, *The Poems of Alexander Pope*, III.i (1950), p. 127.

22 *A Collection of Miscellany Letters Selected out of Mist's Weekly Journal*, IV (1727), p. 210.

23 See for example, in the political sphere, the use made of the figure of Augustus, detailed by Howard D. Weinbrot, *Augustus Caesar in 'Augustan' England* (Princeton, 1978), esp. pp. 53, 76, 182–3.

24 Margaret Anne Doody, *The Daring Muse: Augustan Poetry Reconsidered* (Cambridge, 1985), pp. 177–8. On Hill and allegory see also ch. 5.

25 'Henry Fielding', p. 97.
26 Curtis Price, 'Political Allegory in Late-Seventeenth-Century English Opera', in *Music and Theatre: Essays in honour of Winton Dean*, ed. Nigel Fortune (1987), pp. 1–29, at pp. 12–17, and 'English Traditions in Handel's *Rinaldo*', in *Handel Tercentenary Collection*, ed. Stanley Sadie and Anthony Hicks (1987), pp. 120–37, at p. 131.
27 'English Traditions', pp. 132–3.
28 For an example of the former, Price, 'Political Allegory', pp. 17–19; of the latter, the interpretation by the opera audience of the punishment of the usurper Orontes in Handel's *Floridante* as seditious (Orontes = 'usurping' Hanoverians), see HMC Portland vii, 311, and Winton Dean and J. Merrill Knapp, *Handel's Operas 1704–1726* (1987), pp. 389–90.
29 For *Gustavus Vasa* see below; for *British Enchanters* see Price, 'Political Allegory', p. 26; for *Merlin* see Christine Gerrard, *The Patriot Opposition to Walpole: Politics, Poetry, and National Myth, 1725–1742* (Oxford, 1994), ch. 6; for *Alfred* see below, ch. 12.
30 John Loftis, *The Politics of Drama in Augustan England* (Oxford, 1963), pp. 56–62, 122.
31 Dean, *Oratorios*, pp. 465–6; William C. Smith, *A Handelian's Notebook* (1965), pp. 141–2; Richard Capell, *Daily Telegraph*, 8 April 1939, p. 5.
32 Gerrard, *Patriot Opposition*; for an example of such wishful thinking in semi-opera see Price, 'Political Allegory', pp. 21–2, reading John Old-mixon's and Daniel Purcell's *The Grove* (1700) as a hope for the reconciliation of James II and Anne.
33 Deutsch pp. 481–3, citing Chrysander's suggestion that 'R. W.' was Richard Wesley, one of the subscribers to *Alexander's Feast*.
34 Deutsch p. 497.
35 Patrick Collinson, *The Birthpangs of Protestant England: Religious and Cultural Change in the Sixteenth and Seventeenth Centuries* (1988, repr. 1991), pp. 4–7, 10–11, 18–27, is an excellent introduction.
36 *Britons: Forging the Nation 1707–1837* (New Haven, 1992), pp. 30–3, noting some of the instances I mention here. Colley recognises oratorio as a vehicle of the analogy, but unfortunately repeats the conventional simplistic view of its application.
37 *Critical Observations on Shakespeare* (1746), p. 162; for a modern reading of the poem as political comment see M. A. Radzinowicz, *Towards Samson Agonistes: The Growth of Milton's Mind* (Princeton, 1978), pp. 69, 91–118. On Dryden's political typology see Steven N. Zwicker, *Dryden's Political Poetry: The Typology of King and Nation* (Providence, RI, 1972), ch. 4.
38 *Biblical Drama in England from the Middle Ages to the Present Day* (1968), pp. 69–97, 108, 159–60. See also, on seventeenth-century unacted religious drama, W. E. Stephenson, 'Religious Drama in the Restoration', *PQ* 50 (1971), 599–609, who mentions (p. 606) a 'masque' celebrating the Restoration which 'studs its treatment of Old Testa-

ment material with song after song'. The political meanings of Roger Boyle (Earl of Orrery), *The Tragedy of King Saul* (repr. 1703) and Aaron Hill, *Saul* (unfinished, ptd *Dramatic Works*, 1760), two of the very few biblical dramas of the eighteenth century, would reward exploration.

39 *The Psalms of David, Imitated in the Language of the New Testament, and Apply'd to the Christian State and Worship* (1718), repr. *Works* (1753), IV, 110; see also preface, pp. xi, xiv, and pp. 62, 90, 93, 129, 140, and 'An Essay toward the Improvement of Psalmody: or, An Inquiry how the Psalms of David ought to be Translated into Christian Songs, and how Lawful and Necessary it is to Compose other Hymns according to the Clearer Revelations of the Gospel, for the Use of the Christian Church', appended to *Hymns and Spiritual Songs* (1707), repr. *Works*, IV, 271–91, esp. pp. 277–82. I am grateful to Jeremy Maule for drawing my attention to this aspect of Watts' verse.

40 'The British Fisherman' in *Remnants of Time Employed in Prose and Verse* (1736), repr. *Works*, IV, 609. Paul Korshin, *Typologies in England, 1650–1820* (Princeton, 1982), briefly notices the political analogical use of the Bible in the late seventeenth and late eighteenth centuries (pp. 31, 107, 353–4), but, perhaps because he declines (p. 19) to discuss sermons, he neglects the most substantial eighteenth-century manifestations of it. I disagree with his deduction (p. 108 n. 19) that the use of multiple analogues (classical as well as biblical) for contemporary rulers betokens 'fluctuations and uncertainty'. The preachers' multifarious use of their types has all the confidence of long familiarity – unsurprisingly, since the types are inherited from previous generations: see Barbara Lewalski, *Protestant Poetics and the Seventeenth-Century Religious Lyric* (Princeton, 1979), ch. 4, esp. p. 131, and Zwicker, *Dryden's Political Poetry*, whose account of the sixteenth- and seventeenth-century applications of political typology, or 'sacred history', in devotional writing and secular literature is illuminating for the student of oratorio (pp. 11, 17–22).

41 Thomas Brereton, *An English Psalm, or, a Hymn on the Late Thanksgiving Day: being a Protestant Version of the Second Psalm* (1716). On eighteenth-century British political identity as Protestant and hence anti-Catholic see Colley, *Britons*, pp. 33–6, 42, 46–8.

42 E.g. George Lavington (Bishop of Exeter), *The Nature and Use of a Type* (1724), p. 3; Edward Chandler (Bishop of Coventry and Lichfield), *A Defence of Christianity from the Prophecies of the Old Testament* (1725), pp. 230, 242; Richard Kidder (Bishop of Bath and Wells), *A Demonstration of the Messias. In which the Truth of the Christian Religion is Proved* (1726), p. 32; David Collyer, *The Sacred Interpreter: or, A Practical Introduction towards a Beneficial Reading, and a thorough Understanding, of the Holy Bible* (1732), pp. 241–3.

43 Charles Rollin, *The Method of Teaching and Studying the Belles Lettres* (1734, Dublin, 4/1742), III [= Book IV, *Of History*], 135–7. The account of Joseph occupies pp. 117–37, within Part II, 'Of Sacred

History' (pp. 89–158); it is one of two sections of Scripture selected by Rollin to demonstrate the benefits of studying sacred history (the other, also occupying twenty pages, concerns 'The miraculous deliverance of Jerusalem under Hezekiah').

44 Joseph is a type of Christ in e.g. Samuel Humphreys, *The Sacred Books of the Old and New Testament, Recited at Large* (1735), I, 122; *Joseph Reviv'd: or The Heavenly Favourite*, (1714), a 56–page commentary on his story as evidence of God's grace (esp. pp. 5–8, 31–3); and *The History of Joseph* (Ipswich, 1736), an improving 58–page poem for 'young People' in which the author has 'endeavour'd every where, to shew, what Circumstances in the History, seem to refer to *Jesus Christ*'.

45 Lavington, *The Nature and Use of a Type*, p. 44.

46 On *Robinson Crusoe* as allegory based in scripture see Robert W. Ayers, '*Robinson Crusoe*: "Allusive Allegorick History"', *PMLA* 82 (1967), 399–407.

47 Lavington, *The Nature and Use of a Type*; Rollin, *Method of Teaching*, III, 93–4; Richard Blome, *The History of the Old and New Testament* (1705), p. 69; Isaac Watts, *Hymns and Spiritual Songs, Book II*, in *Works*, IV, 222.

48 Rollin, *Method of Teaching*, III, 93.

49 Key attacks on such reading were Anthony Collins, *A Discourse of the Grounds and Reasons of the Christian Religion* (1724) (see ch. 6), and chs. 10–11 of Collins' *The Scheme of Literal Prophecy Considered* (1727); and Thomas Woolston, *Six Discourses on the Miracles of our Saviour* (1727–30), no less disturbing for being crude and wild (see Jonathan Swift, 'Lines on the Death of Dr Swift', ll. 281–98, and John Leland, *A Short View of the Principal Deistical Writers that have Appeared in England in the Last and Present Century* (1754, 3/1757), I, 108–20, 127). Collins was anticipated by the first major deist bombshell, John Toland's *Christianity not Mysterious: or, A Treatise shewing, that there is Nothing in the Gospel contrary to Reason, nor above it: and that no Doctrine can properly be Called a Mystery* (1696, 1702), pp. 115–16, and by William Whiston's insistence on a solely literal reading, *The Accomplishment of Scripture Prophecies. Being Eight Sermons Preach'd ... at the Lecture Founded by the hon. Robert Boyle esq.* (1706, 1708). Major defences of dual reading included Chandler, *Defence of Christianity*, pp. 162–218; Daniel Waterland, *Scripture Vindicated* (1731–2) in *Works*, VI (Oxford, 1823), pp. 3–21; and John Leland, *The Divine Authority of the Old and New Testament Asserted ... against ... the Moral Philosopher* (2/1739), pp. 107–15. See Henning Graf Reventlow, trans. John Bowden, *The Authority of the Bible and the Rise of the Modern World* (1984), pp. 294–301, 362–72.

50 *Works*, VI (Oxford, 1823), pp. 3–21.

51 Victor Harris, 'Allegory to Analogy in the Interpretation of Scriptures', *PQ* 45 (1966), 1–23, at 15–21.

52 'From Typology to Literature: Hermeneutics and Historical Narrative in Eighteenth-Century England', *The Eighteenth Century: Theory and*

Interpretation 23 (1982), 181–96, at pp. 188–9. On biblical typology see also Korshin, *Typologies*, ch. 3.

53 Of the thousands of eighteenth-century sermons invaluably catalogued in John Cooke, *The Preacher's Assistant* (Oxford, 1783), a selection of those enlarging on the analogy between the biblical Israelites and the British nation is listed in my 'Handel's Israelite Librettos and English Politics, 1732–52', *GHB* 5 (1993), 195–215, at pp. 214–15. David Armitage has pointed out to me that the sermons of 1707 on the Union of the British kingdoms draw a parallel with the union of Judah and Israel, thus laying the ground for comparing united Britain at this date with 'Israel'. D. Napthine and W. A. Speck, 'Clergymen and Conflict 1660–1763', in *The Church and War (Studies in Church History* 20), ed. W. J. Sheils (Oxford, 1983), pp. 231–51, focusing on the Fast and Thanksgiving sermons, show that the ancient Israel/modern Britain parallel continued to be common past the middle of the century; see also F. Deconinck-Brossard, 'The Churches and the '45', in *The Church and War*, pp. 253–62.

54 Noticed and quoted by Dorothea Siegmund-Schultze, 'Zur gesellschaftlichen Situation in London zur Zeit Händels', *HJb* 32 (1986), 85–98, at p. 96. Miller, *The Cause of Britain's being become a Reproach to her Neighbours ... Roehampton ... January 9 1739* (1740); Morell: *The Surest Grounds for Hopes of Success in War ... Kew ... January 9 1739/40* (1740).

55 Napthine and Speck, 'Clergymen and Conflict'.

56 *The Correspondence of Alexander Pope*, ed. George Sherburn (Oxford, 1956), II, 53; [George Berkeley,] *An Essay towards preventing the Ruin of Great Britain* (1721, repr. 1752), in *The Works of George Berkeley, Bishop of Cloyne*, VI, ed. T. E. Jessop (1953), esp. pp. 69, 71.

57 *The Independent*, 25 July 1993.

58 'The Ideology of Jacobitism on the Eve of the Rising of 1745', *History of European Ideas* 6 (1985), 1–18, 173–88, at p. 6.

59 William Cobbett, *The Parliamentary History of England* (1812), X, col. 1323, XI, cols. 1068–9.

60 Quoted Richard Harding, *Amphibious Warfare in the Eighteenth Century: The British Expedition to the West Indies 1740–1742* (Woodbridge, Suffolk, 1991), p. 107.

61 *Gentleman's Magazine* 18 (1748), 78–80, 105–7. On the significance of Louisbourg and the press campaign in favour of retaining it see Robert Harris, *A Patriot Press: National Politics and the London Press in the 1740s* (Oxford, 1993), pp. 189–91, 222–8, 256.

62 *A Chronological and Historical Account of the Most Memorable Earthquakes that have Happened in the World, from the Beginning of the Christian Period to the Present Year 1750. With an Appendix, containing a Distinct Series of those that have been Felt in England. And a Preface, Seriously Address'd to All Christians of Every Denomination. By a Gentleman of the University of Cambridge* (Cambridge, 1750), pp. iv, xiii; among other publications on the subject see particularly Bishop Thomas Sherlock's pastoral letter *To the Clergy and*

People of London and Westminster (1750) and *A Supplement to the Bishop of London's Letter to the Clergy and People of London and Westminster, on occasion of the Late Earthquakes* (1750).

63 Isaac Newton, *Observations upon the Prophecies of Daniel* (1733); Paul Korshin, 'Queuing and Waiting: The Apocalypse in England, 1660–1750', in *The Apocalypse in English Renaissance Thought and Culture*, ed. C.A. Patrides and J. Wittreich (Manchester, 1984), pp. 240–65.

64 *Birthpangs of Protestant England*, pp. 20–7.

65 *Independent on Sunday*, 18 Feb 1990.

66 *Independent Magazine*, 11 Dec 1993, p. 24.

67 Owing to the work of J. G. A. Pocock, e.g. 'Machiavelli, Harrington and English Political Ideologies in the Eighteenth Century', in *Politics, Language and Time: Essays on Political Thought and History* (New York, 1971, repr. London, 1976), pp. 104–47.

68 *The Political Works of James Harrington*, ed. J. G. A. Pocock (Cambridge, 1977), esp. pp. xi–xiii, 78–81, 90–1; Mark Goldie, 'The Civil Religion of James Harrington', in *The Languages of Political Theory in Early-Modern Europe*, ed. Anthony Pagden (Cambridge, 1987), pp. 197–222; Anna Strumia, *L'immaginazione repubblicana: Sparta e Israel nel dibattito filosofico-politico dell'età di Cromwell* (Turin, 1991).

69 Lowman receives a paragraph in Caroline Robbins' *The Eighteenth-Century Commonwealthman* (Cambridge, MA, 1959), p. 242, pointing out the chief ways in which 'The *Dissertation*, while concentrating on the Hebrews, was quite obviously a moral story for the times', but making no connection with contemporary writers other than Harrington. Robbins describes Lowman as a republican, and it may be argued on this basis that few of his readers would have taken his Israel–Britain model seriously. But he gained a second edition, and I think it would have been quite possible to read his implied recommendations as Old Whiggish without having to see in them a call for the abolition of the monarchy.

70 *Dissertation*, pp. 1–2, 4–7, 59–63, 69, 79, 105, 111–16, 126–7, 130–54, 162, 171, 174–5, 178–89, 191–2, 206, 209, 234–5, 240–1, 244–5, 253–4, 284–5.

71 *Dissertation*, p. 162.

72 *Dissertation*, pp. 60–1.

73 *Dissertation*, pp. 272–9.

74 'Of Heroic Virtue', *Five Essays*, ed S.H. Monk (Ann Arbor, 1962) pp. 98–172.

75 *Defoe's Politics: Parliament, Power, Kingship, and 'Robinson Crusoe'* (Cambridge, 1991).

76 *An Enquiry into the Foundation of the English Constitution; or, An Historical Essay upon the Anglo-Saxon Government both in Germany and England* (1745, 2/1753), pp. 45–6, 53, 62–4, 75–9.

77 For other instances see e.g. Dennis, *Vice and Luxury*, pp. 16, 118; [Aaron Hill,] introduction and notes to *Gideon: or, The Patriot. An Epic Poem: in*

Twelve Books. Upon a Hebrew Plan. In honour of the Two Chief Virtues of a People; Intrepidity in Foreign War: and Spirit of Domestic Liberty (1749), taking issue with Harrington's account of the Jewish state as a republic; Leland, *Divine Authority* (many basic arguments in common with Lowman), I, 54, 130–1; William Warburton, *The Divine Legation of Moses* (1737, 1741), as described by Leslie Stephen, *History of English Thought in the Eighteenth Century* (3/1902), I, vii, 14–19; [Samuel Chandler,] *The Old Whig, or, The Consistent Protestant*, 1735–8 (1738), I, 198–200, 244–50.

78 William L. Barcham, *The Religious Paintings of Giambattista Tiepolo: Piety and Tradition in Eighteenth-Century Venice* (Oxford, 1989), pp. 14–27.

79 Michael Talbot, *Vivaldi* (1978), pp. 59–60.

80 *Lord Bolingbroke: Historical Writings*, ed. Isaac Kramnick (Chicago, 1972), pp. xv–xvii; Bolingbroke, *Works*, II, 177, 179, 181–3, 191, 194, 212, 221, 237. For comment on the recommendation of historical study on humanist grounds by another leading writer of the period, Pope, see Howard Erskine-Hill, *The Augustan Idea in English Literature* (1983), ch. X. For other, less prominent, authors of the same period with the same message see e.g. Rollin, *Method of Teaching*, III, 3–9 ('history, when it is well taught, becomes a school of morality for all mankind'), and Michael Meehan, *Liberty and Poetics in Eighteenth-Century England* (1986), p. 75, on John Brown. For early-eighteenth-century ideas about the moral and polemical purposes of history and how it should be written see also Justin Champion, *The Pillars of Priestcraft Shaken: The Church of England and its Enemies, 1660–1730* (Cambridge, 1992), ch. 2.

81 Bolingbroke, *Historical Writings*, pp. xxxix–xlv, and *Remarks*, footnote to Letter 6. In response, Walpole's writers claimed to be representing history fully and reliably rather than as the opposition did, selectively and tendentiously (Simon Targett, 'Sir Robert Walpole's Newspapers, 1722–42: Propaganda and Politics in the Age of Whig Supremacy', Ph.D. diss., University of Cambridge (1991), pp. 388–90).

82 G. B. Hertz (Hurst), *British Imperialism in the Eighteenth Century* (1908), pp. 42–3; Bonamy Dobrée, 'The Theme of Patriotism in the Poetry of the Early Eighteenth Century', *Proceedings of the British Academy* 35 (1949), 49–65; Jeremy Black, *British Foreign Policy in the Age of Walpole* (Edinburgh, 1985), p. 85. On Pope's use of exemplary history in Bolingbroke's manner see e.g. Brean Hammond, *Pope and Bolingbroke: A Study of Friendship and Influence* (Columbia, MO, 1984), p. 117.

83 Morell, 'A chronological table alphabetically digested by TM 1734', in his Commonplace Book, BL Add. MS 28846, fols. 80–135.

84 *The Tears of Music: A Poem to the Memory of Mr Handel* (1760), pp. 14–15.

CHAPTER 10

1 The librettist of *Joshua* has not so far been identified, but Merlin Channon has persuasively conjectured (in conversation) that it was Newburgh Hamilton.

2 Since the Old Testament is no longer common knowledge, some examples may be necessary. For the deity see e.g. Joshua XXIV (God cannot be served as He requires); Judges III (Israel's constant reversion to idolatry and punishment for it with attacks by enemies is intended by God as a way of developing military skills in new generations); Judges XX (on account of a Levite and his concubine, God directs a civil war to take place: 65,130 are killed, an entire tribe and its towns are eliminated); 2 Samuel XXIV (God creates a 'reason' to kill 70,000 with plague). For the Israelites see e.g. Genesis XLVI (Joseph buys up land and forcibly moves the population around or, according to some versions, enslaves them); Numbers XI (the Israelites complain that Egyptian slavery was preferable to the desert because the food was better); Judges XII (Jephtha's triumph leads to civil war in which 42,000 are killed); 2 Samuel XXIX (David as an undercover agent double-crosses the Philistines). For the flavour of the alliance between God and the Israelites see e.g. Numbers XXI (the Israelites offer to destroy the Canaanites if God will give the necessary assistance; God agrees).

3 *Characteristicks of Men, Manners, Opinions, Times* (6/1738), II, 48. Disgust for the Old Testament God and His chosen people is similarly expressed by (notably) Tindal, Chubb, and Morgan; see Henning Graf Reventlow, trans. John Bowden, *The Authority of the Bible and the Rise of the Modern World* (1984), pp. 311–13, 379–80, 383, 400–2.

4 Thomas Stackhouse, *A New History of the Holy Bible from the Beginning of the World to the Establishment of Christianity* (1737, 1752) I, 539–41; for a similarly laboured defence see e.g. Daniel Waterland, *Scripture Vindicated* (1731–2), in *Works*, VI (Oxford, 1823), 114–17.

5 *Oratorios*, p. 226.

6 *The Sacred Books of the Old and New Testament, Recited at Large* (1735), on Judges IV.17 and V.27.

7 John Leland, *An Answer to a Late Book Intituled, Christianity as Old as the Creation* (2/1740), II, 367–70, and *The Divine Authority of the Old and New Testament Asserted ... against ... the Moral Philosopher* (1739–40), I, 48, 118–30.

8 Thomas R. Preston, 'Biblical Criticism, Literature, and the Eighteenth-Century Reader', in *Books and their Readers in Eighteenth-Century England*, ed. I. Rivers (Leicester, 1982), pp. 97–126, esp. pp. 99, 104, 108, provides a fertile starting point for an investigation of connections between the librettos and the way the Bible was read in the eighteenth century. Matthew Henry's *An Exposition of all the Books of the Old and New Testament* reached its fifth edition in 1761.

9 *The History of the Old Testament in Verse* (1715).

10 Trenchard, *Considerations upon the State of our Public Debts* (1720), pp. 10, 28–9, 31; [James Ralph,] *The Remembrancer ... the Twelve First Essays, from the Weekly Paper* (1748), p. 17.

11 Robert Harris, *A Patriot Press: National Politics and the London Press in the 1740s* (Oxford, 1993), pp. 4, 141. On the national sense that George II was not a *British* monarch see Linda Colley, *Britons: Forging the Nation 1707–1837* (New Haven, 1992), pp. 201–4.

12 On internal political instability in the libretto years see e.g. Paul Monod, *Jacobitism and the English People, 1688–1788* (Cambridge, 1990), chs. 4 and 7; Paul Langford, *A Polite and Commercial People: England, 1727–1783* (Oxford, 1989), pp. 210–12; W. A. Speck, *Stability and Strife: England 1714–60* (1977), pp. 235–7; Nicholas Rogers, *Whigs and Cities: Popular Politics in the Age of Walpole and Pitt* (Oxford, 1989), pp. 67–70.

13 David Armitage, 'The Cromwellian Protectorate and the Languages of Empire', *HJ* 35 (1992), 531–55, at pp. 542–6, 553.

14 See e.g. Harris, *Patriot Press*, p. 77.

15 See e.g. Jeremy Black, *British Foreign Policy in the Age of Walpole* (Edinburgh, 1985), pp. 20–1, 27–45; Langford, *A Polite and Commercial People*, pp. 190–4, 219–20; Speck, *Stability and Strife*, pp. 241–7; Uriel Dann, *Hanover and Great Britain 1740–1760* (Leicester, 1991), pp. 30–5, 48, 58, 60, 68–70, 141; Harris, *Patriot Press*, pp. 95–6, 103–5, 108–10, 116, 119–21, 124–6, 167–8, 177–8, 184–9, 210, 244–5.

16 After 1745 the government and opposition were united in wanting war against France for the sake of trade and colonies, but opinion was soon divided on when and on what terms to conclude the war: see e.g. Harris, *Patriot Press*, ch. 7.

17 On the sense of frustration generated in Britain, especially among the public, by military engagements in the 1740s see e.g. Harris, *Patriot Press*, pp. 5, 94, 159, 170, 176, 183, 192, 228–9, 234, 239–41.

18 Cecil A. Moore, 'Whig Panegyric Verse: A Phase of Sentimentalism', *PMLA* 41 (1926), 362–401, repr. in *Backgrounds to English Literature 1700–1760* (Minneapolis, 1953), pp. 104–44, at pp. 110–11.

19 Harris, *Patriot Press*, p. 237.

20 J. G. A. Pocock, *The Machiavellian Moment* (Princeton, 1975), p. 438, citing *The Political and Commercial Works of Dr Charles D'Avenant*, ed. C. Whitworth (1771), I, 15–16.

21 J. A. W. Gunn, *Beyond Liberty and Property: The Process of Self-Recognition in Eighteenth-Century Political Thought* (Kingston and Montreal, 1983), pp. 27–8; Harris, *Patriot Press*, pp. 56, 88, 250.

22 Manuel Schonhorn, *Defoe's Politics: Parliament, Power, Kingship, and 'Robinson Crusoe'* (Cambridge, 1991), pp. 4–5, 93–4.

23 See e.g. Harris, *Patriot Press*, pp. 27–8, 34, 36, 52, 74, 96, 120–2, 125–8, 149–62, 186–9, 218.

24 'Of Commerce', *Political Discourses* (Edinburgh, 1752), p. 9.

25 J. T. Johnson, *Ideology, Reason, and the Limitation of War: Religious and*

Secular Concepts 1200–1740 (Princeton, 1975), p. 129. See also D. Napthine and W. A. Speck, 'Clergymen and Conflict 1660–1763', in *The Church and War (Studies in Church History* 20), ed. W. J. Sheils (Oxford, 1983), pp. 231–51, at pp. 235–6, 245–6; F. Deconinck-Brossard, 'The Churches and the '45', in *The Church and War*, pp. 253–62, at pp. 254–5, 259–60.

26 Murray Roston, *Biblical Drama in England from the Middle Ages to the Present Day* (1968), p. 185.

27 C. F. Pascoe, *Two Hundred Years of the SPG: An Historical Account of the Society for the Propagation of the Gospel in Foreign Parts, 1701–1900* (1901), pp. xvii, 8–135, 196–242, 254, 319, 322, 368, 374, 386, 468, 837, 849, 932; Carl Bridenbaugh, *Mitre and Sceptre: Transatlantic Faiths, Ideas, Personalities, and Politics 1689–1775* (New York, 1962), pp. 30, 77, 88, 109; John Walsh and Stephen Taylor, 'Introduction: The Church and Anglicanism in the "Long" Eighteenth Century', in *The Church of England c. 1689 – c. 1833: From Toleration to Tractarianism*, ed. John Walsh, Colin Haydon and Stephen Taylor (Cambridge, 1993), pp. 1–66, at p. 15.

28 Frederick Madden with David Fieldhouse, eds., *The Classical Period of the First British Empire, 1689–1783 (Select Documents in the Constitutional History of the British Empire and Commonwealth*, II) (Westport, CT, and London, 1985), pp. xxvi–xxix, describe a 'period of relative inertia from the late 1720s to the 1750s' in the British government's concerns for protection of colonial trade and control of colonial self-government: 'there was in practice no *political* subordination of the colonies' and instead 'a policy of *laissez faire*, procrastination and appeasement'. See also P. J. Marshall, 'The Eighteenth-Century Empire' in *British Politics and Society from Walpole to Pitt, 1742–1789*, ed. J. Black (1990), pp. 177–200, at pp. 182, 185–6; Jeremy Black, *A System of Ambition? British Foreign Policy 1660–1793* (1991), pp. 88, 98, 100.

29 [Thomas Gordon] 'The Vanity of Conquerors, and the Calamities attending Conquests', no. 74 (28 April 1722) in [John Trenchard and Thomas Gordon,] *Cato's Letters: or, Essays on Liberty, Civil and Religious, and other Important Subjects* (4/1737), III, 67–74; [Thomas Gordon (trans.)] *The Works of Tacitus ... to which are Prefixed, Political Discourses upon that Author* (1728), I, 124 (Discourse X, 'Of Armies and Conquest'), both cited by David Armitage, 'The British Empire and the Civic Tradition 1656–1742' Ph.D. diss., University of Cambridge (1991), p. 172. Hume, 'Of Luxury' (*Political Discourses*), attributes 'the disorders in the *Roman* state' to 'an ill-model'd government, and the unlimited extent of conquests' (p. 33).

30 1 Kings V. On mid-century British imperialism and its literary reflection see e.g. Margaret Anne Doody, *The Daring Muse: Augustan Poetry Reconsidered* (Cambridge, 1985), pp. 14–16; G. B. Hertz (Hurst), *British Imperialism in the Eighteenth Century* (1908), pp. 1–6, 37–8; Kathleen Wilson, 'Empire, Trade and Popular Politics in Mid-Hanoverian

Britain: The Case of Admiral Vernon', *Past & Present* 121 (1988), 74–109, at pp. 97–103; David S. Shields, *Oracles of Empire: Poetry, Politics, and Commerce in British America, 1690–1750* (Chicago, 1990), pp. 16, 19–20, 24–5, 224–5. *Pace* Shields, the merchant in *Imperium Pelagi* must *be* religious, but Young says nothing about his *spreading* religion.

31 On the librettos' reflection of the British experience of international alliances see ch. 12. On antipathy to them see Harris, *Patriot Press*, pp. 89, 169, 183–4, 193, 243.

32 Jeremy Black, *Natural and Necessary Enemies: Anglo-French Relations in the Eighteenth Century* (1986), pp. 106–7; Harris, *Patriot Press*, pp. 213–14, 233–7, 239, 252.

33 Thus playing to the Patriot antagonism to Spain of the original merchant audiences. The play had ninety-six performances to 1747 and reached its seventh edition in 1740: George Lillo, *The London Merchant*, ed. William H. McBurney (1965).

34 William Cobbett, *The Parliamentary History of England* (1812), XIII, col. 696 (3 April 1744). The same phrase occurs in the other libretto of 1746, Hamilton's *Occasional Oratorio* (the final air, in which tyrants are depicted opposing 'Religion, Liberty, and Law'); Morell's use may derive from Hamilton's. A similar phrase also occurs at an earlier point in *Judas* (Pt I, Simon's second air: 'In defence of your Nation, Religion, and Laws, / The Almighty *Jehovah* will strengthen your Hands'.

35 Thomas Rowe, 'An Ode on Liberty', in *The Miscellaneous Works in Prose and Verse of Mrs Elizabeth Rowe* (1739), II, 303–22.

36 See e.g. Henry, *Exposition*; William Lowth, *Directions for the Profitable Reading of the Holy Scriptures* (1708, multiple editions into nineteenth century), pp. 15, 77.

37 Joseph Hallet, jnr, *Notes on Several Texts of Scriptures* (1736), vol. III of *A Free and Impartial Study of the Holy Scriptures Recommended* (1729–36), pp. 267–357.

38 From Fénelon's *Dialogues concerning Eloquence*, trans. William Stevenson (1722), p. 159, quoted David Norton, *A History of the Bible as Literature* (Cambridge, 1993), II, 25–6.

39 See W. M. Evans, 'From the Land of Canaan to the Land of Guinea: The Strange Odyssey of the Sons of Ham', *American Historical Review* 85 (1980), 15–43, esp. pp. 15–18.

40 *Christianity as Old as the Creation* (3/1732), pp. 84, 237–8, 245–8, his longest critique of a single instance of Old Testament 'immorality'.

41 Leland, *Answer*, II, 358.

42 A loathing he shares with one of his fellow political propagandists of the 1730s, James Thomson, see above, p. 243. Henry St John, Lord Bolingbroke, *Works* (Philadelphia, 1841), II, 210–11, 215. For the context of Bolingbroke's discussion of biblical genealogy see Alun David, 'Christopher Smart and the Hebrew Bible: Poetry and Biblical Criti-

cism in England (1682–1771)', Ph.D. diss., University of Cambridge (1994), pp. 172–9.

43 Pt III, pp. 30–9.

44 I, 258–9, 269; II, 70–6; III, 183.

45 *A Dissertation on the Civil Government of the Hebrews. In which the True Designs, and Nature of their Government Are Explained* (1740, 2/1745), pp. 24–31, 193–4, 213–30. These arguments are of course standard; see also e.g. Isaac Watts, *A Short View of the Whole Scripture History* (1732), repr. *Works* (1753), III, 360; Waterland, *Scripture Vindicated*, in *Works*, VI, 102–4, 117–22.

46 *The State of the Nation, with a General Balance of the Publick Accounts* (1748), p. 21; [Horace Walpole,] *A Second and Third Letter to the Whigs* (1748), pp. 44–5; Wilson, 'Empire'; Black, *British Foreign Policy*, pp. 108–13; Philip Woodfine, 'The Anglo-Spanish War of 1739', in *The Origins of War in Early Modern Europe*, ed. J. Black (Edinburgh, 1987), pp. 185–209, and 'Ideas of Naval Power and the Conflict with Spain, 1737–42', in *The British Navy and the Use of Naval Power in the Eighteenth Century*, ed. J. Black and P. Woodfine (Atlantic Heights, NJ, 1989), pp. 71–90; Harris, *Patriot Press*, pp. 218–37.

47 *The Great Importance of Cape Breton, Demonstrated and Exemplified* (1746), quoted Harris, *Patriot Press*, p. 225. On the debate about continuing the war, the immense value of Cape Breton in the popular mind and the reaction to French victories in the Low Countries see e.g. Harris, *Patriot Press*, pp. 189–91, 222–8, 234–5, 256.

48 *Oceana*, in *The Political Works of James Harrington*, ed. J. G. A. Pocock (Cambridge, 1977), p. 164; see also pp. 174–7, 199, 236.

49 E.g. *Pian Piano*, in *Works*, ed. Pocock, p. 379; *The Art of Lawgiving*, Bk I chs. 1 and 2, in *Works*, pp. 604–9; 632–5.

50 Harrington: *The Prerogative of Popular Government*, in *Works*, ed. Pocock, p. 444, and *The Art of Lawgiving*, in *Works*, pp. 621–36; Lowman, *Dissertation*, pp. 34–46, 50–5, 190, 245.

51 Dom Augustin Calmet, trans. Nicholas Tindal, *Antiquities Sacred and Profane: Or, a Collection of Curious and Critical Dissertations on the Old and New Testament* (1724, 2/1725), pp. 57–8.

52 Black, *British Foreign Policy*, p. 10; Simon Varey, 'The Craftsman 1726–52', Ph.D. diss., University of Cambridge (1976), pp. 58–9, 127, who interestingly suggests further connections between opposition doctrine and the biblical Caleb's exemplary faith and confidence; Michael Harris, 'Print and Politics in the Age of Walpole', in *Britain in the Age of Walpole*, ed. J. Black (1984), pp. 189–210, at p. 204.

53 H. T. Dickinson, *Liberty and Property: Political Ideology in Eighteenth-Century Britain* (1977), p. 159, and on liberty and the constitution in political writing, pp. 61–5, 140–5, 159–62, 172–5; Isaac Kramnick, *Bolingbroke and his Circle: The Politics of Nostalgia in the Age of Walpole* (Cambridge, MA, 1968), pp. 177–80; Pocock, *Machiavellian Moment*, pp. 359, 407–20, 433–6, 450, 482–3; Gunn, *Beyond Liberty and Property*,

pp. 229–37; Reed Browning, *Political and Constitutional Ideas of the Court Whigs* (Baton Rouge, LA, 1982), pp. 52, 70, 144–7, 197, 201–8 (pointing out that the idea of an ancient constitution was not the exclusive preserve of the opposition); Quentin Skinner, 'The Principles and Practice of Opposition: The Case of Bolingbroke versus Walpole', in *Historical Perspectives . . . in honour of J. H. Plumb*, ed. N. McKendrick (1974), pp. 93–128, at pp. 116–26; in contemporary literature, Alan D. McKillop, *The Background of Thomson's 'Liberty'*, Rice Institute Pamphlet: Monograph in English 38/2 (Houston, 1951), and 'Ethics and Political History in Thomson's *Liberty*', in *Pope and his Contemporaries: Essays presented to George Sherburn*, ed. J. L. Clifford and L. A. Landa (Oxford, 1949), pp. 215–29, at pp. 217, 220; Brean Hammond, *Pope and Bolingbroke: A Study of Friendship and Influence* (Columbia, MO, 1984), pp. 87, 89, 94–5, 132–6; Hugh Cunningham, 'The Language of Patriotism', in *Patriotism: The Making and Unmaking of British National Identity*, ed. R. Samuel (1989), I, *History and Politics*, pp. 58–60; Clement Ramsland, 'Britons Never Will Be Slaves: A Study of Whig Political Propaganda in the British Theatre, 1700–1742', *Quarterly Journal of Speech* 28 (1942), 393–9.

54 Given by God to Moses at Horeb (Exodus XXV.10–22) and installed in the temple by Solomon (1 Kings VIII.6–9).

55 *Craftsman* no. 16, 27 January 1727, quoted Maynard Mack, *The Garden and the City: Retirement and Politics in the Later Poetry of Pope 1731–43* (Toronto, 1969), pp. 117–21; letter quoted Kramnick, *Bolingbroke*, p. 30; Bolingbroke, *Works*, II, 391; Letter 2, in *Lord Bolingbroke: Historical Writings*, ed. Isaac Kramnick (Chicago, 1972), p. 163.

56 On Defoe's references to the Covenant and his monarchical interpretation of it in discussions of contractual government, see Schonhorn, *Defoe's Politics*, pp. 28–9, 151. As Patrick Collinson comments, *The Birthpangs of Protestant England: Religious and Cultural Change in the Sixteenth and Seventeenth Centuries* (1988, repr. 1991), p. 11, 'For political and social purposes the covenant was the most protean and formative of all biblical principles.'

57 *Dissertation*, pp. 8–10, 14–15, 56–7, 80, 126, 216, 360.

58 Schonhorn, *Defoe's Politics*, pp. 5–6, distinguishes between Defoe's and Bolingbroke's ideals of a Patriot King: oratorio unites them.

59 Howard D. Weinbrot, *Augustus Caesar in 'Augustan' England* (Princeton, 1978), pp. 47, 52–3, 70, 72, 113, 120–9, and *Britannia's Issue: The Rise of British Literature from Dryden to Ossian* (Cambridge, 1993), pp. 39–47.

60 *Dissertation*, pp. 14–15, 215.

61 Hobbes: *Leviathan* (1651), chs. XIV and XVII; Locke: *Two Treatises of Government* (1690); Hume: 'Of the Original Contract' in *Three Essays* (1748).

62 Samuel Squire, *An Enquiry into the Foundation of the English Constitution; or, An Historical Essay upon the Anglo-Saxon Government both in Germany and England* (1745, 2/1753), pp. 45–6, 53–4, 75–9, 83–94; R. J. Smith, *The*

Gothic Bequest: Medieval Institutions in British Political Thought, 1688–1832 (Cambridge, 1986).

63 *Enquiry*, p. 3.

64 'Principles and Practice of Opposition', pp. 117, 122.

65 *Bolingbroke: Historical Writings*, ed. Kramnick, p. xxiii.

66 See similarly *Judas Macchabæus*, II, 'Victorious hero!'; *Samson*, III.3, 'There shall all *Isr'el*'s valiant Youth resort', 'The Virgins too'; *Deborah*, III.3, 'If, *Jael*, I aright divine', 'The glorious Sun', 'Low at her Feet'; *Belshazzar*, II.3, 'O glorious Prince!'; *Joshua*, III.1, 'Hail! mighty *Joshua*', III.2, 'In bloom of Youth'; *Solomon*, II.3, 'Swell, swell the full Chorus to *Solomon*'s Praise'; *Jephtha*, III.1, 'Happy, *Iphis*', III.2, 'Let me congratulate'.

67 On contemporary performances of Hill's much altered version and Shakespeare's original see below, ch. 14 n.5. Both contain splendid instances of the emotional charge afforded by the 'future perfect' mode in Henry's reply to the French ambassadors and the Agincourt speech. Hill added to these, e.g. the princess at the end of Act III: 'Ages to come, when they shall hear the fame / Of my just act, shall bless my living name' (a formula found elsewhere in Patriot drama and perhaps derived from the Magnificat).

68 *Works*, II, 176; see also II, 373.

69 *Coriolanus* (1749), in *Works* (1766), IV, 272; cf. Queen Eleonora, offering to die to spare her husband's life: 'what am I, with nameless numbers weigh'd? / With myriads yet unborn?' (*Edward and Eleonora*, 1739, *Works*, IV, 36).

70 For *Alfred* see ch. 12.

71 Polybius, *The Histories*, VI.51, 57; Messrs G. Trollope (London), *Gopsall, Leicestershire, Catalogue of ... the Extensive Library*, 14 October 1918.

72 Dennis, *Vice and Luxury Publick Mischiefs* (1724), pp. 16, 118; [Thomas Gordon (trans.),] *Works of Tacitus*, esp. Discourses II–X, and esp. headings to Discourses IV-VII; George, Lord Lyttelton, *Epistle to Mr Pope* (1730), ll. 10–12; Thomson, *Liberty* (1735) (compare Dr Alured Clarke to Mrs Charlotte Clayton, 17 September 1734, *James Thomson (1700–1748): Letters and Documents*, ed. Alan D. McKillop (Lawrence, KS, 1958), pp. 88–9); [Trenchard and Gordon,] *Cato's Letters*, I, 117–23 (no. 18, 25 February 1719/20, 'The terrible Tendency of Publick Corruption to ruin a State, exemplified in that of Rome, and applied to our own'); John Dyer, *The Ruins of Rome* (1740); Thomson, *Winter* (1744), ll. 498–529; Thomas Blackwell, *Memoirs of the Court of Augustus* (1753), I, Bk 3 (and see Michael Meehan, *Liberty and Poetics in Eighteenth-Century England* (1986), pp. 46–7); Dyer, *The Fleece* (1757), II, 328–38. James Sambrook, *The Eighteenth Century: The Intellectual and Cultural Context of English Literature, 1700–1789* (1986), pp. 169–75, in an excellent summary of the lessons drawn from Rome, also notes constant references to its history in parliamentary debates and makes the

connection with the actual ruins of Rome, a central experience of the grand tour.

73 *Works*, II, 397.
74 I, 231.
75 J/H 17 February 1742/3.
76 Kramnick, *Bolingbroke*, pp. 208, 247, 254; Bolingbroke, *Works*, II, 107, 152. For Jennens' *Cyrus* see ch. 13.
77 Lawrence Goldstein, *Ruins and Empire: The Evolution of a Theme in Augustan and Romantic Literature* (Pittsburgh, PA, 1977), pp. 52, 55. For an illuminating contemporary juxtaposition of industry and frugality (leading to strength) with credit and luxury (leading to decay), see [George Berkeley,] *An Essay towards preventing the Ruin of Great Britain* (1721, repr. 1752), in *The Works of George Berkeley, Bishop of Cloyne*, VI, ed. T. E. Jessop (1953), pp. 71–9.
78 'Of Luxury', pp. 35–7.
79 *The Lives of the Roman Poets* (1733), I, 64. Sambrook notes that 'When it was not in practical use, Virgil's *Georgics* provided tags for nearly every eighteenth-century writer on rural subjects' (*Eighteenth Century*, pp. 173–4). As noted above, it also provided the epigraph for *Joshua*.
80 *Dissertation*, p. 216.
81 *Dissertation*, pp. 48–9.
82 *Dissertation*, p. 190.
83 Gunn, *Beyond Liberty and Property*, pp. 110–11, see also p. 12; Hammond, *Pope and Bolingbroke*, p. 67.
84 Dean, *Oratorios*, pp. 40, 250, 251, 331, 560, 564, 566, 594–5, 601. Dean recognises the librettist's disgust for pagan mores in *Theodora*. Rosamond McGuinness and H. Diack Johnstone, 'Concert Life in England I', in *The Blackwell History of Music in Britain: The Eighteenth Century*, ed. Johnstone and Roger Fiske (Oxford, 1990), pp. 31–95, at p. 85, note the 'irresponsibly pagan gaiety' of some of the music Handel gives to the Israelites' 'frivolous or unprincipled enemies' without falling into the error of assuming Handel approves the frivolity.
85 J/H 15 September 1743.
86 See ch. 9.
87 *Virtue Transformed: Political Argument in England, 1688–1740* (Cambridge, 1992), pp. 42–63.
88 Mack, *The Garden and the City*, pp. 141–50, 152; Kramnick, *Bolingbroke*, p. 30; Thomson, *Letters*, ed. McKillop, p. 98 (letter to Aaron Hill); Hill, *Works* (2/1754), II, 2 (letter to Bolingbroke, 25 June 1738). In his *Prompter* of 14 February 1734/5 Hill had praised the second part of Thomson's *Liberty* for its 'sermon against corruption' (Bertrand A. Goldgar, *Walpole and the Wits: The Relation of Politics to Literature 1722–1742* (Lincoln, NE, 1976), p. 144); Miller: *Seasonable Reproof, or, A Satire, in the manner of Horace* (1735).
89 *Dissertation*, pp. 226, 356.
90 *Dissertation*, pp. 56, 216.

91 This account of the position of the government writers William Arnall and James Pitt is taken from Burtt, *Virtue Transformed*, pp. 113–27.

92 Mack, *The Garden and the City*, esp. pp. 65–9, 89–91, 232–3. See also Browning, *Court Whigs*, pp. 13, 28; Dickinson, *Liberty and Property*, p. 173; Pocock, *Machiavellian Moment*, pp. 430–1, 435–6, 458–9, 466, 486; Kramnick, *Bolingbroke*, pp. 223–6; Frank McLynn, 'The Ideology of Jacobitism on the Eve of the Rising of 1745', *History of European Ideas* 6 (1985), 1–18, 173–88, at p. 174.

93 Letter to Elizabeth Young, 29 August 1743, Thomson, *Letters*, ed. McKillop, p. 166.

94 Dean, *Oratorios*, pp. 404, 504.

95 See ch. 9 and Napthine and Speck, 'Clergymen and Conflict', pp. 232, 238–9, 244, 246.

96 *Birthpangs of Protestant England*, p. 18.

97 This was a real possibility for interpreters of the Israel–Britain parallel in the seventeenth century: see Collinson, *Birthpangs of Protestant England*, pp. 18–22.

98 *The Correspondence of Alexander Pope*, ed. George Sherburn (Oxford, 1956), III, 163. See likewise [Berkeley,] *Essay*; John Brown, *An Estimate of the Manners and Principles of the Times* (1757–8), I, 14–16.

99 *Works*, II, 375.

100 Preachers: Napthine and Speck, 'Clergymen and Conflict', pp. 232, 234–5, 238. Moralists: e.g. [Berkeley,] *Essay*, pp. 69–79; Brown, *Estimate*, I, 165. Moral politicians: Bolingbroke's declared aim of moral reform, shared with Swift and Pope and his followers, has been widely noticed, see e.g. Jeffrey Hart, *Viscount Bolingbroke: Tory Humanist* (1965), pp. 96–7, 134–5; Kramnick, *Bolingbroke*, p. 168; Hammond, *Pope and Bolingbroke*, pp. 141–2.

101 Bolingbroke: e.g. *Works*, II, 411, 413; [Berkeley,] *Essay*, pp. 79–84; Brown, *Estimate*, I, 72; preachers: Napthine and Speck, 'Clergymen and Conflict', pp. 234–5.

102 [Berkeley,] *Essay*, pp. 84–5; Brown, *Estimate*, II, 251–9; Bolingbroke, *Works*, II, 396–7, 408.

103 E.g. Hart, *Viscount Bolingbroke*, pp. 96–7; Hammond, *Pope and Bolingbroke*, pp. 141–2. On Pope's projected epic, *Brutus*, as 'pointing the means for redemption or restoration' see Donald T. Torchiana, 'Brutus: Pope's Last Hero', *Journal of English and Germanic Philology* 61 (1962), 853–67, at p. 854.

104 *Dissertation*, p. 187.

105 On anthem in Handelian oratorio see ch. 3.

106 Others include the calling of Barak in *Deborah*, of Abner in *Athalia*, of Judas in *Judas Macchabæus*, and of Jephtha.

CHAPTER 11

1 Geoffrey Brereton, *Jean Racine: A Critical Biography* (1951), pp. 258–9.

2 For Arbuthnot's creative role in these circles see Graydon Beeks, '"A Club of Composers": Handel, Pepusch and Arbuthnot at Cannons', in *Handel Tercentenary Collection*, ed. Stanley Sadie and Anthony Hicks (1987), pp. 209–21.
3 The title page of Elizabeth Legh's copy reads 'The Oratorium. Composed by George Frederick Handel. Esquire, in London 1718' (J. Simon ed., *Handel: A Celebration of His Life and Times* (1985), p. 187). It is universally identified with the 'Oratorium' by Handel listed with the rest of the Cannons music (C. H. Collins Baker and Muriel Baker, *The Life and Circumstances of James Brydges First Duke of Chandos* (Oxford, 1949), p. 139, item 123).
4 Dean, *Oratorios*, p. 197.
5 HMC Egmont MSS, Diary, I, 225; Deutsch pp. 285–6.
6 Deutsch p. 285, citing Baker, *Chandos*, p. 91: 'last winter [i.e. 1731/2] Chandos had been "admitted into the Society of the Gentlemen Performers of Musick"'.
7 Beeks, 'Club of Composers', p. 212.
8 *Daily Journal*, cited Deutsch p. 288.
9 For the contretemps over the *Epistle*, which included mention of 'Mr. Hendel's Noble *Oratories*' for Chandos, and the usefulness to Pope of the public linking of his name with *Esther* in 1732, see George Sherburn, '"Timon's Villa" and Cannons', *Huntington Library Bulletin* 8 (1935), 131–52, esp. pp. 144–6.
10 *Minor Poems*, ed. Norman Ault and John Butt, *The Poems of Alexander Pope*, VI (1954), pp. 423–35: 'The probabilities on the whole seem to be in favour of Pope's authorship' (p. 434); Dean, *Oratorios*, p. 194, opposes their statement that the libretto's debt to Racine 'is not large either in plot or dialogue' by pointing out that nearly every line of the libretto is paraphrased from Racine, though 'the numerous affinities of word and phrase suggest that Brereton rather than the original French was the source'. On Pope's possible authorship see also M. R. Brownell, 'Ears of an Untoward Make: Pope and Handel', *Musical Quarterly* 62 (1976), 554–70, persuasively contesting the notion that Pope was unmusical and had a low opinion of Handel. For Pope's admiration of Handel see also ch. 2.
11 Marie Ruan Hopkinson, *Married to Mercury: A Sketch of Lord Bolingbroke and his Wives* (1936), pp. 137–8. The Marquis died in 1707, and Lady Bolingbroke in 1718.
12 G. Davies and M. Tinling, 'Letters from James Brydges, Created Duke of Chandos, to Henry St John, Created Viscount Bolingbroke', *Huntington Library Bulletin* 9 (1936), 119–66.
13 Angus Ross, 'The Correspondence of Dr John Arbuthnot', Ph.D. diss., University of Cambridge (1956), pp. 614, 700.
14 Dean, *Oratorios*, p. 197, notes that three early Dublin librettos give Arbuthnot as author; so does the posthumous edition of his works (1751). On Arbuthnot's brother Robert's activities as a Jacobite soldier

and banker (for, among others, Chandos) see Ross, 'Correspondence of Arbuthnot', pp. 87, n.6, 803.

15 See ch. 10. For an example of the power of the Esther myth to affect later history, see the *Independent on Sunday*, 27 February 1994 (the Hebron massacre was deliberately carried out during the feast of Purim which celebrates the outcome of the Esther story).

16 *Des révolutions d'Angleterre à la révolution française* (The Hague, 1973), pp. 119–47.

17 On Brydges as a Jacobite supporter see ch. 8, 'Handel'.

18 On the feared invasion see e.g. Jeremy Black, *A System of Ambition? British Foreign Policy 1660–1793* (1991), p. 81.

19 *Daily Journal*, 2 May 1732, cited Deutsch pp. 288–9.

20 Biblical texts: ch. 6; historical record: ch. 9; music theatre: see Christine Gerrard, *The Patriot Opposition to Walpole: Politics, Poetry, and National Myth, 1725–1742* (Oxford, 1994), pp. 119–20, 172–4.

21 Dean, *Oratorios*, p. 205.

22 Norman Sykes, *Edmund Gibson, Bishop of London* (1926), pp. 117–22.

23 Sykes, *Gibson*, pp. 145–6.

24 Deutsch p. 460; Bertrand A. Goldgar, *Walpole and the Wits: The Relation of Politics to Literature 1722–1742* (Lincoln, NE, 1976), pp. 215–16.

25 Sykes, *Gibson*, pp. 131–4.

26 *The Sacred Books of the Old and New Testament, Recited at Large* (1735), on Esther VII. Humphreys also points out that Haman was an Amalekite, and so by birth inevitably at enmity with the Jews; he suggests that this was why Mordecai refused to show Haman respect (on the significance of the Amalekites see ch. 13).

27 Dean, *Oratorios*, p. 642.

28 Howard Erskine-Hill, 'Literature and the Jacobite Cause: Was there a Rhetoric of Jacobitism?' in *Ideology and Conspiracy: Aspects of Jacobitism, 1689–1759*, ed. E. Cruickshanks (Edinburgh, 1982), pp. 49–69; A. H. Shapiro, '"Drama of an Infinitely Superior Nature": The Relationship of Handel's First English Oratorios to Early-Eighteenth-Century Sacred Music Theory and Practice', M.Litt. thesis, University of Cambridge (1988), pp. 107–12.

29 Lutaud, *Des révolutions d'Angleterre. Killing no Murder* (1657) was reissued in 1689, 1708, 1734, 1743 (*recte* 1748) and 1749.

30 *Athaliah, A Tragedy Translated from the French of Monsieur Racine* (1722), cited ch. 2.

31 Humphreys, *Sacred Books*, on 2 Kings XI.1. Humphreys' retelling of the story here amounts to a synopsis of his libretto.

32 Paul Langford, 'Tories and Jacobites 1714–51', in *The History of the University of Oxford*, V: *The Eighteenth Century*, ed. L. S. Sutherland and L. G. Mitchell (Oxford, 1986), pp. 99–127.

33 John, Lord Hervey, *Some Materials towards Memoirs of the Reign of King George II*, ed. Romney Sedgwick (1931), I, 171, cited Shapiro, 'Drama', p. 113.

34 *Athalia*, III.1, 4; Paul Monod, *Jacobitism and the English People 1688–1788* (Cambridge, 1989), pp. 70–2.

35 Philip Brett and George Haggerty, 'Handel and the Sentimental: The Case of *Athalia*', *M&L* 68 (1987), 112–27, at p. 115; Dean, *Oratorios*, p. 256.

36 Shapiro, 'Drama', pp. 120–1; Dean, *Oratorios*, p. 633. Shapiro discusses the possible Nonjuring and Hanoverian readings of the libretto at greater length than is possible here, 'Drama', pp. 113–22.

CHAPTER 12

1 Deutsch pp. 481–3.

2 Deutsch pp. 478–80.

3 On Frederick as opposition figurehead and as patron of the arts see now Christine Gerrard, *The Patriot Opposition to Walpole: Politics, Poetry, and National Myth, 1725–1742* (Oxford, 1994), esp. chs. 2 and 3 and references; for a good summary of his relationship with the opposition see Betty Kemp, 'Frederick, Prince of Wales', in *Silver Renaissance: Essays in Eighteenth-Century English History*, ed. Alex Natan (1961), pp. 38–56.

4 See also chs. 7 and 9.

5 F. G. Stephen, E. Hawkins and M. D. George, *Catalogue of Prints and Drawings in the British Museum*, I, *Political and Personal Satires* III/1 (1877), nos. 2355, 2353 and see also no. 2347.

6 William Cobbett, *The Parliamentary History of England* (1812), X, col. 1042.

7 Deutsch p. 479 (5 April 1739).

8 8 June 1739: *James Thomson (1700–1748): Letters and Documents*, ed. Alan D. McKillop (Lawrence, KS, 1958), p. 83.

9 On the possibility that Brooke aimed at having his play censored so that it could be published by subscription, and on the nature of the subscription, see W. A. Speck, 'Politicians, Peers, and Publication by Subscription 1700 50', in *Books and their Readers in Eighteenth-Century England*, ed. I. Rivers (Leicester, 1982), pp. 47–68, at pp. 58–9, 62.

10 From the evidence of a later work Gerrard infers that Brooke was staunchly Whig, but points out that this did not prevent critics from reading his play as pro-Jacobite (*Patriot Opposition*, ch. 8).

11 James D. Garrison, *Dryden and the Tradition of Panegyric* (Berkeley, 1975), pp. 102–3; Edward Hawkins, *Medallic Illustrations of the History of Great Britain and Ireland to the Death of George II*, ed. A. W. Franks and H. A. Grueber (1885), I, 462–3 and plates XLIV.3–5.

12 Rosamond McGuinness, *English Court Odes 1660–1820* (Oxford, 1971), p. 68.

13 *Poetical Works*, ed. Clarence Tracy (Cambridge, 1962), p. 21.

14 'New Jacobite Songs of the Forty-Five', *Studies in Voltaire and the Eighteenth Century* 267 (1989), 1–75, at p. 31.

15 J/H 10 July 1741.

16 J/H 21 February 1742/3: 'I am not at all surpris'd at the clamours rais'd against Messiah, since I remember a R^t. R. [Right Reverend] took offence at Exodus. I hope this will not engage you in a Quarrel with the bench [of bishops]. They are a terrible body.'

17 J/H 10 July 1741; Donald Burrows, 'Israel in Egypt', *Maryland Handel Festival Programme Booklet* (Bethesda, 1987), p. 33.

18 The libretto as we know it reflects revision and expansion in 1742, see Dean, *Oratorios*, pp. 346–8. A manuscript is among the copies of librettos of Handel's oratorios submitted to the Licenser now in the Larpent Collection, Huntington Library, San Marino, CA; it is in Hamilton's hand.

19 For fuller discussion of *Samson* than is possible here see my 'Intellectual Contexts of Handel's English Oratorios', in *Music in Eighteenth-Century England: Essays in memory of Charles Cudworth*, ed. Christopher Hogwood and Richard Luckett (Cambridge, 1982), pp. 115–33, esp. pp. 116–18.

20 Dustin Griffin, *Regaining Paradise: Milton and the Eighteenth Century* (Cambridge, 1986), pp. 7, 14–16, 279 n. 37.

21 Griffin, *Regaining Paradise*, touches on Hamilton's libretto (pp. 69–70) and Thomson's *Alfred* (pp. 60, 179), but does not mention the similarities between them or between Milton's poem and Thomson's masque.

22 *Alfred: An Epick Poem in Twelve Books, Dedicated to the Illustrious Prince Frederick of Hanover* (1723), dedication and pp. xxxii–xxxiv; 'An Essay upon Epick Poetry', in *Essays upon Several Subjects*, I (1716), pp. 49–51. For modern comment deploring the inactivity of the first two acts of *Samson* see e.g. Dean, *Oratorios*, pp. 326–7, 330.

23 Roger Fiske, *English Theatre Music in the Eighteenth Century* (1973, 2/Oxford, 1986), p. 143, notes that both end with a preview of later English royalty and a tableau of the present royal family in glory and describes the similar ending of *Alfred* (p. 190), but does not make a connection between them. For *Hengist and Horsa* see Hill, *Dramatic Works* (1760).

24 Reed Browning, *Political and Constitutional Ideas of the Court Whigs* (Baton Rouge, LA, 1982), pp. 138–9, 144–7; Alan D. McKillop, 'The Early History of *Alfred*', *PQ* 41 (1962), 311–24, *The Background of Thomson's 'Liberty'*, Rice Institute Pamphlet: Monograph in English 38/2 (Houston, 1951), sec. VI, and 'Ethics and Political History in Thomson's *Liberty*', in *Pope and his Contemporaries: Essays presented to George Sherburn*, ed. J. L. Clifford and L. A. Landa (Oxford, 1949), pp. 215–29, at pp. 227–8. H. T. Dickinson, *Bolingbroke* (1970), notes (p. 259) that, according to Mallet, Bolingbroke wrote the last three stanzas of 'Rule Britannia'. McKillop, 'Early History', and Christine Gerrard, 'The Patriot Opposition to Sir Robert Walpole: A Study of Politics and Poetry, 1725–1742', D.Phil. diss., University of Oxford (1986), p. 272, note that the press widely reported the 1740 Cliveden performance and drew attention to its lesson to Frederick. On English masque tradition as practised by the greatest words-and-music collaborators of the pre-

vious century, Dryden and Purcell, see e.g. Dryden, *Albion and Albanius*, preface, final sentence of main text and final paragraph of postscript.

25 Letter to her sister Sarah Robinson, *The Letters of Mrs Elizabeth Montagu*, ed. Matthew Montagu (1809), II, 66; Paul Monod, *Jacobitism and the English People 1688–1788* (Cambridge, 1989), pp. 70–2.

26 On the textual history of *Alfred* see McKillop, 'Early History', and Michael Burden, *The Masque of Alfred* (Lewiston, NY, 1994).

27 Robert Harris, *A Patriot Press: National Politics and the London Press in the 1740s* (Oxford, 1993), pp. 96–7.

28 On Admiral Vernon as opposition hero see Kathleen Wilson, 'Empire, Trade and Popular Politics in Mid-Hanoverian Britain: The Case of Admiral Vernon', *Past & Present* 121 (1988), 74–109; Gerald Jordan and Nicholas Rogers, 'Admirals as Heroes: Patriotism and Liberty in Hanoverian England', *Journal of British Studies* 28 (1989), 201–24, at pp. 202–11; Nicholas Rogers, *Whigs and Cities: Popular Politics in the Age of Walpole and Pitt* (Oxford 1989), pp. 235–40. For a description of Fielding's mock epic *Vernoniad*, voicing opposition outrage at the government's (supposed) mishandling of Vernon during the war, see Thomas R. Cleary, *Henry Fielding: Political Writer* (Waterloo, Ont., 1984), pp. 147–9. Patriotic outrage on the home front was fuelled by a series of publications during and after the campaign, purportedly or genuinely written by those involved; for these, and for the facts of Vernon's and the government's conduct, see Richard Harding, *Amphibious Warfare in the Eighteenth Century: The British Expedition to the West Indies 1740–1742* (Woodbridge, Suffolk, 1991), pp. 5–6, 106–49.

29 See Harding, *Amphibious Warfare*, pp. 5–6, 106–49. The *Account of the Expedition to Cartagena* (1743) by Charles Knowles, Vernon's chief engineer, casting the blame for Cartagena entirely on Wentworth, circulated in London in MS from late 1741. On the relevance of Strafford's politics see ch. 8, 'Hamilton'.

30 Uriel Dann, *Hanover and Great Britain 1740–1760* (Leicester, 1991), pp. 35–40; Harris, *Patriot Press*, pp. 103–4, 119.

31 Harris, *Patriot Press*, pp. 105, 149.

32 Harris, *Patriot Press*, pp. 120–1, 127–30; Averyl Edwards, *Frederick Louis, Prince of Wales 1707–1751* (1947), pp. 106–7.

33 Rohan Butler, *Choiseul*, I, *Father and Son* (Oxford, 1980), pp. 334–5; Harris, *Patriot Press*, p. 140.

34 Edwards, *Frederick Louis*, pp. 140–1.

35 Harris, *Patriot Press*, pp. 153–66.

36 Howard E. Smither, *A History of the Oratorio*, II, *The Oratorio in the Baroque Era* (Chapel Hill, NC, 1977), p. 298.

37 Dean, *Oratorios*, p. 463.

38 Butler, *Father and Son*, pp. 648–63.

39 Not surprisingly, these sentiments are also the material of the 1745 Fast sermons, which make full use of the Israel–Britain analogy; see D. Napthine and W. A. Speck, 'Clergymen and Conflict 1660–1763',

The Church and War (Studies in Church History 20), ed. W. J. Sheils (Oxford, 1983), pp. 231–51, at p. 242; F. Deconinck-Brossard, 'The Churches and the '45', *The Church and War*, pp. 253–62. On the anxiety generated by the Rebellion, see e.g. Linda Colley, *Britons: Forging the Nation 1707–1837* (New Haven, 1992), p. 86.

40 *Odes on Several Descriptive and Allegoric Subjects* (1747, *recte* 1746).

41 Harris, *Patriot Press*, pp. 223–35. As Harris describes, the situation and opinion changed again in 1747–8.

42 Dean, *Oratorios*, pp. 482–4; see likewise Smither, *Oratorio*, II, 308; Christopher Hogwood, *Handel* (1984), p. 209.

43 *Tatler* no. 82 (18 October 1709), in which Steele shows complete disregard for any connection between character and action.

44 For Morell's classical and other literary work see John Nichols, *Literary Anecdotes of the Eighteenth Century* (1812–15, repr. New York, 1966), I, 652–5.

45 In the introduction to his *Prometheus in Chains, Translated from the Greek of Aeschylus* (1773), Morell endorsed this view. It reflects mainstream thought of the time about Greek tragedy, see ch. 2.

46 E.g. [Horace Walpole,] *A Second and Third Letter to the Whigs* (1748), pp. 45–6, 62, 88. Jeremy Black, 'The Tory View of Eighteenth-Century British Foreign Policy', *HJ* 31 (1988), 469–77, at pp. 473–4. On the 'difficulty of alliance politics' in the pre-war years see e.g. Black, *British Foreign Policy in the Age of Walpole* (Edinburgh, 1985), pp. 7–22; on public criticism of Britain's allies see Harris, *Patriot Press*, pp. 89, 169, 183–4, 193, 243.

47 On the diplomacy of the years of the War of Austrian Succession see e.g. Paul Langford, *The Eighteenth Century, 1688–1815* (1976), pp. 119–30; Jeremy Black, *Natural and Necessary Enemies: Anglo-French Relations in the Eighteenth Century* (1986), pp. 36–51.

48 J. G. A. Pocock, *Virtue, Commerce, and History: Essays on Political Thought and History, chiefly in the Eighteenth Century* (Cambridge, 1985), p. 9. An earlier treatment in English music theatre of the theme of undependable allies – *The Siege of Rhodes* – has also been read as a text for its times, by Curtis Price, 'Political Allegory in Late-Seventeenth-Century English Opera', in *Music and Theatre: Essays in honour of Winton Dean*, ed. Nigel Fortune (1987), pp. 1–29, at pp. 4–5.

CHAPTER 13

1 Lady Irwin to Lord Carlisle, 27 February 1733, HMC Carlisle, 15th Report, App., Pt VI, p. 102.

2 [Thomas Morgan,] *The Moral Philosopher* (1737–40, 2/1738–40), I, 239–41, III, 6–24; Samuel Chandler, 'A Defence of the Prime Ministry and Character of Joseph in answer to the Misrepresentations and Calumnies of the Late Thomas Morgan, M.D. and Moral Philosopher', in *A Vindication of the History of the Old Testament* (1743), pp. 257–610;

John Chapman, *Eusebius: or, The True Christian's Defense against a Late Book Entitul'd The Moral Philosopher*, II (1741), vi–xv; *A Review of the Moral and Political Life and Administration of the Patriarch Joseph: with some Remarks on the Ways and Means by him taken to Enslave the Egyptian Nation, and some Reflections on the Customs and Ceremonies of the Ancient Egyptians and Israelites* (1743), expressing grave anxiety about pro-Joseph works being used in schools and propagating enthusiasm for arbitrary government among the young; Peter Annet, *The History of Joseph Consider'd: or, The Moral Philosopher Vindicated against Mr. Samuel Chandler's Defence of the Prime Ministry and Character of Joseph* (1744).

3 *Oratorios*, pp. 403, 406.

4 Autograph, BL RM 20 e 10; the latter change is evident from the printed libretto, where Miller's wording survives, with a footnote explaining that '*Zaphnath-Paaneah* signifies *Saviour of the World*' (I.4). This naming is a transcription of Genesis XLI.45.

5 Duncan Chisholm, 'New Sources for the Libretto of Handel's *Joseph*', in *Handel Tercentenary Collection*, ed. Stanley Sadie and Anthony Hicks (1988), pp. 182–208.

6 Dean, *Oratorios*, pp. 398–402, 407, Deutsch pp. 586–7, 590. The only modern examination hitherto of the libretto as a political document, Chisholm, 'New Sources', unfortunately misses the possibility of reading *Joseph* as a picture of good government by a virtuous prime minister *contra* Walpole's and his successors' administrations. Chisholm fails to distinguish between court Whig and opposition Whig utterances, and ignores the Patriot opposition literature and Miller's work within it (this also leads to a misreading of Rowe's 'Ode on Liberty' as a picture of the present, whereas Rowe actually locates liberty, in true Patriot opposition style, in *past* ages: see ch. 10, 'Continuity'). Chisholm is unsure of Miller's drift and suggests that Joseph may represent George II, which seems implausible, given that the libretto has an actual king in it in the character of Pharaoh.

7 On Miller's part in the English word-setting lobby see ch. 2.

8 No monarch: *Deborah, Samson, Judas Macchabæus, Joshua, Susanna, Theodora, Jephtha*. Flawed native monarch: *Athalia, Saul*. Foreign monarch: *Esther* (Esther herself is not a *ruler*), *Israel in Egypt, Joseph, Belshazzar, Alexander Balus*.

9 Manuel Schonhorn, *Defoe's Politics: Parliament, Power, Kingship, and 'Robinson Crusoe'* (Cambridge, 1991), pp. 4–8, 93–4, 111–23, 126–7.

10 Saul/Charles I and James II: see below; Haman/Walpole and Joash/Stuart restoration: see ch. 11.

11 Steven N. Zwicker, *Dryden's Political Poetry: The Typology of King and Nation* (Providence, RI, 1972), p. 30 notes that in late sixteeenth-century political typology Queen Elizabeth was Deborah, Judith and Esther. On Elizabeth's eighteenth-century Patriot incarnation, see Christine Gerrard, *The Patriot Opposition to Walpole: Politics, Poetry, and National Myth, 1725–1742* (Oxford, 1994), ch. 6.

12 Rosamond McGuinness, *English Court Odes 1660–1820* (Oxford, 1971). Linda Colley, *Britons: Forging the Nation 1707–1837* (New Haven, 1992), p. 204, points out the dearth of images of the first two Georges as great Old Testament monarchs: they were actually disinclined to have the potentially embarrassing comparison made.

13 On the desire for a leader see e.g. John Trenchard, *Considerations upon the State of our Public Debts* (1720), pp. 10, 28–9, 31; for a restatement in 1748 see e.g. [James Ralph,] *The Remembrancer ... the Twelve First Essays, from the Weekly Paper* (1748), p. 17. On the national sense that George II was not a *British* monarch see Colley, *Britons*, pp. 201–4.

14 This is the context of Patrick Delany's *An Historical Account of the Life and Reign of David, King of Israel* (1740–2), which probably influenced Christopher Smart's *Song to David*; see Arthur Sherbo, *Christopher Smart, Scholar of the University* (East Lansing, MI, 1967), pp. 172–4; Moira Dearnley, *The Poetry of Christopher Smart* (1968), pp. 169–78; Alun David, 'Christopher Smart and the Hebrew Bible: Poetry and Biblical Criticism in England (1682–1771)', Ph.D. diss., University of Cambridge (1994), pp. 148–50.

15 Murray Pittock, 'New Jacobite Songs of the Forty-Five', *Studies in Voltaire and the Eighteenth Century* 267 (1989), 1–75, at p. 45, and *Poetry and Jacobite Politics in Eighteenth-Century Britain and Ireland* (Cambridge, 1994), pp. 68–9.

16 Paul Henry Lang, *George Frideric Handel* (1967), p. 464; Howard E. Smither, *A History of the Oratorio*, II, *The Oratorio in the Baroque Era* (Chapel Hill, NC, 1977), p. 320 (*Solomon* 'would surely have been seen in its time as a glorification of King George II and his England').

17 John Potter (Bishop of Oxford), *A Sermon Preach'd at the Coronation of King George II ... October 11 1727* (1727). J. C. D. Clark, *English Society 1688–1832: Ideology, Social Structure and Political Practice during the Ancien Régime* (Cambridge, 1985), pp. 177–8, points out Potter's insistence on George's divinely appointed, legitimate inheritance of the throne and on the 'entire submission to his authority' thus enjoined on the king's subjects.

18 HMC Egmont MSS, Diary, II, 145–6. I am grateful to Tom McGeary for pointing out Egmont's comment.

19 Maynard Mack, *The Garden and the City: Retirement and Politics in the Later Poetry of Pope 1731–43* (Toronto, 1969), pp. 129–31.

20 Peace negotiations in the War of Austrian Succession began in 1746; Handel began the oratorio in May 1748; the Treaty of Aix la Chapelle was signed October 1748; the oratorio was first performed 17 March 1749.

21 *Works* (Philadelphia, 1841), II, 429.

22 For further examples see Cecil A. Moore, 'Whig Panegyric Verse: A Phase of Sentimentalism', *PMLA* 41 (1926), 362–401, repr. in *Backgrounds to English Literature 1700–1760* (Minneapolis, 1953), pp. 104–44.

23 On which see now David Armitage, 'The British Empire and the Civic

Tradition 1656–1742', Ph.D. diss., University of Cambridge (1991), ch. 5.

24 Slave labour: 1 Kings V.13–15, 20–1; 2 Chron. II.17–18, VIII.7–8; foreign imports: 1 Kings V.6–12, IX.27, X.11–12, 22, 28–9; 2 Chron. I.16–17, II.8–10, 15–16, VIII.18, 9.10–11, 28; paid for with territory, 1 Kings IX.10–14. On the prince's efforts to restrict foreign imports see Gerrard, *Patriot Opposition*, ch. 1.

25 II.1. On the librettos' reflection of the debate about the connection between trade and empire (conquest), see ch. 10.

26 Alan D. McKillop, *The Background of Thomson's 'Liberty'*, Rice Institute Pamphlet: Monograph in English 38/2 (Houston, 1951), pp. 7, 54, 86; Isaac Kramnick, *Bolingbroke and his Circle: The Politics of Nostalgia in the Age of Walpole* (Cambridge, MA, 1968), pp. 68–9; J. G. A. Pocock, *The Machiavellian Moment* (Princeton, 1975), pp. 431, 444–5; J. A. W. Gunn, *Beyond Liberty and Property: The Process of Self-Recognition in Eighteenth-Century Political Thought* (Kingston and Montreal, 1983), pp. 96–119; David S. Shields, *Oracles of Empire: Poetry, Politics, and Commerce in British America, 1690–1750* (Chicago, 1990), pp. 18, 24, 66.

27 For evidence of interest in this theme on the part of Pope, Swift, Addison, Mandeville, Defoe and other leading writers of the period, see Louis A. Landa, 'Pope's Belinda, the General Emporie of the World, and the Wondrous Worm' (1971) and 'Of Silkworms and Farthingales and the Will of God' (1973), both repr. in *Essays in Eighteenth Century English Literature* (Princeton, 1980), pp. 178–98, 199–217.

28 Bertrand A. Goldgar, *Walpole and the Wits: The Relation of Politics to Literature 1722–1742* (Lincoln, NE, 1976), details this charge against Walpole's government fully and sceptically. On the debate about Augustus as patron of the arts and its political implications at this time see Howard D. Weinbrot, *Augustus Caesar in 'Augustan' England* (Princeton, 1978), pp. 68–79; Howard Erskine-Hill, *The Augustan Idea in English Literature* (1983), pp. 249–54; Michael Meehan, *Liberty and Poetics in Eighteenth-Century England* (1986), pp. 46–9, 67–75. On attempts by the Patriot writers, including Aaron Hill, to stimulate government patronage of the arts, see Christine Gerrard, 'The Patriot Opposition to Sir Robert Walpole: A Study of Politics and Poetry, 1725–1742', D.Phil. diss., University of Oxford (1986), ch. 1. On the connection of art, moral truth, national strength and government patronage in this period see also above, ch. 2.

29 *Oratorios*, pp. 88–9.

30 First published 1752 in *Political Discourses*, and retitled 'Of Refinement in the Arts' when it was reissued in 1760.

31 James Thomson, *The Seasons and The Castle of Indolence*, ed. James Sambrook (Oxford, 1972, rev. 1987), 'Autumn', ll. 43–143.

32 For Frederick as encourager of British arts see now Gerrard, *Patriot Opposition*, ch. 3.

33 1 Kings IV.7, XII.1–24; 2 Chron. X.1–19.

34 See chs. 8 and 10 and Jeremy Black, *British Foreign Policy in the Age of Walpole* (Edinburgh, 1985), pp. 20–1, 27–45, and *Natural and Necessary Enemies: Anglo-French Relations in the Eighteenth Century* (1986), pp. 36–51; Graham C. Gibbs, 'English Attitudes towards Hanover and the Hanoverian Succession in the First Half of the Eighteenth Century', in *England und Hannover / England and Hanover*, ed. Adolf M. Birke and Kurt Kluxen (Munich, 1986), pp. 33–51, esp. pp. 35, 43, 46–7; Robert Harris, *A Patriot Press: National Politics and the London Press in the 1740s* (Oxford, 1993), pp. 238–53; Paul Langford, *The Eighteenth Century, 1688–1815* (1976), pp. 123–32, and *A Polite and Commercial People: England, 1727–1783* (Oxford, 1989), pp. 189–94, 209–10, 219–20; Nicholas Rogers, *Whigs and Cities: Popular Politics in the Age of Walpole and Pitt* (Oxford, 1989), pp. 69–70; W. A. Speck, *Stability and Strife: England 1714–60* (1977), pp. 241–54; Philip Woodfine, 'Ideas of Naval Power and the Conflict with Spain, 1737–42', in *The British Navy and the Use of Naval Power in the Eighteenth Century*, ed. J. Black and P. Woodfine (Atlantic Heights, NJ, 1989), pp. 71–90, at p. 71.

35 *The State of the Nation, with a General Balance of the Publick Accounts* (1748), pp. 9, 18, 21, 29, 33, 37, 38–52. For the actual cost of the war see John Brewer, *The Sinews of Power: War, Money and the English State 1688–1783* (1989), p. 30.

36 [Ralph,] *Remembrancer*, pp. 10, 14, 15, 73; [Horace Walpole,] *A Second and Third Letter to the Whigs* (1748), pp. 41–2, 48, 53, 56, 57, 63, 65, 70–3, 84–5, 87, 89.

37 Dean, *Oratorios*, p. 513, though his account is nearer the truth than Lang's (*Handel*, p. 464), which asserts that the librettist 'omitted all adverse nuances'.

38 In his sermon on the anniversary of Queen Anne's accession in 1703 (*Four Sermons*, 1712, pp. 113–51), on 2 Chron. IX.8, William Fleetwood draws attention to the disruption of natural hereditary succession in Solomon's acquisition of the throne, which he conventionally justifies as stemming from God and prompted by His care for His people (the obvious implied parallel being, as often in the sermon literature, the accession of Mary (and then Anne) rather than the Pretender).

39 As Dean suggests in his interpretation of the text as a whole, *Oratorios*, p. 512.

40 Thomas Lediard and John Frederick Lampe, *Britannia* (1732); the title-page description 'An English Opera' owes more to the authors' wish to be nationalistic and modern (see Introduction), advertising the fact that the work is in English but has 'Musick composed after the *Italian* Manner', than to the dramatisation, which seems to me to descend directly from the Jacobean masque. See Roger Fiske, *English Theatre Music in the Eighteenth Century* (1973, 2/Oxford, 1986), pp. 134–5, for further details of its performance, and plate III for the set design, reproduced from the libretto; and on Lediard's spectaculars generally, Richard Southern, 'Lediard and Early Eighteenth-Century

Scene Design', *Theatre Notebook* 2 (1948), 49–54. No student of the curiosities of the eighteenth-century theatre should miss this libretto (BL classmark 11777.cc.3).

41 Thomas Stackhouse, *A New History of the Holy Bible from the Beginning of the World to the Establishment of Christianity* (1737), II, 775, 791.

42 Mack, *The Garden and the City*, pp. 129–31; Herbert M. Atherton, *Political Prints in the Age of Hogarth: A Study of the Iconographic Represen-tation of Politics* (Oxford, 1974), pp. 76, 200–1, 281.

43 1 Kings XI.1–13.

44 Jennens recorded his indebtedness in the printed wordbook with a footnote: 'Xenoph. Cyrop. lib. I'. The moment he annotates, Cyrus' avowed subservience to 'Pow'r divine', corresponds to *Cyropaedia* I.v.14. For *Cyropaedia* as an Oxford (and school) textbook at this period see P. Quarrie, 'The Christ Church Collections Books', in *The History of the University of Oxford*, V, *The Eighteenth Century*, ed. L. S. Sutherland and L. G. Mitchell (Oxford, 1986), pp. 493–512, at p. 494.

45 Andrew Michael Ramsay, *The Travels of Cyrus* (1727, 6/1739); I am indebted to Mark Goldie for information about the continuing influ-ence of this work.

46 George D. Henderson, *Chevalier Ramsay* (Edinburgh, 1952), pp. 121, 124–5.

47 Clark, *English Society*, p. 182. On the deliberate ambivalence of *The Idea of a Patriot King* see Simon Varey, 'Hanover, Stuart, and the *Patriot King*', *BJECS* 6 (1983), 163–72.

48 J. Merrill Knapp, 'The Hall Handel Collection', *Princeton University Library Chronicle* 36 (1974), 3–18, at pp. 9–10.

49 *Poetry and Jacobite Politics*, ch. 2.

50 Moses Lowman, *A Dissertation on the Civil Government of the Hebrews. In which the True Designs, and Nature of their Government Are Explained* (1740, 2/1745), pp. 59–60.

51 *The Nature of the Kingdom or Church of Christ ... A Sermon ... March 31, 1717* ([1717]), p. 9 (the BL catalogue lists fifteen editions in 1717).

52 Described by Justin Champion, *The Pillars of Priestcraft Shaken: The Church of England and its Enemies, 1660–1730* (Cambridge, 1992), ch. 5; see also Henning Graf Reventlow, trans. John Bowden, *The Authority of the Bible and the Rise of the Modern World* (1984), pp. 300–1, 319–27, 330–1, 356–9, 377–9.

53 *Moral Philosopher*, I, 239–47, II, 132, III, 178; see similarly Anthony Ashley Cooper, third Earl of Shaftesbury, *Characteristicks of Men, Manners, Opinions, Times* (6/1738), II, 387–8; Anthony Collins, *A Dis-course of the Grounds and Reasons of the Christian Religion* (1724), pp. 22–3; Matthew Tindal, *Christianity as Old as the Creation* (3/1732), pp. 93–4. For stock rebuttals contemporary with Miller's libretto, see e.g. 'Theo-phanes Cantabrigiensis' [Samuel Squire], *The Ancient History of the Hebrews Vindicated: or, Remarks on Part of the Third Volume of the Moral Philosopher* (Cambridge, 1741) pp. 8–80; Samuel Chandler, 'A Defence

of the Prime Ministry and Character of Joseph', Part II of his *Vindi-cation*, pp. 390–418. See further Reventlow, *Authority of the Bible*, pp. 291–3, 312–13, 395, 399, 401. On earlier freethinkers' associations of Mosaic law with Egyptian practice see Champion, *Pillars of Priestcraft*, pp. 131–2, 145–6, 155–7.

54 John Rogers, *The Necessity of Divine Revelation, and the Truth of the Christian Revelation Asserted, in Eight Sermons. To which is Prefix'd, a Preface with some Remarks on a Late Book Entitled, The Scheme of Literal Prophecy Considered* (2/1729), pp. xlii–liii.

55 *Dissertation*, pp. 2–4, 81–124, 188–9, 195–204, 235, 237, 246–52, 307–33, 339–43. For other defences against anticlericalism see e.g. Samuel Chandler, *Reflections on the Conduct of the Modern Deists* (1727), pp. 29–34; [Joseph Hallet, jnr,] *The Immorality of the Moral Philosopher* (1737), pp. 35–7; and, most nearly anticipating Lowman's main arguments, John Leland, *The Divine Authority of the Old and New Testament Asserted ... against ... the Moral Philosopher* (2/1739), pp. 176–200.

56 *The Political Works of James Harrington*, ed. J. G. A. Pocock (Cambridge, 1977), pp. 77–99; Mark Goldie, 'The Civil Religion of James Harring-ton', in *The Languages of Political Theory in Early-Modern Europe*, ed. Anthony Pagden (Cambridge, 1987), pp. 197–222.

57 *National Corruption and Depravity the Principal Cause of National Disappoint-ment* (York, 1757), quoted D. Napthine and W. A. Speck, 'Clergymen and Conflict 1660–1763', in *The Church and War (Studies in Church History* 20), ed. W. J. Sheils (Oxford, 1983), pp. 231–51, at pp. 240–1.

58 John Walsh and Stephen Taylor, 'Introduction: The Church and Anglicanism in the "Long" Eighteenth Century', in *The Church of England c. 1689 – c. 1833: From Toleration to Tractarianism*, ed. John Walsh, Colin Haydon and Stephen Taylor (Cambridge, 1993), pp. 1–66, at p. 46.

59 See further my 'Intellectual Contexts of Handel's English Oratorios', in *Music in Eighteenth-Century England: Essays in memory of Charles Cudworth*, ed. Christopher Hogwood and Richard Luckett (Cambridge, 1983), pp. 115–33, at pp. 120–1, and Philip Brett and George Haggerty, 'Handel and the Sentimental: The Case of *Athalia*', *M&L* 68 (1987), 112–27.

60 *Letters from a Persian in England, to his Friend at Ispahan* (2/1735), repr. in *George Lyttelton's Political Tracts 1735–1748*, ed. Stephen Parks (New York, 1974), Letters XXIX–XXX.

61 See e.g. H. T. Dickinson, *Liberty and Property: Political Ideology in Eighteenth-Century Britain* (1977), p. 161.

62 *Four Sermons*, pp. 127, 136–7.

63 Weinbrot, *Augustus Caesar*, esp. pp. 47–8, 52–3, 70, 98–9. For an examination of the relation of the king to the law in contemporary drama see e.g. James Thomson's *Tancred and Sigismunda*, discussed by John Loftis, 'Thomson's *Tancred and Sigismunda* and the Demise of the

Drama of Political Opposition', in *The Stage and the Page: London's 'Whole Show' in the Eighteenth-Century Theatre*, ed. George Winchester Stone, jnr (Berkeley, 1981), pp. 34–54, at p. 47.

64 Colley, *Britons*, pp. 47–8.
65 Gerald Straka, *Anglican Reaction to the Revolution of 1688* (Madison, WI, 1962), pp. 112–13; e.g. Anthony Holbrook, *No Security for Protestants under a Popish Prince. A Sermon Preached August the 1st 1715 being the Day of His Majesty's Happy Accession to the Throne* (on 1 Samuel XV.28), (1715), pp. 14–17; Strickland Gough, *Mercy Shewn to the Rebels an Argument for their Conversion, a Sermon Preach'd on the First of August 1716, being the Anniversary of His Majesty King George's Proclamation* (on 1 Samuel XXIV.17–20), (1717), p. 12; Lowman, *Dissertation*, pp. 272–9.
66 John Cooke, *The Preacher's Assistant* (Oxford, 1783), index, 'January 30'; Helen W. Randall, 'The Rise and Fall of a Martyrology: Sermons on Charles I', *Huntington Library Quarterly* 10 (1946–7), 135–67, esp. p. 139; Clark, *English Society*, pp. 158–60.
67 A Stuart family tree ('Genealogie de la Maison Royalle de la Grande Bretagne') originating with James III: Royal Archives, Stuart Papers, vol. 3/101 (I am grateful to Eveline Cruickshanks for this information and for a copy of the tree). On the religious element in the confusion of national identity see e.g. Jeremy Black, 'Introduction: An Age of Political Stability?' in *Britain in the Age of Walpole*, ed. Black (1984), pp. 1–22, at pp. 6, 12–15.
68 Schonhorn, *Defoe's Politics*, pp. 61–6, 95, 111–23.
69 On this play and its authorship see my 'The Achievements of Charles Jennens (1700–1773)', *M&L* 70 (1989), 161–90, at p. 187. Jennens had Orrery's works and memoirs in his library. The libretto has much more in common with the play than with its most frequently cited non-biblical source, Cowley's *Davideis*, but on the latter's themes of monarchical absolutism and divine right (close to Jennens' heart and to his libretto), see Margaret Anne Doody, *The Daring Muse: Augustan Poetry Reconsidered* (Cambridge, 1985), pp. 62–3.
70 See e.g. *A Form of Prayer with Fasting, to be us'd yearly upon the 30th of January, being the Day of the Martyrdom of ... King Charles the First ...* (1685).
71 *The Church of England Man's Companion; or, a Rational Illustration of the Harmony ... and Usefulness of the Book of Common Prayer* (Oxford, 1710, 8/1759), pp. 181–2.
72 *A Collection of Miscellany Letters Selected out of Mist's Weekly Journal*, I (1722), pp. 91–2.
73 Letter from Jennens to Lord Guernsey, 19 September 1738 (in the possession of Lord Aylesford, and consulted by kind permission), printed with some inaccuracies, Deutsch pp. 465–6: 'this Hallelujah Grand as it is, comes in very nonsensically, having no manner of relation to what goes before'. See above, pp. 29–30.
74 Anthony Hicks, 'Handel, Jennens and *Saul*: Aspects of a Collaboration',

in *Music and Theatre: Essays in honour of Winton Dean*, ed. Nigel Fortune (Cambridge, 1987), pp. 203–27, at pp. 211–15.

75 Printed in *A Miscellany of Lyric Poems, the Greatest Part Written for, and Performed in The Academy of Music, held in the Apollo [Tavern]* (1740), pp. 25–32, where it is called an oratorio, as also for a performance in 1737: see Rosamond McGuinness and H. Diack Johnstone, 'Concert Life in England I', in *The Blackwell History of Music in Britain: The Eighteenth Century*, ed. Johnstone and Roger Fiske (Oxford, 1990), pp. 31–95, at p. 80 and n. 85. In the past it has been assumed that the libretto for which Handel thanked Jennens in 1735 (letter of 28 July, Deutsch p. 394) was *Saul*, but it could as well have been *Israel in Egypt*, in which case *Saul* (of which we first have definite evidence when Handel begins to set it on 23 July 1738) could have been written after *David's Lamentation*. On Jennens' authorship of *Israel in Egypt* see ch. 12.

76 McGuinness and Johnstone, 'Concert Life', p. 80; see similarly Ian Bartlett, 'Boyce and Early English Oratorio – I', *MT* 120 (1979), 293–7, at p. 295.

77 Paul Langford, *Public Life and the Propertied Englishman 1689–1798* (Oxford, 1991), p. 126. This alliance with Hanoverian royalty happened some time after the writing of *David's Lament*, but was apparently part of a consistent pattern of allegiance: according to *DNB*, 'He frequently went to court to present his verses to the royal family, and after he became secretary to the British Herring Fishery he tendered gifts of pickled herrings. Both poems and herrings, he declared, "were most graciously accepted".'

78 On Saul and the Amalekites see e.g. Aaron Hill, *Gideon: or, The Patriot* (1749), p. 66; Tindal, *Christianity*, p. 237; Thomas Stackhouse, *A Complete Body of Speculative and Practical Divinity* (1729, 2/1734), p. 465; [Morgan,] *Moral Philosopher*, I (1737), p. 298; [Hallet,] *Immorality of the Moral Philosopher*, pp. 66–7; John Leland, *An Answer to a Late Book Intituled, Christianity as Old as the Creation* (2/1740), II, 359–61; Delany, *Historical Account* I, 1–9; Francis Webber, *The Jewish Dispensation Consider'd and Vindicated, with a View to the Objections of Unbelievers, and particularly of a Late Author Call'd the Moral Philosopher* (Oxford, 1737, 2/1751), p. 39. On Samuel Humphreys' perception of Haman as an Amalekite see ch. 11.

79 Compare 1 Samuel XXVIII.16–18, of which this is an accurate paraphrase; for admiring comment, see Dean, *Oratorios*, pp. 280–1.

80 Hicks, 'Handel, Jennens and *Saul*', p. 211.

81 E.g. *Craftsman* no. 84, 10 February 1727/8: when 'Political jealousy ... happens to seize the Head of a *guilty first Minister* ... he only meditates Revenge; which he attempts by every Method he is capable of pursuing. Worth and Honour and Integrity and Principle, of every Kind, are thrown behind him, and sacrificed to this ignominious and cowardly Passion'.

82 E.g. *Craftsman* no. 168, 20 September 1729.

83 E.g. Dean, *Oratorios*, pp. 537–8.
84 Dean's description, *Oratorios*, p. 538, of *Susanna* as 'a work in which exile and even the Almighty are scarcely mentioned' is baffling. Besides four explicit references to exile in Part I and one in Part III, there are several which, to any informed listener, connote exile (e.g. Joacim's to 'Babylon's proud walls', II.5); and there are sixteen references to God and/or religion.
85 *Oratorios*, pp. 535–6, 538–41.
86 For Susanna and elements of her story as Christian archetypes in the writings of Hyppolytus (Bishop of Rome, early third century), providing precedents for interpreting Susanna as the Church, the Christian soul, and Christ, see Helmut Engel, *Die Susanna-Erzählung*, Orbis Biblicus et Orientalis 61 (Göttingen, 1985), pp. 35–40.

CHAPTER 14

1 James Pitt, in the *London Journal*, 25 September 1731 (no. 639), quoted Simon Targett, 'Sir Robert Walpole's Newspapers, 1722–42: Propaganda and Politics in the Age of Whig Supremacy' Ph.D. diss., University of Cambridge (1991), p. 313; see further pp. 308–25.
2 Henry St John, Lord Bolingbroke, *The Idea of a Patriot King* (1749), *Works* (Philadelphia, 1841), II, 373.
3 For the transmission of Bolingbroke's concept of the ideal leader into plays and verse see now Christine Gerrard, *The Patriot Opposition to Walpole: Politics, Poetry, and National Myth, 1725–1742* (Oxford, 1994), esp. ch. 3.
4 BL Add. MSS 28846, fol. 64r.
5 *King Henry the Fifth. Or, The Conquest of France by the English. A Tragedy* (1723). Written during the opposition's campaign against the British alliance with France, the play was revived in 1735–6 (ten performances), prompting a revival of Shakespeare's play (twelve performances 1738 40, nineteen performances 1744–52).
6 'The Royal Academy of Music and its Directors', in *Handel Tercentenary Collection*, ed. Stanley Sadie and Anthony Hicks (1987), pp. 138–64, at p. 149.
7 The political reading by Ellen T. Harris, *The Librettos of Handel's Operas* (New York, 1989), III, xiii, is unsupported by historical evidence and does not fit the text.
8 Hoadly's libretto is printed in the *Gentleman's Magazine*, 7 (1737), 144–7, where it is attributed to 'Mr Burnet' (hence the puzzlement of Deutsch p. 427, repeated by Dean, *Oratorios*, p. 589), but the index corrects this: 'by Mr Hoadley, not by Mr Burnet'.
9 For example that of Samuel Humphreys, *The Sacred Books of the Old and New Testament, Recited at Large* (1735), which suggests that the story of Jephtha's daughter provided the inspiration for the story of Iphigenia's sacrifice.

10 See [Thomas Morgan,] *The Moral Philosopher*, I (1737), 131–2, II (1739–40), 115–17; [Joseph Hallet, jnr,] *A Letter to the Moral Philosopher, being a Vindication of* [his own] *Pamphlet Entitled The Immorality of the Moral Philosopher* (1737), p. 16; [Thomas Morgan,] *A Defence of the Moral Philosopher* (1737), pp. 9–14. See also David Collyer, *The Sacred Interpreter: or, A Practical Introduction towards a Beneficial Reading, and a thorough Understanding, of the Holy Bible* (1732), I, 249–50; Matthew Tindal, *Christianity as Old as the Creation* (3/1732), pp. 82–4; Thomas Stackhouse, *A Complete Body of Speculative and Practical Divinity* (1729, 2/1734), pp. 459–61.

11 Moses Lowman, *A Dissertation on the Civil Government of the Hebrews. In which the True Designs, and Nature of their Government Are Explained* (1740, 2/1745), p. 69.

12 Besides the one mentioned by Dean, *Oratorios*, p. 593, there is a direct quotation in the quartet (II.3): 'think not God delights / In *Moloch*'s horrid Rites'. At the same point in the story Hoadly has Jephtha contrast the law of God with '*Moloch*'s horrid Rites'.

13 George Buchanan, *Jephthes, sive Votum*, trans. A. Gibb (Edinburgh, 1870); Morell could could have consulted the original, or a recent translation by William Tait, *A Tragedy called Jephthah, or, The Vow . . . by . . . George Buchannan* (Edinburgh, 1750).

14 From MS fol. 35, 'Stet Quicunque volet (Seneca) reversed'; compare Thomson (with reference to Frederick's potential): 'a Prince . . . who knows how to unite the soveraignty of the prince with the liberty of the people, and to found his happiness and Glory on the publick Good. Oh happy as a God he, who has it both in his hand and in his heart to make a people happy!', *James Thomson (1700–1748): Letters and Documents*, ed. Alan D. McKillop (Lawrence, KS, 1958), p. 83 (to Lady Hertford, 10 October 1732).

15 Averyl Edwards, *Frederick Louis, Prince of Wales 1707–1751* (1947), pp. 17–19, 114–19, 161.

16 E.g. Dean, *Oratorios*, p. 594; Christopher Dearnley, *English Church Music 1650–1750* (1970), p. 7.

17 Humphreys, *Sacred Books*, on Judges, ch. 11; see also e.g. Stackhouse, *Complete Body*, pp. 459–61; Daniel Waterland, *Scripture Vindicated* (1731–2), in *Works*, VI (Oxford, 1823), 133–5.

18 Simon Patrick, *A Commentary upon the Books of Joshua, Judges, and Ruth* (1702).

19 *Virtue Transformed: Political Argument in England, 1688–1740* (Cambridge, 1992), pp. 63, 23–4.

20 *Virtue Transformed*, pp. 104–7.

CHAPTER 15

1 Carolyn Gianturco, '*Il trionfo del Tempo e del Disinganno*: Four Case-Studies in Determining Italian Poetic-Musical Genres', *Journal of the Royal Musical Association* 119 (1994), 43–59, at pp. 52–3.

2 The best and fullest account is Thomas W. Perry's forward-looking *Public Opinion, Propaganda, and Politics: A Study of the Jew Bill of 1753* (Cambridge, MA, 1962). The best brief account, especially of the Bill's passage through Parliament, is Allan Peskin's 'England's Jewish Naturalization Bill of 1753', *Historia Judaica* 19 (1957), 3–32. See also Todd M. Endelman, *The Jews of Georgian England* (Philadelphia, 1979), pp. 24–9, 32–3, 36–9, 59–64, 88–91, 100–1; G. A. Cranfield, 'The *London Evening Post* and the Jew Bill of 1753', *HJ* 8 (1965), 16–30; Cecil Roth, *A History of the Jews in England* (Oxford, 3/1964), pp. 212–23, and Edgar R. Samuel, 'The Jews in English Foreign Trade – A Consideration of the "Philo Patriae" Pamphlets of 1753', in *Remember the Days: Essays on Anglo-Jewish History presented to Cecil Roth*, ed. J. M. Shaftesley (1966), pp. 123–43; D. A. Statt, 'The Controversy over the Naturalization of Foreigners in England, 1660–1760', Ph.D. diss., University of Cambridge (1987). On the visual evidence see I. Solomons, 'Satirical and Political Prints on the Jews' Naturalisation Bill, 1753', *Transactions of the Jewish Historical Society of England* 6 (1912), 205–33; Herbert M. Atherton, *Political Prints in the Age of Hogarth: A Study of the Iconographic Representation of Politics* (Oxford, 1974), pp. 162–7; John Miller, *Religion in the Popular Prints* (The English Satirical Print 1600–1832) (Cambridge, 1986), pp. 40–1 and plates. 93–5. The pioneering study by G. B. Hertz (Hurst), '"No Jews; No Wooden Shoes", A Frenzy of 1753', in *British Imperialism in the Eighteenth Century* (1908), pp. 60–109, is still valuable.
3 Perry, *Public Opinion*, pp. 2–3; Roth, *History of the Jews*, p. 217; Hertz, *British Imperialism*, p. 66.
4 *Public Opinion*, pp. 90, 109, 111–17.
5 What follows is based mainly on Perry, *Public Opinion*.
6 Nicholas Rogers, *Whigs and Cities: Popular Politics in the Age of Walpole and Pitt* (Oxford, 1989), pp. 89–91.
7 This linking of the Excise and Jew Bill crises would have had a particular resonance for Handel, whose early oratorio career had been thwarted by the Excise crisis (see ch. 9).
8 Perry, *Public Opinion*, p. 75: rudeness to some Jewish members of a theatre audience.
9 'Of Sacred History', Letter III, *Letters on the Study and Use of History* (1752, written 1735); see ch. 9.
10 Quoted Endelman, *Jews of Georgian England*, p. 90.
11 Cranfield, '"London Evening Post"'.
12 Handel continued performances of existing Israelite oratorios; but this is a different matter from investing in the creation of a new one. According to H. R. S. Van der Veen, *Jewish Characters in Eighteenth-Century Fiction and Drama* (Groningen, 1935), p. 268, during the eighteenth century newly written plays giving hostile portrayals of Jews were least frequent in the period 1736–53 (which corresponds with the oratorio years), and hostility revived with the Naturalisation Bill.

13 *Gentleman's Magazine* 23 (1753), 428–9. For Watts' Christianised psalms see ch. 9.
14 See e.g. Dean, *Oratorios*, pp. 136, 471; Christopher Hogwood, *Handel* (1984), pp. 208, 220.
15 For the 1754 season see the performances at Covent Garden listed Deutsch pp. 746–9.
16 E.g. Dean, *Oratorios*, pp. 527–8, on the 1759 *Solomon*, a revision which (though he does not make the point) omits the bulk of the material identifying Solomon as a *Jewish* king.

APPENDIX 2

1 R. A. Streatfeild, *Handel* (1909), pp. 211–12; Percy Young, *The Oratorios of Handel* (1949), pp. 128–30; Dean, *Oratorios*, pp. 130–43.
2 Thomas Morell, *The Use and Importance of Music in the Sacrifice of Thanksgiving. A Sermon Preach'd at Worcester, September 3, 1746. At the Anniversary Meeting* (1747).
3 Maldwyn Edwards, 'John Wesley', in *A History of the Methodist Church in Britain*, I, ed. Rupert Davies and Gordon Rupp (1965), pp. 35–79, at p. 56; Frank Baker, 'The People Called Methodists – 3. Polity', in *History of the Methodist Church*, I, 211–55, at pp. 219, 228.
4 Edwards, 'John Wesley', pp. 57–9.
5 *George Whitefield's Journals*, ed. Iain Murray (1960), p. 88.
6 John Lawson, 'The People Called Methodists – 2. "Our Discipline"', in *History of the Methodist Church*, I, 181–209, at pp. 191–2, 204–6; A. Raymond George, 'The People Called Methodists – 4. The Means of Grace', in *History of the Methodist Church*, I, 259–73, at p. 266.
7 What follows is based mainly on Nicholas Temperley, 'Music in Church', in *The Blackwell History of Music in Britain: The Eighteenth Century*, ed. H. Diack Johnstone and Roger Fiske (Oxford, 1990), pp. 357–96, at pp. 387–93.
8 Horton Davies, *Worship and Theology in England*, (Princeton, 1961–75), III, *From Watts and Wesley to Maurice, 1690–1850* (1961), pp. 234–5.
9 'Minutes of Several Conversations between the Rev. Mr. Wesley and Others from the Year 1744, to the Year 1789', in *The Works of John Wesley* (1872, repr. Grand Rapids, MI, n.d.), VIII, 318.
10 Edwards, 'John Wesley', pp. 48–50; Rupert Davies, 'The People Called Methodists – 1. "Our Doctrines"', in *History of the Methodist Church*, I, 145–79, at p. 164.
11 Davies, 'Our Doctrines', pp. 150, 159; George, 'The Means of Grace', p. 267.
12 Davies, 'Our Doctrines', pp. 155, 167.
13 Davies, 'Our Doctrines', p. 154.
14 Edwards, 'John Wesley', pp. 38–9; Davies, 'Our Doctrines', p. 166.
15 Davies, 'Our Doctrines', p. 170; Lawson, 'Our Discipline', p. 195; Baker, 'Polity', pp. 216, 224–6.

16 Lawson, 'Our Discipline', p. 188; Davies, 'Our Doctrines', p. 171.
17 Norman Sykes, *Church and State in England in the XVIIIth Century* (Cambridge, 1934), pp. 258–62.

Bibliography of sources cited

Place of publication is London unless otherwise indicated

EIGHTEENTH CENTURY AND EARLIER

For librettos for Handel, see App. 1

MANUSCRIPT SOURCES

Handel, George Frederic: Autograph Scores, British Library
    [Librettists and copyists of]: Oratorio librettos, Larpent Collection, Huntington Library, San Marino, CA
Jennens, Charles and Edward Holdsworth: Correspondence, Coke Collection, Bentley, Hants
Morell, Thomas: Commonplace Book, BL Add. MS 28846
    Letters, King's College, Cambridge, Modern Archives, Coll.34.11
    MSS poems, Osborn Collection, Yale University Library
Synge, Edward, Bishop of Elphin: Plan for an Oratorio, Coke Collection, Bentley, Hants

SERMONS AND TRACTS RELATED TO THEM

A Letter to a Friend ... in Answer to Mr Newte's Sermon (1698)
Abbot, Henry: *The Use and Benefit of Church-Musick, towards Quickening our Devotion. A Sermon preach'd in the Cathedral-Church of Gloucester, at the Anniversary Meeting ... September 9, 1724 ...* (1724)
Allen, Richard: *An Essay to Prove Singing of Psalms with Conjoin'd Voices a Christian Duty* (1696)
Amory, Thomas: *Fast Sermon ... Taunton, 18 December 1745* (2/1745)
Atterbury, Francis: 'The Usefulness of Church Music: A Sermon, Preached on St Cecilia's Day, in the Year 1698', *Sermons and Discourses* (5/1761), IV, 217–41
Banner, Richard: *The Use and Antiquity of Musick in the Service of God. A Sermon Preach'd in the Cathedral-Church at Worcester, September 14 1737 at the Anniversary Meeting* (Oxford, 1737)
Battell, Ralph: *The Lawfulness and Expediency of Church-Musick Asserted, in a Sermon Preach'd at St Brides-Church, upon the 22nd of November 1693* (1694)

Bedford, Arthur: *The Excellency of Divine Musick: or a Sermon Preach'd in the Parish-Church of St Michael's Crooked Lane, in the City of London, on Thursday the Fourth Day of October, and at Sir George Wheeler's Chapel, on Monday the Fifth of November ... 1733. Before Several Members of Such Societies who are Lovers of Psalmody. To which is Added, a Specimen of Easy, Grave Tunes, instead of those which are Used in our Profane and Wanton Ballads* (n.d.)

Bisse, Thomas: *Musick the Delight of the Sons of Men. A Sermon Preached at the Cathedral Church of Hereford, at the Anniversary Meeting ... September 7. 1726* (1726)

A Rationale on Cathedral Worship or Choir-Service: A Sermon Preach'd in the Cathedral Church at Hereford, at the Anniversary Meeting ... Sept. 7. 1720 (1720)

A Sermon Preach'd in the Cathedral Church of Hereford, at the Anniversary Meeting ... September 3, 1729 (1729)

Brady, Nicholas: *Church Musick Vindicated, 1697*, ed. J. E. Philipps, jnr, Augustan Reprint Society 49 (Los Angeles, 1955)

Brooke, James: *The Duty and Advantage of Singing to the Lord. A Sermon Preach'd in the Cathedral Church of Worcester, at the Anniversary Meeting ... Sept. 4. 1728* (n.d.)

Burnet, Gilbert: 'On Church Musick: Occasioned by the Opening of the Organ at St James's Clerkenwell, 1734', Sermon XVI in *Practical Sermons on Various Subjects* (1747), I, 265–80

Burnet, Gilbert (of Coggeshall): *A Defence of Natural and Revealed Religion: being an Abridgement of the Sermons Preached at the Lecture Founded by the Honourable Robert Boyle Esq* (1737)

C[laridge], R[ichard]: *An Answer to Mr Allen's Essay, Vindication and Appendix* (1697)

Coningesby, Edward: *Church-Musick Vindicated; and the Causes of its Dislike Enquir'd into. A Sermon Preach'd at the Cathedral Church of Hereford, at the Anniversary Meeting ... September 6th, 1732* (Oxford, 1732)

Dingley, William: *Cathedral Service Decent and Useful. A Sermon Preach'd before the University of Oxford at St Mary's on Cecilia's Day, 1713* (Oxford, 1713)

Dodwell, Henry: *A Treatise concerning the Lawfulness of Instrumental Musick in Holy Offices to which is Prefix'd, a Preface in Vindication of Mr Newte's Sermon* (1700)

Estwick, Samson: *The Usefulness of Church Musick, 1696*, ed. J. E. Philipps, jnr, Augustan Reprint Society 49 (Los Angeles, 1955)

Fleetwood, William: *Four Sermons* (1712)

Gough, Strickland: *Mercy Shewn to the Rebels an Argument for their Conversion, a Sermon Preach'd on the First of August 1716, being the Anniversary of His Majesty King George's Proclamation* (1717)

Hickman, Charles: *A Sermon Preached at St Bride's Church on St Cecilia's Day November 22nd 1695* (1696)

Hitchin, Edward: *Scripture Proof for Singing of Psalms, Hymns and Spiritual Songs* (1696)

Hoadly, Benjamin: *The Nature of the Kingdom or Church of Christ ... A Sermon ... March 31, 1717* (n.d.)

Holbrook, Anthony: *No Security for Protestants under a Popish Prince. A Sermon Preached August the 1st 1715 being the Day of His Majesty's Happy Accession to the Throne* (1715)

Hughes, William: *The Efficacy and Importance of Musick. A Sermon Preach'd in the Cathedral Church of Worcester ... September 13, 1749* (1749)

Keach, Benjamin: *An Answer to Mr Marlow's Appendix* (1691)
 The Breach Repaired in God's Worship: or, Singing of Psalms, Hymns, and Spiritual Songs, Proved to be an Holy Ordinance of Jesus Christ (1691)

Lavington, George: *The Influence of Church-Music. A Sermon Preached in the Cathedral Church of Worcester, at the Anniversary Meeting ... September 8. 1725* (1725, 3/1753)

Macro, Thomas: *The Melody of the Heart. A Sermon Preach'd at the Opening of an Organ in St Nicholas's Church, in Great Yarmouth, December the 20th 1733* (1734)

Marlow, Isaac: *The Controversie of Singing Brought to an End* (1696)
 Truth Soberly Defended, in a Serious Reply to Mr Benjamin Keach's Book (1692)

Miller, James: *The Cause of Britain's being become a Reproach to her Neighbours ... Roehampton ... January 9 1739* (1740)

Morell, Thomas: *The Surest Grounds for Hopes of Success in War ... Kew ... January 9 1739/40 ...* (1740)
 The Use and Importance of Music in the Sacrifice of Thanksgiving. A Sermon Preach'd at Worcester, September 3, 1746. At the Anniversary Meeting... (1747)

Naish, Thomas: *A Sermon Preach'd at the Cathedral Church of Sarum, November 22 1700, before a Society of Lovers of Musick* (1701)
 A Sermon Preached at the Cathedral Church of Sarum, November the 30th 1727 being the Anniversary Day Appointed for the Meeting of the Society of Lovers of Musick (1727)

Newte, John: *The Lawfulness and Use of Organs in the Christian Church Asserted in a Sermon Preached at Tiverton in the County of Devon upon the Thirteenth of September 1696 on occasion of an Organ's being Erected in that Parish Church* (1696)

Parker, William: *The Pleasures of Gratitude and Benevolence Improved by Church-Musick. A Sermon Preached at the Anniversary Meeting ... Sept. 12, 1753* (1753)

Payne, Thomas: *A Defence of Church Musick. A Sermon Preached in the Cathedral-Church of Hereford at the Meeting of the Three Choirs, September 6, 1738* (Oxford, 1738)

Potter, John: *A Sermon Preach'd at the Coronation of King George II ... October 11 1727* (1727)

Rogers, John: *The Necessity of Divine Revelation, and the Truth of the Christian Revelation Asserted, in Eight Sermons. To which is Prefix'd, a Preface with some Remarks on a Late Book Entitled, The Scheme of Literal Prophecy Considered* (2/1729)

Russell, William: *Some Brief Animadversions upon Mr Allen's Essay* (1696)

S. W., J. C., J. L., Lovers of Truth and Peace: *Truth Vindicated, or Mr Keach's Sober Appeal, Answered* (1691)

Senhouse, Peter: *The Right Use and Improvement of Sensitive Pleasures, and more particularly of Musick. A Sermon Preach'd in the Cathedral Church of Gloucester, at the Anniversary Meeting ... September 20, 1727* (1728)

Sherlock, William: *A Sermon Preach'd at St Paul's Cathedral, November 22 1699 being the Anniversary Meeting of the Lovers of Musick* (1699)

Shuttleworth, John: *A Sermon Preached at Bridgewater in Somersetshire July the Seventeenth, 1700 at the Opening of the* ORGAN *lately Erected there* (1700)

Taswell, William: *The Propriety and Usefulness of Sacred Music. A Sermon Preach'd in the Cathedral Church of Gloucester, at the Anniversary Meeting ... September 8, 1742* (Gloucester, n.d.)

Towerson, Gabriel: *A Sermon concerning Vocal and Instrumental Musick in the Church, as it was Delivered in the Parish Church of St Andrew Undershaft, upon the 31st of May, 1696, being Whit Sunday, and the Day wherein the* ORGAN *there Erected was first made use of* (1696)

Webber, Francis: *The Jewish Dispensation Consider'd and Vindicated, with a View to the Objections of Unbelievers, and particularly of a Late Author Call'd the Moral Philosopher* (Oxford, 1737, 2/1751)

Whiston, William: *The Accomplishment of Scripture Prophecies. Being Eight Sermons Preach'd ... at the Lecture founded by the hon. Robert Boyle esq.* (1706, 1708)

OTHER PUBLICATIONS

Adams, George: *The Tragedies of Sophocles, Translated from the Greek, with Notes Historical, Moral, and Critical ... to which is Prefix'd, a Preface: containing I. A Defence of Tragic Poetry ... II. An Historical Account of its Rise and Progress. III. A Comparison of the Ancient Tragedies with each other* (1729)

Addison, Joseph: *Rosamond* (1707)

and Richard Steele: *The Spectator*, ed. Donald F. Bond (Oxford, 1965)

Annet, Peter: *The History of Joseph Consider'd: or, The Moral Philosopher Vindicated against Mr. Samuel Chandler's Defence of the Prime Ministry and Character of Joseph* (1744)

Aspinall, Edward: *A Collection of Anthems, as the same are now Performed in His Majesty's Chapels Royal, &c* (1724)

Avison, Charles: *An Essay on Musical Expression* (1752, 2/1753)

A Reply to the Author of Remarks on the Essay on Musical Expression (1753)

Baillie, John: *An Essay on the Sublime* (1747)

Bayley, Anselm: *A Collection of Anthems, as the same are now Performed in His Majesty's Chapels Royal, &c* (1749)

Bedford, Arthur: *The Temple Musick: or, an Essay concerning the Method of Singing the Psalms of David, in the Temple, before the Babylonish Captivity. Wherein, the Musick of our Cathedrals is Vindicated, and Supposed to be*

Conformable, not only to that of the Primitive Christians, but also to the Practice of the Church in all Preceding Ages (1706)

The Great Abuse of Musick (1711)

[Berkeley, George:] *An Essay towards Preventing the Ruin of Great Britain* (1721, repr. 1752), in *The Works of George Berkeley, Bishop of Cloyne*, VI, ed. T. E. Jessop (1953)

Blackmore, Sir Richard: *Alfred: an Epick Poem in Twelve Books, dedicated to the Illustrious Prince Frederick of Hanover* (1723)

Creation, a Philosophical Poem (1722)

Essays upon Several Subjects (1716)

A Paraphrase on the Book of Job: As Likewise on the Songs of Moses, Deborah, David, on Six Select Psalms and some Chapters of Isaiah, and the Third Chapter of Habakkuk (1700, 2/1716)

Prince Arthur, an Heroick Poem (1695)

Blackwall, Anthony: *A New Introduction to the Classics* (1718)

Blackwell, Thomas: *An Enquiry into the Life and Writings of Homer* (2/1736)

Memoirs of the Court of Augustus (1753)

Blair, Hugh: *A Critical Dissertation on the Poems of Ossian, Son of Fingal* (1763)

Blome, Richard: *The History of the Old and New Testament* (1705)

Blow, John: *Amphion Anglicus* (1700)

Bolingbroke, Henry St John, Lord: *The Idea of a Patriot King* (1749)

Letters on the Study and Use of History (1752)

Lord Bolingbroke: Contributions to The 'Craftsman', ed. Simon Varey (Oxford, 1982)

Lord Bolingbroke: Historical Writings, ed. Isaac Kramnick (Chicago, 1972)

Remarks on the History of England (1743)

Works (Philadelphia, 1841)

Boyle, Hon. Robert: *The Martyrdom of Theodora and of Didymus* (1687), repr. in *Works* (1744), IV

Some Considerations touching the Style of the Holy Scriptures (1661)

Bramston, James: *The Man of Taste. Occasion'd by an Epistle of Mr Pope's on that Subject* (1733)

Brereton, Thomas: *An English Psalm, or, a Hymn on the Late Thanksgiving Day: being a Protestant Version of the Second Psalm* (1716)

Esther, or Faith Triumphant: A Sacred Tragedy by Mr. Brereton of Brazen-Nose College, Oxford. With a Dedication to the Lord Archbishop of York (1715)

Broughton, Thomas: *Christianity Distinct from the Religion of Nature* (1732)

Brown, John: *A Dissertation on the Rise, Union, and Power, the Progressions, Separations, and Corruptions, of Poetry and Music* (1763)

An Estimate of the Manners and Principles of the Times (1757–8)

Brumoy, Pierre, trans. Charlotte Lennox: *The Greek Theatre of Father Brumoy* (1759)

Buchanan, George: *Jephthes, sive Votum* (1554), trans. William Tait as *A Tragedy Called Jephthah, or, The Vow ... by ... George Buchannan* (Edinburgh, 1750), trans. A. Gibb (Edinburgh, 1870)

Burney, Charles: *Memoirs of Dr Charles Burney 1726–1769*, ed. Slava Klima, Garry Bowers and Kerry S. Grant (Lincoln, NE, 1988)

Butler, Joseph: *The Analogy of Religion, Natural and Revealed, to the Constitution and Course of Nature* (1736)

Calmet, Dom Augustin, trans. Nicholas Tindal: *Antiquities Sacred and Prophane: or, A Collection of Curious and Critical Dissertations on the Old and New Testament* (1724, 2/1725)

Carey, Henry: *The Dragon of Wantley* (1737)
Poems on Several Occasions (3/1729)

Carleton, George: *A Collection of Anthems, as the same are now Performed in His Majesty's Chapels Royal, &c* (1736)

Chandler, Edward: *A Defence of Christianity from the Prophecies of the Old Testament* (1725)

[Chandler, Samuel:] *The Old Whig; or, The Consistent Protestant* [1735–8] (1738)

Chandler, Samuel: *Reflections on the Conduct of the Modern Deists* (1727)
A Vindication of the History of the Old Testament (1743)

Chapman, John: *Eusebius: or, The True Christian's Defense against a Late Book Entitul'd The Moral Philosopher*, II (1741)

A Chronological and Historical Account of the Most Memorable Earthquakes that have Happened in the World, from the Beginning of the Christian Period to the Present Year 1750. With an Appendix, containing a Distinct Series of those that have been Felt in England. And a Preface, Seriously Address'd to All Christians of Every Denomination. By a Gentleman of the University of Cambridge (Cambridge, 1750)

Clarke, Samuel: *A Discourse, concerning the Unchangeable Obligations of Natural Religion, and the Truth and Certainty of the Christian Religion* (1705)

Collier, Jeremy: *Essays upon Several Moral Subjects* (2/1697)
A Short View of the Immorality and Profaneness of the English Stage (1698, 5th corr. edn 1730)

Collins, Anthony: *A Discourse of the Grounds and Reasons of the Christian Religion* (1724)
The Scheme of Literal Prophecy Considered (1727)

Collins, William: *Odes on Several Descriptive and Allegoric Subjects* (1747 [1746])

Collyer, David: *The Sacred Interpreter: or, A Practical Introduction towards a Beneficial Reading, and a thorough Understanding, of the Holy Bible* (1732)

'Columbario, Christopher': *The Pigeon-Pye, or, a King's Coronation, Proper Materials for Forming an Oratorio, Opera or Play, according to the Modern Taste: to be Represented in Opposition to the Dragon of Wantley* (1738)

Cooke, John: *The Preacher's Assistant* (Oxford, 1783)

Cowley, Abraham: *The Complete Works in Verse and Prose*, ed. A.B. Grosart (1881)

Croft, William: *Musica Sacra: or, Select Anthems in Score* (1724, 1730)

Crusius, Lewis: *The Lives of the Roman Poets* (1733)

The Curatical Battle for Q. Chappel: Address to the Reverend Parsons, D--k and M----l (1746)

Dacier, André: *Aristotle's Art of Poetry Translated from the Original Greek according to Mr Theodore Goulston's Edition. Together, with Mr D'Acier's Notes Translated from the French* (1705)

Defoe, Daniel: *Augusta Triumphans* (1728), repr. in *Selected Poetry and Prose of Daniel Defoe*, ed. M. F. Shugrue (New York, 1968)

Delany, Mary: *Autobiography and Correspondence of Mary Granville, Mrs Delany*, ed. Lady Llanover (1861–2)

Delany, Patrick: *An Historical Account of the Life and Reign of David, King of Israel* (1740–2)

  The Present State of Learning, Religion, and Infidelity in Great-Britain. Wherein the Causes of the Present Degeneracy of Taste, and Increase of Infidelity, Are Inquir'd into, and Accounted for (1732)

Dennis, John: *The Critical Works of John Dennis*, ed. Edward Niles Hooker (Baltimore, 1939)

  Vice and Luxury Publick Mischiefs (1724)

Derham, William: *Physico-Theology, or a Demonstration of the Being and Attributes of God from his Works of Creation* (1711–12, 11/1745)

The Devil to Pay at St James's: or a Full and True Account of a Most Horrid and Bloody Battle between Madam Faustina and Madam Cuzzoni ... moreover, how Senesino has taken Snuff, and is going to Leave the Opera, and Sing Psalms at Henley's Oratory ... (1727), repr. in John Arbuthnot, *Miscellaneous Works* (Edinburgh, 1751)

A Dissertation on Patriotism: Shewing, the Use of those Two Great Qualifications of a Patriot, Integrity and Courage (1735)

Do You Know What You Are About? Or, A Protestant Alarm to Great Britain; Proving our Late Theatric Squabble, a Type of the Present Contest for the Crown of Poland; and that the Division between Handel and Senesino has more in it than we Imagine. Also that the Latter is no Eunuch, but a Jesuit in Disguise; with other Particulars of the greatest Importance (1733)

Dryden, John: *The Collected and Miscellaneous Prose Works of John Dryden*, ed. Edmond Malone (1800)

Duncombe, John, ed.: *Letters by Several Eminent Persons Deceased* (1773)

Duncombe, William: *Athaliah, A Tragedy Translated from the French of Monsieur Racine* (1722)

Dyer, John: *The Ruins of Rome* (1740)

Egmont, John Earl of (Viscount Perceval): *Diary*, HMC 63 (1920–3)

Entick, John: *The Evidence of Christianity* (1729)

Evelyn, John: *Diary*, ed. E. S. de Beer (Oxford, 1955)

Felton, Henry: *A Dissertation upon Reading the Classics and Forming a Just Style* (1713, 5/1753)

Fleury, Abbot Claude: 'A Discourse concerning Poetry in General and concerning that of the Hebrews in Particular', in Dom Augustin Calmet, trans. Nicholas Tindal, *Antiquities Sacred and Prophane: or, A Collection of Curious and Critical Dissertations on the Old and New Testament* (1724, 2/1725)

A Form of Prayer with Fasting, to be us'd yearly upon the 30th of January, being the Day of the Martyrdom of ... King Charles the First ... (1685)

Gay, John: *The Beggar's Opera*, ed. P. E. Lewis (Edinburgh, 1973)

Gildon, Charles (attrib.): *A Comparison between the Two Stages*, ed. S. B. Wells (Princeton, 1942)

[Gildon, Charles:] *The Laws of Poetry ... Explained and Illustrated* (1721)

[Gordon, Thomas (trans.):] *The Works of Tacitus ... to which are Prefixed, Political Discourses upon that Author* (1728)

Grassineau, James: *A Musical Dictionary; being a Collection of Terms and Characters, as well Ancient as Modern* (1740)

The Great Importance of Cape Breton, Demonstrated and Exemplified (1746)

Hallet, Joseph, jnr: *A Free and Impartial Study of the Holy Scriptures Recommended* (1729–36)

The Immorality of the Moral Philosopher (1737)

A Letter to the Moral Philosopher, being a Vindication of a Pamphlet Entitled The Immorality of the Moral Philosopher (1737)

Harrington, James: *The Political Works of James Harrington*, ed. J. G. A. Pocock (Cambridge, 1977)

Harris, Thomas: *An Hymn on Christ's Nativity, and Man's Redemption* (1722)

Harris, William: *Practical Discourses on the Principal Representations of the Messiah throughout the Old Testament* (1724)

Hawkins, Sir John: *A General History of the Science and Practice of Music* (1776, repr. New York, 1963)

Hayes, William: *The Art of Composing Music by a Method Entirely New* (1751)

Remarks on Mr Avison's Essay on Musical Expression (1753)

Henry, Matthew: *An Exposition of all the Books of the Old and New Testament* (5/1761)

Hill, Aaron: *Advice to the Poets: A Poem, to which is Prefix'd, an Epistle Dedicatory to the Few Great Spirits of Great Britain* (1731)

Dramatic Works (1760)

Gideon; or, The Patriot. An Epic Poem: in Twelve Books. Upon a Hebrew Plan. In honour of the Two Chief Virtues of a People; Intrepidity in Foreign War: and Spirit of Domestic Liberty (1749)

King Henry the Fifth. Or, The Conquest of France by the English. A Tragedy (1723), repr. in *Dramatic Works*, I

'Preface to Mr Pope concerning the Sublimity of the Ancient Hebrew Poetry', prefixed to *The Creation. A Pindaric Illustration of a Poem originally written by Moses on that Subject* (1720), ed. G. G. Pahl, Augustan Reprint Society ser. 4 no. 2 (Ann Arbor, 1949)

Works (1753, 2/1754)

The History of Joseph (Ipswich, 1736)

Hoadly, John: 'Jephtha', *Gentleman's Magazine* 7 (1737), 144–7

Hogarth, William: *The Analysis of Beauty, Written with a View of Fixing the Fluctuating Ideas of Taste* (1753)

Hooker, Richard [William Webster]: *The Weekly Miscellany. Giving an Account of the Religion, Morality and Learning of the Present Times* (2/1738)

Hughes, John: *Calypso and Telemachus: An Opera* (1712)

'An Essay on Allegorical Poetry', prefixed to *The Works of Spenser*, ed. Hughes (1715, 2/1750)

Poems on Several Occasions (1735)

Six Cantata's or Poems for Musick. After the Manner of the Italians (1710), repr. in *Poems on Several Occasions* (1735)

Hume, David: *Political Discourses* (Edinburgh, 1752)

Three Essays (1748)

Humphreys, Samuel: *The Sacred Books of the Old and New Testament, Recited at Large* (1735)

Husbands, John, ed.: *A Miscellany of Poems by Several Hands* (Oxford, 1731)

Jacob, Hildebrand: 'Of the Sister Arts', in *Works* (1735)

Johnson, Charles: *The Tragedy of Medaea* (1731)

Johnson, Samuel: *A Dictionary of the English Language* (1755)

Lives of the English Poets, ed. G. B. Hill (Oxford, 1905)

Joseph Reviv'd: or The Heavenly Favourite (1714)

Kidder, Richard: *A Demonstration of the Messias. In which the Truth of the Christian Religion is Proved* (1684–99, 2/1726)

Lampe, John Frederick: *The Art of Musick* (1740)

Langhorne, John: *The Tears of Music: A Poem to the Memory of Mr Handel* (1760)

Lavington, George: *The Nature and Use of a Type* (1724)

Law, William: *The Absolute Unlawfulness of the Stage-Entertainment Fully Demonstrated* (1726)

Lediard, Thomas, and John Frederick Lampe: *Britannia* (1732)

Leland, John: *An Answer to a Late Book Intituled, Christianity as Old as the Creation* (1723, 2/1740)

The Divine Authority of the Old and New Testament Asserted . . . against . . . the Moral Philosopher (1739–40)

A Short View of the Principal Deistical Writers that have Appeared in England in the Last and Present Century (1754, 3/1757)

Leslie, Charles: *A Short and Easy Method with the Jews* (1698, 8/1737)

Lillo, George: *The London Merchant*, ed. William H. McBurney (1965)

Lockman, John: *David's Lamentation over Saul and Jonathan* (1736), in *A Miscellany of Lyric Poems* (1740)

Rosalinda: A Musical Drama . . . to which is Prefixed, An Enquiry into the Rise and Progress of Operas and Oratorios. With some Reflections on Lyric Poetry and Music (1740)

'Longinus': *Dionysius Longinus on the Sublime*, trans. and ed. William Smith (1739, 2/1743)

On the Sublime, ed. D. A. Russell (Oxford, 1964)

Lowman, Moses: *A Dissertation on the Civil Government of the Hebrews. In which the True Designs, and Nature of their Government Are Explained* (1740, 2/1745)

Lowth, Robert: *De sacra poesi hebraeorum praelectiones* (Oxford, 1753)

Lowth, William: *Directions for the Profitable Reading of the Holy Scriptures* (1708)

[Lyttelton, George, Lord:] *Letters from a Persian in England, to his Friend at Ispahan* (1735, 2/1735), repr. in *George Lyttelton's Political Tracts 1735–1748*, ed. Stephen Parks (New York, 1974)

Lyttelton, Thomas, Lord (attrib.): *Letters of the Late Lord Lyttelton* (1780, 2/1785)

Malcolm, Alexander: *A Treatise of Musick* (Edinburgh, 1721, London, 1730)

[Mainwaring, John, et al.:] *Memoirs of the Life of the Late George Frederic Handel* (1760)

Middleton, Conyers: *History of the Life of Marcus Tullius Cicero* (1741)

[Miller, James:] *Are These Things So?* and *The Great Man's Answer*, ed. I. Gordon, Augustan Reprint Society 153 (Los Angeles, 1972)

Miller, James: *The Art of Life, in imitation of Horace's Art of Poetry* (1739)
Art and Nature. A Comedy (1738)
The Coffee House (1737)

[Miller, James:] *The H-----r [Hanover] Heroes: or, A Song of Triumph ... By a H---------n [Hanoverian]. Translated from the High German, into English Verse, and the Metre Adapted to Tune of, The Miller of Mansfield* (1744)
Harlequin Horace: or, The Art of Modern Poetry (1731, 2/,3/1735)

Miller, James: *An Hospital for Fools: A Dramatic Fable* (1739)
The Humours of Oxford. A Comedy (1730)
The Man of Taste (1735)
The Mother in Law or, The Doctor the Disease. A Comedy (1734)

[Miller, James:] *Seasonable Reproof, or, A Satire in the manner of Horace* (1735)
The Year Forty-One: Carmen Seculare (1741)

A Miscellany of Lyric Poems, the Greatest Part Written for, and Performed in The Academy of Music, Held in the Apollo (1740)

Mist, Nathaniel: *A Collection of Miscellany Letters Selected out of Mist's Weekly Journal* (1722, 1727)

Montagu, Elizabeth: *The Letters of Mrs Elizabeth Montagu*, ed. Matthew Montagu (1809)

Morell, Thomas: *The Christian's Epinikion* (1743)
Hecuba, Translated from the Greek of Euripides (1749)
Notes and Annotations on Locke on the Human Understanding, Written by order of the Queen (1794)
Poems on Divine Subjects, Original, and Translated from the Latin of Marcus Hieronymus Vida, Bishop of Alba (and M. A. Flaminius) (1732, 2/1736)
Prometheus in Chains, Translated from the Greek of Aeschylus (1773)
'To Stephen Duck: Occasion'd by his Poem on Friendship' in Stephen Duck, *Verses on Several Occasions* (1736)

[Morgan, Thomas:] *A Defence of the Moral Philosopher* (1737)
The Moral Philosopher (1737–40, 2/1738–40)

Newton, Isaac: *Observations upon the Prophecies of Daniel* (1733)

Nichols, John: *Literary Anecdotes of the Eighteenth Century* (1812–15, repr. New York, 1966)

North, Roger: *Roger North on Music*, ed. J. Wilson (1959)

Of the Use and Improvement of the Stage: An Epistle to Charles Fleetwood esq (1737)

Orrery, Roger Boyle, first earl of: *Dramatic Works*, ed. W. S. Clark, jnr (Cambridge, MA, 1937)

Patrick, Simon: *A Commentary upon the Books of Joshua, Judges, and Ruth* (1702)

Parvish, Samuel: *An Inquiry into the Jewish and Christian Revelation, wherein all the Prophecies relating to the Jewish Messiah are Considered, and Compared with the Person and Character of Jesus Christ, and the Times of the Gospel; the Authority of the Canon of Scripture; the Nature and Use of Miracles, etc.* (1739)

Peirce, James: *A Vindication of the Dissenters* (1717)

Pemberton, Henry: *Observations on Poetry, especially the Epic* (1738)

Philips, Ambrose: *The Briton: A Tragedy* (1722)

Playford, John: *A Brief Introduction to the Skill of Musick* (1658, 18/1724)

Pope, Alexander: *The Correspondence of Alexander Pope*, ed. George Sherburn (Oxford, 1956)

The Dunciad, ed. James Sutherland, *The Poems of Alexander Pope*, V (3/1963)

Essay on Man, ed. Maynard Mack, *The Poems of Alexander Pope*, III.i (1950)

Imitations of Horace, ed. John Butt, *The Poems of Alexander Pope*, IV (1939)

Minor Poems, ed. Norman Ault and John Butt *The Poems of Alexander Pope*, VI (1954)

Pastoral Poetry and An Essay on Criticism, ed. E. Audra and Aubrey Williams, *The Poems of Alexander Pope*, I (1961)

Selected Prose of Alexander Pope, ed. Paul Hammond (Cambridge, 1987)

Prior, Matthew: *Literary Works*, ed. H. Bunker Wright and Monroe K. Spears (Oxford, 2/1971)

Poems on Several Occasions ... to which is Prefixed the Life of Mr Prior, by Samuel Humphreys, esq; (3/1733)

Racine, Jean: *Oeuvres*, ed. Pierre Coste (1723)

[Ralph, James:] *The Remembrancer ... the Twelve First Essays, from the Weekly Paper* (1748)

Ramsay, Andrew Michael: *The Travels of Cyrus* (1727, 6/1739)

A Review of the Moral and Political Life and Administration of the Patriarch Joseph: with some Remarks on the Ways and Means by him taken to Enslave the Egyptian Nation, and some Reflections on the Customs and Ceremonies of the Ancient Egyptians and Israelites (1743)

Rollin, Charles: *The Ancient History of the Egyptians, Carthaginians, Assyrians, Babylonians, Medes and Persians, Grecians and Macedonians* (2/1738–40)

The Method of Teaching and Studying the Belles Lettres (1734, 4/Dublin, 1742)

Rowe, Thomas: *Original Poems and Translations by Mr Thomas Rowe* (1738), in *The Miscellaneous Works in Prose and Verse of Mrs Elizabeth Rowe* (1739)

Rymer, Thomas: *Monsieur Rapin's Reflections on Aristotle's Treatise of Poesie . . . made English by Mr Rymer* (1694)

 A Short View of Tragedy (1692)

Saint Evremond, Charles de: 'Of Antient and Modern Tragedy', *Works Made English from the French Original* (1700, 2/1728)

Savage, Richard: *Poetical Works*, ed. Clarence Tracy (Cambridge, 1962)

Say, Samuel: *An Essay on the Harmony, Variety and Power of Numbers* (1745), ed. Paul Fussell, jnr, Augustan Reprint Society 55 (Los Angeles, 1956)

See and Seem Blind; or a Critical Dissertation on the Publick Diversions, &c . . . in a Letter from . . . Lord B----- [Burlington?] to A--- H--- [Aaron Hill?] esq (1732)

Shaftesbury, Anthony Ashley Cooper, third earl of: *Characteristicks of Men, Manners, Opinions, Times* (6/1738)

Sherlock, Thomas: *A Letter to the Clergy and People of London and Westminster . . . on occasion of the Late Earthquakes* (1750)

 The Use and Intent of Prophecy in the Several Ages of the World (1725, 2/1726)

[Shiels, Robert,] rev. Theophilus Cibber: 'The Life of the Revd. Mr. James Millar', in *The Lives of the Poets of Great-Britain and Ireland* (1753), V

Sophocles: *Electra* (English trans.) (1714)

Spence, Joseph: *An Essay on Pope's Odyssey* (1726)

Squire, Samuel: *An Enquiry into the Foundation of the English Constitution; or, An Historical Essay upon the Anglo-Saxon Government both in Germany and England* (1745, 2/1753)

[Squire, Samuel:] 'Theophanes Cantabrigiensis': *The Ancient History of the Hebrews Vindicated: or, Remarks on Part of the Third Volume of the Moral Philosopher* (Cambridge, 1741)

Stackhouse, Thomas: *A Complete Body of Speculative and Practical Divinity* (1729, 2/1734)

 A New History of the Holy Bible from the Beginning of the World to the Establishment of Christianity (1737, 1752)

The State of the Nation, with a General Balance of the Publick Accounts (1748)

Steele, Richard, et al., eds.: *Grammar of the English Tongue* (5/1728)

A Supplement to the Bishop of London's Letter to the Clergy and People of London and Westminster, on occasion of the Late Earthquakes (1750, 4/1750)

Sykes, Arthur Ashley: *An Essay upon the Truth of the Christian Religion: wherein its Real Foundation upon the Old Testament Is Shewn. Occasioned by the Discourse of the Grounds and Reasons of the Christian Religion* (1725, 2/1755)

Temple, Sir William: 'Of Heroic Virtue', in *Five Essays*, ed S.H. Monk (Ann Arbor, 1962)

Theobald, Lewis: *The Censor* (1717, 2/1717)

Thomson, James: *James Thomson (1700–1748): Letters and Documents*, ed. Alan D. McKillop (Lawrence, KS, 1958)

The Seasons and The Castle of Indolence, ed. James Sambrook (Oxford, 1972, rev. 1987)

Works (1766)

and David Mallet: *Alfred, A Masque* (1740)

Tindal, Matthew: *Christianity as Old as the Creation* (1730, 3/1732)

Toland, John: *Christianity not Mysterious: or, A Treatise shewing, that there is Nothing in the Gospel contrary to Reason, nor above it: and that no Doctrine can properly be called a Mystery* (1696, 1702)

Tosi, Pier Francesco: *Opinioni de'cantori antichi e moderni, o sieno osservazioni sopra il canto figurato* (Bologna, 1723), trans. J. E. Galliard as *Observations on the Florid Song* (1742, 2/1743)

The Touch-stone: or, Historical, Critical, Political, Philosophical and Theological Essays on the Reigning Diversions of the Town. Design'd for the Improvement of all Authors, Spectators, and Actors of Operas, Plays, and Masquerades. In which Every Thing Antique, or Modern, relating to Musick, Poetry, Dancing, Pantomimes, Chorusses, Cat-Calls, Audiences, Judges, Criticks, Balls, Ridottos, Assemblies, New Oratory, Circus, Bear-Garden, Gladiators, Prize-Fighters, Italian Strolers, Mountebank Stages, Cock-Pits, Puppet-Shews, Fairs, and Publick Auctions, is occasionally Handled. By a Person of some Taste and some Quality. With a Preface, giving an Account of the Author and the Work (1728)

Trapp, Joseph: *The Aeneis of Virgil Translated into English Blank Verse* (1718)

Lectures on Poetry, trans. W. Bowyer and W. Clarke (1742, first pubd in Latin, Oxford, 1711–19)

Trenchard, John: *Considerations upon the State of our Public Debts* (1720)

[Trenchard, John, and Thomas Gordon:] *Cato's Letters: or, Essays on Liberty, Civil and Religious, and other Important Subjects* (1724, 4/1737)

Upton, John: *Critical Observations on Shakespeare* (1746)

[Walpole, Horace:] *A Letter to the Whigs* (1747, 2/1748)

A Second and Third Letter to the Whigs (1748)

Warburton, William: *The Divine Legation of Moses* (1737, 1741)

Warton, Joseph: *An Essay on the Genius and Writings of Pope* (1756)

Waterland, Daniel: *Scripture Vindicated* (1731–2), in *Works*, VI (Oxford, 1823)

Watson, Richard: *Collection of Theological Tracts* (Cambridge, 1785)

Watts, Isaac: *Horae Lyricae* (1709, 9/1753)

Hymns and Spiritual Songs (1707), repr. in *Works* (1753), IV

The Psalms of David, Imitated in the Language of the New Testament, and Apply'd to the Christian State and Worship (1718), repr. in *Works* (1753), IV

Reliquiae Juveniles: Miscellaneous Thoughts in Prose and Verse, on Natural, Moral, and Divine Subjects, Written chiefly in Younger Years (1734), repr. in *Works* (1753), IV

Remnants of Time Employed in Prose and Verse (1736), repr. in *Works* (1753), IV

A *Short View of the Whole Scripture History* (1732), repr. in *Works* (1753),
III

[Weedon, Cavendish:] *The Oration and Poem at Mr Weedon's Entertainment of
Divine Musick . . . Perform'd at Stationers-Hall, on Tuesday the 6th of Jan.
1702* [new style] (1702)

*Oration, Anthems and Poems, Spoken and Sung at the Performance of Divine
Musick. For the Entertainment of the Lords Spiritual and Temporal and the
honourable House of Commons at Stationers-Hall, January the 31st 1701* [old
style] *Undertaken by Cavendish Weedon Esq* (1602 [recte 1702])

*The Oration, Anthems and Poems, Spoken and Sung at the Performance of Divine
Musick, at Stationers-Hall, for the Month of May, 1702, Undertaken by
Cavendish Weedon, Esq.* (1702)

Wesley, John: *The Works of John Wesley* (1872, repr. Grand Rapids, MI,
n.d.)

Wesley, Samuel: *The History of the Old Testament in Verse* (1715)

Wheatly, Charles: *The Church of England Man's Companion; or, a Rational
Illustration of the Harmony . . . and Usefulness of the Book of Common Prayer*
(Oxford, 1710, 8/1759)

Whitefield, George: *George Whitefield's Journals*, ed. Iain Murray (1960)

Woolston, Thomas: *Six Discourses on the Miracles of our Saviour* (1727–30)

Young, Edward: *Poetical Works* (1741)

NINETEENTH- AND TWENTIETH-CENTURY
PUBLICATIONS

Alderman, William E.: 'Shaftesbury and the Doctrine of Moral Sense',
PMLA 46 (1931), 1087–94

Allen, Brian: *Francis Hayman* (1987)

Armitage, David: 'The British Empire and the Civic Tradition 1656–
1742', Ph.D. diss., University of Cambridge (1991)

'The Cromwellian Protectorate and the Languages of Empire', *HJ* 35
(1992), 531–55

Arnold, Denis and Elsie: *The Oratorio in Venice*, Royal Musical Association
Monographs 2 (1986)

Atherton, Herbert M.: *Political Prints in the Age of Hogarth: A Study of the
Iconographic Representation of Politics* (Oxford, 1974)

Avery, E. L., A. H. Scouten, and G. Winchester Stone, jnr, eds.: *The London
Stage 1660–1800*, II–IV (Carbondale, IL, 1960–2)

Ayers, Robert W.: '*Robinson Crusoe*: "Allusive Allegorick History"', *PMLA*
82 (1967), 399–407

Baker, C. H. Collins and Muriel: *The Life and Circumstances of James Brydges
First Duke of Chandos* (Oxford, 1949)

Baker, David, et al.: *Biographia Dramatica* (3/1812)

Baker, Frank: 'The People Called Methodists – 3. Polity', in *A History of the
Methodist Church in Britain*, I, ed. Rupert Davies and Gordon Rupp
(1965), pp. 211–55

Ball, Terence: 'Party', in *Political Innovation and Conceptual Change*, ed. Terence Ball, James Farr and Russell L. Hanson (Cambridge, 1989), pp. 155–76

Barber, Giles: 'Bolingbroke, Pope, and the *Patriot King*', *The Library*, 5th ser., 19 (1964), 67–89

Barcham, William L.: *The Religious Paintings of Giambattista Tiepolo: Piety and Tradition in Eighteenth-Century Venice* (Oxford, 1989)

Barry, Jonathan: 'Cultural Patronage and the Anglican Crisis: Bristol *c.* 1689–1775', in *The Church of England c. 1689 – c. 1833: From Toleration to Tractarianism*, ed. John Walsh, Colin Haydon and Stephen Taylor (Cambridge, 1993), pp. 191–208

Bartlett, Ian: 'Boyce and Early English Oratorio – I', *MT* 120 (1979), 293–7

Battestin, Martin C., with Ruthe R. Battestin: *Henry Fielding: A Life* (1989, repr. 1993)

Beeks, Graydon: 'The *Chandos Anthems* of Haym, Handel and Pepusch', *GHB* 5 (1993), 161–93

    '"A Club of Composers": Handel, Pepusch and Arbuthnot at Cannons', in *Handel Tercentenary Collection*, ed. Stanley Sadie and Anthony Hicks (1987), pp. 209–21

    'Handel and Music for the Earl of Carnarvon', in *Bach, Handel, Scarlatti: Tercentenary Essays*, ed. Peter Williams (Cambridge, 1985), pp. 1–20

Bennett, G. V.: *The Tory Crisis in Church and State 1688–1730: The Career of Francis Atterbury, Bishop of Rochester* (Oxford, 1975)

Biddle, Leslie J.: 'The Principal Characters of the Royal Arch Story', *Ars Quatuor Coronatorum* 79 (1966), 283–9

Black, Jeremy: *British Foreign Policy in the Age of Walpole* (Edinburgh, 1985)
    The English Press in the Eighteenth Century (1987)
    'Introduction: An Age of Political Stability?', in *Britain in the Age of Walpole*, ed. Black (1984), pp. 1–22
    'Lord Bolingbroke's Operatic Allegory', *The Scriblerian* 16 (1984), 97–9
    Natural and Necessary Enemies: Anglo-French Relations in the Eighteenth Century (1986)
    A System of Ambition? British Foreign Policy 1660–1793 (1991)
    'The Tory View of Eighteenth-Century British Foreign Policy', *HJ* 31 (1988), 469–77

Brereton, Geoffrey: *Jean Racine: A Critical Biography* (1951)

Brett, Philip and George Haggerty: 'Handel and the Sentimental: The Case of *Athalia*', *M&L* 68 (1987), 112–27

Brewer, John: *The Sinews of Power: War, Money and the English State 1688–1783* (1989)

Brewster, Dorothy: *Aaron Hill* (New York, 1913)

Bridenbaugh, Carl: *Mitre and Sceptre: Transatlantic Faiths, Ideas, Personalities, and Politics 1689–1775* (New York, 1962)

Brownell, M. R.: 'Ears of an Untoward Make: Pope and Handel', *Musical Quarterly* 62 (1976), 554–70

Browning, Reed: *Political and Constitutional Ideas of the Court Whigs* (Baton Rouge, LA, 1982)

Broxap, Henry: *The Later Non-Jurors* (Cambridge, 1924)

Burden, Michael: *The Masque of Alfred* (Lewiston, NY, 1994)

Burrows, Donald: 'Handel and Hanover', in *Bach, Handel, Scarlatti: Tercentenary Essays*, ed. Peter Williams (Cambridge, 1985), pp. 35–59

Handel: Messiah (Cambridge, 1990)

'Israel in Egypt', *Maryland Handel Festival Programme Booklet* (Bethesda, 1987)

'Theology, Politics and Instruments in Church: Musicians and Monarchs in London, 1660–1760', *GHB* 5 (1993), 145–60

Burtt, Shelley: *Virtue Transformed: Political Argument in England, 1688–1740* (Cambridge, 1992)

Butler, Rohan: *Choiseul*, I, *Father and Son* (Oxford, 1980)

Buttrey, T. V.: 'Tragedy as Form in Euripides', *Michigan Quarterly Review* 15.2 (Spring 1976), 155–72

Cassidy, G. E.: *The Chapel of St Anne, Kew Green, 1710–1769*, Richmond Historical Society Paper no. 2 (Richmond, 1985)

Castells, F. de P.: *English Freemasonry in its Period of Transition AD 1600–1700* (1931)

Champion, Justin: *The Pillars of Priestcraft Shaken: The Church of England and its Enemies, 1660–1730* (Cambridge, 1992)

Channon, Merlin: 'Handel's Early Performances of *Judas Maccabaeus*: Some New Evidence and Interpretations', *M&L* forthcoming

Chisholm, Duncan: 'New Sources for the Libretto of Handel's *Joseph*', in *Handel Tercentenary Collection*, ed. Stanley Sadie and Anthony Hicks (1987), pp. 182–208

Clark, J. C. D.: *The Dynamics of Change: The Crisis of the 1750s and English Party* (Cambridge, 1982)

English Society 1688–1832: Ideology, Social Structure and Political Practice during the Ancien Régime (Cambridge, 1985)

'A General Theory of Party, Opposition and Government, 1688–1832', *HJ* 23 (1980), 295–325

Clark, Jane: 'For Kings and Senates Fit', *Georgian Group Journal* (1990), 55–63

'"Lord Burlington Is Here": A View without Architecture', in *Lord Burlington: Architecture, Art and Life*, ed. Toby Barnard and Jane Clark (1995)

'The Mysterious Mr Buck', *Apollo*, May, 1989, 317–22

'Palladianism and the Divine Right of Kings', *Apollo*, April, 1992, 224–9

Cleary, Thomas R.: *Henry Fielding: Political Writer* (Waterloo, Ont., 1984)

Cobbett, William: *The Parliamentary History of England* (1812)

Colley, Linda: *Britons: Forging the Nation 1707–1837* (New Haven, 1992)

In Defiance of Oligarchy: The Tory Party 1714–60 (Cambridge, 1982)

Collinson, Patrick: *The Birthpangs of Protestant England: Religious and Cultural Change in the Sixteenth and Seventeenth Centuries* (1988, repr. 1991)

Conolly, L. W.: *The Censorship of English Drama 1737–1824* (San Marino, CA, 1976)

Cox, Howard: 'The Text Selection Process in Handel's Chandos Anthems', *Bach* 24/2 (Spring–Summer 1993), 21–34

Cranfield, G. A.: 'The *London Evening Post* and the Jew Bill of 1753', *HJ* 8 (1965), 16–30

Cruickshanks, Eveline: *Lord Cornbury, Bolingbroke and a Plan to Restore the Stuarts 1731–5*, Royal Stuart Papers 27 (Huntingdon, 1986)
'The Political Management of Sir Robert Walpole, 1720–42', in *Britain in the Age of Walpole*, ed. J. Black (1984), pp. 23–43
Political Untouchables: The Tories and the '45 (1979)

Cuming, Geoffrey: 'The Text of "Messiah"', *M&L* 31 (1950), 226–30

Cunningham, Hugh: 'The Language of Patriotism', in *Patriotism: The Making and Unmaking of British National Identity*, ed. R. Samuel (1989), I, *History and Politics*, pp. 58–60

Curtis, T. C., and W. A. Speck: 'The Societies for Reformation of Manners: A Case Study in the Theory and Practice of Moral Reform', *Literature and History* 3 (1976), 45–64

Dann, Uriel: *Hanover and Great Britain 1740–1760* (Leicester, 1991)

David, Alun: 'Christopher Smart and the Hebrew Bible: Poetry and Biblical Criticism in England (1682–1771)', Ph.D. diss., University of Cambridge (1994)

Davie, Donald: *The Eighteenth-Century Hymn in England* (Cambridge, 1993)
Purity of Diction in English Verse (1952, New York, 1967)

Davies, G., and M. Tinling: 'Letters from James Brydges, Created Duke of Chandos, to Henry St. John, Created Viscount Bolingbroke', *Huntington Library Bulletin* 9 (1936), 119–66

Davies, Horton: *Worship and Theology in England*, (Princeton, 1961–75), III, *From Watts and Wesley to Maurice, 1690–1850* (1961)

Davies, Rupert: 'The People Called Methodists – 1. "Our Doctrines"', in *A History of the Methodist Church in Britain*, I, ed. Rupert Davies and Gordon Rupp (1965), pp. 145–79

Davis, David Brion: *The Problem of Slavery in Western Culture* (Ithaca, NY, 1966)

Dean, Winton: *Handel's Dramatic Oratorios and Masques* (1959)
and J. Merrill Knapp: *Handel's Operas 1704–1726* (1987)

Dearnley, Christopher: *English Church Music 1650–1750* (1970)

Dearnley, Moira: *The Poetry of Christopher Smart* (1968)

Deconinck-Brossard, F.: 'The Churches and the '45', in *The Church and War* (*Studies in Church History* 20), ed. W. J. Sheils (Oxford, 1983), pp. 253–62

Deutsch, Otto Erich: *Handel: A Documentary Biography* (1955)

Dickinson, H. T.: *Bolingbroke* (1970)
'The Eighteenth-Century Debate on the "Glorious Revolution"', *History* 61 (1976), 28–45
Liberty and Property: Political Ideology in Eighteenth-Century Britain (1977)

'The Politics of Pope', in *Alexander Pope: Essays for the Tercentenary*, ed.
C. Nicholson (Aberdeen, 1988), 1–21

'Whiggism in the Eighteenth Century', in *The Whig Ascendancy*, ed. John
Cannon (1981), pp. 28–50

Dixon, Peter: 'Pope and James Miller', *Notes & Queries* 215 (1970), 91–2

Dobrée, Bonamy: 'The Theme of Patriotism in the Poetry of the Early
Eighteenth Century', *Proceedings of the British Academy* 35 (1949),
49–65

Doody, Margaret Anne: *The Daring Muse: Augustan Poetry Reconsidered*
(Cambridge, 1985)

Edwards, Averyl: *Frederick Louis, Prince of Wales 1707–1751* (1947)

Edwards, Maldwyn: 'John Wesley', in *A History of the Methodist Church in
Britain*, I, ed. Rupert Davies and Gordon Rupp (1965), pp. 35–79

Eisen, Walter and Margret, eds.: *Händel-Handbuch Band 4: Dokumente zu
Leben und Schaffen auf der Grundlage von Otto Erich Deutsch, Handel, A
Documentary Biography* (Kassel, 1985)

Emerson, Roger L.: 'Latitudinarianism and the English Deists', in *Deism,
Masonry and the Enlightenment: Essays honoring Alfred Owen Aldridge*, ed.
J. A. Leo Lemay (Newark, NJ, 1987), pp. 19–48

Endelman, Todd M.: *The Jews of Georgian England* (Philadelphia, 1979)

Engel, Helmut: *Die Susanna-Erzählung*, Orbis Biblicus et Orientalis 61
(Göttingen, 1985), pp. 35–40

Erskine-Hill, Howard: 'Alexander Pope: The Political Poet in his Time',
ECS 15 (1981–2), 123–41

The Augustan Idea in English Literature (1983)

'Literature and the Jacobite Cause: Was there a Rhetoric of Jacobitism?'
in *Ideology and Conspiracy: Aspects of Jacobitism, 1689–1759*, ed. E. Cruickshanks (Edinburgh, 1982), pp. 49–69

The Social Milieu of Alexander Pope (New Haven and London, 1975)

Evans, W. M.: 'From the Land of Canaan to the Land of Guinea: The
Strange Odyssey of the Sons of Ham', *American Historical Review* 85
(1980), 15–43

Fellowes, E. H.: *English Cathedral Music* (1941), new edn rev. J.A. Westrup
(1969)

Fiske, Roger: *English Theatre Music in the Eighteenth Century* (1973, 2/Oxford
1986)

Foxon, D. F.: *English Verse 1701–1750: A Catalogue of Separately Printed Poems*
(Cambridge, 1975)

Fritz, Paul S.: *The English Ministers and Jacobitism between the Rebellions of
1715 and 1745* (Toronto, 1976)

Garrison, James D.: *Dryden and the Tradition of Panegyric* (Berkeley, 1975)

George, A. Raymond: 'The People Called Methodists – 4. The Means of
Grace', in *A History of the Methodist Church in Britain*, I, ed. Rupert
Davies and Gordon Rupp (1965), pp. 259–73

Gerrard, Christine: '*The Castle of Indolence* and the Opposition to Walpole',
Review of English Studies new ser. 41 (1990), 44–64

The Patriot Opposition to Walpole: Politics, Poetry, and National Myth, 1725–1742 (Oxford, 1994)

'The Patriot Opposition to Sir Robert Walpole: A Study of Politics and Poetry, 1725–1742', D.Phil. diss., University of Oxford (1986)

'Pope and the Patriots' in *Pope: New Contexts*, ed. David Fairer (Hemel Hempstead, 1990), pp. 25–43

Gianturco, Carolyn: '"Cantate spirituali e morali", with a Description of the Papal Sacred Cantata Tradition for Christmas 1676–1740', *M&L* 73 (1992), 1–31

'*Il trionfo del Tempo e del Disinganno*: Four Case-Studies in Determining Italian Poetic-Musical Genres', *Journal of the Royal Musical Association* 119 (1994), 43–59

Gibbs, Graham C.: 'English Attitudes towards Hanover and the Hanoverian Succession in the First Half of the Eighteenth Century', in *England und Hannover / England and Hanover*, ed. Adolf M. Birke and Kurt Kluxen (Munich, 1986), pp. 33–51

Gibson, Elizabeth: 'The Royal Academy of Music and its Directors', in *Handel Tercentenary Collection*, ed. Stanley Sadie and Anthony Hicks (1987), pp. 138–64

Goldgar, Bertrand A.: *Walpole and the Wits: The Relation of Politics to Literature 1722–1742* (Lincoln, NE, 1976)

Goldie, Mark: 'The Civil Religion of James Harrington', in *The Languages of Political Theory in Early-Modern Europe*, ed. Anthony Pagden (Cambridge, 1987), pp. 197–222

Goldsmith, M. M.: 'Faction Detected: Ideological Consequences of Robert Walpole's Decline and Fall', *History* 64 (1979), 1–19

Private Vices, Public Benefits: Bernard Mandeville's Social and Political Thought (Cambridge, 1985)

Goldstein, Lawrence: *Ruins and Empire: The Evolution of a Theme in Augustan and Romantic Literature* (Pittsburgh, PA, 1977)

Gould, Eliga H.: 'To Strengthen the King's Hands: Dynastic Legitimacy, Militia Reform and Ideas of National Unity in England 1745–1760', *HJ* 34 (1991), 329–48

Gregory, Jeremy: 'Anglicanism and the Arts: Religion, Culture and Politics in the Eighteenth Century', in *Culture, Politics and Society in Britain, 1660–1800*, ed. Jeremy Black and Jeremy Gregory (Manchester, 1991), pp. 82–109

Griffin, Dustin: 'Milton and the Decline of Epic in the Eighteenth Century', *New Literary History* 14 (1982), 143–54

Regaining Paradise: Milton and the Eighteenth Century (Cambridge, 1986)

Grout, Donald J., with Claude V. Palisca: *A History of Western Music* (3/1981)

Guerinot, J. V., and R. D. Jilg: *Contexts 1: The Beggar's Opera* (Hamden, CT, 1976)

Gunn, J. A. W.: *Beyond Liberty and Property: The Process of Self-Recognition in Eighteenth-Century Political Thought* (Kingston and Montreal, 1983)

Factions No More: Attitudes to Party and Government in Eighteenth-Century England (1973)

Halsband, Robert: *Lord Hervey: Eighteenth Century Courtier* (Oxford, 1974)

Hammond, Brean: *Pope and Bolingbroke: A Study of Friendship and Influence* (Columbia, MO, 1984)

Harding, Richard: *Amphibious Warfare in the Eighteenth Century: The British Expedition to the West Indies 1740–1742* (Woodbridge, Suffolk, 1991)

Harris, Ellen T.: *Handel and the Pastoral Tradition* (1980)
  The Librettos of Handel's Operas (New York, 1989)

Harris, George: *The Life of Lord Chancellor Hardwicke* (1847)

Harris, Michael: *London Newspapers in the Age of Walpole: A Study in the Origins of the Modern English Press* (1987)
  'Print and Politics in the Age of Walpole', in *Britain in the Age of Walpole*, ed. J. Black (1984), pp. 189–210

Harris, Robert: *A Patriot Press: National Politics and the London Press in the 1740s* (Oxford, 1993)

Harris, Victor: 'Allegory to Analogy in the Interpretation of Scriptures', *PQ*, 45 (1966), 1–23

Hart, Jeffrey: *Viscount Bolingbroke: Tory Humanist* (1965)

Hawkins, Edward: *Medallic Illustrations of the History of Great Britain and Ireland to the Death of George II*, ed. A. W. Franks and H. A. Grueber (1885)

Henderson, George D.: *Chevalier Ramsay* (Edinburgh, 1952)

Herbage, Julian: *Messiah* (1948)

Herrmann, William, ed.: *George Frideric Handel: Funeral Anthem for Queen Caroline* (New York, 1976)

Hertz (Hurst), G. B.: *British Imperialism in the Eighteenth Century* (1908)

Hicks, Anthony: 'Handel, Jennens and *Saul*: Aspects of a Collaboration', in *Music and Theatre: Essays in honour of Winton Dean*, ed. Nigel Fortune (Cambridge, 1987), pp. 203–27
  'Handel's "La Resurrezione"', *MT* 110 (1969), 145–8

Hill, Christopher: *The English Bible and the Seventeenth-Century Revolution* (1993)

Hogwood, Christopher: *Handel* (1984)
  'Thomas Tudway's History of Music', in *Music in Eighteenth Century England: Essays in memory of Charles Cudworth*, ed. Christopher Hogwood and Richard Luckett (Cambridge, 1983), pp. 19–47

Hollander, John: *The Untuning of the Sky* (New York 1961, repr. 1970)

Holmes, Geoffrey, and Daniel Szechi: *The Age of Oligarchy: Pre-Industrial Britain 1722–1783* (1993)

Hopkinson, Marie Ruan: *Married to Mercury: A Sketch of Lord Bolingbroke and his Wives* (1936)

Hume, Robert D.: 'Handel and Opera Management in London in the 1730s', *M&L* 67 (1986), 347–62
  'Henry Fielding and Politics at the Little Haymarket, 1728–1737', in *The Golden and the Brazen World: Papers in Literature and History, 1650–1800*, ed. J. M. Wallace (Berkeley, 1985), pp. 79–124

'Texts within Contexts: Notes toward a Historical Method', *PQ* 71 (1992), 69–100

Inglesfield, Robert: 'James Thomson, Aaron Hill and the Poetic "Sublime"', *BJECS* 13 (1990), 215–21

Jackson, Keith B.: *Beyond the Craft* (Shepperton, 2/1982)

Jacob, James R., and Timothy Raylor: 'Opera and Obedience: Thomas Hobbes and *A Proposition for Advancement of Moralitie* by Sir William Davenant', *The Seventeenth Century* 6 (1991), 205–50

Jacob, Margaret C.: *The Newtonians and the English Revolution 1689–1720* (Hassocks, Sussex, 1976)

The Radical Enlightenment (1981)

Johnson, J. T.: *Ideology, Reason, and the Limitation of War: Religious and Secular Concepts 1200–1740* (Princeton, 1975)

Jones, Stephen: *Frederick, Prince of Wales and His Circle* (Sudbury, 1981)

Jordan, Gerald, and Nicholas Rogers: 'Admirals as Heroes: Patriotism and Liberty in Hanoverian England', *Journal of British Studies* 28 (1989), 201–24

Keates, Jonathan: *Handel: The Man and his Music* (1985)

Kemp, Betty: 'Frederick, Prince of Wales', in *Silver Renaissance: Essays in Eighteenth-Century English History*, ed. Alex Natan (1961), pp. 38–56

Kenyon, J. P.: *Revolution Principles* (Cambridge, 1977)

Kivy, Peter: 'Mainwaring's *Handel*: Its Relation to English Aesthetics', *Journal of the American Musicological Society* 17 (1964), 170–8

Knapp, J. Merrill: 'The Hall Handel Collection', *Princeton University Library Chronicle* 36 (1974), 3–18

Korshin, Paul: *Typologies in England, 1650–1820* (Princeton, 1982)

'Queuing and Waiting: The Apocalypse in England, 1660–1750', in *The Apocalypse in English Renaissance Thought and Culture*, ed. C. A. Patrides and J. Wittreich (Manchester, 1984), pp. 240–65

Kramnick, Isaac: *Bolingbroke and his Circle: The Politics of Nostalgia in the Age of Walpole* (Cambridge, MA, 1968)

Lam, Basil: 'The Church Music', in *Handel: A Symposium*, ed. Gerald Abraham (1954), pp. 156–78

Landa, Louis A.: 'Pope's Belinda, the General Emporie of the World, and the Wondrous Worm' (1971), repr. in *Essays in Eighteenth Century English Literature* (Princeton, 1980), pp. 178–98

'Of Silkworms and Farthingales and the Will of God' (1973), repr. in *Essays in Eighteenth Century English Literature* (Princeton, 1980), pp. 199–217

Lang, Paul Henry: 'The Composer', in *Man versus Society in Eighteenth-Century Britain*, ed. James L. Clifford (Cambridge, 1968), pp. 85–101

George Frideric Handel (1967)

Langford, Paul: *The Eighteenth Century, 1688–1815* (1976)

The Excise Crisis: Society and Politics in the Age of Walpole (Oxford, 1975)

A Polite and Commercial People: England, 1727–1783 (Oxford, 1989)

Public Life and the Propertied Englishman 1689–1798 (Oxford, 1991)

'Tories and Jacobites 1714–51', in *The History of the University of Oxford*, V: *The Eighteenth Century*, ed. L. S. Sutherland and L. G. Mitchell (Oxford, 1986), pp. 99–127

Larsen, Jens Peter: *Handel's Messiah: Origins, Composition, Sources* (1957)
'Wandlungen der Auffassung von Händels "Messias"', *GHB* 1 (1984), 7–19

Larsson, Roger B.: 'Charles Avison's "Stiles in Musical Expression"', *M&L* 63 (1982), 261–75

Lawson, John: 'The People Called Methodists – 2. "Our Discipline"', in *A History of the Methodist Church in Britain*, I, ed. Rupert Davies and Gordon Rupp (1965), pp. 181–209

Leopold, Silke: '"Israel in Egypt" – ein mißglückter Glücksfall', *GHB* 1 (1984), 35–50

Leranbaum, Miriam: *Alexander Pope's 'Opus Magnum' 1729–1744* (Oxford, 1977)

Lewalski, Barbara: *Protestant Poetics and the Seventeenth-Century Religious Lyric* (Princeton, 1979)

Lightwood, James T.: *Methodist Music in the Eighteenth Century* (1927)

Lincoln, Stoddard: 'Handel's Music for Queen Anne', *Musical Quarterly* 45 (1959), 191–207

Lindgren, Lowell: 'Another Critic Named Samber whose "Particular Historical Significance Has Gone Almost Entirely Unnoticed"', in *Festa Musicologica: Essays in honor of George Buelow* (forthcoming)

Loewenthal [= Smith], Ruth: 'Handel and Newburgh Hamilton: New References in the Strafford Papers', *MT* 112 (1971), 1063–6

Loftis, John: 'Political and Social Thought in the Drama', in *The London Theatre World 1660–1800*, ed. Robert D. Hume (Carbondale, 1980), pp. 263–75
The Politics of Drama in Augustan England (Oxford, 1963)
'Thomson's *Tancred and Sigismunda* and the Demise of the Drama of Political Opposition', in *The Stage and the Page: London's 'Whole Show' in the Eighteenth-Century Theatre*, ed. George Winchester Stone, jnr (Berkeley, 1981), pp. 34–54

Lovell, Percy: '"Ancient" Music in Eighteenth-Century England', *M&L* 60 (1979), 401–15

Lowens, Irving: 'The *Touch-Stone* (1728): a Neglected View of London Opera', *Musical Quarterly* 45 (1959), 325–42

Luckett, Richard: *Handel's Messiah: A Celebration* (1992)

Lutaud, Olivier: *Des révolutions d'Angleterre à la révolution française* (The Hague, 1973)

Lynch, Kathleen M.: *Roger Boyle, First Earl of Orrery* (Knoxville, TN, 1965)

Lysons, D., continued J. Amott, C. Lee and H. Godwin Chance: *Origin and Progress of the Meeting of the Three Choirs of Gloucester, Worcester and Hereford and of the Charity Connected with it* (Gloucester, 1895)

Mace, Dean Tolle: 'The Doctrine of Sound and Sense in Augustan Poetic Theory', *Review of English Studies* new ser. 2 (1951), 129–39

McGeary, Thomas: 'Opera, Satire, and Politics in the Walpole Era', in *The Past as Prologue: Essays to Celebrate the Twenty-Fifth Anniversary of ASECS*, ed. Carla H. Hay with Syndy M. Conger (New York, 1994), pp. 347–72

'Shaftesbury, Handel, and Italian Opera', *HJb* 32 (1986), 99–104

'Shaftesbury on Opera, Spectacle and Liberty', *M&L* 74 (1993), 530–41

'"Warbling Eunuchs": Opera, Gender, and Sexuality on the London Stage, 1705–1742', *Restoration and Eighteenth-Century Theatre Research* 2nd ser. VII/1 (Summer, 1992), 1–22

McGuinness, Rosamond: *English Court Odes 1660–1820* (Oxford, 1971)

and H. Diack Johnstone: 'Concert Life in England I', in *The Blackwell History of Music in Britain: The Eighteenth Century*, ed. Johnstone and Roger Fiske (Oxford, 1990), pp. 31–95

Mack, Maynard: *The Garden and the City: Retirement and Politics in the Later Poetry of Pope 1731–43* (Toronto, 1969)

McKillop, Alan D.: 'The Early History of *Alfred*', *PQ* 41 (1962), 311–24

The Background of Thomson's 'Liberty', Rice Institute Pamphlet: Monograph in English 38/2 (Houston, 1951)

'Ethics and Political History in Thomson's *Liberty*', in *Pope and his Contemporaries: Essays presented to George Sherburn*, ed. J. L. Clifford and L. A. Landa (Oxford, 1949), pp. 215–29

McLynn, Frank: 'The Ideology of Jacobitism on the Eve of the Rising of 1745', *History of European Ideas* 6 (1985), 1–18, 173–88

Madden, Frederick, with David Fieldhouse, eds.: *The Classical Period of the First British Empire, 1689–1783* (*Select Documents in the Constitutional History of the British Empire and Commonwealth*, II) (Westport, CT, and London, 1985)

Mann, Alfred: '*Messiah*: The Verbal Text', in *Festskrift Jens Peter Larsen*, ed. Nils Schiørring, Henrik Glahn and Carsten E. Hatting (Copenhagen, 1972), pp. 181–8

Marshall, Madeleine Forsell, and Janet Todd: *English Congregational Hymns in the Eighteenth Century* (Lexington, KY, 1982)

Marshall, P. J.: 'The Eighteenth-Century Empire', in *British Politics and Society from Walpole to Pitt, 1742–1789*, ed. J. Black (1990), pp. 177–200

Massue, M. H., Marquis de Ruvigny et Raineval: *The Jacobite Peerage* (Edinburgh, 1904)

Matthews, Betty: 'Unpublished Letters concerning Handel', *M&L* 40 (1959), 261–8

Meehan, Michael: *Liberty and Poetics in Eighteenth-Century England* (1986)

Miller, John: *Religion in the Popular Prints* (The English Satirical Print 1600–1832) (Cambridge, 1986)

Monk, Samuel H.: *The Sublime: A Study of Critical Theories in Eighteenth-Century England* (New York, 1935, repr. Ann Arbor, 1960)

Monod, Paul: *Jacobitism and the English People 1688–1788* (Cambridge, 1989)

Moore, Cecil A.: 'Shaftesbury and the Ethical Poets in England', *PMLA* 31 (1916), 264–325

'Whig Panegyric Verse: A Phase of Sentimentalism', *PMLA* 41 (1926), 362–401, repr. in *Backgrounds to English Literature 1700–1760* (Minneapolis, 1953), pp. 104–44

Morehen, John: 'The English Anthem Text, 1549–1660', *Journal of the Royal Musical Association* 117 (1992), 62–85

Morris, David B.: *The Religious Sublime: Christian Poetry and Critical Tradition in Eighteenth-Century England* (Lexington, KY, 1972)

Myers, Robert Manson: *Handel's Messiah: A Touchstone of Taste* (New York, 1948)

'Neoclassical Criticism of the Ode for Music', *PMLA* 62 (1947), 399–421

Napthine, D., and W.A. Speck: 'Clergymen and Conflict 1660–1763', in *The Church and War (Studies in Church History* 20), ed. W. J. Sheils (Oxford, 1983), pp. 231–51

Newman, Gerald: *The Rise of British Nationalism 1740–1830: A Cultural History* (1987)

Nokes, David: *Jonathan Swift: A Hypocrite Reversed* (Oxford, 1985)

Norton, David: *A History of the Bible as Literature* (Cambridge, 1993)

O'Brien, Paula: 'The Life and Works of James Miller', Ph.D. diss., University of London (1979)

Osborn, James M.: 'Pope, the "Apollo of the Arts", and his Countess', in *England in the Restoration and Eighteenth Century*, ed. H. T. Swedenborg, jnr (Berkeley and Los Angeles, 1972), pp. 101–43

Overton, J. H.: *The Nonjurors* (1902)

Parks, Stephen: 'The Osborn Collection: A 4th Biennial Report', *Yale University Library Gazette* 50 (1975–6), 182

Pascoe, C. F.: *Two Hundred Years of the SPG: An Historical Account of the Society for the Propagation of the Gospel in Foreign Parts, 1701–1900* (1901)

Percival, Milton: *Political Ballads illustrating the Administration of Sir Robert Walpole* (Oxford, 1916)

Perry, Thomas W.: *Public Opinion, Propaganda, and Politics: A Study of the Jew Bill of 1753* (Cambridge, MA, 1962)

Peskin, Allan: 'England's Jewish Naturalization Bill of 1753', *Historia Judaica* 19 (1957), 3–32

Pittock, Murray: 'New Jacobite Songs of the Forty-Five', *Studies in Voltaire and the Eighteenth Century* 267 (1989), 1–75

Poetry and Jacobite Politics in Eighteenth-Century Britain and Ireland (Cambridge, 1994)

Platt, Richard: 'Theatre Music I', in *The Blackwell History of Music in Britain: The Eighteenth Century*, ed. H. Diack Johnstone and Roger Fiske (Oxford, 1990), pp. 96–158

Plumb, J. H.: *Sir Robert Walpole*, II, *The King's Minister* (1960, repr. 1972)

Pocock, J. G. A.: 'Machiavelli, Harrington and English Political Ideologies in the Eighteenth Century', in *Politics, Language and Time: Essays on Political Thought and History* (New York, 1971, repr. London, 1976), pp. 104–47

The Machiavellian Moment (Princeton, 1975)

Virtue, Commerce, and History: Essays on Political Thought and History, chiefly in the Eighteenth Century (Cambridge, 1985)

Preston, Thomas R.: 'Biblical Criticism, Literature, and the Eighteenth-Century Reader', in *Books and their Readers in Eighteenth-Century England*, ed. I. Rivers (Leicester, 1982), pp. 97–126

'From Typology to Literature: Hermeneutics and Historical Narrative in Eighteenth-Century England', *The Eighteenth Century: Theory and Interpretation*, 23 (1982), 181–96

Price, Curtis: 'English Traditions in Handel's *Rinaldo*', in *Handel Tercentenary Collection*, ed. Stanley Sadie and Anthony Hicks (1987), pp. 120–37

'Political Allegory in Late-Seventeenth-Century English Opera', in *Music and Theatre: Essays in honour of Winton Dean*, ed. Nigel Fortune (1987), pp. 1–29

Probyn, Clive T.: *The Sociable Humanist: The Life and Works of James Harris 1709–1780* (Oxford, 1991)

Quarrie, P.: 'The Christ Church Collections Books', in *The History of the University of Oxford*, V: *The Eighteenth Century*, ed. L. S. Sutherland and L. G. Mitchell (Oxford, 1986), pp. 493–512

Radzinowicz, M. A.: *Towards Samson Agonistes: The Growth of Milton's Mind* (Princeton, 1978)

Ramsland, Clement: 'Britons Never Will Be Slaves: A Study of Whig Political Propaganda in the British Theatre, 1700–1742', *Quarterly Journal of Speech* 28 (1942), 393–9

Randall, Helen W.: 'The Rise and Fall of a Martyrology: Sermons on Charles I', *Huntington Library Quarterly* 10 (1946–7), 135–67

Redwood, John: *Reason, Ridicule and Religion: The Age of Enlightenment in England* (1976)

Reedy, Gerard: *The Bible and Reason: Anglicans and Scripture in Late Seventeenth Century England* (Philadelphia, 1985)

Reventlow, Henning Graf, trans. John Bowden: *The Authority of the Bible and the Rise of the Modern World* (1984)

Robbins, Caroline: *The Eighteenth-Century Commonwealthman* (Cambridge, MA, 1959)

Roberts, John H.: 'Handel and Jennens' Italian Opera Manuscripts', in *Music and Theatre: Essays in honour of Winton Dean*, ed. Nigel Fortune (Cambridge, 1987), pp. 159–202

Rogers, Nicholas: *Whigs and Cities: Popular Politics in the Age of Walpole and Pitt* (Oxford, 1989)

Rogers, Pat: 'Introduction: The Writer and Society', in *The Eighteenth Century*, ed. Rogers (1978)

Rosenfeld, Sybil: *The Theatre of the London Fairs in the Eighteenth Century* (1960)

Ross, Angus: 'The Correspondence of Dr John Arbuthnot', Ph.D. diss., University of Cambridge (1956)

Roston, Murray: *Biblical Drama in England from the Middle Ages to the Present Day* (1968)

Roth, Cecil: *A History of the Jews in England* (Oxford, 3/1964)

Rumbold, Valerie: 'Pope and the Gothic Past', Ph.D. diss., University of Cambridge (1984)

Rupp, Gordon: *Religion in England 1688–1791* (Oxford, 1986)

Ruttkay, K. G.: 'The Critical Reception of Italian Opera in England in the Early Eighteenth Century', *Angol és Amerikai Filológiai Tanulmányok / Studies in English and American Philology*, ed. L. Kéry and N. J. Szenczi, I (Budapest, 1971), 93–169

Sadie, Stanley: *Handel* (1962)
   ed.: *The New Grove Dictionary of Music and Musicians* (1980)
   ed.: *The New Grove Dictionary of Opera* (1992)

Sambrook, James: *The Eighteenth Century: The Intellectual and Cultural Context of English Literature, 1700–1789* (1986)
   James Thomson, 1700–1748: A Life (Oxford, 1991)

Samuel, Edgar R.: 'The Jews in English Foreign Trade – A Consideration of the "Philo Patriae" Pamphlets of 1753', in *Remember the Days: Essays on Anglo-Jewish History presented to Cecil Roth*, ed. J. M. Shaftesley (1966), pp. 123–43

Scholes, Percy: *The Puritans and Music* (1954)

Schonhorn, Manuel: *Defoe's Politics: Parliament, Power, Kingship, and 'Robinson Crusoe'* (Cambridge, 1991)

Schueller, Herbert M.: 'The Use and Decorum of Music as Described in British Literature, 1700 to 1780', *Journal of the History of Ideas* 13 (1952), 73–93

Shapiro, A. H.: '"Drama of an Infinitely Superior Nature": Handel's Early English Oratorios and the Religious Sublime', *M&L* 74 (1993), 215–45
   '"Drama of an Infinitely Superior Nature": The Relationship of Handel's First English Oratorios to Early-Eighteenth-Century Sacred Music Theory and Practice', M.Litt. thesis, University of Cambridge (1988)

Sharp, Richard: 'New Perspectives in the High Church Tradition: Historical Background 1730–1780', in *Tradition Renewed: The Oxford Movement Conference Papers*, ed. Geoffrey Rowell (1986), pp. 4–23

Shaw, H. Watkins: *Eighteenth Century Cathedral Music*, Church Music Society Occasional Paper 21 (Oxford [1952])

Sherbo, Arthur: *Christopher Smart, Scholar of the University* (East Lansing, MI, 1967)

Sherburn, George: '"Timon's Villa" and Cannons', *Huntington Library Bulletin* 8 (1935), 131–52

Shields, David S.: *Oracles of Empire: Poetry, Politics, and Commerce in British America, 1690–1750* (Chicago, 1990)

Siegmund-Schultze, Dorothea: 'Zur gesellschaftlichen Situation in London zur Zeit Händels', *HJb* 32 (1986), 85–98

Simon, J., ed.: *Handel: A Celebration of his Life and Times* (1985)

Skinner, Quentin: 'The Principles and Practice of Opposition: The Case of Bolingbroke versus Walpole', in *Historical Perspectives . . . in honour of J. H. Plumb*, ed. N. McKendrick (1974), pp. 93–128

Smith, Patrick J.: *The Tenth Muse: A Historical Study of the Opera Libretto* (1971)

Smith, R. J.: *The Gothic Bequest: Medieval Institutions in British Political Thought, 1688–1832* (Cambridge, 1986)

Smith, Ruth: 'The Achievements of Charles Jennens (1700–1773)', *M&L* 70 (1989), 161–90

'The Argument and Contexts of Dryden's *Alexander's Feast*', *SEL: Studies in English Literature* 18 (1978), 465–90

'Handel's Israelite Librettos and English Politics, 1732–52', *GHB* 5 (1993), 195–215

'Intellectual Contexts of Handel's English Oratorios', in *Music in Eighteenth-Century England: Essays in memory of Charles Cudworth*, ed. Christopher Hogwood and Richard Luckett (Cambridge, 1983), pp. 115–33

Smith, William C.: '*Do You Know What You Are About?*: A Rare Handelian Pamphlet', *Music Review*, May 1964, 114–19

Concerning Handel (1948)

A Handelian's Notebook (1965)

'The Text of "Messiah"', *M&L* 32 (1951), 386–7

Smither, Howard E.: *A History of the Oratorio*, I and II, *The Oratorio in the Baroque Era* (Chapel Hill, NC, 1977)

Solomons, I.: 'Satirical and Political Prints on the Jews' Naturalisation Bill, 1753', *Transactions of the Jewish Historical Society of England* 6 (1912), 205–33

Southern, Richard: 'Lediard and Early Eighteenth-Century Scene Design', *Theatre Notebook* 2 (1948), 49–54

Speck, W. A.: 'Politicians, Peers, and Publication by Subscription 1700–50' in *Books and their Readers in Eighteenth-Century England*, ed. I. Rivers (Leicester, 1982), pp. 47–68

Stability and Strife: England 1714–60 (1977)

et al.: '1688 and All That', *BJECS* 15 (1992), 131–49

Statt, D. A.: 'The Controversy over the Naturalization of Foreigners in England, 1660–1760', Ph.D. diss., University of Cambridge (1987)

Stephen, F. G., E. Hawkins and M. D. George: *Catalogue of Prints and Drawings in the British Museum*, I, *Political and Personal Satires* III/1 (1877)

Stephen, Leslie: *History of English Thought in the Eighteenth Century* (1876, 3/1902)

Stephenson, W. E.: 'Religious Drama in the Restoration', *PQ* 50 (1971), 599–609

Straka, Gerald: *Anglican Reaction to the Revolution of 1688* (Madison, WI, 1962)

Streatfeild, R. A.: *Handel* (1909)

Strohm, Reinhard: *Essays on Handel and Italian Opera* (Cambridge, 1985)

Stromberg, Roland N.: *Religious Liberalism in Eighteenth-Century England* (1954)

Strumia, Anna: *L'immaginazione repubblicana: Sparta e Israel nel dibattito filosofico-politico dell'età di Cromwell* (Turin, 1991)

Swanston, Hamish: *Handel* (1990)

Swedenborg, H. T., jnr: *The Theory of the Epic in England 1650–1800* (Berkeley, 1944)

Sykes, Norman: *Church and State in England in the XVIIIth Century* (Cambridge, 1934)

Edmund Gibson, Bishop of London (1926)

Talbot, Michael: *Vivaldi* (1978)

Targett, Simon: 'Sir Robert Walpole's Newspapers, 1722–42: Propaganda and Politics in the Age of Whig Supremacy', Ph.D. diss., University of Cambridge (1991)

Taylor, Carole: 'Handel's Disengagement from the Italian Opera', in *Handel Tercentenary Collection*, ed. Stanley Sadie and Anthony Hicks (1987), pp. 165–81

'Handel and Frederick, Prince of Wales', *MT* 125 (1984), 89–92

Temperley, Nicholas: 'Music in Church', in *The Blackwell History of Music in Britain: The Eighteenth Century*, ed. H. Diack Johnstone and Roger Fiske (Oxford, 1990), pp. 357–96

The Music of the English Parish Church (Cambridge, 1979)

Torchiana, Donald T.: 'Brutus: Pope's Last Hero', *Journal of English and Germanic Philology* 61 (1962), 853–67

Trollope, Messrs G. (London): *Gopsall, Leicestershire, Catalogue of ... the Extensive Library*, 14 October 1918

Trowell, Brian: 'Congreve and the 1744 Semele Libretto', *MT* 111 (1970), 993–4

'Daniel Defoe's Plan for an Academy of Music at Christ's Hospital, with some Notes on His Attitude to Music', in *Source Materials and the Interpretation of Music: A Memorial Volume to Thurston Dart*, ed. Ian Bent (1981), pp. 403–27

'Libretto', in *The New Grove Dictionary of Opera*, ed. Stanley Sadie (1992), II, 1185–1252

Van der Veen, H. R. S.: *Jewish Characters in Eighteenth-Century Fiction and Drama* (Groningen, 1935)

Varey, Simon: '*The Craftsman* 1726–52', Ph.D. diss., University of Cambridge (1976)

'Hanover, Stuart, and the *Patriot King*', *BJECS* 6 (1983), 163–72

Viner, Jacob: *The Role of Providence in the Social Order* (Philadelphia, 1972)

Walsh, John, and Stephen Taylor: 'Introduction: The Church and Anglicanism in the "Long" Eighteenth Century', in *The Church of England c. 1689 – c. 1833: From Toleration to Tractarianism*, ed. John Walsh, Colin Haydon and Stephen Taylor (Cambridge, 1993), pp. 1–66

Weber, William: *The Rise of Musical Classics in Eighteenth-Century England* (Oxford, 1992)

Weinbrot, Howard D.: *Augustus Caesar in 'Augustan' England* (Princeton, 1978)

    Britannia's Issue: The Rise of British Literature from Dryden to Ossian (Cambridge, 1993)

Western, J. R.: *The English Militia in the Eighteenth Century* (Toronto, 1965)

Westrup, J. A.: review of Dean, *Oratorios, M&L* 40 (1959), 366–9

Wilson, Kathleen: 'Empire, Trade and Popular Politics in Mid-Hanoverian Britain: The Case of Admiral Vernon', *Past & Present* 121 (1988), 74–109

Winton, Calhoun: 'Benjamin Victor, James Miller, and the Authorship of *The Modish Couple*', *PQ* 64 (1985), 121–30

Wood, Bruce: 'Cavendish Weedon: Impresario Extraordinary', *The Consort* 33 (1977), 222–4

Woodfine, Philip: 'The Anglo-Spanish War of 1739', in *The Origins of War in Early Modern Europe*, ed. J. Black (Edinburgh, 1987), pp. 185–209

    'Ideas of Naval Power and the Conflict with Spain, 1737–42', in *The British Navy and the Use of Naval Power in the Eighteenth Century*, ed. J. Black and P. Woodfine (Atlantic Heights, NJ, 1989), pp. 71–90

Young, Percy: *The Oratorios of Handel* (1949)

Zwicker, Steven N.: *Dryden's Political Poetry: The Typology of King and Nation* (Providence, RI, 1972)

Index

Collaborative musical works (anthems excepted) are indexed by title

Abraham, patriarch, 143, 150, 247, 249, 253, 256, 257
Acis and Galatea, 6, 11, 14, 15, 16, 17, 19, 21, 25, 60, 78–9, 271, 277–8, 353
Adams, George, 63, 374
Addison, Joseph, 28, 64, 70, 120, 129, 155, 158–60, 212, 342, 343, 376, 387
    see also Rosamond
Aeschylus, 62, 338
    see also drama, Greek
Akenside, Mark, 289
Albion and Albanius, 211, 369, 377, 423
Alcina, 61–2, 138
Alderman, William E., 389
Alexander Balus, 6, 29, 50, 115, 301–3, 307, 336, 352, 363, 425
Alexander's Feast, 5, 11, 17, 22, 32, 34, 46, 77, 82, 192, 353, 367, 390
Alexander's feast, 129
Alfred, 212, 260, 293, 294–5, 299, 368
Alfred the Great, 127, 129, 133, 227, 294–5
allegory
    moral, 60–2, 136, 138, 337
    political, 136, 138, 183, 187–8, chs. 9–14
    religious, 90, 117, 144, 164, 279, 280, 357, 358
    see also typology, biblical
Allegro, il penseroso ed il moderato, L', 3, 5, 11, 18, 22, 25, 37, 38, 50, 61, 271, 353, 390
Allen, Brian, 389
alliances, 175, 236, 241, 245, 297, 301–3, 336
Amalekites, 138, 154, 227, 328, 329–31, 420
Ammonites, 338–40, 342
Amory, Thomas, 220
'ancient constitution' *see under* Britain, constitution
Anglo-Saxons, *see* Alfred the Great; Britain, constitution, 'ancient constitution'
Anne, Princess Royal, 14, 199, 281, 287

Anne, Queen, 15, 79, 199, 326, 404, 428
Annet, Peter, 425
anthems, 16, 47, 48, 92–107, 157–61, 165–6, 233, 274, 282, 284, 355
Apocrypha *see* Bible
Arbuthnot, John, 276, 278–9, 351, 353, 403
Arbuthnot, Robert, 419
Arcadian Academy, 15, 150
Aristotle, 56
Armitage, David, 240, 393, 407, 411–12, 426
army, 176, 184–5, 186, 196–7, 241–2, 252, 297, 298, 300
    see also militia
Arne, Thomas Augustine, 14, 376
    see also Alfred
Arnold, Denis and Elsie, 368
Aspinall, Edward, 381
Athalia, 6, 12, 17, 50, 76, 93, 115, 139, 155, 236, 238–9, 242, 245, 274, 286–7, 291, 307, 323, 324–5, 351, 381, 418, 425
Athaliah, Queen of Judah, 286, 308
Athens, ancient, 56–7, 114, 225, 230, 256
Atherton, Herbert M., 396, 429, 435
Atterbury, Francis, 221
Atterbury Plot, 192
audience reception, *see under* Handel, George Frideric; oratorio, English
Augustine, St, 88
Augustus, Emperor, 138, 255, 262, 263, 312, 326
Austria, *see under* war
Avery, E. L., 367, 369
Avison, Charles, 47–8, 87, 372, 378, 380, 385–6
Ayers, Robert W., 406

Bach, Johann Sebastian, 47, 357
Bacon, Francis, Lord Verulam, 265
Baillie, John, 387

Baker, C. H. Collins and Muriel, 419
Baker, David, 399
Baker, Frank, 436
Bale, John, 215
Ball, Terence, 398
Bangorian Controversy, 320
Banner, Richard, 371, 380
Barber, Giles, 396
Barcham, William L., 409
bards, 139
Barry, Jonathan, 374
Bartlett, Ian, 432
Basil, St, 88
Bathurst, Allen, first Earl of, 294
Battestin, Martin C. and Ruthe R., 204,
    402
battles, engagements, sieges
  Belle Ile, 175
  Bergen op Zoom, 241
  Cape Finisterre, 175
  Cartagena, 174
  Culloden, 177
  Dettingen, 175, 194, 199, 240, 298, 308
  Fontenoy, 175
  Laffeldt, 175, 242
  Panama, 174
  Porto Bello, 174
  Prestonpans, 177
  Rocoux, 175
  Toulon, 175
  see also war
Bayle, Pierre, 308
Bayley, Anselm, 381
Beard, John, 26
Beattie, James, 372
Bedford, Arthur, 46, 86, 90–3, 158, 191,
    392
Beeks, Graydon, 364, 366, 381, 402, 419
Beggar's Opera, The, 20, 188, 398
Belshazzar, 25–8, 30, 31, 33, 37, 38, 79, 94,
    125, 130, 131, 132, 138, 139, 147,
    152–3, 213, 224, 238, 246, 247, 261–3,
    266, 272, 274, 307, 317–19, 323, 352,
    361, 369, 416, 425, 429
Belshazzar, King of Babylon, 129
Bennett, G. V., 398
Bentley, Richard, 155
Berkeley, George, 221, 273, 407, 417–18
Bertolli, Francesca, 19
Bible and Apocrypha
  adaptation and paraphrase of, 4, 16, 27,
    32, 43, 44, 48, 95–6, 102–4, 108,
    113–17, 119, 121–4, 126, 136, 146–53,
    216, chs. 10–14, 346, 349
  authority of, 95, 108–9, 126, 142, 183,
    217–18, 225, 228, 230–1, 243, 327

debated, ch. 6, 170, 217, 219, 226, 228,
    230–1, 234, 236, 248, 321, 331, 338,
    343
books of
  1 Chronicles, 315, 332, 352
  2 Chronicles, 286, 309, 352, 427–8
  1 Corinthians, 111, 351
  Daniel, 106, 133, 134, 193
  Deuteronomy, 235, 275, 357
  Ecclesiasticus, 106, 107, 351
  Esther, 233, 276–7, 279–80, 282, 285,
    351, 420
  Exodus, 89, 146, 147, 331, 351, 352,
    415
  see also Red Sea; Song of Moses
  Ezekiel, 99, 150
  Ezra, 352, 391
  Genesis, 109, 123, 247, 306, 352, 410,
    425
  Habakkuk, 122
  Haggai, 351
  Hebrews, 351
  Hezekiah, 215
  Isaiah, 97, 99–100, 110, 117, 118, 122,
    149, 150, 152, 153, 351, 352, 391
  Jeremiah, 150, 152, 153, 352
  Job, 35, 97, 105–6, 117, 131, 223, 351,
    382
  John, 149, 351
  Joshua, 235, 237, 238, 240, 253, 267,
    275, 410
  Judges, 236, 292, 339, 351, 352, 410
  1 Kings, 250, 315, 352, 415, 427, 429
  2 Kings, 351, 352, 420
  Lamentations, 100–2, 104–6, 351
  Leviticus, 236, 352
  Luke, 99, 102, 149, 351
  1 Maccabees, 352
  Malachi, 351
  Mark, 99, 100, 102, 149
  Matthew, 99, 100, 102, 149, 351,
    382
  Micah, 357
  Numbers, 250, 352, 410
  Philippians, 104, 106, 351
  Psalms, 96, 98, 102, 103, 106, 107, 120,
    122, 123, 161–2, 216–17, 329, 349,
    App. 1, 382
  Revelation, 88, 114, 118, 351, 382
  Romans, 351
  1 Samuel, 351, 431–2
  2 Samuel, 104–6, 314, 328, 331, 351,
    352, 410
  1 Timothy, 151
  Wisdom of Solomon, 107, 351
  Zechariah, 351, 356

see also David, Lament for Saul and
    Jonathan; Song of Deborah; Song of
    Miriam; Song of Moses; Song of
    Solomon; *individual biblical figures*
commentaries on, 83, 109, 116, 118, 120,
    145–6, 148, 190, 230, 236, 237, 285,
    286, 316, 338, 343, 344, 391
style of, 108–9, 114, 116, 118–21, 123–6,
    139, 145–6, 158, 159, 169–70
see also poetry, biblical
see also anthems; drama, biblical,
    religious; Israelites, biblical; poetry,
    biblical; prophecies; typology, biblical
Biddle, Leslie J., 365
Bisse, Thomas, 88, 90, 370–1, 379–80
Black, Jeremy, 230, 394–6, 402, 409,
    411–14, 420, 424, 428, 431
Blackmore, Sir Richard, 111, 114, 123,
    127–9, 131–2, 134, 383, 385, 387
Blackwall, Anthony, 383
Blackwell, Thomas, 130–1, 138, 387–8, 416
Blair, Hugh, 51, 132, 385, 387
Blome, Richard, 406
Blow, John, 97, 157, 161, 379, 381, 391
Boileau, Nicolas, 128
Bolingbroke, Henry St John, Lord, 137,
    142, 176, 179, 181, 183, 195, 205, 206,
    208, 229–31, 239, 248, 254, 255, 257,
    258, 259–60, 262–3, 268, 272–3, 278–9,
    288, 310, 318, 335, 340, 345, 348, 397,
    403, 409, 413, 415, 416–18, 433
    The Idea of a Patriot King, 137, 179, 181,
    183, 239, 254, 255, 262–3, 272–3, 310,
    318, 335, 340
Bononcini, Giovanni, 205, 207
Book of Common Prayer, 16, 94, 98, 103,
    125, 147, 150, 215–16, 217, 277, 291
Bothmer, Caspar von, 48
Boyce, William, 94
    *see also David's Lamentation over Saul and
    Jonathan*
Boyle, Robert, 114–15, 144, 352, 385
    Boyle Lectures, 142, 144, 154–5, 390, 406
Boyle, Roger, *see* Orrery
Brady, Nicholas, 161
Bramston, James, 44
Brereton, Thomas, 68, 165, 216–17, 276–7,
    279, 351, 405, 418
Brett, Philip, 6, 286, 363, 421, 430
Brewer, John, 428
Brewster, Dorothy, 373, 386, 388
Bridenbaugh, Carl, 412
Britain
    analogy with Israel, 10, 90–2, 103, 136–8,
    164, 171, 213–29, chs. 10–14, 348–50,
    357
constitution, 10, 136, 178, 179, 184–5,
    190, 197, 204, 221, 222, 227–8, 253–7,
    259, 269, 284, 286, 294, 321, 325–6,
    332, 347–8
    'ancient constitution', 184, 196, 227–8,
    229, 254, 256–7, 273, 294, 327
    see also liberty
foreign policy, 10, 163, 174–5, 187, 197,
    240–1, 245, 251, 289, 292, 296–7, 300,
    313–14
    see also alliances; war
national art and patronage, 20, 52–6,
    70–80, 82, 127, 133–6, 163–4, 166,
    169, 170, 182, 188, 208, 308, 312, 313
    see also opera, English; oratorio,
    English; poetry, British
national identity, 10, 13, 69, 71–2, 75, 77,
    92, 135, 163, 177, 239, 245, 294
    see also under religion
national pride, 72, 74–6, 127, 164, 175,
    193, 238, 273, 314
national unity, 70, 137, 175, 179, 181,
    183, 186–7, 188, 209–10, 213, 239–40,
    246, 273, 288–9, 292
    see also Patriot literature, opposition,
    theory
reform and regeneration, 52–3, 137, 139,
    164–9, 181–3, 185, 213, 263, 271–4,
    294
    see also under public virtue
union of England and Scotland, 74, 99,
    103
    see also Church of England; corruption;
    empire; faction; Jacobites; liberty;
    Patriot King figure; Patriot literature,
    opposition, theory; patriotism;
    property; public virtue; religion;
    Tories; trade; Whigs
Britannia, 316, 428
British Enchanters, The, 212, 377
Britton, Thomas, 167, 207
Brooke, Henry, 212, 289–90, 291, 295, 336,
    380
Broome, William, 111
Broughton, Thomas, 25, 32, 58, 59, 248
    see also Hercules
Brown, John, 57, 273, 373–4, 397, 418
Brownell, M. R., 419
Browning, Reed, 396, 397, 415, 418, 422
Broxap, Henry, 380
Brumoy, Pierre, 374
Brydges, James, Earl of Carnarvon, Duke of
    Chandos, 14, 15, 25, 93, 190, 199,
    277–9, 281, 365
    see also Cannons
Buchanan, George, 340, 343, 352, 434

Bunyan, John, 219
Burden, Michael, 423
Burlington, Richard Boyle, third Earl of, 25, 197–8, 199, 276, 278, 365
  Burlington House, 15
Burnet, Gilbert (Bishop of Salisbury), 336
Burnet Gilbert (of Coggeshall), 390
Burnet, Mr, 433
Burney, Charles, 14, 16, 281, 368
Burrows, Donald, 147, 200, 363, 366–8, 422
Burtt, Shelley, 268, 344–5, 364, 397, 418
Bush, Alan, 213
Butler, Joseph, 156, 389
Butler, Rohan, 423
Buttrey, T. V., 374

Calmet, Dom Augustin, 91–2, 252, 285, 385, 414
Calver, Clive, 143
Calypso and Telemachus, 15
Campion, Thomas, 158
Canaan, Canaanites, 89, 114, 122, 146, 148, 154, 164, 219, 224, 235, 237, 247–53, 259, 265, 269, 275, 290, 410
Cannons, 14, 15–16, 68, 189, 190, 276, 277, 278, 280
Capell, Richard, 404
Carey, Henry, 71–2, 74–5, 76, 77
  see also *Dragon of Wantley, The*
Carleton, George, 381
Carmarthen, Peregrine, Marquess of, 192
Caroline of Ansbach, Queen of England, 15, 17, 188, 189, 190, 198, 199, 204, 282, 284, 285, 309, 317
  Funeral Anthem for, see under Handel, George Frideric
Carte, Thomas, 191
Carter, Elizabeth, 370
Carteret, John, Earl Granville, 194, 222, 298, 304, 306
Cassidy, G. E., 400
Castells, F. de P., 365
castrati, see under Italy, singers
Cecilia, St, 82
  feast of, celebrations, 45, 84–5, 88, 160, 192
Censor, 110
Champion, Justin, 365, 409, 429–30
Chandler, Edward, 405–6
Chandler, Samuel, 365, 409, 424, 429–30
Chandos, Duke of, see Brydges, James
Channon, Merlin, 31, 365, 368, 410
Chanuka, Feast of, 274, 300
Chapel Royal, 14, 21, 93
Chapman, John, 425
Charles I, 191, 308, 328–30, 332

Charles II, 102, 191, 211, 224, 291
Charles Edward Stuart, Young Pretender, 73, 177, 178, 191, 290, 298, 318, 348
Chaucer, Geoffrey, 197
Chesterfield, Philip Dormer Stanhope, fourth Earl of, 290
  see also *Common Sense*
Chisholm, Duncan, 306, 425
Chiswick, 198
Choice of Hercules, The, 11, 18, 22, 61, 353, 390
chorus, musico-dramatic, 22, 60, 61, 62–9, 83, 159, 160, 161, 166, 170, 271, 342
  see also under oratorio, English
Christianity, see Church of England; religion; typology, biblical
Chronological and Historical Account, 407
Chrysander, Friedrich, 361
Churchill, Sarah, Duchess of Marlborough, 194
Church of England, 8–10, 83–4, 90, 92, 155, 158, 178, 186, 190, 191, 194, 199, 205, 207, 223, 277, 281, 284, 291, 310, 320–1, 323, 325, 347–8, 356
  doctrine, 141, 142, 219, 354
  see also religion
church music, see under music
church–state relations, 9–11, 281–2, 319–25, ch. 15
  see also Church of England; priesthood
Cibber, Susanna Maria (née Arne), 26, 38
Clark, J. C. D., 178, 364, 365, 395, 398, 426, 429, 431
Clark, Jane, 365, 401
Clarke, Samuel, 142, 155, 390
Clayton, Thomas, see *Rosamond*
Cleary, Thomas R., 423
Cliveden, 197
Cobbett, William, 407, 413, 421
Cobham, Sir Richard Temple, Viscount, 294
Colley, Linda, 10, 13, 177, 178, 214, 362, 377, 395, 405, 411, 424, 426, 431
Collier, Jeremy, 46, 52, 69, 84, 161, 374, 376, 379–80
Collins, Anthony, 143, 144, 151, 406, 429
Collins, William, 300
Collinson, Patrick, 223, 271–2, 381, 384, 391, 404, 415, 418
Collyer, David, 148, 405, 434
'Columbario, Christopher', 399
commerce, see trade
Common Sense, 36, 52, 77, 82, 135, 290, 335, 369–70, 372, 377–8
Congreve, William, 353
Conolly, L. W., 379

constitution
  British, *see* Britain, constitution
  Hebraic, *see* Israelites, biblical,
    government
contract, *see* Covenant
Cooke, John, 390, 407, 431
Cornbury Plot, 192
Corneille, Pierre, 15
corruption, national decay, 72, 73, 75, 90,
  92, 137, 168, 183, 185, 193–4, 196,
  203, 220–1, 222–3, 226, 254, 261–74,
  290, 294, 306, 325, 327, 333, 335
Coste, Pierre, 66, 281
country life, *see* frugality
court odes, 308
Covenant, 146, 221, 233, 235, 247, 249,
  253–8, 265, 269, 274, 355–6
Covent-Garden Journal, 370
Covent Garden Theatre, 20, 76
Cowley, Abraham, 111, 114, 123, 124, 133,
  291, 351, 384, 431
Cox, Howard, 381
Craftsman, 176, 195, 197, 202–5, 206, 207,
  208, 210, 211, 229–30, 253, 273, 289,
  292, 293, 294, 332–3, 403, 415, 432
Cranfield, G. A., 349, 435
Crisis, The, 348
Croft, William, 47, 371, 379
Cromwell, Oliver, 240, 292
Crown and Anchor Tavern, 277
Cruickshanks, Eveline, 178, 395, 398–9,
  431
Crusius, Lewis, 264, 290
Cumberland, William Augustus, Duke of,
  31, 189, 195, 198, 213, 231, 299, 317
Cuming, Geoffrey, 390
Cunningham, Hugh, 415
Curtis, T. C., 397
Cuzzoni, Francesca, 205, 206
Cyrus, King of Persia, 12, 130, 152, 153,
  247, 263, 266, 317–18, 391

Dacier, André, 63, 373, 375
Daily Advertiser, 37–8, 370
Daily Journal, 366, 419–20
Daniel, prophet, 139, 150, 152–3, 217, 223,
  261, 266, 323, 333, 334, 351, 352, 391
Dann, Uriel, 411, 423
Davenant, Sir William, 63, 166, 167, 241
David, Alun, 382, 384–5, 426
David, King of Israel, 24, 29, 37, 44, 89, 90,
  114, 122, 136, 137, 143, 145, 146, 154,
  159, 171, 217, 220, 224, 252, 308, 309,
  314–15, 320, 328–30, 332–3, 410, 413
  Lament for Saul and Jonathan, 29, 116,
    122, 328–9, 382–3, 386

Davide e Bersabea, 38
David's Lamentation over Saul and Jonathan, 20,
  329–31
Davie, Donald, 374, 384
Davies, G., 401, 419
Davies, Horton, 436
Davies, Rupert, 436–7
Dawes, Sir William, 277
Dean, Winton, 2, 3, 4, 5–6, 7, 9, 12, 20, 23,
  29, 31, 55, 87, 180, 236, 271, 278, 287,
  301, 305, 313, 333, 361–4, 366–8,
  370–1, 373–4, 377, 379, 381, 402, 404,
  417–25, 428, 432–4, 436
Dearnley, Christopher, 380, 434
Dearnley, Moira, 426
Deborah, 16–17, 26, 76, 93, 115, 118, 120,
  129, 139, 155, 177, 189, 190, 202–4,
  209, 236, 238, 245, 274, 285, 323, 324,
  351, 382, 402, 416, 418, 425
Deborah, Judge of Israel, 24, 154, 246,
  425
  see also Song of Deborah
Deborah and Barak, The Song of, 16, 367
Deconinck-Brossard, F., 407, 412, 424
De Fesch, Willem, *see Joseph*
Defoe, Daniel, 20, 73, 167, 219, 228, 239,
  241, 243, 255, 307, 377
deism, ch. 6, 170, 217, 224, 226, 227, 228,
  230–1, 234, 236, 248–9, 252, 279, 316,
  320–2, 324, 331, 338, 348
Delany, Mary, 25, 32, 36, 37, 94, 145, 368,
  381
Delany, Patrick, 145, 146, 390, 426, 432
Dennis, John, 53, 54, 56, 70, 73, 74, 75,
  81–2, 109–10, 114, 121, 125, 128, 166,
  207, 261, 365, 372, 374, 377, 383, 386,
  408, 416
Derham, William, 155
Desaguliers, John, 365
Denoyer, ?G., ?Philip, dancer, 197
Deutsch, Otto Erich, 32, 125, 361, 366–70,
  372, 375, 376–8, 380–1, 384, 386, 388,
  392–3, 396, 398, 401–4, 419–21, 425,
  431–3, 436
Devil to Pay at St James's, The, 205, 403
Dickinson, H. T., 396–401, 414, 418, 422,
  430
Dido and Aeneas, 377
Dingley, William, 84
Dissenters, 10, 90, 96, 113, 178, 192, 218,
  223, 356–7
Dissertation on Patriotism, 171
Divine Recreations, 392
Dixon, Peter, 399
Dlamini, Rev. Alfred, 224
Dobrée, Bonamy, 230, 409

Doody, Margaret Anne, 44, 109, 113, 135–6, 140, 366, 372, 384, 387–8, 403, 412, 431
Do You Know What You Are About?, 206–7, 403
Dragon of Wantley, The, 71, 367
drama
  biblical, religious, 24, 43, 45, 56–7, 64, 68–9, 113–14, 146, 170, 215, 280, 340
    see also Racine, Jean
  English, 6, 24, 33, 52, 65, 67, 68, 113, 131, 301
  Greek, 56–60, 62, 65, 67–8, 114, 159, 160, 259
  political, 17, 56, 69, 72, 182–3, 188, 193, 202, 211–13, 215, 243, 245, 260, 283, 289–90, 295, 335–7, 341
    see also music theatre; Patriot King figure
druids, 139
Dryden, John, 4, 7, 30, 32, 53, 63, 114, 215, 275, 336, 353
  Alexander's Feast, 17, 32, 46, 82, 192, 353, 367
  on epic, 127, 133, 372, 386
  Song for St Cecilia's Day, 17, 353
  see also Albion and Albanius; *King Arthur*
Dublin, 12, 18, 34, 161
Dublin Journal, 37, 386
Duck, Stephen, 198
Duncombe, John, 375
Duncombe, William, 69, 286
Dupont, John, 323
Dyer, John, 261, 263–4, 416

earthquakes (1750), 222
Eccles, John, *see British Enchanters, The*
Edward III, 230, 294
Edwards, Averyl, 395, 400, 423, 434
Edwards, Maldwyn, 436
Edwards, Thomas, 290
Egmont, John Perceval, second Earl of, 44, 48–9, 277, 309
Eisen, Walter and Margret, 369, 402
Elijah, prophet, 25
Elizabeth I, 184, 308, 425
Emerson, Roger L., 389
empire, 75, 134, 175–7, 182, 213, 243–51, 261, 263–4, 266, 312
Endelman, Todd M., 435
Engel, Helmut, 433
Entick, John, 150–1
epic, 53, 114, ch. 5, 170, 225, 234, 245, 259, 294, 343
Epistle to Mr Handel, 210
Erskine-Hill, Howard, 399, 409, 420, 427

Esther, 6, 13–16, 17, 19, 43, 44, 45, 48, 54, 66, 74, 76, 79, 92, 93, 115, 125, 167, 173, 189, 190, 204, 236, 245, 248, 272, 274, 276–85, 291, 307, 319, 351, 361, 402, 425
Esther, Queen of Persia, 115, 154, 279, 425
Euripides, 57, 67, 302, 338
Evans, W. M., 413
Evelyn, John, 379–80
Excise Bill, 173, 176, 193, 196–7, 200, 202–5, 286, 300, 305, 348
exile, 27, 224, 245, 246, 272, 278, 279, 290, 317, 319, 333, 339, 341
exodus from Egypt, 24, 114, 116, 122, 164, 213–15, 219, 224, 293, 319, 324, 410
  see also Bible, books of, Exodus; Red Sea
Ezio, 43

faction, 10, 69, 78, 137, 178, 183, 186–7, 207–10, 221, 233, 239, 273, 347
Farinelli (Carlo Broschi), 205
Faustina (Faustina Bordoni), 205–6
Fellowes, E. H., 371
Felton, Henry, 124, 386
Fénelon, François de Salignac de la Mothe, 413
Fieldhouse, David, 412
Fielding, Henry, 23, 36–7, 188, 193, 204, 423
Fingal *see* Ossian
Fiske, Roger, 366, 422, 428
Fitzgerald, Edward, 9
Flavio, 210
Fleetwood, Charles, An Epistle to, 69
Fleetwood, William, 326, 428
Fleury, Abbot Claude, 120, 385
Floridante, 404
Flying Post, 253
Form of Prayer with Fasting, 431
Foxon, D. F., 388
France, 174–5, 240–1, 251, 276, 278, 281, 297, 298, 300, 302, 314
Francesina, La (Elisabeth Duparc), 26
Frederick II of Prussia, 174
Frederick Louis, Prince of Wales, 28, 54, 78, 127, 176, 177, 181, 182, 183, 188, 192, 194, 195, 197, 198, 199, 207, 212, 240, 260, 281, 288, 292–5, 298, 299, 300, 308, 311, 313, 318, 330, 335, 338–40, 342, 365
freemasonry, 12
Fritz, Paul S., 399
frugality, 186, 242, 263–6, 269–71, 273, 312, 417

Galliard, John Ernest, 15, 44, 372, 388

see also Calypso and Telemachus
Garrison, James D., 421
Gates, Bernard, 14, 277
Gay, John, *see Acis and Galatea*; *Beggar's Opera, The*
Genest, Charles-Claude, 352
Gentleman's Magazine, 112–13, 117, 121–2, 144, 175, 189, 195, 209, 222, 289, 298, 340, 347, 349, 382, 386, 400, 407, 433, 436
George I, 199, 217, 224, 291
George II, 15, 174, 175–6, 187, 188, 199, 200, 203–4, 206, 220, 232, 239, 240, 255, 284, 306, 307, 308–10, 315, 316–17
George III, 181, 342
George, A. Raymond, 436
George, M. D., 421
Georgia, 242, 250
Gerrard, Christine, 53, 134, 173, 178, 181, 183, 188, 372, 373, 387–9, 393, 395–401, 404, 420–2, 425, 427, 433
Gianturco, Carolyn, 150, 368, 434
Gibbons, Orlando, 99, 102–3
Gibbs, Graham C., 395, 428
Gibson, Edmund, 16, 80, 281–2, 284
Gibson, Elizabeth, 337, 376
Gideon, Samson, 348
Giffard, William, *see Merlin*
Gildon, Charles, 30, 32, 124, 369, 373–5, 383, 386
Gilliver, Lawton, 196
Giulio Cesare, 206, 210
Glover, Richard, 245
God
  creator of universe, 55, 95, 102, 112–13, 120, 123, 128, 153–6, 161, 163, 274
  interest in human affairs, 8–9, 34, 57–8, 92, 95, 102, 122, 128–9, 135, 153–5, 216, 220–4, 234, 249, 263, 268, 271–2, 274, 299, 302, 317–19, 320, 328–33, 338, 343, 345
  see also Israelites, biblical; Israelites, oratorio; miracles; prophecies
Godly Queene Hester, 215
Goldgar, Bertrand, 173, 393, 417, 420, 427
Goldie, Mark, 391, 408, 429–30
Goldsmith, M. M., 396–7
Goldsmith, Oliver, 263
Goldstein, Lawrence, 264, 417
Gordon, Alexander, 19
Gordon, Thomas, 244, 261, 412, 416
Gough, Strickland, 431
Gould, Eliga H., 397
government
  see Britain; Israelites, biblical; Israelites, oratorio; monarchy

Grabu, Louis, *see Albion and Albanius*
Granville, George, Baron Lansdowne, *see British Enchanters, The*
Grassineau, James, 44, 47
Greene, Maurice, 44, 98, 99
  see also Deborah and Barak, The Song of; *Jephtha* (Hoadly and Greene)
Greene, Robert, 215
Gregory, Jeremy, 364, 372
Griffin, Dustin, 293, 387, 422
Grout, Donald, 395
Grove, The, 404
Grub Street Journal, 197
Guerinot, J. V., 398
Guernsey, Henege Finch, Lord, third Earl of Aylesford, 30
Gunn, J. A. W., 266, 396–8, 411, 415, 417, 427
Gunpowder Plot, 277

Haggerty, George, 6, 286, 363, 421, 430
Hallet, Joseph, jnr, 149, 247, 413, 430, 432, 434
Halsband, Robert, 400
Haman, 215
Haman and Mordecai, 351, 366
Hamilton, Newburgh, 24, 25, 32, 36, 44, 192, 199, 200, 369, 410
  see also Alexander's Feast; *Ode for St Cecilia's Day*; *Occasional Oratorio*; *Samson*; *Semele*
Hammond, Brean, 266, 396, 398–9, 409, 415, 417–18
Handel, George Frideric
  audience reception (eighteenth century), 7, 20–1, 24, 32, 48–9, 61, 69–70, 76–8, 80, 85, 87–8, 94, 108–9, 119, 120, 121, 124–5, 135, 167–9, 202–10, 231, 288–9, 377
  autographs, 23–4, 29, 30, 201, 256, 331–2, 381, 425
  career, 7, 10, 13, 33, 36–8, 48, 54, 67, 74, 77, 79–80, 86, 87, 93–4, 150, 170, 199, 200, 202–10, 228, 287, 288, 291, 307, 346, 350, 361
  collaboration with librettists, 3, 6, 9, 12, 16, 23–34, 39, 50, 61, 62, 121, 167, 189, 198, 200–1, 280, 291, 296, 305–6, 329, 378
  correspondence, 25–6, 35, 37–8, 66, 67, 432
  opinions, 2, 6, 7, 9, 15, 22, 25–6, 29, 30, 35, 37–9, 53, 61, 67, 71, 167, 199, 200, 267, 306, 350, 367
  will, 369
  Works:
  anthems, 15, 21, 26, 32, 93, 94, 199

Anthem for the Funeral of Queen
  Caroline, 93–4, 103–7, 199
Anthem for the Wedding of Prince
  Frederick, 199
Anthem for the Wedding of Princess
  Anne, 199
Brockes-Passion, 11, 15
Chandos Anthems, 26, 93–4, 103
Coronation Anthems, 15, 17, 93–4, 103,
  199, 204, 282–4, 285, 287
  'Zadok the Priest', 282–3, 305, 309,
  402
Dettingen Te Deum, 94, 199, 305, 308
Ode for the Birthday of Queen Anne, 15,
  199
operas, Italian, 20, 22, 38, 43, 54, 71,
  173, 190, 200, 203–4, 206, 307, 337–8
  see also under individual titles
oratorios, English
  see under oratorio, English; *see under
  individual titles*
secular English works, 4, 6, 11, 22, 78–9,
  173, 199, 353
  see also under individual titles •
Utrecht Te Deum, 113, 199, 200
Hanover, Hanoverians, 9, 15, 17, 74, 174–9,
  187, 188, 191, 194, 198, 199, 200,
  203–4, 208, 211–12, 217, 220, 224,
  239, 240, 241, 281–4, 287, 290, 291,
  292, 297, 298, 303, 304, 306, 308, 312,
  315, 317, 328, 332, 339, 348
Harding, Richard, 394, 407, 423
Hardwicke, Philip Yorke, first Earl of,
  176
Harley, Edward, second Earl of Oxford,
  157
Harley, Robert, first Earl of Oxford, 157
Harrington, James, 137, 225–6, 228, 251–2,
  257, 265, 322–3, 408
Harris, Ellen T., 367, 433
Harris, George, 395
Harris, Michael, 394, 402, 414
Harris, Robert, 178, 181, 245, 394–6, 407,
  411, 413–14, 423–4, 428
Harris, Thomas, 119
Harris, Victor, 406
Harris, William, 151
Harris, Rev. William, 398
Hart, Jeffrey, 418
Hawkins, Edward, 421
Hawkins, Sir John, 167, 364, 393
Hayes, William, 378, 380, 385
Haym, Niccolò, see *Flavio; Giulio Cesare*
Hayman, Francis, 389
Haymarket, New Theatre in the, 14
Haywood, Eliza, 168–9

heathens, 68, 86, 111, 115–16, 129, 217,
  220, 224, 229, 235, 243–4, 254, 266–7,
  269, 275, 279, 280, 292, 293, 302, 316,
  325, 356, 417
  see also Amalekites; Ammonites; Canaan;
  idolatry; Philistines
Heidegger, John Jacob, 74, 76
Henderson, George, D., 429
Henry V, 231, 294, 308
Henry VIII, 215
Henry, Matthew, 237, 240, 410, 413
Herbage, Julian, 363
Herbert, Edward, first Baron Herbert of
  Cherbury, 141
Herbert, George, 68, 165
Hercules, 6, 11, 18, 22, 27, 58–60, 61, 271,
  342, 353, 361, 363
Herodotus, 153, 352
heroic figures, 129–31
  biblical, 17, 115, 189, 228, 231, 233, 239,
  241, 252, 294, 308, 339
  oratorio, 17, 233, 234, 238, 241, 246, 253,
  258, 260, 268, 274, 275, 280, 285, 290,
  294, 296, 298–9, 308, 317, 339, 341–2
  pagan, 24, 57, 82, 318
Herring, Thomas, 347
Herrmann, William, 381–2
Hersan, Marc-Antoine, 385–6
Hertz (Hurst), G. B., 230, 394, 409, 412,
  435
Hervey, John, Baron, 168, 195, 208, 209
Hesiod, 159
Hickford's Rooms, 20
Hickman, Charles, 84–5, 379
Hicks, Anthony, 30, 329, 366, 369, 431–2
Hill, Aaron, 53–6, 63, 70, 75, 76, 77, 110,
  134–5, 166, 193, 376, 386, 397
  Advice to the Poets, 55–6, 373
  correspondence, 268, 417
  to Handel, 79, 80
  Gideon, 132, 134, 136–8, 225, 386, 408,
  432
  Hengist and Horsa, 295, 422
  Henry V, 212, 259, 336–7, 416
  Ode on Utrecht Te Deum, 113, 168, 209
  paraphrase of Bible, 122, 386
  'Preface to Pope', 112, 123–4
  The Progress of Wit, 211
  Saul, 405
  The Tears of the Muses, 78, 81, 378
  Zara, 243
  see also Plain Dealer; Prompter; Rinaldo
Hill, Christopher, 139
history, national myth
  sense of, 133, 136, 139, 154, 231, 234,
  253, 256–61, 275, 420

use of, 56, 57, 75, 132–3, 136–8, 152, 163, 166, 170, 183, 184, 186, 188, 200, 211, 213, 224, 228–32, 246, 248–50, 256–61, 281, 290, 293–4, 326, 348–9, 357

History of Joseph, 406

history painting, 140, 170, 389

Hoadly, Benjamin, 320

Hoadly, John, *see Jephtha* (Hoadly and Greene)

Hobbes, Thomas, 225, 256, 415

Hogarth, William, 49, 435

Hogwood, Christopher, 46, 361, 364, 371, 401–2, 424, 436

Holbrook, Anthony, 431

Holdsworth, Edward, 24, 27, 33, 61, 151, 191, 291

Hollander, John, 391

Holmes, Geoffrey, 99, 103, 394–5

Homer, 116, 127, 133, 146, 159, 336, 338, 353

Hooker, Edward Niles, 62, 372–3, 383

Hooker, Richard (William Webster), 391

Hopkinson, Marie Ruan, 419

Horace (Quintus Horatius Flaccus), 53, 216, 270

Hughes, John, 15, 69, 110, 117, 138, 353, 369, 378, 388
  see also Acis and Galatea; Calypso and Telemachus; Venus and Adonis

Hulse, John, 117

Hume, David, 242, 244, 256, 264, 313, 412, 415

Hume, Robert D., 18, 211, 361, 367, 398, 403

Humphreys, Pelham, 96

Humphreys, Samuel, 15, 24, 109, 118, 145, 189–90, 200, 236, 343–4, 363, 369, 391, 398, 406, 420, 433–4
  see also Athalia; Deborah; Esther; Ulysses

Husbands, John, 116–17, 119, 384, 385

hymns, 64, 68, 83, 84, 86, 92, 112, 113, 155, 156, 158–9, 162, 165–6, 216, 219, 274, 349, 355, 359

idolatry, 136, 226, 249, 265, 268–9, 274, 316–17, 321, 324, 339, 410

Independent, 407

Independent Magazine, 408

Independent on Sunday, 408

Independent Whig, 144

Inglesfield, Robert, 373, 386

Israel in Egypt, 5, 9, 16, 17–18, 21, 22, 25, 37, 90, 93, 103, 117, 121, 122, 125, 130, 138, 146, 147, 149, 164, 169, 189, 213–14, 219, 224, 238, 246, 249, 250, 288–92, 293, 319, 324, 351, 352, 382, 425, 432

Israelites, biblical, 94, 96, 102, 122, 214–32, 348–50
  and enemies, 95, 136–7, 148, 154, 156, 164, 224, 233, 235, 238, 245, 247, 248, 249–50, 252, 269, 275, 279, 290–1, 293, 410
    see also Amalekites; Ammonites; Canaan; Philistines
  and ethics, 153–4, 156, 234–8, 248, 273, 275
  God's chosen people, 95, 112, 115, 122, 136, 146, 148, 152–4, 156, 164, 219, 220, 222–3, 233–8, 245, 248–53, 258, 265, 269, 274, 277, 330–1, 410
    see also Covenant; miracles; prophecies
  government, 130, 136–8, 156, 224–9, 233, 246, 249, 251–6, 265, 269, 274, 322–3
    see also Covenant; law, Old Testament; monarchy; priests, Old Testament
  land-based, pastoral, *see* frugality
  religious observance, 89–92, 95, 138, 159, 220, 235, 249, 265, 269, 275, 279, 286, 322, 357

Israelites, oratorio
  and enemies, 17, 92, 156, 213–14, 233, 235, 238, 240–7, 250, 267, 272, 274–5, chs. 11–12, 342, 356, 357
    see also Amalekites; Ammonites; Canaan; Philistines
  and ethics, 139, 154, 156, 234–8, 275, 280
  and God, 92, 146–7, 154, 156, 213–14, 216, 233–8, 247, 274, 282, 289, 299, 302, 324, 339, 356–7
    see also Covenant; miracles; prophecies
  government, *see* Covenant; law, Old Testament; monarchy; priests, in oratorio
  land-based, pastoral, *see* frugality
  Law, *see* Covenant; law, Old Testament
  religious observance, 138, 216, 235, 267–8, 272, 274, 300, 325, 332, 339, 341, 356, 357
  unity, 239–40, 275, 310

Italy, 300
  music, 15, 24, 48, 71–2, 150, 207
  singers, 19–20, 37, 43, 44, 71–3, 87, 193, 205–7
    castrati, 19–20, 44, 87, 205–7
    see also opera, Italian

Jackson, Keith B., 365

Jacob, Hildebrand, 113, 378

Jacob, James R., 372, 375, 392

Jacob, Margaret C., 364–5, 391

Jacobites, Jacobitism, 10, 27, 176–7, 178, 179, 185, 188, 190–2, 199, 211, 212, 224, 279–82, 286, 290–2, 295, 301, 308–9, 319, 329, 348
   see also James III; Charles Edward Stuart; Rebellion (1715); Rebellion (1745)
James II, 190, 211, 224, 228, 276, 278–9, 286, 308, 326, 327–8, 332, 391, 404
James III (Old Pretender), 73, 192, 205–6, 211, 212, 224, 286, 308–9
Jennens, Charles, 17, 24, 25, 28, 30, 31, 32–33, 33–4, 35, 39, 110, 118, 145, 150–1, 179, 190–2, 200, 354, 363, 369, 389–91, 431
   correspondence, 24, 27–8, 29, 33, 151, 153, 179, 267, 363–4, 368–9, 374, 391, 417, 421–2
   see also Allegro, il penseroso ed il moderato, L'; *Belshazzar*; *Israel in Egypt*; *Messiah*; *Saul*
Jephtha (Hoadly and Greene), 338–44, 434
Jephtha (Morell and Handel), 6, 12, 61, 115, 117, 138, 147, 148, 173, 232, 238, 239, 245, 248, 268, 272, 274, 324, 336, 337, 338–44, 352, 416, 418, 425
Jephtha, Judge of Israel, 24, 60, 114, 144, 154, 232, 246, 252, 338–40, 342, 343, 410
Jesus, 102, 114, 118, 121, 142, 143, 146–7, 148–52, 156, 169, 217–18, 305, 320, 334, 337, 349, 355, 357–8
   see also Messiah (redeemer)
Jewish Naturalisation Bill, 173, 179, ch. 15
Jews
   biblical, *see* Israelites, biblical; Israelites, oratorio
   conversion of, 91
Jilg, R. D., 398
Johnson, Charles, 374
Johnson, J. T., 243, 411
Johnson, Samuel, 41, 71, 180–1, 210, 230, 294
Johnstone, H. Diack, 417, 432
Jones, Stephen, 401
Jordan, River, 117, 122, 146, 219, 235, 237, 247, 253, 258–9, 275, 394, 423
Joseph, patriarch, 24, 116, 130, 154, 213, 217–18, 305–6, 321, 324, 410
Joseph and his Brethren, 2, 5–6, 20, 23, 31, 50, 115, 116, 130, 139, 155, 193, 194, 217, 236, 245, 255–6, 271, 272, 304–7, 323, 324, 352, 361, 425
Joseph (De Fesch), 20
Joseph Reviv'd, 406
Josephus, 352

Joshua, 25, 50–1, 76, 115, 117, 122, 128, 129, 130, 132, 138, 146, 147, 154, 168, 177, 189, 219, 224, 233–61, 264, 265, 267–8, 269, 271, 274, 275, 324, 352, 386, 416, 425
Joshua, Judge of Israel, 114, 116, 117, 130, 137, 148, 215, 217, 218, 225, 226, 248, 251, 252–3, 255, 256, 258, 269, 323
Judas Maccabeus, 252
Judas Macchabæus, 1, 28, 29, 31, 129, 139, 147, 177, 180, 189, 195, 198, 212–13, 231, 238, 245, 258, 272, 274, 299–301, 323, 324, 352, 361, 365, 413, 416, 418, 425
Juditha Triumphans, 229
justice, *see under* law

Keates, Jonathan, 361, 367
Kemp, Betty, 395, 421
Kenyon, John, 396
Kew, 28, 195, 197, 198
Kidder, Richard, 150, 405
Killing No Murder, 286
King Arthur, 188, 211–12, 284, 377
King's Theatre, 20
Kivy, Peter, 382
Knapp, J. Merrill, 55, 361, 373, 379, 404, 429
Korshin, Paul, 405, 407–8
Kramnick, Isaac, 396–8, 415, 417–18, 427

Lam, Basil, 381
Lamb, Benjamin, 102
Lampe, John Frederick, 14, 393
   see also Britannia; *Dragon of Wantley, The*
land, *see* property
Landa, Louis A., 427
Lang, Paul Henry, 361–2, 364, 374–5, 426, 428
Langford, Paul, 12, 366, 395, 403, 411, 420, 424, 428, 432
Langhorne, John, 231
Larsen, Jens Peter, 9, 21, 361, 364, 368, 371, 381
Larsson, Roger B., 371
Lavington, George, 46, 218, 379, 405–6
law
   justice, 325–7, 333–4
      see also Britain, constitution
   Old Testament, 89–91, 130, 144, 146, 154, 155, 220, 225–8, 236, 245, 251–4, 259, 321–2, 325, 327, 331–2, 357, 415
      see also Covenant; priesthood
Law, William, 52
Lawson, John, 436–7
Lediard, Thomas, *see Britannia*

Leland, John, 128, 144, 236, 248, 406, 409, 410, 413, 430, 432
Lennox, Charles, second Duke of Richmond, 204
Leopold, Silke, 21, 368
Leranbaum, Miriam, 388
Leslie, Charles, 381
Lewalski, Barbara, 405
liberty, 69, 134, 137, 152, 156, 163, 164, 178, 179, 180, 183–6, 194, 196–7, 219, 226, 229, 242, 245–6, 251–4, 257, 261–6, 286, 292, 293, 294, 299, 300, 302, 325, 327, 338, 341, 342
Licensing Act, 84, 182, 290, 292
Lillo, George, 243, 244, 245, 413
Lincoln, Stoddard, 368
Lincoln's Inn, 160
Lincoln's Inn Fields Theatre, 14, 20
Lindgren, Lowell, 375
Locke, John, 148, 198, 256, 285, 401, 415
Lockman, John, 45, 330, 368, 370, 376, 386, 388
    see also David's Lamentation over Saul and Jonathan
Lodge, Thomas, 215
Loftis, John, 173, 188, 379, 393, 398, 404, 430
London Daily Post, 22, 169–70, 213–14, 288–9, 370, 386
London Evening Post, 289, 290, 349
London Journal, 231
London Magazine, 373, 383
Longinus, 108–9, 111, 125
Louis XIV, 217, 278
Louisbourg, 175, 222, 251, 300, 314
Lovell, Percy, 371
Low Countries, 175, 241, 251, 297, 300
Lowens, Irving, 375
Lowman, Moses, 225, 226–8, 249–50, 252, 254–5, 256, 257, 265–6, 269, 273–4, 319–20, 321–3, 340, 429, 431, 434
Lowth, Robert, 91, 119, 353
Lowth, William, 413
Luckett, Richard, 363, 376
Lutaud, Olivier, 279–80, 420
luxury, 137, 138, 159, 185–6, 262, 265–6, 269–70, 312–13, 316, 417
Lyttelton, George, first Baron, 207–8, 325, 388, 403, 416
Lyttelton, Thomas Lord, 198–9

Mace, Dean Tolle, 378
McGeary, Thomas, 66, 72, 375, 377, 394, 403
McGuinness, Rosamond, 417, 421, 426, 432
Machiavelli, Niccolò, 261, 263

Mack, Maynard, 309–10, 397, 399, 415, 417–18, 426, 429
McKillop, Alan D., 415, 422–3, 427
McLynn, Frank, 221, 396, 418
Macpherson, James, *see* Ossian
Macro, Thomas, 86, 380
Madden, Frederick, 412
Madras, 175, 300
Maintenon, Françoise d'Aubigné, Marquise de, 276
Mainwaring, Edward, 48, 109, 167, 361, 364, 368, 371, 378, 382, 385–6, 393, 401
Malcolm, Alexander, 378
Mallet, David, *see Alfred*
Mandeville, Bernard, 186
Manifesto of the Lord Protector, 292–3
Mann, Alfred, 381
Marcilly, Marie-Claire Decamps de, 276, 278
Marshall, Madeleine Forsell, 384
Marshall, P. J., 412
Mary of Modena, Queen of England, 276, 279
Massue, M. H., Marquis de Ruvigny et Raineval, 398
Matthews, Betty, 367
Meehan, Michael, 409, 416, 427
Mellers, Wilfrid, 394
Merlin, 188, 212, 284
Messiah, 1, 4, 5, 6, 9, 16, 18, 22, 25, 26, 27, 31, 33, 34, 35–6, 37, 38, 39, 44, 48, 53, 103, 110, 117, 118, 119, 122, 125, 147, 148–52, 156, 161, 165, 168–9, 192, 217, 267, 291, 351, 356, 357–8, 366, 378, 382, 422
Messiah (redeemer), 24, 114, 118–19, 121, 146, 148–52, 247, 343, 355, 389
    see also Jesus
Methodism, Methodists, 323, App. 2
Middle Temple, 191
Middleton, Conyers, 262
Milhous, Judith, 18
militia, 184–5, 241–2, 244–5, 252, 300, 322
Millar, Andrew, 293
Miller, James, 24, 25, 27, 31, 32, 33, 50, 54, 72, 74, 75, 76, 77, 80, 144, 192–4, 200, 205, 324, 354, 369
    Are These Things So?, 194
    The Art of Life, 76, 377–8
    Hanover Heroes, 194
    Harlequin Horace, 67, 74, 76, 181, 193, 377
    An Hospital for Fools, 193
    Seasonable Reproof, 193, 268–9, 417
    sermons, 193, 220, 407
    The Year Forty-One, 194

see also Joseph and his Brethren
Miller, John, 435
Milton, John, 4, 24, 32, 53, 111, 114, 123, 127, 135–6, 139, 292–3
  L'Allegro, 3, 18, 24, 33, 37, 50, 61, 353
  Areopagitica, 292–3
  Epitaph on the Marchioness of Winchester, 352
  On the Morning of Christ's Nativity, 352
  The Passion, 352
  Paradise Lost, 24, 25, 111–12, 135–6
  Il Penseroso, 3, 18, 24, 33, 37, 50, 61, 353
  psalm paraphrases, 16, 24, 117, 217, 352
  Samson Agonistes, 16, 24, 113, 131, 136, 215, 236, 292, 293, 295, 298–9, 352
  At a Solemn Music, 352
  On Time, 352
miracles, 110, 114, 122, 128, 133, 136, 142, 146–52, 156, 235, 249, 250, 258, 275, 277, 285
Miscellany of Lyric Poems, 432
Mist, Nathaniel, 329, 390, 403, 431
Mist's Weekly Journal, 144, 210–11
monarchy, 73, 136, 137–8, 183, 184, 200, 215, 226–8, 239, 250, 251, 255, ch. 11, 290, 294–5, 301–2, 307–10, 312–13, 314–19, 325–32, 336–8, 348
  see also Hanover; Patriot King figure; *individual monarchs*; Stuart, house of
Monk, Samuel H., 382, 386
Monod, Paul, 178, 395, 411, 421, 423
Montagu, Elizabeth, 295, 423
Monthly Chronicle, 144
Moore, Cecil A., 241, 389, 411, 426
Morehen, John, 381
Morell, Thomas, 24, 28, 31–2, 49, 67–8, 110, 111–12, 144, 147–8, 156, 195–9, 200, 230, 300, 335–6, 338, 354, 363, 369
  The Christian's Epinikion, 141
  Gideon, 346
  Hecuba, 67–8
  Nabal, 346
  Poems on Divine Subjects, 111–12, 147–8
  political affiliation, 195–9
  political poems, 195–7, 341
  Prometheus in Chains, 57
  sermons, 220, 407, 436
  see also Alexander Balus; Choice of Hercules, The; Judas Macchabæus; Theodora; Triumph of Time and Truth, The
Morgan, Thomas, 146, 154, 156, 226, 227, 249, 320–2, 324, 390, 410, 424, 432, 434
Morris, David B., 139, 382–4, 387, 389
Moses, 109, 119, 134, 137, 139, 143, 217, 218, 224, 250, 269, 415

see also exodus from Egypt; Red Sea; Song of Moses
Mosaic Law, *see* law, Old Testament
music
  affectiveness, 34–6, 38–9, 45–9, 63–4, 66, 75, 77, 78, 81–92, 140, ch. 7
  church, 22, 44–8, 66, 73, 83–92, 96, 117, 157–9, 354, 355
    see also anthems; music, sacred; organs; psalms
  instrumental, 81–92
  sacred, 21, 45–9, 57, 64, ch. 3, 117, 121, 150, ch. 7, 170, 209
music theatre, 43, 53, 56, 61–71, 80, 159, 162, 165, 166, 173, 188, 202, 208, 211–12, 260, 281, 284, 293–5, 299, 307, 316, 367–8, 424, 428
Muzio Scevola, 338
Myers, Robert Manson, 1, 118, 362–3, 385, 393

Napthine, D., 407, 412, 418, 423, 430
navy, 174–5, 176, 205, 214, 289, 296, 298
Newman, Gerald, 377
Newton, Isaac, 152, 153–4, 223, 285, 391, 408
Nichols, John, 49, 400, 424
Nokes, David, 400
Nonjurors, 46, 52, 86, 90–1, 161, 179, 190–2, 207, 286, 287, 291, 308, 328, 329
Norris, John, 111
North, Roger, 380
Norton, David, 382, 385, 413

O'Brien, Paula, 192, 373, 375, 377, 399, 403
Occasional Oratorio, 5, 22, 24, 94, 117, 174, 189, 192, 217, 238, 299, 352, 402, 413
Ode for St Cecilia's Day, 5, 11, 17, 22, 163, 353, 390
Oldmixon, George, *see Grove, The; Trionfo del Tempo, e della Verità, Il*
Old Whig, 365, 382, 409
opera
  ballad, 20, 75, 188, 204, 211
  English, 14, 15, 17, 19, 54, 65, 67, 73, 75, 79, 188, 190, 207, 211–13, 284, 295, 376–7, 387, 422
    see also music theatre
  German, 200
  Italian, 14, 15, 18–21, 23, 37, 43, 45, 46, 64, 66, 70–6, 78–82, 87, 188, 193, 203–8
    see also Handel, George Frideric; Opera of the Nobility; Royal Academy; *individual operas*

Opera of the Nobility, 17, 21, 182, 204
opposition, 174, 177, 187, 191, 208, 241,
    251, 253, 266, 273, 282, 297, 300, 303,
    319, 327, 337, 346–8
  see also Jacobites; Patriot literature,
    opposition, theory; Tories; Whigs,
    opposition
oratorio, English
  audience reception (eighteenth century),
    2, 11, 19–20, 22, 34–5, 37, 43–5, 77,
    125–6, 137, 168–70, 188, 202–5, 208,
    213–14, 231, 284, 288–90, 308, 346,
    350, 354
  chorus, 19, 21, 26, 28–30, 35, 38, 61,
    62–4, 68, 77, 83, 88–9, 91–2, 95, 102,
    113, 129, 155, 156, 163, 165, 169, 200,
    216, 245, 259, 272, 274, 275, 304, 305,
    329, 331, 333, 340, 342, 343, 350, 355,
    357–8
  by composers other than Handel, 16, 20,
    24, 329–30, 338–44, 434
  definition, 5, 8, 21–2, 43–4, 74
  development and structure, 13–22, 25,
    38, 43–5, 50–1, 70, 73, 87, 89, 93, 96,
    119, 136, 165, 167, 170, 183, 203, 208,
    287
  moral teaching in, 34, 35, 60–1, 76, 132,
    chs. 10, 14
  nationalism in, 127, 132, 139, 177, 208,
    238–75, 288–99, 356
  performed in theatre, 16, 23, 36–7, 43–5,
    48, 52, 87, 113, 125, 149, 167, 281
  political allusion in, 187, 188, 189, 200,
    204, 210, 213, chs. 10–14
  religion in, 9, 22, 34–6, 38–9, 45, 64, 125,
    129, 135, 139, 152, 167, 183, 243–6,
    265–7, 271–5, 299, 323–4, 345, 356–9
  see also heathens; priests, in oratorio
  singers, 19 21, 26, 37, 44, 206, 207
  sources, 4, 15–18, 24, 26, 32, 68, 91, 93–5,
    102, 104, 109, 113–19, 121–2, 125–6,
    130, 131, 135, 148–51, 153, ch. 10,
    350, App. 1
  subject-matter, 4, 8, 10, 16, 24, 29, 32–6,
    76, 87, 90, 94, 110, 112, 114–23, ch. 5,
    144, 150–1, 154, 156, 173, 177, 182,
    219–21, 227, 233, 257, 287, 346
  see also individual oratorios; Israelites,
    oratorio
oratorio, Italian, 37, 48, 73, 150, 229
organs, organ music, 44, 84–8, 355
Orrery, Roger Boyle, first Earl of, 115, 328,
    351, 384, 405
Osborn, James M., 198, 400
Osborne, Peregrine, second Duke of Leeds,
    192

Ossian, 51, 132, 139, 385
Ottoboni, Pietro, 150
Overton, J. H., 380
Ovid (Publius Ovidius Naso), 353
Oxford, 17, 325

Pamphili, Benedetto, 353
Paradise Lost (Stillingfleet and Smith), 388
paraphrase of Bible, *see under* Bible
Parks, Stephen, 400–1
Parliament, 174, 176, 178, 184–5, 204, 205,
    214, 226–7, 230, 282, 297, 305, 320,
    340, 346–8
  House of Commons, 162, 348
  House of Lords, 162, 245–6, 289
Parnasso in festa, 287
Parvish, Samuel, 151
Pascoe, C. F., 412
Passover, Feast of, 258, 259, 274
Patrick, Simon, 285, 344, 434
Patriot King figure, 27, 130, 134, 138, 186,
    210, 213, 228, 231, 232, 258, 266, 275,
    281, 290, 293–5, 304–5, 306, 308,
    315–19, 327, 335–7, 339–45, 415
  lack of, 238–9, 285, 305, 307–8
  see also under Bolingbroke
Patriot literature, opposition, theory, 134–5,
    137, 176, 178–86, 192–8, 204, 205,
    207, 211, 212, 214, 229–30, 231, 239,
    245, 256, 259, 268, 283, 284, 285,
    288–90, 292–6, 302, 304–10, 312–14,
    318, 332–3, 335–8, 341–2, 344–5
  see also drama, political; poetry, political
patriots, patriotism, 17, 52–3, 55, 56, 69, 73,
    77, 129–30, 135, 139, 163, 171, 177,
    180–4, 190, 210, 215, 240, 242, 243,
    245, 253, 265, 273, 311
Payne, Thomas, 89–90
Peirce, James, 380
Pemberton, Henry, 140
Pendarves, Mary *see* Delany, Mary
Pepusch, Johann Christoph, 15, 44
Perceval, John, *see* Egmont
Percival, Milton, 400
Pergolesi, Giovanni Battista, 48
Pericles, 229
Perry, Thomas W., 347, 435
Peskin, Allan, 435
Philarmonic Society, 14, 277
Philips, Ambrose, 215
Philistines, 215, 220, 296, 297, 298–9, 329,
    410
Pindar, 110, 137
Pitt, James, 335
Pittock, Murray, 291, 319, 426
Plain Dealer, 54, 82, 122, 377–9

Platt, Richard, 366–7
Playford, John, 379
Plumb, J. H., 395
Pocock, J. G. A., 1, 225, 241, 303, 396–8, 408, 411, 415, 418, 424, 427
poetry
 biblical, 35, 87, 91, 108–11, 112, 113, 116–17, 119–25, 159
 British, 17, 24, 32, 49, 53, 54–6, 79, 109–10, 112, 115, 127, 133–9
 classical, 109, 110–11, 112, 115, 116, 118, 127, 129, 132, 135, 138, 159, 216
 moral, religious, 24, 53, 54, 55–6, 109–13, 114–15, 117–19, 121, 127–9, 131–2, 134–6, 155, 159–60, 162–7, 170, 358
 political, 71, 127, 132–9, 162–3, 182–3, 192–7, 202, 209, 213, 215, 230, 241, 244, 245, 246, 263–4, 289, 290–1, 292, 293, 294, 300, 311, 343
 see also Bible, adaptation and paraphrase of; epic
political prints, *see under* press
Polybius, 261
Pope, Alexander, 70, 76, 116, 151, 192–3, 194, 197–8, 268, 272, 279, 319, 351, 353
 Acis and Galatea, 277
 Brutus, 54, 134, 388, 418
 correspondence, 221, 388, 399, 401
 Dunciad, 45, 72, 76–7, 78, 210, 399
 'Epistle to Augustus', 294
 'Epistle to Bolingbroke', 74
 Epistle to Burlington, 277–8, 313, 380
 Essay on Criticism, 86, 112, 380
 Essay on Man, 210, 273
 Esther, 277–82
 Messiah, 111, 118, 383
 Pastorals, 353
 Peri Bathous, 133–4, 135
 Windsor Forest, 244
Popery, *see* Roman Catholicism
Porpora, Nicolà, *see Davide e Bersabea*
Post Angel, 157, 164–6
Potter, John, 309, 315, 426
Prat, Daniel, 87–8, 209, 393
Prayer Book, 1662, *see* Book of Common Prayer
press, 173–4, 175, 176, 185, 205, 211, 251, 292, 296–8, 303, 313–14, 347, 349
 political prints, 289, 316–17, 347–8
 see also individual publications
Preston, Thomas R., 219, 364, 379, 384, 410
Pretender, Young, *see* Charles Edward Stuart
Price, Curtis, 188, 212, 373, 377, 394, 398, 404, 424

priesthood, 10, 155, 156, 225, 227, 286, 320–4, 356–7
priests
 Old Testament, 137, 139, 226, 227, 233, 254, 320–5
 in oratorio, 233, 253, 258, 309, 319–20, 323–5
Prior, Matthew, 111, 117, 157–8, 190, 398
Probyn, Clive T., 368
promised land, *see* Canaan
Prompter, 54, 134, 309, 373, 383, 388, 417
property, 226, 235, 242, 247, 250–2, 254, 257, 263, 265, 275, 302, 310, 321–2
prophecies, 110, 114, 121, 142–4, 148–54, 217, 219, 223, 261, 266, 271–2, 323, 391
prophets, 112, 118, 121, 139, 323, 356
Protestantism, Protestants, 9, 10, 141, 142, 157, 175, 177, 179, 190, 192–3, 205–6, 214, 216, 223–4, 246, 280, 281–2, 284, 302, 428
 see also Church of England; religion
psalms, 16, 24, 35, 68, 83, 86, 87, 90–2, 94–6, 110, 117, 120, 122, 157, 158, 159, 160, 166, 216, 222, 274, 291, 349–50
 see also under Bible, books of
public spirit, 137
public virtue
 civic duty, 182–3, 185–6, 197, 229, 264, 270, 273, 275, ch. 14
 decline/renewal of, 52–3, 68–70, 75, 166, 182, 193–4, 263, 266, 268, 273–4
Pulteney, William, 176, 181, 195–6, 282, 304
Purcell, Daniel, *see Grove, The*
Purcell, Henry, 24, 75
 see also Dido and Aeneas; King Arthur
Purim, Feast of, 274, 279, 420
Puritanism, Puritans, 83, 84, 323

Quarrie, P., 429

Racine, Jean, 15, 68, 276
 Athalie, 17, 68–9, 236, 279, 281, 325, 351
 Esther, 16, 68–9, 165, 276, 278, 279, 280, 281, 286, 351
Radzinowicz, Mary Ann, 404
Raguenet, Abbé François, 66
Ralph, James, 64, 273, 300, 396, 397, 411, 426, 428
Ramsay, Andrew Michael, 318, 429
Ramsland, Clement, 415
Randall, Helen, W., 431
Rawlins, Thomas, 291
Raylor, Timothy, 372, 375, 392

Rebellion (1715), 200, 217, 279, 280
Rebellion (1745), 78, 174, 177, 178, 179,
    181, 185, 189, 192, 198, 213, 220, 224,
    242, 245, 299–300, 319
Rebellion, Great, 321, 328
reception, *see* Handel, George Frideric,
    audience reception; oratorio, English,
    audience reception
Red Sea, 122, 138, 146, 147, 148, 149, 150,
    228, 246, 249, 290–1, 340
    see also exodus from Egypt; Song of Moses
Redwood, John, 389
Reedy, Gerard, 389–90
Reinhold, Thomas, 26
religion
    Christian doctrine defended,
        promulgated, 8, 34–5, 52, 55–6, 58,
        83, 141, 142, 144–5, 147–53, 154–6,
        170, 217, 219, 234, 243, 248–9, 321,
        349, 355–6
    see also typology
    decline/renewal of, 8–9, 52–3, 68–9, 145,
        158–61, 164–8, 186, 193, 220–1, 249,
        266–9, 271–4, 279, 339
    and national identity, 9–10, 57, 69, 73,
        ch. 5, 154, 159, 171, 177, 179, 205–7,
        215–17, 220–1, 223–4, 239, 244–6,
        248, 252, 268, 269, 279, 281–2, 321–4,
        327, 332
    see also Bible; Church of England; deism;
        Methodism; oratorio, English, religion
        in; poetry, moral, religious;
        Protestantism; Roman Catholicism;
        sermons
religious sublime, 64, 90, 92, ch. 4, 127–8,
    130, 135, 139, 145, 157, 163–70
    see also Bible, style of
Remembrancer, 300, 301, 396–7, 411, 426, 428
Resurrezione, La, 11, 15, 366
Reventlow, Henning, Graf, 365, 406, 410,
    429–30
*Review of the Moral and Political Life ...
    Joseph*, 425
Revolution (1688), 74, 179, 184, 211–12,
    213, 220, 242, 253, 286, 321, 326, 328,
    348
Rich, John, 14, 50
Richard II, 230
Richardson, Samuel, 334
Rinaldo, 20, 54, 55, 70, 79, 212
Robbins, Caroline, 408
Roberts, John H., 364
Robinson, Miss, 26
Rogers, John, 430
Rogers, Nicholas, 394, 411, 423, 428, 435
Rogers, Pat, 369

Rolli, Paolo Antonio, 388
    see also Davide e Bersabea; *Muzio Scevola*
Rollin, Charles, 116, 117, 118, 121, 153,
    217–18, 385–6, 405–6, 409
Roman Catholicism, 9–10, 72–3, 142, 175,
    190, 193, 205–7, 214, 216–17, 220–1,
    226, 242–3, 244, 249, 250, 253, 263,
    279–82, 284, 302, 303, 305, 325, 327,
    332
Rome, ancient, 69, 75, 183, 225, 230, 244,
    261–6, 336, 338, 416
Roner, Andreas, 378
Rosamond, 211–12, 295, 376–7
Rosenfeld, Sybil, 368
Ross, Angus, 419–20
Rossi, *see Rinaldo*
Roston, Murray, 177, 215, 384, 412
Roth, Cecil, 435
Rowe, Thomas, 246, 386, 413, 425
Royal Academy, 73, 203, 205, 337
Rumbold, Valerie, 388
Rupp, Gordon, 381, 436
Ruspoli, Francesco Maria, Marchese, 15–16
Russel, William, 191
Ruttkay, K. G., 376
Rymer, Thomas, 373, 375

sacred music, *see under* music
Sadie, Stanley, 366, 375
St Cecilia celebrations, *see under* Cecilia
St Evremond, Charles de, 45, 113–14, 370,
    374
St George's, Hanover Square, 282
St George's, Windsor, 93
St Paul's, 94, 21
Sambrook, James, 112, 372, 374, 391,
    416–17
Samson, 2, 16, 22, 34, 38, 44, 50, 115, 129,
    131, 146, 192, 215, 236, 238, 240, 245,
    258, 267, 272, 292–9, 352, 416, 425
Samson, Judge of Israel, 114, 146, 217, 246,
    252
Samuel, Edgar R., 435
Saul, 17, 20, 29–30, 38, 58, 76, 77, 90, 94,
    114, 115, 116, 129, 138, 139, 145, 146,
    154, 200, 236, 238, 239, 245, 272, 275,
    307–8, 327–33, 351, 357, 361, 363,
    381–2, 425, 432
Saul, King of Israel, 24, 115, 145, 146, 220,
    227–8, 307–8, 309, 328–9, 330–3, 389
Savage, Richard, 137, 291
Say, Samuel, 49
Scarlatti, Alessandro, 150, 364
Scholes, Percy, 379
Schonhorn, Manuel, 228, 307, 328, 411,
    415, 425, 431

Schueller, Herbert M., 370–1, 379
Scouten, A. H., 367, 369
Secker, Thomas, 83
See and Seem Blind, 366, 370
Semele, 6, 11, 18, 22, 23, 38, 60, 79, 271,
  353, 361, 368
Senesino (Francesco Bernardi), 19, 20, 44,
  206–7
Senhouse, Peter, 371
sermons, 8, 10, 45, 83–6, 88–90, 117, 120,
  141, 142, 144, 158, 161, 162, 165,
  193–4, 219–21, 222, 227, 242, 269,
  271–2, 277, 282, 299, 308, 309, 315,
  320, 326, 328, 354, 382, 428
  see also Boyle Lectures
Serwer, Howard, 367
Shadwell, Thomas, 291
Shaftesbury, Anthony Ashley Cooper, third
  Earl of, 66–7, 115–16, 141, 234, 236,
  429
Shaftesbury, Anthony Ashley Cooper,
  fourth Earl of, 66, 367
Shaftesbury, Susannah Noel, Countess of
  (wife of fourth Earl), 44
Shakespeare, William, 24, 110, 212, 259
  Coriolanus, 275
  Henry V, 194, 212, 231, 242, 259, 275,
    336–7
    see also under Hill, Aaron
  Richard II, 289
Shapiro, A. H., 92, 287, 363, 372, 377, 380,
  382, 384, 392–3, 398, 402, 420–1
Sharp, Richard, 381
Shaw, H. Watkins, 47, 371
Sherbo, Arthur, 426
Sherburn, George, 419
Sherlock, Thomas, 385, 407
Sherlock, William, 371
Shields, David S., 394, 413, 427
Shiels, Robert, 399
Sidney, Sir Philip, 117
Siegmund-Schultze, Dorothea, 407
Silesia, 174
Simon, J., 401, 402, 419
Simon, Richard, 141, 390
Skinner, Quentin, 257, 397, 415
slavery, 73, 134, 137, 184, 186, 229, 231,
  246, 247, 250, 252, 259, 289, 291, 292,
  293, 311, 410
Slovo, Joe, 224
Smart, Christopher, 426
Smith, John Christopher, jnr, *see Paradise
  Lost*; *Ulysses*
Smith, John Christopher, snr, 367, 369
  *see also David's Lamentation over Saul and
  Jonathan*

Smith, Patrick J., 366
Smith, R. J., 415
Smith, Ruth, 368–9, 379, 384, 390, 401,
  407, 422, 431
Smith, William, 109, 382
Smith, William C., 6, 36, 369, 390, 403–4
Smither, Howard E., 361, 367–8, 374,
  423–4, 426
Societies for the Reformation of Manners,
  185–6, 268
Society for the Propagation of the Gospel,
  243–4
Solomon, 25, 90–1, 115, 117, 130, 139, 189,
  232, 236, 241, 245, 250, 255, 258, 271,
  307, 309–17, 319–20, 323, 324, 325–7,
  333, 352, 357, 416, 436
Solomon, King of Israel, 12, 24, 89, 90–1,
  117, 120, 130, 143, 154, 220, 227, 232,
  244, 250, 255, 309–10, 311, 313,
  315–17, 320, 326, 415, 428
Solomons, I., 435
Song of Deborah, 110–11, 117, 118, 120,
  122, 136, 382–3
Song of Miriam, 89, 117, 136, 382
Song of Moses, 89–90, 110–11, 112, 117–18,
  121, 122, 130, 136, 324, 382, 383, 386
Song of Solomon, 117, 136
Sophocles, 4, 32, 57, 58–60, 63, 353
Sosarme, 43, 337
Southern, Richard, 428
Spain, 181, 184, 205, 216, 240, 243, 244,
  245, 248
  see also under war
Speck, W. A., 364, 396-8, 407, 411–12, 418,
  421, 423, 428, 430
Spectator, 158–60, 376, 383, 385, 387, 392
Spence, Joseph, 134, 385
Spenser, Edmund, 197, 352
Squire, Samuel, 228, 256, 257, 415, 429
Stackhouse, Thomas, 151, 236, 316, 383,
  385, 391, 410, 429, 432, 434
Stair, John Dalrymple, second Earl of, 298
Stampiglia, Silvio, 150
State of the Nation, 414, 428
Stationers Hall, 160
Statt, D. A., 435
Steele, Sir Richard, 70, 73–4, 301, 376, 424
Stephen, F. G., 421
Stephen, Leslie, 389, 409
Stephenson, W. E., 404
Stillingfleet, Benjamin, see *Paradise Lost*
Stillingfleet, Edward, 390
Stone, G. Winchester, jnr, 367, 369
Strada del Pò, Anna, 206
Straka, Gerald, 431
Streatfeild, R. A., 271, 436

Strohm, Reinhard, 394, 398, 402
Stromberg, Roland N., 389
Strumia, Anna, 408
Stuart, royal house of, 9, 179, 184, 190–2, 208, 220, 257, 283, 284, 290–1, 302, 308, 328–30, 339, 391; *see also* Charles I; Charles Edward Stuart; James II; James III
Supplement to the Bishop of London's Letter, 408
Susanna, 6, 25, 31, 44, 50, 115, 131, 189, 236, 271, 272, 319, 323, 333–4, 352, 361, 368, 425
Susanna, Apocryphal character, 115, 217, 334, 433
Swanston, Hamish, 361
Swedenborg, H. T., jnr, 140, 389
Swift, Jonathan, 196, 210, 272, 276, 278
Swingler, Randall, 213
Sykes, Arthur Ashley, 142, 149
Sykes, Norman, 379, 420, 437
Synge, Edward, 25, 34–5, 37, 110, 125, 165, 378
Szechi, Daniel, 394–5

Tabernacles, Feast of, 274
Talbot, Catherine, 44–5
Talbot, Michael, 409
Tallis, Thomas, 94
Targett, Simon, 394, 397, 409, 433
Taswell, William, 117–18, 375, 382–3
Tate, Nahum, 73, 161, 162–3, 164
    see also Dido and Aeneas
Tatler, 424
Taylor, Carole, 367, 401
Taylor, Stephen, 365, 412, 430
Temperley, Nicholas, 379–81, 392–3, 436
Temple, Sir William, 129–30, 228
Terpander, 77
Theobald, Lewis, 374, 383
Theodora, 6, 22, 68, 111, 115, 131, 156, 266, 346, 350, 352, 358–9, 361, 384, 417, 425
Theodora, martyr, 115
Thompson, Thomas, 143
Thomson, James, 53, 69, 112, 134, 193, 197, 264, 335, 336, 374
    Britannia, 244, 264, 293
    Castle of Indolence, 197, 400
    Coriolanus, 260
    correspondence, 268, 397, 416–18, 421, 434
    Edward and Eleonora, 243, 336
    Liberty, 260, 416–17
    preface to *Areopagitica*, 293
    Seasons, 55, 112, 264, 270, 271, 313, 416, 427

Sophonisba, 17, 336
Tancred and Sigismunda, 336, 430
Three Choirs meetings, 45–6, 88–9, 117, 354, 382
Tiepolo, Giambattista, 228–9
Tillotson, John, 141
Timotheus, 82
Tindal, Matthew, 248, 320, 410, 429, 432, 434
Tindal, Nicholas, 91–2, 385, 414
Tinling, M., 401, 419
Tippett, Michael, 224
Todd, Janet, 384
Toland, John, 142, 151, 406
Torchiana, Donald T., 388, 418
Tories, Toryism, 176, 178, 179, 186, 190, 192, 207, 212, 282, 284, 286, 311, 323, 324, 347
Tosi, Pier Francesco, 48, 372, 375
Touch-stone, The, 64–6, 67, 73, 114, 115
trade, 174, 175, 176, 179, 182, 183, 186, 213, 244, 250–1, 265, 289, 300, 310–12, 326, 347
Trapp, Joseph, 112, 123–4, 127, 132, 382, 384, 387
treaties
    Aix-la-Chapelle, 175, 199, 251, 310, 313–14
    Pardo, Convention of El, 289
    Utrecht, 199
    Vienna, Second Treaty of, 253
Trenchard, John, 239, 244, 411–12, 416, 426
Trionfo del Tempo, e della Verità, Il, 346, 353
Trionfo del Tempo e del Disinganno, Il, 11, 353
Triumph of Time and Truth, The, 5, 11, 18, 61, 346, 353, 390
Trollope (auctioneers), 383, 416
Trowell, Brian, 167, 353, 366, 393
Tudway, Thomas, 46–7
Turner, William, 161, 162
typology, biblical, 146, 147, 150, 217–19, 291, 305, 334, 405

Udall, Nicholas, 215
Ulysses, 190, 284
Universal Spectator, 61–2, 70
Upton, John, 25, 215

Van der Veen, H. R. S., 435
Varey, Simon, 396, 414, 429
Venice, 228–9
Venus and Adonis, 366
Vernon, Admiral Edward, 222, 239, 296–7
verse, *see* poetry
Victor, Benjamin, 169

Villette, Marquis de, 276, 278
Viner, Jacob, 364
Virgil (Publius Vergilius Maro), 24, 112, 118, 132, 133, 138, 151, 255, 264
Vivaldi, Antonio, *see Juditha Triumphans*
Voice of Liberty, The, 289
Voltaire, François Marie Arouet de, 243

Waller, Edmund, 111
Walpole, Horace, 273, 397, 414, 424, 428
Walpole, Sir Robert, 174, 176, 178, 181, 182, 183, 188, 190, 193–4, 196–7, 202–5, 208, 239, 268, 281, 283–4, 285, 288, 289, 296, 304–7, 309, 312, 332, 335
Walsh, John, 365, 412, 430
Wanley, Humphrey, 157
war
  conquest, 130, 137, 240–53, 264
  'just war' theory, 242–3, 248
  of Austrian Succession, 174–6, 187, 222, 240–1, 245–6, 251, 297–8, 300, 302, 303, 314
  of Polish Succession, 174, 178
  of Spanish Succession, 73, 163
  with Spain ('War of Jenkins' Ear'), 174–5, 214, 219, 220, 222, 240, 250, 251, 288–9, 292, 296–7, 298, 314
  see also battles; treaties
Warburton, William, 134, 409
Warton, Joseph, 33, 369
Waterland, Daniel, 219, 406, 410, 414, 434
Watson, Richard, 390
Watts, Isaac, 69, 96, 111, 114, 120, 128, 171, 216, 219, 349, 355, 375–6, 406, 414
Webber, Francis, 154, 391, 432
Weber, William, 371, 381
Webster, William, 209, 391
Weedon, Cavendish, 160–7, 392
Weekly Miscellany, 151, 209, 391
Weinbrot, Howard D., 255, 362, 363, 382, 388, 403, 415, 427, 430
Welchman, Edward, 161, 164
Wentworth, Thomas, third Earl of Strafford, 24, 192, 297
Wentworth, Brigadier-General Thomas, 297
Wesley, Charles, 354, 359
Wesley, John, 354–6, 436
Wesley, Samuel, 111, 237

Western, J. R., 397
West Indies, 174, 240, 248, 296
Westminster Abbey, 21, 93, 94
Westrup, J. A., 363, 371, 374
Wheatly, Charles, 328–9
Whigs, Whiggism, 176, 178–9, 207, 212, 314, 320, 323
  Country, 'Old Whig', 178, 179, 182, 184, 252, 254, 256, 257, 262–3, 273, 286, 294, 322, 326, 327, 335
  Court, administration, 174–87, 195–6, 199, 229, 231, 256, 269–70, 273, 295, 304–6, 310, 327, 335, 346–8
    see also Walpole, Sir Robert
  opposition, 27, 176, 178, 195, 225, 311
    see also Patriot literature, opposition, theory
Whiston, William, 142, 149, 390, 406
Whitefield, George, 354, 356, 436
Whyte, Lawrence, 125–6
Willes, Edward, 103
William III, 190, 211, 215, 224, 228, 277, 281, 291, 327
Wilson, Kathleen, 394, 412, 414, 423
Winton, Calhoun, 399
Wise, Michael, 96, 100
Wolsey, Thomas, 215, 304
Wood, Bruce, 392
Woodfine, Philip, 394, 414, 428
Woolston, Thomas, 406
wordbooks, 12, 23–4, 31, 113, 169, 189, 204, 213, 236, 292, 401
word-setting, 1, 4, 19, 20–1, 28, 29–30, 32–9, 49, 54, 70, 73–80, 84, 88, 93, 157–9, 166, 167, 169–70
Wren, Matthew, 225
Wyndham, Sir William, 197, 222

xenophobia, 20, 72–4, 182, 193, 205–7, 245, 298, 346–9
  see also Israelites, biblical, and enemies; Israelites, oratorio, and enemies
Xenophon, 153, 317–18, 352, 429

York Buildings, 14, 43, 278
Young, Edward, 111, 122, 311, 396, 413
Young, Esther, 23
Young, Percy, 5, 362, 363, 374, 436

Zeno, Apostolo, 306, 352
Zwicker, Steven N., 7, 364, 404–5, 425